SPSS/PC+
4.0 Base Manual
for the IBM PC/XT/AT and PS/2

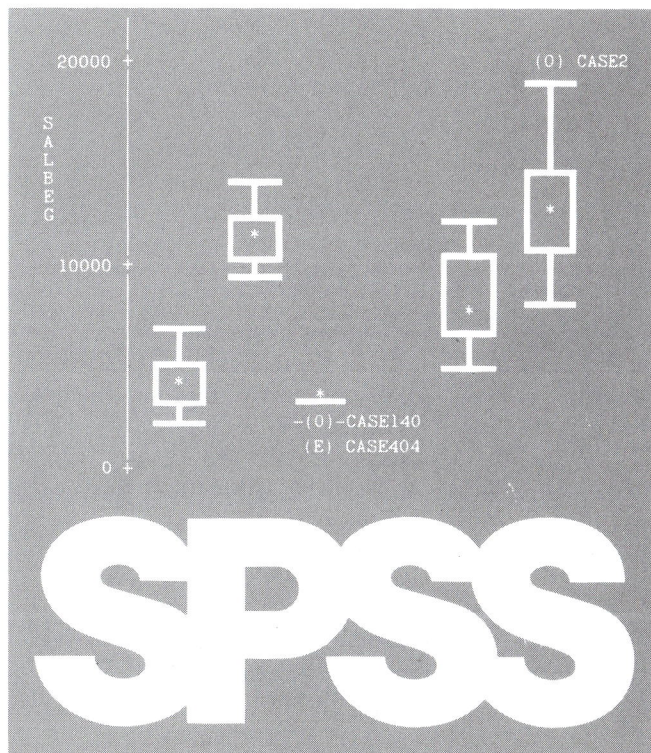

Marija J. Norusis/SPSS Inc.

SPSS Inc.
444 N. Michigan Avenue
Chicago, Illinois 60611
Tel: (312) 329-3500
Fax: (312) 329-3668

SPSS International BV
P.O. Box 115
4200 AC Gorinchem
The Netherlands
Tel: +31.1830.36711
Fax: +31.1830.35839

For more information about SPSS/PC+ and other software produced and distributed by SPSS Inc., please write or call

Marketing Department
SPSS Inc.
444 North Michigan Avenue
Chicago, IL 60611
Tel: (312) 329-3500
Fax: (312) 329-3668

In Europe and the Middle East, please write or call

SPSS International BV
P.O. Box 115
4200 AC Gorinchem
The Netherlands
Tel: +31.1830.36711
Twx: 21019
Fax: +31.1830.35839

SPSS/PC+ 4.0 Base Manual
Copyright © 1990 by SPSS Inc.
All rights reserved.
Printed in the United States of America.

3 4 5 6 7 8 9 0   93 92 91

ISBN 0-923967-11-7

Library of Congress Catalog Card Number: 90-070748

Preface

SPSS/PC+™ 4.0 continues the SPSS line of powerful statistical and information analysis systems running on a wide selection of mainframe and personal computers. As the latest product for the PC-DOS/MS-DOS operating system, it offers new facilities and enhanced flexibility in choosing the portions of the system that meet your needs. SPSS/PC+ 4.0 retains its menu system for building commands and for contextual help, as well as its command-line and batch operation modes. New features in SPSS/PC+ 4.0 are described below. As in previous versions, the SPSS/PC+ 4.0 system is built around the reliable, tested routines developed for SPSS software systems over a period of more than twenty years.

The manuals for SPSS/PC+ have been highly acclaimed. In updating them for SPSS/PC+ 4.0, we have attempted to maintain the balance of operational instructions, statistical guidance, and reference material that has characterized earlier versions. Operational instructions appear in Part A of this manual. In each of the SPSS/PC+ manuals, statistical overviews guide the new user in the rationale behind statistical procedures, their use, and the interpretation of their output. The comprehensive Command Reference in each book remains an essential guide for the experienced user.

This manual describes the base system of SPSS/PC+. Add-on enhancements include SPSS/PC+ Statistics™, SPSS/PC+ Advanced Statistics™, SPSS/PC+ Tables™ for presentation-quality tabular reports, SPSS/PC+ Trends™ for time-series analysis, SPSS/PC+ Categories™ for conjoint analysis and optimal scaling, SPSS Data Entry II™ for data entry and validation, SPSS/PC+ Graphics™ featuring Harvard® Graphics from Software Publishing Corporation, SPSS/PC+ Mapping™ from MapInfo™, and SPSS/PC+ Graph-in-the-Box™ from New England Software.

What's New? Changes since SPSS/PC+ 3.1:

- The new Statistics option combines some of the procedures formerly a part of the base system with FACTOR, CLUSTER, QUICK CLUSTER, and RELIABILITY from the Advanced Statistics option.
- Trends procedures work with Harvard Graphics for high-resolution time-series charts.
- The procedures ADD VALUE LABELS (in the base system), SURVIVAL and PROBIT (in Advanced Statistics), and X11ARIMA (in Trends) have been added.
- The TRANSLATE command reads and writes files in several new formats.
- The existing commands CROSSTABS, FREQUENCIES, GET, and SAVE (in the base system), and REGRESSION (in the Statistics option) offer significant new capabilities.

Compatibility SPSS Inc. warrants that SPSS/PC+ and enhancements are designed for personal computers in the IBM PC and IBM PS/2™ lines with a hard disk and at least 512K of RAM. (Some procedures require 640K of RAM.) These products also function on most IBM-compatible machines. Contact SPSS Inc. for details about specific IBM-compatible hardware.

Serial Numbers Your serial number is your identification number with SPSS Inc. You will need this serial number when you call SPSS Inc. for information regarding support, payment, a defective diskette, or an upgraded system.

The serial number can be found on the diskette labeled U1 in your system. Before using the system, please copy this number to the **registration card.**

Registration Card STOP! Before continuing on, *fill out and send us your registration card.* Until we receive your registration card, you have an unregistered system. Even if you have previously sent a card to us, please fill out and return the card enclosed in your SPSS/PC+ 4.0 package.

Registering your system entitles you to

- Technical support on our customer hotline.
- Favored customer status.
- *Keywords*—the SPSS user newsletter.
- New product announcements.

Of course, unregistered systems receive none of the above, so *don't put it off—send your registration card now!*

Replacement Policy **System Diskettes.** Call the Micro Software Department at 312/329-3300 to report a defective diskette. You must provide us with the serial number of your system. (The normal installation procedure will detect any damaged diskettes.) SPSS Inc. will ship replacement diskettes the same day we receive notification from you. Please return the defective diskettes to the Micro Software Department, SPSS Inc., 444 North Michigan Avenue, Chicago, IL 60611.

Shipping List The shipping list for SPSS/PC+ 4.0 is on a separate sheet in the package.

Training Seminars SPSS Inc. provides both public and onsite training seminars for SPSS/PC+. There is a two-day introductory course to familiarize users with the basics of SPSS/PC+. In addition there is an advanced course, also two days, that deals with more sophisticated aspects of the program. Additional seminars treat specialized topics such as data entry, graphics, report writing, and time series analysis. All seminars feature hands-on workshops.

SPSS/PC+ seminars will be offered in major U.S. and European cities on a regular basis. For further information on these seminars or to schedule an onsite seminar, call the SPSS Inc. Training Department at 312/329-3557.

Additional Documentation Additional copies of all SPSS product manuals may be purchased separately. To order additional manuals, just fill out the Documentation Card included with your system and send it to SPSS Inc. Documentation Sales, 444 N. Michigan Avenue, Chicago, IL, 60611.

Note: In Europe, additional copies of documentation can be purchased by site-licensed customers only. Please contact the European office at the address listed on the copyright page for more information.

Technical Support The SPSS technical hotline is available to registered customers of SPSS/PC+. Customers may call the Techline for assistance in using SPSS products or for installation help for one of the warranted hardware environments.

To reach an SPSS technical support consultant, call 312/329-3410, 9:00 a.m. to 5:00 p.m. CST. Be prepared to identify yourself, your organization, and the serial number of your system.

If you are a Value Plus or Customer EXPress customer, use the priority 800 number you received with your materials. For information on subscribing to the Value Plus or Customer EXPress plan, call SPSS Inc. at 312/329-3313.

Tell Us What You Think   Your comments are important. So send us a letter and let us know about your experiences with SPSS products. We especially like to hear about new and interesting applications using the SPSS/PC+ system. Write to SPSS Inc. Marketing Department, Attn: Micro Software Products Manager, 444 N. Michigan Avenue, Chicago, IL, 60611.

Contacting SPSS Inc.   If you would like to be on our mailing list, write to us at one of the addresses below. We will send you a copy of our newsletter and let you know about SPSS Inc. activities in your area.

SPSS Inc.

444 North Michigan Avenue
Chicago, IL 60611
Tel: (312) 329-3500
Fax: (312) 329-3668

SPSS Federal Systems (U.S.)

800 K St., N.W.
Suite 300
Washington, DC 20001
Tel: (202) 408-7626
Fax: (202) 408-7627

SPSS Latin America

444 North Michigan Avenue
Chicago, IL 60611
Tel: (312) 329-3556
Fax: (312) 329-3668

SPSS Benelux BV

P.O. Box 115
4200 AC Gorinchem
The Netherlands
Tel: +31.1830.36711
Fax: +31.1830.35839

SPSS UK Ltd.

SPSS House
5 London Street
Chertsey
Surrey KT16 8AP
United Kingdom
Tel: +44.932.566262
Fax: +44.932.567020

SPSS GmbH Software

Steinsdorfstrasse 19
D-8000 Munich 22
Germany
Tel: +49.89.2283008
Fax: +49.89.2285413

SPSS Scandinavia AB

Sjöängsvägen 21
S-191 72 Sollentuna
Sweden
Tel: +46.8.7549450
Fax: +46.8.7548816

SPSS Asia Pacific Pte. Ltd.

26-01
78 Shenton Way
Singapore 0207
Singapore
Tel: +65.221.2577
Fax: +65.221.9920

SPSS Japan Inc.

Gyoen Sky Bldg.
2-1-11, Shinjuku
Shinjuku-ku
Tokyo 160
Japan
Tel: +81.3.33505261
Fax: +81.3.33505245

SPSS Australasia

P.O. Box 879
345 Pacific Highway
Crows Nest
Sydney, NSW 2065
Australia
Tel: +61.2.954.5660
Fax: +61.2.954.5616

Introduction

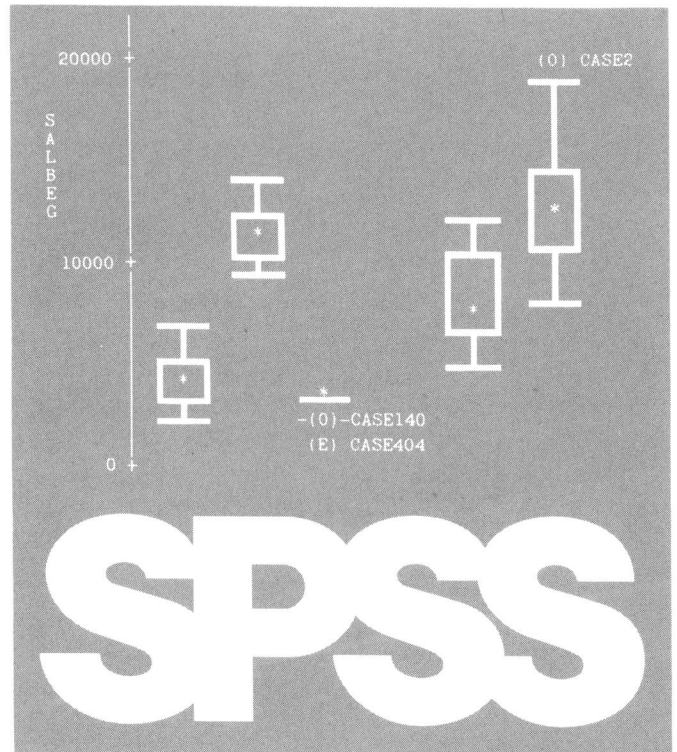

- *About This Manual*
- *Running SPSS/PC+*
- *REVIEW: The SPSS/PC+ Editor*
- *Important DOS Concepts*

Contents

About This Manual

This is a large manual, in part because it documents a large and versatile software system, and in part because it seeks to meet the differing needs of a diverse body of users. For those who have limited experience with statistics, computing, or the IBM PC environment, introductory material and statistical overviews are available. For those who are already familiar with statistical computing, a reference section presents SPSS/PC+ commands without extensive examples. You are likely to find different parts of the manual most valuable as your experience with SPSS/PC+ grows.

If you have just received the system, you should turn first to the Installation Instructions that accompany the system. You need to install SPSS/PC+ only once unless you remove it from your system. (You can, however, remove and reinstall portions of the SPSS/PC+ system; for information, refer to SPSS MANAGER in Part C.)

Introduction. The Introduction (Part A) helps you become familiar with running SPSS/PC+ and using REVIEW, the SPSS/PC+ text editor. *Running SPSS/PC+* describes the system's command-based operation and gives overviews of the three environments available for entering commands. This includes a discussion of the Menu and Help system, a facility introduced with SPSS/PC+ V2.0 that gives you help in building commands by describing each one and guiding you through command syntax. *REVIEW: The SPSS/PC+ Editor* provides an example that shows you step-by-step how to edit files using the fully integrated SPSS/PC+ text editor.

Statistics Guide. The Statistics Guide (Part B) is a complete user's guide to the data definition and analysis facilities of SPSS/PC+. If you are new to computer data analysis, you can start at the beginning of the Guide and progress through introductions to coding and entering data, defining the data to SPSS/PC+, managing it, tabulating it, and analyzing it with the many statistical procedures that SPSS/PC+ makes available. If you are more experienced, you can turn to the Guide whenever you want a more guided approach to certain SPSS/PC+ facilities than you find in the Command Reference or when you want to further your understanding of the statistics calculated by certain procedures. The Guide does not discuss at length the SPSS/PC+ commands that control such things as the destination of output files or the format of the output. For that information, consult Running SPSS/PC+ in the Introduction.

Command Reference. The Command Reference (Part C) is a detailed reference to the syntax and operations of each SPSS/PC+ command. Its opening section, Universals, documents the general characteristics of the system. Following that section, the individual commands are presented in alphabetical order. For each command, the Command Reference provides complete syntax rules plus details of operations.

Examples. The examples presented in Part D illustrate typical uses of SPSS/PC+ analytical procedures. The annotated input and output are arranged not to imitate the progress of an interactive SPSS/PC+ session but to demonstrate a set of commands that carry out a complete data analysis task. You may find that these examples, with their interpretative commentary, extend your understanding of the logic of SPSS/PC+ command structure.

Glossary. The Glossary (Part E) defines terms used in this manual that may be unfamiliar to many users. It does not attempt to cover the full vocabulary of DOS operating manuals or the statistical terms discussed in the Statistics Guide. Remember that the SPSS/PC+ online glossary is available from REVIEW. (Press (F1) and select **Glossary.**)

Appendixes. *Graph-in-the-Box* and *Graph-in-the-Box Executive,* both from New England Software, are frequently used to display SPSS/PC+ results graphically. If you have either of these products, consult the appropriate appendix to find out how best to use it with SPSS/PC+. If your computer has an extended or expanded memory board and RAM-disk software, *Using SPSS/PC+ with RAM Disks* tells you how to use this capability to best advantage in SPSS/PC+. *Files Created by Other Software* gives general suggestions for anyone wanting to use data or command files created by a text editor or other software.

Running SPSS/PC+

OVERVIEW SPSS/PC+ is a system that accesses and analyzes data. The way you communicate with SPSS/PC+ is through the SPSS/PC+ command language. Commands are simply English-like statements. They can be simple, like

```
LIST.
```

They can contain additional specifications, such as

```
LIST CASES FROM 1 TO 100 BY 5.
```

Or commands can contain complex combinations of subcommands, such as

```
FREQUENCIES VARIABLES = SEX JOBCAT /BARCHART /STATISTICS ALL.
```

The command language is easy to understand, and SPSS/PC+ gives you a lot of help in both learning and using it.

You use commands to do three things, usually in the following order:

1 Convert data into a form that can be used by the computer and bring the data into SPSS/PC+. Your data may exist on paper, or they may already exist in some electronic form used by other software (including SPSS, the mainframe version of SPSS/PC+). *Data definition* commands like DATA LIST, TRANSLATE, and GET (among others) tell SPSS/PC+ where and how to read data.

2 Modify data. Once the data are in SPSS/PC+, you might decide, for example, to convert rainfall measured in centimeters to rainfall measured in inches, for which you could use a *data manipulation* command such as

```
COMPUTE RAINFALL = RAINFALL/2.54.
```

3 Process data. When your data are in the form you want, *procedure* commands like FREQUENCIES, MEANS, and REGRESSION tell SPSS/PC+ to do something with your data, such as perform a statistical analysis, produce a report, listing, or plot, sort your cases into a different order, or save your data to a file.

During the course of an SPSS/PC+ session you can repeat any of the three steps above, to use different data, arrange the data differently, or run different analyses on them.

For example, a typical series of commands might resemble the following:

```
GET FILE = 'WEATHER.SYS'.
COMPUTE RAINFALL = RAINFALL/2.54.
MEANS RAINFALL BY MONTH REGION.
```

• The GET FILE command retrieves a *system file* named WEATHER.SYS. (A system file is a special type of SPSS/PC+ file that contains both data and information describing the data.)

• The COMPUTE command converts rainfall in centimeters to rainfall in inches.

• The MEANS command computes the average rainfall for each month and for each region.

SPSS/PC+ can execute these commands one at a time or as a group. The next sections tell you about ways to enter commands and have SPSS/PC+ execute them.

In addition to procedure and data definition and manipulation commands, SPSS/PC+ has *operation* commands such as DISPLAY and SET that you use to find out about and control the SPSS/PC+ environment. For example, notice in the example above that each command must end with a period. If you want to use a different symbol to indicate your commands are complete, you can do so using the SET command.

Table 1 summarizes the commands used in SPSS/PC+.

Table 1   SPSS/PC+ command summary

Function	Commands
Operation commands	
Provide assistance	SHOW, DISPLAY
Specify options for operations and output	SET
Submit SPSS/PC+ commands from a file	INCLUDE
Edit a file	REVIEW
Access DOS or other facilities	DOS, EXECUTE
Data definition and manipulation commands	
Read data	DATA LIST, BEGIN DATA, END DATA, IMPORT GET, TRANSLATE
Transform data	RECODE, COMPUTE, IF, COUNT
Define missing data	MISSING VALUE
Select and weight cases	SELECT IF, PROCESS IF, N, SAMPLE, WEIGHT
Provide labels and formats	TITLE, SUBTITLE, *, VARIABLE LABELS, VALUE LABELS, FORMAT
Procedure commands	
Data display	LIST, PLOT, REPORT, TABLES*
Descriptive statistics	DESCRIPTIVES, FREQUENCIES
Categorical statistics	CROSSTABS, HILOGLINEAR*
Group comparisons	T-TEST, ONEWAY, MEANS, ANOVA
Multivariate statistics	CORRELATION, REGRESSION, CLUSTER*, QUICK CLUSTER*, FACTOR*, DSCRIMINANT*, MANOVA*, RELIABILITY*
Nonparametric statistics	NPAR TESTS
Time series analysis*	ACF, AREG, ARIMA, CASEPLOT, CCF, CURVEFIT, EXSMOOTH, FIT, NPPLOT, PACF, RMV, SPECTRA
Utilities	WRITE, AGGREGATE, SORT CASES, JOIN, EXPORT, SAVE
Graphics	GRAPH*, MAP*, FASTGRAF*

*Available only in SPSS/PC+ options.

Entering Commands into SPSS/PC+

There are three ways to enter commands into SPSS/PC+: at the command prompt, from the integrated text editor REVIEW, or using the Menu and Help system.

- The SPSS/PC+ command prompt. With this method, the system prompts you to enter a command; you enter it; the system evaluates and executes it. This method does not give you a clue as to which command to enter; nor does it provide a great deal of opportunity to edit a command or to change your mind once you've entered it. However, if you already know exactly which commands you want to use, you may prefer to work at the command prompt.

- The REVIEW text editor. This method lets you type your commands into a file instead of at a prompt and then submit them for execution. This method gives you unlimited opportunity to edit and revise the commands before execution. Once you have a set of commands, making minor changes in them to achieve a different analysis can be the fastest way to work.

- The Menu and Help system. REVIEW includes a *Menu and Help system* that allows you to select commands from menus and paste them into the text editor. Along with the menus are descriptions of each command to help you figure out which one to select. The advantage of using the menus is that you don't have to remember the command names or their specifications.

When you first enter SPSS/PC+, you will be in the Menu and Help system.

Getting into SPSS/PC+

Before you can run SPSS/PC+ for the first time, you have to install it, using the installation instructions that accompany the system. Next, you should change your current directory to the one from which you want to execute SPSS/PC+ and in which you want to keep the data and other files used by the system. You may also want to change other DOS environmental parameters. For information about DOS and directories, see *Important DOS Concepts* at the end of Part A, or see your DOS manual.

Once the preliminaries are done, you enter SPSS/PC+ by typing

SPSSPC

at the DOS prompt, and pressing ⏎. This displays the SPSS/PC+ logo screen. Usually, the system then takes you straight into the Menu and Help system. You can change the starting environment by changing the SET commands in your profile. (See the SET command in Part C, and "The SPSSPROF.INI File" in the next chapter, *REVIEW: The SPSS/PC+ Editor.)*

WORKING WITH MENUS

The menu system contains all SPSS/PC+ commands and their keywords. A help system describing the function of commands is built in. You use the Menu and Help system together with the text editor REVIEW to produce your commands.

The menus do not control SPSS/PC+ directly. When you select a command (or a piece of a command) from a menu, it is simply pasted into REVIEW's scratch pad (the scratch pad is discussed below). To execute the commands, you must tell SPSS/PC+ to do so. You can do this whenever you like—you can build a lengthy set of commands and execute them all at once, or you can run them one at a time.

You can take over from the Menu and Help system at any point and use REVIEW to type in commands yourself or to modify commands that you have pasted in. From REVIEW, you can easily recall the Menu and Help system. It appears with information showing and explaining the appropriate options for the command you were typing in REVIEW.

When you enter SPSS/PC+, you are automatically in the Menu and Help system. Your screen looks like the following:

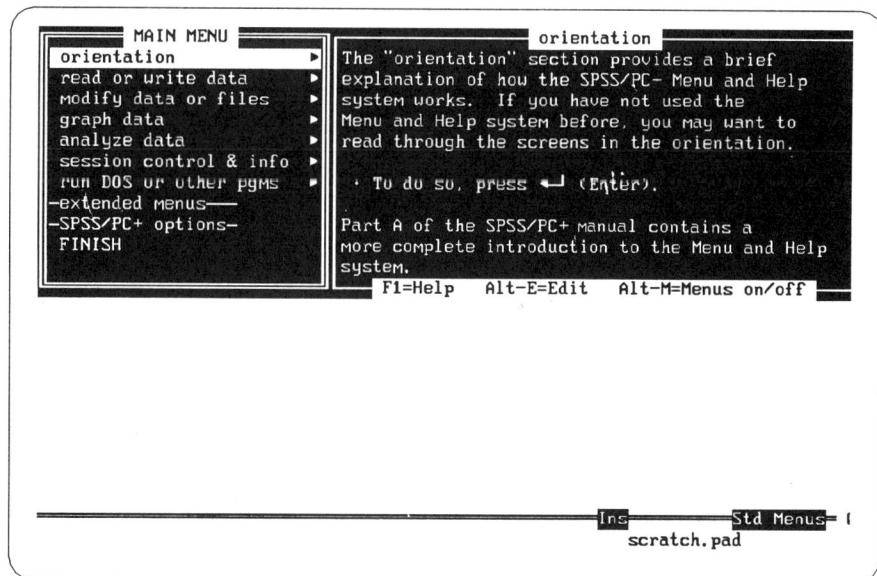

```
╔═══ MAIN MENU ═══╗        ╔════════ orientation ═══╗
║ orientation           ▶║ The "orientation" section provides a brief
║ read or write data    ▶║ explanation of how the SPSS/PC- Menu and Help
║ modify data or files  ▶║ system works. If you have not used the
║ graph data            ▶║ Menu and Help system before, you may want to
║ analyze data          ▶║ read through the screens in the orientation.
║ session control & info▶║
║ run DOS or other pgms ▶║ · To do so, press ◄┘ (Enter).
║ -extended menus-       ║
║ -SPSS/PC+ options-     ║ Part A of the SPSS/PC+ manual contains a
║ FINISH                 ║ more complete introduction to the Menu and Help
║                        ║ system.
                          ╚═══════════════════════════╝
                            F1=Help   Alt-E=Edit   Alt-M=Menus on/off

                                                    ╠Ins═══════╣Std Menus╣ (
                                               scratch.pad
```

Important things to notice are:

- The bottom half of the screen is the *scratch pad,* where REVIEW works as a text editor.
- The top left part of the screen shows a *menu,* in this case the Main Menu, which is the "top" level of the Menu and Help system. The arrowhead characters to the right of each item on the menu indicate that the item has a lower-level menu that you can access to see more detail.
- The top right part of the screen shows a *Help window.* The Help window always describes the highlighted menu item.

When you first enter the system, the top half of the screen—that is, the Menu and Help system—is active.

To see the commands you need to get around in REVIEW and the Menu and Help system, press F1. A "mini-menu" appears at the bottom of the screen. The information you want is **Review help.** Since this item is highlighted, you can select it simply by pressing ⏎. You can also make the selection by pressing the letter that is capitalized for that item, R, instead of ⏎. The following screen will be displayed:

```
                    Guide to Review Function Keys
 Information    F1   Review Help and Menus, Variable and File Lists, Glossary
 Windows        F2   Switch, Change Size, Zoom
 Input Files    F3   Insert File, Edit Different File
 Lines          F4   Insert, Delete, Undelete
 Find&Replace   F5   Find Text, Replace Text
 Go To          F6   Area, Output Page, Line in Error, After Last Line Executed
 Define Area    F7   Mark/Unmark Lines, Rectangle, or Command
 Area Actions   F8   Copy, Move, Delete, Round Numbers, Copy Glossary Entry
 Output File    F9   Write Area or File, Delete File
 Run            F10  Run Commands from Cursor or Marked Area, Exit to Prompt

                       Guide to Menu Commands
 ENTER (⏎)          Paste Selection & Move Down One Level in Menu
 TAB or →           Temporarily Paste Selection & Move Down One Level
 ESC or ←           Remove Last Temporary Paste & Move Up One Level
 Alt-ESC            Jump to Main Menu (also Ctrl-ESC)
 Alt-K              Kill All Temporary Pastes
 Alt-T              Get Typing Window
 Alt-E              Switch to Edit Mode
 Alt-M              Remove Menus
 Alt-V              Get Variables Window
 Alt-C              Run from Cursor
                                                                        01
      Enter command or press F1 for more help or Escape to continue
```

The commands you need to get around the Menu and Help system are shown at the bottom of the screen. As you can see, most of these commands use the Alt key, which you hold down while you press the corresponding command key:

- Alt M (*M* for *M*enu) clears away the Menu and Help system (leaving you in the REVIEW environment) or brings it back if it is not on the screen.
- Alt E allows you to edit the scratch pad but leaves the menus on screen, "frozen," until you press Alt E again (or Esc) to return to the Menu system.

You can also recall the menu system at any time by pressing F1 followed by M.

Exploring the Menus

The easiest way to explore the Menu and Help system is with the cursor arrows on your keyboard.

- ↑ and ↓ move the highlighting up and down the menu. As each menu item is highlighted, the Help window describes what that item does, or how to use it.

- If a menu is too long to fit, up or down arrowheads at the right edge of the menu indicate the presence of items offscreen. As you move the highlighting up and down, the menu scrolls automatically to let you highlight these items. You can also use (PgUp) and (PgDn) to scroll the menus.
- (Home) and (End) take you to, respectively, the first and last items on the menu.
- (→) moves you "deeper" into the menus. For example, if the item **orientation** is highlighted when you press (→), the Orientation menu appears. You know that there is an Orientation menu because of the arrowhead beside **orientation** back on the Main Menu.
- (←) brings you back out of the menus, one level at a time, until you reach the Main Menu.
- If the text in the Help window is too long to fit on the screen, up or down arrowheads at the right edge of the Help window indicate the presence of offscreen text. Hold down the (Alt) key and use (↑), (↓), (PgUp), (PgDn), (Home), or (End) to scroll the text in the Help window (make sure that the (NumLck) key is not active).

Pasting Menu Selections

To use the menu system in SPSS/PC+, you need to do more than just browse around and read it. You use the menus by pasting commands, keywords, variable names, and filenames into REVIEW's scratch pad. The difference between exploring the menus with the cursor arrows, as discussed above, and pasting commands, is simple:

- To *explore* a menu selection without affecting the scratch pad, press (→). The only thing that happens is you move to the lower-level menu associated with the current selection. (The menu selection is held for you, in case you decide to accept it after all.)
- To accept a menu selection and also (if it is part of a command that you are building) to *paste* it into the scratch pad, press (←). The selection appears in the scratch pad, and again you move to the lower-level menu associated with the current selection, if there is one.

Menu selections that are in upper case are either commands or parts of commands. They may be preceded on the menu by either a slash (/) or an exclamation point (!). The slash is a separator that SPSS/PC+ expects between different *subcommands* (parts of commands). The exclamation point indicates a selection that is required: SPSS/PC+ cannot execute the command without that specification.

- You can always paste an uppercase menu selection into the scratch pad by pressing (←).
- Some other selections (such as the symbols +, −, *, and /) will also paste if you select them with (←).
- Selections in lower case do not paste into the Edit window, regardless of whether you use (→) or (←) to select them. You do move to the lower-level menu if there is one.
- When you paste a selection that needs to be "filled in," such as a pair of parentheses ( ) or apostrophes ' ', REVIEW automatically asks you to type the contents, unless selections on a lower-level menu constitute the contents.

You can move to the scratch pad in the bottom half of the screen at any point by simply pressing (Alt) (E). From there, you can

- Edit the commands you've pasted.
- Run them. We'll see below how you pass commands to SPSS/PC+ for execution.
- Save them into a file on disk, to use later. See the next chapter, *REVIEW: The SPSS/PC+ Editor,* for an explanation of saving commands.

To get back to the Menu and Help system, press (Esc).

Pasting after Exploring   If you explore a menu selection by pressing ⟶ and then decide to accept and paste a selection on a lower-level menu, REVIEW goes back to fill in the intermediate step(s) before pasting the lower-level selection.

For example,

- You select the FREQUENCIES command and the /VARIABLES subcommand, and choose the variables for which you want frequency tables. All this is pasted into the scratch pad.

- You aren't sure whether you want to change the default format, so you explore /FORMAT by pressing ⟶. The FORMAT subcommand is not pasted into the scratch pad, but it is moved into a holding area or *buffer* at the bottom of the screen, in case it is needed later:

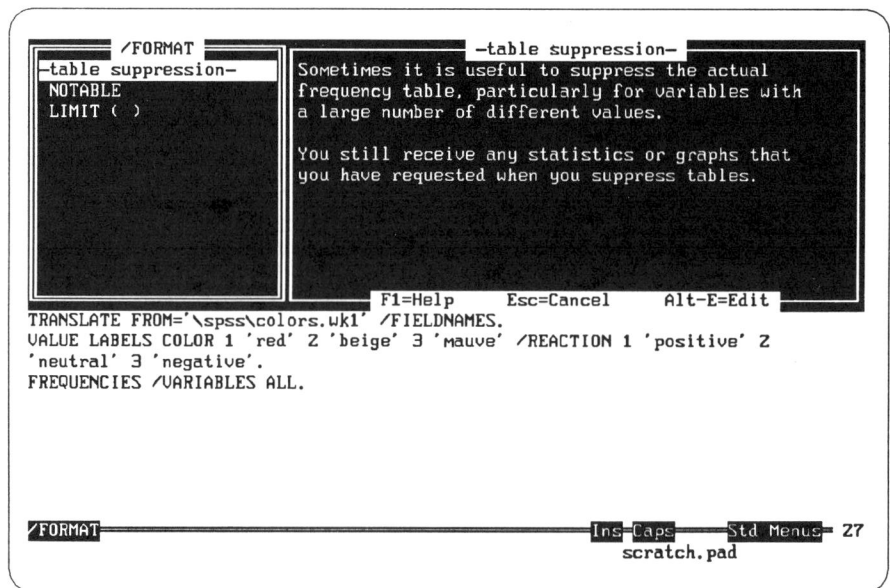

```
╔═ /FORMAT ══════════════╗╔═══════ -table suppression- ══════════╗
║-table suppression-     ║║Sometimes it is useful to suppress the actual
║ NOTABLE                ║║frequency table, particularly for variables with
║ LIMIT ( )              ║║a large number of different values.
║                        ║║
║                        ║║You still receive any statistics or graphs that
║                        ║║you have requested when you suppress tables.
║                        ║║
║                        ║║
║                        ║║
║                        ║║  F1=Help      Esc=Cancel      Alt-E=Edit ║
╚════════════════════════╝╚═════════════════════════════════════════╝
TRANSLATE FROM='\spss\colors.wk1' /FIELDNAMES.
VALUE LABELS COLOR 1 'red' 2 'beige' 3 'mauve' /REACTION 1 'positive' 2
'neutral' 3 'negative'.
FREQUENCIES /VARIABLES ALL.




═/FORMAT═══════════════════════════════════════════Ins═Caps═══════Std Menus═ 27
                                                                scratch.pad
```

- After reading the Help windows for the various FORMAT specifications, you decide that you don't need any of them, so you "back out" by pressing ⟵ (or (Esc), if you prefer). The buffer area and /FORMAT disappear from the bottom of the screen, and the FREQUENCIES menu reappears.

- You move the cursor to /STATISTICS and explore it by pressing ⟶. The STATISTICS menu appears, and /STATISTICS shows up in the buffer. After looking through the various choices on the STATISTICS menu, you decide that you want them all—so you highlight ALL and press ⟵⟞.

- REVIEW first pastes the subcommand /STATISTICS from the buffer, and *then* the keyword ALL that you explicitly pasted.

In this example, REVIEW held the specifications that you explored (/FORMAT and /STATISTICS) in case you decided that you needed them. When you backed out of the /FORMATS menu, it discarded that specification. When you chose a statistics keyword, it filled in /STATISTICS so SPSS/PC+ would know that ALL referred to the STATISTICS subcommand.

- You can clear this holding buffer at any time by pressing (Alt) (K).

- If you don't remember (Alt) (K) (or any other REVIEW command), press (F1), use the cursor arrows to highlight **Review help,** and press ⟵⟞.

Editing Pasted Commands   It's easy to add to or modify the commands you paste into the REVIEW scratch pad.

- Press (Alt) (E) to jump to the scratch pad, or (Alt) (M) to clear the menus completely.
- Then fix the commands. Usually the (Ins) and (Del) keys will be all you need. See the next chapter, *REVIEW: The SPSS/PC+ Editor,* for a discussion of more advanced editing functions.

To return to the menus, press (Alt) (E) again, or, if you cleared the menus completely, press (Alt) (M) again. (You can also press (F1), highlight **Menus** with the cursor arrows, and press (↵).) The Menu and Help window for the specific command or subcommand you're working on in the scratch pad will be displayed. You can paste items from the menu, or you can press (Alt) (E) to continue editing with the Help window to guide you.

Extended Menus   The standard menus do not show all of the keywords you can use to build SPSS/PC+ commands. Seldom-used keywords and options are omitted to reduce the complexity of the menus. To switch to the extended menus that show all available specifications, press (Alt) (X). The message at the right-hand side of the bottom of the screen then changes from **Std Menus** to **Ext Menus.**

Once you are familiar with the system, you may want to place the command

SET MENUS EXTENDED.

in your automatic profile SPSSPROF.INI (see the section on SPSSPROF.INI in the next chapter, *REVIEW: The SPSS/PC+ Editor).* This will cause extended windows to be displayed automatically.

Executing Commands   When you have built a command (or several commands), you can submit those lines to SPSS/PC+ for execution.

1   If you haven't done so already, press (Alt) (E) to move to the REVIEW scratch pad (or (Alt) (M) to clear away the menu system entirely).
2   Put the cursor on the first command, if it's not there already. (You don't have to do these first two steps if you want to execute a single command and the cursor is already on that command in the scratch pad.)
3   Press (F10). On the mini-menu that appears at the bottom of the screen, **run from Cursor** is highlighted, so just press (↵). This tells SPSS/PC+ to run all the commands starting at the one containing the cursor and below.

The screen clears, and your commands appear on the screen one at a time as they are executed. The word **MORE** appears in the corner of the screen when SPSS/PC+ is about to display something else and wants to make sure that you've had time to read what's already there. Press the space bar to continue. After all of the commands and their results have displayed, the system returns you to REVIEW and the Menu and Help system. (You can see the results again whenever you like in the *listing file,* described below.)

Quitting   The FINISH command is at the bottom of the Main Menu. It takes you out of both REVIEW and SPSS/PC+, back to DOS. You can paste and execute it just like any other command.

To leave the Menu and Help system and REVIEW but remain in SPSS/PC+, press (F10) and use the cursor arrows to highlight **Exit to prompt.** Press (↵). (Alternatively, you can just press (F10) followed by (E)). This takes you to the SPSS/PC+ command prompt (see "Working from the Command Prompt," below).

WORKING IN REVIEW

You can also use REVIEW without the menu system. With this method, you type in your commands directly instead of pasting them in from the menus.

To clear away the Menu and Help system after you enter SPSS/PC+, press (Alt) (M). Alternatively, you can go straight to the REVIEW scratch pad when you enter SPSS/PC+ by putting the command

```
SET AUTOMENU OFF
```

in your automatic profile SPSSPROF.INI.

There are several advantages to using REVIEW alone:

- Some commands, particularly DATA LIST and the data transformation commands, are much quicker to type than to select in pieces from the menus.
- When you are repeating or modifying commands, REVIEW gives you the best possible raw material to work with: your previous commands, and their results. It does this through three files: the scratch pad, the listing file, and the log file.

The Scratch Pad

By default, REVIEW's bottom window contains the *scratch pad,* a place where you can play with commands until you're ready to run them. When you leave REVIEW to run commands, this file is saved for you, so that when you return to REVIEW (assuming you didn't leave SPSS/PC+), all your commands are still there. If you want to run them again, perhaps with some alterations to try a different approach or correct errors, they're easy to edit (see the next chapter, *REVIEW: The SPSS/PC+ Editor*).

The Listing File

The *listing file* contains a copy of all the output produced by your commands. The main use for the listing file is to review your work or to edit the output. When the session is over, you can print the listing file from DOS (it's named SPSS.LIS by default).

The listing file is displayed in REVIEW's upper window, which is initially covered by the Menu and Help system. When you clear the menus by pressing (Alt) (M), you see the listing file in the top half of the screen. (If you haven't yet executed any commands, you won't have any output, so the top half of the screen will be blank.)

If you want to see the Menu and Help system while using the listing file, you can call the menus by pressing (F1), using the cursor arrows to highlight **Menus,** and pressing (⏎) (or just by pressing (F1) followed by (M)). The menus appear in the bottom half of your screen:

Value Label	Value	Frequency	Percent	Valid Percent	Cum Percent
positive	1	5	27.8	27.8	27.8
neutral	2	8	44.4	44.4	72.2
negative	3	5	27.8	27.8	100.0
TOTAL		18	100.0	100.0	

Valid Cases   18   Missing Cases   0

```
Page   5                          SPSS/PC+                              10/9/87
╔══ MAIN MENU ══╗                              ╔═══ orientation ═══╗
║ orientation       ►║           The "orientation" section provides a brief
║ read or write data  ►║         explanation of how the SPSS/PC+ Menu and Help
║ modify data or files ►║        system works.  If you have not used the
║ graph data          ►║         Menu and Help system before, you may want to
║ analyze data        ►║         read through the screens in the orientation.
║ session control & info ►║
║ run DOS or other pgms  ►║        · To do so, press ⏎ (Enter).
║─extended menus──║
║─SPSS/PC+ options─║             Part A of the SPSS/PC+ manual contains a
                                 F1=Help   Alt-E=Edit   Alt-M=Menus on/off
                                              Ins        Std Menus
                                        spss.lis
```

When you switch back to editing the bottom window, the Menu and Help system reappears in the top window.

While you're in SPSS/PC+, it's often helpful to examine your commands vs. the output they produce by getting the scratch pad or the log file (described below) in the bottom window and the listing file in the top window. You can scroll whichever window is active (whichever one contains the cursor). To switch the cursor from one window to the other, press (F2) and then press (↵) to select the highlighted item **Switch windows** from the mini-menu at the bottom of the screen.

The Log File

The log file contains a copy of all the commands that SPSS/PC+ has executed during your current session, in the order in which they were submitted. From within REVIEW, it's easy to access the log file:

1. Press (F3), and then press (↵) to select the highlighted item **Edit different file** from the mini-menu that appears at the bottom of the screen (or just press (F3) followed by (E)).

2. Type the name of the file to edit, SPSS.LOG, in the box at the bottom of the screen, and press (↵).

The log file is a useful record of what you've already done since, in addition to the commands you've run, it also contains

- Error messages about commands that couldn't be executed.
- Notes that direct you to the location of output in the listing file.

Note that the log file contains a record of all the commands you submit in the session. For example, if you run a set of commands twice, the second time with modifications, the log file will contain both sets. The scratch pad, however, will only contain the modified set.

Working Faster

The following features can help you work in REVIEW more quickly:

- To select an item from a mini-menu, you can press the letter capitalized for that item, instead of using the cursor arrows to highlight the item and pressing (↵). For example, to delete a line, you can just press (D) after pressing (F4). For commonly used selections, if you know the letter for item you want, you can bypass the mini-menu altogether by simply holding down the (Alt) key while pressing the letter. For example, to insert a line, you can just press (Alt)(I) rather than pressing (F4) and then selecting **Insert after.** For the functions for which this shortcut is available, see REVIEW in Part C. Or, if you know that the selection you want is the highlighted one, you can just press the function key followed by (↵).
- When you press (F1) and select **Menus,** REVIEW displays the menu for the command under the cursor, rather than the Main Menu.
- When the Menu and Help system is active, you can use incremental search to move the cursor to a menu item—just type in the first letter or letters of the item you want to select to make the cursor jump to that item.
- When you are in the scratch pad, you can quickly place the cursor at specified locations by pressing (F6) and selecting the location you want— **Error line,** or **after executed Line.** (Note: For **Error line** to be displayed, you must set RUNREVIEW to AUTO; see SET in Part C.)
- When you are in the listing file, you can quickly move to the output page you want by pressing (F6), selecting **Output page** from the mini-menu, and entering the number of the page you want.

Special Features

REVIEW has several special features that make your work easier. These features are available even when you aren't using the Menu and Help system:

- To see lists of files, press (F1), move the cursor arrows to highlight **File list,** press (↵), and then either specify particular types of files or press (↵) again to see all files in your current directory. SPSS/PC+ then displays a list of the files you requested. In the list, one of the files is highlighted; more detailed information about this file appears in the narrow box below the list. If you press ⏎, the name will be pasted into the scratch pad. Or you can use the cursor arrows to highlight another file.

• After you have brought data into your computer with a command like DATA LIST or GET, you can see a list of the variables in the active file by pressing F1, highlighting **Var list,** and pressing ⏎. SPSS/PC+ then displays a list of the currently defined variables. In the list, one of the variables is highlighted; more detailed information about this variable appears in the narrow box below the list. If you press ⏎ again, the variable name will be pasted into the scratch pad. You can also highlight a group of variables by pressing F7 at the first variable and moving the cursor arrows over the other variables you want. To paste the highlighted group into the edit window, press ⏎.

• SPSS/PC+ contains an online glossary that defines the terms used in commands and their output. To look up a term in the glossary, press F1, use the cursor arrows to highlight **Glossary,** and press ⏎. The system displays a box containing the term currently under the cursor. To look up this term, just press ⏎; to look up a different term, type it in the box and then press ⏎. The system then displays the definition you requested. For more information about the Glossary, see "Getting Help," below.

Quitting

To leave REVIEW, press F10, use the cursor arrows to highlight **Exit to prompt,** and press ⏎. This takes you to the SPSS/PC+ prompt. To leave SPSS/PC+, at the prompt type

FINISH

and press ⏎. You will be returned to DOS.

WORKING FROM THE COMMAND PROMPT

If you like the speed of working directly with commands and you know the command you want to use, you can ignore both REVIEW and the Menu and Help system altogether and work from the SPSS/PC+ command prompt. To go to the command prompt as soon as you enter SPSS/PC+, change the SET RUNREVIEW command in the profile SPSSPROF.INI to MANUAL. To reach the command prompt when you are already in REVIEW in SPSS/PC+, press F10, use the cursor arrows to highlight **Exit to prompt,** and press ⏎.

The command prompt works like this:

• SPSS/PC+ prompts for a command.
• You enter a command.
• SPSS/PC+ responds to your command.
• SPSS/PC+ prompts for another command.

This process continues until you end your SPSS/PC+ session.

The SPSS/PC+ Command Prompt and Terminator

SPSS/PC+ tells you it is ready for a command by displaying a command prompt. The default command prompt is **SPSS/PC:**. Whenever SPSS/PC+ displays the prompt, you can begin entering a command on that line.

You must end every command with a command terminator to tell SPSS/PC+ that the command is complete. The default command terminator is a period (.). *Do not type any other characters after the command terminator.* To submit the command to SPSS/PC+, just press ⏎.

If a command is too long to fit on one line, type whatever fits on the line and press ⏎. As long as you do not include a command terminator, SPSS/PC+ will respond with a continuation prompt. This signals you to continue the command on that line. The default continuation prompt is seven spaces followed by a colon.

Use as many lines as each command requires, pressing ⏎ to submit each line of the command. SPSS/PC+ gives continuation prompts until you enter the command terminator. When the command specifications are complete, enter the terminator and press ⏎. SPSS/PC+ responds with the output for the command, if any, and prompts for another command.

If you enter a complete command and forget to include the command terminator, simply enter the terminator in response to the continuation prompt. You can also terminate the command by simply pressing ⏎ again—that is, entering a completely empty line. (Failing to end a command with a period, or whatever character you have specified as the command terminator, is a common oversight when just beginning with SPSS/PC+. Be alert for a continuation prompt when you think you have finished entering a command. Enter a period, or an empty line, to complete the command.)

You can use the SET command to change the default prompts and terminator (see SET in Part C).

SPSS/PC+ Error Detection

As you enter each command, SPSS/PC+ checks it for proper syntax. If you misspell or improperly specify a command or subcommand, SPSS/PC+ immediately displays an error message. It also checks to make sure that you do not use variables that are not defined.

For example, the VARIABLE LABELS command below is mistyped as **vriable labels**. SPSS/PC+ displays an appropriate error message and prompts for a new command.

```
                                                            █ MORE █




DATA LIST FILE 'phys1.dat'/phys 1-3 studied 5 avstay 7-10(1) avstay2 12-15(1).
URIABLE LABELS PHYS'' /STUDIED 'Total Patients Studied' /AVSTAY 'Average Stay'

ERROR       1, Text: URIABLE LABELS
INVALID COMMAND—Check spelling.  If it is intended as a continuation of a
previous line, the terminator must not be specified on the previous line.
If a DATA LIST is in error, in-line data can also cause this error.
This command not executed.
```

Since you are allowed to abbreviate SPSS/PC+ keywords to their first three characters, you will not get an error message if you misspell a keyword after the first three characters.

Correcting Errors

Several special keys on the keyboard help you correct simple errors you make in entering commands. If you have made an error on the line you are typing, just backspace over the incorrect characters and type the rest of the line correctly before you press the enter key.

If you want to cancel an entire line, press the escape key. SPSS/PC+ then displays a backslash (\) at the end of the line and places the cursor on the next line. You can then retype the line correctly and continue with your session by pressing ⏎. After you enter the corrected line, SPSS/PC+ prompts you for the next command. If you were in the middle of entering a multi-line command, you would retype only the line that you canceled with the escape key and then continue typing the command.

For information on using function keys to edit input lines, look up "Editing Keys" in the index of your DOS manual. On the IBM and most compatible machines, the function keys (F1), (F2), and (F3) work at the SPSS/PC+ command prompt as described in the DOS manual.

Running Commands   As described at the beginning of this chapter, there are three basic types of SPSS/PC+ commands:

- Operation commands.
- Data definition and manipulation commands.
- Procedure commands.

SPSS/PC+ executes an operation command as soon as you enter it. As you enter a data definition or manipulation command, SPSS/PC+ checks that it follows the language rules for the command. However, SPSS/PC+ does not actually execute any data definition commands until you enter a *procedure* command, which reads the data.

When you enter a procedure command, SPSS/PC+ first executes all preceding data definition and manipulation commands. These commands construct the active data file of your cases. The active file contains the data you tell SPSS/PC+ to read, the results of any transformations you request, and a dictionary of information you have provided about each variable (names, labels, missing values, and so forth), all in a format that the computer can understand.

The SPSS/PC+ system is divided into several interlinked modules, each of which contain a small number of procedures. When you enter a procedure command, SPSS/PC+ checks whether that procedure is part of the current module. If not, SPSS/PC+ displays the message **MODULE SWAP** in the status area. Then it automatically loads the module containing the procedure. This can take several seconds.

As SPSS/PC+ processes cases, it displays a case counter in the status area in the upper right-hand corner of the screen, as shown in the following:

```
                                                        CASE      552




VARIABLE LABELS PHYS'' /STUDIED 'Total Patients Studied' /AVSTAY 'Average Stay'
/AVSTAYZ 'Average Stay for Matching Patients'.
CROSSTABS /TABLES PHYS BY AVSTAY.


***** Given WORKSPACE allows for  5554 Cells with
      2 Dimensions for CROSSTAB problem *****
```

When the procedure is complete, SPSS/PC+ displays the message **MORE** in the status area. Press any key to display the procedure results.

You can specify different types of analyses for the same active file, and you can modify the active file. For example, you can use a CROSSTABS command after a FREQUENCIES command to explore the same variables with different analyses. Or you might follow a FREQUENCIES command with a RECODE command and another FREQUENCIES command to compare the results of the same analysis on a recoded variable.

Quitting

To exit from SPSS/PC+, at the command prompt simply type

`FINISH`

and press ⏎. This returns you to the DOS prompt.

GETTING HELP

SPSS/PC+ provides two kinds of online assistance: a contextual help system, and an online glossary.

The Help System

Contextual help for building commands is supplied by the Menu and Help system. Any time you activate the menus, REVIEW attempts to identify the command on which the cursor is located and to display the appropriate menu. If you are typing commands into REVIEW and your memory fails you, activate the menus to see what your options are.

The Online Glossary

SPSS/PC+ contains an online glossary to help you understand the terms used in commands and in their output.

To use the glossary, you must first be in a file in REVIEW (not in the Menu and Help system).

1 Place the cursor under the term you want to look up. (To look up a command or keyword from the Menu system, first paste it into the scratch pad.)
2 Press F1, use the cursor arrows to highlight **Glossary** on the mini-menu, and press ⏎. The system then displays a search string box at the bottom of the screen, filled in with the word that's under the cursor.
3 If the displayed word isn't the one you want to look up, type the desired word over the one that appears in the box. Otherwise, just press ⏎.

If the word is in the glossary, the system then displays its definition. If the word isn't in the glossary, the system displays the closest alphabetic match.

• The bottom line of the display shows the terms that precede and follow the displayed one in the glossary. Press Ctrl PgUp or Ctrl PgDn to display these definitions.
• If you don't understand a word used in the definition, you can *paste* the whole definition into the editing window, put the cursor on the problem word, and ask for *its* definition. F8 copies the definition into the active editing window. The definition appears in the window as a marked area, so that you can easily copy or move it to another place.
• You can also paste the definition into the listing file to annotate your output for later reference. (Remember to save the listing file if you make editing changes like this.)

MANAGING FILES

SPSS/PC+ writes six types of files: the scratch pad, listing files, log files, system files, portable files, and results from procedures.

• The *scratch pad* contains the commands you type or paste into it. Its name is SCRATCH.PAD. This file is saved automatically whenever you leave REVIEW, and when you leave SPSS/PC+.
• The *listing file* contains your display output. By default, this output is sent to the screen and to the SPSS.LIS file on disk. You can specify a different disk file. You can also have this output sent to the printer.

- The *log file* contains a log of the commands executed by SPSS/PC+, together with messages about commands that caused errors, and about the location of command output in the listing file. The default log file is SPSS.LOG.
- A *system file* saves data and a data dictionary for use in subsequent SPSS/PC+ sessions, after you use the SAVE command. The default system file, when you use the SAVE command without specifying another filename, is SPSS.SYS.
- The *portable file* is used to transport data and a data dictionary across machines, when you use the EXPORT command. There is no default portable file.
- The *results file* includes results (matrix materials, new data, etc.) from specific commands: WRITE, CORRELATION, CLUSTER, QUICK CLUSTER, FACTOR, REGRESSION, ONEWAY, DSCRIMINANT, and MANOVA. The default results file is SPSS.PRC.

At the beginning of each session, the default files SCRATCH.PAD, SPSS.LIS, and SPSS.LOG are reinitialized. This means that the scratch pad, listing, and log files from any previous session are lost unless they were directed to a file other than the default (see Command Reference: SET) or unless they have been renamed using the DOS *RENAME* command (see "DOS Commands" in your DOS manual). The default system file SPSS.SYS and results file SPSS.PRC are not automatically reinitialized. However, each time you write to these files, any existing contents are *replaced* by the new material. To avoid this, you can specify a name explicitly on the SAVE command (OUTFILE='filename') or you can specify SET RESULTS= 'filename'. Alternatively, you can use the DOS *RENAME* command at the end of a session to give these files a new name that will not be overwritten.

SPSS/PC+ reads from and writes to the current directory unless you specify otherwise. To specify a file in a different directory, you must follow DOS conventions for directory names (see "Using Tree-Structured Directories" in your DOS manual). Portable files and the results file must always be in the current directory.

REVIEW: The SPSS/PC+Editor

REVIEW is the SPSS/PC+ text editor. As explained in the previous chapter, it is particularly designed to give you special help for entering SPSS/PC+ commands and for viewing their output, by means of the Menu and Help system, and the scratch pad, listing, and log files. But it is also very useful simply for standard editing tasks, such as creating, editing, or browsing through *any* text file. This section shows you how to perform standard text-editing tasks with REVIEW.

Note that not all REVIEW commands are described in this chapter. For a complete list, see REVIEW in Part C.

WORKING WITH A DATA FILE

A text file can serve a variety of purposes. One common use of a text file is to hold the data that you want to analyze with SPSS/PC+. For this session, we'll enter data from a fictitious survey of people's reactions to various colors for the SPSS/PC+ manual cover.

Getting into REVIEW

When you want to use REVIEW simply as a text editor, you can get into it directly from DOS, without using SPSS/PC+ at all. To do this, at the DOS prompt you simply type SPSSPC/RE followed by a space and the name of the file you want to edit. If you want to edit two files—one in the top window and one in the bottom—you simply enter both filenames; the file entered first appears in the top window. (You can also get into REVIEW from within SPSS/PC+ by typing the word REVIEW followed by the filename(s) *in apostrophes* at the SPSS/PC+ command prompt. This overrides the default scratch pad and listing files, and gives you the file(s) you named.)

For this example, at the DOS prompt type:

```
SPSSPC/RE COLORS.DAT
```

When you press ⏎, you see the SPSS/PC+ logo screen and then the REVIEW screen, with the cursor positioned at the top. (The screen is initially blank, since we are creating a new file.) Since we're only editing one file, REVIEW shows only one window, which takes up the whole screen.

Entering Data

The data we want to enter in this file consist simply of numbered codes representing colors and respondents' reactions to them. We'll put the color codes in the first column of each line, and the reaction codes in the third column of each line. Type the data shown below. Press ⏎ to start each new line. If you make mistakes, ignore them for now; we'll see in a minute how to make corrections.

```
1 1
1 1
1 2
1 2
1 3
1 3
2 2
2 2
2 2
2 2
2 2
3 1
3 1
3 1
3 3
3 3
3 3
```

Moving around the Screen

When you have entered the data (mistakes and all), you can experiment with moving the cursor around the screen. To do this, use the cursor-movement keys on the right side of your keyboard: (Home), (End), (↑), (↓), (←), and (→). These keys will operate correctly only when they are not locked into *numerical mode,* a mode that is indicated by the appearance of **Num** in the bottom-right corner of your screen. To get out of numerical mode, press (NumLck); the **Num** message then disappears from your screen.

As you move the cursor, notice that the column number in the lower-right corner of the screen changes to correspond to the cursor location. Notice also that the cursor will not move right of the last character in any line. If your file had lines of unequal length and you moved the cursor up or down, you would find that the cursor always tried to stay in the column in which it started—but if the line it was moving onto had fewer columns, it would move left to the last column in that line and then move back to the right when it reached a longer line.

The following keys allow quick cursor movement. (Since your file isn't very large at the moment, you won't be able to experiment with all of them now, but you'll certainly find them useful later.)

- (Tab) moves the cursor right to the next tab stop on the line. A tab stop occurs every eight characters. However, the cursor won't move to a tab stop that's beyond the last character in a line.
- (⇧) (Tab) moves the cursor left to the preceding tab stop on the line.
- (Ctrl) (→) moves the cursor to the end of the line.
- (Ctrl) (←) moves the cursor to the beginning of the line.
- (↵) moves the cursor to the start of the next line when you are in *overtype mode* (see "Insert Mode versus Overtype Mode," below).
- (PgDn) moves the cursor down one screen.
- (PgUp) moves the cursor up one screen.
- (Ctrl) (Home) moves the cursor to the top of the file.
- (Ctrl) (End) moves the cursor to the bottom of the file.

Making Changes

It's easy to make changes or corrections in your file using REVIEW. The following section shows you a variety of ways of doing this.

Deleting Characters and Joining Lines

To delete unwanted characters, you either put the cursor on the character and press the (Del) key, or put the cursor immediately to the right of the character and press the backspace key. Try this on anything you mistyped while entering the data. (If you didn't make any mistakes, type some characters at the end of the file.) You'll find that the character under or to the left of the cursor disappears and the rest of the text on the line moves over one space to fill in.

If you press (Del) when the cursor is on the space at the end of a line, the next line jumps up to join the line the cursor is on. Try this by putting the cursor at the end of the first line and pressing (Del). (We'll see below how to split these lines again.)

Insert Mode versus Overtype Mode

There are two modes of editing in REVIEW: insert mode and overtype mode. In *insert mode,* the text you type is inserted to the left of the current character, and the text to the right of the cursor moves over to make room for the new text. In *overtype mode,* the text you type replaces text in the current line.

When you are in insert mode, the message **Ins** displays in the lower-right corner of your screen. In overtype mode, the **Ins** message disappears. Press (Ins) to switch from one editing mode to the other.

It's easy to see how this works. Press (Home) to move to the top of the screen. Make sure you're in insert mode; then type

jjjj

The numeric codes that were already there move over to make room for the letters.

Now press (Ctrl) (←) to get back to the beginning of the line. Press (Ins) to get into overtype mode; then type

ssss

Because you're in overtype mode, the s's replace the j's.

Only one editing key behaves differently depending on the mode. In overtype mode, (←) moves the cursor to the beginning of the next line. In insert mode, (←) splits the line the cursor is currently on, at the cursor location. To try this, make sure you're still in overtype mode, and press (←); the cursor simply moves down to the next line. Now put the cursor under the **1** on the first line, and get into insert mode by pressing (Ins). This time when you press (←), the line splits, with the part that was to the right of the cursor moving down to become the next line. Use this same method to split the line joined above with the (Del) key, putting the second set of codes back on their own line.

While it is impossible to enter more than 80 characters on a line, you can create lines longer than 80 characters by joining two lines together. However, the only way to view the part of the line that extends past the 80th column is to split the line again. It is good practice to avoid such long lines. SPSS/PC+ does not read commands past the 80th column.

Editing Functions

You perform many editing functions in REVIEW by pressing a function key and then making a selection from a mini-menu that appears at the bottom of the screen. For example, when you press (F4) you get a small menu that says:

```
lines: Insert after    insert Before    Delete    Undelete
```

- The most likely choice is highlighted. Just press (←) to select and execute it. To select a different command on the menu, use the cursor arrows to move the highlighting, and then press (←).
- To avoid executing any of the commands on a mini-menu, press (Esc).
- Only relevant commands appear in the mini-menu.
- One letter (usually the first) of each menu item is capitalized. Instead of selecting an item by highlighting it and pressing (←), you can select it by just pressing its capitalized letter. For example, to insert a line after the one where the cursor is, press (I); to delete the current line, press (D), and so on.
- As alternatives to the mini-menus themselves, some commands let you use a combination of the (Alt) key and the selection key from the mini-menu. For example, to insert a line, you can hold down (Alt) and press (I), instead of pressing (F4) and selecting **Insert after** from the menu. See REVIEW in Part C for these commands and key combinations.
- If you are an experienced SPSS/PC+ user, you can still use all the old key combinations if you have learned them. For example, (Ctrl) (F4) deletes the current line without going through the mini-menu. Only the unmodified function keys call up the mini-menus.
- Function keys that perform editing functions (such as (F4)) are not available when the Menu and Help system is active. Press (Alt) (E) before using one of these function keys if you need to.

Put the cursor anywhere you like and try some editing functions. Note that if you accidentally delete a line you wanted to keep, REVIEW gives you a chance to get it back—by pressing (F4) and selecting **Undelete.** However, you can restore only the most recently deleted line. If you accidentally delete several lines, you can restore only the last one deleted.

Working with Areas

Some REVIEW editing functions operate on entire areas of lines or parts of lines. In this section we'll illustrate how to perform editing tasks—copying, moving, and deleting—on areas.

To mark an area for editing, you press (F7) at one boundary of the area, select the type of area you want to work with, and press (F7) again at the other boundary. It doesn't matter whether you start at the beginning or ending location.

For example, let's work with an area consisting of the last six lines of your data file.

1   Press (End) to move the cursor to the last line.
2   Press (F7) followed by (↵) to select the highlighted item, **Lines,** marking this line as one boundary of the area. The line begins to flash. On IBM PCs and some other computers, it will also be highlighted. The message

    ```
    Waiting for second line mark
    ```

    appears at the bottom of the screen.
3   Move the cursor up six lines to the first line that contains **3 1.**
4   Press (F7) to mark this as the first line of the area.

The message **Area marked - 6 lines** appears at the bottom of the screen. If your computer has highlighting, the entire six-line area will be highlighted. We can now invoke any of the REVIEW commands that operate on areas.

Copying Areas.   First, let's put a copy of the area at the end of the file. Move the cursor to the last line of the file by pressing (Ctrl) (End). To insert the copy of the area starting on the line following the cursor, press (F8) followed by (↵) to select **Copy.** The copy then appears. Since the copy took more lines than were left on the screen, the screen instantly scrolls to make room for them.

Notice that the original area is still marked. Another area command would affect this original area, not the copy.

Moving Areas.   Now let's move the original area to another location, at the top of the file. First move the cursor to the top of the file by pressing (Ctrl) (Home). Then move the block to the line following the cursor by pressing (F8), using the right cursor arrow to highlight **Move,** and pressing (↵). The original marked area moves from its location and reappears just below the first line of the file. The copy that we made is still at the end of the file.

Note that the original area is still marked, even after its move to the top of the file. We can therefore continue to work with this same area in its new location.

Deleting Areas.   This time, let's try deleting it: to do this, press (F8), highlight **Delete,** and press (↵). Notice that, while the original area at the top of the file disappeared, the copy that we made at the end of the file did not. The Delete Area command, like all the area commands, applies only to the currently marked area, not to copies.

Unmarking Areas.   When you're done working with an area, press (F7) a third time. When a marked area already exists, (F7) unmarks it. You can try this by marking any area of lines you like (press (F7) followed by (↵) at one line, and (F7) again at the other line); then press (F7) once again. The highlighting of the marked area disappears and the message **Area cancelled** appears at the bottom of the screen.

Rectangular Areas.   The area that you mark does not need to consist of complete lines. Instead, it can be a rectangle made up only of selected columns within lines. Marking a rectangle is similar to marking lines—you place the cursor at one corner of the rectangle, press (F7) and select **Rectangle.** Then place the cursor at the diagonally opposite corner of the rectangle and press (F7) again.

All of the area commands work for rectangles. To copy or move a rectangle, you place the cursor at the *top left* corner of the area to which you want to copy or move it, press (F8) and then select **Copy** or **Move.** If REVIEW is in *insert* mode, copying or moving the rectangle pushes existing text to the right. If REVIEW is in *overtype* mode, copying or moving overlays existing text, replacing it. If the copy or move location is to the right of existing lines, REVIEW adds spaces as needed to the ends of existing lines to keep the rectangle aligned.

Working with Two Files

When you are editing two files, the copy and move functions—including those for areas—can operate between the files. That is, you can copy or move an area from one file into the other. The procedure is the same as working within one file—mark the area in one file, position the cursor in the other file (by pressing F2 followed by ← to select **Switch windows**), and press the appropriate function key.

If you want to see more text in one window than in the other, you can change the size of the windows. Press F2, highlight **Change window size**, and press ←. Then fill in the number of lines you want to see in the upper window (the smallest number allowed is 7). After you press ← again, the system adjusts both windows accordingly.

The Help Displays

If you don't remember which function key does what, you can press F1 and select **Review help** to see the following help screen:

```
╔══════════════════ Guide to Review Function Keys ══════════════════╗
║ Information   F1   Review Help and Menus, Variable and File Lists, Glossary ║
║ Windows       F2   Switch, Change Size, Zoom                       ║
║ Input Files   F3   Insert File, Edit Different File                ║
║ Lines         F4   Insert, Delete, Undelete                        ║
║ Find&Replace  F5   Find Text, Replace Text                         ║
║ Go To         F6   Area, Output Page, Line in Error, After Last Line Executed ║
║ Define Area   F7   Mark/Unmark Lines, Rectangle, or Command        ║
║ Area Actions  F8   Copy, Move, Delete, Round Numbers, Copy Glossary Entry ║
║ Output File   F9   Write Area or File, Delete File                 ║
║ Run           F10  Run Commands from Cursor or Marked Area, Exit to Prompt ║
╚════════════════════════════════════════════════════════════════════╝
╔═══════════════════ Guide to Menu Commands ═══════════════════╗
║ ENTER (←)    Paste Selection & Move Down One Level in Menu     ║
║ TAB or →     Temporarily Paste Selection & Move Down One Level ║
║ ESC or ←     Remove Last Temporary Paste & Move Up One Level   ║
║ Alt-ESC      Jump to Main Menu (also Ctrl-ESC)                 ║
║ Alt-K        Kill All Temporary Pastes                         ║
║ Alt-T        Get Typing Window                                 ║
║ Alt-E        Switch to Edit Mode                               ║
║ Alt-M        Remove Menus                                      ║
║ Alt-V        Get Variables Window                              ║
║ Alt-C        Run from Cursor                                   ║
╚════════════════════════════════════════════════════════════════╝
                                                              01
    Enter command or press F1 for more help or Escape to continue
```

The top half of this display shows the functions associated with each key. You can call up this screen whenever you aren't sure which function key to press. (For full descriptions of all of REVIEW's functions, see REVIEW in Part C.)

Commands are grouped by function so that related commands are all accessed with the same function key. For example, all the line commands (inserting, deleting, and undeleting lines) are accessed with F4.

If you press F1 again while viewing the help screen, you see a second help display showing the keys that allow you to move around in REVIEW.

A number of commands prompt you for additional information when you issue them. These prompts always appear at the bottom of your screen. You can press F1 in response to any prompt to get a fuller description of the prompt. REVIEW will tell you exactly what information it is requesting and will list possible responses.

Entering Extended ASCII Characters

You can enter extended ASCII characters by activating NumLck and holding down the Alt key while you type the character's ASCII numeric code on the numeric key pad. The character appears when you release the Alt key.

Saving the File

After you've entered the data and made any corrections, you can save the file. (If you were to leave REVIEW without saving the file, everything you've typed would be lost.) To save the file, press (F9) and select **write Whole file.** REVIEW asks for confirmation that you want to save the file under the same name you started with; to do so, just press (←). (If you wanted to give the file a different name, you could just type it in.) REVIEW then saves the file and displays a message when it's done.

OTHER FILES

In this session we've used REVIEW to create and edit a data file. However, REVIEW is also useful for editing *any* medium-sized (up to several hundred lines) file, including:

• Files that hold commands, like the scratch pad and log files, or any other file into which you've entered commands. However, when you run REVIEW outside of SPSS/PC+ you can't *execute* commands in the file, and you can't see a variable list, since there is no active file.

• The listing file, which holds SPSS/PC+ output.

The SPSSPROF.INI File

Another file you may want to create and edit with REVIEW is the file called SPSSPROF.INI, which is the *automatic profile.* This file contains commands that are automatically executed whenever you get into SPSS/PC+. Usually these are SET commands, which control the way SPSS/PC+ operates. Since these commands are executed automatically when you enter the system, they allow you to begin with the environment you prefer. You can learn about SET commands in Part C or under the Main Menu selection **session control & info**.

To edit the automatic profile, specify its name as you get into REVIEW, and then use any of REVIEW's editing functions to add or change the commands you want, or delete the ones you don't want.

File Limitations

In general, REVIEW can edit ASCII files that are small enough to fit into the available memory (RAM) of your computer. Note that REVIEW itself—and any other software currently loaded into memory—occupies some of your computer's RAM. REVIEW *cannot* edit

• Binary files. If a file has graphics characters in it when you use the DOS *TYPE* command to display it on your screen, it is probably a binary file. (SPSS/PC+ system files are binary files.)

• Files too large to fit in the working memory (RAM) available to REVIEW. REVIEW tells you if it does not have enough memory. (Operations such as scrolling may slow down noticeably as REVIEW runs out of memory.)

Important DOS Concepts

SPSS/PC+ is specifically tailored to the IBM PC/XT, PC/AT, and closely compatible computers running Release 2.0 or later of DOS. To use such a computer effectively, you must acquire a basic familiarity with the concepts and commands of DOS. You should not rely on this manual for such information. Read at least the chapters in your DOS manual on files and filenames, and on using directories. Browse through the descriptions of important commands such as *COPY, DEL, RENAME, TYPE, BACKUP,* and *DISKCOPY.* After reading about directories, note how to work with them using the *MKDIR* (or *MD*) and *CHDIR* (or *CD*) commands. The *CHKDSK* command provides useful information about both disk space and memory (RAM).

In this chapter, you will find information on DOS as it is used with SPSS/PC+. This discussion is *not* adequate to make you proficient in the use of your computer. You do not need to be an expert on DOS to use SPSS/PC+, but a little time invested in learning basic concepts from the DOS manual will make your work easier and more efficient. If you are already familiar with DOS, you may wish to skim this section to see how the SPSS/PC+ system fits in.

DOS is an operating system, a control program that manages the hardware functions of your computer such as accepting commands from the keyboard, writing to the screen, and managing the creation and use of files on disk. When you use an application program such as SPSS/PC+, the most important concepts to understand are those involving disk files.

DOS FILENAMES

The files that contain information stored on your hard disk, or on floppy diskettes, are referred to by name. When you create a file yourself, you assign a name to it. When SPSS/PC+ creates a file it assigns a name, either according to your specifications or using a built-in default. A complete file specification can contain any or all of the following parts, although you rarely have to specify them all.

drive name A single letter indicating which of the disk drives connected to your computer holds the disk on which the file is stored. When you specify this, follow it immediately by a colon (:) to show that it is a drive name. Drive names vary, but by far the most common convention is for A: (and perhaps B:) to be the names of floppy-diskette drives, and for C: to be the drive containing the hard disk.

pathname A specification for the directory containing the file. Pathnames are discussed in "The Path Command," below.

filename A name from one to eight characters that identifies the file. This is also called the "primary filename," since you must always include the extension (perhaps using a wildcard) when specifying a file whose name has an extension. Letters and numbers are allowed in filenames. Blank spaces are not allowed *in the middle* of a filename. See your DOS manual for a complete discussion of the characters that are permitted in filenames.

extension A specification from one to three characters, typically used to indicate what kind of information the file contains. The extension is always separated from the filename by a period. For example, SPSS.LIS has filename SPSS and extension LIS.

In fact, most references to files use only the filename and extension. This is understood to mean that the file is on your *default drive* and in your *current directory,* as explained below.

Wildcards
You can often use DOS "wildcard" characters when specifying filenames or extensions. Use of these characters, the asterisk and the question mark, is explained in the DOS manual. Basically, the asterisk represents *any* character or characters at the end of a filename or extension, and the question mark represents any single character in a filename or extension. Thus,

```
erase *.bak
```

erases all files with the extension BAK in the current directory, and

```
copy a:*.* c:
```

copies all files (any name, any extension) from the floppy diskette in the A: drive onto the hard disk in C:. Consult the DOS manual for more information on these shortcuts.

THE DEFAULT DRIVE

When you are running DOS or a DOS program (including SPSS/PC+), a "default drive" is always assigned to you. DOS displays the letter associated with this drive in its command prompt and assumes that any file for which you do not explicitly specify a drive resides on the default drive. If your default drive is A:, the DOS command prompt may look like this (perhaps with some additional information):

```
A>
```

To make another drive the default, simply type in its letter followed by a colon, and DOS will confirm what you have done by using the new drive in its command prompt:

```
A> c:

C>
```

DIRECTORIES AND PATHS

A DOS directory is simply a subset of the contents of a disk. Directories are particularly convenient on hard disks, which can contain hundreds of files: They are less often used on floppy diskettes, although they are perfectly legal. Since directories can be nested inside other directories, you have to specify a "path," *either explicitly or implicitly,* to tell DOS where to find a particular directory. Advantages of using directories include:

- A directory listing of a group of related files will often fit on a single screen, while a listing of all the files on a hard disk would be too extensive to be useful.
- You can use the same name (for example, SPSS.LIS) for different files as long as they are in different directories.
- Different people can share a machine without getting in each other's way by establishing individual directories to hold their files.
- Valuable software, such as SPSS/PC+, can be saved in a directory that is never used as anyone's default directory, to reduce the likelihood of accidental damage. To delete a file that is not in your default directory, you have to include a pathname on the DEL or ERASE command.

Directories can contain not only files but also other directories (which can contain other directories, and so on).

The Current Directory
Just as you always have a default drive in DOS, you always have a *current directory.* If you name a file without specifying a directory, DOS assumes that the file is in your current directory. When you start up a system that initially assigns the hard disk as your default drive, you will be in its "root directory," which is the main directory of the whole disk. Operating from the root directory, you do not even need to be aware that directories exist. When your disk contains a large number of files, as all hard disks eventually do, you should create and work from one or more smaller directories.

It is a good idea always to be aware of your current directory. If you enter the DOS command,

```
prompt $p$g
```

then the DOS command prompt will always remind you of your current directory. See "Using Batch Files to Avoid DOS," below, to find out how to have this command entered for you automatically so that you don't have to remember it.

DOS Commands for Directories

The most important DOS commands for using directories are

MKDIR or MD   *Make directory.* Use this command to create a new directory. The short form, *MD,* is easier to spell and works just as well.

CHDIR or CD   *Change directory.* Use this command anytime you want to change your current directory. Unlike other directory commands, *CD* is typically used at least once in a session.

RMDIR or RD   *Remove directory.* This command deletes a directory. It can only be used after everything in the directory has been deleted.

Example. Here the DOS prompts are in upper case, while commands entered by the user are shown in lower case:

```
A>c:

C>prompt $p$g

C:\>md myfiles

C:\>cd myfiles

C:\MYFILES>
```

- The first command sets the default drive to C:
- The *PROMPT* command changes the command prompt to show the current directory. Since the user is still in the root directory, the current directory is simply represented by a backslash (\), as discussed in the next section.
- The *MD* command creates a new directory named MYFILES.
- The *CD* command establishes MYFILES as the current directory. Notice that the final prompt from DOS displays the current directory.

Paths

A path specification is simply a way to indicate a particular directory. You use path specifications on the directory commands discussed above, or whenever you need to name a file that is not in your current directory. The basic rules are simple, but you should consult your DOS manual for more information.

- A path specification consists of one or more directory names, separated by backslashes (\). If you name more than one directory, they are nested, with the one named first including them all.
- The directories in a path specification must already exist (except, of course, on the *MD* command that creates them).
- A path specification does not include any blank spaces.
- If the first character of the path specification is a backslash, DOS understands the path to begin at the root directory.
- If the first character of the path specification is not a backslash, DOS understands the path to begin in your current directory (see the example below). This means that the path can only indicate directories *inside* your current directory. (If your current directory is the root, a backslash in the first character of a path specification is optional.)
- If you are using the path specification to identify a particular *file* rather than a directory, put a backslash after the name of the directory that contains the file and follow this immediately with the filename and the extension, if any.

Example. This example first shows the *DEL* (delete) command using a complete file specification, including drive, path, primary filename, and extension. As before, the DOS prompt is shown in upper case, while the command is shown in lower case. The file is in a directory named DATA, which in turn is in a directory named WORK. Since this is a complete specification, it means the same thing regardless of what your default drive or current directory is:

```
A>del c:\work\data\employ.dat
```

If the default drive is C: but the root is still the current directory, the specification is:

```
C:\>del work\data\employ.dat
```

If, instead, the current directory is WORK, the same command can be entered like this:

```
C:\WORK>del data\employ.dat
```

Finally, suppose that the current directory is the DATA directory inside the WORK directory:

```
C:\WORK\DATA>del employ.dat
```

As long as you are working with files in your current directory on your default drive, you do not need to specify anything but the filename and extension. For most people, this is the typical situation.

THE PATH COMMAND

The *PATH* command enables you to dispense with the effort of specifying (and remembering) the paths to commonly used files in other directories. Often the most convenient way to issue this command is through the AUTOEXEC.BAT file discussed below in "Using Batch Files to Avoid DOS."

Normally, if you enter the name of a program, a batch file, or one of the DOS disk-based commands, DOS searches for it only in your current directory and will not find it if it is somewhere else. (The error message is "Bad command or filename.")

One solution to this problem is to always specify paths; another is to copy the SPSSPC.COM file along with the disk-based DOS command files and other frequently used programs and batch files to your working directory so that you can access them directly.

A better solution to the problem is to use the DOS *PATH* command, which permits you to define other directories that should be searched to find programs, batch files, or disk-based DOS commands that do not exist in your current directory. You can enter paths to several directories, separated by semicolons, on the *PATH* command. (If you enter a second *PATH* command, the directories listed on it completely replace the list of directories on the first *PATH* command.) Directories are searched in the order you list them on the *PATH* command. For example,

```
path \;\spss;\dos
```

will permit you to execute programs, batch files, and disk-based DOS commands that are in the root directory, the \SPSS directory, or the \DOS directory without explicitly specifying a path.

THE SPSS/PC+ SYSTEM DIRECTORY

The SPSS/PC+ system must be installed in a specific directory on your system. You must specify which directory to use when you install the system. The installation procedure then creates this directory and saves the program modules into it.

Normally, you should use a directory named \SPSS. If you choose a directory other than \SPSS, you must issue the DOS command:

```
SET SPSS=path
```

to indicate where the modules can be found. (This is a DOS system environment command, not an SPSS/PC+ command.) For example, to indicate that SPSS/PC+ is installed in a directory named \PCPLUS, specify:

SET SPSS=\PCPLUS

(You can place such a command into your AUTOEXEC.BAT file. You might also wish to put a path to this directory on your *PATH* command. See the next section.)

If the SPSS/PC+ system is on a drive other than your default drive, you must indicate this also:

SET SPSS=E:\PCPLUS

This DOS command specifies that the SPSS/PC+ system is on the E: drive, in a directory named \PCPLUS.

USING BATCH FILES TO AVOID DOS

You cannot avoid DOS entirely. The more you learn about DOS, the easier your work will be. However, there is always a point when remembering command syntax becomes more trouble than it is worth. Some people reach this point quickly when studying operating-system commands. Batch files, which contain DOS commands or groups of DOS commands that can be invoked with a single word, provide a convenient way to avoid memorizing the names or syntax of DOS commands.

You can create a batch file with any editor or word processor, for example EDLIN, which comes with DOS and is described in the DOS manual, or REVIEW, which comes with SPSS/PC+ and is described in this manual. You simply enter some commands into a file just as you would enter them directly; or if you like, you can use some of the simple programming facilities that DOS supports in batch files.

After you have saved these commands into an ASCII file (a file containing ordinary letters, numbers, and punctuation, rather than special binary codes used only by computer programs), you can execute them simply by typing the filename. The file extension for a batch file must be BAT. You do not need to type this extension when invoking a batch file.

AUTOEXEC.BAT

One batch file, AUTOEXEC.BAT, is particularly useful in conjunction with SPSS/PC+. If you create an AUTOEXEC.BAT file in the root directory of your initial default disk, it is executed automatically whenever you start up your system. As explained in the DOS manual, there are a number of useful commands you can put into this file. Two commands are especially helpful when you are running SPSS/PC+.

PROMPT PG As explained above, this command sets the DOS command prompt to include the path to your current directory. The specification PG is not particularly easy to remember, so this command is well placed in this batch file, where you do not need to remember it.

PATH \SPSS The SPSS/PC+ system is stored in a directory that is usually named \SPSS. If you include this directory on a PATH command in your AUTOEXEC.BAT file, you will be able to run both SPSS/PC+ and REVIEW from any directory, without entering a pathname to it. You may wish to define paths to other directories also; if so, enter all of the paths on the same *PATH* command, separated by semicolons.

Since AUTOEXEC.BAT is searched for and executed immediately after you start up (or "boot") your system, it must be on the startup disk from which DOS is loaded. In most systems with built-in hard disks, this is the hard disk. Systems that require a floppy diskette to be inserted at startup must have the AUTOEXEC.BAT file on that floppy diskette. AUTOEXEC.BAT must always be in the root directory, since that is the current directory at system startup.

SETTING SYSTEM PARAMETERS

When you boot or reboot your system, DOS reads a special file named CONFIG.SYS (if it exists) to customize the system configuration. You can set a number of parameters by creating a CONFIG.SYS file, as explained in your DOS manual. To run SPSS/PC+, you should set up this file to include at least the following two parameters:

FILES Specify FILES=20. This parameter controls the maximum number of open files allowed. The default number, 8, is insufficient when using SPSS/PC+.

BUFFERS Specify BUFFERS=8 to increase the number of file buffers that the system allocates. This can significantly speed up the performance of SPSS/PC+.

Use any editor, such as EDLIN or REVIEW, to create the CONFIG.SYS file. After creating it, reboot the system (hold the Ctrl and Alt keys down and press Del) so that the new parameters will take effect.

Statistics Guide

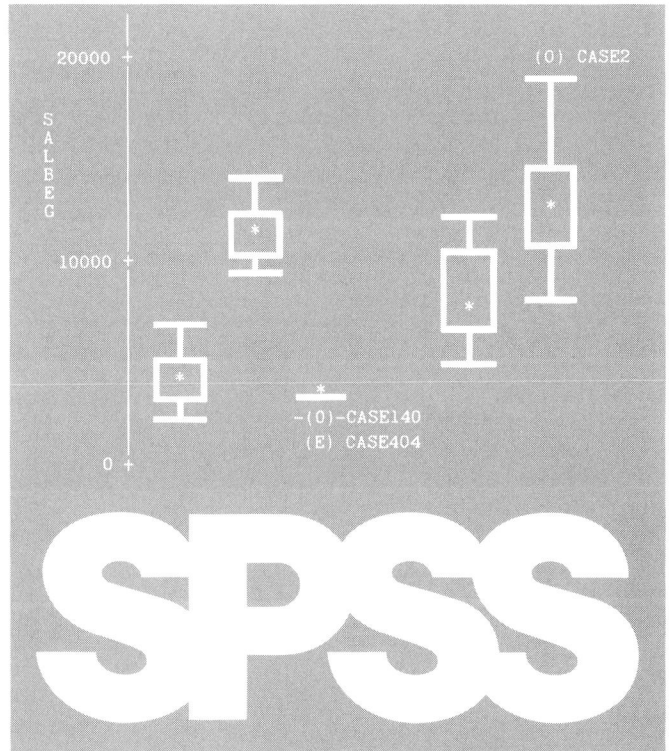

Contents

1 The SPSS/PC+ System

Many purchases come with suggestions for use. Children's blocks, microwave ovens, and woodcutting tools are all accompanied by colorful booklets describing results that can be obtained with them. What should a book accompanying a statistical software package contain? Although the results of statistical analyses are not as photogenic as block structures, gourmet meals, and fine furniture, data analysis is a creative process that can result in important contributions to many different undertakings. Increased profits in business, improved treatments for disease, as well as insights into social phenomena, are often attributable to the careful acquisition and analysis of data.

In this part of your SPSS/PC+ manual, we illustrate the application of various statistical procedures to solve a variety of real problems. The problems and their solutions range from the simple—counting the number of people who die on Mondays, to the complex—searching for salary discrimination. The goal is to introduce the building blocks that can be used alone or in many combinations to analyze and display data.

Before proceeding to a detailed discussion of the hows and whys of data analysis with SPSS/PC+, let's take a quick overview of the types of analyses that can be produced. The data we will use are from a recent *Consumer Reports* evaluation of 35 beers. The beers were rated on overall quality and a variety of other attributes, such as price, calories, sodium, and alcohol content.

1.1 PREPARING A REPORT

One of the first steps in examining the beer data may be to prepare a report that contains detailed information about each of the beers. Figure 1.1 is an excerpt from output produced by the SPSS/PC+ REPORT procedure. Reports may contain additional information, such as summary statistics. Chapter 14 describes the REPORT procedure in detail.

Figure 1.1   Excerpt from a report produced by REPORT

```
             CONSUMER REPORTS BEER RATING - JULY 1983

   RATING    BEER                  6-PACK   AVAILABLE   PRICE CLASS
                                   PRICE    IN U.S.

   VERY GOOD MILLER HIGH LIFE        2.49   NATIONAL    PREMIUM
             BUDWEISER               2.59   NATIONAL    PREMIUM
             SCHLITZ                 2.59   NATIONAL    PREMIUM
             LOWENBRAU               2.89   NATIONAL    SUPER-PREMIUM
             MICHELOB                2.99   NATIONAL    SUPER-PREMIUM
             HENRY WEINHARD          3.65   REGIONAL    SUPER-PREMIUM
             ANCHOR STEAM            7.19   REGIONAL    SUPER-PREMIUM
     MEAN                           $3.48

   GOOD      OLD MILWAUKEE           1.69   REGIONAL    POPULAR
             SCHMIDTS                1.79   REGIONAL    POPULAR
             PABST BLUE RIBBON       2.29   NATIONAL    PREMIUM
             AUGSBERGER              2.39   REGIONAL    SUPER-PREMIUM
             STROHS BOHEMIAN STYLE   2.49   REGIONAL    PREMIUM
             COORS                   2.65   REGIONAL    PREMIUM
             OLYMPIA                 2.65   REGIONAL    PREMIUM
     MEAN                           $2.28

   FAIR      BLATZ                   1.79   REGIONAL    POPULAR
             ROLLING ROCK            2.15   REGIONAL    PREMIUM
             HAMMS                   2.59   REGIONAL    PREMIUM
             HEILEMANS OLD STYLE     2.59   REGIONAL    PREMIUM
             TUBORG                  2.59   REGIONAL    PREMIUM
     MEAN                           $2.34
```

1.2
DESCRIBING THE DATA

A simple report just displays the data values. It does not attempt to organize or summarize the data. Several SPSS/PC+ procedures are designed especially for summarizing data. For example, a frequency table contains counts of the number of times a response occurs—the number of men and women in a sample, the number of children in families, or the number of visits to the dentist in a year by the head of the household. Figure 1.2a, which was produced by the SPSS/PC+ FREQUENCIES procedure, is a frequency table of the number of beers rated very good, good, and fair by the *Consumer Reports* panel. Of the 35 beers, 11 (31.4%) were rated very good, 14 (40%) good, and the remaining 10 (28.6%) fair.

Figure 1.2a Frequency table from FREQUENCIES

RATING

Value Label	Value	Frequency	Percent	Valid Percent	Cum Percent
VERY GOOD	1	11	31.4	31.4	31.4
GOOD	2	14	40.0	40.0	71.4
FAIR	3	10	28.6	28.6	100.0
	TOTAL	35	100.0	100.0	

The information presented in a frequency table can also be displayed in a bar chart. Figure 1.2b shows a bar chart of the beer ratings. Each value in the table is represented by a bar whose length is proportional to the number of times the value occurs in the data. The FREQUENCIES procedure can also be used to produce bar charts as well as various statistics that are useful for describing data. FREQUENCIES is described in Chapter 7.

Figure 1.2b Bar chart from FREQUENCIES

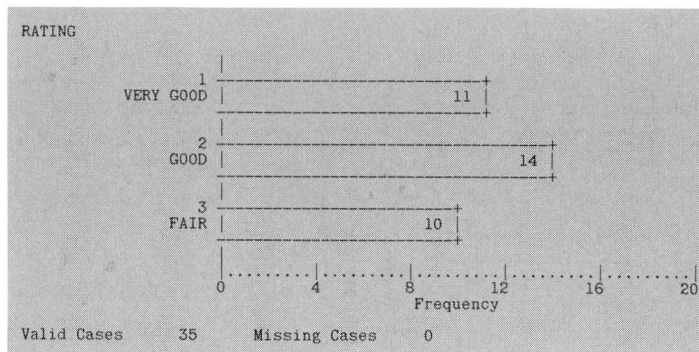

```
RATING

            1 |
    VERY GOOD |-------------------------------+
              |                            11 |
              |-------------------------------+
            2 |
         GOOD |--------------------------------+
              |                             14 |
              |--------------------------------+
            3 |
         FAIR |-----------------------+
              |                    10 |
              |-----------------------+
              |.........|.........|.........|.........|.........|
              0         4         8        12        16        20
                                    Frequency

Valid Cases     35     Missing Cases    0
```

1.3
COUNTING COMBINATIONS OF RESPONSES

A frequency table just counts the number of times various responses occur to a single item. Often, however, it is useful to count the number of times certain combinations of responses occur. For example, you might want to know how many men and how many women answered yes, no, or maybe to a survey question. Or you might want to know the number of fatal, serious, or minor accidents involving standard, compact, and subcompact cars.

Figure 1.3 shows a table that tabulates two items together—the rating of the beer and whether it was light or not. From this table, one can see that no light beers were rated as very good, 4 were rated as good, and 3 were rated as fair. This type of table, known as a crosstabulation or contingency table, is available with the CROSSTABS procedure. CROSSTABS can also compute a variety of percentages and statistics that indicate how closely two (or more) variables are related. The CROSSTABS procedure is described in Chapter 10.

Figure 1.3 Crosstabulation from CROSSTABS

```
Crosstabulation:        LIGHT
                     By RATING

                        RATING
               Count
                       VERY      GOOD      FAIR      Row
                       GOOD                          Total
                           1I        2I        3I
   LIGHT            ---------+--------+--------+--------+
                    0 |    11  |    10  |     7  |    28
     NO               |       |        |        |    80.0
                    ---------+--------+--------+--------+
                    1 |       |     4  |     3  |     7
     YES              |       |        |        |    20.0
                    ---------+--------+--------+--------+
                Column      11       14       10       35
                Total      31.4     40.0     28.6    100.0

Number of Missing Observations =         0
```

1.4 SUMMARIZING RESPONSES

Both frequency tables and crosstabulation tables summarize the data by counting the number of times each response occurs. When a response can have many possible values—age, weight, or income—counting the number of times each possible individual response occurs may result in very large tables which are not very useful. Instead of looking at all responses, you might want to group values that are close to one another and see how often such groups of values (people in their twenties, individuals over 250 pounds) occur.

Figure 1.4 shows the distribution of alcohol content for the 35 beers. Each row of asterisks represents a range of alcohol values. As in the bar chart, the length of the row is proportional to the number of times the values occur. For example, the longest row corresponds to alcohol values between 4.25 and 4.75 and represents 17 beers. Such figures, called histograms, can be obtained from the SPSS/PC+ FREQUENCIES procedure.

Figure 1.4 Histogram of alcohol content from FREQUENCIES

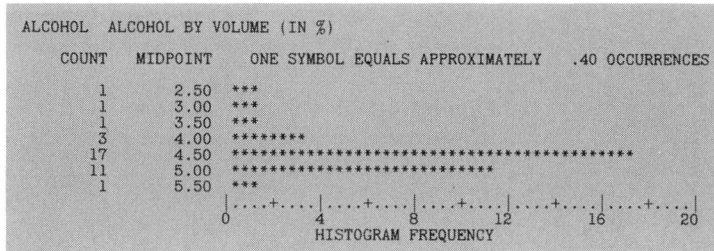

```
ALCOHOL   ALCOHOL BY VOLUME (IN %)

    COUNT    MIDPOINT    ONE SYMBOL EQUALS APPROXIMATELY    .40 OCCURRENCES

        1       2.50     ***
        1       3.00     ***
        1       3.50     ***
        3       4.00     ********
       17       4.50     *************************************************
       11       5.00     *******************************
        1       5.50     ***
                         |....+....|....+....|....+....|....+....|....+....|
                         0        4        8       12       16       20
                                    HISTOGRAM FREQUENCY
```

1.5 SUMMARY STATISTICS

It is possible to summarize the information contained in a histogram even further by calculating single numbers that represent an average or typical value and the amount of spread or variability in the data. Figure 1.5a contains the mean, the mode (the most frequently occurring value), the median (the value above which half the values fall), the variance (a measure of how spread out the values are), and the smallest and largest values for the alcohol content of the beers in the survey. These statistics and many others are calculated in the SPSS/PC+ FREQUENCIES and MEANS procedures.

Figure 1.5a Some summary statistics available from FREQUENCIES

```
Mean        4.577
Mode        4.700
Median      4.700
Variance     .364
Minimum     2.300
Maximum     5.500
```

Although it is informative to know that the average alcohol content of all the beers is 4.58%, you may also want to see if alcohol content is similar for the three beer rating groups. Figure 1.5b shows the average alcohol content for the three ratings. Beers rated as very good had the highest alcohol content (4.9%), while those rated fair had the lowest (4.2%). The good beers were in the middle, with an average alcohol content of 4.6%. This type of table, which shows the means of a variable for subgroups of cases, can be obtained from the SPSS/PC+ MEANS procedure (see Chapter 11).

Figure 1.5b   Table from MEANS

```
Summaries of   ALCOHOL      ALCOHOL BY VOLUME (IN %)
By levels of   RATING

Variable       Value  Label                    Mean      Std Dev    Cases

For Entire Population                          4.5771      .6030      35

RATING             1   VERY GOOD               4.9000      .1789      11
RATING             2   GOOD                    4.5786      .4300      14
RATING             3   FAIR                    4.2200      .8954      10

    Total Cases =     35
```

1.6
PLOTTING THE DATA

When you want to examine the relationship between two variables, both of which can have many values, plotting the two variables may be helpful. Figure 1.6a, which was produced by the SPSS/PC+ PLOT procedure, is a plot of the price of the beer and the alcohol content. Each point is also identified by its *Consumer Reports* rating. Note that there does not appear to be a strong relationship between price and alcohol content since there is beer in various price ranges for the values of alcohol content. No "pattern" between cost and alcohol content appears to exist.

Examining plots of several variables together is a valuable step in many analyses. Plots of sales with advertising expenditures, blood pressure with weight, and birth rates with GNP all reveal interesting relationships between the two variables. The PLOT procedure produces a variety of plots that can be used to examine relationships among variables and is described in Chapter 12.

Figure 1.6a   Sample output from PLOT

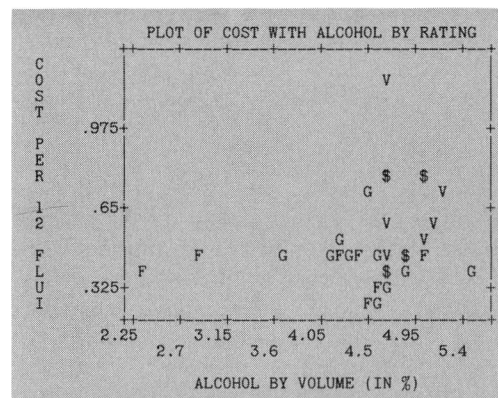

Another way to examine the strength of association between two variables is through indexes such as the correlation coefficient. Figure 1.6b contains correlation coefficients between price, alcohol content, and sodium content. Since these values are small (close to 0), there appears to be no linear association between the pairs of variables. (A linear association is one in which points cluster around a straight line.) The SPSS/PC+ CORRELATION procedure can be used to calculate correlation coefficients and various associated statistics. CORRELATION is described in the *SPSS/PC+ Statistics* manual.

Figure 1.6b   Correlation coefficients available from CORRELATION

```
Correlations:    PRICE       ALCOHOL      SODIUM

     PRICE        1.0000        .1961       -.0897
                 (     0)      (    35)     (    35)
                  P= .         P= .129      P= .304

     ALCOHOL       .1961       1.0000        .2050
                 (    35)      (     0)     (    35)
                  P= .129      P= .         P= .119

     SODIUM       -.0897        .2050       1.0000
                 (    35)      (    35)     (     0)
                  P= .304      P= .119      P= .

(Coefficient / (Cases) / Significance)

" . " is printed if a coefficient cannot be computed
```

1.7
TESTING HYPOTHESES AND BUILDING MODELS

SPSS/PC+ also provides statistical tests for evaluating the likelihood of actual differences in a population based on observed differences in a sample. For example, we may test the hypothesis that beers rated very good and fair differ in price or alcohol content—not just for beers in the survey but for all beers. Or we may hypothesize that beers in the three rating categories differ in sodium content. The SPSS/PC+ T-TEST procedure can be used to test the hypothesis that two population means are equal, while the SPSS/PC+ procedures ONEWAY and ANOVA are useful for testing hypotheses about several population means. For a discussion of T-TEST, ONEWAY, and ANOVA, see the *SPSS/PC+ Statistics* manual.

Since beers are known to vary considerably in cost, it may be interesting to try to predict the cost of a beer based on variables such as alcohol content, number of calories, availability, and origin. The SPSS/PC+ REGRESSION procedure (see *SPSS/PC+ Statistics*) is used to develop a model that examines the relationship between a dependent variable, in this case cost, and a set of independent variables. Special facilities for selecting variables to be included in a model as well as testing the adequacy of fit of the model are also available.

You may want to study the associations among categorical variables; that is, variables whose values are categories—such as beer rating, class, and availability. The SPSS/PC+ procedure available for this type of analysis is HILOGLINEAR, a hierarchical loglinear technique. Loglinear models are a class of statistical techniques that model the number of cases in a cell of a multidimensional crosstabulation as a function of the variables used for classification.

Suppose that a number of individuals rated the beer on a number of characteristics, such as lightness, body, color, head, taste when drunk from a bottle, can, or glass, packaging, sizes available, and so on. You would expect that the responses to different items would be correlated. One explanation for the observed correlations is the idea that the items are related because they tap some of the same dimensions on which people rate beer. These dimensions may be quality, value, and accessibility. Factor analysis is one of the statistical techniques that is used to search for these underlying common dimensions, called *factors*. The SPSS/PC+ FACTOR procedure provides several methods for estimating the factors and for making their interpretation easier.

Although there are many different brands of beer in the world, one may wonder whether they are all that different from one another or whether the beers can be lumped into several fairly homogeneous categories. Since there are many attributes which can be used to describe the beers, any subset of these might serve as the basis for looking for similarities. The SPSS/PC+ CLUSTER procedure can be used to calculate "distances" between pairs of beers and then, based on these distances, group the beers into similar categories, called clusters. Several different ways of defining distances between items and forming clusters are available.

When you know in advance the number of clusters to expect, you can use the SPSS/PC+ QUICK CLUSTER procedure instead. QUICK CLUSTER is less flexible than CLUSTER. However, it can process large files efficiently, while the number of cases you can process with CLUSTER is limited by the amount of memory available.

Sometimes you already know the way your cases are grouped, but you want to know why the groupings came out that way. The beers were rated as "very good," "good," or "fair" in the *Consumer Reports* evaluation. Is there any way to predict these ratings from the other variables available? The SPSS/PC+ DSCRIMINANT procedure can be used to predict how the beers were rated in quality, on the basis of their price, alcohol content, sodium content, and so on. If the prediction works well for the beers actually rated, you could then use the DSCRIMINANT procedure to try and predict how other beers would have been rated if they had been included in the evaluation.

Sometimes the tests available in procedures ANOVA and ONEWAY are not general enough for a complex analysis. The SPSS/PC+ MANOVA procedure lets you test a wide variety of hypotheses about the effects of categorical or continuous variables on one or more dependent variables. It can handle most types of linear models, including "repeated measures" analyses in which dependent variable(s) have been measured on several occasions.

For more information on FACTOR, CLUSTER, and QUICK CLUSTER, see the *SPSS/PC+ Statistics* manual. For more information on HILOGLINEAR, DSCRIMINANT, and MANOVA, see the *SPSS/PC+ Advanced Statistics* manual.

1.8 SUMMARY

The SPSS/PC+ product contains many facilities for analyzing and reporting data. For most problems, you will probably want to explore your data using several different techniques. Although it may be tempting to run a lot of different procedures with which you are not very familiar in the hope of making sense of the data, this is not a very good tactic. Instead, you should think about the problem you want to solve, spend some time considering the statistical techniques that may be helpful in arriving at a solution, and only then proceed with the analysis. You should also keep in mind the caveat that the most complicated procedure is not necessarily the best. A little common sense and thought will not only save time but give better results as well.

Contents

2 Preparing Data for Analysis

Before information can be analyzed by SPSS/PC+, it must be entered into a disk file. This entails two steps—arranging the data into a suitable format and entering the data into the computer. You can use an editor program to create the file and enter the data. If you are not already familiar with an editor, you may wish to use REVIEW, which is included with your system (see Part A: REVIEW). It is also possible to enter data directly into an SPSS/PC+ command file or to bring in a file that already exists on a mainframe computer. In this chapter we will consider only the first step—taking data which are stored in some form that a computer cannot read and preparing it for analysis.

2.1
CASES, VARIABLES, AND VALUES

Consider Table 2.5a, which contains an excerpt from the *Consumer Reports* report on beers discussed in Chapter 1. Each line in the table represents a *case,* or observation, for which *values* are available for a set of *variables.*

For the first case, MILLER HIGH LIFE beer, the value of the cost variable is 42 cents, and of the alcohol variable, 4.7%. For each beer, the same variables— rating, origin, availability, price, cost, calories, sodium, alcohol content, class, and light (type of beer)—are recorded. What differs are the actual values of the variables. Each case has one and only one value for each variable. "Unknown" and "missing" are acceptable values for a variable, although these values require special treatment during analysis.

The case is the basic unit for which measurements are taken. In this analysis, the case is a brand of beer. In studies of political opinion or brand preference, the case is most likely the individual respondent to a questionnaire. A case may be a larger unit, such as a school, county, or nation; it may be a time period, such as a year or month in which measurements are obtained; or it may be an event, such as an auto accident.

For any single analysis, the cases must be the same. If the unit of analysis is a county, all cases are counties and the values of each variable are for individual counties. If the unit is a state, all cases are states and the values for each variable are for states.

2.2
Identifying Important Variables

A critical step in any study is the selection of variables to be included. For example, an employee can be described using many variables, such as place of residence, color of hair and eyes, years of education, work experience, and so forth. The variables that are relevant to the problem under study must be chosen from the vast array of information available. If important variables are excluded from the data file, the results will be of limited use. This point may seem obvious, but it is all too easy to overlook an important variable until you need it for analysis, when it is too late to get the information. For example, if a variable such as years of work experience is excluded from a study of salary discrimination, few—if any—correct conclusions can be drawn. All potentially relevant variables should be included in the study, since it is much easier to exclude unnecessary variables from analysis than to gather additional information.

2.3
Recording the Data

Once the variables have been selected, you must decide how they will be recorded. Do you need to record the actual date of birth, or can you simply record the age in years? Is it sufficient to know if someone is a high-school or college graduate, or do you need to know the actual number of years of education? It is usually a good idea to record the data in as much detail as possible. For example, if you record actual ages, cases can be grouped later into age categories. But if you just record each case as over 50 years or under 50 years of age, you can never analyze your data using any other age categories.

2.4
Coding the Variables

One way to simplify data entry is to assign numbers or symbols to represent responses. This is known as *coding* the data. For example, instead of typing "light" or "regular" as the values for the type-of-beer variable, the codes *1* and *0* can be used. If only numbers are included in a coding scheme, it is called *numeric*. If letters or a mixture of numbers, letters, and special symbols are chosen, the code is termed *alphanumeric* or *string*. By coding, you substantially decrease the number of symbols that you need to type, especially for variables whose values are originally recorded as words (such as class of beer). If you want the coded values to be labeled on the output, a few instructions in SPSS/PC+ will take care of it.

Coding schemes are arbitrary by their very nature. The type-of-beer variable could also be coded *R* for regular and *L* for light. All that is necessary is that each possible response have a distinct code. For example, coding the states by their first letter is unacceptable since there are many states that begin with the same letter. Maine, Massachusetts, Michigan, Maryland, Minnesota, Mississippi, Missouri, and Montana would be indistinguishable.

It is usually helpful to have one variable that uniquely identifies each case. For the beer data, that variable is the name of the beer. Sometimes it is useful to identify cases with an ID number. This identifier can help you easily locate the data lines for cases with unusual values or missing information.

2.5
An Example

Table 2.5a shows a portion of the uncoded data from the beer study. A possible coding scheme for this data is shown in Table 2.5b. Figure 2.5a contains data for the first three beers coded according to this scheme. Once the data are coded, a format for arranging the data in a computer file must be determined. Each data line (usually entered from a terminal) is also known as a *record*. Each line is composed of columns in which the numbers or characters are stored. Two decisions that must be made are how many lines will be needed for each case and in what column locations each variable will be stored.

Table 2.5a   Excerpt from uncoded data for the beer study

Rating	Beer	Origin	Avail	Price	Cost
Very good	MILLER HIGH LIFE	USA	National	2.49	.42
Very good	BUDWEISER	USA	National	2.59	.43
Very good	SCHLITZ	USA	National	2.59	.43
Very good	LOWENBRAU	USA	National	2.89	.48
Good	OLD MILWAUKEE	USA	Regional	1.69	.28
Good	DOS EQUIS	Mexico	Regional	4.22	.70
Fair	PABST EXTRA LIGHT	USA	National	2.29	.38

Calories	Sodium	Alchohol	Class	Light
149	17	4.7	Premium	Regular
144	15	4.7	Premium	Regular
151	19	4.9	Premium	Regular
157	15	4.9	Super-premium	Regular
145	23	4.6	Popular	Regular
145	14	4.5	Not given	Regular
68	15	2.3	Not given	Light

Table 2.5b   Coding scheme for beer data form

Variable	Coding scheme
RATING	1 = Very good 2 = Good 3 = Fair
BEER	Actual name of the beer
ORIGIN	1 = USA 2 = Canada 3 = France 4 = Holland 5 = Mexico 6 = Germany 7 = Japan
AVAIL	1 = National 2 = Regional
PRICE	price per six-pack of 12-ounce containers
COST	cost per 12 fluid ounces
CALORIES	calories per 12 fluid ounces
SODIUM	sodium per 12 fluid ounces in mg
ALCOHOL	alcohol by volume (in %)
CLASS	0 = Not given 1 = Super-premium 2 = Premium 3 = Popular
LIGHT	0 = Regular 1 = Light

Figure 2.5a   Coded data

```
RATING    BEER              ORIGIN AVAIL PRICE COST CALORIES SODIUM ALCOHOL CLASS LIGHT
   1    MILLER HIGH LIFE      1     1     249   42    149      17     47      2     0
   1    BUDWEISER             1     1     259   43    144      15     47      2     0
   1    SCHLITZ               1     1     259   43    151      19     49      2     0
```

Figure 2.5b   One-record file

```
         1         2         3         4         5
1234567890123456789012345678901234567890123456789 0  Columns

1 MILLER HIGH LIFE       1 1 249  42 149 17 47 2 0
1 BUDWEISER              1 1 259  43 144 15 47 2 0
1 SCHLITZ                1 1 259  43 151 19 49 2 0
```

Figure 2.5b shows a listing of a file in which one line is used for each case. The column locations for the variables are also indicated. Rating is in column 1, the name of the beer in columns 3 through 22, origin in column 25, the availability of the beer in column 27, the price in columns 29–31, the cost in columns 33–35, calories in columns 37–39, the sodium content in columns 41–42, the alcohol content in columns 44–45, class in column 47, and the light or regular designation in column 49. The numbers are positioned in each field so that the last digit is in the last column of the field for the variable. For example, a calorie count of 72 would have the number 7 in column 38; leading blanks or zeros occupy the

Statistics Guide

beginning columns. This is known as *fixed-column format.* (Freefield input is discussed in Section 2.6.) The decimal points for the price, cost, and alcohol variables are not included in the file. The decimal point does not need to be included since SPSS/PC+ commands can be used to indicate its location. If the decimal point is included, it occupies a column like any other symbol.

When there are many variables for each case, more than one line may be necessary to store the information. For example, if your screen width is 80, you may prefer to enter information that requires more than 80 columns on two or more lines. It is usually recommended that you enter an identification number for each case and a record number onto each line if it takes more than one line to record the data for a case. You can then easily locate missing or out-of-order data lines.

It is important to allocate a sufficient number of columns for each variable. For example, if only two columns are used to record a weight variable, only weights less than 100 pounds will fit. Always allocate the maximum number of columns that you might need. Don't worry if your observed data do not actually require that many columns.

All data files considered in this manual are *rectangular.* That is, all cases have the same variables and the same number of lines per case. Some data files are not rectangular. For instance, every case may not have the same variables recorded. So, in a study of adverse drug reactions, cases that are alive will not have a data line detailing autopsy findings. Another nonrectangular file might not define all cases as the same unit, as in a file containing some lines with data about families and some lines with data about individual members within families. Currently, SPSS/PC+ does not contain facilities for handling these kinds of files.

2.6
Freefield Format

Sometimes it is more convenient not to have to worry about arranging variables in particular column locations. Instead, for each case, variables are entered in the same order with at least one blank separating values. Figure 2.6 shows how a freefield data file for the first three cases of the beer data might look.

Figure 2.6   Beer data in freefield format

```
1 'MILLER HIGH LIFE' 1 1 2.49 .42 149 17 4.7 2 0
1 BUDWEISER 1 1 2.59 .43 144 15 4.7 2 0
1 SCHLITZ 1 1 2.59 .43 151 19 4.9 2 0
```

Figure 2.5b differs from Figure 2.6 in several ways. Whenever there is a blank within the name, the name of the beer is enclosed in apostrophes (or quotation marks). This indicates that the blanks are part of the value. Decimal points must be included in the data. Freefield data are discussed in greater detail in the Command Reference under DATA LIST FREE.

2.7
DESIGNING FORMS

When a study is based on data already gathered, there is not much that can be done about the forms on which data reside or how the information is recorded. For example, if education is recorded in categories, the actual number of years cannot be entered into the data file. However, when a study is planned in advance, special forms can be designed that indicate both the type of information to be collected and where it will reside on the computer file. This type of form makes data entry much easier. You can enter the information directly from the form onto a disk using a terminal.

Sometimes data collection forms are designed with space for miscellaneous comments. These comments can be analyzed only if they are coded. For example, if undergraduate major is listed in the comments section, it must be coded into a variable. A coding scheme such as 1=physical sciences, 2=social sciences, 3=humanities, 4=engineering, and so forth could be used. Unless the comment section has specific codable information, it cannot be analyzed in any reasonable manner.

2.8
THE DATA FILE

The data file is the most crucial component of any analysis. Unless the data have been carefully gathered, recorded, and entered, all subsequent analyses will be of limited use. Always try to obtain as much of the necessary information as possible for all of the cases that are to be included in a study. A special code standing for missing information should be reserved only for cases where it is impossible to ascertain a certain value. Once the data have been coded and entered, make sure to check the values. Any suspicious values should be confirmed. They may be the result of coding or data-entry errors. Subsequent chapters show how you can use SPSS/PC+ to help locate errors in a data file.

2.9
THE SPSS/PC+
SESSION

After you have prepared your data, you are ready to run the SPSS/PC+ program. The way in which you start the program and enter commands to read, modify, and analyze your data, or to obtain help about the system itself, were described in Running SPSS/PC+, earlier in this manual.

The SPSS/PC+ commands for carrying out analyses follow a simple progression. At the start of a session, you need to tell the system how to interpret (and perhaps where to find) your data. You might want to add some labels and print formats to make the output more readable and identify values that stand for missing data. These commands are discussed in Chapter 3. Next, you might wish to make some modifications to the data file. For example, if you have recorded age in years (as you were advised to do above), you might want to create a new variable that gives age categories. The commands for this type of operation are in Chapter 4. For a given analysis, you might want to select a particular subset of cases or perhaps a random sample. Commands for selecting and sampling cases are discussed in Chapter 5. Finally, you can use one of many procedure commands to produce a report or a statistical analysis. Chapters 7 through 14 contain detailed information about the procedures available in SPSS/PC+. You can continue modifying the data and running procedures until you end the session with the FINISH command.

Contents _____

3 Defining Data

The data definition commands in SPSS/PC+ answer the following questions:

• Where is the collection of data stored on your machine?
• How many lines are there for each case?
• What are the names of the variables, and where are they located on the data file?
• What labels should be attached to variables and values?
• What values are used to represent missing information?

3.1
DESCRIBING THE DATA FILE

The SPSS/PC+ commands in Figure 3.1 define and produce a listing of data from the beer data. Assume that the data are entered in fixed format. That is, variables are stored in the same column locations for all of the cases. Section 3.7 discusses data definition when data are entered using freefield format.

The first data definition command is DATA LIST, which tells SPSS/PC+ where to find the data and how to read it.

Figure 3.1 Command file for the beer data

```
DATA LIST /RATING 1 BEER 3-22(A) ORIGIN 25 AVAIL 27
    PRICE 29-31(2) COST 33-35(2) CALORIES 37-39 SODIUM 41-42
    ALCOHOL 44-45(1) CLASS 47 LIGHT 49.

VARIABLE LABELS AVAIL 'AVAILABILITY IN THE U.S.' /
    PRICE 'PRICE PER 6-PACK' /
    COST 'COST PER 12 FLUID OUNCES' /
    CALORIES 'CALORIES PER 12 FLUID OUNCES' /
    SODIUM 'SODIUM PER 12 FLUID OUNCES IN MG' /
    ALCOHOL 'ALCOHOL BY VOLUME (IN %)' /
    CLASS 'PRICE CLASS'.

VALUE LABELS RATING 1 'VERY GOOD' 2 'GOOD' 3 'FAIR' /
    ORIGIN 1 'USA' 2 'CANADA' 3 'FRANCE' 4 'HOLLAND'
    5 'MEXICO' 6 'GERMANY'  7 'JAPAN' /
    AVAIL 1 'NATIONAL' 2 'REGIONAL' /
    CLASS 0 'NOT GIVEN' 1 'SUPER-PREMIUM'
    2 'PREMIUM' 3 'POPULAR'/
    LIGHT 0 'REGULAR' 1 'LIGHT'.

MISSING VALUE CLASS(0).
BEGIN DATA.
1  MILLER HIGH LIFE      1 1 249   42 149 17 47 2 0
1  BUDWEISER             1 1 259   43 144 15 47 2 0
1  SCHLITZ               1 1 259   43 151 19 49 2 0
.....        Remainder of cases not shown
END DATA.

LIST VARIABLES=RATING TO PRICE CALORIES ALCOHOL /CASES=10.
FINISH.
```

3.2
Locating the Data

You can enter data along with your SPSS/PC+ commands or read data from a separate file. If the data are in a file other than the SPSS/PC+ command file, name the file in which the data are stored with the FILE subcommand, as in

```
DATA LIST FILE='BEER.DAT'
```

BEER.DAT is the name SPSS/PC+ uses to locate the file on which the data are stored. You specify the name of the file in apostrophes (or quotes). If the file is not stored in the current directory, you can give the path name within the apostrophes (see Part A: Running SPSS/PC+). If you enter the data in the same file as the SPSS/PC+ commands, you do not need to use a FILE subcommand (see Section 3.14).

3.3
Choosing Variable Names

After you have identified the data file, you assign names to each of the variables and give their location on the file. You use the assigned variable name to refer to a variable throughout the SPSS/PC+ session. For example, a variable that describes father's occupation might be named PAOCCUP. Keep in mind the following rules when you name variables:

- The name must begin with a letter or the @ symbol. The remaining characters in the name can be any letter, any digit, a period, or the symbols _, $, #, or @.
- The length of the name cannot exceed eight characters.
- Blanks and special symbols such as &, !, ?, /, ', cannot occur in a variable name.
- Each variable must have a unique name—duplication is not allowed.
- The reserved keywords in Table 3.3 cannot be used as variable names since they have special meaning in SPSS/PC+.

The following are all valid variable names: LOCATION, LOC@5, X_1, and OVER$500.

You can create a set of variable names by using the keyword TO. When you are assigning new names, as in DATA LIST specifications, ITEM1 TO ITEM5 is equivalent to five names: ITEM1, ITEM2, ITEM3, ITEM4, and ITEM5. The prefix can be any valid name and the numbers can be any integers, so long as the first number is smaller than the second, and the full variable name, including the number, does not exceed eight characters.

Table 3.3   SPSS/PC+ reserved keywords

ALL	AND	BY	EQ	GE	GT	LE
LT	NE	NOT	OR	TO	WITH	

It is a good idea to assign names that help you identify the variables. You could give the names X and Z to variables for age and sex, but the names AGE and SEX give you a much better idea of the nature of each variable. The variable names assigned to the beer data include RATING for the rating of the beer, ALCOHOL for the alcohol content, PRICE for the price of a six-pack, and CALORIES for caloric content.

3.4
Indicating Column Locations

Along with a variable's name, you specify its column location on the data file. All variables on the same line are identified at the same time. For example, the command

```
DATA LIST FILE='BEER.DAT'
/RATING 1 BEER 3-22(A) ORIGIN 25 AVAIL 27.
```

describes four variables. Variable definition begins with the first slash. The numbers after the variable names give their column locations. For example, RATING is in column 1, and BEER is in columns 3 through 22 (and is alphanumeric; see Section 3.8).

Although variables from the same data line must be defined together, they do not need to be defined in any particular sequence within that line. That is, variables at the end of a line can be defined before those at the beginning of the same line. It is the order in which you define variables that determines their order on your SPSS/PC+ active file, not necessarily their original order on your file.

If several variables are recorded in adjacent columns of the same line and have the same width and format type (numeric or string), you can use an abbreviated format to define them on DATA LIST. List all of the variable names followed by the beginning column location of the first variable in the list, a dash, and the ending column location of the last variable in the list. For example, in the command

```
DATA LIST FILE='HUB.DAT' /
  DEPT82 19 SEX 20 MOHIRED YRHIRED 12-15
```

MOHIRED and YRHIRED form a list of variables, and 12–15 is the column specification for both. (The second slash is needed for this file to skip a second line of data not being defined; see Section 3.6). The DATA LIST command divides the total number of columns specified equally among the variables in the list. Thus, MOHIRED is in columns 12–13 and YRHIRED is in columns 14–15. Be careful to use variables of equal width when defining data this way. If you use variables of different widths, and SPSS/PC+ can divide the number of columns by the number of variables equally, your data will be read incorrectly. If the total number of columns is not an even multiple of the number of variables listed, SPSS/PC+ displays an error message and does not read the file.

3.5
Establishing Display Formats

Whenever you see the values of a variable displayed, SPSS/PC+ knows what format to use because it knows the variable's width and type from the DATA LIST specifications. This information, along with the variable name, labels, and missing values (see Sections 3.10 and 3/11), forms the *dictionary* portion of your SPSS/PC+ active file. Any time that you want to change the format of a numeric variable (string variable formats cannot be changed), use the FORMAT command (see Command Reference: FORMAT).

3.6
Specifying Data Recorded on Multiple Lines

Sometimes your data are located on more than one line or record for each case. To read more than one line for each case, enter a slash and define the variables recorded on the first line, and then enter a slash followed by the the variable definitions for the next data line. Repeat this procedure until you have defined all lines for each case in your data file. For example, the following DATA LIST command defines a personnel file that was entered with two lines per case:

```
DATA LIST FILE='HUB.DAT' /
  DEPT82 19 SEX 20 MOHIRED YRHIRED 12-15
  /SALARY82 21-25.
```

This DATA LIST reads variables DEPT82, SEX, MOHIRED, and YRHIRED from the first line and SALARY82 from the second line.

3.7
Freefield Data Input

With freefield format, successive data values are simply separated by one or more blanks or one comma. Variables must be in the same order for each of the cases, but they need not be in the same columns (see Chapter 2). If you choose this manner of entering data, specify the keyword FREE after the DATA LIST command. In this case, column locations are not specified after the variable names. However, you must indicate the length of long string variables using the A notation (see Section 3.8). It is probably a good idea to also give the length of short strings so the dictionary format will be correct (the default for short strings is A8). For example,

```
DATA LIST FREE /
    RATING BEER (A20) ORIGIN AVAIL PRICE COST CALORIES
    SODIUM ALCOHOL CLASS LIGHT.
```

can be used to define the variables for the beer example. Note that if values of string variables include blanks (such as Miller High Life for the BEER variable), they must be enclosed within apostrophes in the data file. Otherwise, the blanks are read as indicating a new variable.

The advantage of freefield format is obvious: data entry is much simpler since variables do not have to be put in particular locations. The major disadvantage of freefield data entry is that if you inadvertently omit a data value, all values for subsequent variables and cases are incorrect. For example, if the rating variable is omitted for the second case, the value for the type of beer is taken as the rating (which will cause an error since it is a string value), and everything that follows is wrong. A similar problem can arise if you mistakenly enter an extra value. Therefore, it is particularly important to list and check the data values after input with freefield format.

Another disadvantage of freefield input is that all numeric variables are assigned dictionary formats of width eight and two decimal places. However, you can use the FORMAT command to assign proper formats following the DATA LIST command.

3.8
Types of Variables

You can define two types of variables with SPSS/PC+: numeric and string (alphanumeric). A numeric variable contains only numbers. Numeric variables can be either decimals (such as 12.345) or integers (such as 1234). A string variable can contain a combination of letters, numbers, and special characters. There are two types of string variables—short strings and long strings. A string variable whose values contain eight characters or less is considered a short string. The variable SEX, coded as F or M, is a short string. In the beer data example, the name of the beer is a long string. The difference is that short strings can be used in several data transformation and procedure commands where long strings cannot. String variables are identified with the letter A in parentheses following the column specification on the DATA LIST command, as in:

```
DATA LIST FILE='BEER.DAT' /BEER 3-22(A).
```

where variable BEER is defined as a string variable.

When using freefield format, you should also indicate the width of the string variable, as in BEER (A20). Use the maximum string-value length for a variable as the width. Count all characters and blanks in calculating the width. For example, "Miller High Life" has a width of 16 with blanks included.

3.9
Indicating Decimal Places

By default, DATA LIST assumes that the data format type is numeric and that the numbers are integers, or that any decimal points are explicitly coded. To indicate noninteger values when the decimal point is not actually coded in the data, specify the number of *implied* decimal places by enclosing the intended number in parentheses following the column specification. The specification

```
DATA LIST FILE='BEER.DAT' /ALCOHOL 44-45(1).
```

locates the variable that measures alcohol content in columns 44 through 45. The last digit of ALCOHOL is stored as a decimal position.

For example, if the number 47 is stored in columns 44–45, the specification ALCOHOL 44–45 (1) results in the number 4.7. The specification ALCOHOL 44–45 (2) results in the number 0.47. The dictionary format is also affected by the implied decimal. The two-column designation 44–45 (1) results in a three-column dictionary format in order to accommodate the decimal point. If the number is stored in the data file with the decimal point, the decimal point overrides the DATA LIST format specification (but the dictionary format might have to be adjusted). Implied decimals can only be used with fixed-format data.

3.10
VARIABLE AND VALUE LABELS

The VARIABLE LABELS and VALUE LABELS commands supply information that is used for labeling the output of SPSS/PC+ sessions. These labels are optional, but using them often makes the output more readable. Some variables that have many values, such as age or weight, do not need value labels since the values themselves are meaningful.

The VARIABLE LABELS command assigns variables an extended descriptive label. Specify the variable name, followed by at least one comma or blank, and the label enclosed in apostrophes or quotation marks. Multiple label specifications are optionally separated by slashes, as in:

```
VARIABLE LABELS AVAIL 'AVAILABILITY IN THE U.S.' /
   PRICE 'PRICE PER 6-PACK' /
   COST 'COST PER 12 FLUID OUNCES' /
   CALORIES 'CALORIES PER 12 FLUID OUNCES' /
   SODIUM 'SODIUM PER 12 FLUID OUNCES IN MG' /
   ALCOHOL 'ALCOHOL BY VOLUME (IN %)' /
   CLASS 'PRICE CLASS'.
```

This command assigns variable labels to the variables AVAIL through CLASS. A variable label applies to only one variable. The variable must have been previously defined on a DATA LIST, GET, or IMPORT command, or on one of the transformation commands that create new variables. The label can be up to 40 characters long and can include blanks and any other characters.

To use an apostrophe as part of a label, enclose the label in quotation marks, as in:

```
VARIABLE LABELS SALARY82 "EMPLOYEE'S 1982 SALARY".
```

Quotation marks are entered in a label in the same manner.

The VALUE LABELS command assigns descriptive labels to values. The VALUE LABELS command is followed by a variable name, or variable list, and a list of values with associated labels. The command

```
VALUE LABELS RATING 1 'VERY GOOD' 2 'GOOD' 3 'FAIR' /
   ORIGIN 1 'USA' 2 'CANADA' 3 'FRANCE' 4 'HOLLAND'
   5 'MEXICO' 6 'GERMANY'  7 'JAPAN' /
   AVAIL 1 'NATIONAL' 2 'REGIONAL' /
   CLASS 0 'NOT GIVEN' 1 'SUPER-PREMIUM' 2 'PREMIUM' 3 'POPULAR' /
   LIGHT 0 'REGULAR' 1 'LIGHT'.
```

assigns labels to the values for the variables RATING, ORIGIN, AVAIL, CLASS, and LIGHT. The labels for each variable are separated from the labels for the preceding variable by a slash. You can assign labels for values of any variable already defined. If the variable is a string, the value must be enclosed in apostrophes. Value labels can be up to 20 characters long and can contain any characters, including blanks.

The VALUE LABELS command completely replaces all of the value labels for the variables named on it. If you want to add one or more new value labels or replace some of the existing labels without entering the whole set of labels, use the ADD VALUE LABELS command. This command leaves unchanged the labels for values that are not mentioned.

3.11
IDENTIFYING
MISSING VALUES

Sometimes information for a particular variable is not available for a case. When information about the value of a variable is unknown, a special code is used to indicate that the value is missing. For example, if a patient's age is not known, this can be indicated by a code such as −1 to indicate that the information is missing.

The MISSING VALUE command identifies the value that represents missing information. Specify the variable name or variable list and the specified missing value in parentheses, as in:

```
MISSING VALUE CLASS(0).
```

This command assigns the value 0 as missing for variable CLASS.

User-missing values specified on the MISSING VALUE command are distinguished from the *system-missing* value (which is indicated on output by a period). SPSS/PC+ assigns the system-missing value when it encounters a value other than a number for a variable declared as numeric on the DATA LIST command. For example, blanks are set to system-missing for numeric variables. An alternative to entering a special value, then, is to leave a field blank. However, you will find that assigning a user-missing value gives you more control in tables and other results from SPSS/PC+.

System-missing values are also assigned when new variables created with data transformation commands are undefined, as when an attempt is made to divide by 0 or when a case is missing a value for a variable used in computing the new variable.

3.12
THE ACTIVE FILE

The DATA LIST command defines an *active file*. This is the file you work with during your session. The active file exists only temporarily unless you use the SAVE command. It consists of a dictionary of variable names and labels, value labels, and missing-value specifications; it also contains the actual data, whether you entered them interactively or read them in from another file. At any time in your session, you can modify the labels (by entering new labels) or the data (with the commands discussed in the next chapter). You can use the SAVE command to write a copy of the active file to disk for later use. When saved to disk in this way, it is called a *system file*.

In addition to modifying the data values or the labels in your active file, you can completely replace it with another active file, or you can combine it with system files that you have previously saved to disk. Any command which defines a new active file will replace the existing active file. (DATA LIST, GET, IMPORT, JOIN, and sometimes AGGREGATE do this.) Use the JOIN command to combine the active file with existing system files.

3.13
LISTING DATA

Once you have defined the data file, you are ready to specify an SPSS/PC+ procedure. SPSS/PC+ procedures are used to tabulate the data, to calculate statistics, and to generate reports and plots. The session in Figure 3.1 requests a listing of the data values for the first 10 cases. The LIST command for this session is:

```
LIST VARIABLES=RATING TO PRICE CALORIES ALCOHOL /CASES=10.
```

The subcommand VARIABLES indicates which of the variables are to be displayed (the default is to list all variables). The CASES subcommand indicates the number of observations for which the values are to be listed (the default is to list all cases). LIST uses the dictionary formats to display the variable's values. Therefore, it is a good check on whether a new variable has the proper width and number of decimal places.

Figure 3.13 shows the listing of the first 10 cases. This listing is useful for spotting errors in data entry or data definition. For example, if the wrong columns have been given for the AVAIL variable, strange values will probably appear in the listing. From this listing, you might decide to assign a DOLLAR format to PRICE (see Command Reference: FORMAT).

Figure 3.13   Output from LIST

```
RATING BEER              ORIGIN AVAIL PRICE CALORIES ALCOHOL

     1    MILLER HIGH LIFE      1     1   2.49    149      4.7
     1    BUDWEISER             1     1   2.59    144      4.7
     1    SCHLITZ               1     1   2.59    151      4.9
     1    LOWENBRAU             1     1   2.89    157      4.9
     1    MICHELOB              1     1   2.99    162      5.0
     1    LABATTS               2     2   3.15    147      5.0
     1    MOLSON                2     2   3.35    154      5.1
     1    HENRY WEINHARD        1     2   3.65    149      4.7
     1    KRONENBOURG           3     2   4.39    170      5.2
     1    HEINEKEN              4     1   4.59    152      5.0

NUMBER OF CASES READ =     10    NUMBER OF CASES LISTED =      10
```

You can use the TO convention on a procedure command to refer to variables that are adjacent in your SPSS/PC+ active file (the order in which they were defined on your DATA LIST command). Thus, if you specify VARA TO VARD on a procedure, VARA, VARD, and any variables that have been defined between VARA and VARD are analyzed. For example, the command

```
LIST VARIABLES=RATING TO PRICE CALORIES ALCOHOL.
```

requests a listing for variables RATING, BEER, ORIGIN, AVAIL, and PRICE, plus variables CALORIES and ALCOHOL. See Figure 3.1 for the DATA LIST command that defines these variables.

3.14
INLINE DATA

Sometimes, instead of keeping your data in an external file (that you refer to with the FILE subcommand), you may prefer to enter your data along with your SPSS/PC+ commands. When this is the case, separate the *inline data* from the other lines in the command file with the BEGIN DATA and END DATA commands. The BEGIN DATA command follows the data-definition commands and precedes the data, and the END DATA command follows the last line of the data (see Figure 3.1).

3.15
READING MATRICES

For the SPSS/PC+ procedures FACTOR, REGRESSION, ONEWAY, and CLUSTER (discussed in *SPSS/PC+ Statistics*), instead of reading the original cases you can enter certain summary statistics such as means, sample sizes, correlations, covariances, or distance coefficients. This results in a considerable decrease in processing time. All statistical computations are based on the summary statistics. (The results you get are the same as if you had entered the original cases, since all of the necessary information is contained in the summary statistics.)

Reading intermediate values instead of the actual cases is useful when you have used SPSS/PC+ procedures to write a file with summary results or when the summary results are available from some other source, such as journals.

When you enter summary statistics, special specifications are required on the DATA LIST command (see Command Reference: DATA LIST—Matrix Materials).

3.16
USING AN SPSS/PC+ SYSTEM FILE

Once you have defined your data file in SPSS/PC+, you do not need to repeat the data definition process. Information from the data definition commands described in this chapter can be permanently saved along with the data on specially formatted files called the SPSS/PC+ *system file* and the *portable file*. Variables created or altered by data transformations and the descriptive information for these variables can also be saved on these files.

The system file is used in subsequent SPSS/PC+ sessions without requiring respecification of variable locations, formats, missing values, or variable and value labels. You can update the system file, altering the descriptive information or modifying the data, and you can save the updated version in a new system file. See the SAVE and GET commands in the Command Reference.

The portable file is used to transport your data plus definitions between SPSS/PC+ and SPSS-X on a mainframe computer without having to redefine them each time. See the EXPORT and IMPORT commands in the Command Reference.

3.17
USING SPREADSHEET OR DATABASE FILES

If your data are already in a spreadsheet or database file, you may be able to use the TRANSLATE command to read them directly into SPSS/PC+. TRANSLATE reads

• Spreadsheet files from Lotus 1-2-3 or Symphony.
• Spreadsheet files saved in SYLK format by Multiplan or other programs.
• Database files from dBase-II, dBase-III, or dBase-III Plus.

TRANSLATE can also write your data into a spreadsheet or database file.

It is inefficient to translate the file format each time you use the data, so you should save it in the form of an SPSS/PC+ system file if you plan to analyze the same data repeatedly.

See Command Reference: TRANSLATE for details on using the TRANSLATE command.

Contents_____

4 Transforming Data

In the beer data (see Chapter 1), 35 brands of beer are rated on a three-point scale with the categories "very good," "good," and "fair." Suppose you want to compare the beers on their ratings, but are interested only in making a dichotomous distinction between ratings of "good" and "fair." To do this, you would want to collapse the rating categories of "very good" and "good" into a single category.

Or suppose you have done a survey of political attitudes, and you have five "yes" or "no" questions on the topic of women's rights. You might want to create a new variable that counts the total number of "yes" responses to the five items.

Operations such as these, where you take existing variables and alter their values or use them to create new variables, are called *data transformations.*

There are four commands in SPSS/PC+ that allow you to perform a wide variety of data transformations. Use the RECODE command to alter the values of an existing variable. Typical reasons for recoding variables include combining several values into one, rearranging the order of categories, or carrying out simple data checks. You would use RECODE to collapse the rating categories in the beer data.

The COMPUTE command creates new variables through numeric transformations of existing ones. For instance, the beer data contain a variable that is the number of calories in 12 ounces of beer. You might want to use COMPUTE to figure out how many calories there would be in an eight-ounce glass of each brand.

The COUNT command creates a new variable that, for each case, counts the occurrences of certain values across a list of variables. You would use COUNT to add the "yes" responses to the women's rights questions on the political survey.

You can use the IF command to transform data differently for subsets of cases. For example, a company may award vacation time on the basis of length of employment. The IF command could be used to calculate vacation time for employees who have been with the company for varying lengths of time.

4.1
RECODING VALUES
OF VARIABLES

The RECODE command tells SPSS/PC+ to make specified changes in a variable's values as the data are being read. Take the availability variable from the beer data as an example. The command

```
RECODE AVAIL (1=2)(2=1).
```

reverses values 1 and 2 for variable AVAIL (i.e., if a case has value 1, it is changed to 2, and vice versa).

To be recoded, a variable must already exist in your data file. The variable's name precedes the list of value specifications on the RECODE command. You can create as many new values for a variable as you wish, as long as each specification is enclosed in parentheses. A single specification can be used to recode several values as one new value. Thus, the command

```
RECODE RATING (1,2=1)(3,4=2).
```

changes RATING variable values to 1 for cases with original ratings of 1 or 2, and to 2 for cases originally rated as 3 or 4.

You cannot list more than one *new* value in a single value specification. Thus, specifications like (2,3=0,1) or (1=5,6) cannot be used.

The value specifications on a RECODE command are evaluated from left to right, and the value of a case is recoded only once in a single RECODE command. For example, if a case has the value 0 for the variable SEX, the command

```
RECODE SEX (0=1)(1=0)(3=99).
```

recodes SEX as 1 for that case. This value is not recoded back to 0 by the second value specification. Variable values that you do not mention on a RECODE command are left unchanged.

If you want to recode several variables in the same way, you can use a single RECODE command to do so, as in the command:

```
RECODE SEX RACE SURGERY (0=1)(1=0)(3=99).
```

In addition, you can use one RECODE command to perform different recodes for different variables by separating the variable names and their specifications with a slash, as in the command:

```
RECODE SODIUM (10 THRU 15=1)(15 THRU 20=2) /
   COST (.28 THRU .39=1)(.40 THRU .50=2)(.51 THRU 1.20=3).
```

You can use the TO keyword to refer to several consecutive variables in the file. For example, the command

```
RECODE SCORE1 TO SCORE5 (5=1)(6=2)(7=3).
```

recodes SCORE1, SCORE5, and all the variables between them in the file.

4.2 Recoding Numeric Variables

Several keywords are available to facilitate recoding of numeric variables. Use the keywords THRU, LOWEST, and HIGHEST to recode a range of variables. Thus, the command

```
RECODE CALORIES (68 THRU 100=1)(101 THRU 170=2).
```

recodes all the values between 68 and 100 (inclusive) as 1 and all the values between 101 and 170 (inclusive) as 2 for the CALORIES variable. The LOWEST (or LO) keyword specifies the lowest value of a variable, while HIGHEST (or HI) specifies the highest value. The command

```
RECODE CALORIES (LO THRU 100=1)(101 THRU HI=2).
```

is equivalent to the previous command. When you use LOWEST or HIGHEST to specify a range, user-missing values in the range are recoded, but system-missing values are not changed.

You can use the ELSE keyword to recode all values not previously mentioned into a single category. Thus, the command

```
RECODE CALORIES (LO THRU 100=1)(ELSE=2).
```

is equivalent to the previous two commands. ELSE should be the last specification for a variable, since RECODE will ignore subsequent specifications for that variable. ELSE does recode system-missing values.

You can also use ELSE as a data-cleaning device. For example, if the variables SCORE1 to SCORE5 have only 5, 6, and 7 as legitimate values, you might use the command

```
RECODE SCORE1 TO SCORE5 (5=1)(6=2)(7=3)(ELSE=SYSMIS).
```

to recode the valid values to new values and recode the nonvalid values as system-missing.

4.3
Recoding Missing Values

The MISSING keyword is useful for recoding all missing values (user- or system-missing) to a single value. For example, if -99 is the missing value you have declared for the AGE variable, the command

```
RECODE AGE (MISSING=-1).
```

recodes -99 and any system-missing values for AGE to -1, while leaving the other AGE values unchanged.

You can use the SYSMIS keyword as either an input or output specification. The command

```
RECODE AGE (SYSMIS=-1).
```

recodes the system-missing value to -1.

The SYSMIS keyword as an output specification recodes specified values to system-missing, as in the commands

```
RECODE AGE (MISSING=SYSMIS).
```

and

```
RECODE AGE (-99=SYSMIS).
```

Both commands recode the AGE missing values to system-missing.

You *cannot* use the MISSING keyword as an output specification on RECODE to recode values as user-missing. Thus, SPSS/PC+ does not accept a recode specification like (17=MISSING) for the variable AGE. To classify value 17 for AGE as missing, use the MISSING VALUE command, as in

```
MISSING VALUE AGE(17).
```

When you use the MISSING and SYSMIS keywords to recode missing values to a single new value, that value is not automatically considered a missing value. The MISSING VALUE command is required to define it as such, as in the following example:

```
RECODE AGE (MISSING=-1).
MISSING VALUE AGE(-1).
```

4.4
Recoding Continuous Value Ranges

If a variable has noninteger values, some values may escape recoding unless you make certain they are included in a value range. For example, the command

```
RECODE AGE (0 THRU 17=1)(18 THRU 65=2)(66 THRU 99=3).
```

does not recode values between 17 and 18 and between 65 and 66. Thus, values like 17.2 and 65.8 would be left unchanged. You can avoid this problem by using overlapping endpoint values in the specifications, as in the command:

```
RECODE AGE (66 THRU 99=3)(18 THRU 66=2)(0 THRU 18=1).
```

Note that the order of the recode specifications has been reversed, since a value is recoded only once into the first specification it meets. Thus, the value 66 is coded as a 3 and is not altered further, even though it serves as an endpoint on the following specification.

4.5
Recoding String Variables

You can use the RECODE command to recode string variables. Only short strings (those containing eight or fewer characters) can be recoded. The keywords LOWEST or LO, HIGHEST or HI, THRU, SYSMIS and MISSING do not apply to recoding string variables.

When recoding string variables, you must enclose all values in apostrophes (or quotation marks). For example, the command

```
RECODE LIGHT ('Y'='A')('N'='B').
```

recodes *Y* into *A* and *N* into *B* for the string variable LIGHT.

When recoding string variables, the values in a specification must be of equal length and must have the same length that you have defined for the alphanumeric variable being recoded. Use blanks to specify the exact string-value length. For example, the command

```
RECODE GRADES ('ABC '='ABCD').
```

recodes the value *ABC* into *ABCD* for the four-character string variable GRADES.

4.6
Automatic Recoding

Sometimes it's useful to have consecutive numbers as codes for a variable. Some statistical procedures require numeric data, and it's often more efficient if the numeric codes are consecutive numbers (1, 2, 3 rather than 152, 2002, 9314.5). If you know what all the existing codes are, you can do this with RECODE, but it might take quite a bit of typing. The AUTORECODE command is designed to do this automatically.

```
AUTORECODE CITY INTO CITYCODE.
```

This command looks at all the existing values of CITY and creates a new variable named CITYCODE. CITYCODE will have the value 1 for all cases that have the first value of CITY (in ascending order if CITY is numeric, or in alphabetical order if CITY is string). CITYCODE will have the value 2 for all cases with the second value of CITY, and so on.

You can automatically recode several variables by naming them before the keyword INTO, and providing the same number of new names after INTO. If you'd rather assign new codes in descending numeric order, or reverse alphabetical order, use the DESCENDING subcommand after the list of new variable names. And if you want to see a table of old and new values, specify PRINT.

```
AUTORECODE PRODUCT, SALESREP INTO PRODNUM, REP /
    DESCENDING /PRINT.
```

AUTORECODE assigns value labels to the new variables that it creates. If the existing variables have value labels, they are copied to the new variables. If not, the *values* of the existing variables are converted into value labels for the new ones.

By using AUTORECODE on a long string variable, you can obtain a numeric variable that's accepted by SPSS/PC+ transformation commands.

4.7
COMPUTING NEW VARIABLES

The COMPUTE command creates new variables through numeric transformations of already existing variables. COMPUTE names the variable you want to create (the *target variable*) followed by an *expression* defining the variable. For example, the command

```
COMPUTE TOTSCORE=MIDTERM+FINAL+HOMEWORK.
```

defines the new variable TOTSCORE as the sum of the variables MIDTERM, FINAL, and HOMEWORK.

The target variable can be a variable that already exists or a new variable. If the target variable already exists, its values are replaced with those produced by the specified transformation. If it is a new variable, it is added to the end of the dictionary in your active file.

The expression on the COMPUTE command can use existing numeric variables, constants, arithmetic operators (such as + and −), numeric functions such as SQRT (square root) and TRUNC (truncate), the missing value function (VALUE), the cross-case function (LAG), random-number functions, and the date function (YRMODA). For example, the command

```
COMPUTE GRADESCR=.35*MIDTERM+.45*FINAL+.2*HOMEWORK.
```

creates a new variable, GRADESCR, that is the weighted average of the variables MIDTERM, FINAL, and HOMEWORK.

4.8
Transforming String Variables

You can use COMPUTE to create or modify short string variables. A variable can be set equal to an existing string variable or to a string constant, as in the command

```
COMPUTE STATE='IL'.
```

which creates variable STATE with the value *IL* for all cases.

String values and constants must be enclosed in apostrophes or quotation marks.

When you create a new string variable by setting a variable name equal to a string constant, the new string variable is assigned a dictionary format equal to the width of the string constant. Thus, the previous command creates STATE as a two-character string variable. When you create a string variable by setting a variable name equal to an existing string variable, the new variable's dictionary format is the same as that of the original variable.

Leading or trailing blanks must be specified. Once you have created a string variable, all subsequent transformations on the variable must use the width first specified.

4.9
Specifying Arithmetic Operations

The following arithmetic operators are available for transforming numeric variables with COMPUTE:

+ *Addition.*
− *Subtraction.*
* *Multiplication.*
/ *Division.*
** *Exponentiation.*

Arithmetic operators must be explicitly specified. You cannot, for example, write (PROPTAX)(100) instead of (PROPTAX)*100.

You can include blanks in an arithmetic expression to improve readability, as in the command:

```
COMPUTE TAXTOTAL = PROPTAX + FICA + STATETAX + FEDTAX.
```

Since fairly complex expressions are possible, it is important to keep in mind the order in which operations are performed. Functions (see Sections 4.10 through 4.11) are evaluated first, then exponentiation, then multiplication and division, and, finally, addition and subtraction. Thus, if you specify

```
COMPUTE NEWRATE=SQRT(RATE1)/SQRT(RATE1)+SQRT(RATE3).
```

the square roots (SQRT) are calculated first, then the division is performed, and the addition is performed last.

You can control the order in which operations are performed by enclosing the operation you want executed first in parentheses. Thus, the command

```
COMPUTE NEWRATE=SQRT(RATE1)/(SQRT(RATE1)+SQRT(RATE3)).
```

produces different results from the previous command, since addition is performed before division.

Operations at the same level, as far as order of execution is concerned, are evaluated from left to right. For example, the command

```
COMPUTE SCORE=( A/B * C ).
```

results in a different value than the command

```
COMPUTE SCORE=( A/ (B * C) ).
```

since in the first command *A* is divided by *B*, and the resulting quantity multiplied by *C*, while the second command first multiplies *B* times *C* and then divides *A* by the resulting quantity.

If you are uncertain about the order of execution, you should use parentheses to make the order you want explicit.

4.10
Specifying Numeric Functions

You can specify numeric functions such as square roots, logarithms, and trigonometric functions in a COMPUTE expression. The quantity to be transformed by such a function is called the *argument* and is specified in parentheses after the function keyword. For example, in the command

```
COMPUTE TOTLCOST=RND(COST * 6).
```

the function RND (round to the nearest integer) acts on the argument COST * 6 to create the new variable TOTLCOST.

The argument can be a variable name, a number, or an expression involving several variables. A numeric function can have only one argument.

The following numeric function keywords are available:

ABS   *Absolute value.* For example, ABS(-4.7) is 4.7; ABS(4.7) is 4.7.

RND   *Argument rounded to the nearest integer.* For example, RND(-4.7) is -5.

TRUNC   *Argument truncated to its integer part.* For example, TRUNC(-4.7) is -4.

MOD10   *Remainder resulting when the argument is divided by 10.* For example, MOD(198) is 8.

SQRT   *Square root.*

EXP   *Exponential. e is raised to the power of the argument.*

LG10   *Base 10 logarithm.*

LN   *Natural or Naperian logarithm.*

ARTAN   *Arctangent.*

SIN   *Sine.* The argument must be in radians.

COS   *Cosine.* The argument must be in radians.

For example, in the command

```
COMPUTE LOGINCOM=LN(INCOME+1).
```

LOGINCOM is the natural logarithm of the expression INCOME+1.

4.11
Other Functions

Also available on COMPUTE are two random-number functions (UNIFORM and NORMAL), the cross-case function (LAG), and the date function (YRMODA).

UNIFORM(arg)   *A uniform pseudo-random number.* The number is drawn from a distribution having values uniformly distributed between zero and the value of the argument.

NORMAL(arg)   *A normal pseudo-random number.* The number is drawn from a normal distribution with a mean of zero and a standard deviation equal to the argument.

LAG(arg)   *Get the value of the previous case for the variable named.*

YRMODA(arg list)   *Convert the year, month, and day in the argument list into a day number.* The year, month, and day are specified in that order. The number computed is the number of days since October 15, 1582 (the first day of the Gregorian calendar).

All of these functions can be used with numeric variables. Only the LAG function is available for short string variables.

4.12
The YRMODA Function

The YRMODA function converts a given date into the number of days since October 15, 1582. For example the expression YRMODA(1582,10,15) returns a value of 1. YRMODA(1800,1,1) returns 79337, indicating that January 1, 1800 is 79,336 days after the beginning of the Gregorian calendar.

The time interval between two dates can be calculated by converting each of the dates to day numbers and then subtracting the earlier day from the later one. For example, to calculate an individual's age in years on July 4, 1982, specify

```
AGE=(YRMODA(1982,7,4) - YRMODA(BYR,BMO,BDAY)) /365.25
```

where BYR is the year, BMO the month, and BDAY the day of birth.

The YRMODA function has three arguments, which can be variables, constants, or expressions that result in integer values.

- The first argument can be any year from 1582 to 47516. If you specify a number between 00 and 99, SPSS/PC+ will interpret it to mean 1900 to 1999.
- The second argument is the month, coded from 1 to 13. Month 13 refers to the first month of the subsequent year. For example, YRMODA(84,13,1) specifies January 1, 1985.
- The third argument is a day from 0 through 31. Day 0 specifies the last day of the previous month, regardless of whether it was 28, 29, 30, or 31. Thus, (84,2,0) refers to the last day of January in 1984. This is equivalent to (84,1,31), since January has 31 days.

4.13
Using Functions in Complex Expressions

You can specify more than one function in an argument as well as combine functions with arithmetic operators. Such arguments will be evaluated in the order described in Section 4.9 or in the order specified by parentheses. For example, if the command

```
COMPUTE PCTTAXES=RND((TAXES/INCOME)*100).
```

is used, TAXES is first divided by INCOME, the result is multiplied by 100, and this result is rounded off to the nearest integer to get the new variable PCTTAXES.

4.14
Missing Values

If a case has missing values for any of the variables used in a COMPUTE expression, the case is assigned the system-missing value for the computed variable. For example, if the command

```
COMPUTE AGECUBE=AGE**3.
```

is used, the AGECUBE variable will not be computed for any case with a missing value for AGE.

A case is also assigned the system-missing value for a computed variable when the specified operation is not defined for that case. For example, if the command

```
COMPUTE PCTTAXES=(TAXES/INCOME)*100.
```

is used, a case with the value 0 for INCOME is assigned the system-missing value for PCTTAXES because division by 0 is not defined. If the result of an expression cannot be represented on the computer (even when valid values are used in the expression itself), the system-missing value is assigned to the new variable. The following errors will result in assignment of the system-missing value:

**	A negative number to a noninteger power.
/	A divisor of 0.
SQRT	A negative argument.
EXP	An argument that produces a result too large to be represented on the computer.
LG10	A negative or 0 argument.
NORMAL	A negative or 0 argument.
YRMODA	Arguments that do not form a valid date.

Some arithmetic operations involving 0 produce the same result whether any of the arguments have missing values or not. These operations are shown in Table 4.14a.

Table 4.14a   Missing-value exceptions in numeric expressions

Expression	Computed value
0 * missing	= 0
0 / missing	= 0
missing ** 0	= 1
0 ** missing	= 0

SPSS/PC+ tries to evaluate a function using all the information it has, assigning the system-missing value only when there is insufficient information to compute the new variable. Table 4.14b summarizes the ways in which the system-missing value is assigned.

Table 4.14b   Missing values in arguments to functions

Function	Assigns system-missing value if
ABS (x)	x is missing
ARTAN (x)	
COS (x)	
EXP (x)	
LG10 (x)	
LN (x)	
NORMAL (x)	
RND (x)	
SIN (x)	
SQRT (x)	
TRUNC (x)	
UNIFORM (x)	
VALUE (x)	x is system-missing
YRMODA (x1,x2,x3)	any x is missing
MOD (x)	x is missing
LAG (x)	x is missing

4.15
Including User-Missing Values

The VALUE function on COMPUTE allows you to include user-missing values in a transformation.

VALUE *Ignore user-missing values for the variable specified.* The argument must be a variable name.

Thus, the command

```
COMPUTE TOTAL=VALUE(SCORE1)+VALUE(SCORE2)+VALUE(SCORE3).
```

includes user-missing values in computing TOTAL.

4.16
COUNTING VALUES
ACROSS VARIABLES

Use the COUNT command to create a variable that records, for each case, the number of times some value or list of values occurs in a list of variables. For example, the command

```
COUNT FEMINISM=ERA JOBEQUAL POLEQUAL (1).
```

creates the variable FEMINISM, which indicates the number of times in a case the value 1 occurs for ERA, JOBEQUAL, and POLEQUAL. Thus, the value of FEMINISM is 0, 1, 2, or 3. You can count across more than one variable list and more than one value, as in the command

```
COUNT FEMINISM=ERA JOBEQUAL POLEQUAL(1) VOTE CAMPAIGN(3,4).
```

which counts the number of times the value 1 occurs in the variables ERA, JOBEQUAL, and POLEQUAL, and the values 3 or 4 in VOTE and CAMPAIGN.

The criterion variable list can include both string and numeric variables, provided they have separate value specifications. String values must be enclosed in apostrophes.

You can specify adjacent variables with the TO keyword and ranges of numeric values with the LOWEST, HIGHEST, and THRU keywords. (You cannot specify any keywords with string variables). More than one variable can be created with a single COUNT command by separating the specifications with a slash, as in the command

```
COUNT PSYCHTIC=PTEST1 TO PTEST10(51 THRU HIGHEST) /
   SCHIZPHR=STEST1 TO STEST10(LOWEST THRU 20).
```

The COUNT command counts user-missing values. For example, the command

```
COUNT RACISM=SCALE1 TO SCALE12(LOWEST THRU 5).
```

counts the value of −99 even though it has been defined by the user as missing.

If you want to count missing values, in order to deduct them from your previous sum of the values, specify the SYSMIS or MISSING keyword in parentheses after the numeric variable list. For example, the command

```
COUNT PHYSMISS=AGE WEIGHT HEIGHT(SYSMIS).
```

creates the new variable PHYSMISS, which records the number of system-missing values each case has for these variables. The MISSING keyword stands for both user- and system-missing values.

4.17
SPECIFYING
CONDITIONAL
TRANSFORMATIONS

The IF command allows you to make transformations in your data contingent on logical conditions. IF consists of a *logical expression* in parentheses followed by a *target variable* and an *assignment expression*. For example, the command

```
IF (AGE GE 18) VOTER=1.
```

uses the logical expression "(AGE GE 18)" and the assignment expression "VOTER=1" to assign the value 1 to the target variable VOTER for all cases with AGE values greater than or equal to 18. You construct the assignment expression in the same way as the expression in a COMPUTE statement (see Section 4.7). Thus, you can specify conditional operations like:

```
IF (INCOME GE 25000) TAXES=INCOME * .33.
```

SPSS/PC+ evaluates logical expressions as true or false and executes the specified assignment only when the expression is true; otherwise, the system-missing value is assigned.

B

Statistics Guide

You can use string variables in IF transformations, as in the command:

```
IF (AGE GE 18) AGEGRP='ADULTS'
```

The same conditions that apply to using string variables with COMPUTE (see Sections 4.5 and 4.8) also apply when using them with IF.

4.18
Specifying Conditions for Transformations

The logical expression on the IF command can be a complex statement involving variables, constants, functions, nested parentheses, and so on. You must include either a relational operator (such as EQ or GE) or a missing-value function (MISSING or SYSMIS) in the logical expression. Other operations and functions are optional. (See Sections 4.9 through 4.13 for a description of other available operators and functions.)

4.19
Comparing Values in a Logical Expression

A *relation* is a logical expression that compares two values using a *relational operator*. For example, the command

```
IF (COST EQ .43) NEWCOST=2.
```

compares the equivalence of the variable COST and the value .43. The following relational operators are available:

EQ *Equal to.* The logical expression is true if the expression on the left is equal to the expression on the right.

NE *Not equal to.* The logical expression is true if the left and right expressions are not equal.

LT *Less than.* The logical expression is true if the expression on the left is less than the expression on the right.

LE *Less than or equal to.* The logical expression is true if the expression on the left is less than or equal to the expression on the right.

GT *Greater than.* The logical expression is true if the expression on the left is greater than the expression on the right.

GE *Greater than or equal to.* The logical expression is true if the expression on the left is greater than or equal to the expression on the right.

The expressions in a relation can be variables, constants, arithmetic expressions, or functions, as in the commands:

```
IF (SCORE1+SCORE2 GT TESTA) NEWSCORE=1.
```

and

```
IF (LOGINCOM GE 5) CLASS=1.
```

Use blanks to separate the relational operator from the expressions. You can use parentheses and extra blanks to make a command more readable, as in the command:

```
IF ( (SCORE1 + SCORE2)  GE 90) GRADE=4.
```

Parentheses are required around the logical expression.

4.20
Joining Relations

You can join two or more relations by using the logical operators AND and OR. For example, the command

```
IF (HOMEWORK GE 85 AND MIDTERM GE 90 AND FINAL GE 90) GRADE=4.
```

assigns GRADE the value 4 only when HOMEWORK is at least 85 and

MIDTERM and FINAL are at least 90. When AND is used, the logical expression is true only when *all* relations joined by AND are true. When OR is used, the logical expression is true when *any* of the relations joined by OR are true. Thus, the command

```
IF ((A EQ 4 AND B EQ 3) OR (A EQ 3 AND B EQ 4)) C=1
```

assigns the value 1 to *C* for any case that has a value of 4 for *A* and 3 for *B* *or* to any case with the value 3 for *A* and 4 for *B*.

You must specify operators and expressions explicitly; the specification (X EQ 1 OR 2) in place of (X EQ 1 OR X EQ 2) is invalid.

4.21
Reversing the Logic of an Expression

The NOT logical operator reverses the true or false status of the expression that immediately follows it. For example, the command

```
IF (NOT RACE EQ 1 AND SEX EQ 0) GROUP=1.
```

assigns value 1 to GROUP for cases where RACE does not equal 1 and SEX *is* equal to 0. This is not equivalent to the command

```
IF (NOT(RACE EQ 1 AND SEX EQ 0)) GROUP=1.
```

which assigns value 1 to GROUP for cases where RACE does not equal 1 and SEX does *not* equal 0.

4.22
The Order of Evaluation

IF evaluates arithmetic operators and functions in a logical expression in the same order as does the COMPUTE command (see Section 4.9). Functions and arithmetic operators are evaluated first, then relational operators, then NOT, then AND, and then OR. In the expression (NOT SCORESUM/5 EQ 10), the value of SCORESUM is divided by 5, the result compared to 10, and the true-false status of this comparison reversed by NOT.

If you specify both AND and OR, AND is executed before OR. For example, in the command

```
IF (HOMEWORK GE 90 AND MIDTERM GE 90 OR FINAL GE 95) GRADE=4.
```

the logical expression is true for a case with HOMEWORK and MIDTERM values of at least 90, or for a FINAL value of at least 95. You can use parentheses to clarify or change the order of evaluation. Thus, the command

```
IF ((HOMEWORK GE 90 AND MIDTERM GE 90) OR FINAL GE 95) GRADE=4.
```

is equivalent to the previous command. The command

```
IF (HOMEWORK GE 90 AND (MIDTERM GE 90 OR FINAL GE 95)) GRADE=4.
```

is not equivalent. In this statement, a case must have a score of at least 90 for HOMEWORK, as well as a value of at least 90 for MIDTERM *or* 95 for FINAL, to be assigned the grade 4.

4.23
Missing Values

If the truth of a logical expression cannot be determined because of missing values, the command is not executed. In a relation with only one relational operator, the logical expression is indeterminate if the expression on either side of the operator has a missing value. For example, if you specify

```
IF (FINAL GT MIDTERM) TEST=1.
```

and either FINAL or MIDTERM is missing for a case, SPSS/PC+ cannot tell whether one variable is greater than the other. In such a case, SPSS/PC+ leaves the target variable unchanged if it is an existing variable. If it is a new variable, it retains its initialized sytem-missing value.

When several relations are joined by AND or OR, SPSS/PC+ automatically returns the missing value if *any* of the relations in the expression have missing values determined to be true or false.

4.24
Missing-Value Logical Functions

You can use the functions MISSING and SYSMIS to specify missing values as criteria for performing or not performing transformations.

MISSING *Return 1 if the value is missing and 0 otherwise.*
SYSMIS *Return 1 if the value is system-missing and 0 otherwise.*

For example, the command

```
IF (SYSMIS(SCORE1)) GRADE=0.
```

determines if SCORE1 is system-missing. If it is, GRADE is assigned the value 0.
The command

```
IF (NOT(MISSING(GRADE))) GRAD=1.
```

evaluates whether the value of GRADE is not equal to the user- or system-missing values. Each case that has a valid value for GRADE is assigned the value 1 for GRAD.

You can also use the VALUE function on an IF command to ignore the user-missing status of values. For example, the commands

```
RECODE AGE (5 THRU 20 = 1) (20 THRU 65 = 2) (65 THRU HI = 3).
MISSING VALUE AGE (3).
IF (VALUE(AGE) GT 0 ) GRPAGE=1.
```

collapse the values of AGE into three values and designate the value 3 as user-missing. The IF command specifies that any case with a value greater than 0 on AGE be given the value 1 on GRPAGE. Because the VALUE keyword on the IF command tells SPSS/PC+ to ignore user-missing values, cases with value 3 on AGE are given the value 1 on GRPAGE.

The VALUE function should always be used in conjunction with a relational operator in a logical expression on the IF command.

4.25
EXECUTING DATA TRANSFORMATIONS

When the data are read, transformation commands are evaluated and executed in the order in which they appear. Thus, the order in which you specify your commands can be important. For the commands

```
RECODE POLACT1 POLACT2 (1 THRU 2=1)(3 THRU 4=2)(ELSE=SYSMIS).
COUNT POLACT=POLACT1,POLACT2(1).
```

the order of execution is critical, since the COUNT command assumes that the RECODE command has already been executed.

Transformations are not carried out until the data are read. You must include a procedure command (or another command that causes SPSS/PC+ to read the data) for the transformations to be executed. Additionally, unless a system file is saved or the data are written out in some way, the transformations are in effect only for a single SPSS/PC+ session.

4.26
USING DATA
DEFINITIONS WITH
TRANSFORMATIONS

You can use the data-definition commands VARIABLE LABELS, VALUE LA-BELS, MISSING VALUE, and so on, to describe any variable created or altered by transformations, as in the commands:

```
RECODE SEX RACE SURGERY (1=0)(0=1)(ELSE=SYSMIS).
COMPUTE LOGAGE=LN(AGE).
VARIABLE LABELS LOGAGE 'NATURAL LOG OF AGE'.
VALUE LABELS SEX 1 'FEMALE' 0 'MALE'
             RACE 1 'BLACK' 0 'WHITE'
             SURGERY 1 'SURGERY PERFORMED' 0'NO SURGERY'.
```

Since a variable must already exist in your active file before it can be defined, the data-definition commands must follow the transformation commands that create the variable.

Contents _____

5 Selecting, Weighting, and Ordering Cases

Suppose you are interested in plotting the relationship between cost and alcohol content in the beer data, but you want the plot to include only domestic beers. Or you wish to examine the distribution of calories only for the beers that have been assigned ratings of "very good." These are two examples of situations where you want to select a subset of cases from a file, based on some particular criterion. You can use the SELECT IF command to select a subset of cases for an entire SPSS/PC+ session. The PROCESS IF command selects a subset of cases only for the following instruction.

When there are many cases in a file, you may want to select a random sample of them for processing. This decreases the time needed for analysis, and may provide you with useful preliminary results. For example, if you had information on 10,000 cases, you might want to obtain plots or histograms for a random subset of them. These plots should reflect the overall trends present in the data. The SAMPLE command selects a random sample of cases from a file.

To restrict analysis to the first *n* cases in a data set, use the N command. This command is particularly useful if you want to get an idea of the output produced by a procedure without having to wait for all cases to be processed. For example, if you are preparing a report and want to make sure that you have included all the necessary information in an appropriate format, running it on a small number of "test" cases is an efficient strategy.

The WEIGHT command allows you to assign different "weights" to cases for an analysis. For example, if your sample does not reflect the true proportion of cases with particular attributes in the population, you can assign appropriate weights to adjust for this when estimating certain statistics. However, the sample sizes and significance levels associated with such weighted analyses cannot be interpreted in the usual fashion.

On occasion, you may wish to sort the observations in a file based on values of certain variables. For example, you might want to sort the beers in ascending order on the basis of alcohol content. Use the SORT CASES command to do this. You can then list the cases in this order or prepare reports using the sorted file (see Chapter 14).

5.1
SELECTING CASES PERMANENTLY

The SELECT IF command selects cases for analysis if they meet criteria you specify. You specify these criteria in a logical expression that SPSS/PC+ can evaluate as true or false. For example, the command

```
SELECT IF (SEX EQ 1).
```

selects cases with the value 1 for SEX for analysis.

You can include the SELECT IF command anywhere in an SPSS/PC+ session, except between the BEGIN DATA and END DATA commands. Once you use SELECT IF, the selection specified is in effect for all subsequent procedures. If you use another SELECT IF command, it selects a subset of cases from the first selected subset rather than from the original data set.

Multiple SELECT IF commands should be used with caution, as you can end up selecting no cases. For example, if the commands

```
SELECT IF (SEX EQ 1).
FREQUENCIES VARIABLES=TEMP FIRSTEKG SECNDEKG.
SELECT IF (SEX EQ 2).
FREQUENCIES VARIABLES=TEMP FIRSTEKG SECNDEKG.
```

are used, there will be no cases for the second FREQUENCIES procedure to analyze, since SEX cannot equal both 1 and 2. If you want to temporarily select cases for one procedure, use the PROCESS IF command (see Section 5.3).

5.2
Specifying the Logical Expression

The logical expression on SELECT IF is specified in the same way as the logical expression on the IF command (see Chapter 4). The logical expression must be enclosed in parentheses and include either a relational operator or a missing-value function. You can construct complex selection criteria by using the logical operators AND, OR, and NOT in the logical expression. If the logical expression cannot be determined for a case because of missing values, that case is not selected.

To select cases with missing values for analysis, use the SYSMIS and MISSING functions. For example, the command

```
SELECT IF (MISSING(AGE)).
```

selects all cases with missing values for AGE.

You can use the VALUE function to include cases with user-missing values in a selection of cases. A SELECT IF logical expression containing the VALUE function should also contain a relational operator. Thus, the command

```
SELECT IF (VALUE(SCORE) LE 40).
```

selects all cases with SCORE values less than or equal to 40, including values that have been defined as missing. (See Chapter 4 for more information on missing values in logical expressions.)

5.3
SELECTING CASES TEMPORARILY

The PROCESS IF command temporarily selects cases for analysis by the immediately following procedure. Like SELECT IF, its specification consists of a logical expression, and it can use any of the relational operators (EQ, NE, GT, GE, LT, or LE). However, the logical operators AND, OR, and NOT cannot be used with PROCESS IF. Thus, a specification like (SALES GE 10000 AND DIVISION EQ 3) is not valid on this command.

If you specify several PROCESS IF commands immediately before a procedure command, only the last one takes effect. For example, if the commands

```
PROCESS IF (SEX EQ 1).
PROCESS IF (SEX EQ 2).
FREQUENCIES VARIABLES=TEMP FIRSTEKG SECNDEKG.
```

are used, the second PROCESS IF command overrides the first, and the FREQUENCIES procedure will analyze all cases for which SEX equals 2.

5.4
DRAWING A TEMPORARY SAMPLE

The SAMPLE command draws a random subsample of cases for analysis in the immediately following procedure. You can include SAMPLE anywhere in an SPSS/PC+ session except between the BEGIN DATA and END DATA commands.

To sample a proportion of cases, specify the proportion on the SAMPLE command, as in

```
SAMPLE .25.
```

This command samples approximately one-fourth of the cases.

If you know the total number of cases, you can specify the number of cases to be sampled, as in the command

```
SAMPLE 50 FROM 200.
```

This command draws a random sample of 50 cases only if there are exactly 200 total cases. If there are fewer than 200 cases, proportionately fewer cases are sampled. If there are more than 200 cases, the subsample is taken only from the first 200 cases.

If SAMPLE follows a SELECT IF or PROCESS IF command, the sample is drawn from the selected subset of cases. Conversely, if SAMPLE precedes SELECT IF or PROCESS IF, the specified subset of cases is selected from the sample. If you specify more than one SAMPLE command prior to a procedure, only the last SAMPLE command is executed.

5.5
SELECTING THE FIRST n CASES

The N command is used to select the first *n* cases in a file. For example, if your file has 1000 cases, but you want to analyze only the first 100 cases, specify

```
N 100.
```

You can enter the N command at any point in an SPSS/PC+ session. Once specified, it limits the number of cases analyzed by all subsequent procedures. More than one N command can be used in a single session, but once you execute a procedure using a given *n*, you cannot increase the number of cases for subsequent procedures; you can only decrease the number of cases in the working data set.

The commands PROCESS IF, SELECT IF, and SAMPLE are executed before N if the commands occur together (even if N is specified first). For example, if you specify

```
N 100.
SAMPLE .5.
```

approximately half of the total cases are sampled, and then the first 100 of these are selected for analysis.

5.6
WEIGHTING CASES

You can adjust the weighting of cases for analysis by using the WEIGHT command. For example, if you have a sample in which males have been oversampled (i.e., there is a much higher proportion of males in the sample than in the population), you may want to give the data for males less weight in your computations. The WEIGHT command is also useful for entering data that have been crosstabulated (see Chapter 10).

The only specification on WEIGHT is the name of the variable to be used for weighting, as in the command

```
WEIGHT BY WGHTVAR.
```

Only one weighting variable can be specified on the command, and it must be numeric. The values of the weighting variable need not be integers, but missing or negative values are treated as zeros. Most SPSS/PC+ procedures can handle noninteger weights, with the exception of PLOT and NPAR TESTS. When weighting is used, files that are saved retain the weighting in the system-variable $WEIGHT.

The weighting variable can be an already existing variable or a variable created through transformation statements. For example, suppose men have been oversampled by a factor of 2. To compensate for this, you can weight male cases by one half, as in the commands

```
COMPUTE WT=1.
IF (SEX EQ 2) WT=.5.
WEIGHT BY WT.
```

If you create a weighting variable with an IF command, it is important to first initialize its weight with a COMPUTE command. Otherwise, cases not covered by the IF command will have missing values for the weighting variable. A case weighted by 1 is unaffected when WEIGHT is executed, but a case weighted by 0 or by a missing value is eliminated.

A WEIGHT command stays in effect for the entire job unless followed by another WEIGHT command or turned off with the command

```
WEIGHT OFF.
```

Weighting is *not* cumulative. That is, a new WEIGHT command reweights the sample rather than altering previously weighted values. For example, if the commands

```
WEIGHT BY WT1.
DESCRIPTIVES ALL.
WEIGHT BY WT2.
DESCRIPTIVES ALL.
```

are used, the first DESCRIPTIVE procedure computes summary statistics based on cases weighted by WT1, and the second DESCRIPTIVES procedure computes summary statistics based on cases weighted by WT2.

When weighting is in effect, significance tests are usually based on the weighted sample size. If the weighted number of cases exceeds the sample size, the p-values given for these tests will be too small. If the weighted number of cases is smaller than the actual sample size, the p-values calculated will be too large. You can avoid these problems by using weight factors that add up to the sample size.

5.7
SORTING DATA

You can use the SORT CASES command to reorder your data according to the values of a specified variable or variables. Specify SORT CASES with the BY keyword, followed by the name(s) of the variable(s) to be used for sorting. The variables specified can be numeric or string. String variables are sorted by alphabetical order.

Cases can be sorted in ascending or descending order. Ascending order is the default. To sort cases in descending order (in which the values for the sorting variable are ordered from highest to lowest), you specify (D) after the variable name, as in the command

```
SORT CASES BY SALES(D).
```

(D) is also used to reverse the alphabetical order of string variables.

You can specify (A) after a variable name to explicitly request ascending order. When (D) or (A) appears after a list of otherwise unspecified variables, all are sorted in the order specified. For example, the command

```
SORT CASES BY PRODUCT DEPT SALES(D).
```

requests that PRODUCT, DEPT, and SALES all be sorted in descending order.

When several sorting variables are listed, cases are first sorted according to the first variable named. Cases with the same value for the first sorting variable are then sorted according to the second sorting variable, and so on. For example, the command

```
SORT CASES BY PRODUCT(D) DEPT(A) SALES(D).
```

produces the following sorted values for PRODUCT, DEPT, and SALES:

```
4 1  $9,750
4 2 $18,083
4 2 $15,608
4 2 $15,132
4 2 $12,438
4 2 $11,240
4 2 $10,050
3 1 $17,051
3 2 $39,000
3 2 $19,682
3 2 $13,650
3 2  $9,777
3 2  $9,507
3 2  $8,872
3 2  $8,239
1 1 $35,750
1 1 $17,111
1 1 $13,910
```

Contents _____

6 Restructuring Files: Procedures JOIN, AGGREGATE, and FLIP

SPSS/PC+ provides two commands for restructuring files. Procedure JOIN combines the contents of system files and creates a new active file. AGGREGATE creates a system file with cases containing summary measures for groups of cases. In this chapter, we will use school enrollment records to illustrate the use of JOIN and AGGREGATE to update and summarize the information in your SPSS/PC+ files.

6.1
OVERVIEW

Consider a simple class roster compiled at pre-registration time. As more students join the class during the first week, their records need to be added to the existing roster. A simple addition of cases, as illustrated in Figure 6.1a, is all that's needed. In SPSS/PC+, this simple addition of cases from one file to another file is accomplished with the JOIN command specifying keyword ADD. Sections 6.2 through 6.3 discuss adding files together.

Figure 6.1a Adding cases to a file

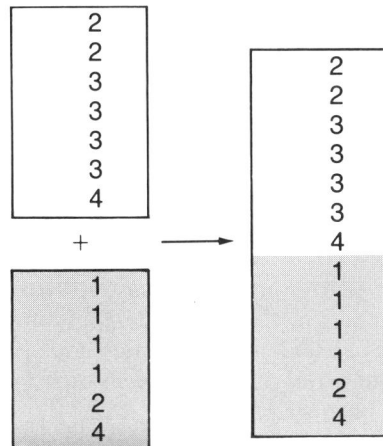

Suppose the instructor wants the new cases added according to a particular order of some variable, such as class year. He could either perform a simple addition and then sort the file or specify that the addition of cases should use the values of a key variable for interleaving, as shown in Figure 6.1b. Interleaving cases from one file with cases in another file is accomplished with JOIN ADD specifying a key variable on the BY subcommand. Section 6.4 discusses the BY subcommand and how to use it.

Figure 6.1b   Interleaving cases with a key

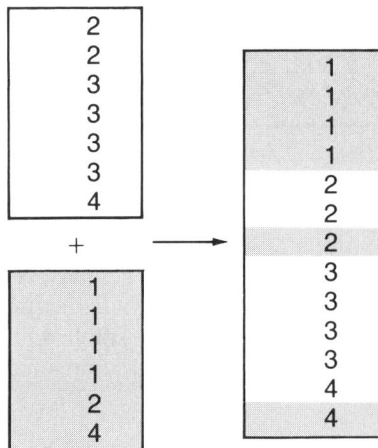

Once the instructor has a class roster, he might decide to add data related to the course to each student record. If the instructor has files that contain exactly the same cases sorted in the same order, he can perform a simple parallel match of files, shown in Figure 6.1c. Procedure JOIN specifying keyword MATCH combines the contents of the first record from each input file, then the contents of the second record from each input file, and so on. Section 6.10 describes how JOIN MATCH combines variables from parallel files.

Figure 6.1c   Matching parallel data files

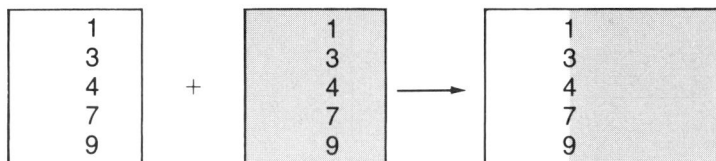

As the quarter progresses, an instructor can use the class roster as a grade book, appending test scores, grades on term papers, and so forth. By using a key variable such as student identification number, he can ensure that the correct test score is matched to the student who took the test. Figure 6.1d shows matching files with a key variable.

By using the key variable, the instructor doesn't have to worry about having test scores for each student in the roster file. For example, students who have dropped the course won't have a grade and are absent from the grade file. These students are assigned a missing value in the resulting file. In addition, each unique value of the key variable is retained in the resulting file. Thus, if a student was not on the class roster but took the exam, the grade is retained in the resulting file. Section 6.11 discusses matching nonparallel files with key variables.

Figure 6.1d Matching nonparallel data files with a key

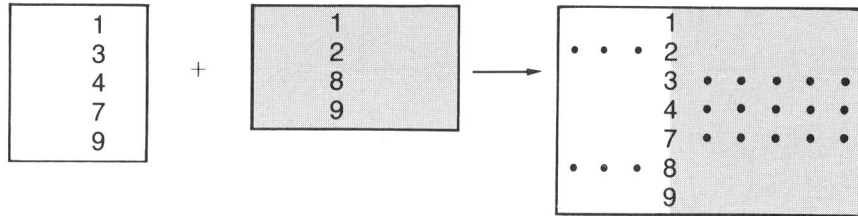

Files containing different types of data can be combined by using JOIN MATCH with a key and designating one file a TABLE file. For example, the instructor might build one file combining the grade-book files for each class he taught that year. He might also build a table file containing one case for each class, with summary information such as the number of exams, the final exam average, high and low grades, etc., recorded for each class. By using the class variable as a key and designating the file with the summary information a table, he can append the summary variables to individual student records. Figure 6.1e shows cases from one file combined with variables from a table. A table match adds variables from the table file to cases only when there is a match on a key variable. Section 6.13 discusses the use of file and table matches.

Figure 6.1e Matching table data to a file with a key

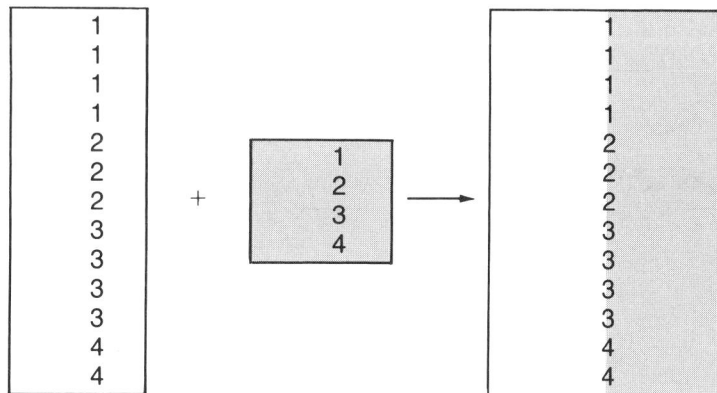

To create the table file of summary information described in the preceding example, the instructor could use his hand calculator to compute class averages and scan the file for the highest and lowest scores for each class. This process would have to be repeated for each class. Or the instructor could have SPSS/PC+ build the table file using procedure AGGREGATE.

Figure 6.1f   Aggregating cases

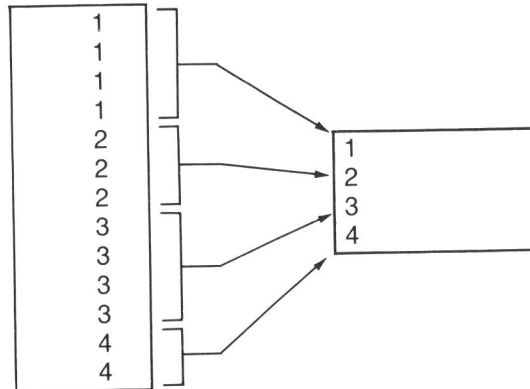

The ADD and MATCH keywords on procedure JOIN are mutually exclusive and must be specified before any other keywords or subcommands. JOIN ADD combines cases from two to five input files. JOIN MATCH combines variables from two to five input files. JOIN MATCH and JOIN ADD combine variables and cases from SPSS/PC+ *system files,* one of which can be the most recently defined active file. JOIN always creates a new active file for use by other commands. Procedure AGGREGATE groups cases and creates variables from an active file and either replaces the active file or writes an SPSS/PC+ system file.

When you use JOIN to interleave cases or to match variables based on values of keys, each input file must be sorted in ascending order of each key variable (see Section 6.12). AGGREGATE does not require that the active file be sorted.

6.2
ADDING FILES

You can use JOIN with keyword ADD to combine the cases from two to five system files into a rectangular file. Instead of using only previously saved SPSS/PC+ system files, one of the files can be the current active file.

6.3
Adding Cases to the Active File

Students who show up at the first day of class can be added to a previously defined system file containing students who have pre-registered for a course. The file SOC100.LAT (Figure 6.3a) contains data on students who showed up for the first day of class and are not included in the pre-registration file. This file contains the same variables as the pre-registration system file but on different students. The commands

```
DATA LIST FILE='SOC100A.LAT'/COURSE 1-3 SECTION 5
   (A) MEETTIME 7-10    DAYS 12-14(A) STUNUM 16-20
   LASTNAME 22-33(A) FSTNAME 35-44(A) CLASSYR 46.
VARIABLE LABELS CLASSYR 'Class'.
VALUE LABELS CLASSYR 1 'Freshman' 2 'Sophmore' 3 'Junior' 4 'Senior'.

TITLE 'Combined Soc100 Section A Roster'.
```

provide definitions for an active file with just the late-registering students.

Figure 6.3a   Data to add to pre-registration file

```
100 a 0900 mwf 10009 Atmore       Samuel     1
100 a 0900 mwf 24365 McDowell     Denise     1
100 a 0900 mwf 27111 Hutchinson   Christine  1
100 a 0900 mwf 55287 Swift        Jennifer   1
100 a 0900 mwf 62432 Jamieson     Bailey     1
100 a 0900 mwf 89765 Paulsen      Patrick    2
100 a 0900 mwf 54338 Darfler      Marleena   4
```

To add cases for students who pre-registered for the course, issue the command:

```
JOIN ADD FILE=*
  /FILE='S100A.PSF'.
LIST.
SAVE OUTFILE='SOC100A.NSF'.
```

The JOIN ADD command adds cases from the system file S100A.PSF to the active file of late-registering students (the asterisk refers to the active file). Note that the order of cases in the resulting active file is determined by the order in which files are named on the FILE subcommands.

After the JOIN command is executed, the active file contains the combined set of cases. The LIST command produces a listing of the contents of this file, shown in Figure 6.3b. The SAVE command creates an SPSS/PC+ system file containing all the cases. The title "Combined Soc100 Section A Roster" specified on the TITLE command is also included in the system file.

Figure 6.3b   Listing of combined files

```
COURSE SECTION MEETTIME DAYS STUNUM LASTNAME      FSTNAME    CLASSYR

   100 a          900  mwf   10009 Atmore         Samuel        1
   100 a          900  mwf   24365 McDowell       Denise        1
   100 a          900  mwf   27111 Hutchinson     Christine     1
   100 a          900  mwf   55287 Swift          Jennifer      1
   100 a          900  mwf   62432 Jamieson       Bailey        1
   100 a          900  mwf   89765 Paulsen        Patrick       2
   100 a          900  mwf   54338 Darfler        Marleena      4
   100 a          900  mwf   43289 Sweeney        John          2
   100 a          900  mwf   23763 Baker          Catherine     2
   100 a          900  mwf   22304 Jones          Barbara       3
   100 a          900  mwf   27001 Jacobsen       Richard       3
   100 a          900  mwf   35760 Roberts        Elizabeth     3
   100 a          900  mwf   64352 Atkinson       Thomas        3
   100 a          900  mwf   79885 Klein          Janet         4


Number of cases read =      14   Number of cases listed =     14
```

6.4
Interleaving Cases

You can use JOIN ADD to interleave cases in ascending order of one or more variables by naming one or more key variables on the BY subcommand. You can specify up to ten variables as keys for interleaving cases on BY. Cases must be sorted in ascending order of the key variable before they can be interleaved. Thus, you should use SORT prior to saving system files or sort the current active file (see Section 6.12).

For example, you can create a combined file that contains students from the two files described in Section 6.3 grouped according to class year. Both the system file SOC100A.PSF and the raw data set SOC100A.LAT must be sorted in ascending order of variable CLASSYR. To interleave cases on the basis of CLASSYR, use the following command:

```
JOIN ADD FILE=*
  /FILE='S100A.PSF'
  /BY=CLASSYR.

LIST.
SAVE OUTFILE='SOC100A.SF'.
```

Figure 6.4 shows the results of the LIST command, with all the cases in order of variable CLASSYR.

Figure 6.4 Interleaved cases on the active file

```
COURSE SECTION MEETTIME DAYS STUNUM LASTNAME    FSTNAME    CLASSYR

  100 a           900 mwf  10009 Atmore      Samuel         1
  100 a           900 mwf  24365 McDowell    Denise         1
  100 a           900 mwf  27111 Hutchinson  Christine      1
  100 a           900 mwf  55287 Swift       Jennifer       1
  100 a           900 mwf  62432 Jamieson    Bailey         1
  100 a           900 mwf  89765 Paulsen     Patrick        2
  100 a           900 mwf  43289 Sweeney     John           2
  100 a           900 mwf  23763 Baker       Catherine      2
  100 a           900 mwf  22304 Jones       Barbara        3
  100 a           900 mwf  27001 Jacobsen    Richard        3
  100 a           900 mwf  35760 Roberts     Elizabeth      3
  100 a           900 mwf  64352 Atkinson    Thomas         3
  100 a           900 mwf  54338 Darfler     Marleena       4
  100 a           900 mwf  79885 Klein       Janet          4


Number of cases read =      14     Number of cases listed =     14
```

When you combine cases from two or more files and name a BY variable for interleaving, you can expect a warning message whenever there are duplicate values of the key variable across files. The example above produces such a message because the active file and the system file, S100A.SF, both contain cases with values 2 and 4 for the variable CLASSYR. If your input files do not contain duplicate values, no warning message is issued.

6.5
Managing Variables

Sometimes you will want to include only a subset of variables from your input files in the file you create with JOIN. Or you may have a situation where the same variable has different names on different files that you want to combine.

With the DROP and KEEP subcommands on JOIN, you can select a subset of variables for inclusion in the resulting file. With the RENAME subcommand, you can supply new names for any variables in the resulting file. In addition, you can use the MAP subcommand to produce a table of the variables in all input files and in the resulting file after any subsetting or renaming.

Sections 6.6 through 6.8 show you how to use MAP to see what's in the files you create with JOIN and how to manage the variables within them using DROP, KEEP, and RENAME.

6.6
Viewing the Active File Dictionary

The MAP subcommand produces a listing of the current status of the active file dictionary. Included in the listing are the names of each input file and of the variables from each file.

Consider the following JOIN command, which combines cases from five previously saved system files:

```
JOIN ADD FILE='SOC100A.SF'
  /FILE='SOC100B.SF'
  /FILE='SOC222A.SF'
  /FILE='SOC310A.SF'
  /FILE='HDS444A.SF'
  /MAP.

LIST.
SAVE OUTFILE='ALLSTUD.S85'.
```

This example creates an active file that contains all students registered in every class and all variables that exist in any of the input files. Figure 6.6a shows the map produced by the MAP subcommand. Variables DEPT, CLASSTYP, and PASSFAIL from the input file HDS444A.SF are present in the resulting active file. If a case comes from an input file that does not contain a particular variable, SPSS/PC+ assigns the system-missing value (numeric variables) or a blank (string variables).

Figure 6.6a   Map of concatenated system files

RESULT	SOC100A.SF	SOC100B.SF	SOC222A.SF	SOC310A.SF	HDS444A.SF
COURSE	COURSE	COURSE	COURSE	COURSE	COURSE
SECTION	SECTION	SECTION	SECTION	SECTION	SECTION
MEETTIME	MEETTIME	MEETTIME	MEETTIME	MEETTIME	MEETTIME
DAYS	DAYS	DAYS	DAYS	DAYS	DAYS
STUNUM	STUNUM	STUNUM	STUNUM	STUNUM	STUNUM
LASTNAME	LASTNAME	LASTNAME	LASTNAME	LASTNAME	LASTNAME
FSTNAME	FSTNAME	FSTNAME	FSTNAME	FSTNAME	FSTNAME
CLASSYR	CLASSYR	CLASSYR	CLASSYR	CLASSYR	CLASSYR
DEPT					DEPT
CLASSTYP					CLASSTYP
PASSFAIL					PASSFAIL

Figure 6.6b shows a listing of the cases in the file. Cases from SOC100A.SF come first, followed by cases from the next named file, and so on. Each case contains a value for variables DEPT, CLASSTYP, and PASSFAIL, even though these variables occur in only one of the five original files.

Figure 6.6b   Listing of concatenated system files

```
S
C  E              S
O  C              T
U  T     D        U                                    D
R  I     A        N                                    E
S  O     Y        U                                    P
E  N MEETTIME S   M LASTNAME   FSTNAME   CLASSYR T  CLASSTYP PASSFAIL

100 a     900 mwf 10009 Atmore     Samuel     1          .        .
100 a     900 mwf 24365 McDowell   Denise     1          .        .
100 a     900 mwf 27111 Hutchinson Christine  1          .        .
100 a     900 mwf 55287 Swift      Jennifer   1          .        .
100 a     900 mwf 62432 Jamieson   Bailey     1          .        .
100 a     900 mwf 89765 Paulsen    Patrick    2          .        .
100 a     900 mwf 43289 Sweeney    John       2          .        .
100 a     900 mwf 23763 Baker      Catherine  2          .        .
100 a     900 mwf 22304 Jones      Barbara    3          .        .
100 a     900 mwf 27001 Jacobsen   Richard    3          .        .
100 a     900 mwf 35760 Roberts    Elizabeth  3          .        .
100 a     900 mwf 64352 Atkinson   Thomas     3          .        .
100 a     900 mwf 54338 Darfler    Marleena   4          .        .
100 a     900 mwf 79885 Klein      Janet      4          .        .
100 b    1100 mwf 10229 Smithe     Peter      1          .        .
100 b    1100 mwf 34365 Farroro    Dennis     1          .        .
100 b    1100 mwf 25111 Huber      Joan       1          .        .
100 b    1100 mwf 55587 Westerman  David      1          .        .
100 b    1100 mwf 62442 Mount      Sigrid     1          .        .
100 b    1100 mwf 89763 Harris     Emily      4          .        .
100 b    1100 mwf 70395 Jones      James      2          .        .
100 b    1100 mwf 53763 Halley     Beth       2          .        .
100 b    1100 mwf 82224 Manova     Svetlana   2          .        .
100 b    1100 mwf 97291 Sullivan   Linda      3          .        .
100 b    1100 mwf 50762 Dexter     Richard    3          .        .
100 b    1100 mwf 62752 Colby      Jeffrey    3          .        .
100 b    1100 mwf 54358 Fiorello   Francis    3          .        .
222 a    1200 tth 12239 Smith      Patricia   1          .        .
222 a    1200 tth 35467 Freiberg   Gerhardt   1          .        .
222 a    1200 tth 65141 Mills      Charles    2          .        .
222 a    1200 tth 53287 West       James      2          .        .
222 a    1200 tth 39742 Maus       Mickey     2          .        .
222 a    1200 tth  9763 Herrmann   Monty      2          .        .
222 a    1200 tth 48364 Daveport   Joyce      2          .        .
222 a    1200 tth 81043 Hill       Robert     2          .        .
222 a    1200 tth 42524 Mason      Perry      2          .        .
222 a    1200 tth 95591 Evans      Linda      3          .        .
222 a    1200 tth 61932 Bates      Oliver     3          .        .
222 a    1200 tth 93132 Hughes     Olivia     3          .        .
222 a    1200 tth 44359 Bates      Lucy       4          .        .
310 a    1400 mwf 42305 O'Kane     Stanley    1          .        .
310 a    1400 mwf 60611 Hallet     Robin      2          .        .
310 a    1400 mwf 14420 Robinson   Thomas     2          .        .
310 a    1400 mwf  4901 Nace       Laura      3          .        .
310 a    1400 mwf 99999 Liebmann   Geoffrey   3          .        .
310 a    1400 mwf 43995 Countryman Katharyn   3          .        .
310 a    1400 mwf 60618 Adams      William    3          .        .
310 a    1400 mwf 14520 Stephenson Lynn       4          .        .
310 a    1400 mwf 22112 Jensen     Lars       4          .        .
444 a    1430 tth 25851 Smith      Jack       3  hds sem          1
444 a    1430 tth 87034 Cobbleigh  Nicholas   4  hds sem          1
444 a    1430 tth 13792 Heisenhuer Jane       4  hds sem          2
444 a    1430 tth 89763 Harris     Emily      4  hds sem          1
444 a    1430 tth 91913 Chambers   Dianne     4  hds sem          2

Number of cases read =     54    Number of cases listed =     54
```

**6.7
Selecting a Subset of
Variables**

You can create an active file that contains all the variables from each input file or select a subset of variables from each file. The subcommands DROP and KEEP indicate which variables from an input file should be omitted or retained on the resulting active file. DROP and KEEP apply only to the immediately preceding named file. For example,

```
JOIN ADD FILE='SOC100A.SF'/DROP=SECTION, MEETTIME, DAYS
    /FILE='SOC100B.SF'/DROP=SECTION, MEETTIME, DAYS
    /FILE='SOC222A.SF'/DROP=SECTION, MEETTIME, DAYS
    /FILE='SOC310A.SF'/DROP=SECTION, MEETTIME, DAYS
    /FILE='HDS444A.SF'/KEEP=COURSE STUNUM LASTNAME FSTNAME CLASSYR
    /BY CLASSYR
    /MAP.
```

joins five system files, interleaving cases on the basis of values of CLASSYR. All variables except SECTION, MEETTIME, and DAYS are taken from the first four system files. Only variables COURSE, STUNUM, LASTNAME, FSTNAME, and CLASSYR are included from the fifth system file. The output from the MAP subcommand is shown in Figure 6.7a. It is placed last so that it will show the status at the end of the JOIN ADD operation. The listing of the contents of the active file from the LIST command is shown in Figure 6.7b.

Figure 6.7a   Map of combined system files with specific variables

RESULT	SOC100A.SF	SOC100B.SF	SOC222A.SF	SOC310A.SF	HDS444A.SF
COURSE	COURSE	COURSE	COURSE	COURSE	COURSE
STUNUM	STUNUM	STUNUM	STUNUM	STUNUM	STUNUM
LASTNAME	LASTNAME	LASTNAME	LASTNAME	LASTNAME	LASTNAME
FSTNAME	FSTNAME	FSTNAME	FSTNAME	FSTNAME	FSTNAME
CLASSYR	CLASSYR	CLASSYR	CLASSYR	CLASSYR	CLASSYR

Figure 6.7b   Listing of interleaved cases after variables are dropped

COURSE	STUNUM	LASTNAME	FSTNAME	CLASSYR
100	10009	Atmore	Samuel	1
100	24365	McDowell	Denise	1
100	27111	Hutchinson	Christine	1
100	55287	Swift	Jennifer	1
100	62432	Jamieson	Bailey	1
100	10229	Smithe	Peter	1
100	34365	Farroro	Dennis	1
100	25111	Huber	Joan	1
100	55587	Westerman	David	1
100	62442	Mount	Sigrid	1
222	12239	Smith	Patricia	1
222	35467	Freiberg	Gerhardt	1
310	42305	O'Kane	Stanley	1
100	89765	Paulsen	Patrick	2
100	43289	Sweeney	John	2
100	23763	Baker	Catherine	2
100	70395	Jones	James	2
100	53763	Halley	Beth	2
100	82224	Manova	Svetlana	2
222	65141	Mills	Charles	2
222	53287	West	James	2
222	39742	Maus	Mickey	2
222	9763	Herrmann	Monty	2
222	48364	Daveport	Joyce	2
222	81043	Hill	Robert	2
222	42524	Mason	Perry	2
310	60611	Hallet	Robin	2
310	14420	Robinson	Thomas	2
100	22304	Jones	Barbara	3
100	27001	Jacobsen	Richard	3
100	35760	Roberts	Elizabeth	3
100	64352	Atkinson	Thomas	3
100	97291	Sullivan	Linda	3
100	50762	Dexter	Richard	3
100	62752	Colby	Jeffrey	3
100	54358	Fiorello	Francis	3
222	95591	Evans	Linda	3
222	61932	Bates	Oliver	3
222	93132	Hughes	Olivia	3
310	4901	Nace	Laura	3
310	99999	Liebmann	Geoffrey	3
310	43995	Countryman	Katharyn	3
310	60618	Adams	William	3
444	25851	Smith	Jack	3
100	54338	Darfler	Marleena	4
100	79885	Klein	Janet	4
100	89763	Harris	Emily	4
222	44359	Bates	Lucy	4
310	14520	Stephenson	Lynn	4
310	22112	Jensen	Lars	4
444	87034	Cobbleigh	Nicholas	4
444	13792	Heisenhuer	Jane	4
444	89763	Harris	Emily	4
444	91913	Chambers	Dianne	4

Number of cases read =   54   Number of cases listed =   54

6.8
Renaming Variables

Sometimes, variables containing the same information have different variable names in different files. For example, the student's identification number might be called STUDNUM in one file and ID in another. You can reconcile such differences during a JOIN ADD with the RENAME subcommand, as in:

```
GET FILE='SOC100.ASF'.

JOIN ADD FILE='SOC100.BSF'/RENAME (STUDNUM=ID)
  /FILE=* /KEEP=LASTNAME FSTNAME ID CLASSYR
  /MAP.
```

The GET command retrieves the system file SOC100.ASF and makes it the active file. JOIN ADD specifies SOC100.BSF as the first input file. The RENAME subcommand changes the name of variable STUDNUM in SOC100.BSF to ID in the resulting active file. The values of LASTNAME, FSTNAME, ID and CLASSYR for cases in the active file (*) are added to SOC100.BSF. The MAP display is shown in Figure 6.8.

The RENAME subcommand ensures that values are contained under the same variable name. If RENAME had not been specified in the example above, the combined file would contain both variables STUDNUM and ID. Cases from the first input file SOC100.BSF would have the system-missing value for ID, while cases from the file SOC100.ASF would be system-missing for STUDNUM.

Figure 6.8   Map of case additions with renamed variable

```
RESULT        SOC100.BSF    *
--------      ----------    ----------
ID            ID            ID
LASTNAME      LASTNAME      LASTNAME
FSTNAME       FSTNAME       FSTNAME
CLASSYR       CLASSYR       CLASSYR
MAJOR         MAJOR
```

The RENAME subcommand can also be used to distinguish variables that record different attributes but have the same name on different files. For example, two files might each contain a variable called CLASS. In one file CLASS refers to course name, and in the second file it refers to the student's year in school. To avoid confusing one variable with the other, you could rename CLASS in the second file to SCHLYEAR. Cases in the second file would then have missing values for CLASS.

6.9
MATCHING FILES

Once a class roster has been developed, you can use JOIN MATCH to append variables with test grades or other information to each student's record. If each input file contains corresponding cases in the same order but with different variables, the files are *parallel* (see Figure 6.1c). A parallel or sequential match combines the variables from the first case from each input file, then the second case from each input file, and so on, without regard to any identifying values that may be present.

Nonparallel files have more or less overlapping sets of cases (see Figure 6.1d). Often cases in one input file are missing from another, or cases may be duplicated in one or the other files. You can append variables to particular cases by specifying that cases be combined according to a common value on one or more key variables (such as an identification number) present in each input file. The BY subcommand names the key variables.

Parallel and nonparallel files contain cases with the same kinds of observations or units of analysis. For example, one file can contain a student roster while another file contains student grades. Each file has individual students as the unit of analysis. Matching the two files results in a student gradebook file.

You can also use JOIN MATCH to combine two files containing different types of data. For example, one file contains test and final grades for students enrolled in five different classes. Another file contains the number of students enrolled in each course and the average final grade for each course offered in the college. By designating the course file a *table* and using the course as a key variable, SPSS/PC+ "looks up" the data in the table file and matches variables to cases in the other input file. A table file contributes variables only from cases that contain corresponding values on key variables. The table file can contain records that don't necessarily correspond to cases in the other input files.

You can use the DROP, KEEP, RENAME, and MAP subcommands described in Sections 6.6 through 6.8 with JOIN MATCH. Up to five input files can be matched, one of which may be the active file. Sections 6.10 through 6.13 describe applications using parallel, nonparallel, and table look-up matches.

6.10
Parallel Files—Same Cases, Different Variables

After assembling a student roster, an instructor receives additional information on each student, such as the student's major and whether the course is required for graduation. The instructor can define an active file containing these variables and add them to an existing system file containing the roster. If each input file contains corresponding cases in the same order, a parallel match can be specified.

Figure 6.10a shows a raw data file containing information on students' majors and required course status. These variables can be added to the class roster saved in Section 6.4 using the following commands:

```
TITLE 'Grade Book'.
DATA LIST FILE='MAJINFO.DAT'/STUNUM 7-10 LASTNAME 13-24 (A)
    FSTNAME 26-35 (A) REQUIRED 39 MAJOR 41-43 (A).
VALUE LABELS REQUIRED 1 'Must Pass'.

JOIN MATCH FILE='SOC100A.SF'/FILE=*.

LIST.

SAVE OUTFILE='SOC100A.GRA'.
```

The DATA LIST command defines an active file with variables STUNUM, LASTNAME, FSTNAME, REQUIRED, and MAJOR. The JOIN MATCH command joins cases from the system file SOC100A.SF with the variables from the active file, represented by an asterisk.

Figure 6.10a   Raw data to be added to class roster

```
100 a 10009 Atmore      Samuel     1
100 a 24365 McDowell    Denise     1
100 a 27111 Hutchinson  Christine  1
100 a 55287 Swift       Jennifer   1
100 a 62432 Jamieson    Bailey     1
100 a 89765 Paulsen     Patrick    2 1 psy
100 a 43289 Sweeney     John       2 1 soc
100 a 23763 Baker       Catherine  2   adm
100 a 22304 Jones       Barbara    3 1 adm
100 a 27001 Jacobsen    Richard    3 1 pol
100 a 35760 Roberts     Elizabeth  3 1 his
100 a 64352 Atkinson    Thomas     3   csi
100 a 79885 Klein       Janet      4 1 che
100 a 54338 Darfler     Marleena   4 1 che
```

The order in which files are named determines the order of variables in the resulting active file. Variables from the first-named file are first, followed by variables from the next-named file, and so on. When two or more files have a variable with the same name, values in the resulting file are taken from the first file named on the JOIN command. Figure 6.10b shows the listing of the active file after the parallel match has been performed.

Figure 6.10b   Listing of active file after parallel match

```
                          D                                                      M
                          A                                                      A
                          Y                                                      J
     COURSE SECTION MEETTIME S    STUNUM LASTNAME      FSTNAME    CLASSYR REQUIRED R

       100 a         900  mwf     10009 Atmore        Samuel         1          1    .
       100 a         900  mwf     24365 McDowell      Denise         1          1    .
       100 a         900  mwf     27111 Hutchinson    Christine      1          1    .
       100 a         900  mwf     55287 Swift         Jennifer       1          1    .
       100 a         900  mwf     62432 Jamieson      Bailey         1          1    .
       100 a         900  mwf     89765 Paulsen       Patrick        2          1  psy
       100 a         900  mwf     43289 Sweeney       John           2          1  soc
       100 a         900  mwf     23763 Baker         Catherine      2          .  adm
       100 a         900  mwf     22304 Jones         Barbara        3          1  adm
       100 a         900  mwf     27001 Jacobsen      Richard        3          1  pol
       100 a         900  mwf     35760 Roberts       Eliazbeth      3          1  his
       100 a         900  mwf     64352 Atkinson      Thomas         3          .  csi
       100 a         900  mwf     54338 Darfler       Marleena       4          1  che
       100 a         900  mwf     79885 Klein         Janet          4          1  che

  Number of cases read =        14     Number of cases listed =        14
```

6.11
Nonparallel Files—Different Cases, Different Variables

In many circumstances input files do not contain corresponding cases. Some cases may be present in one file and not in another. For example, students are not always present in class on the day of an examination: some may have overslept, others may have dropped the class. The instructor might have one file with records for all students who registered for the class and another file with records for students who took the exam. By using a key variable such as student number, the instructor can append test scores to the appropriate student record.

Up to ten variables can be named as keys. The key variables must be present in each input file, and each file must be sorted in ascending order on the key variables. The key variables are named on the BY subcommand, which follows all other input file specifications.

For example, the raw data file containing the student identification number (STUNUM) and exam grades is shown in Figure 6.11a. To combine this file with the student roster created in Section 6.10, you must first sort each file in order of the key variable:

```
GET FILE='SOC100A.GRA'/DROP=MEETTIME DAYS.
SORT CASES BY STUNUM.

SAVE OUTFILE='SORTS100.ASF'.

DATA LIST FILE='TEST1.DAT'/STUNUM 1-5 SCORE1 7-8.
SORT CASES BY STUNUM.

TITLE 'GRADES THROUGH EXAM1'.
JOIN MATCH FILE='SORTS100.ASF'/FILE= *
  /BY STUNUM
  /MAP.
LIST.
SAVE OUTFILE='GRAS1AOS.SYF'.
```

The GET subcommand retrieves the system file containing the roster, omitting variables MEETTIME and DAYS. The SORT command sorts cases in ascending order of STUNUM. The SAVE command saves the sorted version of the file for use with JOIN MATCH. The DATA LIST command defines the raw data file, TEST1.DAT, which contains two variables, STUNUM and SCORE. The second SORT command ensures that cases are in the same order as the roster file.

The FILE subcommands on the JOIN command specify system file SORTS100.ASF as the first file and the active file as the second file. The BY subcommand indicates that cases from the two input files are to be matched only when they have the same value on key variable STUNUM. The MAP subcommand requests a map of the variables contained on each file (Figure 6.11b), and the

LIST command shows the data saved into the system file GRAS1A0S.SYF (Figure 6.11c). Note that students who did not take the exam have the system-missing value for variable SCORE1.

Figure 6.11a   Student number and exam grade file

```
10009 76
24365 86
27111 68
62432 91
43289 86
23763 55
22304 76
35760 84
64352 85
79885 78
54338 80
```

Figure 6.11b   Map from nonparallel match

RESULT	SORTS100.ASF	*
COURSE	COURSE	
SECTION	SECTION	
STUNUM	STUNUM	STUNUM
LASTNAME	LASTNAME	
FSTNAME	FSTNAME	
CLASSYR	CLASSYR	
REQUIRED	REQUIRED	
MAJOR	MAJOR	
SCORE1		SCORE1

Figure 6.11c   Active file listing from nonparallel match

```
Page  10   GRADES THROUGH EXAM1                                         6/28/85

COURSE SECTION STUNUM LASTNAME      FSTNAME      CLASSYR REQUIRED MAJOR SCORE1

   100 a        10009 Atmore        Samuel           1       .    adm      76
   100 a        22304 Jones         Barbara          3       1    adm      76
   100 a        23763 Baker         Catherine        2       .    adm      55
   100 a        24365 McDowell      Denise           1       .             86
   100 a        27001 Jacobsen      Richard          3       1    pol      .
   100 a        27111 Hutchinson    Christine        1       .             68
   100 a        35760 Roberts       Eliazbeth        3       1    his      84
   100 a        43289 Sweeney       John             2       1    soc      86
   100 a        54338 Darfler       Marleena         4       1    che      80
   100 a        55287 Swift         Jennifer         1       .             .
   100 a        62432 Jamieson      Bailey           1       .             91
   100 a        64352 Atkinson      Thomas           3       .    csi      85
   100 a        79885 Klein         Janet            4       1    che      78
   100 a        89765 Paulsen       Patrick          2       1    psy      .

Number of cases read =      14     Number of cases listed =      14
```

When you match files with the BY subcommand, the resulting active file contains values for every variable on each input file. If a variable is not a key variable but is contained on more than one input file, the value from the first-named file is used in the resulting active file. If two variables have the same name but represent different information, you can use the RENAME subcommand to ensure that no information is lost (see Section 6.8).

If an input file contains cases with the same value or combination of values for key variables, variables from the other input files are matched only to the first case. Each subsequent duplicate case is assigned system-missing values for the remaining variables from the other input files. If values should be appended to all matching cases, use a TABLE match (see Section 6.13).

6.12
Sorting Key Variables

When a BY subcommand is used on JOIN, all input files must be sorted in ascending order of the key variables. The best way to ensure that files are sorted in the correct order is to sort each input file with the SORT command prior to issuing the JOIN command. For all input files except the active file, you will need to resave the file as a system file after specifying SORT, as shown in the example in Section 6.11.

When multiple keys are specified, an easy rule of thumb is to specify the variables on the SORT command in the same order as they are named on the BY subcommand. For example,

```
GET FILE='PREREG.SYF'.
SORT BY DEPT COURSE.
SAVE OUTFILE='PREREGS.SYF'.

GET FILE='LATEREG.SYF'.
SORT BY DEPT COURSE.

JOIN MATCH FILE='PREREGS.SYF'/ FILE=* /BY DEPT COURSE
```

sorts both files in ascending order of COURSE within categories of DEPT. Table 6.12 illustrates values of the variables sorted in ascending order.

Table 6.12   Sorting order for DEPT COURSE

DEPT	COURSE
hds	100
hds	101
hds	444
mat	100
mat	222
soc	100
soc	222
soc	310

6.13
Table and Case Files—Group and Case Data

A *table lookup* match joins variables from one file designated as a table to groups of corresponding cases based on common values of one or more key variables. The table file should contain only one case for each combination of key variables.

For example, an instructor might create a system file containing summary information on each class. Figure 6.13a shows a listing from this system file. Each case contains a unique combination of values for department, course number, and section. The instructor also has a system file containing all grades for all students he taught that year. A listing of this file is shown in Figure 6.13b. Each line contains individual student grades.

Figure 6.13a   Listing of ALLCOURS.SYF file

DEPT	COURSE	SECTION	EXAMS	CLASSAV
hds	272	a	4	92.02
hds	444	a	2	87.00
soc	100	a	4	86.82
soc	100	b	4	85.62
soc	222	a	6	84.92
soc	310	a	4	87.75
soc	444	a	3	94.35

Figure 6.13b Listing of GRADES84.SYF file

D E P T	COURSE	SECTION	STUNUM	LASTNAME	T E S T 1	TEST2	TEST3	TEST4	TEST5	TEST6	GRADE
hds	444	a	25851	Smith	81	93	.	.	.	.	87
hds	444	a	87034	Cobbleigh	91	96	.	.	.	.	94
hds	444	a	13792	Heisenhuer	93	94	.	.	.	.	94
hds	444	a	89763	Harris	66	85	.	.	.	.	76
hds	444	a	91913	Chambers	93	75	.	.	.	.	84
soc	100	a	10009	Atmore	97	95	95	92	.	.	95
soc	100	a	24365	McDowell	96	87	76	99	.	.	90
soc	100	a	27111	Hutchinson	73	81	91	75	.	.	80
soc	100	a	55287	Swift	.	.	.	.	.	.	.
soc	100	a	62432	Jamieson	89	84	81	87	.	.	85
soc	100	a	89765	Paulsen	.	.	.	.	.	.	.
soc	100	a	43289	Sweeney	95	75	76	82	.	.	82
soc	100	a	23763	Baker	86	79	90	99	.	.	89
soc	100	a	22304	Jones	67	95	98	78	.	.	85
soc	100	a	27001	Jacobsen	.	.	.	.	.	.	.
soc	100	a	35760	Roberts	94	88	87	95	.	.	91
soc	100	a	64352	Atkinson	68	82	90	85	.	.	81
soc	100	a	54338	Darfler	86	90	92	85	.	.	88
soc	100	a	79885	Klein	96	79	85	96	.	.	89
soc	100	b	10229	Smithe	81	71	85	86	.	.	81
soc	100	b	34365	Farroro	88	71	94	96	.	.	87
soc	100	b	25111	Huber	71	83	81	78	.	.	78
soc	100	b	55587	Westerman	76	96	91	98	.	.	90
soc	100	b	62442	Mount	87	84	77	98	.	.	87
soc	100	b	89763	Harris	95	98	84	100	.	.	94
soc	100	b	70395	Jones	68	95	98	90	.	.	88
soc	100	b	53763	Halley	91	91	92	81	.	.	89
soc	100	b	82224	Manova	92	82	97	81	.	.	88
soc	100	b	97291	Sullivan	67	80	89	80	.	.	79
soc	100	b	50762	Dexter	80	90	85	98	.	.	88
soc	100	b	62752	Colby	88	72	79	77	.	.	79
soc	100	b	54358	Fiorello	65	84	95	96	.	.	85
soc	222	a	12239	Smith	84	100	80	96	83	93	89
soc	222	a	35467	Freiberg	75	98	80	95	86	95	88
soc	222	a	65141	Mills	74	78	94	76	81	90	82
soc	222	a	53287	West	73	99	77	75	80	91	83
soc	222	a	39742	Maus	70	95	82	83	79	80	82
soc	222	a	9763	Herrmann	87	82	78	.	.	.	.
soc	222	a	48364	Daveport	84	76	94	93	97	77	87
soc	222	a	81043	Hill	71	87	87	98	91	80	86
soc	222	a	42524	Mason	69	78	84	85	82	93	82
soc	222	a	95591	Evans	80	76	92	83	93	77	84
soc	222	a	61932	Bates	93	75	86	97	82	85	86
soc	222	a	93132	Hughes	80	88	84	92	99	81	87
soc	222	a	44359	Bates	70	89	84	96	85	74	83
soc	310	a	42305	O'Kane	75	87	84	87	.	.	83
soc	310	a	60611	Hallet	75	85	91	88	.	.	85
soc	310	a	14420	Robinson	69	87	89	97	.	.	86
soc	310	a	4901	Nace	91	96	97	82	.	.	92
soc	310	a	99999	Liebmann	92	92	81	82	.	.	87
soc	310	a	43995	Countryman	80	80	85	93	.	.	85
soc	310	a	60618	Adams	72	.	.	.	.	.	.
soc	310	a	14520	Stephenson	94	90	96	87	.	.	92
soc	310	a	22112	Jensen	80	91	98	100	.	.	92

Number of cases read =   54   Number of cases listed =   54

With these two files, the instructor can use JOIN to match variables from the course file to individual student records and compute a variable showing how each student did in relation to the class averages:

```
JOIN MATCH FILE='GRADES84.SYF'/TABLE='ALLCOURS.SYF'
  /BY DEPT COURSE SECTION
  /MAP.

COMPUTE GRADDIFF=GRADE-CLASSAV.

LIST VAR=DEPT COURSE SECTION STUNUM LASTNAME GRADE GRADDIFF.
```

The FILE subcommand on JOIN names the student file, and the TABLE subcommand designates the course file a table. The BY subcommand names the three key variables, and the MAP subcommand requests a map of the variables in each file (see Figure 6.13c). The COMPUTE command creates a new variable based on the difference between GRADE, which comes from the GRADES84.SYF file, and CLASSAV, which comes from the ALLCOURS.SYF file.

To perform the match, JOIN reads a case in the student file and "looks up" a match of key variables in the table file. When a match is found, the values from the table file are appended to the case. Nonmatching cases from the table file are ignored. Nonmatching cases from other input files are assigned system-missing values for variables named in the TABLE file. When JOIN finds more than one case in the student file for a particular combination of DEPT, COURSE, and SECTION, a warning message indicating there are duplicate cases is issued. Usually this message can be ignored.

The results of the LIST command, shown in Figure 6.13d show some of the variables in the resulting active file. Note that no cases appear for courses in the table file that did not have matches in the gradebook file.

Figure 6.13c   Map from file and table match

```
RESULT          GRADES84.SYF  ALLCOURS.SYF

COURSE          COURSE        COURSE
SECTION         SECTION       SECTION
STUNUM          STUNUM
LASTNAME        LASTNAME
DEPT            DEPT          DEPT
TEST1           TEST1
TEST2           TEST2
TEST3           TEST3
TEST4           TEST4
TEST5           TEST5
TEST6           TEST6
GRADE           GRADE
EXAMS                         EXAMS
CLASSAV                       CLASSAV
```

Figure 6.13d   Listing of cases from table look-up match

```
DEPT COURSE SECTION STUNUM LASTNAME      GRADE GRADDIFF

hds   444 a    25851 Smith         87    0.0
hds   444 a    87034 Cobbleigh     94    7.00
hds   444 a    13792 Heisenhuer    94    7.00
hds   444 a    89763 Harris        76   -11.00
hds   444 a    91913 Chambers      84    -3.00
soc   100 a    10009 Atmore        95    8.18
soc   100 a    24365 McDowell      90    3.18
soc   100 a    27111 Hutchinson    80   -6.82
soc   100 a    55287 Swift          .     .
soc   100 a    62432 Jamieson      85   -1.82
soc   100 a    89765 Paulsen        .     .
soc   100 a    43289 Sweeney       82   -4.82
soc   100 a    23763 Baker         89    2.18
soc   100 a    22304 Jones         85   -1.82
soc   100 a    27001 Jacobsen       .     .
soc   100 a    35760 Roberts       91    4.18
soc   100 a    64352 Atkinson      81   -5.82
soc   100 a    54338 Darfler       88    1.18
soc   100 a    79885 Klein         89    2.18
soc   100 b    10229 Smithe        81   -4.62
soc   100 b    34365 Farroro       87    1.38
soc   100 b    25111 Huber         78   -7.62
soc   100 b    55587 Westerman     90    4.38
soc   100 b    62442 Mount         87    1.38
soc   100 b    89763 Harris        94    8.38
soc   100 b    70395 Jones         88    2.38
soc   100 b    53763 Halley        89    3.38
soc   100 b    82224 Manova        88    2.38
soc   100 b    97291 Sullivan      79   -6.62
soc   100 b    50762 Dexter        88    2.38
soc   100 b    62752 Colby         79   -6.62
soc   100 b    54358 Fiorello      85    -.62
soc   222 a    12239 Smith         89    4.08
soc   222 a    35467 Freiberg      88    3.08
soc   222 a    65141 Mills         82   -2.92
soc   222 a    53287 West          83   -1.92
soc   222 a    39742 Maus          82   -2.92
soc   222 a     9763 Herrmann       .     .
soc   222 a    48364 Daveport      87    2.08
soc   222 a    81043 Hill          86    1.08
soc   222 a    42524 Mason         82   -2.92
soc   222 a    95591 Evans         84    -.92
soc   222 a    61932 Bates         86    1.08
soc   222 a    93132 Hughes        87    2.08
soc   222 a    44359 Bates         83   -1.92
soc   310 a    42305 O'Kane        83   -4.75
soc   310 a    60611 Hallet        85   -2.75
soc   310 a    14420 Robinson      86   -1.75
soc   310 a     4901 Nace          92    4.25
soc   310 a    99999 Liebmann      87    -.75
soc   310 a    43995 Countryman    85   -2.75
soc   310 a    60618 Adams          .     .
soc   310 a    14520 Stephenson    92    4.25
soc   310 a    22112 Jensen        92    4.25

Number of cases read =     54   Number of cases listed =     54
```

6.14
OBTAINING GROUP DATA: PROCEDURE AGGREGATE

Procedure AGGREGATE computes summary measures such as the sum and mean across groups of cases and produces either an SPSS/PC+ system file or a new active file containing one case per group. The variables on the resulting aggregated file are summary measures.

For example, consider a file of grades for each student enrolled in each class taught by an instructor. AGGREGATE can be used to create a class file containing such items as mean grade for each class, number of students completing the class, and percentage of students failing a class. In the new file, each case is a class and the values are aggregated information on students.

AGGREGATE often is used in conjuction with JOIN MATCH. For example, once you have obtained class averages with AGGREGATE, you can add the average grade for the class to each student's record and compare each student's grade to the average. In this operation, the aggregated file is used as a table file in the JOIN command.

To use AGGREGATE, you must specify three sets of information: the aggregated file, the variables that define groups, and the functions that create the aggregated variables. Optionally, you can specify missing-value treatments and whether the input file has been sorted according to the grouping variables.

6.15
Specifying the File Destination

The file produced by AGGREGATE either replaces the active file or is written as an SPSS/PC+ system file. The OUTFILE subcommand determines the destination of the aggregated file and must be the first specification.

To create and save a system file, specify a DOS filename enclosed in apostrophes on the OUTFILE subcommand. For example, assume you are creating an aggregated file from a class roster file. The sequence of commands is:

```
GET FILE='ALLCLASS.SYF'.
AGGREGATE OUTFILE="ENROLLN.SYF"
  /BREAK=DEPT COURSE SECTION
  /NUMSTU=NU.
```

In this example, the new aggregated system file is written to the file ENROLLN.SYF, and the active file remains unchanged. To replace the active file with the aggregated file, specify an asterisk instead of the filename on the OUTFILE subcommand, as in:

```
GET FILE='ALLCLASS.SYF'.
AGGREGATE OUTFILE=*
  /BREAK=DEPT COURSE SECTION
  /NUMSTU=NU.
```

When you specify the active file on OUTFILE, the aggregated file is not permanently saved unless you use the SAVE command after the AGGREGATE procedure.

6.16
Grouping Cases

Procedure AGGREGATE summarizes groups of cases. A *break group* is a set of cases on the input file that have the same values for a variable or set of variables. Each break group defines one case on the new aggregated file.

For example, in a file of students registered for different classes, each case is a student and includes variables for class name, course number, department, student identification number, major, year in school, and other attributes. Each of these variables can be used individually or jointly to group the students. If you were to aggregate by course number, all cases with the same course number would constitute a group. If you were to aggregate by department and course number, all students taking Sociology 100 would be in one group, all students taking Sociology

200 would be in another, all students in Human Development 100 in another, and so forth. Each combination of department and course number is a break group.

The BREAK subcommand defines the break group variables and must follow the OUTFILE subcommand. You can name as many variables as you want on the BREAK subcommand, and you can use keyword TO to refer to a set of adjacent variables on the file. For example, to name variables DEPT, COURSE, and SECTION as the grouping variables, specify:

```
GET FILE='ALLCLASS.SYF'.
AGGREGATE OUTFILE=*
  /BREAK=DEPT COURSE SECTION
  /NUMSTU=NU.

LIST.
```

The GET command names the ALLCLASS.SYF system file, which contains information on all students in all classes. The AGGREGATE command directs the aggregated file to the active file and uses values for variables DEPT and COURSE to group cases. By default, AGGREGATE arranges cases in ascending order on each variable named on the BREAK subcommand. Figure 6.16a shows the contents of the resulting active file from the LIST command. The aggregated file contains five cases, one for each unique combination of DEPT and COURSE. Note that AGGREGATE saves all variables named on the BREAK subcommand on the resulting aggregated file. Each break variable retains all dictionary information from the input file.

Figure 6.16a   Aggregated file in default order

```
DEPT COURSE SECTION  NUMSTU

hds    444   a          5
soc    100   a         14
soc    100   b         13
soc    222   a         13
soc    310   a          9


Number of cases read =       5    Number of cases listed =        5
```

The BREAK subcommand also lets you specify the arrangement of cases on the resulting file. For example, the following AGGREGATE command specifies that the aggregated active file is to be sorted in descending order of variable DEPT, in ascending order of variable COURSE, and descending order of variable SECTION:

```
GET FILE='ALLCLASS.SYF'.
AGGREGATE OUTFILE=*
  /BREAK=DEPT (D) COURSE (A) SECTION (D)
  /NUMSTU=NU.

LIST.
```

Figure 6.16b shows the resulting active file sorted in the designated order.

Figure 6.16b   Sorted aggregated file

```
DEPT COURSE SECTION  NUMSTU

soc    100   b         13
soc    100   a         14
soc    222   a         13
soc    310   a          9
hds    444   a          5


Number of cases read =       5    Number of cases listed =        5
```

You can specify sorting order for any variable named on the BREAK subcommand. The sort designation applies to all preceding undesignated variables. In the absence of a designation, the resulting aggregated file is sorted in ascending order on each variable. String values sorted in ascending order follow the ASCII code value sequence: first numbers, then uppercase letters, and finally lowercase letters (see the Appendix in your IBM *BASIC Reference* manual). Sorting strings in descending order reverses the sequence, starting with lowercase letters.

6.17
Using a Presorted Active File

When your active file is already sorted in the order you want your aggregated file, you can use the PRESORTED subcommand. When you specify PRESORTED, each time a *different* value or combination of values is encountered on variables named on the BREAK subcommand, a new aggregate case is created. If the input file is not sorted and PRESORTED is specified, AGGREGATE produces multiple cases for combinations of the break variables.

For example, the commands

```
GET FILE='ALLCLASS.SYF'.
AGGREGATE OUTFILE=*
  /PRESORTED
  /BREAK=DEPT COURSE SECTION
  /NUMSTU=NU.

LIST.
```

tell SPSS/PC+ that the ALLCLASS.SYF system file is already sorted by DEPT, COURSE, and SECTION.

When it is used, PRESORTED must be specified between the OUTFILE and BREAK subcommands. You cannot specify sort order for the resulting aggregated file by designating (A) or (D) for variables named on the BREAK subcommand (see Section 6.16). If the PRESORTED subcommand is used and sort order is specified on the BREAK subcommand, the aggregated file is sorted in the order of the input file and a warning is issued stating that the sort directions specified on BREAK are ignored.

6.18
Creating Aggregated Variables

Each variable on an aggregated file is created by applying an aggregate function to a variable on the active file. The simplest specification is a *target variable list* followed by an equals sign, the function keyword, and the list of *source variables* in parentheses. The aggregate functions available are listed in Section 6.19.

For example, using the data shown in Figure 6.18a, the commands

```
DATA LIST FILE='ALLGRADE.DAT'/ COURSE 2-4 SECTION 6 (A)
    STUNUM 8-12 LASTNAME 14-25 (A) DEPT 27-29 (A) EXAMS 31
    TEST1 TO TEST6 33-56.
FORMATS TEST1 TO TEST6 (F2.0).
COMPUTE FINGRADE=RND((TEST1+TEST2+TEST3+TEST4+TEST5+TEST6)/EXAMS).
FORMATS FINGRADE (F3).

AGGREGATE OUTFILE='CLASSAV1.TOT'
    /BREAK=DEPT COURSE SECTION
    /CLASSAV=MEAN(FINGRADE).
```

define an active file and then use it to create a new variable CLASSAV as the mean of variable FINGRADE for each section of a course within in each department. CLASSAV is the target variable for mean values of FINGRADE for each break group.

Figure 6.18a   ALLGRADE.DAT data set

```
100 a 10009 Atmore      soc 4  97  95  95  92   0   0
100 a 24365 McDowell    soc 4  96  87  76  99   0   0
100 a 27111 Hutchinson  soc 4  73  81  91  75   0   0
100 a 55287 Swift       soc 4                   0   0
100 a 62432 Jamieson    soc 4  89  84  81  87   0   0
100 a 89765 Paulsen     soc 4                   0   0
100 a 43289 Sweeney     soc 4  95  75  76  82   0   0
100 a 23763 Baker       soc 4  86  79  90  99   0   0
100 a 22304 Jones       soc 4  67  95  98  78   0   0
100 a 27001 Jacobsen    soc 4                   0   0
100 a 35760 Roberts     soc 4  94  88  87  95   0   0
100 a 64352 Atkinson    soc 4  68  82  90  85   0   0
100 a 54338 Darfler     soc 4  86  90  92  85   0   0
100 a 79885 Klein       soc 4  96  79  85  96   0   0
100 b 10229 Smithe      soc 4  81  71  85  86   0   0
100 b 34365 Farroro     soc 4  88  71  94  96   0   0
100 b 25111 Huber       soc 4  71  83  81  78   0   0
100 b 55587 Westerman   soc 4  76  96  91  98   0   0
100 b 62442 Mount       soc 4  87  84  77  98   0   0
100 b 89763 Harris      soc 4  95  98  84 100   0   0
100 b 70395 Jones       soc 4  68  95  98  90   0   0
100 b 53763 Halley      soc 4  91  91  92  81   0   0
100 b 82224 Manova      soc 4  92  82  97  81   0   0
100 b 97291 Sullivan    soc 4  67  80  89  80   0   0
100 b 50762 Dexter      soc 4  80  90  85  98   0   0
100 b 62752 Colby       soc 4  88  72  79  77   0   0
100 b 54358 Fiorello    soc 4  65  84  95  96   0   0
222 a 12239 Smith       soc 6  84 100  80  96  83  93
222 a 35467 Freiberg    soc 6  75  98  80  95  86  95
222 a 65141 Mills       soc 6  74  78  94  76  81  90
222 a 53287 West        soc 6  73  99  77  75  80  91
222 a 39742 Maus        soc 6  70  95  82  83  79  80
222 a  9763 Herrmann    soc 6  87  82  78       0   0
222 a 48364 Daveport    soc 6  84  76  94  93  97  77
222 a 81043 Hill        soc 6  71  87  87  98  91  80
222 a 42524 Mason       soc 6  69  78  84  85  82  93
222 a 95591 Evans       soc 6  80  76  92  83  93  77
222 a 61932 Bates       soc 6  93  75  86  97  82  85
222 a 93132 Hughes      soc 6  80  88  84  92  99  81
222 a 44359 Bates       soc 6  70  89  84  96  85  74
310 a 42305 O'Kane      soc 4  75  87  84  87   0   0
310 a 60611 Hallet      soc 4  75  85  91  88   0   0
310 a 14420 Robinson    soc 4  69  87  89  97   0   0
310 a  4901 Nace        soc 4  91  96  97  82   0   0
310 a 99999 Liebmann    soc 4  92  92  81  82   0   0
310 a 43995 Countryman  soc 4  80  80  85  93   0   0
310 a 60618 Adams       soc 4  72               0   0
310 a 14520 Stephenson  soc 4  94  90  96  87   0   0
310 a 22112 Jensen      soc 4  80  91  98 100   0   0
444 a 25851 Smith       hds 2  81  93   0   0   0   0
444 a 87034 Cobbleigh   hds 2  91  96   0   0   0   0
444 a 13792 Heisenhuer  hds 2  93  94   0   0   0   0
444 a 89763 Harris      hds 2  66  85   0   0   0   0
444 a 91913 Chambers    hds 2  93  75   0   0   0   0
```

The target and source variable lists must be of equal length, as in:

```
AGGREGATE OUTFILE='CLASSAV2.TOT'
  /BREAK=DEPT COURSE SECTION
  /CLASSAV TEST1AVE =MEAN(FINGRADE TEST1).
```

This specification creates two aggregated variables: CLASSAV is the mean of FINGRADE, and TEST1AVE is the mean of TEST1.

You can use keyword TO in both the target and source variable lists. For example, to create averages for each test, specify:

```
AGGREGATE OUTFILE='CLASSAV3.TOT'
  /BREAK=DEPT COURSE SECTION
  /TESTAVE1 TO TESTAVE6=MEAN(TEST1 TO TEST6).
```

Any number of functions can be used to create variables. You can define up to 200 variables, including the break variables. Separate each function specification with a slash, as in:

```
AGGREGATE OUTFILE='CLASSAVE.TOT'
  /BREAK=DEPT COURSE SECTION
  /TESTAVE1 AVEFINAL=MEAN(TEST1 FINGRADE)
  /TESTSD1 SDFINAL=SD(TEST1 FINGRADE).

GET FILE='CLASSAVE.TOT'.
LIST.
```

Figure 6.18b shows the results from the LIST command.

Figure 6.18b   Listing of aggregated variables and values

```
DEPT COURSE SECTION TESTAVE1 AVEFINAL  TESTSD1  SDFINAL

hds   444 a           84.80    87.00    11.63    7.55
soc   100 a           86.09    86.82    11.53    4.64
soc   100 b           80.69    85.62    10.40    4.91
soc   222 a           77.69    84.92     7.60    2.54
soc   310 a           80.89    87.75     9.28    3.69


Number of cases read =        5   Number of cases listed =        5
```

6.19
Functions

The following functions are available in procedure AGGREGATE:

SUM(varlist)	*Sum across cases.* Dictionary formats are F8.2.
MEAN(varlist)	*Mean across cases.* Dictionary formats are F8.2.
SD(varlist)	*Standard deviation across cases.* Dictionary formats are F8.2.
MAX(varlist)	*Maximum value across cases.* Complete dictionary information is copied from the source variables to the target variables.
MIN(varlist)	*Minimum value across cases.* Complete dictionary information is copied from the source variables to the target variables.
PGT(varlist,value)	*Percentage of cases greater than value.* Dictionary formats are F5.1.
PLT(varlist,value)	*Percentage of cases less than value.* Dictionary formats are F5.1.
PIN(varlist,value1,value2)	*Percentage of cases between value1 and value2 inclusive.* Dictionary formats are F5.1.
POUT(varlist,value1,value2)	*Percentage of cases not between value1 and value2.* Cases where the source variable equals value1 or value2 are not counted. Dictionary formats are F5.1.
FGT(varlist,value)	*Fraction of cases greater than value.* Dictionary formats are F5.3.
FLT(varlist,value)	*Fraction of cases less than value.* Dictionary formats are F5.3.
FIN(varlist,value1,value2)	*Fraction of cases between value1 and value2 inclusive.* Dictionary formats are F5.3.
FOUT(varlist,value1,value2)	*Fraction of cases not between value1 and value2.* Cases where the source variable equals value1 or value2 are not counted. Dictionary formats are F5.3.
N(varlist)	*Weighted number of cases in break group.* Dictionary formats are F7.0 for unweighted files and F8.2 for weighted files.
NU(varlist)	*Unweighted number of cases in break group.* Dictionary formats are F7.0.
NMISS(varlist)	*Weighted number of missing cases.* Dictionary formats are F7.0 for unweighted files and F8.2 for weighted files.
NUMISS(varlist)	*Unweighted number of missing cases.* Dictionary formats are F7.0.
FIRST(varlist)	*First nonmissing observed value in break group.* Complete dictionary information is copied from the source variables to the target variables.
LAST(varlist)	*Last nonmissing observed value in break group.* Complete dictionary information is copied from the source variables to the target variables.

The percentage functions (PGT, PLT, PIN, and POUT) return values between 0 and 100, inclusive. The fraction functions (FGT, FLT, FIN, and FOUT) return values between 0 and 1, inclusive.

6.20
Function Arguments

Only numeric variables can be used with SUM, MEAN, and SD. Both long and short string variables can be used with all other functions. For example, to obtain the percentage of females when SEX is coded M and F, specify either

```
PCTFEM=PLT(SEX,"M")
```

or

```
PCTFEM=PIN(SEX,"F","F")
```

Blanks and commas can be used interchangeably to separate arguments to functions.

Functions PGT, PLT, PIN, POUT, FGT, FLT, FIN, and FOUT take values as arguments. PGT, PLT, FGT, and FLT have one argument that is a value. PIN, POUT, FIN, and FOUT have two value arguments. For example, the specification

```
LOQUART1 LOFINAL=PLT(TEST1 FINGRADE,75)
```

assigns the percentage of cases with values less than 75 for TEST1 to LOQUART1 and for FINGRADE to LOFINAL. The specification

```
CGRADE=FIN(FINGRADE,70,79)
```

assigns the fraction of cases having final grade scores of 70 to 79 to CGRADE. For PIN, POUT, FIN, and FOUT, the first argument should be lower than the second argument. If the first argument is higher, AGGREGATE automatically reverses them and displays a warning message.

The N and NU functions do not require arguments. Without arguments they return the number of weighted and unweighted cases in a break group. If you supply a variable list, they return the weighted and unweighted number of nonmissing cases for the variables specified.

6.21
Labels and Formats

With the exception of the functions MAX, MIN, FIRST, and LAST, which copy complete dictionary information from the source variable, new variables created by AGGREGATE have the default dictionary formats described in Section 6.19 and no labels. To label a new variable, specify a label in apostrophes immediately following the variable name, as in:

```
AGGREGATE OUTFILE='CLASSAV2.TOT'
 /BREAK=DEPT COURSE
 /CLASSAV "Final Average"
  TEST1AVE '1st Test Average'=MEAN(FINGRAE TEST1).
```

The label applies only to the immediately preceding variable.

If you are specifying the aggregated file as the new active file, you can also use the VARIABLE LABELS command to add labels, as in:

```
AGGREGATE OUTFILE=*
 /BREAK=DEPT COURSE
 /CLASSAV TEST1AVE=MEAN(FINGRADE TEST1).
VARIABLE LABELS CLASSAV "Final Average" / TEST1AVE "1st Test Av-
erage".
```

Use the FORMATS command to change dictionary formats for an active file created from AGGREGATE, as in:

```
AGGREGATE OUTFILE=*
 /BREAK=DEPT COURSE
 /CLASSAV TEST1AVE=MEAN(FINGRADE TEST1).
VARIABLE LABELS CLASSAV 'Final Average' / TEST1AVE '1st Test Av-
erage'.
FORMATS CLASSAV TEST1AVE (F4.1).
```

The formats for CLASSAV and TEST1AVE are changed from the default width of eight with two decimal places (F8.2) to a width of four columns with one decimal digit (F4.1).

If the aggregate file is saved as a system file, the file must be retrieved with a GET command before the FORMATS and VARIABLE LABELS commands can be issued.

6.22
Missing Data

By default, all nonmissing cases are used in the computation of aggregate variables. To force target variables to system-missing if any of the cases in the group are missing on the source variable, use the MISSING subcommand. The MISSING subcommand has one keyword specification, COLUMNWISE.

The MISSING subcommand follows the OUTFILE subcommand, as in:

```
AGGREGATE OUTFILE='CLASSREP.SYF'
  /MISSING=COLUMNWISE
  /BREAK=DEPT COURSE
  /TESTAVE1 AVEFINAL=MEAN(TEST1 FINGRADE).
  /TESTSD1 SDFINAL=SD(TEST1 FINGRADE).

GET FILE='CLASSREP.SYF'.
LIST.
```

The results of the LIST command are shown in Figure 6.22. You can compare these values with those shown in Figure 6.18b.

Figure 6.22 Listing of aggregated values with columnwise treatment

```
DEPT COURSE SECTION TESTAVE1 AVEFINAL  TESTSD1  SDFINAL

hds   444  a        84.80    87.00     11.63    7.55
soc   100  a          .        .         .        .
soc   100  b        80.69    85.62     10.40    4.91
soc   222  a        77.69      .        7.60      .
soc   310  a        80.89      .        9.28      .


Number of cases read =     5   Number of cases listed =      5
```

The MISSING subcommand has no effect on the N, NU, NMISS, or NUMISS functions. For example, N(TEST1) returns the same result for the default and for columnwise deletion.

6.23
Including Missing Values

To force a function to treat user-missing values as valid, follow the function name with a period, as in:

```
LOFINAL=PLT.(FINGRADE,75)
```

LOFINAL will equal the percentage of cases within the group with values less than 75 for FINGRADE even if some of the values are defined as missing.

To obtain the first value of AGE in a break group whether it is missing or not, specify:

```
FIRSTAGE = FIRST.(AGE)
```

If the first case in a break group has a user-missing value on AGE, FIRSTAGE is set to that value. Since variables created with FIRST have the same dictionary information as their source variables, the value for FIRSTAGE is still treated as user-missing on the aggregated file.

The period is ignored when used with N, NU, NMISS, and NUMISS if these functions have no argument. On the other hand, NMISS.(AGE) gives the number of cases on which AGE has the system-missing value. The effect of specifying the period on N, NU, NMISS, and NUMISS is illustrated by the following:

$$N = N. = N(AGE)+NMISS(AGE) = N.(AGE)+NMISS.(AGE)$$

$$NU = NU. = NU(AGE)+NUMISS(AGE) = NU.(AGE)+NUMISS.(AGE)$$

That is, the function N (the same as N. with no argument) is equal to the sum of cases with valid and with missing values for AGE, which is also equal to the sum of cases with either valid or user-missing values and with system-missing values for AGE. The same holds for the NU, NMISS, and NUMISS functions.

Table 6.23 demonstrates the effect of the MISSING subcommand and of including user-missing values. Each entry in the table is the number of cases used to compute the specified function for a particular break group of variable EDUC. The BREAK group has 10 nonmissing cases, 5 user-missing cases, and 2 system-missing cases. With the exception of the MEAN function, columnwise treatment produces the same results as the default for every function.

Table 6.23   Alternative missing-value treatments

Function	Default	Columnwise
N	17	17
N.	17	17
N(EDUC)	10	10
N.(EDUC)	15	15
MEAN(EDUC)	10	0
MEAN.(EDUC)	15	0
NMISS(EDUC)	7	7
NMISS.(EDUC)	2	2

6.24
EXAMPLE FOR JOIN AND AGGREGATE

At the end of the semester, an instructor puts together a report outlining the individual performance of each student. The commands below use JOIN and AGGREGATE to combine class grade books into a single file, develop summary variables of overall class performance, combine class and student variables, and then produce a listing of individual performance compared to class averages:

```
JOIN ADD FILE='SOC100A.FSF'
  /FILE='SOC100B.FSF'
  /FILE='SOC222A.FSF'
  /FILE='SOC310A.FSF'
  /FILE='HDS444A.FSF'
  /MAP.

SORT BY DEPT COURSE SECTION.

AGGREGATE OUTFILE='AVERAGE.FSF'
  /PRESORTED
  /BREAK=DEPT COURSE SECTION
  /AVEGRADE=MEAN(FINGRADE)
  /SDGRADE=SD(FINGRADE)
  /PCTFAIL=PLT(FINGRADE,65).

JOIN MATCH FILE=* /TABLE='AVERAGE.FSF'
  /BY DEPT COURSE SECTION.

COMPUTE GRADEDEV=FINGRADE-AVEGRADE.

LIST VARS=DEPT COURSE SECTION LASTNAME STUNUM FINGRADE GRADEDEV.

SAVE OUTFILE='YEAREND.FSF'.
```

• The JOIN ADD command combines cases from each of five system files. Variables from the files and in the resulting active file are listed with the MAP subcommand.

• The SORT command orders cases in ascending order of SECTION within categories of COURSE within categories of DEPT.

• The OUTFILE subcommand on AGGREGATE indicates that the aggregated file should be directed to system file AVERAGE.FSF. The PRESORTED specification states that the file is already sorted.

• The BREAK subcommand creates one case for each distinct combination of DEPT, COURSE, and SECTION. Each case contains values of the break variables, as well as three variables produced with three different aggregate functions, MEAN, SD, and PLT.

- The JOIN command matches cases in the active file with cases in the aggregate file, which is designated a table file. Cases are matched based on the key variables DEPT, COURSE, and SECTION. A new active file is available for other SPSS/PC+ commands.
- The COMPUTE command creates a variable based on the difference between the student's grade and the class average.
- The LIST command produces a simple listing of the named variables from the current active file.
- The SAVE command saves the active file for use in subsequent sessions.

Figure 6.24a Map of variables in input and resulting files

RESULT	SOC100A.FSF	SOC100B.FSF	SOC222A.FSF	SOC310A.FSF	HDS444A.FSF
COURSE	COURSE	COURSE	COURSE	COURSE	COURSE
SECTION	SECTION	SECTION	SECTION	SECTION	SECTION
STUNUM	STUNUM	STUNUM	STUNUM	STUNUM	STUNUM
LASTNAME	LASTNAME	LASTNAME	LASTNAME	LASTNAME	LASTNAME
DEPT	DEPT	DEPT	DEPT	DEPT	DEPT
EXAMS	EXAMS	EXAMS	EXAMS	EXAMS	EXAMS
TEST1	TEST1	TEST1	TEST1	TEST1	TEST1
TEST2	TEST2	TEST2	TEST2	TEST2	TEST2
TEST3	TEST3	TEST3	TEST3	TEST3	TEST3
TEST4	TEST4	TEST4	TEST4	TEST4	TEST4
TEST5	TEST5	TEST5	TEST5	TEST5	TEST5
TEST6	TEST6	TEST6	TEST6	TEST6	TEST6
FINGRADE	FINGRADE	FINGRADE	FINGRADE	FINGRADE	FINGRADE

Figure 6.24b LISTING of cases after table look-up JOIN MATCH

DEPT	COURSE	SECTION	LASTNAME	STUNUM	FINGRADE	GRADEDEV
hds	444	a	Smith	25851	87	0.0
hds	444	a	Cobbleigh	87034	94	7.00
hds	444	a	Heisenhuer	13792	94	7.00
hds	444	a	Harris	89763	76	-11.00
hds	444	a	Chambers	91913	84	-3.00
soc	100	a	Atmore	10009	95	8.18
soc	100	a	McDowell	24365	90	3.18
soc	100	a	Hutchinson	27111	80	-6.82
soc	100	a	Swift	55287	.	.
soc	100	a	Jamieson	62432	85	-1.82
soc	100	a	Paulsen	89765	.	.
soc	100	a	Sweeney	43289	82	-4.82
soc	100	a	Baker	23763	89	2.18
soc	100	a	Jones	22304	85	-1.82
soc	100	a	Jacobsen	27001	.	.
soc	100	a	Roberts	35760	91	4.18
soc	100	a	Atkinson	64352	81	-5.82
soc	100	a	Darfler	54338	88	1.18
soc	100	a	Klein	79885	89	2.18
soc	100	b	Smithe	10229	81	-4.62
soc	100	b	Farroro	34365	87	1.38
soc	100	b	Huber	25111	78	-7.62
soc	100	b	Westerman	55587	90	4.38
soc	100	b	Mount	62442	87	1.38
soc	100	b	Harris	89763	94	8.38
soc	100	b	Jones	70395	88	2.38
soc	100	b	Halley	53763	89	3.38
soc	100	b	Manova	82224	88	2.38
soc	100	b	Sullivan	97291	79	-6.62
soc	100	b	Dexter	50762	88	2.38
soc	100	b	Colby	62752	79	-6.62
soc	100	b	Fiorello	54358	85	-.62
soc	222	a	Smith	12239	89	4.08
soc	222	a	Freiberg	35467	88	3.08
soc	222	a	Mills	65141	82	-2.92
soc	222	a	West	53287	83	-1.92
soc	222	a	Maus	39742	82	-2.92
soc	222	a	Herrmann	9763	.	.
soc	222	a	Daveport	48364	87	2.08
soc	222	a	Hill	81043	86	1.08
soc	222	a	Mason	42524	82	-2.92
soc	222	a	Evans	95591	84	-.92
soc	222	a	Bates	61932	86	1.08
soc	222	a	Hughes	93132	87	2.08
soc	222	a	Bates	44359	83	-1.92
soc	310	a	O'Kane	42305	83	-4.75
soc	310	a	Hallet	60611	85	-2.75
soc	310	a	Robinson	14420	86	-1.75
soc	310	a	Nace	4901	92	4.25
soc	310	a	Liebmann	99999	87	-.75
soc	310	a	Countryman	43995	85	-2.75
soc	310	a	Adams	60618	.	.
soc	310	a	Stephenson	14520	92	4.25
soc	310	a	Jensen	22112	92	4.25

Number of cases read =   54   Number of cases listed =   54

6.25
SWAPPING CASES AND VARIABLES: PROCEDURE FLIP

SPSS/PC+ assumes a file structure in which the variables are the columns and the cases are the rows. This is the file structure required to correctly read and analyze your data. Sometimes, however, data are recorded in just the opposite fashion: the cases are the columns and each variable is a row. You might find this to be the case with spreadsheet data that you have read with TRANSLATE.

To get this kind of file into the structure required by SPSS/PC+, you need to use the FLIP command. FLIP switches the columns and rows of your data so that what was in column 1, row 2, is now in column 2, row 1. For example, suppose you have two products, each with quarterly sales, and the data are structured like this:

```
        Q1    Q2    Q3    Q4    Q5    Q6
PROD1   24    36    78    48    53    65
PROD2   39    82    31    49    22    48
```

The transposed file looks like this:

```
      PROD1 PROD2
Q1    24     39
Q2    36     82
Q3    78     31
Q4    48     49
Q5    53     22
Q6    65     48
```

If you need to use FLIP to reorganize your file, do so as soon as possible in the session, ideally right after you read the data with TRANSLATE. This is so you can be sure that any commands you issue apply to the new, corrected active file. For additional information on transposing your file, see Command Reference: FLIP.

6.26
When FLIP Won't Help

A typical format for spreadsheet files containing time series data is shown in Figure 6.26. This file contains a single time series that begins in January, 1980, and ends in December, 1984.

Figure 6.26   A possible spreadsheet file structure

	A	B	C	D	E	F	G	H	. . .	M
1	YEAR	JAN	FEB	MAR	APR	MAY	JUN	JUL	. . .	DEC
2	1980	22	27	21	31	34	33	39	. . .	29
3	1981	31	33	33	34	41	42	44	. . .	35
4	1982	33	34	31	37	43	51	49	. . .	41
5	1983	43	49	49	55	57	62	61	. . .	54
6	1984	57	63	70	68	74	79	83	. . .	71

Reading this file into SPSS/PC+ Trends with TRANSLATE would give you 13 variables (YEAR through DEC) and five cases (1980 through 1984). However, swapping the columns and rows with FLIP would give you 5 separate series, one for each year, instead of one continuous series. To get a structure like this into the proper format, you need to read the data twice: once with TRANSLATE and once with DATA LIST. The commands that would be used for the file in Figure 6.26 are:

```
TRANSLATE FROM='SPREAD.DAT' /TYPE=WK1 /FIELDNAMES /DROP=YEAR.
WRITE.
DATA LIST FILE='SPSS.PRC' FREE /SERIES1.
DATE Y 1980 M 1.
```

- The TRANSLATE command reads the spreadsheet data from file SPREAD.DAT, using the first row as variable names and dropping the YEAR variable.
- The raw data are then written to an ASCII file with the WRITE command. By default, the file is named SPSS.PRC.
- DATA LIST reads the raw data in freefield format as one continuous series named SERIES1.
- The DATE command (available with the SPSS/PC+ Trends option) reassigns the correct year and month information to the data.

Contents _____

7 Data Tabulation: Procedure FREQUENCIES

Few people would dispute the effects of "rainy days and Mondays" on the body and spirit. It has long been known that more suicides occur on Mondays than other days of the week. Recently an excess of cardiac deaths on Mondays has also been noted (Rabkin et al., 1980). This chapter looks at data from the Western Electric study, in which the incidence of coronary heart disease in 2,017 men was monitored for 20 years. Here, the day of the week on which deaths occurred is examined to see if an excess of deaths occurred on Mondays.

7.1 A FREQUENCY TABLE

A first step in analyzing data on day of death might be to count the number of deaths occurring on each day of the week. Figure 7.1a contains this information.

Figure 7.1a   Frequency of death by day of week

DAYOFWK	DAY OF DEATH				
Value Label	Value	Frequency	Percent	Valid Percent	Cum Percent
SUNDAY	1	19	7.9	17.3	17.3
MONDAY	2	11	4.6	10.0	27.3
TUESDAY	3	19	7.9	17.3	44.5
WEDNESDAY	4	17	7.1	15.5	60.0
THURSDAY	5	15	6.3	13.6	73.6
FRIDAY	6	13	5.4	11.8	85.5
SATURDAY	7	16	6.7	14.5	100.0
MISSING	9	130	54.2	MISSING	
	TOTAL	240	100.0	100.0	

Each row of the frequency table describes a particular day of the week. The last row represents cases for which the day of death is not known or that have not died. For the table in Figure 7.1a, there are 110 cases for which day of death is known. The first column (**Value Label**) gives the name of the day, while the second column (**Value**) contains the value given to the computer to represent the day.

The number of people dying on each day is in the third column (**Frequency**). Monday is the least-frequent death day with 11 deaths. These 11 deaths are 4.6% (11/240) of all cases. This percentage is in the fourth column, labeled **Percent**. However, of the 240 people, 130 had no day of death. The 11 deaths on Monday are 10.0% of the total deaths for which death days are known (11/110). This percentage is in the fifth column, labeled **Valid Percent**.

The last column of the table (**Cum Percent**) contains the cumulative percentage. For a particular day, this percentage is the sum of the valid percentages of that day and all other days that precede it in the table. For example, the cumulative percentage for Tuesday is 44.5, which is the sum of the percentage of deaths that occurred on Sunday, Monday, and Tuesday. It is calculated as

$$\frac{19}{110} + \frac{11}{110} + \frac{19}{110} = \frac{49}{110} = 44.5\%$$

Equation 7.1

Figure 7.1b is a frequency table of day of death for cases who experienced sudden coronary death. This is a particularly interesting category, since it is thought that sudden death may be related to stressful events such as return to the work environment. In Figure 7.1b there does not appear to be a clustering of deaths on any particular day. Sunday has 22.2% of the deaths, while Thursday has 8.3%. Since the number of sudden deaths in the table is small, the magnitude of the observed fluctuations is not very impressive.

Figure 7.1b Frequency of sudden cardiac death by day of the week

```
DAYOFWK    DAY OF DEATH


                                                        Valid      Cum
       Value Label                Value  Frequency  Percent  Percent  Percent
   SUNDAY                          1         8       22.2     22.2     22.2
   MONDAY                          2         4       11.1     11.1     33.3
   TUESDAY                         3         4       11.1     11.1     44.4
   WEDNESDAY                       4         7       19.4     19.4     63.9
   THURSDAY                        5         3        8.3      8.3     72.2
   FRIDAY                          6         6       16.7     16.7     88.9
   SATURDAY                        7         4       11.1     11.1    100.0
                                          --------  -------  -------
                         TOTAL              36      100.0    100.0

   Valid Cases      36     Missing Cases      0
```

7.2
Visual Displays

While the numbers in the frequency table can be studied and compared, it is often useful to present results in a visually interpretable form. Figure 7.2a is a pie chart of the data displayed in Figure 7.1a. Each slice represents a day of the week. The size of the slice depends on the frequency of death for that day. Monday is represented by 10.0% of the pie chart, since 10.0% of the deaths for which the day is known occurred on Monday.

**Figure 7.2a Frequency of death by day of week
(From SPSS Graphics, a mainframe product)**

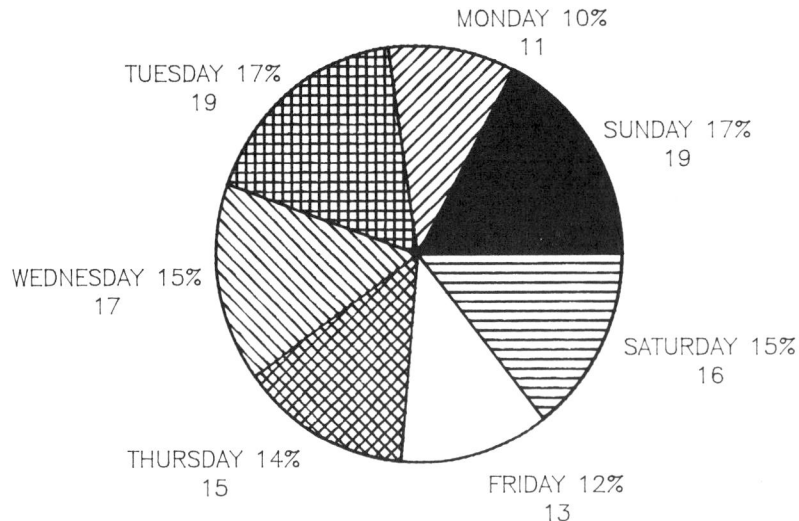

Another way to represent the data is with a bar chart, as shown in Figure 7.2b. There is a bar for each day, and the length of the bar is proportional to the number of deaths observed on that day. Inside each bar is the number of cases occurring on that day.

**Figure 7.2b Frequency of death by day of the week
(Bar chart from SPSS procedure FREQUENCIES)**

```
DAYOFWK    DAY OF DEATH

        SUNDAY ***************************************************** 19
        MONDAY ***************************** 11
       TUESDAY ***************************************************** 19
     WEDNESDAY *********************************************** 17
      THURSDAY ***************************************** 15
        FRIDAY *********************************** 13
      SATURDAY ******************************************** 16

Valid Cases       110      Missing Cases    130
```

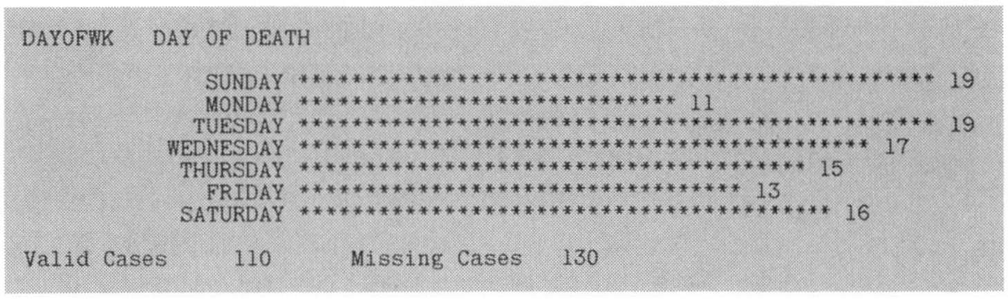

Only values that actually occur in the data are represented in the bar chart from procedure FREQUENCIES. For example, if no deaths took place on Thursday, no space would be left for Thursday and the bar for Wednesday would be followed by the one for Friday. If you chart the number of cars per family, the bar describing 6 cars may be next to the one for 25 cars if no family has 7 to 24 cars. Therefore, you should pay attention to where categories with no cases may occur.

Although the basic information presented by frequency tables, pie charts, and bar charts is the same, the visual displays enliven the data. Differences among the days of the week are apparent at a glance, eliminating the need to pore over columns of numbers.

7.3
What Day?

Although the number of sudden cardiac deaths is small in this study, the data in Figure 7.1b indicate that the number of deaths on Mondays is not particularly large. In fact, Sunday has the most deaths, slightly over 22%. A recent study of over a thousand sudden cardiac deaths in Rochester, Minnesota, also found a slightly increased incidence of death on weekends for men (Beard et al., 1982). The authors speculate that for men, this might mean "the home environment is more stressful than the work environment." But one should be wary of explanations that are not directly supported by data. It is only too easy to find a clever explanation for any statistical finding. (For further analysis of these data, see *SPSS/PC+ Statistics.*)

7.4
Histograms

A frequency table or bar chart of all values for a variable is a convenient way of summarizing a variable that has a relatively small number of distinct values. Variables such as sex, country, and astrological sign are necessarily limited in the number of values they can have. For variables that can take on many different values, such as income to the penny or weight in ounces, a tally of the cases with each observed value may not be very informative. In the worst situation, when all cases have different values, a frequency table is little more than an ordered list of those values.

Variables that have many values can be summarized by grouping the values of the variables into intervals and counting the number of cases with values within each interval. For example, income can be grouped into $5,000 intervals such as 0–4999, 5000–9999, 10000–14999, and so forth, and the number of observations in each group can be tabulated. Such grouping should be done using SPSS/PC+ during the actual analysis of the data. As indicated in Chapter 2, the values for variables should be entered into the data file in their original, ungrouped form.

A histogram is a convenient way to display the distribution of such grouped values. Consider Figure 7.4, which is a histogram for body weight in pounds of the sample of 240 men from the Western Electric study. The first column indicates the number of cases with values within the interval, while the second column gives the midpoint, or middle value, for the interval. Each row of symbols represents the number of cases with values in the interval. For example, the second row of the histogram has 10 symbols, which represent 10 men who weighed between 130 and 140 pounds in 1958. The number of cases represented by each symbol depends on the size of the sample and the maximum number of cases falling into an interval. Intervals that have no observations are included in the histogram but no symbols are displayed. This differs from a bar chart, which does not leave space for the empty categories.

A histogram can be used in any situation in which it is reasonable to group adjacent values. Histograms should not be used to display variables in which there is no underlying order to the values. For example, if 100 different religions are arbitrarily assigned codes of 1 to 100, grouping values into intervals is meaningless. Either a bar chart or a histogram in which each interval corresponds to a single value should be used to display such data.

Figure 7.4 A histogram of body weight

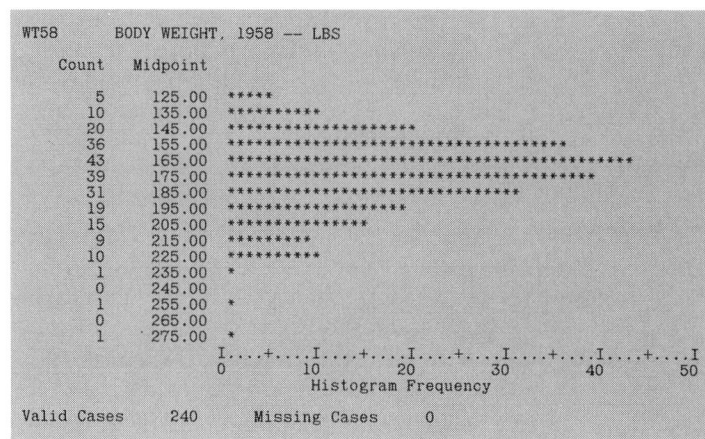

```
WT58      BODY WEIGHT, 1958 -- LBS

    Count   Midpoint

        5    125.00   *****
       10    135.00   **********
       20    145.00   ********************
       36    155.00   ************************************
       43    165.00   ******************************************
       39    175.00   **************************************
       31    185.00   ******************************
       19    195.00   *******************
       15    205.00   ***************
        9    215.00   *********
       10    225.00   **********
        1    235.00   *
        0    245.00
        1    255.00   *
        0    265.00
        1    275.00   *
                      I....+....I....+....I....+....I....+....I....+....I
                      0        10        20        30        40        50
                                    Histogram Frequency

Valid Cases     240     Missing Cases     0
```

7.5
Screening Data

Frequency tables, bar charts, and histograms can serve purposes other than summarizing data. Unexpected codes in the tables may indicate errors in data entry or coding. Cases with death days coded as 0 or 8 are in error if the numbers 1 through 7 represent the days of the week and 9 stands for unknown. Since errors in the data should be eliminated as soon as possible, it is a good idea to run frequency tables as the first step in analyzing data.

Frequency tables and visual displays can also help you identify cases with values that are unusual but possibly correct. For example, a tally of the number of cars in families may show a family with 25 cars. Although such a value is possible, especially if the survey did not specify cars in working condition, it raises suspicion and should be examined to ensure that it is really correct.

Incorrect data values distort the results of statistical analyses, and correct but unusual values may require special treatment. In either case, early identification is valuable.

7.6
RUNNING PROCEDURE FREQUENCIES

The FREQUENCIES procedure produces frequency tables, bar charts (for discrete variables), histograms (for continuous variables), and various descriptive statistics (means, standard deviations, percentiles, and so forth).

FREQUENCIES operates via subcommands. Only one, the VARIABLES subcommand, is required.

7.7
Specifying the Variables

The VARIABLES subcommand names the variables to be analyzed. Simply specify the names of the variables you want to analyze, as in the command

```
FREQUENCIES VARIABLES=RAISE82 AGE DEPT.
```

No other specification or subcommand is needed when only frequency tables are desired. You can use the keyword ALL to name all variables in the file, and the keyword TO to refer to consecutive variables in the file.

7.8
Formatting Options

Several formatting options are available via the FORMAT subcommand. You can control the formatting of tables and the sorting of categories within a table. The FORMAT subcommand affects all of the variables listed on the VARIABLES subcommand. You can use only one FORMAT subcommand per FREQUENCIES command, but you can request several formatting options per FORMAT subcommand.

7.9
Table Formats

The following FORMAT keywords are used to control the formatting of tables:

NOLABELS *Do not display value labels.* By default, FREQUENCIES displays the value labels defined by the VALUE LABELS command (see Chapter 3).

DOUBLE *Double-space frequency tables.*

NEWPAGE *Begin each table on a new page.* By default, FREQUENCIES displays as many tables on a page as it can.

CONDENSE *Use condensed format.* Frequency counts are displayed in three columns. Value labels and percentages are not displayed, and valid and cumulative percentages are rounded off to integers.

ONEPAGE *Use conditional condensed format.* ONEPAGE requests condensed format for tables that would require more than one page with the default format. All other tables are displayed in the default format. If CONDENSE and ONEPAGE are both specified, all tables are displayed in condensed format.

For example, the command

```
FREQUENCIES VARIABLES=RAISE82 AGE DEPT
  /FORMAT=NEWPAGE.
```

requests frequency tables for variables RAISE82, AGE, and DEPT. Each table begins on a new page.

7.10
The Order of Values

By default, numeric values in a frequency table are listed in ascending order and string values in alphabetical order. Three other methods of sorting values can be requested by using one of the following keywords on the FORMAT subcommand:

DVALUE *Sort values in descending order.*

AFREQ *Sort values in ascending order of frequency.*

DFREQ *Sort value in descending order of frequency.*

If more than one sorting method is requested, the last one specified is used.

7.11
Suppressing Tables

If you have a lot of variables with many values, or if you want only descriptive statistics (or histograms or bar charts), you may want to suppress the display of frequency tables. Use the following FORMAT keywords to do this:

LIMIT(n) *Do not display tables for variables with more categories than the specified value.*

NOTABLE *Suppress all frequency tables.*

If LIMIT and NOTABLE are both specified, no tables are displayed. When tables are suppressed, the number of cases with missing values and the number of cases with valid values are still displayed.

7.12
Requesting Bar Charts and Histograms

Both bar charts and histograms can be requested with one FREQUENCIES command. Use the BARCHART subcommand to obtain bar charts for all variables listed on the VARIABLES subcommand, and the HISTOGRAM subcommand to obtain histograms for all numeric variables. If you want only those bar charts that will fit on one page and histograms for all other numeric variables, use the HBAR subcommand.

7.13
BARCHART Subcommand

To obtain bar charts, use subcommand BARCHART, as in the command

```
FREQUENCIES VARIABLES=DAYOFWK/BARCHART.
```

which was used to produce Figure 7.2b. No further specifications are required.

By default, all tabulated values are plotted. The scale for the horizontal axis is in terms of frequencies and is determined by the largest frequency in the data. With optional BARCHART specifications you can specify minimum and maximum bounds for plotting and request a horizontal scale based on percentages. You can also specify the maximum frequency to be used for the horizontal scale.

MIN(n)   *Use the lowerbound* n. Values below this minimum are not plotted.
MAX(n)   *Use the upperbound* n. Values above this maximum are not plotted.
PERCENT(n) *Scale the horizontal axis in percentages.* n specifies the maximum percentage for any value and is not required. If *n* is too small or not specified, SPSS/PC+ uses 5, 10, 25, 50, or 100, depending on the largest percentage in the data.
FREQ(n)   *Scale the horizontal axis in frequencies, with* n *as the maximum frequency.* If no *n* is specified, or if *n* is too small, SPSS/PC+ uses 10, 20, 50, 100, 200, 500, 1000, 2000, and so on, depending on the largest frequency in the data.

These optional specifications can be entered in any order. For example, the command

```
FREQUENCIES VARIABLES=DAYOFWK/BARCHART MAX(5) MIN(2).
```

could be used to request a barchart for the variable DAYOFWK with values from 2 through 5.

7.14
HISTOGRAM Subcommand

Histograms are obtained by specifying the HISTOGRAM subcommand. No further specifications are required, although several formatting options are available. In the default format, all tabulated values are included, the horizontal axis is scaled by frequencies, and the scale is determined by the largest frequency in the data. The default number of intervals is 21 (or fewer if the range of values is less than 21).

All of the BARCHART formatting specifications described in Section 7.13 can be used with HISTOGRAM to alter the histogram format. In addition, you can specify the interval width and have a normal curve superimposed on the histogram by using the following optional specifications:

INCREMENT(n) *Use an interval width equal to* n.
NORMAL   *Superimpose a normal curve.* A normal curve with the same mean and variance as the plotted variable is superimposed on the histogram. All valid values, including those excluded by MIN and MAX, are used in calculating the mean and variance.

The HISTOGRAM specifications can be entered in any order. For example, the command

```
FREQUENCIES  VARIABLES=WT58/ FORMAT=NOTABLE
  /HISTOGRAM MIN(120) MAX(280) INCREMENT(10).
```

was used to produce the output in Figure 7.4.

7.15
HBAR Subcommand

When the HBAR subcommand is used, bar charts are displayed for numeric variables if the chart will fit on one page; otherwise, HBAR produces a histogram. HBAR produces bar charts for short string variables and for the short-string portion of long string variables, regardless of the number of values.

All of the HISTOGRAM formatting options can be used with HBAR.

7.16
Requesting Percentiles and Ntiles

Use the PERCENTILES and NTILES subcommands to obtain percentiles for all variables specified on the VARIABLES subcommand. If more than one PERCEN-TILES or NTILES subcommand is specified, one table with the values for all requested percentiles is displayed.

Percentiles, the values below which given percentages of cases fall, are obtained by specifying PERCENTILES, followed by an optional equals sign and a list of percentages. For example, the command

```
FREQUENCIES VARIABLES=VARZ/PERCENTILES=10 25 33.3 66.7 75.
```

requests the values for percentiles 10, 25, 33.3, 66.7, and 75 for variable VARZ. When a requested percentile cannot be calculated, a period is displayed.

Ntiles, the values that divide the sample into groups with equal numbers of cases, are obtained by specifying NTILES, followed by an optional equals sign and an integer indicating the number of subgroups. For example, the command

```
FREQUENCIES VARIABLES=VARZ/NTILES=4.
```

requests quartiles (percentiles 25, 50, and 75) for variable VARZ.

7.17
Optional Statistics

The STATISTICS subcommand is used to request various statistics for all variables listed on the VARIABLES subcommand. Use the keywords shown below to obtain these statistics.

MEAN *Mean.*

SEMEAN *Standard error of the mean.*

MEDIAN *Median.* The median is not available if AFREQ or DFREQ is specified in the FORMAT subcommand.

MODE *Mode.*

STDDEV *Standard deviation.*

VARIANCE *Variance.*

SKEWNESS *Skewness.*

SESKEW *Standard error of the skewness statistic.*

KURTOSIS *Kurtosis.*

SEKURT *Standard error of the kurtosis statistic.*

RANGE *Range.*

MINIMUM *Minimum.*

MAXIMUM *Maximum.*

SUM *Sum.*

DEFAULT *Mean, standard deviation, minimum, and maximum.*

ALL *All available statistics.*

NONE *No statistics.*

You can specify as many keywords as you wish on the STATISTICS subcommand. For example, the command

```
FREQUENCIES VARIABLES=RAISE82 AGE
  /STATISTICS=MEAN SKEWNESS RANGE SUM.
```

requests the mean, skewness, range, and sum for variables RAISE82 and AGE.

If STATISTICS is specified without any keywords, the default statistics are displayed.

7.18
Missing Values

Both user-missing and system-missing values are included in frequency tables. They are labeled as missing and are not included in the valid or cumulative percentages. They are also not used in calculating descriptive statistics and do not appear in bar charts or histograms.

One optional missing-value treatment is available. This option is requested with the keyword INCLUDE on the MISSING subcommand.

INCLUDE *Include cases with user-missing values.* Cases with user-missing values are included in the percentages, statistics, and plots.

7.19
Example

The following commands produced the output in Figure 7.1a.

```
DATA LIST / DAYOFWK 1 WT58 2-4.
VARIABLE LABELS DAYOFWK 'DAY OF DEATH'
                /WT58 'BODY WEIGHT, 1958 -- LBS'.
VALUE LABELS DAYOFWK 1 'SUNDAY' 2 'MONDAY' 3 'TUESDAY' 4 'WEDNESDAY'
                5 'THURSDAY' 6 'FRIDAY' 7 'SATURDAY' 9
'MISSING'.
MISSING VALUE DAYOFWK (9).
BEGIN DATA.
data records
END DATA.
FREQUENCIES  VARIABLES=DAYOFWK/BARCHART.
FINISH.
```

- The DATA LIST command defines the variable names and column locations for the variables used in the analysis.
- The VARIABLE LABELS and VALUE LABELS commands assign descriptive labels for the variables.
- The MISSING VALUE command defines the value 9 as missing for the variable DAYOFWK.
- The FREQUENCIES command requests a frequency table and a bar chart for the variable DAYOFWK.

Contents

8 Descriptive Statistics: Procedures FREQUENCIES and DESCRIPTIVES

Survey data that rely on voluntary information are subject to many sources of error. People deliberately distort the truth, inadvertently fail to recall events correctly, or refuse to participate. Refusals influence survey results by failing to provide information about a particular type of person—one who refuses to answer surveys at all or avoids certain types of questions. For example, if college graduates tend to be unwilling to answer polls, results of surveys will be biased.

One possible way to examine the veracity of responses is to compare them to official records. Systematic differences between the two sources jeopardize the usefulness of the survey. Unfortunately, for many sensitive questions such as illicit drug use, abortion history, or even income, official records are usually unavailable.

Wyner (1980) examined the differences between the true and self-reported numbers of arrests obtained from 79 former heroin addicts enrolled in the Vera Institute of Justice Supported Employment Experiment. As part of their regular quarterly interviews, participants were asked about their arrest histories in New York City. The self-reported value was compared to arrest record data coded from New York City Police Department arrest sheets. The goal of the study was not only to quantify the extent of error but also to identify factors related to inaccurate responses.

8.1 EXAMINING THE DATA

Figure 8.1a shows histograms for the three variables—true number of arrests, reported arrests, and the discrepancy between the two. From a histogram it is possible to see the *shape* of the distribution; that is, how likely the different values are, how much spread or *variability* there is among the values, and where typical values are concentrated. Such characteristics are important because of the direct insight they provide into the data and because many statistical procedures are based on assumptions about the underlying distributions of variables.

**Figure 8.1a   Reported and true arrests
(Histograms from SPSS/PC+ FREQUENCIES Command)**

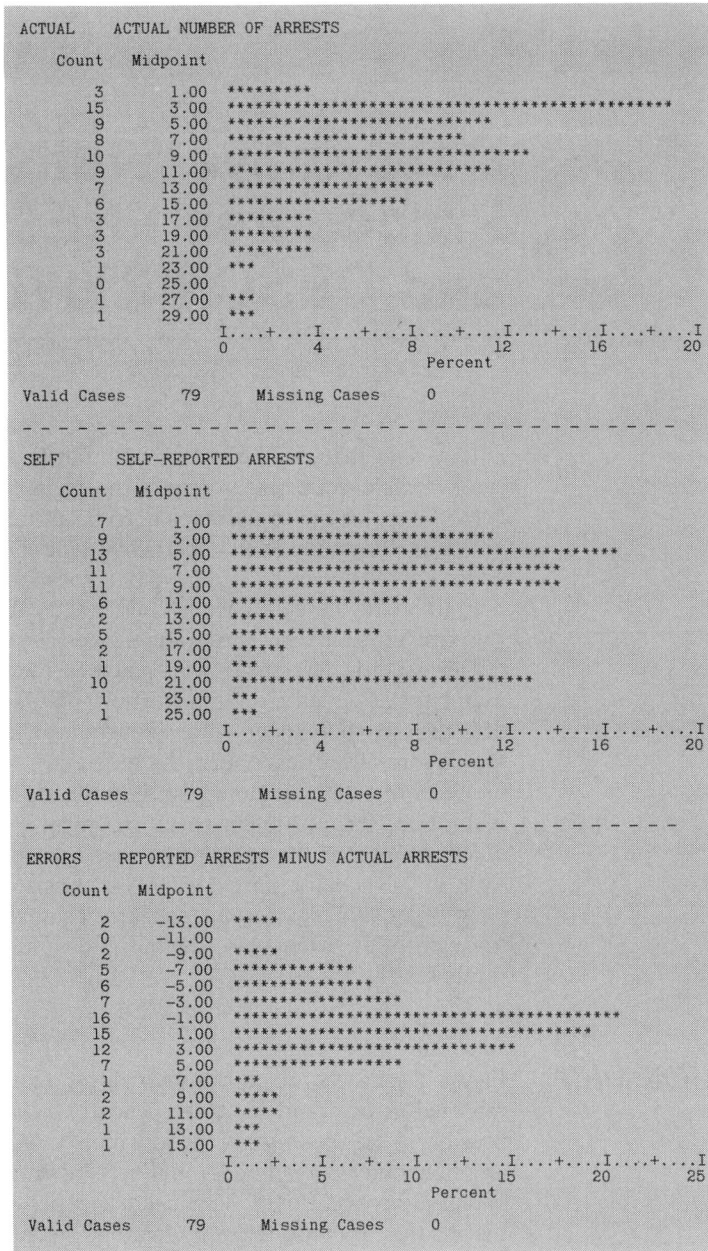

```
ACTUAL     ACTUAL NUMBER OF ARRESTS

   Count   Midpoint
       3      1.00   *********
      15      3.00   ********************************************************
       9      5.00   *****************************
       8      7.00   **************************
      10      9.00   *********************************
       9     11.00   *****************************
       7     13.00   **********************
       6     15.00   *******************
       3     17.00   *********
       3     19.00   *********
       3     21.00   *********
       1     23.00   ***
       0     25.00
       1     27.00   ***
       1     29.00   ***
                     I....+....I....+....I....+....I....+....I....+....I
                     0        4        8       12       16       20
                                               Percent

Valid Cases      79      Missing Cases      0
```

- -

```
SELF       SELF-REPORTED ARRESTS

   Count   Midpoint
       7      1.00   ************************
       9      3.00   *****************************
      13      5.00   ***********************************************
      11      7.00   **************************************
      11      9.00   **************************************
       6     11.00   ********************
       2     13.00   ******
       5     15.00   *****************
       2     17.00   ******
       1     19.00   ***
      10     21.00   **********************************
       1     23.00   ***
       1     25.00   ***
                     I....+....I....+....I....+....I....+....I....+....I
                     0        4        8       12       16       20
                                               Percent

Valid Cases      79      Missing Cases      0
```

- -

```
ERRORS     REPORTED ARRESTS MINUS ACTUAL ARRESTS

   Count   Midpoint
       2    -13.00   *****
       0    -11.00
       2     -9.00   *****
       5     -7.00   **************
       6     -5.00   **************
       7     -3.00   ******************
      16     -1.00   *********************************************
      15      1.00   ****************************************
      12      3.00   ********************************
       7      5.00   ******************
       1      7.00   ***
       2      9.00   *****
       2     11.00   *****
       1     13.00   ***
       1     15.00   ***
                     I....+....I....+....I....+....I....+....I....+....I
                     0        5       10       15       20       25
                                               Percent

Valid Cases      79      Missing Cases      0
```

The distributions of the reported and true numbers of arrests have a somewhat similar shape. Neither distribution has an obvious central value, although the self-reported values have the tallest peak at 4 to 5 arrests, while the actual number of arrests has its peak at 2 to 3 arrests. The distribution of self-reported arrests also has a peak at 20 to 21 arrests. The peaks corresponding to intervals which contain 5, 15, and 20 arrests arouse the suspicion that people may be more likely to report their arrest records as round numbers. Examination of the true number of arrests shows no corresponding peaks at multiples of five.

The distribution of the differences between reported and true number of arrests is not as irregularly shaped as the two distributions from which it is derived. It has two adjacent peaks with midpoint values of -1 and $+1$. Most cases cluster around the peak values, and cases far from these values are infrequent. Figure 8.1b is a condensed frequency table for the response errors (the adjusted and cumulative percentages are rounded to the nearest integer). Almost 47% of the sample (37 cases) reported their arrest record to within two arrests of the true value. Only 22% (17 cases) misrepresented their records by more than 5 arrests. Underreporting is somewhat more likely than exaggeration, with 39% of the cases overestimating and 48% of the cases underestimating.

Figure 8.1b   Error in reported arrests
(Condensed frequency table from SPSS/PC+ FREQUENCIES)

```
ERRORS     REPORTED ARRESTS MINUS ACTUAL ARRESTS


                      CUM                        CUM                         CUM
   VALUE  FREQ PCT PCT    VALUE  FREQ PCT PCT     VALUE  FREQ PCT PCT
     -14     2    3   3      -2     6    8  35        7     1   1  92
      -9     2    3   5      -1    10   13  48        8     1   1  94
      -8     3    4   9       0    10   13  61        9     1   1  95
      -7     2    3  11       1     5    6  67       10     1   1  96
      -6     1    1  13       2     6    8  75       11     1   1  97
      -5     5    6  19       3     6    8  82       12     1   1  99
      -4     3    4  23       4     4    5  87       15     1   1 100
      -3     4    5  28       5     3    4  91

Valid Cases     79      Missing Cases     0
```

8.2
Percentile Values

Percentiles are values above and below which certain percentages of the cases fall. For example, 95% of the cases have values less than or equal to the 95th percentile. From the cumulative percentage column in the frequency table in Figure 8.1b, the value for the 95th percentile is 9.

Figure 8.2 contains some commonly used percentiles for the distributions in Figure 8.1a. The three percentiles (25%, 50%, and 75%) divide the observed distributions into approximately four equal parts. The actual and self-reported numbers of arrests have the same 25th percentile, the value 4. This means that about 75% of the values are greater than or equal to 4, and 25% less than 4.

Figure 8.2   Percentiles for reported and actual arrests and errors

```
ACTUAL     ACTUAL NUMBER OF ARRESTS

Percentile     Value     Percentile     Value     Percentile     Value
   25.00       4.000       50.00        8.000       75.00        13.000

Valid Cases    79      Missing Cases     0

- - - - - - - - - - - - - - - - - - - - - - - - - - - - - - - -

SELF       SELF-REPORTED ARRESTS

Percentile     Value     Percentile     Value     Percentile     Value
   25.00       4.000       50.00        7.000       75.00        14.000

Valid Cases    79      Missing Cases     0

- - - - - - - - - - - - - - - - - - - - - - - - - - - - - - - -

ERRORS     REPORTED ARRESTS MINUS ACTUAL ARRESTS

Percentile     Value     Percentile     Value     Percentile     Value
   25.00      -3.000       50.00         0.0        75.00         3.000

Valid Cases    79      Missing Cases     0
```

8.3
SUMMARIZING THE DATA

Although frequency tables and bar charts are useful for summarizing and displaying data (see Chapter 7), further condensation and description is often desirable. A variety of summary measures that convey information about the data in single numbers can be computed. The choice of summary measure, or *statistic,* as it is often called, depends upon characteristics of the data as well as of the statistic. One important characteristic of the data that must be considered is the *level of measurement* of each variable being studied.

8.4
Levels of Measurement

Measurement is the assignment of numbers or codes to observations. Levels of measurement are distinguished by ordering and distance properties. A computer does not know what measurement underlies the values it is given. You must determine the level of measurement of your data and apply appropriate statistical techniques.

The traditional classification of levels of measurement into nominal, ordinal, interval, and ratio scales was developed by S. S. Stevens (1946). This remains the basic typology and is the one used throughout this manual. Variations exist, however, and issues concerning the statistical effect of ignoring levels of measurement have been debated (see, for example, Borgatta & Bohrnstedt, 1980).

8.5
Nominal Measurement

The nominal level of measurement is the "lowest" in the typology because no assumptions are made about relations between values. Each value defines a distinct category and serves merely as a label or name (hence, "nominal" level) for the category. For instance, the birthplace of an individual is a nominal variable. For most purposes, there is no inherent ordering among cities or towns. Although cities can be ordered according to size, density, or air pollution, a city thought of as "place of birth" is a concept that is normally not tied to any order. When numeric values are attached to nominal categories, they are merely identifiers. None of the properties of numbers such as relative size, addition, or multiplication can be applied to these numerically coded categories. Therefore, statistics that assume ordering or meaningful numerical distances between the values do not ordinarily give useful information about nominal variables.

8.6
Ordinal Measurement

When it is possible to rank or order all categories according to some criterion, the ordinal level of measurement is achieved. For instance, classifying employees into clerical, supervisory, and managerial categories is an ordering according to responsibilities or skills. Each category has a position lower or higher than another category. Furthermore, knowing that supervisory is higher than clerical and that managerial is higher than supervisory automatically means that managerial is higher than clerical. However, nothing is known about how much higher; no distance is measured. Ordering is the sole mathematical property applicable to ordinal measurements, and the use of numeric values does not imply that any other property of numbers is applicable.

8.7
Interval Measurement

In addition to order, interval measurements have the property of meaningful distance between values. A thermometer, for example, measures temperature in degrees which are the same size at any point on the scale. The difference between 20°C and 21°C is the same as the difference between 5°C and 6°C. However, an interval scale does not have an inherently determined zero point. In the familiar Celsius and Fahrenheit systems, 0° is determined by an agreed-upon definition, not by the absence of heat. Consequently, interval-level measurement allows us to study differences between items but not their proportionate magnitudes. For example, it is incorrect to say that 80°F is twice as hot as 40°F.

8.8
Ratio Measurement

Ratio measurements have all the ordering and distance properties of an interval scale. In addition, a zero point can be meaningfully designated. In measuring physical distances between objects using feet or meters, a zero distance is naturally defined as the absence of any distance. The existence of a zero point means that ratio comparisons can be made. For example, it is quite meaningful to say that a 6-foot-tall adult is twice as tall as a 3-foot-tall child or that a 500-meter race is five times as long as a 100-meter race.

Because ratio measurements satisfy all the properties of the real number system, any mathematical manipulations appropriate for real numbers can be applied to ratio measures. However, the existence of a zero point is seldom critical for statistical analyses.

8.9
Summary Statistics

Figure 8.9 contains a variety of summary statistics that are useful in describing the distributions of reported arrests, true number of arrests, and the discrepancy between the two. The statistics can be grouped into three categories according to what they quantify: central tendency, dispersion, and shape.

Figure 8.9   Statistics describing arrest data

```
ACTUAL    ACTUAL NUMBER OF ARRESTS

Mean         9.253    Std Err      .703    Median      8.000
Mode         3.000    Std Dev     6.248    Variance   39.038
Kurtosis      .597    S E Kurt     .535    Skewness     .908
S E Skew      .271    Range      28.000    Minimum     1.000
Maximum     29.000    Sum       731.000
```

```
SELF      SELF-REPORTED ARRESTS

Mean         8.962    Std Err      .727    Median      7.000
Mode         5.000    Std Dev     6.458    Variance   41.704
Kurtosis     -.485    S E Kurt     .535    Skewness     .750
S E Skew      .271    Range      25.000    Minimum      0.0
Maximum     25.000    Sum       708.000

Valid Cases     79    Missing Cases     0
```

```
ERRORS    REPORTED ARRESTS MINUS ACTUAL ARRESTS

Mean         -.291    Std Err      .587    Median       0.0
Mode        -1.000    Std Dev     5.216    Variance   27.209
Kurtosis     1.102    S E Kurt     .535    Skewness     .125
S E Skew      .271    Range      29.000    Minimum   -14.000
Maximum     15.000    Sum       -23.000

Valid Cases     79    Missing Cases     0
```

8.10
Measures of Central Tendency

The mean, median, and mode are frequently used to describe the location of a distribution. The *mode* is the most frequently occurring value (or values). For the true number of arrests, the mode is 3 (see Figure 8.9); for the self-reported values, it is 5. The distribution of the difference between the true and self-reported values is multimodal. That is, it has more than one mode since the values −1 and 0 occur with equal frequency. SPSS/PC+, however, displays only one mode, as shown in Figure 8.9. The mode can be used for data measured at any level. It is usually not the preferred measure for interval and ordinal data since it ignores much of the available information.

The *median* is the value above and below which one half of the observations fall. For example, if there are 79 observations, the median is the 40th largest observation. When there is an even number of observations, no unique center value exists, so the mean of the two middle observations is usually taken as the median value. For the arrest data, the median is 0 for the differences, 8 for the true arrests, and 7 for reported arrests. For ordinal data the median is usually a good measure of central tendency since it uses the ranking information. The median should not be used for nominal data since ranking of the observations is not possible.

The *mean*, also called the arithmetic average, is the sum of the values of all observations divided by the number of observations. Thus,

$$\bar{X} = \sum_{i=1}^{N} \frac{X_i}{N}$$

Equation 8.10

where N is the number of cases and X_i is the value of the variable for the ith case. Since the mean utilizes the distance between observations, the measurements should be interval or ratio. Mean race, religion, and auto color are meaningless. For dichotomous variables coded as 0 and 1, the mean has a special interpretation: it is the proportion of cases coded 1 in the data.

The three measures of central tendency need not be the same. For example, the mean number of true arrests is 9.25, the median is 8, and the mode is 3 (see Figure 8.9). The arithmetic mean is greatly influenced by outlying observations, while the median is not. Adding a single case with 400 arrests would increase the mean from 9.25 to 14.1, but it would not affect the median. Therefore, if there are values far removed from the rest of the observations, the median may be a better measure of central tendency than the mean.

For symmetric distributions, the observed mean, median, and mode are usually close in value. For example, the mean of the differences between reported and true arrest values is -0.291, the median is 0, and the modes are -1 and 0. All three measures give similar estimates of central tendency in this case.

8.11
Measures of Dispersion

Two distributions can have the same values for measures of central tendency and yet be very dissimilar in other respects. For example, if the true number of arrests for five cases in two methadone clinics is

CLINIC A: 0, 1, 10, 14, 20
CLINIC B: 8, 8, 9, 10, 10

the mean number of arrests (9) is the same in both. However, even a cursory examination of the data indicates that the two clinics are different. In the second clinic, all cases have fairly comparable arrest records, while in the first the records are quite disparate. A quick and useful index of dissimilarity, or dispersion, is the *range*. It is the difference between the *maximum* and *minimum* observed values. For clinic B the range is 2, while for clinic A it is 20. Since the range is computed only from the minimum and maximum values, it is sensitive to extremes.

Although the range is a useful index of dispersion, especially for ordinal data, it does not take into account the distribution of observations between the maximum and minimum. A commonly used measure of variation that is based on all observations is the *variance*. For a sample, the variance is computed by summing the squared differences from the mean for all observations and then dividing by one less than the number of observations. In mathematical notation this is

$$S^2 = \sum_{i=1}^{N} \frac{(X_i - \bar{X})^2}{N - 1}$$

Equation 8.11

If all observations are identical—that is, if there is no variation—the variance is 0. The more spread out they are, the greater the variance. For the methadone clinic example above, the sample variance for Clinic A is 73, while for Clinic B it is 1.

The square root of the variance is termed the *standard deviation*. While the variance is in units squared, the standard deviation is expressed in the same units of measurement as the observations. This is an appealing property since it is much clearer to think of variability in terms of the number of arrests instead of the number of arrests squared.

8.12
The Normal Distribution

For many variables, most observations are concentrated near the middle of the distribution. As distance from the central concentration increases, the frequency of observation decreases. Such distributions are often described as "bell-shaped." An example is the *normal* distribution (see Figure 8.12a). A broad range of observed phenomena in nature and in society are approximately normally distributed. For example, the distributions of variables such as height, weight, and blood pressure are approximately normal. The normal distribution is by far the most important theoretical distribution in statistics and serves as a reference point for describing the form of many distributions of sample data.

Figure 8.12a   A normal curve

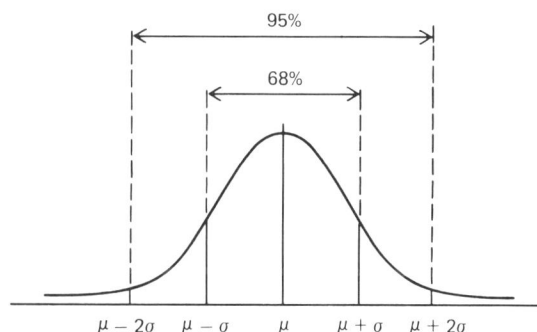

The normal distribution is symmetric: when it is folded in the center, the two sides are identical. The three measures of central tendency—the mean, median, and mode—coincide exactly (see Section 8.10). As shown in Figure 8.12a, 95% of all observations in the normal distribution fall within two standard deviations (σ) of the mean (μ), and 68% within one standard deviation. The exact theoretical proportion of cases falling into various regions of the normal curve can be found in tables given in most introductory statistics textbooks.

In SPSS/PC+, you can superimpose a normal distribution on a histogram. For example, in Figure 8.12b, which contains a histogram of differences in arrest records, the colons and periods indicate what the distribution of cases would be if the variable had a normal distribution with the same mean and variance.

Figure 8.12b Histogram of errors with the normal curve superimposed

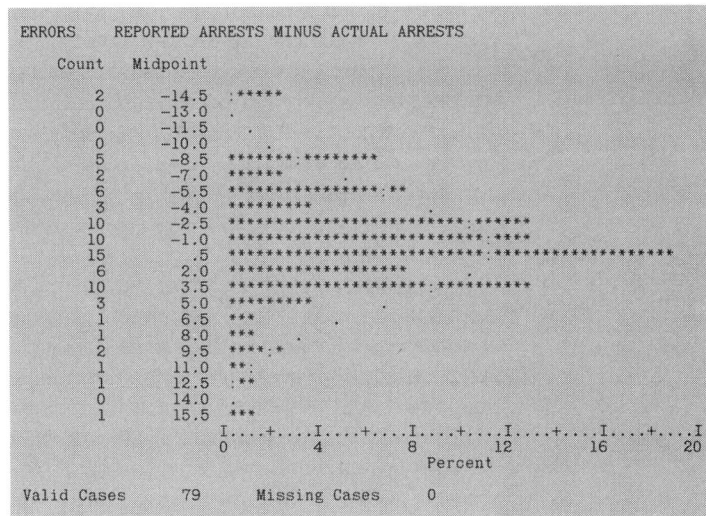

```
ERRORS    REPORTED ARRESTS MINUS ACTUAL ARRESTS

    Count   Midpoint
        2    -14.5  :*****
        0    -13.0  .
        0    -11.5    .
        0    -10.0
        5     -8.5  *******:********
        2     -7.0  ******    .
        6     -5.5  *****************:**
        3     -4.0  *********          .
       10     -2.5  ***************************:******
       10     -1.0  ******************************:****
       15      .5   *******************************:********************
        6     2.0   ******************:***
       10     3.5   ***********************:**********
        3     5.0   *********          .
        1     6.5   ***         .
        1     8.0   ***    .
        2     9.5   ****:*
        1    11.0   **:
        1    12.5   :**
        0    14.0   .
        1    15.5   ***
                    I....+....I....+....I....+....I....+....I....+....I
                    0        4        8        12       16       20
                                        Percent

Valid Cases    79    Missing Cases    0
```

**8.13
Measures of Shape**

A distribution that is not symmetric but has more cases, or more of a "tail," toward one end of the distribution than the other is called *skewed*. If the tail is toward larger values, the distribution is positively skewed or skewed to the right. If the tail is toward smaller values, the distribution is negatively skewed or skewed to the left.

Another characteristic of the form of a distribution is called *kurtosis*, the extent to which, for a given standard deviation, observations cluster around a central point. If cases within a distribution cluster more than those in the normal distribution (that is, the distribution is more peaked), the distribution is called *leptokurtic*. A leptokurtic distribution also tends to have more observations straggling into the extreme tails than does a normal distribution. If cases cluster less than in the normal distribution (that is, it is flatter), the distribution is termed *platykurtic*.

Although examination of a histogram provides some indication of possible skewness and kurtosis, it is often desirable to compute formal indexes that measure these properties. Values for skewness and kurtosis are 0 if the observed distribution is exactly normal. Positive values for skewness indicate a positive skew, while positive values for kurtosis indicate a distribution that is more peaked than normal. For samples from a normal distribution, measures of skewness and kurtosis typically will not be exactly 0 but will fluctuate about 0 because of sampling variation.

**8.14
Standard Scores**

It is often desirable to describe the relative position of an observation within a distribution. Knowing that a person achieved a score of 80 in a competitive examination conveys little information about performance. Judgment of performance would depend on whether 80 is the lowest, the median, or the highest score.

One way of describing the location of a case in a distribution is to calculate its *standard score*. This score, sometimes called the Z score, indicates how many standard deviations above or below the mean an observation falls. It is calculated by finding the difference between the value of a particular observation X_i and the mean of the distribution, and then dividing this difference by the standard deviation:

$$Z_i = \frac{X_i - \overline{X}}{S}$$

Equation 8.14

The mean of Z scores is 0, and the standard deviation is 1.

For example, a participant with 5 actual arrests would have a Z score of $(5-9.25)/6.25$, or -0.68. Since the score is negative, the case had fewer arrests than the average for the individuals studied.

Standardization permits comparison of scores from different distributions. For example, an individual with Z scores of -0.68 for actual arrests and 1.01 for the difference between reported and actual arrests had fewer arrests than the average but exaggerated more than the average.

When the distribution of a variable is approximately normal and the mean and variance are known or are estimated from large samples, the Z score of an observation provides more specific information about its location. For example, if actual arrests and response error were normally distributed, 75% of cases would have more arrests than the example individual but only 16% would have exaggerated as much (75% of a standard normal curve lies above a Z score of -0.68, and 16% lies above a score of 1.01).

8.15
Who Lies?

The distribution of the difference between reported and actual arrests indicates that response error exists. Although observing a mean close to 0 is comforting, misrepresentation is obvious. What then are the characteristics that influence willingness to be truthful?

Wyner identifies three factors that are related to inaccuracies: the number of arrests before 1960, the number of multiple-charge arrests, and the perceived desirability of being arrested. The first factor is related to a frequently encountered difficulty—the more distant an event in time, the less likely it is to be correctly recalled. The second factor, underreporting of multiple-charge arrests, is probably caused by the general social undesirability of serious arrests. Finally, persons who view arrest records as laudatory are likely to inflate their accomplishments.

8.16
STATISTICS AVAILABLE WITH PROCEDURE FREQUENCIES

In addition to frequency tables, bar charts, and histograms, procedure FREQUENCIES calculates univariate statistics for all variables named on the VARIABLES subcommand. To request statistics, use the STATISTICS subcommand followed by an equals sign and the keywords that correspond to the statistics you want. For example, the command

```
FREQUENCIES  VARIABLES=ACTUAL SELF ERRORS/FORMAT=NOTABLE
  /STATISTICS=ALL.
```

produces the output in Figure 8.9. See Chapter 7 for a complete list of the statistics available with FREQUENCIES.

8.17
Percentiles

You can use FREQUENCIES to request percentiles for all variables specified on the VARIABLES subcommand. Include the PERCENTILES subcommand followed by an equals sign and a list of percentiles between 0 and 100. For example, the command

```
FREQUENCIES  VARIABLES=ACTUAL SELF ERRORS/FORMAT=NOTABLE
  /PERCENTILES=25 50 75.
```

produces Figure 8.2.

In SPSS/PC+, percentiles are calculated by sorting the values from the smallest to the largest and finding the values below and above which the requisite number of cases fall. Therefore, it is possible for several percentiles to have the same value. For example, if the values are

0 1 1 1 1

all percentiles greater than the 20th are 1.

If you have collapsed your data into discrete codes, you can use the GROUPED subcommand to inform SPSS/PC+ that this is so. It will then be able to make more accurate estimates of percentiles. Before using this subcommand, recode the collapsed values so that each code equals the midpoint of the range it represents. For example, if AGE is collapsed so that the value 2 represents ages in the twenties, recode 2 to 25, the midpoint of the range.

The GROUPED subcommand affects the statistics calculated by the PER-CENTILES and NTILES subcommands, as well as the MEDIAN statistic available on the STATISTICS subcommand. Examples of its use are given in the Command Reference.

8.18
RUNNING PROCEDURE DESCRIPTIVES

Procedure DESCRIPTIVES calculates all of the statistics provided by procedure FREQUENCIES, except the median and the mode, and provides a compact table of statistics. Because it does not sort values into a frequency table and displays summaries of several variables on a page, it is an efficient procedure for computing descriptive statistics.

Procedure DESCRIPTIVES requires a list of variables for which statistics are to be computed. The optional STATISTICS subcommand indicates the statistics to be computed, and the OPTIONS subcommand specifies treatment of missing values and formatting options.

Descriptive statistics can be computed only for numeric variables. If a string variable is specified in the variable list, a warning is issued and no statistics are displayed for that variable.

8.19
Specifying the Variables

The VARIABLES subcommand names the variables for which statistics are to be calculated. For example, to calculate the default statistics (mean, standard deviation, minimum, and maximum) for variables TRUE, SELF, and ERRORS, specify

```
DESCRIPTIVES VARIABLES=TRUE SELF ERRORS.
```

The actual keyword VARIABLES can be omitted, as in the command

```
DESCRIPTIVES TRUE SELF ERRORS.
```

You can also use the TO keyword to refer to a set of consecutive variables on the active file, and keyword ALL to refer to all user-defined variables.

8.20
Optional Statistics

By default the DESCRIPTIVES procedure calculates the mean, standard deviation, minimum, and maximum. Additional statistics can be requested with the STATISTICS subcommand:

Statistic 1 *Mean.*
Statistic 2 *Standard error of mean.*
Statistic 5 *Standard deviation.*
Statistic 6 *Variance.*
Statistic 7 *Kurtosis.*
Statistic 8 *Skewness.*

Statistic 9   *Range.*

Statistic 10 *Minimum.*

Statistic 11 *Maximum.*

Statistic 12 *Sum.*

Statistic 13 *Mean, standard deviation, minimum, and maximum.* This is the same as the default.

ALL   *All available statistics.*

If the STATISTICS subcommand is used, only the statistics requested are displayed. Thus, if you are using the STATISTICS subcommand, you must specify Statistic 13 to get the default statistics.

8.21
Missing Values

By default, DESCRIPTIVES includes only cases with valid values for a variable in the calculation of statistics for that variable. Use one of the following options on the OPTIONS subcommand for alternative treatments of missing values.

Option 1 *Include user-missing values.* Cases that have user-missing values are included in the calculation of statistics for all variables named on the command.

Option 5 *Exclude missing values listwise.* A case with missing values for any of the variables is excluded from computations for all of the variables.

8.22
Formatting Options

By default, DESCRIPTIVES displays the statistics and a 40-character variable label for each variable on one line. If the statistics requested do not fit within the available width, DESCRIPTIVES will first truncate the variable label and then use serial format. (You can use the SET command to change the width of the display; see SET in the Command Reference). Serial format provides larger field widths and permits more decimal places for very large or very small numbers than does the default format.

Optionally, you can request any of the following on the OPTIONS subcommand:

Option 2 *Suppress variable labels.*

Option 6 *Serial format.* The requested statistics are displayed below each variable name.

Option 7 *Narrow format.* Use narrow format, regardless of the width defined on SET.

Option 8 *Suppress variable names.* The variable name will be displayed only if there is no variable label.

8.23
Example

Figure 8.23 shows the default statistics produced by the DESCRIPTIVES command in the following SPSS/PC+ command file:

```
DATA LIST   FIXED / ACTUAL 1-2 SELF 3-4 ERRORS 5-7.
VARIABLE LABELS   ACTUAL 'ACTUAL NUMBER OF ARRESTS'
                  /SELF 'SELF-REPORTED ARRESTS'
                  /ERRORS 'REPORTED ARRESTS MINUS ACTUAL ARRESTS'.
BEGIN DATA.
data records
END DATA.
DESCRIPTIVES  ACTUAL SELF ERRORS.
FINISH.
```

• The DATA LIST command reads one record per case with three variables. The variable named ACTUAL is recorded in columns 1 and 2, the variable named SELF is in columns 3 and 4, and the variable named ERRORS is in columns 5 through 7.

• The VARIABLE LABELS command assigns labels to all three variables.

• The DESCRIPTIVES command requests descriptive statistics for the three variables.

Figure 8.23 Default statistics available with DESCRIPTIVES

```
Number of Valid Observations (Listwise) =        79.00

Variable       Mean    Std Dev   Minimum   Maximum     N  Label

ACTUAL         9.25      6.25      1.00     29.00      79  ACTUAL NUMBER OF ARRESTS
SELF           8.96      6.46      0.0      25.00      79  SELF-REPORTED ARRESTS
ERRORS         -.29      5.22    -14.00     15.00      79  REPORTED ARRESTS MINUS ACTUAL ARRESTS
```

Contents

9 Looking First: Procedure EXAMINE

The first step of data analysis should always be a detailed examination of the data. It doesn't matter whether the problem you're solving is simple or complex, whether you're planning to do a t-test or a multivariate repeated measures analysis of variance. First you should take a careful look at the data. In this chapter, we'll consider some methods for exploring data using the SPSS/PC+ EXAMINE procedure.

9.1 REASONS FOR EXAMINING DATA

There are several important reasons for examining your data carefully before you begin your analysis. Let's start with the simplest.

9.2 Identifying Mistakes

Data must make a hazardous journey before they find final rest in a computer file. First a measurement is made or a response elicited, sometimes with a faulty instrument or by a sleepy experimenter. The result is then recorded, often barely legibly, in a lab notebook, medical chart, or personnel record. Often this information is not actually coded and entered onto a data form until much later. From this form the numbers must yet find their way into their designated slot in the computer file. Then they must be properly introduced to a computer program. Their correct location and missing values must be specified.

Errors can be introduced at any step. Some errors are easy to spot. For example, forgetting to declare a value as missing, using an invalid code, or entering the value 701 for age will be apparent from a frequency table. Other errors, like entering an age of 54 instead of 45, may be difficult, if not impossible, to spot. Unless your first step is to carefully check your data for mistakes, errors may contaminate all of your analyses.

9.3 Exploring the Data

After the commotion of data acquisition, entry, and checking, it's time to actually look at the data—not to search frantically for statistical significance, but to examine the data carefully using simple exploratory techniques. Why bother, you might ask? Why not just begin your analysis?

Data analysis has often been compared to detective work. Before the actual trial of a hypothesis there is much evidence to be gathered and sifted. Based on the clues, the hypothesis itself may be altered, or the methods for testing it may have to be changed. For example, if a display of the distribution of data values reveals a "gap," that is, there are no values in a particular range, we must ask why. If there are some values far removed from the others, we must also ask why. If the pattern of numbers is strange, for example if all values are even, we must determine why. If we see unexpected variability in the data, we must look for possible explanations. Perhaps there are additional variables that might explain some of the variability.

9.4
Preparing for Hypothesis Testing

Looking at the distribution of the values is also important for evaluating the appropriateness of the statistical techniques we are planning to use for hypothesis testing or model building. Perhaps the data must be transformed so that the distribution is approximately normal, or so that the variances in the groups are similar. Or perhaps a nonparametric technique is needed.

9.5
WAYS OF DISPLAYING DATA

Now that we've established why it's important to look at data, we'll consider some of the techniques that are available for exploring data. To illustrate the methods, we'll use the Western Electric data, which are described in Chapter 7 of the *SPSS/PC+ V2.0 Base Manual*, and the bank salary data, which are described in Chapter 10 of that manual.

9.6
The Histogram

The histogram is a commonly used display. The range of observed values is subdivided into equal intervals and then the number of cases in each interval is obtained. Each row of symbols in a histogram represents the number of cases with values within the interval.

Figure 9.6 is a histogram of diastolic blood pressure for a sample of 239 men from the Western Electric study. The first column, labeled **Frequency**, is the number of cases with values in the intervals. The second column, **bin center**, is the midpoint of each of the bins. For example, the midpoint of the first bin is 65. The text underneath the histogram shows that the length of each bin is 10. Thus, the first interval contains cases with diastolic blood pressures in the 60's. Cases with diastolic blood pressures in the 70's go into the next interval. The last bin center is labeled **125** and includes cases with values in the 120's.

Figure 9.6 Histogram of diastolic blood pressure

```
GET FILE='ELECTRIC.SYS'.
EXAMINE VARIABLES=DBP58 /PLOT=HISTOGRAM.
```

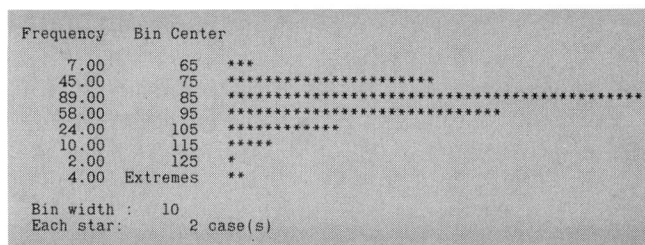

```
 Frequency    Bin Center

      7.00        65   ***
     45.00        75   **********************
     89.00        85   ********************************************
     58.00        95   *****************************
     24.00       105   ************
     10.00       115   *****
      2.00       125   *
      4.00    Extremes  **

 Bin width :    10
 Each star:      2 case(s)
```

The last row of this histogram is for cases whose values are much larger than the rest. These are labeled **extremes.** The reason the histogram is not extended to accommodate these cases is to avoid having too many intervals, or intervals that are very wide. For example, if there is a person with a diastolic blood pressure of 200, the histogram would have a lot of empty bins between the bin centers of 125 and 205. Of course, we could have fewer bins and make them wider, but this would obscure potentially interesting information. That's why the histogram contains special bins for very large and very small values.

9.7
The Stem-and-Leaf Plot

A display closely related to the histogram is the stem-and-leaf plot. The stem-and-leaf plot provides more information about the actual values than does a histogram. Consider Figure 9.7a, which is a stem-and-leaf plot of the diastolic blood pressures. As in a histogram, the length of each row corresponds to the number of cases that fall into a particular interval. However, instead of representing all cases with the same symbol—say, a star—the stem-and-leaf plot represents each case with a symbol that corresponds to the actual observed value. This is done by dividing observed values into two components—the leading digit or digits, called the stem, and a trailing digit, called the leaf. For example, the value 75 has a stem of 7 and a leaf of 5. In the plot, each row represents a stem and each case is represented by its leaf value.

Figure 9.7a Stem-and-leaf plot of diastolic blood pressure

```
SET LENGTH=59.
EXAMINE VARIABLES=DBP58 /PLOT=STEMLEAF.
```

```
Frequency    Stem &  Leaf
      .00      6   *
     7.00      6   .  5558889
    13.00      7   *  0000111223344
    32.00      7   .  55555555566777777777777788888889999
    44.00      8   *  00000000000000000000001111122222333333334444
    45.00      8   .  555555555566666666777777777777778888899999999999
    31.00      9   *  0000000001111111112222222222333334
    27.00      9   .  55666666777777788888888888899999
    13.00     10   *  0000122233333
    11.00     10   .  55555577899
     5.00     11   *  00003
     5.00     11   .  55789
     2.00     12   *  01
     4.00 Extremes      (125), (133), (160)

 Stem width:    10
 Each leaf:      1 case(s)
```

In this example, each stem is subdivided into two rows. The first row of each pair has cases with leaves of 0 through 4, while the second row has cases with leaves of 5 through 9. Consider the two rows that correspond to the stem of 11. From the first of these rows, we can see that there are four cases with diastolic blood pressures of 110, and one case with a pressure of 113. Similarly, there are two cases with values of 115, and one each with values of 117, 118, and 119. Notice also that Figure 9.7a uses a SET LENGTH command before EXAMINE. It is sometimes useful to increase the page length to obtain a more detailed plot than that obtained by default.

The last row of the stem-and-leaf plot is for cases with values removed from the rest. Again, the actual values are given. From the frequency column we see that there are four extreme cases. Their values are 125, 133, and 160. Only distinct values are listed.

To identify cases with extreme values, you can display a table containing identifying information for cases with the largest and smallest values. Figure 9.7b shows the five cases with the largest and smallest values for diastolic blood pressure. When the data file contains names or other information that can be used to identify cases, this can be listed. Otherwise, the sequence of the case in the data file is reported.

Figure 9.7b Extreme cases

```
EXAMINE VARIABLES=DBP58 /STATISTICS=EXTREME.
```

```
                              Extreme Values
                          -------  -------

     5    Highest    Case #          5    Lowest    Case #
         160        CASE120             65       CASE155
         133        CASE56              65       CASE156
         125        CASE162             65       CASE73
         125        CASE42              68       CASE174
         121        CASE26              68       CASE34
```

9.8
Other Stems

In Figure 9.7a each stem was subdivided into two parts—one for leaves of 0 thru 4, the other for leaves of 5 thru 9. When there are few stems, it is sometimes useful to subdivide each stem even further. Consider Figure 9.8, which is a stem-and-leaf plot of cholesterol levels for the men in the Western Electric study. In this figure stems are divided into five parts—each is used to represent two leaf values. The first, designated by an asterisk, is for leaves of 0 and 1; the next, designated by "t," is for leaves of 2's and 3's; the "f" is for leaves of 4's and 5's; "s" for 6's and 7's; and "." for 8's and 9's.

This stem-and-leaf plot differs from the previous in yet another way. Since cholesterol values have a wide range, in this example from 106 to 515, using the first two digits for the stem would result in an unnecessarily detailed plot. To avoid this, we will use only the hundreds digit as the stem instead of the first two digits. The line after the stem-and-leaf plot tells us that the stems are in hundreds. The leaf is then the tens digit. The last digit is ignored. Thus, from this stem-and-leaf plot it is not possible to determine the exact cholesterol level for a case. Instead, each case is classified only by its first two digits.

Figure 9.8   Stem-and-leaf plot of cholesterol levels

```
SET LENGTH=59.
EXAMINE VARIABLES=CHOL158 /PLOT=STEMLEAF.
```

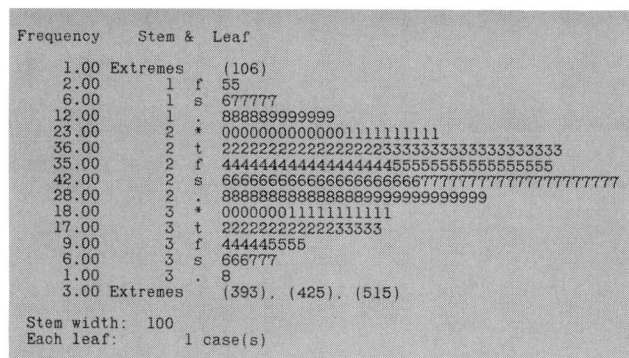

```
Frequency    Stem &  Leaf

    1.00  Extremes    (106)
    2.00      1   f   55
    6.00      1   s   677777
   12.00      1   .   888889999999
   23.00      2   *   00000000000001111111111
   36.00      2   t   222222222222222223333333333333333333
   35.00      2   f   44444444444444444455555555555555555
   42.00      2   s   666666666666666666666777777777777777777777
   28.00      2   .   8888888888888889999999999999
   18.00      3   *   000000011111111111
   17.00      3   t   22222222222233333
    9.00      3   f   444445555
    6.00      3   s   666777
    1.00      3   .   8
    3.00  Extremes    (393), (425), (515)

Stem width:   100
Each leaf:         1 case(s)
```

9.9
The Boxplot

Both the histogram and the stem-and-leaf plot provide useful information about the distribution of observed values. We can see how tightly cases cluster together. We can see if there is a single peak or several peaks. We can determine if there are extreme values.

A display that further summarizes information about the distribution of the values is the boxplot. Instead of plotting the actual values, a boxplot displays summary statistics for the distribution. It plots the median, the 25th percentile, the 75th percentile, and values that are far removed from the rest.

Figure 9.9a shows an annotated sketch of a boxplot. The lower boundary of the box is the 25th percentile, and the upper boundary is the 75th percentile. (These percentiles are sometimes called Tukey's hinges and are calculated a little differently from ordinary percentiles.) The asterisk in the box represents the median. Fifty percent of the cases have values within the box. The length of the box corresponds to the interquartile range, which is the difference between the 75th and 25th percentiles.

Figure 9.9a   Annotated sketch of a boxplot

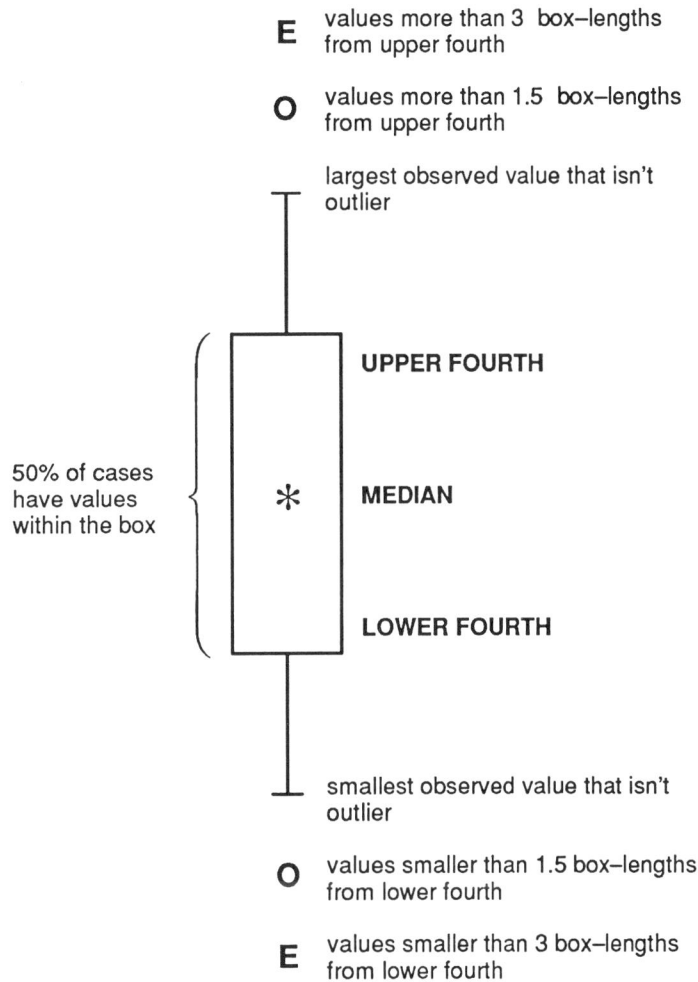

E — values more than 3 box–lengths from upper fourth

O — values more than 1.5 box–lengths from upper fourth

largest observed value that isn't outlier

UPPER FOURTH

50% of cases have values within the box

* MEDIAN

LOWER FOURTH

smallest observed value that isn't outlier

O — values smaller than 1.5 box–lengths from lower fourth

E — values smaller than 3 box–lengths from lower fourth

The boxplot includes two categories of cases with outlying values. Cases with values more than 3 box-lengths from the upper or lower edge of the box are called extreme values. On the boxplot these are designated with the letter E. Cases with values between 1.5 and 3 box-lengths from the edge of the box are called outliers and are designated with the letter O. The largest and smallest observed values that aren't outliers are also shown. Lines are drawn from the ends of the box to these values. (These lines are sometimes called whiskers and the plot is called a box-and-whiskers plot.)

What can you tell about your data from a boxplot? From the median you can determine the central tendency, or location. From the length of the box you can see the spread, or variability, of your observations. If the median is not in the center of the box you know that the observed values are skewed. If the median is closer to the bottom of the box than the top, the data are positively skewed. There is a tail with large values. If the median is closer to the top of the box than the bottom, the opposite is true. The distribution is negatively skewed. The length of the tail is shown by the whiskers and the outlying and extreme points.

Boxplots are particularly useful for comparing the distribution of values in several groups. For example, suppose you want to compare the distribution of beginning salaries for people employed in several different positions at a bank.

Figure 9.9b contains boxplots of the bank salary data. From this plot you can see that the first two job categories have similar distributions for salary, although the first has several extreme values. The third job category has little variability. All 27 people in this category earn similar amounts of money. The last two groups have much higher median salaries than the other groups, and larger spread as well.

Figure 9.9b   Boxplots for bank salary data

```
GET FILE 'BANK.SYS'.
SELECT IF (JOBCAT LE 5).
EXAMINE VARIABLES=SALBEG BY JOBCAT /PLOT=BOXPLOT.
```

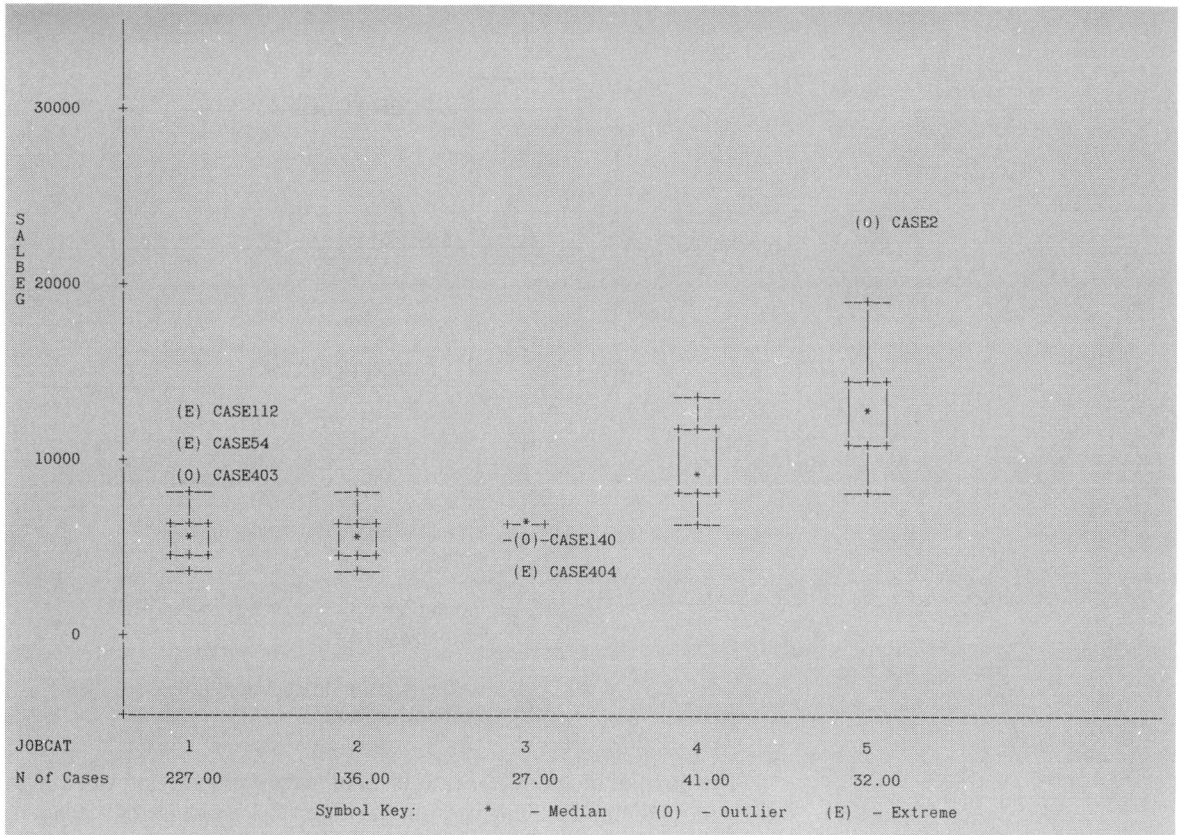

9.10
EVALUATING
ASSUMPTIONS

Many statistical procedures, such as analysis of variance, require that all groups come from normal populations with the same variance. Therefore, before using them, we often wish to test the hypothesis that all the group variances are equal or that the samples are from normal populations. If it appears that the assumptions are violated, we may want to determine appropriate transformations.

9.11
The Levene Test

There is a wide variety of tests available for evaluating the assumption that all groups come from populations with equal variances. Many of these tests, however, are heavily dependent on the data being samples from normal populations. Analysis of variance procedures, on the other hand, is reasonably robust to departures from normality. The Levene test is a homogeneity of variance test that is less dependent on the assumption of normality than most tests and thus is particularly useful with analysis of variance. It is obtained by computing for each case the absolute difference from its cell mean and then performing a one-way analysis of variance on these differences.

From Figure 9.11 you can see that, for the salary data, the null hypothesis that all group variances are equal is rejected. We should consider transforming the data if we plan to use a statistical procedure which requires equality of variance. Next we'll consider how to select a transformation.

Figure 9.11   The Levene test

```
Test of homogeneity of variance                     df1      df2      Significance
   Levene Statistic                     28.9200        4      458            .0000
```

9.12
Spread-and-Level Plots

Often there is a relationship between the average value, or level, of a variable, and the variability or spread associated with it. For example, we can see in Figure 9.9b that as salaries increase, so does the variability.

One way of studying the relationship between spread and level is to plot the values of spread and level for each group. If there is no relationship, the points should cluster around a horizontal line. If this is not the case, we can use the observed relationship between the two variables to choose an appropriate transformation.

9.13
Determining the Transformation

A power transformation is frequently used to stabilize variances. All a power transformation does is raise each data value to a specified power. For example, a power transformation of two squares all of the data values. A transformation of one-half indicates that the square root of all the values be taken. If the power is 0, the log of the numbers is used.

To determine an appropriate power for transforming the data we can plot, for each group, the log of the median against the log of the interquartile range. Figure 9.13 shows such a plot for the salary data shown in Figure 9.9b. You see that there is a fairly strong linear relationship between spread and level. From the slope of the line, we can estimate the power value that will eliminate or lessen this relationship. The power is obtained by subtracting the slope from one. That is,

Power $= 1 -$ slope

Although this formula can result in all sorts of powers, for simplicity and interpretability we usually choose the closest powers that are multiples of one-half. Table 9.13 shows the most commonly used transformations.

Figure 9.13 Spread-and-level plot of bank data

```
EXAMINE VARIABLES=SALBEG BY JOBCAT /PLOT SPREADLEVEL.
```

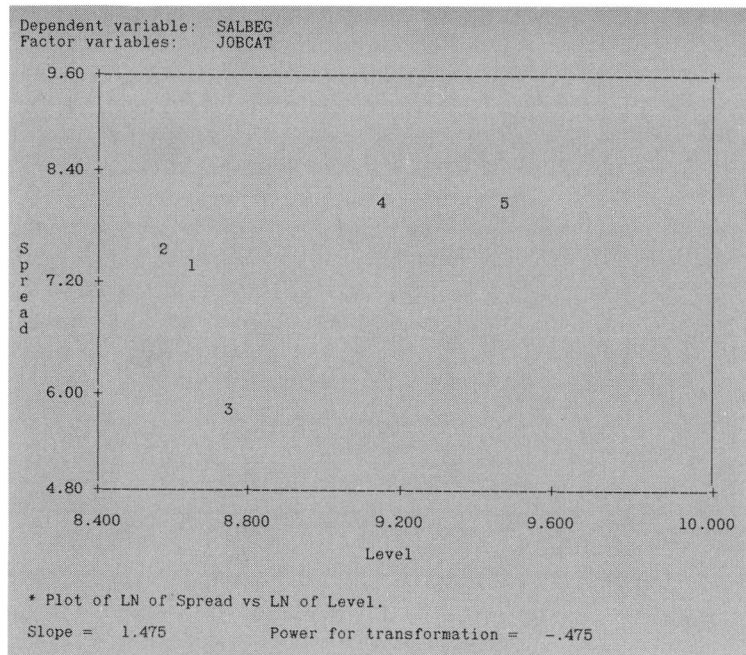

Dependent variable: SALBEG
Factor variables: JOBCAT

* Plot of LN of Spread vs LN of Level.
Slope = 1.475   Power for transformation = -.475

Table 9.13 Commonly used transformations

Power	Transformation
3	Cube
2	Square
1	No change
1/2	Square root
0	Logarithm
-1/2	Reciprocal of the square root
-1	Reciprocal

As shown in Figure 9.13, the slope of the least-squares line for the bank data is 1.475, so the power for the transformation is −.475. Rounding to the nearest multiple of a half, we will use the reciprocal of the square root.

After applying the power transformation, it is wise to obtain a spread-and-level plot for the transformed data. From this plot you can judge the success of the transformation.

9.14
Tests of Normality

Since the normal distribution is very important to statistical inference, we often want to examine the assumption that our data come from a normal distribution. One way to do this is with a normal probability plot. In a normal probability plot, each observed value is paired with its expected value from the normal distribution. (The expected value from the normal distribution is based on the number of cases in the sample and the rank order of the case in the sample.) If the sample is from a normal distribution, we expect that the points will fall, more or less, on a straight line.

Figure 9.14a is a normal probability plot of a sample of 200 points from a normal distribution. Note how the points cluster about a straight line. You can also plot the actual deviations of the points from a straight line. This is called a detrended normal plot and is shown in Figure 9.14b. If the sample is from a normal population, the points should cluster around a horizontal line through 0 and there should be no pattern. A striking pattern suggests departure from normality.

Figure 9.14a   Normal probability plot

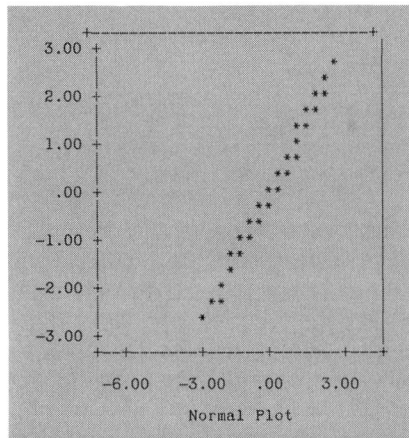

Figure 9.14b   Detrended normal plot

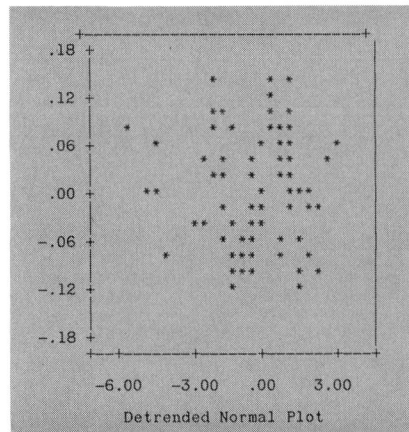

Figure 9.14c shows a normal probability plot and a detrended plot for data from a uniform distribution. The points do not cluster around a straight line, and the deviations from a straight line are not randomly distributed about 0.

Figure 9.14c   Normal plots for a uniform distribution

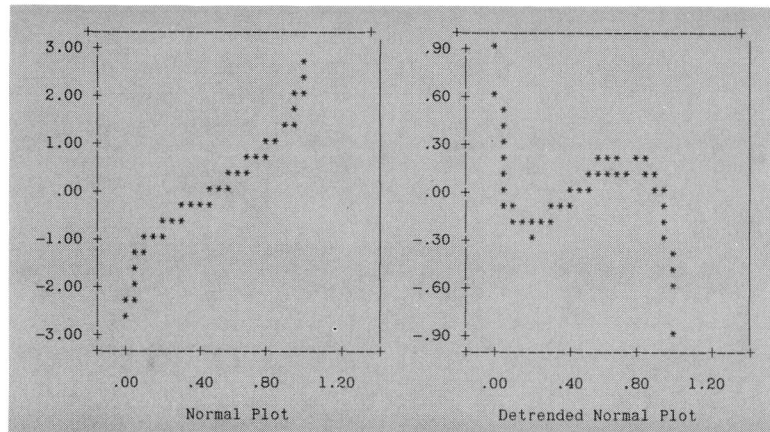

Although normal probability plots provide a visual basis for checking normality, it is often desirable to compute a statistical test of the hypothesis that the data are from a normal distribution. Two commonly used tests are the Shapiro-Wilks and the Lilliefors. The Lilliefors test is based on a modification of the Kolmogorov-Smirnov test for the situation when means and variances are not known but must be estimated from the data. The Shapiro-Wilks test has been found to have good power in many situations when compared to other tests of normality (Conover, 1980).

Figure 9.14d contains normal probability plots and tests of normality for the diastolic blood pressure data. From the small observed significance levels, you see that the hypothesis of normality can be rejected. However, it is important to remember that whenever the sample size is large almost any goodness-of-fit test will result in rejection of the null hypothesis. It is almost impossible to find data that are *exactly* normally distributed. For most statistical tests, it is sufficient that the data are approximately normally distributed. Thus, for large data sets you should look not only at the observed significance level but also at the magnitude of the departure from normality.

Figure 9.14d   Normal plots for diastolic blood pressure

```
EXAMINE VARIABLES=DBP58 /PLOT=NPPLOT.
```

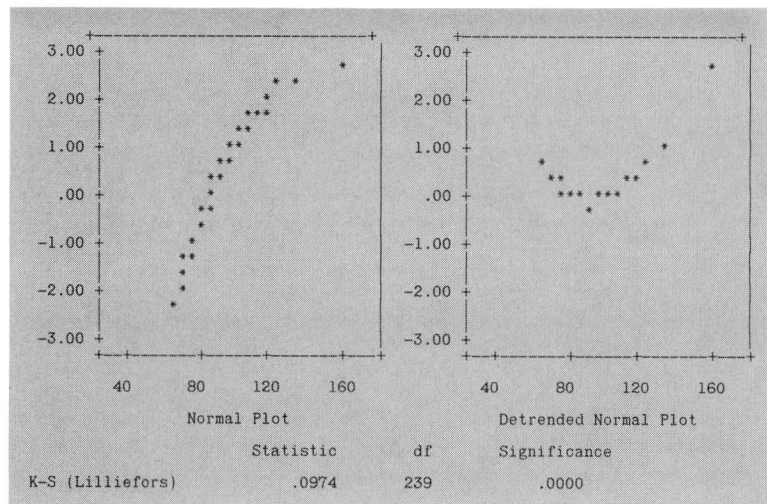

	Statistic	df	Significance
K-S (Lilliefors)	.0974	239	.0000

9.15
ESTIMATING
LOCATION WITH
ROBUST ESTIMATORS

We often use the arithmetic mean to estimate central tendency, or location. We know, however, that the mean is heavily influenced by outliers. One very large or very small value can change the mean dramatically. The median, on the other hand, is insensitive to outliers. Addition or removal of extreme values has little effect on the median. The median is called a *resistant* measure, since its value depends on the "main body" of the data and not on outliers. The advantage of resistant measures are easy to see. Their values are not unduly influenced by a few observations. They don't change much if small amounts of data are added or removed.

Although the median is an intuitive, simple measure of location, there are better estimators of location if we are willing to make some assumptions about the population from which our data originate. Estimators that depend on simple, fairly nonrestrictive assumptions about the underlying distribution and are not sensitive to these assumptions are called *robust* estimators. We will now consider some robust estimators of central tendency that depend only on the assumption that the data are from a symmetric population.

9.16
The Trimmed Mean

A simple robust estimator of location can be obtained by "trimming" the data to exclude values that are far removed from the others. For example, a 20% trimmed mean disregards the smallest 20% and the largest 20% of all observations. The estimate is based only on the 60% of data values that are in the middle. What's the advantage of the trimmed mean? Like the median, it results in an estimate that is not influenced by extreme values. However, unlike the median it is not based solely on a single value, or two values, that are in the middle. It is based on a much larger number of "middle" values. (The median can be considered a 50% trimmed mean, since half of the values above and below the median are ignored!) In general a trimmed mean makes better use of the data than does the median.

9.17
M-Estimators

When calculating a trimmed mean, we subdivide our cases into two groups—those that are included and those that are excluded from the computation of the mean. We can consider the trimmed mean as a weighted mean in which cases have weights of 0 or 1, depending on whether they are included or excluded from the computations. (A weighted mean is calculated by assigning to each case a weight and then using the formula $\overline{X} = \Sigma w_i x_i / \Sigma w_i$.) In the trimmed mean we treat observations that are far from most of the others pretty harshly. We exclude them altogether. A more lenient alternative is to include them but give them smaller weights than cases that are closer to the center. An estimator that does this is the M-estimator. (The M stands for generalized *m*aximum-likelihood estimator.)

Since there are many different schemes that can be used to assign weights to cases, there are many different M-estimators. (The usual mean can be viewed as an M-estimator with all cases having a weight of 1.) All commonly used M-estimators assign weights so that they decrease as distance from the center of the distribution increases. Figures 9.17a through 9.17d show the weights used by four common M-estimators.

Common M-estimators

Figure 9.17a Huber's (c=1.339)

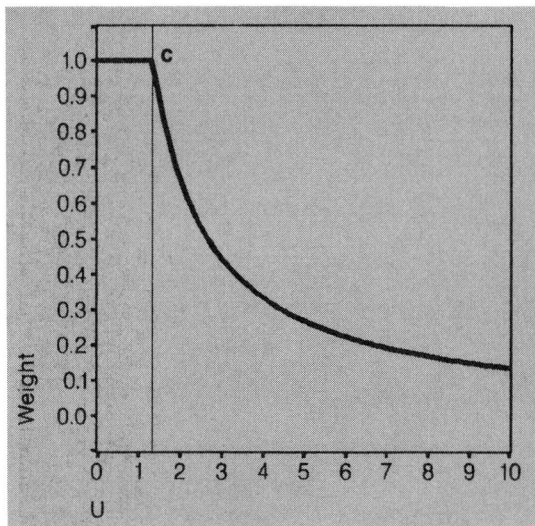

Figure 9.17b Tukey's biweight (c=4.685)

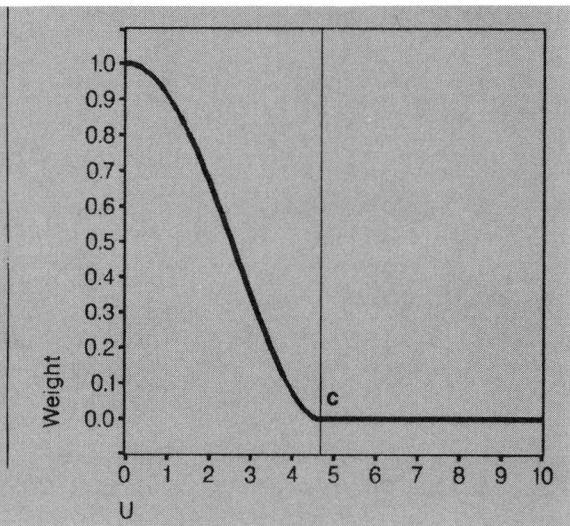

Figure 9.17c Hampel's (a=1.7, b=3.4, c=8.5)

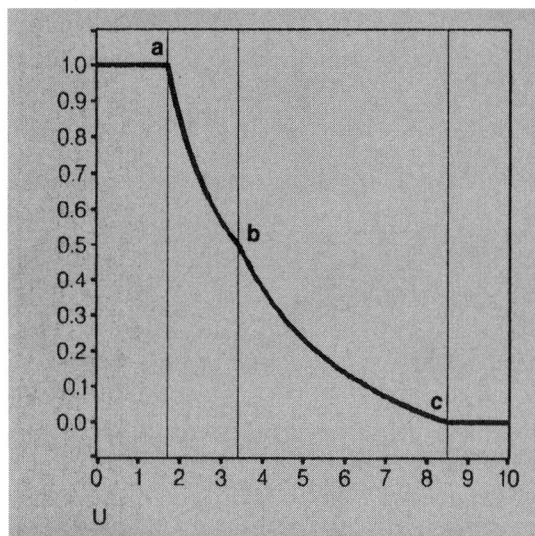

Figure 9.17d Andrew's (c=1.339π)

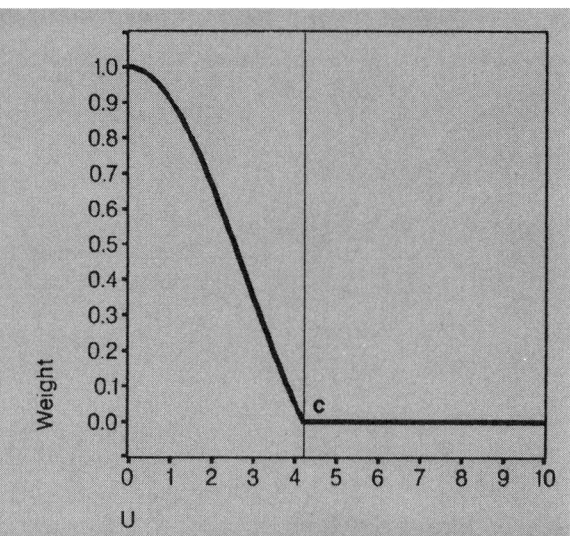

Consider Figure 9.17a, which is for Huber's M-estimators. The value on the horizontal axis is a standardized distance from the estimate of location. It is computed using the following formula:

$$u_i = |\text{value for } i\text{th case} - \text{estimate of location}|/\text{estimate of spread}$$

The estimate of spread used is the median of the absolute deviations from the sample median, commonly known as MAD. It is calculated by first finding the median for the sample and then for each case computing the absolute value of the deviation from the median. The MAD is then the median of these absolute values.

Since the weights for cases depend on the value of the estimate of central location, M-estimators must be computed iteratively.

From Figure 9.17a, you can see that cases with small values for the absolute value of the standardized distance from the estimate have large weights. Up to a certain critical point, cases have weights of 1. After the critical point, the weights decrease as the distance increases. (The SPSS/PC+ default values for these critical points are given in parentheses in Figures 9.17a through 9.17d)

The four M-estimators in Figures 9.17a through 9.17d differ from each other in the way they assign weights. Tukey's biweight estimators (Figure 9.17b) look much like Huber's estimators (Figure 9.17a). They differ in that the Tukey biweight does not have a point at which weights shift abruptly from 1. Instead, weights gradually decline to 0. Cases with values greater than c standardized units from the estimate are assigned weights of 0.

Hampel's three-part redescending M-estimator (Figure 9.17c) has a more complicated weighting scheme than the Huber or Tukey biweight. It uses four schemes for assigning weights. Cases with values less than a receive a weight of 1, cases with values between a and b receive a weight of a/u, while cases between b and c receive a weight of

$$\frac{a}{u} \cdot \frac{c-u}{c-b}$$

Cases with values greater than c receive a weight of 0. Andrew's M-estimator (Figure 9.17d) looks similar to Huber's. The difference is that there is no abrupt change in the assignment of weights. A smooth function replaces the separate pieces.

Figure 9.17e contains basic descriptive statistics and values for the M-estimators for the diastolic blood pressure data. As expected, the estimates of location differ for the various methods. The mean produces the largest estimate, 88.79. That's because we have a positively skewed distribution and the mean is heavily influenced by the large values. Of the M-estimators, the Huber and Hampel estimates have the largest values. They too are influenced by the large data values. The remaining two M-estimates are fairly close in value.

Figure 9.17e   M-estimates for blood pressure variable

```
EXAMINE VARIABLES=DBP58 /MESTIMATORS.
```

```
   DBP58

   Valid cases:       239.0   Missing cases:        1.0   Percent missing:      .4

   Mean           88.7908  Std Err        .8441  Min         65.0000  Skewness    1.2557
   Median         87.0000  Variance   170.3006  Max        160.0000  S E Skew     .1575
   5% Trim        88.0065  Std Dev     13.0499  Range       95.0000  Kurtosis    3.5958
                                                 IQR         17.0000  S E Kurt     .3137

                                     M-Estimators
                                     ------------

   Huber  (1.339)              87.1219   Tukey  (4.685)              86.4269
   Hampel (1.700,3.400,8.500)  87.1404   Andrew (1.340 * pi)         86.4105
```

In summary, M-estimators are good alternatives to the usual mean and median. The Huber is a good estimator when the distribution is close to normal but is not recommended if there are extreme values. For further discussion of robust estimators, see Hogg (1979) and Hoaglin, Mosteller, and Tukey (1983).

9.18
SUMMARY

Examination of the data is the most essential step of good data analysis. This chapter has shown a variety of descriptive statistics and displays that is useful as a preliminary step in data analysis. All of these statistics and displays are available in the SPSS/PC+ EXAMINE procedure. With EXAMINE, you can screen your data, visually examine the distributions of values for various groups, and test for normality and homogeneity of variance.

9.19
RUNNING PROCEDURE EXAMINE

The EXAMINE procedure provides a variety of descriptive plots and statistics, including stem-and-leaf plots, boxplots, normal probability plots, and spread-and-level plots. Also available are the Levene test for homogeneity of variance, the Shapiro-Wilks and Lilliefors tests for normality, and several robust maximum-likelihood estimators of location. Cases can be subdivided into groups and statistics obtained for each group.

9.20
Specifying the Variables

The only required specification is the VARIABLES subcommand and a list of variables for which descriptive statistics are to be calculated. For example, to obtain descriptive statistics for the variables SALBEG and EDUC, specify:

```
EXAMINE VARIABLES=SALBEG EDUC.
```

The VARIABLES subcommand can be specified only once.

9.21
Specifying the Cells

To subdivide cases into cells based on their values for grouping (factor) variables, specify the factor variables after keyword BY. String variables can be used as factors, but only the first eight characters are used.

For example, to obtain summary statistics for SALBEG and EDUC when cases are subdivided into employment categories (JOBCAT), specify:

```
EXAMINE VARIABLES=SALBEG EDUC BY JOBCAT.
```

If several variables are listed after keyword BY, separate analyses are obtained for each factor variable. For example, the command

```
EXAMINE VARIABLES=SALBEG EDUC BY JOBCAT SEX.
```

will produce summary statistics for salary and education for categories of JOBCAT and for categories of SEX. To obtain summary statistics for cells based on the combination of values of JOBCAT and SEX, use the keyword BY to separate the factor names. The command

```
EXAMINE VARIABLES=SALBEG EDUC BY JOBCAT BY SEX.
```

will produce descriptive statistics for cells formed by the combination of values of sex and job category. That is, there will be cells for males and females within each job category. If there are five job categories, you will obtain 11 analyses: one for all cases combined, and one for each of the ten cells formed by the combinations of JOBCAT and SEX. Note that you will not obtain analyses for each individual job category and for each sex. To obtain this additional output, specify:

```
EXAMINE VARIABLES=SALBEG EDUC BY SEX JOBCAT JOBCAT BY SEX.
```

Note that specifying many cells will generate a large amount of output. Be sure to request only the analyses that you need.

9.22
Identifying Cases in the Output

Individual cases can be identified in the output according to their values for a selected variable specified on the ID subcommand. For example, to identify cases by their values for EMPLNO, specify:

```
EXAMINE VARIABLES=SALBEG BY JOBCAT /ID=EMPLNO.
```

If the ID subcommand is not specified, the system variable $CASENUM is used.

9.23
Obtaining Basic Descriptive Statistics

Use the STATISTICS subcommand to control the output of basic descriptive statistics. The following keywords can be specified:

DESCRIPTIVE *Basic descriptive statistics only.* This includes the mean, median, mode, 5% trimmed mean, standard error, variance, standard deviation, minimum, maximum, range, interquartile range, skewness, and kurtosis; standard errors are displayed for the last two. Interquartile range computations are based on the method specified with the PERCENTILES subcommand.

EXTREMES (n) *The cases with the* n *largest and* n *smallest values.* If *n* is omitted, the cases with the five largest and five smallest values are displayed. Cases are identified by their values for the variable specified on the ID subcommand. If the ID subcommand is not used, cases are identified by their values for the system variable $CASENUM.

ALL *Basic descriptive statistics and extreme values.* All statistics available with DESCRIPTIVE and EXTREMES are displayed. The default *n* of 5 is used for EXTREMES.

NONE *Neither basic descriptive statistics nor extreme values.*

9.24
Obtaining Robust Maximum-Likelihood Estimators

Use the MESTIMATORS subcommand to obtain robust maximum-likelihood estimators of location. If the MESTIMATORS subcommand is specified without keywords, all four M-estimators are calculated. Individual estimators and values for weighting constants can be selected with the following keywords:

HUBER(c) *Huber's M-estimator with weighting constant* c. By default, $c=1.339$.

ANDREWS(c) *Andrews' wave estimator with weighting constant* c. The constant is multiplied by pi. By default, $c=1.34$.

HAMPEL(a,b,c) *Hampel's redescending M-estimator with constants* a, b, *and* c. By default, $a=1.7$, $b=3.4$, and $c=8.5$.

TUKEY(c) *Tukey's biweight estimator with constant* c. By default, $c=4.685$.

ALL *All four M-estimators.* This is the default when MESTIMATORS is specified without a keyword.

NONE *No M-estimators.* This is the default if MESTIMATORS is omitted.

For example, to calculate all four M-estimators for the variable DBP58, specify:

```
EXAMINE VARIABLES=DBP58 /MESTIMATORS.
```

To obtain only the Andrew's estimator with a weighting constant of 2 pi, specify:

```
EXAMINE VARIABLES=DBP58 /MESTIMATORS ANDREWS(2).
```

9.25
Obtaining Frequency Tables

Use the FREQUENCIES subcommand to obtain frequency tables. You can specify starting values and increment sizes. For example, to obtain a frequency table for DBP58 using increments of 5 and starting at 70, specify:

```
EXAMINE VARIABLES=DBP58 /FREQUENCIES FROM (70) BY (5).
```

If you do not specify a starting value or increment, EXAMINE will select a value based on the data. If you specify an increment of 0, a frequency table for each distinct value is produced.

9.26
Obtaining Percentiles

Use the PERCENTILES subcommand to obtain percentiles. You can also select the method of estimation. For example, to calculate the 25th, 50th, and 75th percentiles using the default method of estimation, specify:

```
EXAMINE VARIABLES=DBP58 /PERCENTILES(25,50,75).
```

If you specify the PERCENTILES subcommand without percentile values in parentheses, the default percentiles are 5, 10, 25, 50, 75, 90, and 95.

The following methods are available for calculating the percentiles, where W is the sum of weights for all nonmissing cases, p is the percentile divided by 100, i is the rank of the case when cases are sorted in ascending order, and X_i is the value for the ith case.

HAVERAGE   *Weighted average at $X_{(W+1)p}$.* The percentile value is the weighted average of X_i and X_{i+1} using the formula $(1-f)X_i + fX_{i+1}$, where $(W+1)p$ is decomposed into an integer part i and fractional part f. This is the default if PERCENTILES is specified without a keyword.

WAVERAGE   *Weighted average at X_{Wp}.* The percentile value is the weighted average of X_i and X_{i+1} using the formula $(1-f)X_i + fX_{i+1}$, where i is the integer part of Wp.

ROUND   *Observation closest to Wp.* The percentile value is X_i, where i is the integer part of $(Wp + .5)$.

EMPIRICAL   *Empirical distribution function.* The percentile value is X_i when the fractional Wp is equal to 0 and i is the integer part. The percentile value is X_{i+1} when the fractional part of Wp is greater than 0.

AEMPIRICAL   *Empirical distribution with averaging.* The percentile value is $(X_i + X_{i+1})/2$ when the fractional part of Wp equals 0. The percentile value is X_{i+1} when the fractional part of Wp is greater than 0.

NONE   *No percentile output.* This is the default if PERCENTILES is omitted.

The keyword for the method to be used for calculating the percentiles follows the list of percentile values, as in:

```
EXAMINE  VARIABLES=DBP58 /PERCENTILES(25 50 75)=WAVERAGE.
```

To obtain default percentiles using the empirical estimates, specify:

```
EXAMINE VARIABLES=DBP58 /PERCENTILES EMPIRICAL.
```

9.27
Plotting the Data

EXAMINE produces boxplots, stem-and-leaf plots, histograms, normal probability plots, and spread-and-level plots. The Shapiro-Wilks and/or Lilliefors tests of normality are calculated if normal probability plots are requested. The Levene test for homogeneity of variance is displayed if a spread-and-level plot is requested. If the PLOT subcommand is specified without any keywords or if the subcommand is omitted, stem-and-leaf plots and boxplots are produced. If any plots are specified on PLOT, only the requested plots are displayed.

The following keywords can be used with the PLOT subcommand:

BOXPLOT   *Boxplot.* The boundaries of the box are Tukey's hinges. The median is identified by an asterisk. The length of the box is the interquartile range (IQR) based on Tukey's hinges. Values more than 3 IQR's from the end of the box are labeled as extreme (**E**). Values more than 1.5 IQR's from the end of the box but less than 3 IQR's are labeled as outliers (**O**). This is produced by default.

STEMLEAF   *Stem-and-leaf plot*, in which each observed value is divided into two components—the leading digits (stem) and trailing digits (leaf). This is produced by default.

HISTOGRAM   *Histogram.*

SPREADLEVEL(p) *Spread-and-level plot.* If the keyword appears alone, for each cell, the natural log of the interquartile range is plotted against the log of the median. If the power for transforming the data (p) is supplied, the power transformation is performed and the IQR and median of the transformed data are plotted. If p=0 is specified, a natural log transformation of the data is done. The slope of the regression line and Levene's test for homogeneity of variance are also displayed. Levene's test is based on the original data if no transformation is specified and on the transformed data if a transformation is done.

NPPLOT *Normal probability and detrended probability plots.* The Shapiro-Wilks statistic and the Kolmogorov-Smirnov statistic with a Lilliefors significance level for testing normality are calculated. The Shapiro-Wilks statistic is not calculated when the sample size exceeds 50.

ALL *All available plots.*

NONE *No plots.*

For example, to request stem-and-leaf plots and normal probability plots, specify:

```
EXAMINE VARIABLES=DBP58 /PLOT STEMLEAF NPPLOT.
```

To determine an appropriate transformation of the data based on a plot of the logs of the interquartile ranges against the logs of the medians, specify:

```
EXAMINE VARIABLES=DBP58 /PLOT SPREADLEVEL.
```

To obtain a plot of interquartile ranges against medians when the data values are squared, specify:

```
EXAMINE VARIABLES=DBP58 /PLOT SPREADLEVEL(2).
```

To obtain a plot of the interquartile ranges against the medians after the data have been log transformed, specify:

```
EXAMINE VARIABLES=DBP58 /PLOT SPREADLEVEL(0).
```

9.28
Boxplot Display

Use the COMPARE subcommand to control how boxplots are displayed. Two methods are available. For each variable you can display the boxplots for all cells side by side, or you can display all of the boxplots for a cell together. (You will only have several boxplots for a single cell if you specify more than one dependent variable.)

Let's consider the advantage of each method. If you display the boxplots for all cells together, you can see how the distribution of a particular variable differs for the cells. For example, suppose you have variables SAL1, SAL2, SAL3, and SAL4, containing yearly salaries for the first four years of employment. If you specify

```
EXAMINE VARIABLES=SAL1 SAL2 SAL3 SAL4 BY JOBCAT BY SEX
  /COMPARE GROUPS.
```

you could easily compare each of the yearly salaries for the groups, since the distribution of SAL1 would be shown for all groups, followed by the distribution of SAL2 for all groups, and so forth. However, if you specify

```
EXAMINE VARIABLES=SAL1 SAL2 SAL3 SAL4 BY JOBCAT BY SEX
  /COMPARE VARIABLES.
```

for each cell the boxplots for the four salaries will be grouped together. This allows you to examine salary changes over time for each group.

9.29
Controlling the Scale

By default, the histogram and stem-and-leaf scale are based on the values of the cases in a particular plot. You can, however, use the same scale for all plots for each dependent variable by specifying the SCALE subcommand. The following keywords are available:

PLOTWISE   *Scales are based on the values of cases in each plot.* This is the default.
UNIFORM   *All plots for each dependent variable use the same scale.*

For example, if you specify

```
EXAMINE VARIABLES=SAL1 BY JOCBCAT /SCALE UNIFORM.
```

the same scale is used for all stem-and-leaf plots. If histograms are requested, they will also be on the same scale.

9.30
Missing Values

By default, cases with either system- or user-missing values for any variable specified on the VARIABLES subcommand are excluded from the analysis. You can specify other missing-value treatments using the MISSING subcommand. The following keywords are available:

LISTWISE   *Cases with any missing values are deleted.* This is the default.
PAIRWISE   *Cases with nonmissing values for a cell are included in the analysis of that cell.* The case may have missing values for variables used in other cells.
REPORT   *Missing values for factor variables are treated as a separate category.* All output is produced for this additional category. Frequency tables include categories for missing values.
INCLUDE   *Cases with user-missing values are included.* Only cases with system-missing values are excluded from the analysis. This keyword can be used together with LISTWISE, PAIRWISE, or REPORT.

For example, the command

```
EXAMINE VARIABLES=SALBEG EDUC BY JOBCAT /MISSING PAIRWISE.
```

will exclude cases from the analysis of SALBEG only if they have missing values for SALBEG or JOBCAT. It doesn't matter whether the value of EDUC is missing or not. Only cases with missing values for EDUC or JOBCAT will be excluded from the analysis of EDUC.

Contents

10 Crosstabulation and Measures of Association: Procedure CROSSTABS

Newspapers headline murders in subway stations, robberies on crowded main streets, suicides cheered by onlookers. All are indications of the social irresponsibility and apathy said to characterize city residents. Since overcrowding, decreased sense of community, and other urban problems are usually blamed, you might ask whether small-town residents are more responsible and less apathetic than their urban counterparts.

Hansson and Slade (1977) used the "lost letter technique" to test the hypothesis that altruism is higher in small towns than in cities, unless the person needing assistance is a social deviant. In this technique, stamped and addressed letters are "lost," and the rate at which they are returned is examined. A total of 216 letters were lost in Hansson and Slade's experiment. Half were dropped within the city limits of Tulsa, Oklahoma, the others in 51 small towns within a 50-mile radius of Tulsa. The letters were addressed to three fictitious people at a post-office box in Tulsa: M. J. Davis; Dandee Davis, c/o Pink Panther Lounge; and M. J. Davis, c/o Friends of the Communist Party. The first person is considered a normal "control," the second a person whose occupation is questionable, and the third a subversive or political deviant.

10.1 CROSSTABULATION

To see whether the return rate is similar for the three addresses, the letters found and mailed and those not mailed must be tallied separately for each address. Figure 10.1 is a *crosstabulation* of address type and response. The number of cases (letters) for each combination of values of the two variables is displayed in a *cell* in the table, together with various percentages. These cell entries provide information about relationships between the variables.

Figure 10.1 Crosstabulation of status of letter by address

```
CROSSTABS TABLES=RETURNED BY ADDRESS
    /CELLS.
```

```
RETURNED  FOUND AND MAILED  by  ADDRESS  ADDRESS ON LETTER

                    ADDRESS                    Page 1 of 1
            Count
            Row Pct |CONTROL  DANDEE   COMMUNIS
            Col Pct |                     T       Row
            Tot Pct |    1  |    2  |    3  | Total
RETURNED    --------+-------+-------+-------+
                1   |   35  |   32  |   10  |   77
   YES          45.5 | 41.6 | 13.0 |  35.6
                48.6 | 44.4 | 13.9 |
                16.2 | 14.8 |  4.6 |
            --------+-------+-------+-------+
                2   |   37  |   40  |   62  |  139
   NO           26.6 | 28.8 | 44.6 |  64.4
                51.4 | 55.6 | 86.1 |
                17.1 | 18.5 | 28.7 |
            --------+-------+-------+-------+
            Column     72      72      72      216
             Total    33.3    33.3    33.3   100.0

        Chi-Square                  Value          DF          Significance
    ---------------------------     -----------    ----        ------------

    Pearson                         22.56265        2            .00001
    Likelihood Ratio                24.68684        2            .00000
    Mantel-Haenszel test for        18.83234        1            .00001
        linear association
    Minimum Expected Frequency -    25.667


    Number of Missing Observations:  0
```

In Figure 10.1, the address is called the *column* variable since each address is displayed in a column of the table. Similarly, the status of the letter, whether it was returned or not, is called the *row* variable. With three categories of the column variable and two of the row, there are six cells in the table.

10.2
Cell Contents and Marginals

The first entry in the table is the number of cases, or *frequency*, in that cell. It is labeled **Count** in the key displayed in the upper-left corner of the table. For example, 35 letters addressed to the control were returned, and 62 letters addressed to the Communist were not returned. The second entry in the table is the *row percentage* (**Row Pct**). It is the percentage of all cases in a row that fall into a particular cell. Of the 77 letters returned, 45.5% were addressed to the control, 41.6% to Dandee, and 13.0% to the Communist.

The *column percentage* (**Col Pct**), the third item in each cell, is the percentage of all cases in a column that occur in a cell. For example, 48.6% of the letters addressed to the control were returned and 51.4% were not. The return rate for Dandee is similar (44.4%), while that for the Communist is markedly lower (13.9%).

The last entry in the table is the *table percentage* (**Tot Pct**). The number of cases in the cell is expressed as a percentage of the total number of cases in the table. For example, the 35 letters returned to the control represent 16.2% of the 216 letters in the experiment.

The numbers to the right and below the table are known as *marginals*. They are the counts and percentages for the row and column variables taken separately. In Figure 10.1, the row marginals show that 77 (35.6%) of the letters were returned, while 139 (64.4%) were not.

10.3
Choosing Percentages

Row, column, and table percentages convey different types of information, so it is important to choose carefully among them.

In this example, the row percentage indicates the distribution of address types for returned and "lost" letters. It conveys no direct information about the return rate. For example, if twice as many letters were addressed to the control, an identical return rate for all letters would give row percentages of 50%, 25%, and 25%. However, this does not indicate that the return rate is higher for the control. In addition, if each category had the same number of returned letters, the row percentages would have been 33.3%, 33.3%, and 33.3%, regardless of whether one or all letters were returned.

The column percentage is the percentage of letters returned and not returned for each address. By looking at column percentages across rows, you can compare return rates for the address types. Interpretation of this comparison would not be affected if unequal numbers of letters had been addressed to each category.

Since it is always possible to interchange the rows and columns of any table, general rules about when to use row and column percentages cannot be given. The percentages to use depend on the nature of the two variables. If one of the two variables is under experimental control, it is termed an *independent variable*. This variable is hypothesized to affect the response, or *dependent variable*. If variables can be classified as dependent and independent, the following guideline may be helpful: If the independent variable is the row variable, select row percentages; if the independent variable is the column variable, select column percentages. In this example the dependent variable is the status of the letter, whether it was mailed or not. The type of address is the independent variable. Since the independent variable is the column variable in Figure 10.1, column percentages should be used for comparisons of return rates.

10.4
Adding a Control Variable

Since Figure 10.1 combines results from both the city and the towns, differences between the locations are obscured. Two separate tables, one for the city and one for the towns, are required. Figure 10.4 shows crosstabulations of response and address for each of the locations. SPSS/PC+ produces a separate table for each value of the location (control) variable.

Figure 10.4 Crosstabulations of status of letter by address controlled for location

```
CROSSTABS TABLES=RETURNED BY ADDRESS BY LOCATION
  /CELLS=COUNT COLUMN /STATISTICS=CHISQ.
```

```
RETURNED  FOUND AND MAILED  by  ADDRESS  ADDRESS ON LETTER
Controlling for..
LOCATION  LOCATION LOST  Value = 1  CITY

                       ADDRESS                        Page 1 of 1
              Count
              Col Pct |CONTROL DANDEE  COMMUNIS
                      |                     T
                      |                            Row
                      |    1  |    2  |    3  |  Total
RETURNED      --------+-------+-------+-------+
           1  |   16  |   14  |    9  |    39
  YES        |   44.4 |  38.9 |  25.0 |  36.1
             +-------+-------+-------+
           2  |   20  |   22  |   27  |    69
  NO         |   55.6 |  61.1 |  75.0 |  63.9
             +-------+-------+-------+
      Column       36      36      36     108
      Total      33.3    33.3    33.3   100.0

     Chi-Square                 Value          DF        Significance
------------------------------------------------------------------------

Pearson                       3.13043           2          .20904
Likelihood Ratio              3.21259           2          .20063
Mantel-Haenszel test for      2.92252           1          .08735
    linear association
Minimum Expected Frequency -  13.000


RETURNED  FOUND AND MAILED  by  ADDRESS  ADDRESS ON LETTER
Controlling for..
LOCATION  LOCATION LOST  Value = 2  TOWN

                       ADDRESS                        Page 1 of 1
              Count
              Col Pct |CONTROL DANDEE  COMMUNIS
                      |                     T
                      |                            Row
                      |    1  |    2  |    3  |  Total
RETURNED      --------+-------+-------+-------+
           1  |   19  |   18  |    1  |    38
  YES        |   52.8 |  50.0 |   2.8 |  35.2
             +-------+-------+-------+
           2  |   17  |   18  |   35  |    70
  NO         |   47.2 |  50.0 |  97.2 |  64.8
             +-------+-------+-------+
      Column       36      36      36     108
      Total      33.3    33.3    33.3   100.0

     Chi-Square                 Value          DF        Significance
------------------------------------------------------------------------

Pearson                      24.92932           2          .00000
Likelihood Ratio             31.25343           2          .00000
Mantel-Haenszel test for     19.54962           1          .00001
    linear association
Minimum Expected Frequency -  12.667


Number of Missing Observations:  0
```

These tables show interesting differences between cities and towns. Although the overall return rates are close, 36.1% for the city and 35.2% for the towns, there are striking differences between the addresses. Only 2.8% of the Communist letters were returned in towns, while 25.0% of them were returned in Tulsa. (At least two of the Communist letters were forwarded by small-town residents to the FBI for punitive action!) The return rates for both the control (52.8%) and Dandee (50.0%) are higher in towns.

The results support the hypothesis that, in small towns, suspected social deviance influences the response more than in big cities, although it is surprising that Dandee and the Pink Panther Lounge were deemed worthy of as much assistance as they received. If the Communist letter is excluded, inhabitants of small towns are somewhat more helpful than city residents, returning 51% of the other letters, in comparison to the city's 42%.

10.5 GRAPHICAL REPRESENTATION OF CROSSTABULATIONS

As with frequency tables, visual representation of a crosstabulation often simplifies the search for associations. Figure 10.5 is a bar chart of letters returned from the crosstabulations shown in Figure 10.4. In a bar chart, the length of each bar represents the frequencies or percentages for each category of a variable. In Figure 10.5, the percentages plotted are the column percentages shown in Figure 10.4 for the returned letters only. This chart clearly shows that the return rates for the control and Dandee are high compared to the return rate for the Communist. Also, it demonstrates more vividly than the crosstabulation that the town residents' return rates for the control and Dandee are higher than city residents' return rates, but that the reverse is true for the Communist.

Figure 10.5   Status of letter by address by location (bar chart from SPSS/PC+ Graphics)

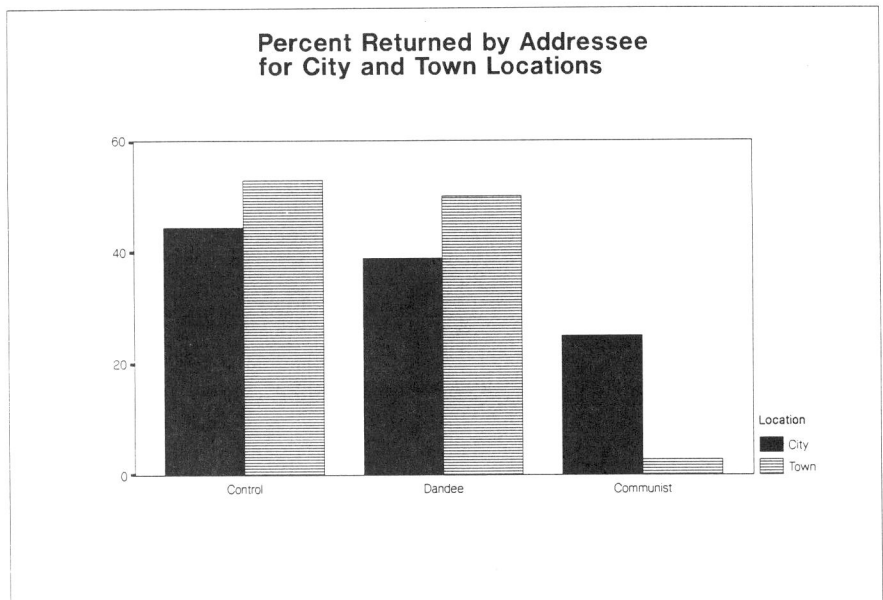

10.6 USING CROSSTABULATION FOR DATA SCREENING

Errors and unusual values in data entry that cannot be spotted with FREQUEN-CIES can sometimes be identified using crosstabulation. For example, a case coded as a male with a history of three pregnancies would not be identified as suspicious in FREQUENCIES tables of sex and number of pregnancies. When considered separately, the code for male is acceptable for variable sex and the value 3 is acceptable for number of pregnancies. Jointly, however, the combination is unexpected.

Whenever possible, crosstabulations of related variables should be obtained so that anomalies can be identified and corrected before further statistical analysis of the data.

10.7
CROSSTABULATION STATISTICS

Although examination of the various row and column percentages in a crosstabulation is a useful first step in studying the relationship between two variables, row and column percentages do not allow for quantification or testing of that relationship. For these purposes, it is useful to consider various indexes that measure the extent of association as well as statistical tests of the hypothesis that there is no association.

10.8
The Chi-Square Test of Independence

The hypothesis that two variables of a crosstabulation are *independent* of each other is often of interest to researchers. Two variables are by definition independent if the probability that a case falls into a given cell is simply the product of the marginal probabilities of the two categories defining the cell.

For example, in Figure 10.1 if returns of the letter and address type are independent, the probability of a letter being returned to a Communist is the product of the probability of a letter being returned and the probability of a letter being addressed to a Communist. From the table, 35.6% of the letters were returned and 33.3% of the letters were addressed to a friend of the Communist party. Thus, if address type and status of the letter are independent, the probability of a letter being returned to the Communist is estimated to be

$P(\text{return})\ P(\text{Communist})=0.356 \times 0.333 = 0.119$

The *expected* number of cases in that cell is 25.7, which is 11.9% of the 216 cases in the sample. From the table, the *observed* number of letters returned to the Communist is 10 (4.6%), nearly 16 fewer than expected if the two variables are independent.

To construct a statistical test of the independence hypothesis, you repeat the above calculations for each cell in the table. The probability under independence of an observation falling into cell (ij) is estimated by

$$P(\text{row} = i \text{ and column} = j) = \left(\frac{\text{count in row } i}{N}\right) \left(\frac{\text{count in column } j}{N}\right) \quad \textbf{Equation 10.8a}$$

To obtain the expected number of observations in cell (ij), the probability is multiplied by the total sample size.

$$E_{ij} = N\left(\frac{\text{count in row } i}{N}\right) \left(\frac{\text{count in column } j}{N}\right) \quad \textbf{Equation 10.8b}$$

$$= \frac{(\text{count in row } i)\ (\text{count in column } j)}{N}$$

Figure 10.8 contains the observed and expected frequencies and the *residuals*, which are the observed minus the expected frequencies for the data in Figure 10.1.

Figure 10.8   Observed, expected, and residual values

```
CROSSTABS TABLES=RETURNED BY ADDRESS
   /CELLS=COUNT EXPECTED RESID
   /STATISTICS=CHISQ.
```

```
RETURNED   FOUND AND MAILED  by  ADDRESS   ADDRESS ON LETTER

                  ADDRESS                        Page 1 of 1
            Count
            Exp Val  CONTROL  DANDEE   COMMUNIS
            Residual                      T          Row
                        1   |    2   |    3   |    Total
RETURNED   -----------+--------+--------+--------+
  YES         1         35       32       10        77
                       25.7     25.7     25.7      35.6%
                        9.3      6.3    -15.7
                      +--------+--------+--------+
  NO          2         37       40       62       139
                       46.3     46.3     46.3      64.4%
                       -9.3     -6.3     15.7
                      +--------+--------+--------+
            Column      72       72       72       216
            Total     33.3%    33.3%    33.3%    100.0%
Number of Missing Observations:   0
```

A statistic often used to test the hypothesis that the row and column variables are independent is the *Pearson chi-square*. It is calculated by summing over all cells the squared residuals divided by the expected frequencies.

$$\chi^2 = \sum_i \sum_j \frac{(O_{ij} - E_{ij})^2}{E_{ij}}$$

Equation 10.8c

The calculated chi-square is compared to the critical points of the theoretical chi-square distribution to produce an estimate of how likely (or unlikely) this calculated value is if the two variables are in fact independent. Since the value of the chi-square depends on the number of rows and columns in the table being examined, you must know the *degrees of freedom* for the table. The degrees of freedom can be viewed as the number of cells of a table that can be arbitrarily filled when the row and column totals (marginals) are fixed. For an $r \times c$ table, the degrees of freedom are $(r - 1) \times (c - 1)$, since once $(r-1)$ rows and $(c-1)$ columns are filled, frequencies in the remaining row and column cells must be chosen so that marginal totals are maintained.

In this example, there are two degrees of freedom (1×2), and the Pearson chi-square value is 22.56 (see Figure 10.8). If type of address and return rate are independent, the probability that a random sample would result in a chi-square value of at least that magnitude is less than 0.00001. This probability is also known as the *observed significance level* of the test. If the probability is small enough (usually less than 0.05 or 0.01), the hypothesis that the two variables are independent is rejected.

Since the observed significance level in Figure 10.1 is very small (based on the combined city and town data), the hypothesis that address type and return rate are independent is rejected. When the chi-square test is calculated for the city and town data separately (Figure 10.4), different results are obtained. The observed significance level of the city data is 0.209, so the independence hypothesis is not rejected. For the towns, the observed significance level is less than 0.000005, and the hypothesis that address and return rate are independent is rejected. These results support the theory that city and town residents respond differently.

An alternative to the commonly used Pearson chi-square is the likelihood ratio chi-square (see Figure 10.8). This test is based on maximum likelihood theory and is often used in the analysis of categorical data. For large samples, the Pearson and likelihood ratio chi-square statistics give very similar results. (The test labeled **Mantel-Haenszel** is discussed in section 10.15.)

The chi-square test is a test of independence; it provides little information about the strength or form of the association between two variables. The magnitude of the observed chi-square depends not only on the goodness of fit of the independence model but also on the sample size. If the sample size for a particular table increases *n*-fold, so does the chi-square value. Thus, large chi-square values can arise in applications where residuals are small relative to expected frequencies but where the sample size is large.

Certain conditions must be met for the chi-square distribution to be a good approximation of the distribution of the statistic in the equation given above. The data must be random samples from multinomial distributions and the expected values must not be too small. While it has been recommended that all expected frequencies be at least 5, recent studies indicate that this is probably too stringent and can be relaxed (Everitt, 1977). CROSSTABS displays the number of cells with expected frequencies less than 5 and the minimum expected cell value.

To improve the approximation for a 2×2 table, *Yates' correction for continuity* is sometimes applied. Yates' correction for continuity involves subtracting 0.5 from positive differences between observed and expected frequencies (the residuals) and adding 0.5 to negative differences before squaring. For a discussion of some of the controversy regarding the merits of this correction, see Conover (1974) and Mantel (1974).

An alternative test for the 2×2 table is based on the hypergeometric distribution. Exact probabilities of obtaining the observed results if the two variables are independent and the marginals fixed are calculated. This is called *Fisher's exact test*. It is most useful when the total sample size and the expected values are small. SPSS/PC+ calculates Fisher's exact test if any expected cell value in a 2×2 table is less than 5.

10.9
Measures of Association

In many research situations, the strength and nature of the dependence of variables is of central concern. Indexes that attempt to quantify the relationship between variables in a cross-classification are called *measures of association*. No single measure adequately summarizes all possible types of association. Measures vary in their interpretation and in the way they define perfect and intermediate association. These measures also differ in the way they are affected by various factors such as marginals. For example, many measures are "margin sensitive" in that they are influenced by the marginal distributions of the rows and columns. Such measures reflect information about the marginals along with information about association.

A particular measure may have a low value for a given table, not because the two variables are not related, but because they are not related in the way to which the measure is sensitive. No single measure is best for all situations. The type of data, the hypothesis of interest, as well as the properties of the various measures must all be considered when selecting an index of association for a given table. It is not, however, reasonable to compute a large number of measures and then to report the most impressive as if it were the only one examined.

The measures of association available in CROSSTABS are computed only from bivariate tables. For example, if three dichotomous variables are specified in the table, two sets of measures are computed, one for each subtable produced by the values of the controlling variable. In general, if relationships among more than two variables are to be studied, examination of bivariate tables is only a first step. For an extensive discussion of various more sophisticated multivariate procedures for the analysis of qualitative data, see Feinberg (1977), Everitt (1977), and Haberman (1978).

10.10
Nominal Measures

Consider measures that assume only that both variables in the table are nominally measured. As such, these measures can only provide some indication of the strength of association between variables; they cannot indicate direction or anything about the nature of the relationship. The measures provided are of two types: those based on the chi-square statistic and those that follow the logic of proportional reduction in error, denoted PRE.

10.11
Chi-Square-Based Measures

As explained above, the chi-square statistic itself is not a good measure of the degree of association between two variables. But its widespread use in tests of independence has encouraged the use of measures of association based upon it. Each of these measures based on the chi-square attempts to modify the chi-square statistic to minimize the influence of sample size and degrees of freedom as well as to restrict the range of values of the measure to those between 0 and 1. Without such adjustments, comparison of chi-square values from tables with varying dimensions and sample sizes is meaningless.

The *phi-coefficient* modifies the Pearson chi-square by dividing it by the sample size and taking the square root of the result:

$$\phi = \sqrt{\frac{\chi^2}{N}}$$

Equation 10.11a

For tables in which one dimension is greater than 2, phi may not lie between 0 and 1 since the chi-square value can be greater than the sample size. To obtain a measure that must lie between 0 and 1, Pearson suggested the use of

$$C = \sqrt{\frac{\chi^2}{\chi^2 + N}}$$

Equation 10.11b

which is called the *coefficient of contingency*. Although the value of this measure is always between 0 and 1, it cannot generally attain the upper limit of 1. The maximum value possible depends upon the number of rows and columns. For example, in a 4×4 table, the maximum value of C is 0.87.

Cramér introduced the following variant:

$$V = \sqrt{\frac{\chi^2}{N(k - 1)}}$$

Equation 10.11c

where k is the smaller of the number of rows and columns. This statistic, known as *Cramér's V*, can attain the maximum of 1 for tables of any dimension. If one of the table dimensions is 2, V and phi are identical.

Figure 10.11 shows the values of the chi-square-based measures for the letter data. The test of the null hypothesis that a measure is 0 is based on the Pearson chi-square probability.

Figure 10.11 Chi-square-based measures

```
CROSSTABS TABLES=RETURNED BY ADDRESS
  /STATISTICS=PHI CC.
```

```
RETURNED  FOUND AND MAILED  by  ADDRESS  ADDRESS ON LETTER

                 ADDRESS                      Page 1 of 1
          Count
                 CONTROL  DANDEE  COMMUNIS
                                      T
                    1   |    2   |    3   | Row
RETURNED     --------+--------+--------+ Total
             1  |   35   |   32   |   10   |   77
  YES           |        |        |        |  35.6
             ---+--------+--------+--------+
             2  |   37   |   40   |   62   |  139
  NO            |        |        |        |  64.4
             ---+--------+--------+--------+
          Column     72       72       72      216
          Total     33.3     33.3     33.3    100.0
```

```
                                                       Approximate
       Statistic              Value     ASE1  T-value  Significance
                             --------          -------
Phi                           .32320                    .00001 *1
Cramer's V                    .32320                    .00001 *1
Contingency Coefficient       .30753                    .00001 *1

*1 Pearson chi-square probability

Number of Missing Observations:  0
```

The chi-square-based measures are hard to interpret. Although when properly standardized they can be used to compare strength of association in several tables, the "strength of association" being compared is not easily related to an intuitive concept of association.

10.12
Proportional Reduction in Error

Common alternatives to chi-square-based measurements are those based on the idea of *proportional reduction in error* (PRE), introduced by Goodman and Kruskal (1954). With PRE measures, the meaning of association is clearer. These measures are all essentially ratios of a measure of error in predicting the values of one variable based on knowledge of that variable alone and the same measure of error applied to predictions based on knowledge of an additional variable.

For example, Figure 10.12 is a crosstabulation of depth of hypnosis and success in treatment of migraine headaches by suggestion (Cedercreutz, 1978). The best guess of the results of treatment when no other information is available is the outcome category with the largest proportion of observations (the modal category). In Figure 10.12, "no change" is the largest outcome category, with 45% of the subjects. The estimate of the probability of incorrect classification is 1 minus the probability of the modal category:

$$P(1) = 1 - 0.45 = 0.55 \qquad \text{Equation 10.12a}$$

Figure 10.12 Depth of hypnosis and success of treatment

```
CROSSTABS TABLES=HYPNOSIS BY MIGRAINE
  /CELLS=COUNT COLUMN TOTAL
  /STATISTICS=LAMBDA.
```

```
HYPNOSIS  DEPTH OF HYPNOSIS  by  MIGRAINE  OUTCOME

                    MIGRAINE                        Page 1 of 1
             Count
             Tot Pct  CURED    BETTER   NO
                                        CHANGE   Row
                        1        2        3    | Total
HYPNOSIS    --------+--------+--------+--------+
          1 |   13   |    5   |        |    18
   DEEP       |   13.0 |    5.0 |        |    18.0
            +--------+--------+--------+
          2 |   10   |   26   |   17   |    53
   MEDIUM     |   10.0 |   26.0 |   17.0 |    53.0
            +--------+--------+--------+
          3 |        |    1   |   28   |    29
   LIGHT      |        |    1.0 |   28.0 |    29.0
            +--------+--------+--------+
           Column     23       32       45       100
           Total    23.0     32.0     45.0    100.0

      Chi-Square                    Value          DF           Significance
  ------------------                -----          --           ------------

  Pearson                         65.52526          4               .00000
  Likelihood Ratio                73.37559          4               .00000
  Mantel-Haenszel test for        50.95032          1               .00000
      linear association
  Minimum Expected Frequency -     4.140
  Cells with Expected Frequency < 5 -     1 OF     9 ( 11.1%)

                                                                Approximate
       Statistic                  Value      ASE1    T-value    Significance
  ------------------              -----      ----    -------    ------------

  Phi                             .80948                            .00000 *1
  Cramer's V                      .57239                            .00000 *1
  Contingency Coefficient         .62918                            .00000 *1


  Lambda :
      symmetric                   .35294     .11335   2.75267
      with HYPNOSIS dependent     .29787     .14702   1.72276
      with MIGRAINE dependent     .40000     .10539   3.07580
  Goodman & Kruskal Tau :
      with HYPNOSIS dependent     .29435     .06304              .00000 *2
      with MIGRAINE dependent     .34508     .04863              .00000 *2
  Uncertainty Coefficient :
      symmetric                   .35514     .05083   6.48252    .00000 *3
      with HYPNOSIS dependent     .36537     .04950   6.48252    .00000 *3
      with MIGRAINE dependent     .34547     .05298   6.48252    .00000 *3


  *1 Pearson chi-square probability
  *2 Based on chi-square approximation
  *3 Likelihood ratio chi-square probability
  Number of Missing Observations:  0
```

Information about the depth of hypnosis can be used to improve the classification rule. For each hypnosis category, the outcome category that occurs most frequently for that hypnosis level is predicted. Thus, no change is predicted for participants achieving a light level of hypnosis, better for those achieving a medium level, and cured for those achieving a deep level. The probability of error when depth of hypnosis is used to predict outcome is the sum of the probabilities of all the cells that are not row modes:

$$P(2)=0.05+0.10+0.17+0.01=0.33$$

Equation 10.12b

Goodman and Kruskal's *lambda*, with outcome as the predicted (dependent) variable, is calculated as

$$\lambda_{\text{outcome}} = \frac{P(1) - P(2)}{P(1)} = \frac{0.55 - 0.33}{0.55} = 0.40$$

Equation 10.12c

Thus, a 40% reduction in error is obtained when depth of hypnosis is used to predict outcome.

Lambda always ranges between 0 and 1. A value of 0 means the independent variable is of no help in predicting the dependent variable. A value of 1 means that the independent variable perfectly specifies the categories of the dependent variable (perfection can occur only when each row has at most one nonzero cell). When the two variables are independent, lambda is 0; but a lambda of 0 need not imply statistical independence. As with all measures of association, lambda is constructed to measure association in a very specific way. In particular, lambda reflects the reduction in error when values of one variable are used to predict values of the other. If this particular type of association is absent, lambda is 0. Other measures of association may find association of a different kind even when lambda is 0. A measure of association sensitive to every imaginable type of association does not exist.

For a particular table, two different lambdas can be computed, one using the row variable as the predictor and the other using the column variable. The two do not usually have identical values, so care should be taken to specify which is the dependent variable, that is, the variable whose prediction is of primary interest. In some applications, dependent and independent variables are not clearly distinguished. Then, a symmetric version of lambda, which predicts the row variable and column variable with equal frequency, can be computed. When the lambda statistic is requested, SPSS/PC+ displays the symmetric lambda as well as the two asymmetric lambdas.

10.13
Goodman and Kruskal's Tau

When lambda is computed, the same prediction is made for all cases in a particular row or column. Another approach is to consider what happens if the prediction is randomly made in the same proportion as the marginal totals. For example, if you're trying to predict migraine outcome without any information about the depth of the hypnosis, you can use the marginal distributions in Figure 10.12 instead of the modal category to guess cured for 23% of the cases, better for 32% of the cases, and no change for 45% of the cases.

Using these marginals, you would expect to correctly classify 23% of the 23 cases in the cured category, 32% of the 32 cases in the better category, and 45% of the 45 cases in the no change category. This results in the correct classification of 35.78 out of 100 cases. When additional information about the depth of hypnosis is incorporated into the prediction rule, the prediction is based on the probability of the different outcomes for each depth of hypnosis. For example, for those who experienced deep hypnosis, you would predict cure 72% of the time (13/18) and better 28% of the time (5/18). Similarly, for those with light hypnosis, you would predict better 3% of the time and no change 97% of the time. This results in correct classification for about 58 of the cases.

Kruskal and Goodman's tau is computed by comparing the probability of error in the two situations. In this example, when predicting only from the column marginal totals, the probability of error is 0.64. When predicting from row information the probability of error is 0.42. Thus:

tau (migraine|hypnosis) = (0.64 − 0.42)/0.64 = 0.34   **Equation 10.13**

By incorporating information about the depth of hypnosis, we have reduced our error of prediction by about 34%.

A test of the null hypothesis that tau is 0 can be based on the value of $(N\text{-}1)(c - 1)$ tau (col|row), which has a chi-square distribution with $(c - 1) \times (r - 1)$ degrees of freedom. In this example, the observed significance level for tau is very small, and you can reject the null hypothesis that tau is 0. The asymptotic standard error for the statistic is shown in the column labeled **ASE1**. The asymptotic standard error can be used to construct confidence intervals.

10.14
Measuring Agreement

Measures of agreement allow you to compare the ratings of two observers for the same group of objects. For example, consider the data reported in Bishop et al. (1975), shown in Figure 10.14.

Figure 10.14 Student teachers rated by supervisors

```
CROSSTABS TABLES=SUPRVSR1 BY SUPRVSR2
   /CELLS=COUNT TOTAL
   /STATISTICS=KAPPA.
```

```
SUPRVSR1  Supervisor 1  by  SUPRVSR2  Supervisor 2

                        SUPRVSR2                      Page 1 of 1
                Count
                Tot Pct  Authorit Democrat Permissi
                         arian    ic       ve          Row
                            1.00|    2.00|    3.00|   Total
SUPRVSR1        --------+--------+--------+--------+
                   1.00 |    17  |     4  |     8  |    29
    Authoritarian       |  23.6  |   5.6  |  11.1  |  40.3
                        +--------+--------+--------+
                   2.00 |     5  |    12  |        |    17
    Democratic          |   6.9  |  16.7  |        |  23.6
                        +--------+--------+--------+
                   3.00 |    10  |     3  |    13  |    26
    Permissive          |  13.9  |   4.2  |  18.1  |  36.1
                        +--------+--------+--------+
                Column       32       19       21        72
                Total      44.4     26.4     29.2     100.0


                                                          Approximate
         Statistic                 Value      ASE1     T-value  Significance
         ---------                 -----      ----     -------  ------------


Kappa                             .36227     .09144   4.32902

Number of Missing Observations:  0
```

Two supervisors rated the classroom style of 72 teachers. You are interested in measuring the agreement between the two raters. The simplest measure that comes to mind is just the proportion of cases for which the raters agree. In this case it is 58.3%. The disadvantage of this measure is that no correction is made for the amount of agreement expected by chance. That is, you would expect the supervisors to agree sometimes even if they were assigning ratings by tossing dice.

To correct for chance agreement you can compute the proportion of cases that you would expect to be in agreement if the ratings are independent. For example, Supervisor 1 rated 40.3% of the teachers as authoritarian, while Supervisor 2 rated 44.4% of the teachers as authoritarian. If their rankings are independent, you would expect that 17.9% (40.3% $\times$ 44.4%) of the teachers would be rated as authoritarian by both. Similarly, 6.2% would be rated as democratic (23.6% $\times$ 26.4%) and 10.5% (36.1% $\times$ 29.2%) as permissive. Thus, 34.6% of all the teachers would be classified the same merely by chance.

The difference between the observed proportion of cases in which the raters agree and that expected by chance is 0.237 (0.583 − 0.346). *Cohen's kappa* (1960) normalizes this difference by dividing it by the maximum difference possible for the marginal totals. In this example, the largest possible "non-chance" agreement is 1 − 0.346 (the chance level). Therefore:

$$\text{kappa} = 0.237/(1 - 0.346) = 0.362$$ **Equation 10.14**

The test of the null hypothesis that kappa is 0 can be based on the *t* statistic shown in Figure 10.14. (See Benedetti & Brown, 1978, for further discussion of standard errors for measures of association as well as discussion of the degrees of freedom for the *t* statistic.) The *t* value is the ratio of the value of kappa to its asymptotic standard error when the null hypothesis is true. (This asymptotic error is not the one shown on the output. The asymptotic standard error on the output, ASE1, does not assume that the true value is 0.)

Since the kappa statistic measures agreement between two raters, the two variables that contain the ratings must have the same range of values. If this is not true, CROSSTABS will not compute kappa.

10.15
Ordinal Measures

Although relationships among ordinal variables can be examined using nominal measures, other measures reflect the additional information available from ranking. Consideration of the kind of relationships that may exist between two ordered variables leads to the notion of direction of relationship and to the concept of *correlation*. Variables are positively correlated if cases with low values for one variable also tend to have low values for the other and cases with high values on one also tend to be high on the other. Negatively correlated variables show the opposite relationship: the higher the first variable, the lower the second tends to be.

The Spearman correlation coefficient is a commonly used measure of correlation between two ordinal variables. For all of the cases, the values of each of the variables are ranked from smallest to largest and the Pearson correlation coefficient is computed on the ranks. The Mantel-Haenszel chi-square is another measure of linear association between the row and column variables in a crosstabulation. It is computed by multiplying the squared Pearson correlation coefficient by the number of cases minus 1. The resulting statistic has one degree of freedom (Mantel & Haenszel, 1959). (Although the Mantel-Haenszel statistic is displayed whenever chi-square is requested, it should not be used for nominal data.)

10.16
Ordinal Measures Based on Pairs

For a table of two ordered variables, several measures of association based on a comparison of the values of both variables for all possible *pairs* of cases or observations are available. Cases are first compared to determine if they are *concordant, discordant,* or *tied.* A pair of cases is *concordant* if the values of both variables for one case are higher (or both are lower) than the corresponding values for the other case. The pair is *discordant* if the value of one variable for a case is larger than the corresponding value for the other case, and the direction is reversed for the second variable. When the two cases have identical values on one or on both variables, they are *tied.*

Thus, for any given pair of cases with measurements on variables X and Y, the pair may be concordant or discordant, or tied in one of three ways: they may be tied on X but not on Y, they may be tied on Y but not on X, or they may be tied on both variables. When data are arranged in crosstabulated form, the number of concordant, discordant, and tied pairs can be easily calculated since all possible pairs can be conveniently determined.

If the preponderance of pairs is concordant, the association is said to be positive: as ranks of variable X increase (or decrease), so do ranks of variable Y. If the majority of pairs is discordant, the association is negative: as ranks of one variable increase, those of the other tend to decrease. If concordant and discordant pairs are equally likely, no association is said to exist.

The ordinal measures presented here all have the same numerator: the number of concordant pairs (P) minus the number of discordant pairs (Q) calculated for all distinct pairs of observations. They differ primarily in the way in which $P-Q$ is normalized. The simplest measure involves subtracting Q from P and dividing by the total number of pairs. If there are no pairs with ties, this measure (Kendall's tau-a) is in the range from -1 to $+1$. If there are ties, the range of possible values is narrower; the actual range depends on the number of ties. Since all observations within the same row are tied, so also are those in the same column, and the resulting tau-a measures are difficult to interpret.

A measure that attempts to normalize $P-Q$ by considering ties on each variable in a pair separately but not ties on both variables in a pair is tau-b:

$$\tau_b = \frac{P - Q}{\sqrt{(P + Q + T_X)(P + Q + T_Y)}}$$ Equation 10.16a

where T_X is the number of pairs tied on X but not on Y, and T_Y is the number of pairs tied on Y but not on X. If no marginal frequency is 0, tau-b can attain $+1$ or -1 only for a square table.

A measure that can attain, or nearly attain, $+1$ or -1 for any $r \times c$ table is tau-c:

$$\tau_c = \frac{2m(P - Q)}{N^2(m - 1)}$$ Equation 10.16b

where m is the smaller of the number of rows and columns. The coefficients tau-b and tau-c do not differ much in value if each margin contains approximately equal frequencies.

Goodman and Kruskal's *gamma* is closely related to the tau statistics and is calculated as

$$G = \frac{P - Q}{P + Q}$$ Equation 10.16c

Gamma can be thought of as the probability that a random pair of observations is concordant minus the probability that the pair is discordant, assuming the absence of ties. The absolute value of gamma is the proportional reduction in error between guessing concordant and discordant ranking of each pair depending on which occurs more often and guessing ranking according to the outcome of the toss of a fair coin. Gamma is 1 if all observations are concentrated in the upper-left to lower-right diagonal of the table. In the case of independence, gamma is 0. However, the converse (that a gamma of 0 necessarily implies independence) need not be true except in the 2×2 table.

In the computation of gamma, no distinction is made between the independent and dependent variable; the variables are treated symmetrically. Somers (1962) proposed an asymmetric extension of gamma that differs only in the inclusion of the number of pairs not tied on the independent variable (X) in the denominator. Somers' d is

$$d_Y = \frac{P - Q}{P + Q + T_Y}$$ Equation 10.16d

The coefficient d_Y indicates the proportionate excess of concordant pairs over discordant pairs among pairs not tied on the independent variable. The symmetric variant of Somers' d uses for the denominator the average value of the denominators of the two asymmetric coefficients.

These ordinal measures for the migraine data are shown in Figure 10.16. All of the measures indicate that there is a fairly strong linear association between the two variables.

Figure 10.16 Ordinal measures

```
CROSSTABS TABLES=HYPNOSIS BY MIGRAINE
  /FORMAT=NOTABLE
  /STATISTICS=CORR BTAU CTAU GAMMA D.
```

```
HYPNOSIS  DEPTH OF HYPNOSIS  by  MIGRAINE  OUTCOME

Number of valid observations = 100


                                                            Approximate
         Statistic                Value     ASE1    T-value  Significance
    ----------------------        ------    ------  -------  ------------


 Kendall's Tau-b                  .67901    .04445  11.96486
 Kendall's Tau-c                  .63360    .05296  11.96486
 Gamma                            .94034    .02720  11.96486
 Somers' D :
    symmetric                     .67866    .04443  11.96485
    with HYPNOSIS dependent       .65774    .05440  11.96485
    with MIGRAINE dependent       .70096    .03996  11.96486


 Pearson's R                      .71739    .04484  10.19392    .00000
 Spearman Correlation             .72442    .04317  10.40311    .00000



 Number of Missing Observations:  0
```

10.17
Measures Involving Interval Data

If the two variables in the table are measured on an interval scale, various coefficients that make use of this additional information can be calculated. A useful symmetric coefficient that measures the strength of the *linear* relationship is the Pearson correlation coefficient, or *r*. It can take on values from -1 to $+1$, indicating negative or positive linear correlation.

The *eta* coefficient is appropriate for data in which the dependent variable is measured on an interval scale and the independent variable on a nominal or ordinal scale. When squared, eta can be interpreted as the proportion of the total variability in the dependent variable that can be accounted for by knowing the values of the independent variable. The measure is asymmetric and does not assume a linear relationship between the variables.

10.18
Estimating Risk in Cohort Studies

Often you want to identify variables that are related to the occurrence of a particular event. For example, you may want to determine if smoking is related to heart disease. A commonly used index that measures the strength of the association between presence of a factor and occurence of an event is the *relative risk ratio*. It is estimated as the ratio of two incidence rates, for example, the incidence rate of heart disease in those who smoke and the incidence rate of heart disease in those who do not smoke.

For example, suppose you observe for five years 1000 smokers without a history of heart disease and 1000 nonsmokers without a history of heart disease, and you determine how many of each group develop heart disease during this time period. (Studies in which a group of disease-free people are studied to see who develops the disease are called *cohort* or *prospective* studies.) Figure 10.18 contains hypothetical results from such a cohort study.

Statistics Guide

Figure 10.18 Hypothetical cohorts

```
CROSSTABS TABLES=SMOKING BY HDISEASE
   /STATISTICS=RISK.
```

```
SMOKING  Smoking  by  HDISEASE  Heart Disease

                 HDISEASE         Page 1 of 1
          Count
                 Yes      No
                                    Row
                   1.00|    2.00| Total
SMOKING   -------+------+------+
            1.00 |  100 |  900 |  1000
 Yes             |      |      |  50.0
          -------+------+------+
            2.00 |   50 |  950 |  1000
 No              |      |      |  50.0
          -------+------+------+
          Column    150   1850    2000
          Total     7.5   92.5   100.0




     Statistic               Value        95% Confidence Bounds
-----------------------------------------------------------------
Relative Risk Estimate (SMOKING 1.0 / SMOKING 2.0) :
   case control             2.11111        1.48544      3.00032
   cohort (HDISEASE 1.0 Risk)  2.00000     1.44078      2.77628
   cohort (HDISEASE 2.0 Risk)   .94737      .92390       .97143

Number of Missing Observations:  0
```

The five-year incidence rate for smokers is 100/1000, while the incidence rate for nonsmokers is 50/1000. The relative risk ratio is 2 (100/1000 divided by 50/1000). This indicates that, in the sample, smokers are twice as likely to develop heart disease as nonsmokers.

The estimated relative risk and its 95% confidence interval are in the row labeled **cohort (HDISEASE 1.0 Risk)** in Figure 10.18. In CROSSTABS, the ratio is always computed by taking the incidence in the first row and dividing it by the incidence in the second row. Since either column can represent the event, separate estimates are displayed for each column. The 95% confidence intervals do not include the value of 1, so you can reject the null hypothesis that the two incidence rates are the same.

10.19
Estimating Risk in Case-Control Studies

In the cohort study described above, we took a group of disease-free people (the cohort) and watched what happened to them. Another type of study that is commonly used is called a retrospective, or *case-control*, study. In this type of study, we take a group of people with the disease of interest (the cases) and a comparable group of people without the disease (the controls) and see how they differ. For example, we could take 100 people with documented coronary heart disease and 100 controls without heart disease and establish how many in each group smoked. The hypothetical results are shown in Figure 10.19.

Figure 10.19   Hypothetical Smoking Control

```
CROSSTABS TABLES=GROUP BY SMOKING
    /CELLS=COUNT ROW
    /STATISTICS=RISK.
```

```
GROUP  by  SMOKING

                        SMOKING         Page 1 of 1
                 Count
                 Row Pct  Yes      No
                                                 Row
                          1.00|    2.00| Total
        GROUP    ---------+--------+--------+
                    1.00|     30|     70|    100
        Cases            |   30.0|   70.0|   50.0
                         +--------+--------+
                    2.00|     10|     90|    100
        Controls         |   10.0|   90.0|   50.0
                         +--------+--------+
                 Column      40     160     200
                 Total     20.0    80.0   100.0



        Statistic                    Value        95% Confidence Bounds
    -----------------------------    -------      ---------------------
    Relative Risk Estimate (GROUP 1.0 / GROUP 2.0) :
        case control                 3.85714       1.76660     8.42156
        cohort (SMOKING 1.0 Risk)    3.00000       1.55083     5.80334
        cohort (SMOKING 2.0 Risk)     .77778        .67348      .89823

    Number of Missing Observations:  0
```

From a case-control study we cannot estimate incidence rates. Thus, we cannot compute the relative risk ratio. Instead, we estimate relative risk using what is called an *odds ratio.* We compute the odds that a "case" smokes and divide it by the odds that a control smokes.

For example, from Figure 10.19, the odds that a case smokes are 30/70. The odds that a control smokes are 10/90. The odds ratio is then 30/70 divided by 10/90, or 3.85. The odds ratio and its confidence interval are in the row labeled **case control** in Figure 10.19. The CROSSTABS procedure expects the cases to be in the first row and the controls in the second. Similarly, the event of interest must be in the first column. For further discussion of measures of risk, see Kleinbaum et al. (1982).

10.20
RUNNING PROCEDURE CROSSTABS

Procedure CROSSTABS produces two-way to *n*-way crosstabulations and related statistical measures for variables with numeric or string values. In addition to cell counts, you can obtain cell percentages and expected values. You can alter the handling of missing values, reorder rows, request an index of tables, and write cell frequencies to a file.

10.21
TABLES Subcommand

The only required subcommand for CROSSTABS is the TABLES subcommand. The minimum specification for the TABLES subcommand is a list of one or more variables followed by the keyword BY and a second list of one or more variables, as in:

```
CROSSTABS TABLES=RETURNED BY ADDRESS.
```

The first variable list specifies the *row variables*, and the variable list following the first BY keyword specifies the *column variables*.

Optionally, you can specify *control variables* with additional BY keywords and variable lists, as in:

```
CROSSTABS TABLES=RETURNED BY ADDRESS BY LOCATION.
```

A separate subtable is generated for each value of the control variable(s). In this example, the control variable LOCATION has two values, producing two subtables (as in Figure 10.4).

You can specify more than one variable in each dimension. Use the TO keyword to imply consecutive variables on the active system file, as in:

```
CROSSTABS  TABLES=CONFINAN TO CONARMY BY SEX TO REGION.
```

This command will produce CROSSTABS tables for all the variables between and including CONFINAN and CONARMY by all the variables between and including SEX and REGION.

You can specify multiple TABLES subcommands. Each subcommand should be separated by a slash.

10.22
VARIABLES Subcommand

To run CROSSTABS in *integer mode*, use the VARIABLES subcommand. Integer mode requires more memory than general mode if the table has many empty cells, but less if the data values fall within narrow ranges. You must specify an integer value range enclosed in parentheses for each variable, as in:

```
CROSSTABS VARIABLES=RETURNED(1,2) ADDRESS(1,3)
  /TABLES=RETURNED BY ADDRESS.
```

Since only values within the specified range will be included, you can use the VARIABLES subcommand to select subsets of cases for analysis. If multiple variables have the same range, you need to specify the range only once, as in:

```
CROSSTABS VARIABLES=ADDRESS(1,3) RETURNED LOCATION(1,2)
  /TABLES=RETURNED BY ADDRESS BY LOCATION.
```

which specifies the same range for variables RETURNED and LOCATION.

If used, the VARIABLES subcommand must be the first subcommand specified, and it must include all variables specified on subsequent TABLES subcommands. The TO keyword on subsequent TABLES subcommands refers to the order of variables on the VARIABLES subcommand, not the order of variables on the active system file.

10.23
CELLS Subcommand

By default, CROSSTABS displays only the number of cases in each cell. Use the CELLS subcommand to display row, column, or total percentages, expected values, and residuals. These items are calculated separately for each bivariate table or subtable.

You can specify the CELLS subcommand by itself, or with one or more keywords. If you specify the CELLS subcommand by itself, CROSSTABS displays cell counts plus row, column, and total percentages for each cell. If you specify keywords, CROSSTABS displays only the cell information you request.

The following keywords can be specified on the CELLS subcommand:

COUNT   *Cell counts.* This is the default if you omit the CELLS subcommand.

ROW   *Row percentages.* Row percentages are the number of cases in each cell in a row expressed as a percentage of all cases in that row.

COLUMN   *Column percentages.* Column percentages are the number of cases in each cell in a column expressed as a percentage of all cases in that column.

TOTAL   *Two-way table total percentages.* This is the number of cases in each cell of a subtable expressed as a percentage of all cases in that subtable.

EXPECTED   *Expected frequencies.* Expected frequencies are the number of cases expected in each cell if the two variables in the subtable were statistically independent.

RESID   *Residuals.* The residual is the value of the observed cell count minus the expected value.

SRESID   *Standardized residuals.* (Haberman, 1978.)

ASRESID   *Adjusted standardized residuals.* (Haberman, 1978.)

ALL   *All cell information.* This includes cell counts, row, column, and total percentages, expected values, residuals, standardized residuals, and adjusted standardized residuals.

NONE   *No cell information.* Use NONE to write tables to a file without displaying any tables. This has the same effect as specifying FORMAT=NOTABLES (see Section 10.26).

For example, the command

```
CROSSTABS TABLES=RETURNED BY ADDRESS
  /CELLS.
```

produces Figure 10.1, and the command

```
CROSSTABS TABLES=RETURNED BY ADDRESS
  /CELLS=COUNT EXPECTED RESID.
  /STATISTICS=CHISQ.
```

produces Figure 10.8.

10.24
STATISTICS Subcommand

CROSSTABS can calculate a number of summary statistics for each subtable. Unless you specify otherwise, it calculates statistical measures of association for the cases with valid values included in the subtable. If you include user-missing values with the MISSING subcommand, cases with user-missing values are included in the tables as well as in the calculation of statistics.

The STATISTICS subcommand requests summary statistics. You can specify the STATISTICS subcommand by itself, or with one or more keywords. If you specify STATISTICS by itself, CROSSTABS calculates CHISQ. If you include a keyword or keywords on the STATISTICS subcommand, CROSSTABS calculates all the statistics you request.

Asymptotic standard errors (ASE1) that are not based on the assumption that the true value is 0 are also calculated. The t statistics displayed are the ratio of the measure to an asymptotic standard error which assumes the true coefficient is 0.

The following keywords can be specified on the STATISTICS subcommand:

CHISQ   *Chi-square.* The output includes the Pearson chi-square, likelihood-ratio chi-square, and Mantel-Haenszel linear association chi-square. For 2×2 tables, Fisher's exact test is computed when a table that does not result from missing rows or columns in a larger table has a cell with an expected frequency less than 5; Yates' corrected chi-square is computed for all other 2×2 tables. This is the default if STATISTICS is specified without keywords.

PHI   *Phi and Cramer's* V.

CC   *Contingency coefficient.*

LAMBDA   *Lambda, symmetric and asymmetric, and Goodman and Kruskal's tau.*

UC   *Uncertainty coefficient, symmetric and asymmetric.*

BTAU   *Kendall's tau*-b.

CTAU   *Kendall's tau*-c.

GAMMA   *Gamma.* Partial and zero-order gammas for 3-way to 8-way tables are available in integer mode only (see Section 10.22). Zero-order gammas are displayed for 2-way tables and conditional gammas are displayed for 3-way to 10-way tables in general mode.

D   *Somers' d, symmetric and asymmetric.*

ETA   *Eta.* Available for numeric data only.

CORR   *Pearson's* r, *and Spearman's correlation coefficient.* Available for numeric data only.

KAPPA   *Kappa coefficient.* Kappa can only be computed for square tables in which the row and column values are identical. If there is a missing row or column, use integer mode to specify the square table, since a missing column or row in general mode would keep the table from being square (see Section 10.22). (Kraemer, 1982.)

RISK   *Relative risk.* Relative risk can be calculated only for 2×2 tables. (Kleinbaum et al., 1982).

ALL   *All available statistics.*

NONE   *No summary statistics.* This is the default if STATISTICS is omitted.

For example, the command

```
CROSSTABS TABLES=RETURNED BY ADDRESS
 /STATISTICS=PHI CC.
```

produces Figure 10.11.

10.25
MISSING Subcommand

By default, CROSSTABS deletes cases with missing values on a table-by-table basis. A case missing on any of the variables specified for a table is not used either in the table or in the calculation of the statistics. Missing values are handled separately for each TABLES subcommand. The number of missing cases is displayed at the end of the table, following the last subtable and after any requested statistics.

    The MISSING subcommand controls missing values. The following keywords can be specified on the MISSING subcommand:

TABLE   *Delete cases with missing values on a table-by-table basis.* This is the default if you omit the MISSING subcommand.

INCLUDE   *Include cases with user-missing values.*

REPORT   *Report missing values in the tables.* This option includes missing values in tables but not in the calculation of percentages or statistics. The letter **M** is used to indicate that cases within a cell are missing. REPORT is available only in integer mode (see Section 10.22).

10.26
FORMAT Subcommand

Use the FORMAT subcommand to modify the default formats. The following keywords can be specified:

LABELS   *Display both variable and value labels for each table.* This is the default. The values for the row variables are displayed in order from lowest to highest. CROSSTABS uses only the first 16 characters of the value labels. Value labels for the columns are displayed on two lines with eight characters per line.

NOLABELS   *Suppress variable and value labels.*

NOVALLABS   *Suppress value labels but display variable labels.*

AVALUE   *Display row variables ordered from lowest to highest.* This is the default.

DVALUE   *Display row variables ordered from highest to lowest.*

NOINDEX   *Suppress a table index.* This is the default.

INDEX   *Display an index of tables.* The index lists all tables produced by the CROSSTABS command and the page number where each table begins. The index follows the last page of tables produced by the tables list.

TABLES   *Display the crosstabulation tables.* This is the default.

NOTABLES   *Suppress table display.* If you use the STATISTICS subcommand (see Section 10.24) and specify NOTABLES, only the statistics are displayed. If you do not use the STATISTICS subcommand and specify NOTABLES, the CROSSTABS command produces no output.

BOX   *Use box-drawing characters around every cell.* This is the default.

NOBOX   *Suppress the box-drawing characters around each cell.* The banner and stub are still separated from the table by box-drawing characters.

10.27
WRITE Subcommand

The WRITE subcommand writes cell frequencies to the resulting file (specified on the SET RESULTS command), for subsequent use by SPSS/PC+ or some other program. The output file contains one record per cell.

NONE *Do not write the cell counts to the file.* This is the default if you omit the WRITE subcommand.

CELLS *Write the cell count for nonempty cells to a file.*

ALL *Write the cell count for all cells to a file.* This is only available in integer mode. (See the VARIABLES subcommand, Section 10.22.)

For more information about the WRITE subcommand, see Command Reference: CROSSTABS.

10.28
Entering Crosstabulated Data

You can use the CROSSTABS procedure to calculate statistics for a pre-existing crosstabulation without entering the individual case data. Each cell of the table is considered a case. The variables for each case are the cell count and the values of the row, column, and control variables.

Define this file as you would any other file. Then use the WEIGHT command to count each case as many times as the value of the cell count variable. For example, Figure 10.18 was produced from a table, rather than raw data, using the following commands:

```
DATA LIST FREE /SMOKING HDISEASE COUNT.
BEGIN DATA.
1 1 100
1 2 900
2 1 50
2 2 950
END DATA.
VARIABLE LABELS
    SMOKING 'Smoking'
    HDISEASE 'Heart Disease'.
VALUE LABELS SMOKING HDISEASE 1 'Yes' 2 'No'.
WEIGHT BY COUNT.
CROSSTABS TABLES=SMOKING by HDISEASE
    /STATISTICS=RISK.
```

- The DATA LIST command names three variables: SMOKING is the row variable, HDISEASE is the column variable, and COUNT is the cell count.

- The optional VARIABLE LABELS and VALUE LABELS commands identify the variables and values in the tables.

- The WEIGHT command weights each case by the cell count.

- The CROSSTABS command recreates the table, and the STATISTICS subcommand provides summary statistics not provided with the original table.

Contents

11 Describing Subpopulation Differences: Procedure MEANS

The 1964 Civil Rights Act prohibits discrimination in the workplace based on sex or race. Employers who violate the act by unfair hiring or advancement practices can be prosecuted. Numerous lawsuits have been filed on behalf of women, blacks, and other groups offered equal protection under the law.

The courts have ruled that statistics can be used as *prima facie* evidence of discrimination, and many lawsuits depend heavily on complex statistical analyses, which attempt to demonstrate that similarly qualified individuals are not treated equally. Identifying and measuring all variables that legitimately influence promotion and hiring is difficult, if not impossible, especially for nonroutine jobs. Years of schooling and prior work experience can be quantified, but what about the more intangible attributes such as enthusiasm and creativity? How are they to be objectively measured so as not to become convenient smoke screens for concealing discrimination?

11.1
SEARCHING FOR DISCRIMINATION

In this chapter, employee records for 474 individuals hired between 1969 and 1971 by a bank engaged in Equal Employment Opportunity (EEO) litigation are analyzed. Two types of unfair employment practices are of particular interest: shunting (placing some employees in lower job categories than others with similar qualifications) and salary and promotion inequities.

Although extensive and intricate statistical analyses are usually involved in studies of this kind (see, for example, Roberts, 1980), the discussion here is necessarily limited. The SPSS/PC+ MEANS procedure is used to calculate average salaries for groups of employees based on race and sex. Additional grouping variables are introduced to help "explain" some of the observed variability in salary.

11.2
Who Does What?

Figure 11.2 is a crosstabulation of job category at the time of hiring with sex and race characteristics. The first three job classifications contain 64% of white males (adding column percentages), 94% of both nonwhite males and white females, and 100% of nonwhite females. Among white males, 17% are in the college trainee program, compared to 4% of white females.

Although these observations are interesting, they do not imply discriminatory placement into beginning job categories because the qualifications of the various groups are not necessarily similar. If women and nonwhites are more qualified than white males in the same beginning job categories, discrimination may be suspected.

Figure 11.2   Crosstabulation of job category by sex-race

```
Crosstabulation:        JOBCAT      EMPLOYMENT CATEGORY
                     By SEXRACE

                  Count |WHITE    |MINORITY|WHITE    |MINORITY|
SEXRACE->         Col Pct|MALES    |MALES   |FEMALES  |FEMALES |
                  Tot Pct|     1.0 |    2.00|    3.00 |    4.00| Row
JOBCAT            -------+---------+--------+---------+--------+ Total
              1   |      75 |      35 |      85 |      32 |     227
    CLERICAL      |    38.7 |    54.7 |    48.3 |    80.0 |    47.9
                  |    15.8 |     7.4 |    17.9 |     6.8 |
                  +---------+--------+---------+--------+
              2   |      35 |      12 |      81 |       8 |     136
    OFFICE TRAINEE|    18.0 |    18.8 |    46.0 |    20.0 |    28.7
                  |     7.4 |     2.5 |    17.1 |     1.7 |
                  +---------+--------+---------+--------+
              3   |      14 |      13 |         |         |      27
    SECURITY OFFICER|   7.2 |    20.3 |         |         |     5.7
                  |     3.0 |     2.7 |         |         |
                  +---------+--------+---------+--------+
              4   |      33 |       1 |       7 |         |      41
    COLLEGE TRAINEE|   17.0 |     1.6 |     4.0 |         |     8.6
                  |     7.0 |      .2 |     1.5 |         |
                  +---------+--------+---------+--------+
              5   |      28 |       2 |       2 |         |      32
    EXEMPT EMPLOYEE|   14.4 |     3.1 |     1.1 |         |     6.8
                  |     5.9 |      .4 |      .4 |         |
                  +---------+--------+---------+--------+
              6   |       3 |       1 |       1 |         |       5
    MBA TRAINEE   |     1.5 |     1.6 |      .6 |         |     1.1
                  |      .6 |      .2 |      .2 |         |
                  +---------+--------+---------+--------+
              7   |       6 |         |         |         |       6
    TECHNICAL     |     3.1 |         |         |         |     1.3
                  |     1.3 |         |         |         |
                  +---------+--------+---------+--------+
          Column       194       64      176       40         474
          Total       40.9     13.5     37.1      8.4       100.0

Number of Missing Observations =          0
```

11.3
Level of Education

One easily measured employment qualification is years of education. Figure 11.3a shows the average years of education for the entire sample (labeled **For Entire Population**), for each of the two sexes (labeled **SEX** and **MALES** or **FEMALES**), and for each of the two race categories within each sex category (labeled **MINORITY** and **WHITE** or **NONWHITE**).

Figure 11.3a   Education broken down by race within sex

```
Summaries of    EDLEVEL     EDUCATIONAL LEVEL
By levels of    SEX         SEX OF EMPLOYEE
                MINORITY    MINORITY CLASSIFICATIONS


Variable        Value Label                 Sum       Mean    Std Dev   Variance   Cases

For Entire Population                  6395.0000    13.4916    2.8848    8.3223     474

SEX             0     MALES            3723.0000    14.4302    2.9793    8.8764     258
  MINORITY      0     WHITE            2895.0000    14.9227    2.8484    8.1132     194
  MINORITY      1     NONWHITE          828.0000    12.9375    2.8888    8.3452      64

SEX             1     FEMALES          2672.0000    12.3704    2.3192    5.3785     216
  MINORITY      0     WHITE            2172.0000    12.3409    2.4066    5.7917     176
  MINORITY      1     NONWHITE          500.0000    12.5000    1.9081    3.6410      40

  Total Cases =      474
```

The entire sample has an average of 13.49 years of education. Males have more years of education than females—an average of 14.43 years compared to 12.37. White males have the highest average level of education, almost 15 years, which is 2 years more than nonwhite males and approximately 2.5 years more than either group of females.

Figure 11.3b   Education by sex-race and job category

```
Summaries of    EDLEVEL      EDUCATIONAL LEVEL
By levels of    JOBCAT       EMPLOYMENT CATEGORY
                SEXRACE


Variable        Value  Label                    Mean    Std Dev   Cases

For Entire Population                          13.4916   2.8848    474

JOBCAT             1   CLERICAL                12.7753   2.5621    227
  SEXRACE       1.00   WHITE     MALES         13.8667   2.3035     75
  SEXRACE       2.00   MINORITYMALES           13.7714   2.3147     35
  SEXRACE       3.00   WHITE     FEMALES       11.4588   2.4327     85
  SEXRACE       4.00   MINORITYFEMALES         12.6250   2.1213     32

JOBCAT             2   OFFICE TRAINEE          13.0221   1.8875    136
  SEXRACE       1.00   WHITE     MALES         13.8857   1.4095     35
  SEXRACE       2.00   MINORITYMALES           12.5833   2.6097     12
  SEXRACE       3.00   WHITE     FEMALES       12.8148   1.9307     81
  SEXRACE       4.00   MINORITYFEMALES         12.0000   0.0        8

JOBCAT             3   SECURITY OFFICER        10.1852   2.2194     27
  SEXRACE       1.00   WHITE     MALES         10.2857   2.0542     14
  SEXRACE       2.00   MINORITYMALES           10.0769   2.4651     13

JOBCAT             4   COLLEGE TRAINEE         17.0000   1.2845     41
  SEXRACE       1.00   WHITE     MALES         17.2121   1.3407     33
  SEXRACE       2.00   MINORITYMALES           17.0000   0.0        1
  SEXRACE       3.00   WHITE     FEMALES       16.0000   0.0        7

JOBCAT             5   EXEMPT EMPLOYEE         17.2813   1.9713     32
  SEXRACE       1.00   WHITE     MALES         17.6071   1.7709     28
  SEXRACE       2.00   MINORITYMALES           14.0000   2.8284      2
  SEXRACE       3.00   WHITE     FEMALES       16.0000   0.0        2

JOBCAT             6   MBA TRAINEE             18.0000   1.4142      5
  SEXRACE       1.00   WHITE     MALES         18.3333   1.1547      3
  SEXRACE       2.00   MINORITYMALES           19.0000   0.0        1
  SEXRACE       3.00   WHITE     FEMALES       16.0000   0.0        1

JOBCAT             7   TECHNICAL               18.1667   1.4720      6
  SEXRACE       1.00   WHITE     MALES         18.1667   1.4720      6

 Total Cases =    474
```

In Figure 11.3b, the cases are further subdivided by their combined sex-race characteristics and by their initial job category. For each cell in the table, the average years of education, the standard deviation, and number of cases are displayed. White males have the highest average years of education in all job categories except MBA trainees, where the only nonwhite male MBA trainee has nineteen years of education. From this table, it does not appear that females and nonwhites are overeducated when compared to white males in similar job categories. However, it is important to note that group means provide information about a particular class of employees. While discrimination may not exist for a class as a whole, some individuals within that class may be victims (or beneficiaries) of discrimination.

11.4
Beginning Salaries

The average beginning salary for the 474 persons hired between 1969 and 1971 is $6,806. The distribution by the four sex-race categories is shown in Figure 11.4a.

Figure 11.4a   Beginning salary by sex-race

```
Summaries of   SALBEG     BEGINNING SALARY
By levels of   SEXRACE

Variable       Value  Label              Sum         Mean     Std Dev    Variance      Cases

For Entire Population                  3226250.00  6806.4346  3148.2553  9911511.19     474

SEXRACE       1.00   WHITE    MALES    1675680.00  8637.5258  3871.1017  14985428.4     194
SEXRACE       2.00   MINORITYMALES      419424.000  6553.5000  2228.1436  4964624.00      64
SEXRACE       3.00   WHITE    FEMALES   939926.000  5340.4886  1225.9605  1502979.07     176
SEXRACE       4.00   MINORITYFEMALES    191220.000  4780.5000   771.4188   595086.923      40

 Total Cases =    474
```

White males have the highest beginning salaries—an average of $8,638—followed by nonwhite males. Since males are in higher job categories than females, this difference is not surprising.

Figure 11.4b Beginning salary by sex-race and job category

```
Summaries of    SALBEG       BEGINNING SALARY
By levels of    JOBCAT       EMPLOYMENT CATEGORY
                SEXRACE


Variable        Value  Label                        Mean

For Entire Population                             6806.4346

JOBCAT            1    CLERICAL                    5733.9471
  SEXRACE      1.00    WHITE    MALES              6553.4400
  SEXRACE      2.00    MINORITYMALES               6230.7429
  SEXRACE      3.00    WHITE    FEMALES            5147.3176
  SEXRACE      4.00    MINORITYFEMALES             4828.1250

JOBCAT            2    OFFICE TRAINEE              5478.9706
  SEXRACE      1.00    WHITE    MALES              6262.2857
  SEXRACE      2.00    MINORITYMALES               5610.0000
  SEXRACE      3.00    WHITE    FEMALES            5208.8889
  SEXRACE      4.00    MINORITYFEMALES             4590.0000

JOBCAT            3    SECURITY OFFICER            6031.1111
  SEXRACE      1.00    WHITE    MALES              6102.8571
  SEXRACE      2.00    MINORITYMALES               5953.8462

JOBCAT            4    COLLEGE TRAINEE             9956.4878
  SEXRACE      1.00    WHITE    MALES             10467.6364
  SEXRACE      2.00    MINORITYMALES              11496.0000
  SEXRACE      3.00    WHITE    FEMALES            7326.8571

JOBCAT            5    EXEMPT EMPLOYEE            13258.8750
  SEXRACE      1.00    WHITE    MALES             13255.2857
  SEXRACE      2.00    MINORITYMALES              15570.0000
  SEXRACE      3.00    WHITE    FEMALES           10998.0000

JOBCAT            6    MBA TRAINEE               12837.6000
  SEXRACE      1.00    WHITE    MALES             14332.0000
  SEXRACE      2.00    MINORITYMALES              13992.0000
  SEXRACE      3.00    WHITE    FEMALES            7200.0000

JOBCAT            7    TECHNICAL                 19996.0000
  SEXRACE      1.00    WHITE    MALES             19996.0000

  Total Cases =    474
```

Figure 11.4b shows beginning salaries subdivided by race, sex, and job category. For most of the job categories, white males have higher beginning salaries than the other groups. There is a $1,400 salary difference between white males and white females in the clerical jobs and a $1,000 difference in the general office trainee classification. In the college trainee program, white males averaged over $3,000 more than white females. However, Figure 11.3b shows that white females in the college trainee program had only an undergraduate degree, while white males had an average of 17.2 years of schooling.

11.5
Introducing More Variables

The differences in mean beginning salaries between males and females are somewhat suspect. It is, however, unwise to conclude that salary discrimination exists, since several important variables, such as years of prior experience, have not been considered. It is necessary to control (or to adjust statistically) for other relevant variables. Using procedure MEANS to crossclassify cases by the variables of interest and compare salaries across the subgroups is one way of achieving control. However, as the number of variables increases, the number of cases in each cell rapidly diminishes, making statistically meaningful comparisons difficult. To circumvent these problems, regression methods, which achieve control by specifying certain statistical relations that may describe what is happening, are used. Regression methods are described in *SPSS/PC+ Statistics.*

11.6
RUNNING PROCEDURE MEANS

MEANS calculates the means, sums, standard deviations, and variances of a variable for subgroups defined by other variables (the independent variables). Optional specifications on MEANS provide one-way analysis of variance and a test of linearity. MEANS operates via the TABLES, OPTIONS, and STATISTICS subcommands.

11.7
Specifying the Tables

The minimum specification required by the MEANS procedure is the TABLES subcommand with a single tables list. The tables list must specify at least one dependent variable, the keyword BY, and at least one independent variable, as in the command

```
MEANS TABLES=SALBEG BY SEXRACE.
```

used to produce the output in Figure 11.4a.

The actual keyword TABLES can be omitted. For example, the output in Figure 11.4a could also have been obtained with the command:

```
MEANS SALBEG BY SEXRACE.
```

Although the dependent variable must be numeric, independent variables can be numeric or string. Long strings are truncated to short strings to define categories. More than one dependent variable and independent variable can be specified, and the TO keyword can be used to name a set of adjacent variables in the active file, as in the command:

```
MEANS RAISE80 TO RAISE83 BY DEPT TO AGE.
```

This command produces MEANS tables for all variables between (and including) RAISE80 and RAISE83 in the file, broken down first by DEPT, then by each of the variables between DEPT and AGE in the file, and finally by AGE.

When several BY keywords are used in the tables list, the variable after the last BY changes most quickly. (This is the opposite of the CROSSTABS format, in which the last variable changes most slowly.) For example, the command

```
MEANS TABLES=SALBEG BY JOBCAT BY SEXRACE.
```

produces the table shown in Figure 11.4b, which shows beginning salary (SALBEG) for value 1 of JOBCAT broken down by each of the four values of SEXRACE. Then beginning salary for value 2 of JOBCAT is shown, again broken down by the four values of SEXRACE, and so forth.

When you specify multiple variables in a dimension of a table, they will be processed from left to right. For example, the command

```
MEANS RAISE82 RAISE83 BY DEPT AGE BY SEX RACE.
```

produces eight tables. The first is RAISE82 by DEPT by SEX, the second is RAISE82 by DEPT by RACE, the third is RAISE82 by AGE by SEX, and so on. The last table is RAISE83 by AGE by RACE.

More than one tables list can be specified on a single MEANS command if they are separated by a slash. For example, the command

```
MEANS TABLES=RAISE81 BY SEX/EDLEVEL BY RACE.
```

requests two tables, RAISE81 by SEX and EDLEVEL by RACE.

11.8
Optional Statistics

By default, procedure MEANS displays means, standard deviations, and the number of cases for subgroups. You can modify the display by specifying the following options on the OPTIONS subcommand:

Option 5 *Suppress group counts.* The number of cases in each group is not displayed.
Option 6 *Display group sums.*
Option 7 *Suppress group standard deviations.*
Option 11 *Suppress group means.*
Option 12 *Display group variances.*

You can also obtain a one-way analysis of variance and a test of linearity by specifying the following on the STATISTICS subcommand:

Statistic 1 *One-way analysis of variance including eta and eta^2.*

Statistic 2 *Test of linearity.* Includes the sums of squares, mean squares, and degrees of freedom associated with the linear and nonlinear components, as well as the F ratio, Pearson's r, and Pearson's r^2. The linearity test is not calculated if the grouping variable is a string variable.

ALL *Display all statistics.* Produces the same display as Statistic 2.

If a two-way or higher-order breakdown is specified, the second and subsequent grouping variables are ignored in the analysis of variance table. For example, the command

```
MEANS SALBEG BY JOBCAT BY SEXRACE
   /STATISTICS=1.
```

produces a breakdown of SALBEG by JOBCAT within SEXRACE, but an analysis of variance is calculated only for the SALBEG by JOBCAT table. Two-way and higher-order analyses of variance can be obtained by using the ANOVA procedure, and a more complete one-way analysis of variance can be obtained by using the ONEWAY procedure (for a detailed discussion of both procedures, see *SPSS/PC+ Statistics*).

11.9
Missing Values

By default, MEANS deletes cases with missing values on a table-by-table basis: a case with missing values for any of the variables specified for a table is not used in building that table.

You can specify two alternative missing-value treatments on the OPTIONS subcommand:

Option 1 *Include cases with user-missing values.* Cases with user-missing values are included in all tables and statistics.

Option 2 *Exclude cases with user-missing dependent values.* Any case with missing values for the independent variables but with a valid value for the dependent variable is included in the analysis.

11.10
Formatting Options

By default, MEANS displays variable names and variable labels at the beginning of each table. Within the table, groups defined by the independent variables are identified by variable name, values, and value labels. Use the OPTIONS subcommand to change these defaults.

Option 3 *Suppress all labels.* No variable or value labels are displayed.

Option 8 *Suppress value labels.* No value labels are displayed for independent variables.

Option 9 *Suppress independent variable names.*

Option 10 *Suppress independent variable values.*

11.11

Example

The following SPSS/PC+ commands were used to obtain the output in Figure 11.4a:

```
DATA LIST / MINORITY 8 SEX 16 JOBCAT 24 EDLEVEL 31-32 SALBEG 36-40.
VARIABLE LABELS MINORITY 'MINORITY CLASSIFICATIONS'
                /SEX 'SEX OF EMPLOYEE'
                /JOBCAT 'EMPLOYMENT CATEGORY'
                /EDLEVEL 'EDUCATIONAL LEVEL'
                /SALBEG 'BEGINNING SALARY'.
VALUE LABELS MINORITY 0 'WHITE' 1 'NONWHITE'
                /SEX 0 'MALES' 1 'FEMALES'
                /JOBCAT 1 'CLERICAL' 2 'OFFICE TRAINEE' 3 'SECURITY OFFICER'
                    4 'COLLEGE TRAINEE' 5 'EXEMPT EMPLOYEE'
                    6 'MBA TRAINEE' 7 'TECHNICAL'.

COMPUTE SEXRACE=1.
IF              (MINORITY EQ 1 AND SEX EQ 0) SEXRACE=2.
IF              (MINORITY EQ 0 AND SEX EQ 1) SEXRACE=3.
IF              (MINORITY EQ 1 AND SEX EQ 1) SEXRACE=4.
VALUE LABELS    SEXRACE 1 'WHITE    MALES' 2 'MINORITYMALES'
                3 'WHITE   FEMALES' 4 'MINORITYFEMALES'.
BEGIN DATA.
data records
END DATA.
MEANS TABLES=SALBEG BY SEXRACE
  /OPTIONS=6,12.
FINISH.
```

- The DATA LIST command gives the variable names and column locations for the variables used in the analysis.
- The VARIABLE LABELS and VALUE LABELS commands give descriptive labels to the variables and the values.
- The COMPUTE command and the three IF commands create a new variable, SEXRACE, that combines the sex and race variables already in the file. COMPUTE sets the initial value of SEXRACE to 1; this will be the white-male category. The IF commands then specify the value 2 for nonwhite males, the value 3 for white females, and the value 4 for nonwhite females.
- The VALUE LABELS command defines labels for the values of the new SEXRACE variable. These labels are formatted to avoid awkward breaks when displayed in the CROSSTABS table in Figure 11.2 (see Chapter 10).
- The MEANS command requests a table of SALBEG broken down by SEXRACE. Options 6 and 12 request the display of group sums and group variances.

Contents_____

12 Plotting Data: Procedure PLOT

Today the quest for the Fountain of Youth has been replaced by the Search for Slimness. It's almost acceptable to grow old, as long as one remains trim and fit. Programs for weight loss are gaining ever-increasing attention, and behavioral psychologists are studying the effectiveness of many different weight-loss strategies. Black and Sherba (1983) studied the effects of two different types of behavior programs on weight loss. One group of subjects was taught behavioral weight-loss techniques, while the second was taught weight-loss techniques and problem-solving behavior. Their data set is examined in this chapter.

12.1
DESCRIBING WEIGHT LOSS

As discussed in Chapter 7, a histogram is a convenient method for displaying the distribution of a variable that can have many values. Figure 12.1a shows the percentage of excess weight actually lost during the treatment for each of the twelve cases in the study. From this figure, we can see that about one third of the participants lost 20% or more of the required weight during treatment. To see if weight loss is maintained, consider Figure 12.1b, which shows the percentage of weight loss one year after treatment. It appears that subjects did not gain back the weight but maintained weight loss.

Figure 12.1a Histogram of weight loss during treatment

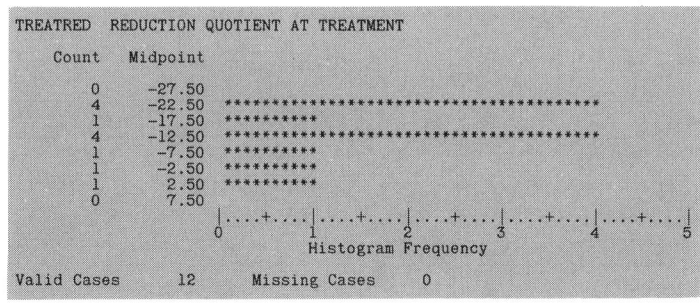

```
TREATRED   REDUCTION QUOTIENT AT TREATMENT

    Count    Midpoint
       0     -27.50
       4     -22.50   ****************************************
       1     -17.50   **********
       4     -12.50   ****************************************
       1      -7.50   **********
       1      -2.50   **********
       1       2.50   **********
       0       7.50
                      |....+....|....+....|....+....|....+....|....+....|
                      0         1         2         3         4         5
                                     Histogram Frequency

Valid Cases      12      Missing Cases      0
```

Figure 12.1b Histogram of weight loss after one year

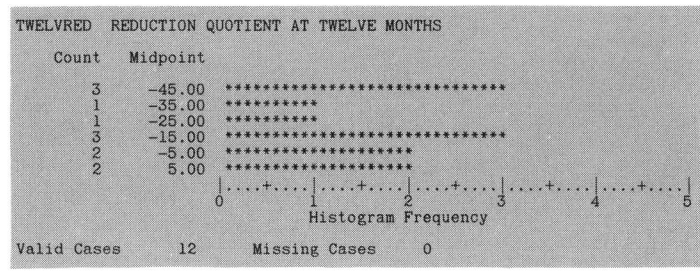

```
TWELVRED   REDUCTION QUOTIENT AT TWELVE MONTHS

    Count    Midpoint
       3     -45.00   ******************************
       1     -35.00   **********
       1     -25.00   **********
       3     -15.00   ******************************
       2      -5.00   ********************
       2       5.00   ********************
                      |....+....|....+....|....+....|....+....|....+....|
                      0         1         2         3         4         5
                                     Histogram Frequency

Valid Cases      12      Missing Cases      0
```

Although the histograms provide information about the weight loss during treatment and weight loss after twelve months, they reveal nothing about the relationship between the two variables since they each describe single variables. To determine whether lost weight during treatment is maintained or replaced at twelve months, the two variables must be studied together.

Figure 12.1c is a scatterplot of the percentage of weight loss during treatment and at one year for the twelve cases. Each symbol 1 on the plot represents one case, showing the values for that case on two variables—loss during treatment and loss at one year. For example, the circled point represents a case with a treatment loss of 25% and a twelve-month value of −18%.

Figure 12.1c   Scatterplot for weight loss during treatment and after one year

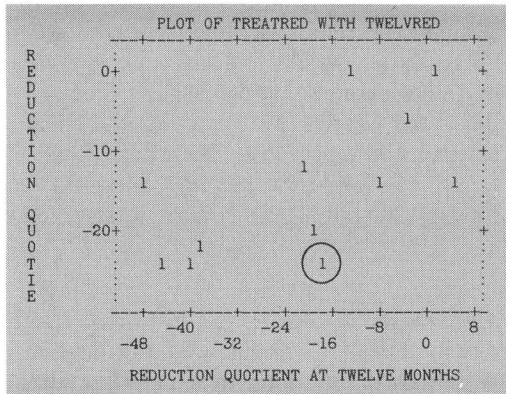

Since plots generated for terminals and printers have a limited number of positions in which to display points, it may not be possible to distinguish cases with similar values for the two variables. When two or more cases with similar values fall on the same point on the scatterplot, a number is displayed indicating how many cases overlap at that point. The scale of the plot depends on the minimum and maximum values for the two variables plotted. If the values for a few cases are far removed from the others, the majority of cases may appear bunched together in order to permit the outlying cases to appear on the same plot.

Figure 12.1d contains the symbols used to represent multiple cases at each point. For example, the symbol D is used when there are 13 coincident points.

Figure 12.1d   Scatterplot symbols for multiple cases

12.2
Controlled Scatterplots

Often it is informative to identify each point on a scatterplot by its value on a third variable. For example, cases may be designated as males or females, or as originating from the West, Midwest, or East. Figure 12.2 is the same plot as Figure 12.1c except each case is identified as being a participant in the behavior program (the value 1) or the problem-solving program (the value 2). A dollar sign is displayed if cases from different groups coincide.

Figure 12.2   Scatterplot identifying the two programs

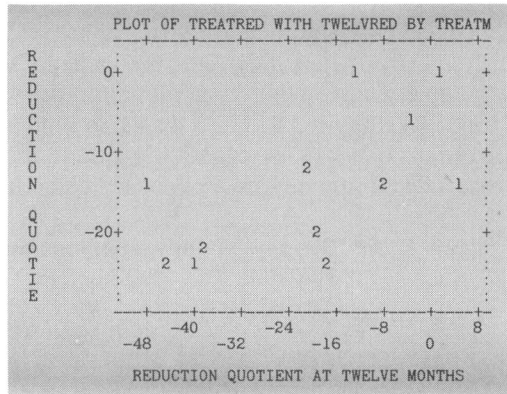

```
        PLOT OF TREATRED WITH TWELVRED BY TREATM
     --+----+----+----+----+----+----+----+----+--
  R   :                                           :
  E  0+                         1          1     +
  D   :                                           :
  U   :                              1            :
  C   :                                           :
  T -10+                                          +
  I   :                                           :
  O   :  1            2          2      1         :
  N   :                                           :
      :                                           :
  Q -20+              2                           +
  U   :       2                                   :
  O   :   2  1        2                           :
  T   :                                           :
  I   :                                           :
  E   --+----+----+----+----+----+----+----+----+--
          -40       -24        -8        8
       -48       -32       -16        0

          REDUCTION QUOTIENT AT TWELVE MONTHS
```

By examining Figure 12.2, one can see if the weight-loss-maintenance relationships are similar for the two groups.

12.3
Plotting Multiple Variables

Weight-loss maintenance may be associated with many variables, including age. Figure 12.3a is a plot of age with weight loss during treatment while Figure 12.3b is a plot of weight loss at twelve months with age. There appears to be a somewhat negative relationship between age and weight loss. Older people appear to have lost a greater percentage of weight than younger ones.

Figure 12.3a   Scatterplot of age with weight loss during treatment

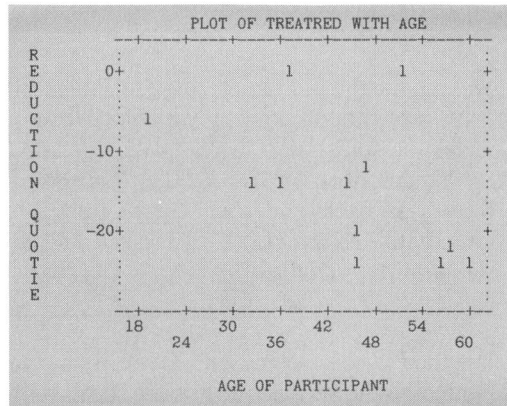

```
          PLOT OF TREATRED WITH AGE
     --+----+----+----+----+----+----+----+----+--
  R   :                                           :
  E  0+              1          1                 +
  D   :                                           :
  U   :   1                                       :
  C   :                                           :
  T -10+                              1           +
  I   :                                           :
  O   :            1   1       1                  :
  N   :                                           :
  Q -20+                       1                  +
  U   :                              1            :
  O   :                       1       1   1       :
  T   :                                           :
  I   :                                           :
  E   --+----+----+----+----+----+----+----+----+--
          18       30        42        54
             24        36        48        60

              AGE OF PARTICIPANT
```

Figure 12.3b   Scatterplot of age with weight loss at twelve months

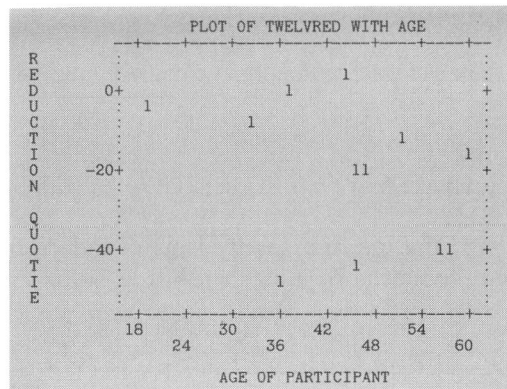

```
          PLOT OF TWELVRED WITH AGE
     --+----+----+----+----+----+----+----+----+--
  R   :                                           :
  E   :                      1                    :
  D  0+    1           1                          +
  U   :                                           :
  C   :                1                          :
  T   :                           1               :
  I   :                                    1      :
  O -20+                      11                  +
  N   :                                           :
  Q   :                                           :
  U   :                                           :
  O -40+                              11          +
  T   :                      1                    :
  I   :                                           :
  E   :            1                              :
      --+----+----+----+----+----+----+----+----+--
          18       30        42        54
             24        36        48        60

              AGE OF PARTICIPANT
```

Figures 12.3a and 12.3b can be combined into a single plot as shown in Figure 12.3c. Each case appears twice on Figure 12.3c: once with treatment weight loss (denoted as **1**) and once with twelve-month loss (denoted as **2**). When there are several cases with similar ages, one cannot tell which are the matching points. For example, at age 36 there are four points, since there are two cases with similar ages (one is 36, one is 35). The $ displayed represents multiple occurrences at a given location. However, we cannot tell if these are the two values for the same case or one value from one case and one from another.

Figure 12.3c   Overlay plot of weight loss during treatment and at twelve months

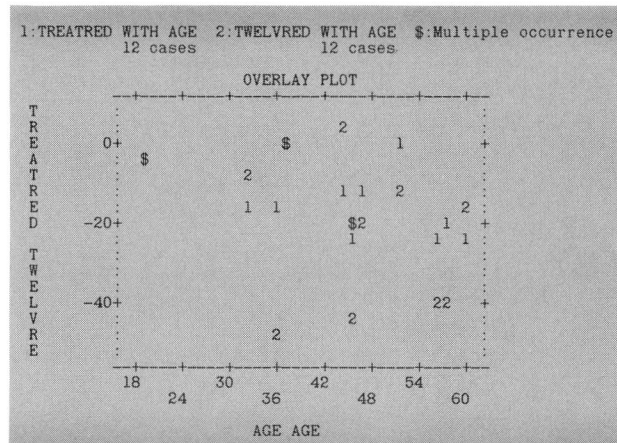

12.4
RUNNING
PROCEDURE PLOT

You can use the PLOT procedure to obtain bivariate scatterplots or regression plots (with or without control variables), contour plots, overlay plots, and some regression statistics. (For complete regression analysis, use procedure REGRESSION, described in *SPSS/PC+ Statistics*.) Formatting options enable you to control axis size and scale, the plotting symbols used, and the frequency they represent. You can also label the plot and axes, request reference lines, and plot standardized variables.

12.5
Specifying the Variables

Use the PLOT subcommand to specify the variables to be plotted. Variables to be plotted on the vertical (*Y*) axis are specified first, followed by the WITH keyword, followed by the variables to be plotted on the horizontal (*X*) axis.

By default, PLOT produces bivariate scatterplots. For example, the following command produces the output in Figure 12.1c:

```
PLOT PLOT=TREATRED WITH TWELVRED.
```

You can produce multiple plots with one PLOT subcommand. For example, the command

```
PLOT PLOT=IQ GRE WITH GPA SAT.
```

produces four plots: IQ with GPA, IQ with SAT, GRE with GPA, and GRE with SAT.

You can also specify plots of individual pairs of variables on one PLOT subcommand by using the PAIR keyword. For example, the command

```
PLOT PLOT=IQ GRE WITH GPA SAT (PAIR).
```

produces two plots: IQ with GPA and GRE with SAT.

Multiple plot lists can be specified on the PLOT subcommand if they are separated by semicolons, as in the command:

```
PLOT PLOT=IQ WITH GPA EDUC;GRE WITH SAT.
```

This produces three plots: IQ with GPA, IQ with EDUC, and GRE with SAT. You can also specify multiple PLOT subcommands on one PLOT command.

A control variable or contour variable (see Section 12.6) can be specified on the PLOT subcommand by naming it after the BY keyword following the list of horizontal-axis variables. For example, the command

```
PLOT PLOT=TREATRED WITH TWELVRED BY TREATMNT.
```

was used to obtain the plot in Figure 12.2. Only one control or contour variable can be specified on a plot list. PLOT uses the first character of a control variable's value label as a plotting symbol. For example, if SEX is the control variable, with value labels FEMALE and MALE, the observations for females are represented by F and those for males by M. If a variable has no value labels, the first character of the actual value is used as the plotting symbol. When cases with different values for the control variable fall in the same position on the plot, they are represented by a single $.

12.6
Choosing the Type of Plot

Use the FORMAT subcommand to specify the type of plot you want to produce. Four types of plots are available: scatterplots, regression plots, contour plots, and overlay plots. If FORMAT is not used, or is used without further specification, scatterplots are displayed. To specify plot type, use the following keywords on the FORMAT subcommand.

DEFAULT   *Bivariate scatterplot.* When there are no control variables, each symbol represents the case count at that plot position. When a control variable is specified, each symbol represents the first character of the value label of the control variable.

REGRESSION   *Scatterplot plus regression statistics.* The vertical-axis variable is regressed on the horizontal-axis variable, and the regression line intercepts on each axis are indicated with the letter R. In a control plot, regression statistics are pooled over all categories.

CONTOUR(n)   *Contour plot with* n *levels.* Contour plots use a continuous variable as the control variable. The control variable is specified after BY on the PLOT subcommand. The contour variable is recoded into *n* intervals of equal width. Up to 35 contour levels can be specified. If *n* is omitted, the default is 10 levels.

OVERLAY   *Overlay plots.* All plots specified on the next PLOT subcommand are displayed in one plot frame. A unique plotting symbol is used for each overlaid plot. An additional symbol indicates multiple plot points at the same position. Control plots cannot be overlaid.

For more information on these keywords, refer to Command Reference: PLOT.

Specify the FORMAT subcommand before the PLOT subcommand to which it refers. One FORMAT subcommand can be specified before each PLOT subcommand.

For example, the command

```
PLOT FORMAT=OVERLAY
  /PLOT=TREATRED TWELVRED WITH AGE.
```

produces the overlay plot in Figure 12.3c.

Overlay plots are useful when several variables represent the same type of measurement or when the same variable is measured at different times. For example, the command

```
PLOT  SYMBOLS='MD'
  /VSIZE=30 /HSIZE=70
  /FORMAT=OVERLAY
  /TITLE 'MARRIAGE AND DIVORCE RATES  1900-1981'
  /VERTICAL='RATES PER 1000 POPULATION'
  /HORIZONTAL='YEAR' REFERENCE (1918,1945) MIN (1900) MAX (1983)
  /PLOT=MARRATE DIVRATE WITH YEAR.
```

produces the overlay plot of marriage and divorce rates over time shown in Figure 12.6a (data taken from the *Information Please Almanac,* 1983).

Figure 12.6a An overlay plot

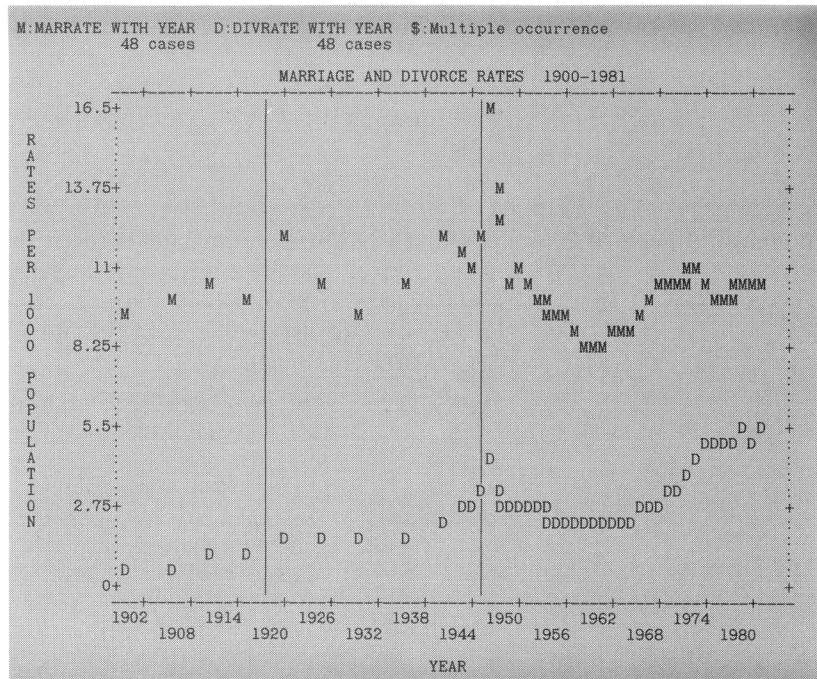

Contour plots evaluate the effect of a continuous variable as a control variable. If you use symbols with different degrees of density, you can produce a visual representation of the density of your contour variable. For example, the command

```
PLOT FORMAT=CONTOUR (10)
  /HSIZE=100/VSIZE=60
  /SYMBOLS='.-=*+OXOXM',' '      -OW'
  /TITLE='SOLUBILITY OF AMMONIA IN WATER'
  /HORIZONTAL='ATMOSPHERIC PRESSURE'
  /VERTICAL='TEMPERATURE'
  /PLOT=TEMP WITH PRESSURE BY CONCENT.
```

produces the output in Figure 12.6b, representing the concentration of ammonia in water under varying conditions of temperature and atmospheric pressure.

Figure 12.6b   A contour plot

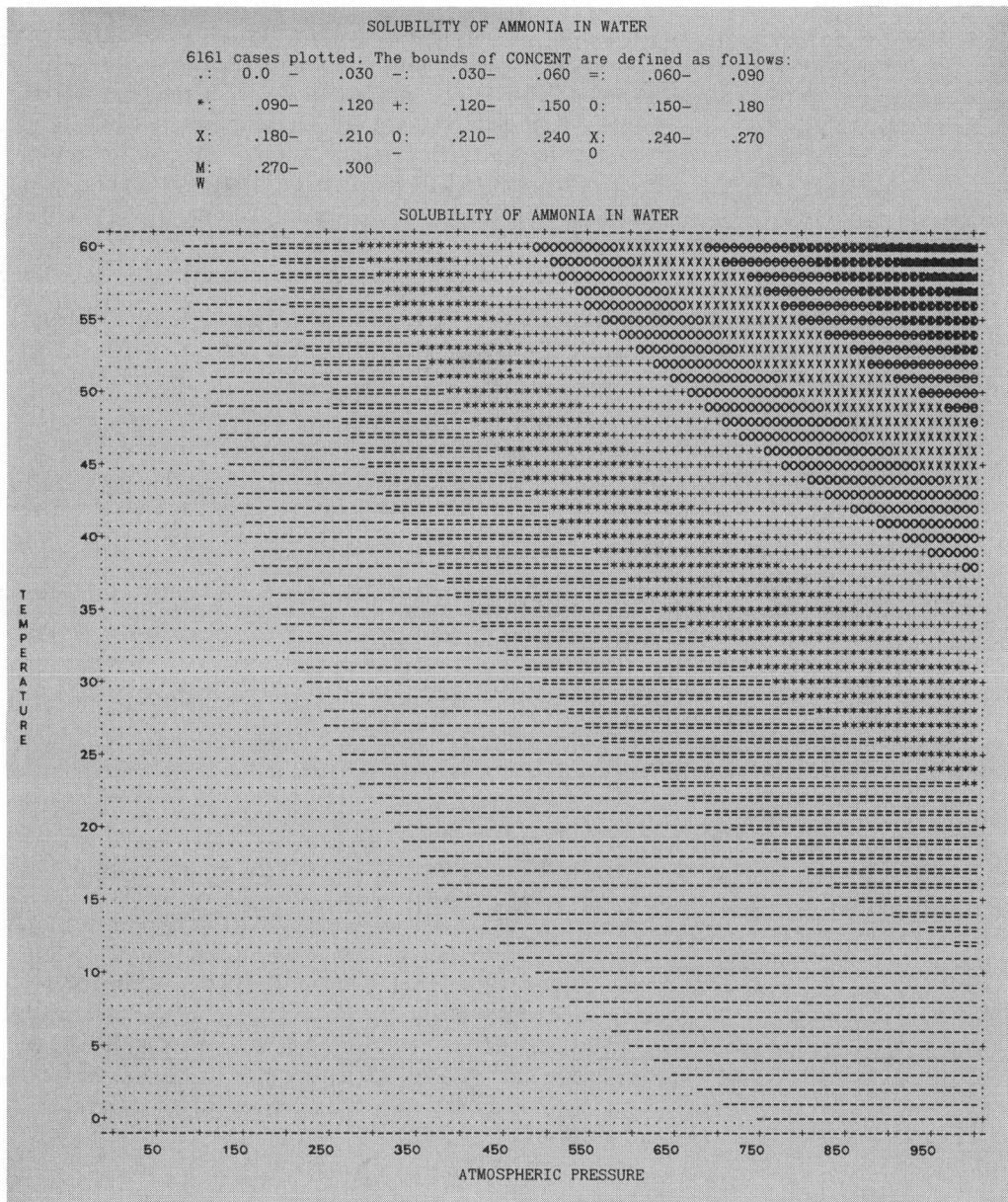

Plots with regression statistics are described and shown in *SPSS/PC+ Statistics.*

12.7
Setting Plot Symbols

A wide range of alphabetical, numeric, and special ASCII graphic characters are available as plot symbols. Use the CUTPOINT and SYMBOLS subcommands to control the display of plot symbols.

The CUTPOINT subcommand specifies the number of cases represented by plotting symbols. For example, you can have the symbol 1 represent one case at a position, the symbol 2 represent two cases at a position, and the symbol 3 represent three or more cases at a position. CUTPOINT can be used only once on a PLOT command and applies to all plots requested. The CUTPOINT subcommand cannot be used for control plots, overlay, or contour plots.

The following specifications are available with CUTPOINT:

EVERY(n) *Frequency intervals of width* n. Assign the first symbol when the number of cases at a position is between 1 and *n*, the second symbol when the number of cases at a position is between $n+1$ and $2n$, and so on. The default symbols used are 1, 2, 3, ... X, Y, Z, with a default *n* of 1. An asterisk (*) represents 36 or more cases.

(value list) *Each value defines a cutpoint.* Assign the first symbol when the number of cases at a position is less than or equal to the first value, the second symbol when the number of cases at a position is greater than the first value and less than or equal to the second value, and so on. Specify values separated by blanks or commas. Up to 35 cutpoints can be specified.

For example, if the command

```
PLOT CUTPOINT=EVERY(4)
  /PLOT=SCORE WITH ANXIETY.
```

is used, one to four cases in the same position are represented by a 1, five to eight cases by a 2, and so on. If the command

```
PLOT CUTPOINT=(5,10,25)
  /PLOT=SCORE WITH ANXIETY.
```

is used, one to five cases in the same position are represented by a 1, six to ten cases by a 2, 11 to 25 cases by a 3, and more than 25 cases by a 4.

The SYMBOLS subcommand allows you to choose other plotting symbols to represent a plot position. For scatterplots and regression plots, each symbol represents the number of cases at a plot position. For overlay plots, each symbol represents one of the overlaid plots. For contour plots, each symbol represents one level of the contour variable. SYMBOLS cannot be used with control plots. Use the VALUE LABELS command to define appropriate labels when control plots are requested. The SYMBOLS subcommand can be used only once on a PLOT command and applies to all plots requested. You can request one of the following options with the SYMBOLS subcommand:

ALPHANUMERIC *Alphanumeric plotting symbols.* The characters 1 through 9, A through Z, and * are used, in that order. Thus, in a scatterplot, 1 indicates one case at a position, and * represents 36 or more cases at a position. This is the default if the SYMBOLS subcommand is not specified.

NUMERIC *Numeric plotting symbols.* The characters 1 through 9 and * are used, with * indicating 10 or more cases at a position in a scatterplot.

'symbols'['ovprnt'] *List of plot symbols.* In the list of symbol values, the characters specified are not separated by blanks or commas. The list of overprinting symbols is enclosed in a separate set of apostrophes or quotation marks and is separated from the first symbols list with a blank or comma. When overprint symbols are displayed on the screen, only the second overprinting symbol list will be displayed. You can select any special ASCII graphic characters available on your PC as symbols. Look under "ASCII" in the index of your DOS manual for further reference.

If the SYMBOLS subcommand is specified, a table of symbols and their equivalents like the one shown in Figure 12.1d is displayed. If the SYMBOLS subcommand is omitted, the default alphanumeric symbol set is used.

For example, the command

```
PLOT CUTPOINTS=(1,2,3,4)
  /SYMBOLS='.:x*X'
  /PLOT=INCOME WITH ASTRSIGN.
```

requests a scatterplot with a period (.) representing one case at a position, a colon (:) representing two cases, x representing three cases, an asterisk (*) representing four cases, and X representing five or more cases.

12.8
Specifying Plot Titles

Use the TITLE subcommand to specify a plot title. The title can contain up to 60 characters and must be enclosed in single quotation marks, as in the command:

```
PLOT TITLE='CORPORATE TAKEOVERS 1975-1983'
  /PLOT=TAKEOVER WITH YEAR.
```

TITLE can be specified once before each PLOT subcommand and applies only to the following PLOT subcommand. Titles longer than the horizontal axis are truncated. If the TITLE subcommand is not used, a default title is displayed, consisting of the names of the variables plotted for scatterplots or the type of the plot requested on FORMAT.

12.9
Scaling and Labeling Plot Axes

The VERTICAL and HORIZONTAL subcommands allow you to control the scaling and labeling of the vertical and horizontal axes, obtain reference lines at specified positions, specify minimum and maximum values, and obtain plots of standardized variables. Resetting minimum or maximum values is especially useful when you want to focus on a subset of a larger plot. Standardized plots are appropriate when you want to overlay plots of variables with very different scales.

The VERTICAL and HORIZONTAL subcommands can be used once before each PLOT subcommand and apply to all plots specified in the following PLOT subcommand. You can request the following specifications on these subcommands:

'label'
: *Use the axis label specified (up to 40 characters).* The default label is the variable label or, if there is no variable label, the variable name. Labels longer than the axis are truncated.

MIN(n)
: *Use the minimum value* n *on the axis.* The default is the minimum observed value for the plotted variable.

MAX(n)
: *Use the maximum value* n *on the axis.* The default is the maximum observed value for the plotted variable or, sometimes, a slightly larger number (to obtain equal-width integer scaling).

UNIFORM
: *Use the same scaling for all plots.* This keyword is unnecessary when MIN and MAX are specified. If UNIFORM is specified instead of the MIN and MAX keywords, PLOT determines the minimum and maximum observed values across all plotted variables on the PLOT subcommands.

REFERENCE(values)
: *Draw reference lines at the values specified.* Specify values separated by blanks or commas. The default is no reference lines.

STANDARDIZE
: *Plot standardized variables.* The default is to plot observed values.

12.10
Setting the Plot Size

The VSIZE and HSIZE subcommands control the height and width, respectively, of the plot. The default size of the PLOT depends on the current page size (for defaults, see Command Reference: PLOT). These subcommands override the page size set on the SET command. For example, the command

```
PLOT VSIZE=30/HSIZE=45
  /PLOT=SALES WITH REP DISTRICT.
```

requests a height of 30 lines and a width of 45 positions for the plots of SALES with REP and SALES with DISTRICT.

The VSIZE and HSIZE subcommands can be used only once: all plots requested are then drawn to the specified size.

12.11
Missing Values

The MISSING subcommand controls the treatment of missing values. The subcommand can be used only once on each PLOT command. You can request the following options on the MISSING subcommand:

PLOTWISE *Exclude cases with missing values plotwise.* Cases that are missing for any variable within a single plot are not included. In an overlay plot, plotwise deletion applies to each plot that is overlaid. This is the default if no missing-value treatment is specified.

LISTWISE *Exclude cases with missing values listwise.* Cases with missing values for any variable named on the PLOT subcommand are excluded from all plots.

INCLUDE *Include cases with user-defined missing values.* INCLUDE can be used with either PLOTWISE or LISTWISE to include cases with user-missing values while deleting cases with system-missing values according to one or the other treatment.

12.12
Example

The following commands were used to obtain the output in Figure 12.3c:

```
DATA LIST FREE /
   TREATMNT SEX AGE INITWT PEROVRWT TREATLOS THREELOS SIXLOSS
TWELVLOS
   TREATRED THREERED SIXRED TWELVRED.
VARIABLE LABELS
   TREATMNT 'TREATMENT GROUP'/SEX 'SEX OF PARTICIPANT' /
   AGE 'AGE OF PARTICIPANT'/INITWT 'INITAL WEIGHT IN POUNDS' /
   PEROVRWT 'INITIAL PERCENT OVERWEIGHT' /
   TREATLOS 'WEIGHT LOSS AT TREATMENT' /
   THREELOS 'WEIGHT LOSS AT THREE MONTHS' /
   SIXLOSS 'WEIGHT LOSS AT SIX MONTHS' /
   TWELVLOS 'WEIGHT LOSS AT TWELVE MONTHS' /
   TREATRED 'REDUCTION QUOTIENT AT TREATMENT' /
   THREERED 'REDUCTION QUOTIENT AT THREE MONTHS' /
   SIXRED 'REDUCTION QUOTIENT AT SIX MONTHS' /
   TWELVRED 'REDUCTION QUOTIENT AT TWELVE MONTHS'.
VALUE LABELS   SEX 1 'FEMALE' 2 'MALE'.
BEGIN DATA.
data records
END DATA.
PLOT FORMAT=OVERLAY
  /PLOT=TREATRED TWELVRED WITH AGE.
FINISH.
```

- The DATA LIST command tells SPSS/PC+ that the variables are to be read in freefield format. It also gives the variable names.
- The VARIABLE LABELS command assigns descriptive labels to the variables.
- The VALUE LABELS command assigns labels to the values of the variable SEX.
- The PLOT command asks for an overlay plot of TREATRED and TWELVRED with AGE.

Contents

13 Establishing Order: Procedure RANK

Ranks are sometimes the most natural way to collect data. Market researchers ask us to rank products from least favorite to most favorite; sportscasters give us their lists of the top twenty basketball or football teams. Ranks are also useful for interpreting measurements when we have reason to suspect that the underlying scale is not really interval. Registrars often convert grade-point averages to class ranks, perhaps suspecting that grades aren't really measured on a consistent interval scale. Similarly, when you have reason to suspect that your data are not measured on a nice interval scale or do not have the kind of distribution required for many statistical techniques, you might choose to analyze them using a nonparametric procedure which requires very limited assumptions about the underlying distribution. Many nonparametric procedures replace data values with ranks.

13.1
COMPUTING RANKS

The basic idea of rank assignment is straightforward. We order the data values and then assign sequential integers, from 1 to the number of cases, to the ordered values. If our data values are sorted from smallest to largest—that is, the data are in ascending order—the smallest value receives the rank of 1. If the data are sorted in descending order, from largest to smallest, the largest value receives a rank of 1.

Difficulties with the assignment of ranks occur when there are tied values. For example, if our data values are 10, 10, 11, and 20, several different schemes can be used to assign ranks to the tied values of 10. The most frequently used method assigns the average of the ranks for which they are tied. If we are assigning ranks based on ascending data values, the two cases with values of 10 are tied for ranks of 1 and 2, so we assign them a rank of 1.5, ((1+2)/2). If we had three values of 10, each of them would receive a rank of 2 ((1+2+3)/3). The SPSS/PC+ RANK procedure offers several other possibilities for the treatment of ties. For example, in Figure 13.1, class ranks are assigned in descending order (so that the highest grade-point average receives rank 1) with the lowest rank assigned to all students tied with the same grade-point average (so that the two students tied for second both receive rank 2).

Figure 13.1   Class ranks using descending order and low scores for ties

```
DATAT LIST / NAME 1-24 (A) GPA 26-28 (2).
BEGIN DATA.
MARK ANDERSON           325
ANDREW BROWN            400
YVONNE HIRSCHFIELD      275
HAROLD THOMPSON         400
SALLY WILSON            425
END DATA.
RANK GPA (D) /TIES=LOW.
SORT CASES BY RGPA.
LIST.
```

NAME	GPA	RGPA
SALLY WILSON	4.25	1.000
ANDREW BROWN	4.00	2.000
HAROLD THOMPSON	4.00	2.000
MARK ANDERSON	3.25	4.000
YVONNE HIRSCHFIELD	2.75	5.000

13.2
ORDERING THE DATA INTO CATEGORIES

Based on the ranks assigned to cases, we can classify them into several distinct groups. For example, we may subdivide our cases into quartiles—that is, classify the cases into four groups of approximately equal size based on the values of their ranks. You can subdivide the cases into as many groups as you like using the RANK procedure.

Figure 13.2 shows average weights of the men in the Western Electric Study (see Chapter 9) when they are grouped into quartiles based on their diastolic blood pressure. (Quartiles are determined by the RANK procedure and saved in the variable NDBP58, which is then used as the BY variable in the MEANS procedure.) You can see that the average weights increase across the quartiles. The four groups are not exactly of the same size since there are many tied values for diastolic blood pressure (see the stem-and-leaf plots in Chapter 9). All tied values are assigned to the same quartile group.

Figure 13.2   Mean weight of subjects within quartiles

```
GET FILE='ELECTRIC.SYS'.
RANK VARIABLES=DBP58 /NTILES(4).
VALUE LABELS NDBP58 1 "FIRST QUARTILE OF DBP58"
    2 "SECOND QUARTILE" 3 "THIRD QUARTILE" 4 "FOURTH QUARTILE".
MEANS WT58 BY NDBP58.
```

```
                DESCRIPTION    OF   SUBPOPULATIONS

CRITERION VARIABLE    WT58       BODY WEIGHT, 1958 -- LBS
   BROKEN DOWN BY     NDBP58     NTILES OF DBP58


VARIABLE       VALUE  LABEL                    MEAN      STD DEV   CASES

FOR ENTIRE POPULATION                          173.4812   24.7644   239

NDBP58            1    FIRST QUARTILE OF DB    167.0962   22.2994    52
NDBP58            2    SECOND QUARTILE         171.8525   24.0720    61
NDBP58            3    THIRD QUARTILE          176.4697   25.9847    66
NDBP58            4    FOURTH QUARTILE         177.3833   25.4313    60

   TOTAL CASES=240
MISSING CASES=1 or     .4 PCT
```

13.3
PROGRAMMING STATISTICAL TESTS BASED ON RANKS

The SPSS/PC+ NPAR TESTS procedure contains most of the commonly used nonparametric tests. However, you may want to use a test which is not yet available. Using the RANK procedure and some other simple SPSS procedures, you should be able to implement most nonparametric tests.

13.4
Conover's Test for Equality of Variance

Conover (1980) describes a nonparametric test for the hypothesis that two samples come from populations with equal variance. He describes a food packaging company that wants to compare two methods for packaging cereal. Table 13.4 contains data for the two methods, conveniently designated as "present" and "new."

Table 13.4   Conover cereal packaging data

Amount in box	
Present	**New**
10.8	10.8
11.1	10.5
10.4	11.0
10.1	10.9
11.3	10.8
	10.7
	10.8
Mean **10.74**	**10.79**

The test statistic for evaluating the null hypothesis of equal variances is:

$$T = \frac{T_1 - n\,\overline{R^2}}{\sqrt{\dfrac{nm}{N(N-1)}\Sigma R_i^4 - \dfrac{nm}{(N-1)}(\overline{R^2})^2}}$$

Equation 13.4a

where T_1 is the sum of squared ranks for the smaller group, and n and m are the group sizes. In this test the ranks are based not on the original data but on the absolute value of the deviation from the group mean. To calculate the test statistic, we enter the data as two variables, one containing the measurements of amounts of cereal in the box and the other indicating the group for each measurement. A preliminary run of the MEANS procedure provides the means for each group. We can then proceed, as in Figure 13.4, to compute the absolute values of the differences from the group means, rank them, and then square the ranks and raise them to the fourth power. Descriptive statistics from the MEANS procedure for the new variables then give us the needed information to compute the test statistic.

Figure 13.4   Calculating numbers for equality of variance test

```
IF (GROUP EQ 1) ABSDIF=ABS(AMOUNT-10.74).
IF (GROUP EQ 2) ABSDIF=ABS(AMOUNT-10.79).
RANK ABSDIF/RANK INTO R.
COMPUTE R2=R**2.
COMPUTE R4=R**4.
VARIABLE LABELS R2 'SQUARED RANKS' r4 'RANKS TO THE FOURTH POWER'.
MEANS R2 R4 BY GROUP / OPTIONS 6 7.
```

```
         D E S C R I P T I O N   O F   S U B P O P U L A T I O N S

CRITERION VARIABLE      R2          SQUARED RANKS
    BROKEN DOWN BY      GROUP


VARIABLE        VALUE  LABEL                      SUM        MEAN      CASES

FOR ENTIRE POPULATION                           648.00    54.0000       12

GROUP            1.00  PRESENT                   462.00    92.4000        5
GROUP            2.00  NEW                       186.00    26.5714        7

   TOTAL CASES=12


         D E S C R I P T I O N   O F   S U B P O P U L A T I O N S

CRITERION VARIABLE      R4          RANKS TO THE FOURTH POWER
    BROKEN DOWN BY      GROUP


VARIABLE        VALUE  LABEL                      SUM        MEAN      CASES

FOR ENTIRE POPULATION                         60660.00  5055.0000       12

GROUP            1.00  PRESENT                 52194.00 10438.8000        5
GROUP            2.00  NEW                      8466.00  1209.4286        7

   TOTAL CASES=12
```

From the numbers in Figure 13.4, we calculate:

$$T = \frac{462 - 5\,(54)}{\sqrt{\dfrac{5\times7}{12\times11}\times 60{,}660 - \dfrac{5\times7}{11}\times(54)^2}} = 2.3273$$

Equation 13.4b

The observed significance level is obtained from tables available in Conover (1980). In this case, the observed significance level is less than 0.05, so we reject the null hypothesis that both methods have equal variability.

13.5
Spearman Correlation Coefficient

The RANK procedure can also be used to calculate the Spearman Rank Correlation Coefficient. This is a nonparametric correlation coefficient based on ranks. In fact, it is just the usual Pearson correlation coefficient applied to ranks. For example, to calculate the Spearman correlation coefficient between diastolic blood pressure and weight in the Western Electric men, we would use the RANK procedure to rank the two variables and then calculate a correlation coefficient on the ranks (Figure 13.5).

Figure 13.5 Calculating the Spearman correlation coefficient

```
GET FILE='ELECTRIC.SYS'.
RANK VARIABLES=DBP58 WT58/RANK.
CORRELATION VARIABLES=RDBP58 RWT58.
```

```
                    RDBP58        RWT58

    RDBP58         1.0000         .1474
                  (   239)       (   239)
                   P= .          P= .011


    RWT58           .1474        1.0000
                  (   239)       (   240)
                   P= .011       P= .


   (COEFFICIENT / (CASES) / 1-TAILED SIG)
   " . " IS PRINTED IF A COEFFICIENT CANNOT BE COMPUTED
```

13.6
Normal Scores in Statistical Tests

When analyzing ranks, we ignore the actual distance between observations. For example, if we have the values 1, 3, 9, and 10, or the values 1, 2, 70, and 100, we will assign them the same ranks. The distance between the observations doesn't matter; only their order matters. There is a class of statistical tests which attempts to replace the ranks with other numbers that more closely resemble the observations from a particular distribution. For example, if we have five observations, instead of analyzing the ranks from 1 to 5, we can replace the ranks by quartiles from a particular distribution, usually the normal. That is, we find the five numbers which divide the area of a normal distribution into six equal parts and then analyze them. In this case, we would analyze the scores -0.9674, -0.4307, 0, 0.4307, and 0.9674. If we analyze the normal scores instead of the ranks, the resulting statistical tests will have, under certain conditions, somewhat better statistical properties, even if the population from which the sample is obtained is not normal.

13.7
The van der Waerden Test for Several Independent Samples

To see how normal scores can be used to test the null hypothesis that all population distributions are identical, let's consider the van der Waerden test for several independent samples. The test statistic is:

$$T = \frac{\sum n_i \bar{A}_i^2}{S^2}$$

Equation 13.7

where n_i is the number of cases in group i, $\bar{A}_i$ is the average normal score in group i, and S^2 is the variance of all of the normal scores. To compute this statistic, we must compute the average score in each group, square these averages, multiply them by the sample size in each group, and then sum them across all groups. Finally, we divide this sum by the variance of the scores.

Conover (1980) presents data for comparing four methods of growing corn. Figure 13.7a contains the SPSS/PC+ session to calculate the van der Waerden test for the hypothesis that the four populations from which the samples were taken are in fact identical. Figure 13.7b, the output from the LIST procedure, shows the data, the ranks, and the normal scores for all four methods. Figure 13.7c contains the relevant portions of the output from the two DESCRIPTIVES commands. The first gives the variance for all the cases; the second gives the sum of the squared means multiplied by the sample sizes. Dividing that sum by the variance yields the test statistic:

$$21.31 / .846 = 25.19$$

The significance level is based on the chi-squared distribution with degrees of freedom equal to one less than the number of groups. The observed significance level is less than 0.001, so the null hypothesis is rejected.

Figure 13.7a SPSS/PC+ commands for van der Waerden test

```
DATA LIST FREE/ GROUP YIELD.
BEGIN DATA.
1 83 1 91 1 94 1 89 1 89 1 96 1 91 1 92 1 90
2 91 2 90 2 81 2 83 2 84 2 83 2 88 2 91 2 89 2 84
3 101 3 100 3 91 3 93 3 96 3 95 3 94
4 78 4 82 4 81 4 77 4 79 4 81 4 80 4 81
END DATA.
FORMATS YIELD GROUP(F3.0).
RANK YIELD /RANK /NORMAL INTO VWSCORE /FRACTION VW.
LIST.
DESCRIPTIVES VARIABLES=VWSCORE /STATISTICS=6.
AGGREGATE OUTFILE=*/BREAK=GROUP
  /MEAN=MEAN(VWSCORE) /COUNT=N(VWSCORE).
COMPUTE PRODUCT=MEAN**2 * COUNT.
DESCRIPTIVES VARIABLES=PRODUCT /STATISTICS=12.
```

Figure 13.7b Data, ranks, and normal scores for Conover data

GROUP	YIELD	RYIELD	VWSCORE
1	83	11.000	-.4837
1	91	23.000	.4047
1	94	28.500	.8938
1	89	17.000	-.0358
1	89	17.000	-.0358
1	96	31.500	1.2816
1	91	23.000	.4047
1	92	26.000	.6522
1	90	19.500	.1437
2	91	23.000	.4047
2	90	19.500	.1437
2	81	6.500	-.8938
2	83	11.000	-.4837
2	84	13.500	-.2905
2	83	11.000	-.4837
2	88	15.000	-.1800
2	91	23.000	.4047
2	89	17.000	-.0358
2	84	13.500	-.2905
3	101	34.000	1.9022
3	100	33.000	1.5792
3	91	23.000	.4047
3	93	27.000	.7436
3	96	31.500	1.2816
3	95	30.000	1.0676
3	94	28.500	.8938
4	78	2.000	-1.579
4	82	9.000	-.6522
4	81	6.500	-.8938
4	77	1.000	-1.902
4	79	3.000	-1.368
4	81	6.500	-.8938
4	80	4.000	-1.204
4	81	6.500	-.8938

Figure 13.7c Output from DESCRIPTIVES

Variable	Variance	Valid N	Label
VWSCORE	.846	34	NORMAL of YIELD using VW

Variable	Sum	Valid N	Label
PRODUCT	21.314	4	

13.8
Graphical Tests of Normality

Normal scores can also be used to examine the hypothesis that data come from a normal distribution. We can generate normal scores for each of the cases based on their ranks and then plot the observed values against the normal scores. If the underlying distribution is normal, we expect the points to cluster around a straight line. Figure 13.8 is a plot of the observed diastolic blood pressures for the Western Electric men against the normal scores. (In this case, instead of using the normal scores proposed by van der Waerden, we use a modification suggested by Blom which results in scores that are somewhat closer to the exact expected values for the order statistics.) From this plot, we see that our observed distribution differs somewhat from normal. Similar normal probability plots can also be obtained with the EXAMINE procedure (see Chapter 9).

Figure 13.8 Normal probability plot

```
GET FILE='ELECTRIC.SYS'.
RANK VARIABLES=DBP58 /NORMAL INTO NORMAL.
PLOT PLOT=NORMAL WITH DBP58.
```

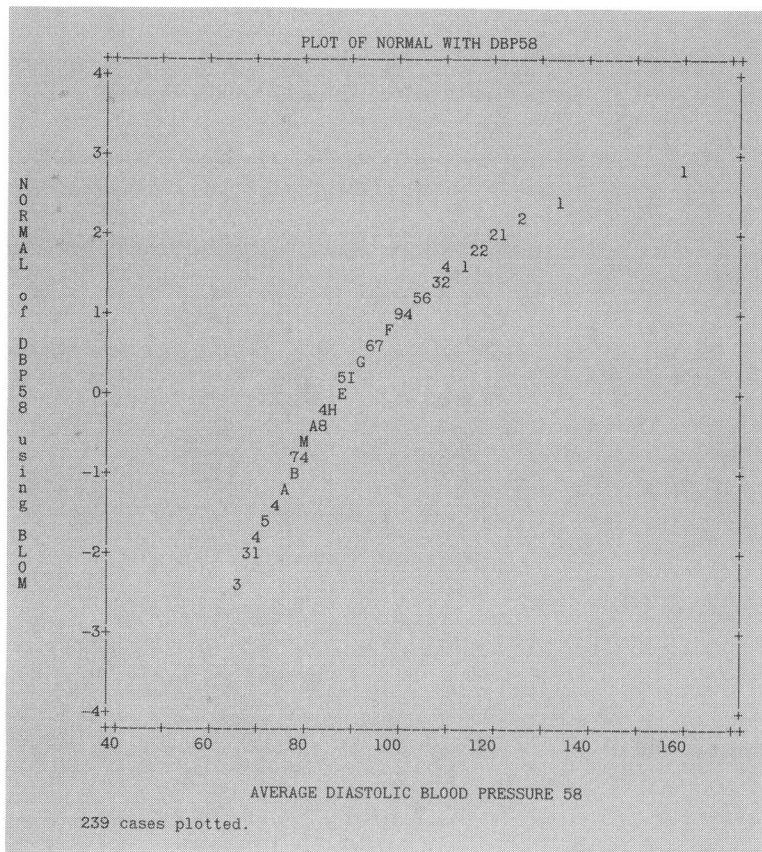

13.9
Scores for an Exponential Distribution

If we have reason to believe that our data are a sample from an exponential distribution, instead of computing normal scores we can compute scores based on the exponential distribution. These scores are sometimes called Savage scores. (The length of time between consecutive events, when the events occur randomly in time, follows an exponential distribution.) To see whether a sample of data might originate from an exponential distribution, we can plot Savage scores against the observed values. Again, if the data are from an exponential distribution, the points should cluster around a straight line. Figure 13.9 is a plot of data values which appear to come from an exponential distribution.

Figure 13.9   Savage scores (Problem 5 from Conover, p. 367)

```
DATA LIST FREE/DISTANCE.
BEGIN DATA.
0.3 6.1 4.3 3.3 1.9 4.8 .3 1.2 .8 10.3 1.2 .1 10 1.6 27.6
12 14.2 19.7 15.5
END DATA.
RANK VARIABLES=DISTANCE /SAVAGE INTO SAVDIST.
PLOT PLOT=SAVDIST WITH DISTANCE.
```

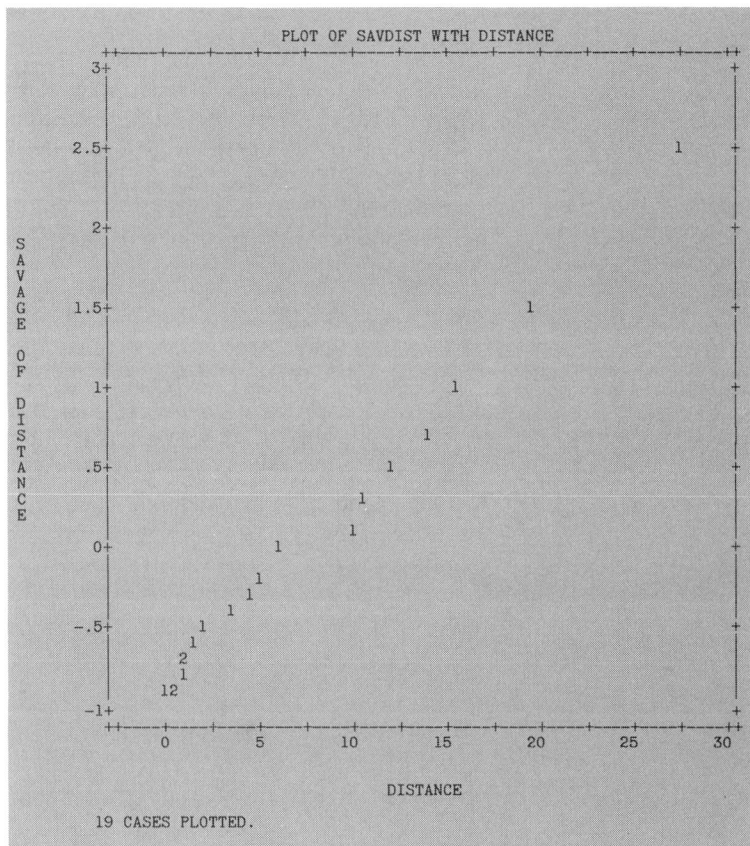

```
                          PLOT OF SAVDIST WITH DISTANCE
             ++---+---+---+---+---+---+---+---+---+---+---+---+---++
          3+                                                         +
           |                                                         |
           |                                                         |
        2.5+                                             1         + |
           |                                                         |
           |                                                         |
          2+                                                       + |
     S     |                                                         |
     A     |                                                         |
     V  1.5+                                    1                   + |
     A     |                                                         |
     G     |                                                         |
     E    1+                                 1                      + |
           |                                                         |
     O     |                             1                           |
     F      |                                                        |
         .5+                         1                             + |
     D     |                                                         |
     I     |                       1                                 |
     S    0+                    1                                   + |
     T     |                 1                                       |
     A     |               1                                         |
     N  -.5+            1                                          + |
     C     |           1                                             |
     E     |          1                                              |
           |          2                                              |
           |          1                                              |
         -1+         12                                            + |
            ++---+---+---+---+---+---+---+---+---+---+---+---+---++
             0       5      10      15      20      25      30

                              DISTANCE

       19 CASES PLOTTED.
```

13.10
RUNNING PROCEDURE RANK

The RANK procedure computes ranks, normal and Savage scores, and related statistics. It can also be used to classify cases into groups based on percentile values. Ranks, scores, and group memberships are saved as variables on the active file. The procedure does not require that the file be sorted.

13.11
Specifying the Variables

Variables for which ranks are to be computed are specified after the VARIABLES subcommand. For example,

```
RANK VARIABLES=INCOME.
```

creates a new variable, RINCOME, which contains ranks based on ascending values of INCOME. (Ascending order means that the rank of 1 goes to the case with the smallest value and the rank of n, where n is the number of cases, goes to the case with the largest value.)

If you want ranks to be assigned to cases in descending order, so that the case with the largest value is assigned a rank of 1, specify (D) after the variable name. The command

```
RANK VARIABLES=INCOME(D).
```

assigns ranks based on descending values of the variable.

Statistics Guide

13.12
Specifying Groups

If you wish to classify cases into groups based on values of a factor variable and then rank cases within each of the groups, specify the grouping variable following the keyword BY. For example,

```
RANK VARIABLES=INCOME BY JOBCAT.
```

ranks the cases separately for each of the values of JOBCAT.

13.13
Treatment of Ties

By default, cases with the same values for a variable are assigned the average of the ranks for the tied values. For example, consider a data set of six cases with the values 10, 15, 15, 15, 16, and 20. If we are assigning ranks in ascending order of the values, the case with the value of 10 is assigned a rank of 1. The next three cases, all with values of 15, are tied for the ranks of 2, 3, and 4. By default, we assign each of them the rank $(2+3+4)/3$, which is 3. The last two cases are assigned ranks of 5 and 6. Options for the treatment of ties are selected with the TIES subcommand. The following keywords are available:

MEAN   *Average rank assigned to tied values.* This is the default.
LOW   *Lowest rank assigned to tied values.*
HIGH   *Highest rank assigned to tied values.*
CONDENSE *Only distinct values of the variable are ranked.* That is, ranks are assigned from 1 to D, where D is the number of distinct values. Cases with the same values receive the same ranks.

To understand how the methods handle ties, consider the data set previously described. Table 13.13 shows the ranks assigned to the cases for each of the methods.

Table 13.13   Options for handling ties in ranks

Case	Value	MEAN	LOW	HIGH	CONDENSE
1	10	1	1	1	1
2	15	3	2	4	2
3	15	3	2	4	2
4	15	3	2	4	2
5	16	5	5	5	3
6	20	6	6	6	4

To request ranking for values in descending order, with the lowest value assigned to ties, specify:

```
RANK VARIABLES=INCOME(D)/TIES=LOW.
```

13.14
Computing Other Statistics

By default, the RANK procedure computes ranks for each of the variables listed on the VARIABLES subcommand. Other functions are also available. Each of the following keywords can be specified once:

RANK   *Assign ranks as described in previous sections.*
RFRACTION *Divide each rank by the number of cases with valid values,* or by the sum of weights if the WEIGHT command is used.
PERCENT   *Divide each rank by the number of cases with valid values* and multiply by 100.
N   *Sum of case weight.* The value of the variable is a constant for all cases in the same group.
NTILES(n) *Divide the cases into* n *approximately equal groups based on the values of the variable.* Cases are assigned to groups from 1 to *n*, where the lowest values are in the first group and the largest values are in the *n*th group. Cases are assigned to groups using the formula $group_i =$

$TRUNCATE(1 + (R_i \times n / (W+1)))$, where TRUNCATE signifies the integer part of the result, R_i is the rank of case i, n is the number of groups, and W is the sum of case weights.

PROPORTION   Estimate of the cumulative proportion (area) of the distribution corresponding to a particular rank. Several different methods are available for estimating the cumulative proportion. See Section 13.16.

NORMAL   Normal scores computed from the ranks. The new variable contains the z-score from the standard normal which corresponds to the estimated cumulative proportion. For example, if the estimated cumulative proportion for an observation is 0.50, its normal score is 0. Several different methods are available for estimating the cumulative proportion. See Section 13.16.

SAVAGE   Scores based on an exponential distribution.

13.15
Assigning Names to Variables Created by RANK

By default, new variable names are created by adding the first letter of the function name to the first seven characters of the variable name. For example, the variable RINCOME is used for the ranks of the variable INCOME, the variable NINCOME for the normal scores of INCOME. If you are saving the results from several functions which start with the same letter (for example, PERCENT and PROPORTION), the first new variable is named by prefixing the first letter to the variable name. Subsequent variables are named XXXnnn, where XXX is the first three letters of the function name and nnn is a sequence number assigned to the variable. If PERCENT is specified first, the name PINCOME is assigned to the percent function, and the name PRO001 to the proportion function. If this scheme results in non-unique names, variables are assigned the names RNKXXnn, where XX is the first two letters of the function and nn is a sequence number. Descriptive labels are assigned to each new variable, so it is easy to see what the resulting names are.

If you wish to assign your own variable names, use the INTO keyword with each of the functions used. For example,

```
RANK VARIABLES=INCOME/RANK INTO RANKINC.
```

assigns the name RANKINC to the ranks of the INCOME variable. Similarly,

```
RANK VARIABLES=INCOME/RANK INTO RANKINC/NORMAL INTO NORMINC.
```

also assigns the name NORMINC to the normal scores for INCOME.

13.16
Estimating the Cumulative Proportion

The functions NORMAL and PROPORTION require an estimate of the cumulative proportion corresponding to each rank. Four methods are available for estimating this cumulative proportion: BLOM, RANKIT, TUKEY, and VW. The default is BLOM. For a description of these methods, see Command Reference: RANK.

13.17
Display of Summary Table

By default, a summary table describing the newly created variables is displayed. Use the PRINT subcommand with the keyword NO to suppress this table.

13.18
Missing Values

By default, if a case has a system-missing value or a user-missing value, it is assigned a rank of system-missing. If you wish to treat user-missing values as valid values, use the MISSING subcommand. For example,

```
RANK VARIABLES=INCOME/MISSING=INCLUDE.
```

treats user-missing values as valid values. System-missing values are still assigned system-missing values for any variable created by the RANK procedure.

Contents_____

14 Reporting Results: Procedure REPORT

Case listings and descriptive statistics are basic tools for studying and presenting data. You can obtain case listings with LIST, frequency counts and descriptive statistics with FREQUENCIES and DESCRIPTIVES, and subpopulation statistics with MEANS. Each of these procedures uses a format designed to make the information clear, but if that format isn't what you need for presentation, there is little you can do to change it. REPORT gives you the control you need over data presentation.

REPORT is a formatting tool. It allows you to present case listings and summary statistics (including frequencies) in report format. Your report can be one page long, or it can be hundreds of pages long. With REPORT's subcommands and keywords, you can specify the variables you want to summarize or list and organize them into subgroups. You can calculate summary statistics on the report variables and also calculate cross-variable statistics that are unavailable in other procedures, such as the ratio of two means.

14.1 BASIC REPORT CONCEPTS

This section introduces you to the two basic elements of a report: its contents, and the organization of those contents. To illustrate these concepts (and others in this chapter), we'll use information from a retail company's personnel file. The file contains data such as employees' names, salaries, employment grades, length of time in grade, overall length of employment, store branch and department, shift, and so forth.

14.2 Report Contents: Summaries and Listings

Reports contain summary statistics calculated for groups of cases, listings of individual cases, or a combination of both statistics and listings.

14.3 Summary Reports

Summary reports display summary statistics but do not display case listings. The summary information consists of the statistic or statistics you request for the report variables. Each statistic displays in a separate row on the report, referred to as a *summary line.* The cells within the summary line display the statistical values. Figure 14.3 shows a summary report presenting means as the summary statistics.

Figure 14.3 Summary personnel report

```
Personnel Data

                          Tenure     Tenure
                            in         in
  Division       Age     Company     Grade      Salary—Annual
  --------       ---     -------     -----      -------------

  Carpeting
  Mean          30.75      4.04       3.31         $11,754

  Appliances
  Mean          31.11      3.81       3.54         $12,508

  Furniture
  Mean          36.87      4.79       4.08         $13,255

  Hardware
  Mean          36.20      4.60       4.57         $17,580
```

14.4
Listing Reports

Listing reports list individual cases. The case listings comprise the values and/or labels recorded for each of the report variables. In addition to listing cases, a listing report can display as many summary statistics as a summary report. Figure 14.4a presents a report that contains case listings, and 14.4b shows one that contains both listings and summaries.

Figure 14.4a Personnel report with case listings

```
Personnel Data

                          Tenure     Tenure
                            in         in
  Division       Age     Company     Grade      Salary—Annual
  --------       ---     -------     -----      -------------

  Carpeting     22.00      3.92       3.08         $10,900
                27.00      3.67       2.17          $9,200
                23.00      3.92       3.08         $10,900
                35.00      6.00       5.33         $19,500
                36.00      3.83       3.25         $10,000
                24.00      4.00       3.25         $10,000
                44.00      4.83       4.33         $15,690
                33.00      3.75       3.25         $10,000
                27.00      4.33       3.17         $10,000
                33.00      2.67       2.67          $9,335
                35.00      3.50       3.00         $15,520
                30.00      4.08       3.08         $10,000

  Appliances    42.00      6.50       6.50         $18,000
                26.00      2.92       2.08          $8,000
                24.00      3.17       3.17          $8,975
                21.00      2.67       2.67          $8,700
                38.00      5.00       4.42         $28,300
                33.00      3.42       2.92          $8,900
                30.00      2.67       2.67          $7,500
                32.00      2.92       2.92          $8,900
                34.00      5.08       4.50         $15,300
```

Figure 14.4b   Personnel report with case listings and summaries

```
Personnel Data

                          Tenure      Tenure
                            in          in
     Division      Age    Company      Grade    Salary--Annual

     Carpeting    22.00     3.92        3.08        $10,900
                  27.00     3.67        2.17         $9,200
                  23.00     3.92        3.08        $10,900
                  35.00     6.00        5.33        $19,500
                  36.00     3.83        3.25        $10,000
                  24.00     4.00        3.25        $10,000
                  44.00     4.83        4.33        $15,690
                  33.00     3.75        3.25        $10,000
                  27.00     4.33        3.17        $10,000
                  33.00     2.67        2.67         $9,335
                  35.00     3.50        3.00        $15,520
                  30.00     4.08        3.08        $10,000

     Mean         30.75     4.04        3.31        $11,754

     Appliances   42.00     6.50        6.50        $18,000
                  26.00     2.92        2.08         $8,000
                  24.00     3.17        3.17         $8,975
                  21.00     2.67        2.67         $8,700
                  38.00     5.00        4.42        $28,300
                  33.00     3.42        2.92         $8,900
                  30.00     2.67        2.67         $7,500
                  32.00     2.92        2.92         $8,900
                  34.00     5.08        4.50        $15,300

     Mean         31.11     3.81        3.54        $12,508
```

14.5
Report Organization

A report is organized into columns and rows. Each column is defined by a variable. The columns on the left are the *break variables*—those whose values divide the report into subgroups. In Figures 14.3, 14.4a, and 14.4b, DIVISION is the break variable. The other columns, on the right, are the *report variables*—those whose values are listed or summarized. The order of the columns is the order in which you specify the variables.

The rows consist of case listings or summary statistics. The order of the rows is the order of the cases in the file. (See Section 14.14 for more information about the order of cases.)

14.6
BUILDING THE REPORT

Four basic subcommands determine the appearance of reports:

FORMAT   Determines the report's general page layout and whether cases are listed. If it is specified, FORMAT precedes all other subcommands on the REPORT command.

VARIABLES   Specifies the *report variables* that are listed and/or summarized in columns in the report. The order in which you list variables on the VARIABLES subcommand determines the order in which columns appear on the report. The VARIABLES subcommand is required.

BREAK   Specifies the *break variable(s)* that break the report rows into subgroups. Break variables always display as the leftmost columns on the report.

SUMMARY   Names a statistic or set of statistics to calculate.

The VARIABLES subcommand is required on every REPORT command. In addition, a listing report requires the FORMAT subcommand with the LIST keyword, while a summary report requires the BREAK and SUMMARY subcommands.

Each subcommand, when used, must follow the order above: FORMAT followed by VARIABLES, BREAK, and SUMMARY. You can specify multiple BREAK and SUMMARY subcommands.

REPORT has other subcommands, but the four above are the ones you'll use most often. They are described in more detail below.

14.7
Choosing Formats and Obtaining Listings

Use the FORMAT subcommand to specify whether AUTOMATIC or MANUAL default formats are implemented. The AUTOMATIC keyword, new in SPSS/PC+ V2.0, facilitates report design by automatically implementing the basic format features you are most likely to use. MANUAL implements the defaults that were used in earlier versions of SPSS/PC+. MANUAL is the default. See REPORT in Part C for a table that compares the default settings for AUTOMATIC and MANUAL.

The FORMAT subcommand also determines whether a report contains summaries or listings, or both. Summaries are the default. To produce a listing report, add the keyword LIST to the FORMAT subcommand. For example,

```
REPORT FORMAT=AUTOMATIC LIST /
```

The keyword LIST applies to all variables named on the VARIABLES subcommand.

14.8
Specifying Report Variables

The required VARIABLES subcommand determines the variables that appear in the report columns. The minimum VARIABLES specification is a list of variables, as in

```
VARIABLES=LNAME AGE TENURE JTENURE
```

which instructs REPORT to list or summarize data for the variables LNAME, AGE, TENURE, and JTENURE.

14.9
Defining Break Groups

The BREAK subcommand specifies the variable whose values break the report rows into subgroups. For example, the REPORT subcommand

```
BREAK=DIVISION /
```

specifies a subgroup for each value of DIVISION.

The BREAK subcommand is required on all summary reports but is optional on listing reports. If you do not want to break a listing report into subgroups, omit the BREAK subcommand.

The REPORT command does not organize data itself, so you must first use the SORT command to organize cases into the break groups you intend to specify on the BREAK subcommand (see Section 14.14).

14.10
Requesting Summary Statistics

To request statistics for subgroups of cases on either a summary or listing report, specify the statistic on a SUMMARY subcommand immediately after a BREAK subcommand. You cannot use a SUMMARY subcommand without a corresponding BREAK subcommand, and the BREAK subcommand must precede its associated SUMMARY subcommands.

For example, the commands

```
SORT CASES BY DIVISION.
REPORT FORMAT=AUTOMATIC /
       VARS=AGE TENURE JTENURE SALARY /
       BREAK=DIVISION /
       SUMMARY=MEAN.
```

request the mean values for AGE, TENURE, JTENURE, and SALARY at each break of the variable DIVISION, as shown in Figure 14.3.

For a list of the summaries available in REPORT, see the REPORT command in Part C.

B

Statistics Guide

14.11
Adding Statistics

To add more summaries, you simply add more SUMMARY subcommands. For example, the following commands

```
SORT CASES BY DIVISION.
REPORT FORMAT=AUTOMATIC /
       VARS=AGE TENURE JTENURE SALARY /
       BREAK=DIVISION /
       SUMMARY=MEAN /
       SUMMARY=MIN /
       SUMMARY=MAX.
```

request the minimum and maximum values in addition to the means for variables AGE, TENURE, JTENURE, and SALARY. Each summary appears on its own line on the report.

14.12
Adding Break Levels

Beyond breaking data into subgroups, you might want to further subdivide it into multiple break levels, adding break columns on the left of the report. To do this, specify multiple BREAK subcommands. Successive BREAK subcommands group the data within preceding BREAK subcommands.

Before specifying a report with multiple break levels, use SORT CASES to sort the break variables into the order you intend to use them (see Section 14.14). Then specify successive BREAK subcommands, as in:

```
SORT CASES BY DIVISION STORE.
REPORT FORMAT=AUTOMATIC /
       VARS=AGE TENURE SALARY /
       BREAK=DIVISION /
       SUMMARY=MEAN /
       SUMMARY=VALIDN /
       BREAK=STORE /
       SUMMARY=MEAN.
```

Figure 14.12 shows a portion of the report. The DIVISION and STORE columns are defined by the break variables. Only the means are shown for each level of store branch within a division. Both means and the number of valid cases are shown for each division.

Figure 14.12   Personnel report with multiple breaks

```
Personnel Data

                               Tenure
                 Branch          in
Division         Store     Age   Company   Salary—Annual
----------       --------  ----  -------   -------------

Carpeting        Suburban

                 Mean      26.75   4.37     $12,625

                 Downtown

                 Mean      32.75   3.87     $11,318
Mean                       30.75   4.04     $11,754
N                          12      12       12
```

When you specify a SUMMARY subcommand, REPORT calculates the statistic you request for the specified break level only. If you want the same statistic for multiple break levels, you must request it at each desired level (see Section 14.32 for a shorthand way of doing this). If you don't want any summary statistics at a given break level, omit the SUMMARY subcommand at that level.

14.13
Breaks Defined by More than One Variable

To combine break groups in a single column, list multiple variables on the same BREAK subcommand. For example, the commands

```
TITLE Personnel Data.
SORT CASES BY DIVISION SHIFT.
REPORT FORMAT=AUTOMATIC /
      VARS=AGE TENURE SALARY /
      BREAK=DIVISION SHIFT "Division" "and" "Shift" /
      SUMMARY=MEAN.
```

combine break variables DIVISION and SHIFT in the same column. By default, REPORT uses the heading from the first variable on the BREAK subcommand. To include both variable names, another column heading is specified in apostrophes (see Section 14.20).

Figure 14.13 shows that REPORT displays the value labels of both break variables in the same column, with the specified column heading, and calculates the mean for AGE, TENURE, and SALARY any time the value of either DIVISION or SHIFT changes. (Only two divisions are shown in FIGURE 14.13.) Note that REPORT does not calculate overall means for each division. To obtain means by division, specify DIVISION and SHIFT on separate BREAK subcommands (see Section 14.12).

Figure 14.13   Report with stacked break variables

```
Personnel Data

Division                 Tenure
and                        in
Shift            Age     Company    Salary—Annual
————————        ————    ————————    —————————————


Carpeting
First

Mean            30.57     3.80        $11,649

Carpeting
Second

Mean            24.00     4.00        $10,000

Carpeting
Weekend

Mean            32.75     4.48        $12,375

Appliances
First

Mean            31.17     3.75        $13,062

Appliances
Second

Mean            42.00     6.50        $18,000

Appliances
Weekend

Mean            25.50     2.67         $8,100
```

14.14
Preparing Data for REPORT

REPORT does not organize the data itself as it reads the cases and computes the summaries. Instead, it simply reads cases in the order they reside in the file, listing them (if you request a listing) while keeping track of information you requested for summaries.

For example, when REPORT calculates a statistic, it calculates it for the subgroup defined by the first value of the break variable. When the value of the break variable changes in the data, REPORT calculates and displays the statistics you requested. It then displays the next value of the break variable and resumes reading cases until the value of the break variable changes again. It displays the requested summary statistics every time it reads a change in the value for the break variable.

Therefore, before you run REPORT, the data must be organized in the file in such a way that all cases with the same value for the break variable reside together. It doesn't matter if the values are in ascending, descending, or some other order—only that all the cases in the same group are together.

To organize data in the file, use the SORT command immediately before the REPORT command. For example, the command

```
SORT BY DIVISION.
```

organizes the data in Figure 14.3 by the subgroups Carpeting, Appliances, Furniture, and Hardware. If you wanted to further subdivide these divisions according to the subgroupings of other variables, you would name additional variables on the SORT command. For example, the command

```
SORT BY DIVISION STORE.
```

groups the data into the divisions of Carpeting, Appliances, Furniture, and Hardware and then organizes the data within each of the divisions according to the subgroups of the variable STORE, which are Suburban and Downtown.

14.15
Trial Runs

Because REPORT is so flexible and its output can have so many components, you may want to experiment with the report layout before you run the final report. If you have a large data file, you can experiment with a subset of the data until you obtain your intended format.

To process a subset of the data, use one of the following techniques:

- Use the N command to limit the number of cases read. The system does not attempt to read more cases than the number specified on the N command. For example, if the file contains 10,000 cases and you specify 10 on the N command, REPORT reads only the first 10 cases.
- If the REPORT contains break variables, and the labeling and spacing of breaks are important considerations, you can obtain a subset of the entire file containing cases from several breaks by using the SAMPLE command.

14.16
REFINING THE REPORT

In addition to specifying the basic report structure as described above, REPORT gives you the ability to refine various report components. These include the following:

- Titles and footnotes
- Margins and alignment
- Column contents and labeling
- Horizontal spacing
- Summary statistics
- String variables
- Missing values

These topics are discussed in Sections 14.17 through 14.36.

14.17
Adding Titles and Footnotes

The optional TITLE and FOOTNOTE subcommands in REPORT enable you to place titles and footnotes on the left, in the center, and on the right of each page of a report. Enclose each line of the title or footnote in apostrophes, separating lines by a comma or a space. To include an apostrophe in a title, either enclose the string in quotation marks or use double apostrophes not separated by a space. For example,

```
SORT CASES BY DIVISION.
REPORT FORMAT=AUTOMATIC LIST /
       VARS=LNAME AGE TENURE SALARY /
       BREAK=DIVISION /
       SUMMARY=MEAN /
       TITLE= "Personnel Report" 'Employees" Profile'.
```

specifies a two-line title. *Personnel Report* displays on the first title line, and *Employee's Profile* displays beneath it on the second title line. The quotation marks enclosing the second title line assure that the apostrophe will display in the title.

If you don't specify a title, SPSS/PC+ uses its system title as a default when the REPORT width is greater than or equal to the system title's width plus 12. To specify a blank title line, type a space between apostrophes. There is no default footnote.

To specify the left, right, or center positions for either titles or footnotes, use the following conventions:

```
TITLE=
    LEFT   '      '      Left-justified title
    RIGHT  '      '      Right-justified title
    CENTER '      '/     Centered title

FOOTNOTE=
    LEFT   '      '      Left-justified note
    RIGHT  '      '      Right-justified note
    CENTER '      '/     Centered note
```

Using TITLE or FOOTNOTE with no reference to a position is equivalent to specifying the center position. However, if you specify a left or right position on the same subcommand, you must use the keyword CENTER to specify the center position. To specify multiple title and footnote lines in any given position, specify each line in apostrophes. Do not repeat the positional keywords. For example,

```
TITLE=LEFT  'Personnel Report' 'As of January 1, 1987'
      RIGHT 'ACME Products' '2201 LaSalle Park'
            'Chicago, Illinois 60611'
```

produces a two-line left title and a three-line right title. Notice that LEFT, RIGHT, and CENTER are not separated by slashes.

Titles and footnotes display on each page of a multiple-page report. The LEFT, RIGHT, and CENTER alignments are relative to the report's margins. If you specify a title or footnote that is wider than the report width, REPORT generates an error message.

You can specify titles and footnotes anywhere after the FORMAT subcommand (except between BREAK and SUMMARY) as long as all title subcommands precede all footnote subcommands. There is no fixed limit to the number of title or footnote lines you can define on a report.

Three special arguments are available in titles and footnotes:

)PAGE   *Print the page number right-justified in a five-character field.*

)DATE   *Print the current date in the form* dd/mmm/yy *right-adjusted in a nine-character field.*

)variable *Print this variable's value label in this relative position.*

You can use all three arguments in as many titles and footnotes as you like on a single report. The following are typical examples:

```
TITLE=LEFT  'Personnel Report' 'Prepared on )DATE" /
      RIGHT 'Page )PAGE" /
FOOTNOTE=RIGHT 'Regional Manager: )MGRNM" /
```

The left title includes the current date, and the right title includes the current page numbers. The footnote includes the value label for MGRNM.

Each variable you specify with *)variable* must be one you've defined in the active file, though it does not need to be a variable you've included as a column on your report. If you specify a variable that has no value label, the value itself will display, formatted according to its print format. You cannot specify a system variable or a variable you create with the STRING subcommand (see Section 14.33).

One label or value from each variable specified in a *)variable* argument displays on every page of the report. The label that REPORT displays for each varies from page to page and is chosen from cases as follows:

• If a new page starts with a case listing, REPORT takes the labeled value from the first case listed.

• If a new page starts with a BREAK line, REPORT takes the labeled value from the first case of the new break group.

• If a new page starts with a summary line, REPORT takes the labeled value from the last case of the break group being summarized.

• If you specify the same variable in both a title and a footnote, REPORT takes the title value from the top case on the page and the footnote value from the last case on the page.

You cannot use variables named DATE or PAGE in the *)variable* argument because they will only display the current date or a page number. If you want to use a variable named DATE or PAGE, change the variable's name with the MODIFY VARIABLES command before you use it in the *)variable* argument.

14.18
Margins and Report Alignment

Report margins determine the maximum width allowed for a report. (The finished report may be narrower, however.) REPORT uses a default left margin of 1, and a default right margin equal to your system's defined width. To change the margins, use the MARGINS keyword on the FORMAT subcommand (see REPORT in Part C).

Report alignment refers to a report's position relative to its defined margins. For example, report margins of (1,80) allow for an 80-character report. If the finished report is only 50 characters wide, the report's alignment refers to whether the report is left-justified against column 1 of the margins, right-justified against column 80, or centered between columns 1 and 80. The default is left-justified. To change the default, use the ALIGNMENT keyword on the FORMAT subcommand (see REPORT in Part C).

14.19
Column Contents and Labeling

Sections 14.20 through 14.24 discuss options for controlling the contents, layout, and labeling of columns.

14.20
Column Headings

Each column in a report has a heading. By default, REPORT uses the variable label for the heading. If there is no label, REPORT uses the variable name.

REPORT wraps default column headings within their column widths, using as many lines as necessary and attempting to split lines meaningfully at spaces. With FORMAT=AUTOMATIC, REPORT centers each column heading within the width of its column. However, when value labels or string values exceed the width of the longest word in the heading, REPORT left-justifies the heading.

To specify a column heading, enclose the heading in apostrophes or quotation marks following the variable name on either the VARIABLES or BREAK subcommands. With automatic format, REPORT does not wrap a heading you specify; it displays the heading exactly as you arrange it in your specification. To display the heading on multiple lines, enclose each line within its own set of apostrophes or quotation marks. To include an apostrophe in the heading, use quotation marks around the heading. For example,

```
SORT CASES BY DIVISION
REPORT FORMAT=AUTOMATIC LIST
    /VARIABLES=LNAME 'Employee'
                AGE "Employee's Age" TENURE JTENURE
    /BREAK=DIVISION 'Company' 'Division'
    /SUMMARY=MEAN
```

produces the report in Figure 14.20 (only the first few lines of the report are shown). Each heading is centered, except for Company Division and Employee. Because DIVISION and LNAME are string variables with values wider than the longest word in the column heading, the column headings are left-justified.

Figure 14.20 Column headings

```
Personnel Data

                                              Tenure     Tenure
Company                                         in          in
Division       Employee       Employee's Age  Company     Grade
-----------    -----------    --------------  -------     ------

Carpeting      Ford               27.00        3.67        2.17
               Cochran            22.00        3.92        3.08
               Hoawinski          23.00        3.92        3.08
               Gates              24.00        4.00        3.25
               Mulvihill          30.00        4.08        3.08
               Lavelle            27.00        4.33        3.17
               Mahr               33.00        2.67        2.67
```

14.21
Column Widths and Spacing

When you don't specify a column width for a variable, REPORT determines a default width, using the *larger* of the following for each variable:

• The widest print format in the column, whether it is a variable print format or a summary print format.

• The width of any temporary variable you define with REPORT's STRING subcommand.

• If you assign a column heading, the length of the longest title line in that heading. For example, VARS = TENURE 'Tenure in Company' 'Measured' 'in Months' specifies 'Tenure in Company' as the longest line in a three-line heading.

• When no column heading is specified, the length of the longest word in the variable label, or the length of the variable name. (If FORMAT=MANUAL, variable labels are not evaluated.)

• If you specify (LABEL), the length of the variable's longest value label. (With FORMAT=AUTOMATIC, (LABEL) is the default for break variables.) REPORT reads value labels from the dictionary, so it's possible for you to exclude a value from your report, yet still have that value's label determine the width of a column. (If FORMAT=MANUAL, REPORT uses the length of the variable's longest value label, up to 20 characters; 20 is the largest value it uses for this criterion with MANUAL format.)

To override the default, specify a column width in parentheses following the variable name on the VARIABLES or BREAK subcommand, as in:

```
REPORT FORMAT = AUTOMATIC /
    VARIABLES = LNAME (10) AGE /
    BREAK = DIVISION (5) /
    SUMMARY = MEAN.
```

Intercolumn Spacing. REPORT subtracts the combined column widths of the break and report variables from the REPORT margins. It then divides the result by the number of columns minus 1. It uses this value or 4, whichever is least, as the space between each column.

Automatic Fit. When the above criteria result in a report that is too wide for the report margins, AUTOMATIC format shrinks the report. It performs the following steps, stopping as soon as the report fits within the margins:

- It reduces intercolumn spacing incrementally until it reaches a minimum intercolumn space of 1. It will never reduce it to 0.
- It shortens strings, begining with the longest string from a string variable at least 15 characters wide. It shortens the string as much as needed—up to 40% of its length. If necessary it repeats the step, using different string variables. It will not shorten the same string twice.

REPORT does not implement the *automatic fit* criteria unless FORMAT= AUTOMATIC.

14.22
Labels versus Values

When running a listing report, you frequently want to see value labels for the report variables rather than the values themselves. For example, if you want to run a personnel report that includes an employee's sex, you would prefer to see the labels Female and Male rather than the values 1 and 2 on the report. By specifying the keyword (LABEL) after the variable name on the VARIABLES subcommand, you instruct REPORT to display labels rather than values for that variable.

For example, to produce a listing report that shows the sex, age, job grade, and work shift for each employee, you would use the following commands:

```
SORT CASES BY LNAME
REPORT FORMAT=AUTOMATIC LIST
        /VARS=LNAME SEX(LABEL) AGE JOBGRADE(LABEL) SHIFT(LABEL)
```

The keyword (LABEL) generates a descriptive report, as you can see in Figure 14.22 (only part of the report is shown).

Figure 14.22   Personnel report with keyword (LABEL)

```
Personnel Data

Last Name        Sex          Age     Job Grade          Shift
-----------      ------       ------  -----------        ------
Baker            Male         42.00   Sales Staff        Weekend
Blount           Male         41.00   Sales Staff        Weekend
Carlyle          Female       40.00   Sales Staff        Weekend
Cochran          Female       22.00   Sales Staff        First
Cochran          Male         39.00   Sales Staff        Second
Dan              Male         36.00   Sales Staff        Weekend
Farkas           Male         37.00   Sales Staff        First
Ford             Female       27.00   Support Staff      First
Ford             Female       36.00   Sales Staff        Weekend
Gates            Female       24.00   Sales Staff        Second
Golden           Female       42.00   Sales Staff        First
Gonzales         Female       42.00   Support Staff      First
Hoawinski        Female       23.00   Sales Staff        First
Jacobesen        Male         44.00   Supervisory Staff  Second
Johnson          Female       42.00   Sales Staff        Second
```

If the variable list contains a set of inclusive variables implied by the keyword TO, (LABEL) applies to the entire set of variables in the list. However, (LABEL) cannot be implied for a set of variables named individually. For example, in

```
/VARIABLES=V1 TO V5(LABEL)
```

(LABEL) applies to all variables implied by V1 TO V5. But in

```
/VARIABLES=V1 V2 V3 V4 V5(LABEL)
```

(LABEL) applies only to V5.

14.23
Stacking Report Variables

When FORMAT=LIST, REPORT permits you to stack report variables together in a single column by linking them with + signs on the VARIABLES subcommand. For example,

```
TITLE Personnel Data.
SORT CASES BY DIVISION LNAME.
REPORT FORMAT=AUTOMATIC LIST/
        VARS=LNAME
        TENURE p STORE(LABEL) "Tenure" "and" "Location"
        AGE SALARY/
        BREAK=DIVISION/
        SUMMARY=MEAN.
```

stacks the variables TENURE and STORE in a single column, as shown in Figure 14.23 (only one division is shown). LNAME, AGE, and SALARY are unaffected. The stacked variables each start a new line on the report and are listed in the order they are defined on the VARIABLES subcommand. REPORT will not split the values for a single case across page breaks in the report.

Figure 14.23   Report with stacked report variables

```
Personnel Data

                                 Tenure
                                  and
   Division       Last Name     Location      Age      Salary--Annual
   --------       ---------     --------      ---      --------------

   Carpeting      Cochran           3.92     22.00         $10,900
                                Suburban
                  Dan               3.83     36.00         $10,000

                  Ford              3.67     27.00          $9,200
                                Suburban
                  Gates             4.00     24.00         $10,000
                                Downtown
                  Hoawinski         3.92     23.00         $10,900
                                Suburban
                  Jones             4.83     44.00         $15,690
                                Downtown
                  Katz              3.75     33.00         $10,000
                                Downtown
                  Lavelle           4.33     27.00         $10,000
                                Downtown
                  Mahr              2.67     33.00          $9,335
                                Downtown
                  McAndrews         3.50     35.00         $15,520
                                Downtown
                  Mulvihill         4.08     30.00         $10,000
                                Downtown
                  Tygielski         6.00     35.00         $19,500
                                Suburban

   Mean                             4.04     30.75         $11,754
```

REPORT reads values from all the stacked variables when it determines column widths. However, REPORT uses the default heading from the first variable on the stacked list (if you don't specify a heading), and it uses only values from the first variable on the stacked list to calculate summaries.

14.24
Creating Empty Columns

You can add space between columns by creating a dummy variable on the VARIABLES subcommand. Since a dummy variable has no values, its column will be blank. To insert this blank column between other variables' columns, specify the variable name followed by the keyword (DUMMY) between the names of the variables whose columns are to be separated by the blank column. For example,

```
/VARIABLES = AGE TENURE XX(DUMMY) (7) ' ' SALARY
```

places a blank column 7 spaces wide between the columns for TENURE and SALARY. The blank title specified between apostrophes overrides the default column heading.

The space created by dummy variables is also useful for holding the results of composite functions (see Section 14.31).

14.25
Horizontal Spacing

The keyword LIST on FORMAT has an optional argument, (n), that controls the spacing of cases in listing reports. By default, there are no blank lines between cases. An integer value in parentheses specifies a blank line after every *n* cases. For example, LIST(1) produces a double-spaced listing and LIST(3) lists cases in sets of three. The spacing option makes it easier to read reports with many cases.

The following commands generate the report shown in Figure 14.25 (only part of the report is shown):

```
SORT CASES BY LNAME
REPORT FORMAT=AUTOMATIC LIST(3)
       /VARS=LNAME AGE TENURE JTENURE
```

To insert a blank line between several variables that are stacked in one column (see Stacking Report Variables, above), either specify (DUMMY) after a nonexistent variable name, or specify a blank space between two plus signs.

Figure 14.25   Personnel report with optional spacing

```
Personnel Data

                              Tenure       Tenure
                                in           in
   Last Name          Age     Company      Grade
   ---------          ---     -------      -----

   Baker              42.00    5.25         3.75
   Blount             41.00    5.25         3.75
   Carlyle            40.00    6.00         6.00

   Cochran            22.00    3.92         3.08
   Cochran            39.00    5.50         5.50
   Dan                36.00    3.83         3.25

   Farkas             37.00    4.42         3.67
   Ford               27.00    3.67         2.17
   Ford               36.00    4.50         3.67
```

Other keywords in REPORT allow you to control spacing between titles and column headings, between headings and listings, between individual rows within the body of the report, and between the body of the report and footnotes. These keywords are listed in Table 14.37 and described under REPORT in Part C.

14.26
Summary Statistics

REPORT gives you precise control over the types of summaries to be displayed and their appearance on the report. Sections 14.27 through 14.32 describe summary specifications.

14.27
Selecting Variables for Statistics

A statistic specified on the SUMMARY subcommand is calculated for all the variables named on the VARIABLES subcommand. If you want the statistic to be calculated only for selected report variables, name the desired variables in parentheses on the SUMMARY subcommand, as in

```
SORT CASES BY DIVISION.
REPORT FORMAT=AUTOMATIC LIST /
       VARIABLES=LNAME AGE TENURE JTENURE SALARY /
       BREAK=DIVISION /
       SUMMARY=MEAN(JTENURE, SALARY).
```

You cannot use the TO keyword on SUMMARY to imply a set of variables.

14.28
Summaries across Break Groups (Report Totals)

The keyword (TOTAL) on the BREAK subcommand calculates summary statistics for all the cases on the report. These totals display at the end of the report. You can specify (TOTAL) for both listing and summary reports.

To generate a report that has break level summaries plus total summaries, specify (TOTAL) after the variable named on the BREAK subcommand that precedes the summary whose totals you want, as in:

```
SORT CASES BY STORE DIVISION.
REPORT FORMAT=AUTOMATIC /
       VARIABLES=AGE TENURE JTENURE SALARY /
       BREAK=STORE(TOTAL) /
       SUMMARY=VALIDN (AGE) /
       BREAK=DIVISION /
       SUMMARY=MEAN.
```

The first set of BREAK and SUMMARY subcommands calculates the number of employees who work at each branch store and the total number of employees who work for the company by counting those that have valid values for AGE. The second set calculates a mean for each division but does not calculate a mean for the entire company because (TOTAL) is not specified at this break level. Figure 14.28a shows the report.

Figure 14.28a Summary report with totals

Personnel Data					
Branch Store	Division	Age	Tenure in Company	Tenure in Grade	Salary—Annual
Suburban	Carpeting				
	Mean	26.75	4.37	3.42	$12,625
	Appliances				
	Mean	30.20	4.05	3.77	$14,395
	Furniture				
	Mean	35.29	4.71	4.32	$12,975
	Hardware				
	Mean	32.00	4.33	4.33	$22,500
N		17			
Downtown	Carpeting				
	Mean	32.75	3.87	3.25	$11,318
	Appliances				
	Mean	32.25	3.52	3.25	$10,150
	Furniture				
	Mean	38.25	4.86	3.86	$13,500
	Hardware				
	Mean	37.25	4.67	4.62	$16,350
N		24			
TOTAL					
N		41			

When the statistics you want REPORT to calculate for the totals differ from those you want it to calculate at the various break levels, specify (TOTAL) on a BREAK subcommand and do not name a variable; then use as many SUMMARY subcommands as you need to specify the summary totals you want REPORT to calculate. Name your break variables on subsequent BREAK subcommands. For example, when you specify

```
SORT CASES BY DIVISION.
REPORT FORMAT=AUTOMATIC /
      VARIABLES=AGE TENURE JTENURE SALARY /
      BREAK=(TOTAL) /
      SUMMARY=VALIDN (AGE) /
      BREAK=DIVISION /
      SUMMARY=MEAN.
```

REPORT calculates the total number of employees in the company but does not calculate the number of employees within each division. It calculates a mean for each division but does not calculate a mean for the entire company (see Figure 14.28b).

Figure 14.28b   Totals that differ from break level summaries

```
Personnel Data

                            Tenure     Tenure
                              in         in
     Division      Age     Company     Grade     Salary—Annual
     --------      ---     -------     -----     -------------
     Carpeting
     Mean         30.75     4.04        3.31        $11,754
     Appliances
     Mean         31.11     3.81        3.54        $12,508
     Furniture
     Mean         36.87     4.79        4.08        $13,255
     Hardware
     Mean         36.20     4.60        4.57        $17,580

     N             41
```

You can specify (TOTAL) on a BREAK subcommand that does not name a variable to obtain totals for a listing report that does not contain break levels. Use as many SUMMARY subcommands as you need to specify the totals you want REPORT to calculate, as in:

```
SORT CASES BY LNAME.
REPORT FORMAT=AUTOMATIC LIST/
      VARIABLES=LNAME AGE TENURE JTENURE SALARY /
      BREAK=(TOTAL) /
      SUMMARY=MEAN /
      SUMMARY=VALIDN (JTENURE).
```

Each statistic specified on a SUMMARY subcommand is calculated for all the cases in the report. Though the file is sorted by LNAME to alphabetize the listing, SORT CASES is optional since the report has no break variables.

Figure 14.28c   Listing report with totals

```
Personnel Data

                            Tenure     Tenure
                              in         in
     Last Name     Age     Company     Grade     Salary—Annual
     ---------     ---     -------     -----     -------------
       .
       .
     Sedowski     30.00     2.67        2.67         $7,500
     Shavilje     32.00     2.92        2.92         $8,900
     Snolik       34.00     5.08        4.50        $15,300
     Syms         32.00     4.33        4.33        $22,500
     Totman       41.00     4.50        3.50        $13,300
     Tygielski    35.00     6.00        5.33        $19,500
     Wajda        26.00     3.17        3.17         $8,975
     Washington   32.00     4.42        3.67        $14,400
     White        25.00     3.92        3.33        $11,000
     Wilson       36.00     4.42        3.75        $14,000

     Mean
                  33.73     4.34        3.79        $13,179
     N
                                         41
```

Figure 14.28c shows the last lines of the report. The mean values are those for the entire 41 employees. The summary titles *Mean* and *N* begin in the left-most column and are left-justified. The values for each statistic display one row beneath their title, allowing you to specify a summary title that spans as far as the right margin of the report (see Section 14.29).

14.29
Summary Titles

By default, REPORT uses its own summary titles (listed in Part C) on a report to identify each statistic you request on the SUMMARY subcommand. It displays the summary title in the column corresponding to the break being summarized, aligning the titles with the labels or values in the column. The title displays in mixed case or upper case, depending upon your system's default specifications.

You can change the default summary title by enclosing a one-line title in apostrophes or quotation marks, as in

```
SUMMARY=STDDEV 'Standard Deviation'
```

Use leading blanks to indent summary titles within the break column.

If you specify a summary title wider than its break column, the title extends into the break column to its right. If the width of the available break columns is insufficient to display the full summary title, the title is truncated.

REPORT allows you to move summary titles between break columns. To do so, specify in parentheses the number of the break column in which you want the summary title to appear, counting the first specified BREAK subcommand as 1. For example, the commands

```
REPORT FORMAT=AUTOMATIC LIST /
       VARIABLES=LNAME AGE TENURE JTENURE SALARY /
       BREAK=STORE /
       SUMMARY=MEAN(JTENURE)
       BREAK=DIVISION /
       SUMMARY=MEAN(SALARY) 'Average Salary' (1)
```

display the title Average Salary in the column for the first break, STORE, rather than in the column for DIVISION.

Although summary titles can only be one line long, when you use multiple SUMMARY subcommands you can continue a summary title from one summary line to another. For example,

```
SUMMARY=SUM 'Sums and Averages' /
SUMMARY=MEAN 'Based on 1986 5% Sample'
```

produces a two-line summary with a title continuing from the first to the second line. You can also specify a blank title for any summary line.

14.30
Print Formats for Summary
Statistics

Every summary function has a default display format. For example, the PERCENT function uses a width of 6 places, including one decimal place. For the default formats, see REPORT in Part C.

You can specify COMMA and DOLLAR formats when they are not the default, or PLAIN to override those formats when they are the default. You can also specify an alternative number of decimal digits by enclosing the desired number in a separate set of parentheses. For example, in the subcommand

```
SUMMARY = MEAN(SALARY(COMMA)(2))
```

SUMMARY displays the mean of SALARY without a dollar sign and with two decimal digits.

If the column is not wide enough to display the specified decimal digits for a given function, REPORT displays fewer decimals. REPORT uses scientific notation or displays asterisks if the column is not wide enough to display the integer portion of the number.

14.31
Composite Functions

A composite function operates on simple aggregate statistics and their arguments to produce a single result. For example, say you want to run a listing report that shows the average age, tenure, and salary of employees, and also reflects what the average salary will be when next year's 7% across-the-board salary increase takes effect. The following commands produce such a report:

```
SORT CASES BY DIVISION LNAME
REPORT FORMAT=AUTOMATIC LIST /
       VARS=LNAME AGE TENURE SALARY /
       BREAK=DIVISION /
       SUMMARY=MEAN /
       SUMMARY=MULTIPLY(MEAN(SALARY)1.07) "7% Raise"
```

Note that the summary title is specified after the final parentheses enclosing the arguments, not between the function name (MULTIPLY) and its arguments.

Figure 14.31 shows one division from the report. Note that the composite function computes only one result.

Figure 14.31   Report with composite function

```
Personnel Data

                                     Tenure
                                       in
   Division    Last Name      Age    Company    Salary—Annual
   ---------   ----------     ----   --------   -------------

   Carpeting   Cochran       22.00     3.92        $10,900
               Dan           36.00     3.83        $10,000
               Ford          27.00     3.67         $9,200
               Gates         24.00     4.00        $10,000
               Hoawinski     23.00     3.92        $10,900
               Jones         44.00     4.83        $15,690
               Katz          33.00     3.75        $10,000
               Lavelle       27.00     4.33        $10,000
               Mahr          33.00     2.67         $9,335
               McAndrews     35.00     3.50        $15,520
               Mulvihill     30.00     4.08        $10,000
               Tygielski     35.00     6.00        $19,500

   Mean                      30.75     4.04        $11,754
   7% Raise                                        $12,577
```

By default, REPORT displays the result of the composite function calculation in the column defined by the first variable in the function that is also named on the VARIABLES subcommand. To move the result to another variable's column, specify that variable's name in parentheses after you completely define the composite function's argument. For example,

```
SUMMARY=MULTIPLY(MEAN(SALARY)1.07) (LNAME)
```

places the result in the column defined by LNAME. Without (LNAME), this summary would appear in the column for SALARY. Unlike simple functions, the composite function result can be placed in any report column, including those defined by dummy variables or string variables.

It is often advisable to specify the format and number of decimal digits you want to display. Specify print formats for composites within parentheses following the name of the variable in whose column the result is to be displayed. For example, in the subcommand

```
SUMMARY=MULTIPLY(MEAN(SALARY)1.07) (SALARY(2))
```

(SALARY(2)) specifies that the increased average salary be displayed with 2 decimal places in the SALARY column.

You can use any numeric SPSS/PC+ variables, not just REPORT variables, as arguments to composite functions. You do not have to name a variable on the VARIABLES subcommand to use it in a composite function. You cannot use a composite function as an argument to a composite function. You can only use simple functions, variables, and constants.

There are three basic reasons for using composite functions:

1   To place a summary statistic in a column other than the one for which it is calculated. For example, the sum of VARA is normally displayed in the column corresponding to VARA. It can, however, be placed in any other column by using a composite such as

```
SUMMARY=ADD(SUM(VARA)) (VARB)
```

which adds the sum of VARA to nothing and places it in VARB's column. The SUBTRACT, GREAT, LEAST, and AVERAGE composite functions can achieve the same result.

2 To manipulate statistics and change the unit of analysis. Certain arithmetic operations between variables produce the same result at either the case level or the subpopulation level. You can subtract the sum of variable A from the sum of variable B and obtain the same answer as subtracting A from B for each case and summing the result. However, dividing the sum of A by the sum of B is not the same as dividing A by B for each case and averaging the results.

3 To manipulate variables not named on the VARIABLES subcommand so that these variables are not allocated a column in the report. For example, you might want to adjust dollar figures by some index when displaying means but not to allocate a column for the index.

For a complete list of the composite functions available in REPORT, see Part C.

14.32
Repeating Summary Specifications

The keyword PREVIOUS on SUMMARY references a set of SUMMARY subcommands defined for a previous BREAK subcommand. For example,

```
REPORT   FORMAT=LIST/
         VARIABLES=NAME AGE TENURE /
         BREAK=DIVISION /
         SUMMARY=MEAN /
         SUMMARY=VALIDN(AGE) /
         BREAK=STORE /
         SUMMARY=PREVIOUS.
```

displays means and the valid number of cases for AGE for each STORE within the DIVISION.

PREVIOUS accepts an optional argument in parentheses to point to the particular set of summaries to be copied. For example, PREVIOUS(1) copies all the SUMMARY subcommands applying to the first BREAK subcommand, and PREVIOUS(2) copies summary specifications for the second BREAK subcommand. No other specification can be used on a SUMMARY subcommand using PREVIOUS.

14.33
Using Strings

The STRING subcommand enables you to link together SPSS/PC+ variables and constants to create new temporary variables you can use in REPORT. You can link together both alphanumeric and numeric variables and also intermix them.

For example, the subcommand

```
STRING= PHONE (AREA '/' EXCH '-' NUM)
```

creates a string variable named PHONE, which comprises three variables and two constants.

• The STRING subcommand must precede the VARIABLES subcommand.

• New STRING variables are temporary and available to the REPORT procedure only. The name you assign them must be unique and must follow SPSS/PC+ variable-naming conventions.

• You cannot use the keyword TO to imply a list of variables on the STRING subcommand.

You can use STRING variables on both the VARIABLES and BREAK subcommands, specifying column headings for them as you do for any other variables.

14.34
A STRING Application

One use of the STRING subcommand is to separate report columns with a column of special characters, such as asterisks or vertical bars. For example,

```
TITLE Personnel Data.
REPORT FORMAT=AUTOMATIC LIST /
      STRING=FILL ('*') /
      VARS=LNAME AGE TENURE FILL(1) " " SALARY.
```

defines a string variable FILL with the value "*" for each case. Naming FILL between TENURE and SALARY on the VARIABLES subcommand displays a vertical column of asterisks between those two columns on a listing report. The (1) after FILL on VARIABLES specifies a column width of 1; the space between apostrophes specifies a blank column heading. Figure 14.34 shows the first few lines of the report.

Figure 14.34   Column of special characters

```
Personnel Data


                        Tenure
                          in
Last Name        Age    Company          Salary--Annual


Ford            27.00    3.67      *         $9,200
Cochran         22.00    3.92      *        $10,900
Hoawinski       23.00    3.92      *        $10,900
Gates           24.00    4.00      *        $10,000
Mulvihill       30.00    4.08      *        $10,000
Lavelle         27.00    4.33      *        $10,000
Mahr            33.00    2.67      *         $9,335
Katz            33.00    3.75      *        $10,000
Jones           44.00    4.83      *        $15,690
    .
    .
    .
```

14.35
Handling Missing Values

The MISSING subcommand within REPORT controls the treatment of missing values. You can specify one MISSING subcommand per REPORT command. It must follow the VARIABLE subcommand and precede BREAK.

The MISSING subcommand has three options:

VAR   *Treat missing values separately for each variable named on the VARIA-BLES subcommand.* Missing values are indicated in case listings but are not included in calculating summary statistics. MISSING=VAR is the default.

LIST(varlist n)   *Eliminate any case with missing values on n or more of the variables named on the variable list.*

NONE   *Handle all user-missing values as though they were not missing.* The keyword NONE applies to the entire set of variables named on the VARIABLES subcommand. It cannot be used to ignore missing-data indicators for some variables selectively.

For example, the subcommand

```
MISSING=LIST (AGE TENURE SALARY 2)
```

deletes any case with missing values on two or more of the variables AGE, TENURE and SALARY from case listings and from summaries. If a case is missing for just one or for none of the variables listed, it is not deleted from case listings but is deleted from summaries for those variables for which it is missing. If no number is specified, the default is 1.

MISSING specifications apply to REPORT-generated strings, as well as to other variables. If one variable in a REPORT-generated string is missing, the string is missing.

Only variables named on the VARIABLES and SUMMARY subcommands are checked for missing values. You must use a SELECT IF command to eliminate cases missing on break variables.

14.36
Changing the Missing-Value
Indicator

REPORT uses a period to indicate missing values in case listings, break values, and summary statistics.

The MISSING keyword on the FORMAT subcommand enables you to change the default missing-value indicator from a period (.) to any other character, including a blank. To do so, specify any one-character symbol, including a blank, in apostrophes, as in:

```
FORMAT=AUTOMATIC LIST MISSING "m" /
```

14.37
SUMMARY

REPORT has a full range of keywords that allow you to control the format and layout of a report. Table 14.37 will help you determine the subcommands and keywords to use to achieve the results you want. You can then consult the REPORT in Part C to quickly locate full descriptions of each.

Table 14.37

Function	Subcommand	Keyword
Adjusting margins	FORMAT	MARGINS(l,r)
Aligning columns	FORMAT	ALIGN(LEFT,CENTER,RIGHT)
Aligning report contents	VARIABLES, BREAK	(OFFSET(n|CENTER))
Determining column contents	FORMAT	LIST NOLIST MISSING ' '
	VARIABLES, BREAK	(VALUE LABEL)
	BREAK	NAME NONAME
Moving summary titles	SUMMARY	( ) col number
Page lengths	FORMAT	LENGTH(*|n)
	BREAK	(PAGE(RESET))
Page numbers	FORMAT	PAGE1(n)
Shifting column headings	FORMAT	CHALIGN(TOP,BOTTOM) TSPACE(n)
	VARIABLES, STRING, BREAK	' ' literal
	VARIABLES, BREAK	(CENTER, LEFT, RIGHT)
Spacing between columns	FORMAT	COLSPACE (4 n)
	VARIABLES	(DUMMY)
Spacing between rows	FORMAT	TSPACE(n) CHDSPACE(n) LIST(n) BRKSPACE(n) SUMSPACE(n) FTSPACE(n)
	VARIABLES	(DUMMY)
	BREAK, SUMMARY	(SKIP(n))
Specifying column widths	VARIABLES, STRING, BREAK	(n) following varname
Totals on listing reports	BREAK	(TOTAL)
Underscores between listings and summaries	BREAK	UNDERSCORE
Underscoring column headings	FORMAT	UNDERSCORE(ON OFF)

Bibliography

Beard, C. M., V. Fuster, and L. R. Elveback. 1982. Daily and seasonal variation in sudden cardiac death, Rochester, Minnesota, 1950–1975. *Mayo Clinic Proceedings* 57: 704–706.

Black and Sherba. 1983. Contracting to problem-solve to lose weight. *Behavior Therapy* 14: 105–109.

Blalock, H. M. 1979. *Social statistics.* New York: McGraw-Hill.

Blom, G. 1958. *Statistical estimates and transformed beta variables.* New York: John Wiley & Sons.

Borgatta, E. F., and G. W. Bohrnstedt. 1980. Level of measurement once over again. *Sociological methods and research* 9(2): 147–160.

Brown, M. B., and J. K. Benedetti. 1977. Sampling behavior of tests for correlation in two-way contingency tables. *Journal of the American Statistical Association* 72: 309–315.

Cedercreutz, C. 1978. Hypnotic treatment of 100 cases of migraine. In *Hypnosis at its bicentennial,* ed. F. H. Frankel and H. S. Zamansky. New York: Plenum Press.

Churchill, G. A., Jr. 1979. *Marketing research: Methodological foundations.* Hinsdale, Ill.: Dryden Press.

Cohen, J. 1960. A coefficient of agreement for nominal scales. *Educational and Psychological Measurement* 20: 37–46.

Conover, W. J. 1974. Some reasons for not using the Yates continuity correction on 2 × 2 contingency tables. *Journal of the American Statistical Association* 69: 374–376.

——. 1980. *Practical nonparametric statistics,* 2nd ed. New York: John Wiley & Sons.

Consumer Reports. 1983. Beer. *Consumer Reports* (July): 342–348.

Everitt, B. S. 1977. *The analysis of contingency tables.* London: Chapman & Hall.

Freund, R. J. 1980. The case of the missing cell. *The American Statistician* 34: 94–98.

Goodman, L. A., and W. H. Kruskal. 1954. Measures of association for cross-classification. *Journal of the American Statistical Association* 49: 732–764.

Hansson, R. O., and K. M. Slade. 1977. Altruism toward a deviant in city and small town. *Journal of Applied Social Psychology* 7(3): 272–279.

Hays, W. L. 1981. *Statistics for the social sciences,* 3rd ed. New York: Holt, Rinehart & Winston.

Hoaglin, D. C., F. Mosteller, and J. W. Tukey. 1983. *Understanding robust and exploratory data analysis.* New York: John Wiley & Sons.

Hogg, R. V. 1979. An introduction to robust estimation. *Robustness in Statistics,* 1–18.

Kleinbaum, D. G., L. L. Kupper, and H. Morgenstern. 1982. *Epidemiological research: Principles and quantitative methods.* Belmont, Calif.: Wadsworth, Inc.

Lehmann, E. L. 1975. *Nonparametrics: Statistical methods based on ranks.* San Francisco: Holden-Day.

Loether, H. J., and D. G. McTavish. 1976. *Descriptive and inferential statistics: An introduction.* Boston: Allyn & Bacon.

Mantel, N., and W. Haenszel. 1959. Statistical aspects of the analysis of data from retrospective studies of disease. *Journal of the National Cancer Institute* 22: 719–748.

Mantel, N. 1974. Comment and a suggestion on the Yates continuity correction. *Journal of the American Statistical Association* 69: 378–380.

Paul, O., et al. 1963. A longitudinal study of coronary heart disease. *Circulation* 28: 20–31.

Rabkin, S. W., F. A. Mathewson, and R. B. Tate. 1980. Chronobiology of cardiac sudden death in men. *Journal of the American Medical Association* 244(12): 1357–1358.

Somers, R. H. 1962. A new symmetric measure of association for ordinal variables. *American Sociological Review* 27: 799–811.

Wyner, G. A. 1980. Response errors in self-reported number of arrests. *Sociological Methods and Research* 9(2): 161–177.

Command Reference

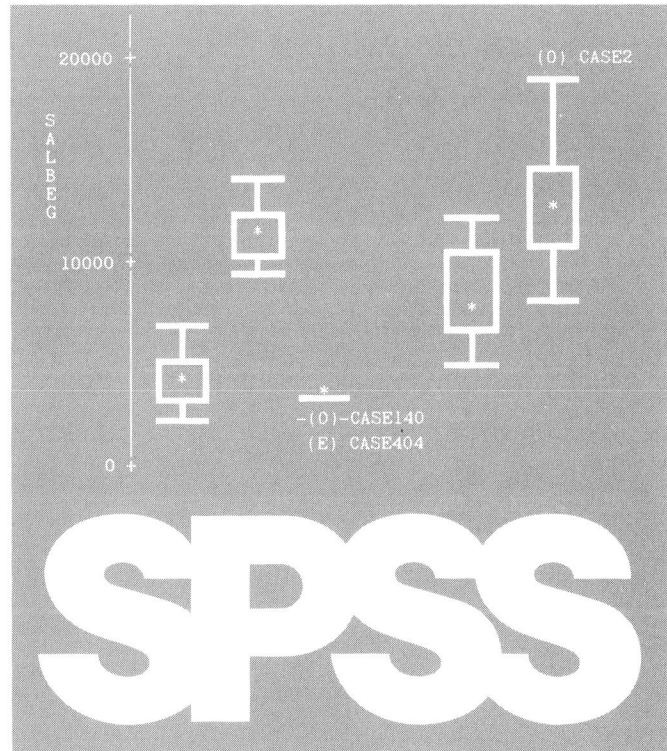

```
         20000 +                                      (O) CASE2
             S
             A
             L
             B                            ┬
             E                           ┌┴┐         ┬
             G                           │*│        ┌┴┐
                                         └┬┘        │*│
         10000 +                          ┴        ┌┴┐
                                                   │*│┬
                       ┬                           │*│
                      ┌┴┐                          └─┘
                      │*│                          ┴
                      └┬┘         *
                       ┴         -(O)-CASE140
                                  (E) CASE404
             0 +
```

■ *Universals*
■ *Commands*

Contents

Universals

Syntax

Using SPSS/PC+ means becoming familiar with its language. Every effort has been made to keep the language natural, consistent, and straightforward.

Syntax Diagrams

Each SPSS/PC+ command described in this Command Reference includes a syntax diagram that shows all the subcommands, keywords, and specifications allowed for that command. The syntax diagram is used to show all the specifications for a command. By remembering the following rules, you can use the syntax diagram as a quick reference for each command.

• Elements shown in capital letters are keywords.

• Elements in lower case describe specifications supplied by the user.

• Elements in boldface type are defaults. Some defaults are indicated with **.

• Special delimiters, such as parentheses, apostrophes, or quotation marks, are required where indicated.

• Elements enclosed in square brackets ([ ]) are optional. When brackets would confuse the format, they are omitted. The command description explains which specifications are required or optional.

• Braces ({ }) indicate a choice between elements.

• The word *varlist* stands for a list of variable names.

• The command terminator is not shown in the syntax diagram.

Command Order

There are few formal rules regarding the order in which SPSS/PC+ commands should be specified. Understanding how SPSS/PC+ works will make it easy to specify commands in the right order.

• Variables must be defined before they can be used in procedures or assigned missing values or labels. You must use at least one DATA LIST, GET, JOIN, AGGREGATE, IMPORT, or TRANSLATE command to define variables for a session. (You can also define variables using the DE command available with SPSS Data Entry II.) IF, COUNT, COMPUTE, and CREATE commands also define variables.

• The logical outcome of command processing frequently determines the order: although data transformations are not carried out until the data are read, the result is as though the commands were executed when encountered.

Commands

Commands are the instructions that you give SPSS/PC+ to initiate an action. The following rules apply to all SPSS/PC+ commands:

• Commands begin with a keyword that is the name of the command and often have additional specifications, such as subcommands and user specifications. Refer to the discussion of each command to see which subcommands and additional specifications are required.

• Each command ends with a command terminator. The default command terminator is a period (.).

• The command terminator must be the last non-blank character in a line.

• Commands can begin in any column of a command line and continue for as many lines as needed. The exception is the END DATA command, which must begin in the first column of the first line after the end of data.

• The maximum length of any line in a command is 80 characters, including the prompt and the command terminator.

• Spaces can be added or lines broken at any point where a single blank is allowed. The only exceptions are the END DATA command, which can have only one space between words, and TITLE and SUBTITLE specifications, which cannot be broken across two lines.

- Commands and any command specifications can be entered in upper and lower case. Commands, subcommands, keywords, and variable names are translated to upper case before processing. All user specifications, including labels and data values, preserve upper and lower case.
- Most two-word commands—such as BEGIN DATA, SORT CASES, or VALUE LABELS—can be abbreviated to their first word. END DATA is an exception: you must enter both words. If the first specification on the command, such as a variable name, begins with the same three letters as the second word of a two-word command, you must enter the second word of the command explicitly before entering the specification. If two commands begin with the same three letters, such as DATE (in SPSS/PC+ Trends) and DATA LIST, you must specify the second word of the two-word command.

Subcommands

Many commands include additional specifications called *subcommands* for locating data, handling data, and formatting the output display.

- Subcommands begin with a keyword that is the name of the subcommand. Some subcommands include additional specifications.
- A subcommand keyword is separated from its specifications, if any, by an equals sign. The equals sign is optional unless the first three characters of the specification conflict with a variable name.
- Most subcommands can be named in any order. However, some commands require a specific subcommand order.
- Subcommands are separated from one another by a slash.

Keywords

Keywords are words specially defined by SPSS/PC+ to identify commands, subcommands, functions, operators, and other specifications.

- Keywords, including commands and subcommands, can be truncated to the first three characters of each word. The only exception is the keyword WITH, which must be spelled in full.
- Some keywords are reserved and cannot be used as variable names. Logical operators (AND, OR, and NOT), relational operators (EQ, GE, GT, LE, LT, and NE), and ALL, BY, TO, and WITH are the reserved keywords.
- Keyword ALL refers to all user-defined variables in the active file.
- Keyword THRU between two values specifies a range. The range includes the specified values.
- Keyword TO between two variable names specifies an inclusive list of variables.

Values

Values refer to specifications in commands or the data points processed by SPSS/PC+.

- A number specified as an argument to a subcommand can be entered with or without leading zeros.
- Data values of numeric variables can be specified as integers or real numbers, with or without leading zeros.
- Whenever values of string (alphanumeric) variables are used in commands, they must be specified within apostrophes or quotation marks, including all blanks.
- String values in data files or entered between BEGIN DATA and END DATA commands do not need to be enclosed in special delimiters (see DATA LIST: Freefield Format for exceptions).
- Blanks within apostrophes or quotation marks are significant.

Delimiters

Delimiters are used to separate data values, keywords, arguments, and specifications.

- The blank is usually used to delimit one specification from another, except when another delimiter serves the same purpose or where the comma is required.

• Commas are required to separate arguments to functions. Otherwise, commas are generally valid substitutes for blanks and vice versa.

• Arithmetic operators (+, −, *, and /) serve as delimiters in expressions. Blanks before and after arithmetic operators are optional.

• Special delimiters include parentheses, apostrophes, quotation marks, the slash, the equals sign, and so forth. Blanks before and after special delimiters are optional.

• The slash is used primarily to separate subcommands and lists of variables. Although slashes are sometimes optional, entering them as shown in the syntax diagrams is good practice.

• The equals sign is used between a subcommand and its specifications, as in FILE='filename', and to show equivalence, as in old variable list=new variable list. Equals signs following subcommands are frequently optional, but it is best to enter them.

Strings

The term *string* is used to refer to alphanumeric data or specifications such as titles and labels.

• The values of string variables can contain alphabetical characters as well as numbers.

• String variables whose values contain 8 or fewer characters are referred to as *short string variables.* String variables that contain more than 8 characters are referred to as *long string variables.* The maximum number of characters in a long string is 255. Strings longer than 130 are essentially useless, however.

• Only short string variables or values can be used in SPSS/PC+ transformation commands. To transform the data based on the values of a long string variable, use AUTORECODE to create a numeric variable from the long string variable.

• Each string specified in a command should be enclosed in a set of either apostrophes or quotation marks.

• String specifications cannot be broken across command lines.

• Missing values cannot be generated for string variables read from a raw data file, since any character is a legal string value.

• When a transformation command on a string variable yields a missing or undefined result, a blank value is assigned.

• Blank is therefore defined as the user-missing value for string variables created by transformation commands. If you compute one string variable equal to another, user-missing values will be converted to blanks (but will remain user-missing).

Files

SPSS/PC+ uses a number of files in its operation. This section provides an overview to the types of files you can use, as well as a discussion of the active file.

Types of Files

The files that you can use in a session are:

active file   *A file specially formatted for use in SPSS/PC+, containing the data and a data dictionary.* The active file is initially defined by the DATA LIST, GET, IMPORT, JOIN, or TRANSLATE command, or the SPSS Data Entry II DE command. It is available until you replace it with a new active file or until you enter FINISH. You can modify the active file using transformations, analyze it using any of the procedures, and save it with SAVE or EXPORT. You can replace it with a new active file using a DATA LIST, GET, JOIN, AGGREGATE, TRANSLATE, DE, or IMPORT command. The active file is stored in SPSS/PC+ workspace and in temporary files on disk, and it cannot be named.

command file   *A file that contains SPSS/PC+ commands.* You can use the INCLUDE command to process the commands in a command file as an alternative to entering commands interactively, or you can submit a command file directly from REVIEW.

data file   *A file that contains only raw data.* The data file is the file you specify on the DATA LIST command (unless the data are inline). Data files can be arranged in fixed or freefield format. In fixed-format files, the values of each variable for each case are recorded in the same location on each record. In freefield format, the values of each variable are recorded in the same order but not necessarily in the same location (see DATA LIST: Fixed Format and DATA LIST: Freefield Format).

listing file   *A file containing output from SPSS/PC+ procedures.* Filenames for listing files can be specified on the SET command.

log file   *A file created by SPSS/PC+ that contains a copy of all the commands that are executed during a session.* Filenames for log files can be specified on the SET command. You can use a log file as a command file in subsequent sessions.

results file   *A file that contains procedure data output.* This file can contain a rectangular data set produced by the WRITE command or matrix materials produced by CLUSTER, CORRELATION, DSCRIMINANT, FACTOR, MANOVA, ONEWAY, QUICK CLUSTER, or REGRESSION. Filenames for results files can be specified on the SET command.

scratch pad   *A file used by REVIEW as a work area for building commands.* The scratch pad is used as a command file.

system file   *A binary file that is a copy of the active file and is saved on disk for later use.* In later runs, processing a system file is considerably more efficient than recreating the active file from raw data. You create system files with the SAVE command and read system files with the GET command.

portable file   *A portable ASCII file containing data and a dictionary.* A portable file can be created with the EXPORT command. Portable files are read using the IMPORT command.

• All filenames must be enclosed in apostrophes.

• Unless otherwise specified, file specifications default to the current drive and directory.

• Command files, data files, and system files can be read from any drive and directory; system files, log files, and listing files can be written to any drive and directory. When using a file on another drive or directory, you must explicitly specify the drive or path in the file specification.

• The results file cannot be written to a directory other than the current directory.

• A portable file can neither be written to nor read from a directory other than the current directory. It can be written to a floppy drive.

SPSS/PC+ Active File

When SPSS/PC+ processes data definition commands, it builds an internal file called the *active file*. The active file contains data and an associated data dictionary (stored in memory) of variable names, variable and value labels, missing-value flags, and format specifications. Data in the active file are stored in temporary files kept on the current default drive or on the drive specified with SET WORKDEV. The active file data can be altered by transformation commands and is used as input for SPSS/PC+ procedures.

• The active file is initially defined with a DATA LIST, GET, JOIN, IMPORT, TRANSLATE, or SPSS Data Entry II DE command.

• The active file can contain up to 200 variables.

• Each 8-character portion of a long string variable counts toward the system limit of 200 variables. For example, a 20-character string variable counts as 3 toward the system limit of 200 variables.

• The active file is available for use with SPSS/PC+ commands until the FINISH command is entered or until a new active file is built.

• The data contained in the active file are always read when a procedure is executed.

• Data transformation commands cause the active file data to be altered prior to processing data for a procedure. When these commands are entered prior to a procedure, the data are passed twice: once to incorporate the instructions from the transformation commands, and then to perform the SPSS/PC+ procedure.

• The N command limits the number of cases processed from the active file. The SELECT IF command limits the number of cases processed based upon some logical criteria. SELECT IF and N permanently affect the number of cases in the active file.

• The SAMPLE and PROCESS IF commands affect the number of cases only for the next procedure.

• The FORMATS, VALUE LABELS, VARIABLE LABELS, and MISSING VALUES commands affect the active file dictionary, not the data. No transformation pass occurs.

• The WEIGHT command affects the value of the existing system variable, $WEIGHT. No transformation pass occurs.

• The active file is replaced with a new active file when a new DATA LIST, GET, DE, JOIN, IMPORT, TRANSLATE (with FROM), or AGGREGATE (with OUTFILE=*) command is issued. The SPSS/PC+ Trends commands CREATE and RMV also replace the active file. MODIFY VARS may replace the active file.

Variables

This section describes rules for defining variables in SPSS/PC+.

Variable-Naming Conventions

Variable-naming conventions are the rules used to establish variable names in the active file dictionary and to refer to variables in commands.

• Variable names have a maximum of eight characters. The first character of user-defined variables must be an alphabetical letter or the @ character.

• The period, underscore, and the characters $, #, and @ can be used *within* variable names. For example, A._$@#1 is a valid variable name.

• Variable names ending with a period should be avoided, since the period will be interpreted as a command terminator when the variable name comes at the end of a command line.

• SPSS/PC+ creates special system variables that begin with a dollar sign ($). Such variables cannot be named on the DATA LIST, GET, or IMPORT commands.

• Variable names can be established on the DATA LIST, COMPUTE, COUNT, and IF commands. They can be changed with MODIFY VARS.

• You can establish the names of a set of variables on DATA LIST using the TO convention. Specify a character prefix with a numeric suffix before and after the keyword TO. The prefix can be any valid name and the number suffixes can be any integers, so long as the first number is smaller than the second. Each variable name, including the number, must not exceed eight characters. For example, ITEM1 TO ITEM5 establishes five variables named ITEM1, ITEM2, ITEM3, ITEM4, and ITEM5.

• With the TO convention, leading zeros used in suffixes are included in the variable name. For example, V001 TO V100 establishes 100 variables, V001, V002, V003, . . . , V100. V1 TO V100 establishes 100 variables, V1, V2, V3, . . . , V100.

• The TO keyword can also be used on commands other than DATA LIST to refer to a set of consecutive variables on the active file. AVAR TO VARB refers to the variables AVAR and all other variables up to and including VARB on the active file. Use the DISPLAY command or the Variables menu ((Alt) (V)) in REVIEW to see the order of variables on the active file.

• Reserved keywords that cannot be used as variable names are

ALL   AND   BY   EQ   GE   GT   LE
LT   NE   NOT OR   TO   WITH

System Variables   SPSS/PC+ provides three system variables that are included as part of each case in the active file. The three variables are $DATE, $CASENUM, and $WEIGHT.

- System variables begin with a dollar sign ($).
- System variables cannot be named on a DATA LIST, GET, or IMPORT command.
- System variables cannot be named as target variables on COUNT, COMPUTE, and IF commands.
- $DATE and $CASENUM are established when data are read with a DATA LIST or IMPORT command.
- The value of $DATE is the date a case was read in on the DATA LIST command or created in SPSS Data Entry II.
- The value of $CASENUM is the sequence number of each case as it is read by SPSS/PC+ during execution of a DATA LIST or IMPORT command, or as it is created by SPSS Data Entry II.
- The value of $CASENUM remains unchanged, even after SORT, SELECT IF, SAVE, and GET commands, so you can always identify the original case number.
- The initial value of $WEIGHT for each case is 1.00.
- The value of $WEIGHT is changed using the WEIGHT transformation.
- When a file is written using SAVE, the current values of each system variable are written to the file.
- When a file is written using EXPORT, $WEIGHT is the only system variable written to the file.
- When a file is written using WRITE, $CASENUM and $WEIGHT can be included. $DATE cannot be included.

Variable Format   Values are stored internally in double precision. They are displayed according to a format specification. This format specification is used to display values in procedures and to write data to other files. The format specification *does not* affect the precision of data values stored in memory. You can use the DISPLAY command specifying VARIABLES=ALL to see the format of each of your variables.

Variable formats have two components, the variable type and the variable width. Variables can be one of two types, numeric or string. Numeric variables can contain numbers, decimal points, and optional leading plus or minus signs. String variable values can contain numbers, letters, and punctuation characters (see Strings).

The format of a variable is defined on the DATA LIST command or is assigned by SPSS/PC+ on an IF, COUNT, or COMPUTE command. You can change the format of numeric variables with the FORMATS command. You cannot change the format of string variables.

Variable Type
- By default, the DATA LIST command assumes variables are numeric. String variables are indicated by the A format specification.
- Variables created by COMPUTE or IF commands are assigned a format type based on specifications in the assignment expression (see COMPUTE and IF).

Variable Width
- The width determines how the values are displayed in the output.
- Variables defined with DATA LIST using keyword FIXED use the column specifications to calculate the maximum width of data values. If a decimal place is implied on DATA LIST, one column is added to the width required to display the value to allow for the decimal point.
- Numeric variables read with DATA LIST FREE are assigned a display width of eight characters.
- String variables read with DATA LIST FREE are assigned a width of eight characters, including a decimal point and two decimal digits. If the actual width is greater than eight columns, you must specify the maximum number of characters after the format specification, as in NAME (A20).

- Numeric variables created with COMPUTE or IF are assigned a width of eight characters, including a decimal point and two decimal digits.
- String variables created with COMPUTE or IF are assigned a width based on the assignment expression. When the assignment expression creates a variable by equating it to an existing variable, the width of the new variable is equal to the width of the existing variable. When the assignment expression creates a new string variable by equating it to a string constant, the width of the new string variable has a width equal to the initial specification of the string constant.

Format Specifications   The FORMATS command allows you to change the print and write width, display additional decimal values, and add a dollar sign and commas to values of numeric variables.

- You cannot change the variable type from string to numeric or vice versa.
- The FORMATS command changes only the print and write formats, not the internal representation, of a variable.
- If you do not allow enough room to display the values of a variable, SPSS/PC+ displays the value without decimal values, commas, or dollar signs. When the value cannot be reasonably represented in the width provided, SPSS/PC+ rounds it, uses scientific notation, or displays asterisks (**) in the available space.

Transformation Expressions

Transformation expressions are used in COMPUTE, IF, PROCESS IF, and SELECT IF commands. The following sections describe the different types of operators and functions that can be used in transformation expressions.

Arithmetic Operators

Arithmetic operators are used with numeric variables in expressions on COMPUTE, IF, and SELECT IF commands. String variables and string constants cannot be used with arithmetic operators. The arithmetic operators are:

+   Addition   −   Subtraction
*   Multiplication   /   Division
** Exponentiation

Syntax
- No two operators can appear consecutively.
- Arithmetic operators cannot be entered before or after relational and logical operators (see Logical Expressions).
- Blanks (not commas) can be inserted before and after an operator to improve readability.

Operations
- Arithmetic operators are executed after functions (see Functions).
- The order of operations is exponentiation, then multiplication and division, and then addition and subtraction.
- Operators at the same level are executed from left to right.
- Use parentheses to override the order of operation. Execution begins with the innermost set of parentheses and progresses out.
- If any variables or values in an arithmetic or logical expression are missing, the result is always system-missing. The only exceptions are values used as arguments to the missing-value functions VALUE, SYSMIS, and MISSING.
- A negative number raised to a noninteger power is system-missing.

Functions   Functions are used on COMPUTE, IF, and SELECT IF command expressions. All functions are available for use with numeric variables. Only the LAG function can be used with short string variables. No functions can be used with long string variables. For examples using functions, see COMPUTE, IF, and SELECT IF commands.

The expression that is transformed by a function is called the *argument*. Most functions have a variable name or a list of variable names as arguments. You can substitute constants for variable names. Arguments are always enclosed in parentheses. For example, to generate the square root of variable X, specify X as the argument to the SQRT function, as in SQRT(X).

Arguments can include arithmetic and exponential operators and numeric constants to form a complex expression. The expression VARA + VARB, enclosed in parentheses, forms an argument that can be used by most functions. You can use sets of parentheses in complex expressions used as arguments. For functions that take multiple arguments, such as a list of of variables, each argument is separated by a comma and the entire list of arguments is enclosed in parentheses.

- By default, functions in expressions are evaluated before arithmetic, relational, and logical operators. The default order of evaluation is numeric functions, then exponentiation, then arithmetic operators, then relational operators, and then logical operators.
- Operations at the same level are executed from left to right.
- Use parentheses to override the default order of operation. Execution begins with the innermost set of parentheses and progresses out.

Numeric Functions
- Numeric functions always return numbers (or the system-missing value whenever the result is indeterminate).
- All numeric functions take one argument enclosed in parentheses. The argument can be either a variable name or an expression.

ABS(arg)   *Absolute value.* ABS(−4.7) is 4.7; ABS(4.7) is 4.7. The argument can be an expression or a variable name. Returns system-missing if the argument is missing.

RND(arg)   *Round the absolute value to an integer and reaffix the sign.* RND(−4.7) is −5. The argument can be an expression or a variable name. Returns system-missing if the argument is missing.

TRUNC(arg)   *Truncate to an integer.* TRUNC(−4.7) is −4. The argument can be an expression or a variable name. Returns system-missing if the argument is missing.

MOD10(arg)   *Remainder (modulus) when the argument is divided by 10.* MOD10(198) is 8; MOD10(−198) is −8. The argument can be an expression or a variable name. Returns 0 if the argument is 0 and system-missing if the argument is missing.

SQRT(arg)   *Square root.* The argument can be an expression or a variable name. Returns system-missing if the argument is negative or missing.

EXP(arg)   *Exponential. e* is raised to the power of the argument. The argument can be an expression or a variable name. Returns system-missing if the argument is missing or if the argument produces a result too large to be represented.

LG10(arg)   *Base 10 logarithm.* The argument can be an expression or a variable name. Returns system-missing if the argument is negative, 0, or missing.

LN(arg)   *Natural or Naperian logarithm (base* e*).* The argument can be an expression or a variable name and must be positive and greater than 0. Returns system-missing if the argument is missing.

ARTAN(arg)   *Arctangent* (alias ATAN). The argument can be an expression or a variable name. The result is given in radians. Returns system-missing if the argument is missing.

SIN(arg)   *Sine.* The argument can be an expression or a variable name but it must yield radians. Returns system-missing if the argument is missing.

COS(arg)   *Cosine.* The argument can be an expression or a variable name but it must yield radians. Returns system-missing if the argument is missing.

The arc sine function is not directly available but can be computed easily as the following:

```
COMPUTE ARCSINX = ARTAN(X/SQRT(1-X*X)).
```

Note: this identity is valid only if X is greater than −1 and less than 1.

Missing-Value Functions • Each missing-value function takes one variable name enclosed in parentheses as an argument.

VALUE(arg) *Returns the numeric value of valid or user-missing data in a form that is not considered missing in expressions.* The argument must be a single variable name. Use this function to test for user-missing values in IF and SELECT IF logical expressions. For example, if 999 was declared as a user-missing value for VAR1, the expression IF (VALUE(VAR1) EQ 999) is evaluated as *true* for cases where VAR1 has that value; the expression IF (VAR1 EQ 999) would be evaluated as *missing,* since this expression contains a variable with a missing value.

MISSING(arg) *Return 1 (true) if the value is either system-missing or user-missing and return 0 (false) otherwise.* The argument must be a single variable name.

SYSMIS(arg) *Return 1 (true) if the value is system-missing and 0 (false) otherwise.* The argument must be a single variable name.

Cross-Case Function **LAG(arg)** *The value of the variable one case before.* The argument must be a numeric variable. LAG(GNP) returns the value of GNP for the case before the current one. If you are selecting cases from a file, LAG returns the value for the case previously selected. Returns system-missing for the first case.

Random-Number Functions • The seed value used for random number functions can be changed using the SEED specification on the SET command.

UNIFORM(arg) *A uniform pseudo-random number.* The random number is uniformly distributed with values varying between 0 and the value of the argument. The argument must be a numeric constant or variable name.

NORMAL(arg) *A normal pseudo-random number.* The random number is randomly distributed with a mean of 0 and a standard deviation equal to the argument. The argument must be a numeric constant or variable name. Returns system-missing if the argument is 0 or negative.

Date Function **YRMODA(arg list)** *Convert year, month, and day to a day number.* The number returned is the number of days since October 15, 1582 (day 1 of the Gregorian calendar).

• Arguments for YRMODA can be variables, constants, or any other type of numeric expression but must yield integers.

• Year, month, and day must be specified in that order.

• The first argument can be any year between 0 and 99, or between 1582 to 47516.

• If the first argument yields a number between 00 and 99, 1900 through 1999 is assumed.

• The month can range from 1 through 13. Month 13 yields the last day of the year—as in YRMODA(YEAR,13,0)—or the first month of the next year—as in YRMODA(YEAR,13,DAY).

• The day can range from 0 through 31. Day 0 is the last day of the previous month. For example, YRMODA(YEAR,MONTH + 1,0) is the last day of MONTH.

• Returns missing if any of the three arguments is missing.

• Returns missing if the arguments do not form a valid date after October 15, 1582.

C

Command Reference

Logical Expressions

A logical expression is an expression that can be evaluated as true, false, or missing, based upon conditions found in the data. Logical expressions can be simple logical relations among variables, or they can be complex logical tests involving variables, constants, functions, relational operators, and logical operators. Logical expressions can be used on the IF, SELECT IF, and PROCESS IF commands. However, logical expressions used with PROCESS IF can contain only the relational operators, not the logical operators.

Relational operators used in expressions are:

EQ or =	Equal to	NE or ~= or <>	Not equal to
LT or <	Less than	LE or <=	Less than or equal to
GT or >	Greater than	GE or >=	Greater than or equal to

Logical operators are

AND or &   OR or | NOT or ~

Syntax

- Parentheses enclosing a logical expression are required.
- Blanks (not commas) must separate the relational and logical operators from the expressions.
- String values must be enclosed in apostrophes or quotation marks.
- The operators EQ and NE must compare one string variable to another or one numeric value to another.
- Only strings of the same length are compared using EQ or NE.
- Long string values cannot be used in logical expressions or transformations. Use AUTORECODE if necessary.

Operations

- In expressions, functions and arithmetic operators are executed before relational and logical operators.
- Relational operators are executed before logical operators.
- Logical NOT is executed first, then AND, and then OR.
- Operators at the same level are executed from left to right.
- Use parentheses to override the order of operation. Execution begins with the innermost set of parentheses and progresses out.

Limitations

- The complexity of a logical expression is limited by available memory.

AND and OR

- AND returns true if both expressions are true.
- OR returns true if either expression is true.

NOT

- NOT reverses the outcome of the expression.
- NOT affects only the expression that immediately follows (unless otherwise indicated by parentheses.)

Logical Outcomes

- Logic is indeterminate and the outcome is missing if the expression on either side of a relational operator is missing.

Commands

ADD VALUE LABELS

```
ADD VALUE LABELS varlist value 'label' value 'label'...
                 [/varlist...]
```

Example:

```
ADD VALUE LABELS JOBGRADE 'P' 'Parttime Employee'
                          'C' 'Customer Support'.
```

Overview

ADD VALUE LABELS adds or alters value labels without affecting the value labels that have already been defined for that variable. In contrast, VALUE LABELS adds or alters value labels but deletes all existing value labels for that variable when it does so.

Basic Specification

- The basic specification is a variable name and individual values with associated labels.

Syntax Rules

- Labels can be assigned to values of any previously defined variable. It is not necessary to enter value labels for all of a variable's values.
- Each value label must be enclosed in apostrophes or quotation marks.
- When an apostrophe occurs as part of a label, enclose the label in quotation marks.
- Value labels cannot exceed 60 characters.
- Value labels can contain any characters, including blanks.
- The same labels can be assigned to the same values of different variables by specifying a list of variable names. For string variables, the variables must be of equal length.
- Multiple sets of variable names and value labels can be specified on one ADD VALUE LABELS command as long as each set is separated by slashes.

Operations

- ADD VALUE LABELS takes effect as soon as it is encountered in the command sequence, unlike most transformations, which do not take effect until the data are read.
- The added value labels are automatically displayed on the output from many procedures and are stored in the active system file dictionary.
- ADD VALUE LABELS can be used for variables that have no previously assigned value labels.
- Labels added to values do not affect those labels previously assigned to other values.
- In the specification, if a value is specified that is longer than the format of the associated variable, SPSS will be unable to read the full value and may not be able to associate the value labels correctly. This occurs even though the values named on ADD VALUE LABELS and the actual values agree.
- If the value specifications for string variables are shorter than the variable being labeled, the value specifications are right-padded without warning.

Limitations

- Each value label can be up to 60 characters long, although most procedures display only 20 characters.
- Some procedures display fewer than 20 characters in labels.
- The TABLES procedure (available in SPSS Tables) will display all 60 characters of a label.

C

Command Reference

Example

```
ADD VALUE LABELS V1 TO V3 1 'Officials & Managers'
                          6 'Service Workers'
             /V4 'N' 'New Employee'.
```

- Labels are assigned to the values 1 and 6 of the variables between and including V1 and V3 on the active system file.

- Following the required slash, a label for value N of V4 is specified. N is a string value and must be enclosed in apostrophes or quotation marks.

- If labels exist for values 1 and 6 on V1 TO V3 and value N on V4, they are changed in the dictionary. If labels do not exist for these values, new labels are added to the dictionary.

- Existing labels for values other than 1 and 6 on V1 TO V3 and value N on V4 are unaffected.

String Value Labels

- Both the values and the labels for short string variables must be enclosed in apostrophes or quotation marks. Value labels cannot be assigned to long string variables.

- The values of a short string variable cannot be longer than the format of the associated variable.

- If labels are to be assigned to a set of string variables, the variables must be of equal length.

Example

```
ADD VALUE LABELS  STATE 'TEX' "Texas" 'TEN' "Tennessee"
                        'MIN' "Minnesota".
```

- The GET command gets the system file CITY.

- The ADD VALUE LABELS command assigns labels to three values of variable STATE. Each value and each label is specified in either apostrophes or quotation marks.

- The format for variable STATE must be three characters wide because values TEX, TEN, and MIN are three characters long.

Example

```
ADD VALUE LABELS STATE REGION 'U' "Unknown".
```

- Label UNKNOWN is assigned to value U for both STATE and REGION.

- STATE and REGION must be string variables of length 1 character. If STATE and REGION have *unequal* lengths, a separate specification must be made for each, as in

```
ADD VALUE LABELS STATE 'U  ' "Unknown" / REGION 'U' "Unknown".
```

AGGREGATE

```
AGGREGATE OUTFILE={'filename'}
                  {*         }

[/PRESORTED]

/BREAK=varlist [{(A)}] [varlist [{(A)}]] ...
               {(D)}            {(D)}

[/MISSING=COLUMNWISE]

/aggvar ['label'] aggvar ['label'] ...
     =function(varlist[,arguments])

[/aggvar ...]
```

Example:
```
AGGREGATE OUTFILE='AGGEMP.SYS'
   /BREAK=LOCATN82 DEPT82
   /COUNT=N
   /AVGSAL AVGRAISE=MEAN(SALARY82 RAISE82)
   /SUMSAL SUMRAISE=SUM(SALARY82 RAISE82)
   /BLACKPCT 'Percentage Black'=PIN(RACE,1,1)
   /WHITEPCT 'Percentage White'=PIN(RACE,5,5).
```

Overview

Procedure AGGREGATE creates a new active or system file from the current active file by aggregating groups of cases into single cases. The values of one or more variables in the active file define the case groups. A series of aggregate functions creates new variables that have one value for each case group. Each function operates on a *source variable* in the active file to create an *aggregated variable* for the new active or system file.

Defaults

By default, AGGREGATE excludes missing values from all aggregate variable calculations except those involving functions N, NU, NMISS, and NUMISS. Unless otherwise specified, AGGREGATE sorts the aggregated cases in ascending order of the values of the case-grouping variables.

Tailoring

Output File. You can produce either a new active file or a system file with AGGREGATE. You can specify any legal DOS filename as the name of the system file.

Case Grouping. You can group cases according to the values of any one or more of the variables in your active file. Variables that you use to group cases are called *break variables*. A set of cases in the file with identical values for each break variable is called a *break group*. AGGREGATE calculates a single value for each new variable for each break group.

Sorting. You can sort the aggregated cases into either ascending or descending order of the values of each break variable. If the file is already sorted by the break variables, you can instruct AGGREGATE to skip this final pass through the file.

Aggregated Variables. You can create aggregated variables using any of 19 aggregate functions. Functions SUM, MEAN, and SD can take only numeric variables as arguments, but all other aggregate functions will accept both numeric and string variables.

Labels and Formats. You can specify variable labels for the aggregated variables on the AGGREGATE command. Variables created with functions MAX, MIN, FIRST, and LAST will assume the formats and value labels of their respective source variables. All other variables will assume the default print formats described under Aggregate Functions, below.

Missing Values. By default, AGGREGATE declares a value of a new variable missing only if all values of the source variable are missing in the relevant break group. Optionally, you can declare a new variable missing if there is a single missing value for the source variable among any cases in the break group. You can also include user-missing values in the calculation of an aggregate function.

C

Command Reference

Syntax
- The minimum specification is the OUTFILE subcommand with a filename or asterisk, the BREAK subcommand with a single variable name, and an aggregate function that creates a new aggregated variable.
- The OUTFILE subcommand must be specified first.
- The aggregate functions must be specified last.
- If specified, the PRESORTED subcommand must precede the BREAK subcommand.
- Subcommands and variable definition statements must be separated by slashes.

Operations
- AGGREGATE causes the data to be read.
- The system files that AGGREGATE produces are, like all system files, binary files designed to be read and written by SPSS/PC+ only. They cannot be edited.
- When AGGREGATE produces a system file, the active file remains unchanged and is still available for analysis.
- AGGREGATE places the new system file in the current DOS directory.
- When AGGREGATE creates a new active file, it erases the old active file. Only the new active file is available for analysis.
- AGGREGATE includes the break variables in the file it creates.
- If the active file is already sorted in the order you want your aggregated file, use the PRESORTED subcommand. If you specify PRESORTED, a new aggregate case is created each time a different value or combination of values is encountered on variables named on the BREAK subcommand.

OUTFILE Subcommand

The OUTFILE subcommand specifies whether AGGREGATE should create a new system file or replace the active file.

- An asterisk following the equals sign tells AGGREGATE to replace the active file.
- A name in single quotes following the equals sign tells AGGREGATE to create a new system file with the given name.
- Names for system files must adhere to the DOS restrictions on filenames.

Example

```
AGGREGATE OUTFILE='AGGEMP.SYS'
  /BREAK=LOCATN82
  /AVGSAL=MEAN(SALARY82).
```

- This example creates a system file called AGGEMP.SYS in the current DOS directory.
- The new system file will contain variables LOCATN82 and AVGSAL.

BREAK Subcommand

The BREAK subcommand lists the *break variables*. Each unique combination of values of the break variables defines one break group. A *break group* consists of cases with identical values for each break variable.

- The variables named on the BREAK subcommand can be any combination of variables from the active file.
- Unless it encounters the PRESORTED subcommand (see below), AGGREGATE sorts cases after aggregating. By default, cases are sorted in ascending order of the values of the break variables.
- You can control the sort order by specifying an A (for ascending) or D (for descending) in parentheses after any break variables.
- The designations (A) and (D) apply to all preceding undesignated variables.
- AGGREGATE sorts first on the first-named variable, then on the second-named variable within the groups created by the first, and so on.
- Subcommand PRESORTED overrides all sorting specifications.

Example   /BREAK=LOCATN82 DEPT82 (A) TENURE (D)

- This subcommand names variables LOCATN82, DEPT82, and TENURE as the break variables.
- Cases are sorted in ascending order of LOCATN82, in ascending order of DEPT82 within LOCATN82, and in descending order of TENURE within LOCATN82 and DEPT82.

PRESORTED Subcommand

The PRESORTED subcommand indicates that cases in the active file are sorted according to the values of the break variables. This prevents AGGREGATE from sorting cases that have already been sorted.

- If specified, the PRESORTED subcommand must precede the BREAK subcommand.
- When you specify PRESORTED, SPSS/PC+ forms an aggregate case out of each group of *adjacent* cases with the same values for the break variable(s).
- If the active file is not sorted by the break variables in ascending order and PRESORTED is specified, a warning message is generated but the procedure is executed. Each group of adjacent cases with the same values for break variables forms a case in the output file, which may produce multiple cases with the same values for the break variables. In this case, the output file will not be sorted by the break variables.

Example   /PRESORTED
/BREAK=LOCATN82 DEPT82

- In this example, the PRESORTED subcommand tells AGGREGATE that the cases are already sorted by variables LOCATN82 and DEPT82.
- AGGREGATE does not make an extra data pass to sort the cases.

Aggregate Functions

An aggregated variable is created by applying an aggregate function to a variable in the active file. The variable in the active file is the *source* variable, and the new aggregated variable is called the *target* variable.

- The simplest specification is a target variable list, followed by an equals sign, the function keyword, and a list of source variables.
- The number of target variables named must match the number of source variables.
- When several aggregate variables are defined at once, the first-named target variable is a function of the first-named source variable, the second-named target is a function of the second-named source, and so on.
- You can optionally specify variable labels for the target variables. A label is specified in single quotation marks after the target variable to which it applies. Value labels cannot be assigned on the AGGREGATE command.
- Print formats are automatically assigned to target variables according to the function it is based on (see list of functions below).
- If you are creating a system file, it will not be possible to change print formats or add value labels immediately. However, you can do so later by calling the system file into the active file, specifying the new labels and formats, and resaving.

The following functions are available:

SUM(varlist)	*Sum across cases.* Dictionary formats are F8.2.
MEAN(varlist)	*Mean across cases.* Dictionary formats are F8.2.
SD(varlist)	*Standard deviation across cases.* Dictionary formats are F8.2.
MAX(varlist)	*Maximum value across cases.* Complete dictionary information is copied from the source variables to the target variables.

MIN(varlist)	*Minimum value across cases.* Complete dictionary information is copied from the source variables to the target variables.
PGT(varlist,value)	*Percentage of cases greater than value.* Dictionary formats are F5.1.
PLT(varlist,value)	*Percentage of cases less than value.* Dictionary formats are F5.1.
PIN(varlist,value1,value2)	*Percentage of cases between value1 and value2 inclusive.* Dictionary formats are F5.1.
POUT(varlist,value1,value2)	*Percentage of cases not between value1 and value2.* Cases where the source variable equals value1 or value2 are not counted. Dictionary formats are F5.1.
FGT(varlist,value)	*Fraction of cases greater than value.* Dictionary formats are F5.3.
FLT(varlist,value)	*Fraction of cases less than value.* Dictionary formats are F5.3.
FIN(varlist,value1,value2)	*Fraction of cases between value1 and value2 inclusive.* Dictionary formats are F5.3.
FOUT(varlist,value1,value2)	*Fraction of cases not between value1 and value2.* Cases where the source variable equals value1 or value2 are not counted. Dictionary formats are F5.3.
N(varlist)	*Weighted number of cases in break group.* Dictionary formats are F7.0 for unweighted files and F8.2 for weighted files.
NU(varlist)	*Unweighted number of cases in break group.* Dictionary formats are F7.0.
NMISS(varlist)	*Weighted number of missing cases.* Dictionary formats are F7.0 for unweighted files and F8.2 for weighted files.
NUMISS(varlist)	*Unweighted number of missing cases.* Dictionary formats are F7.0.
FIRST(varlist)	*First nonmissing observed value in break group.* Complete dictionary information is copied from the source variables to the target variables.
LAST(varlist)	*Last nonmissing observed value in break group.* Complete dictionary information is copied from the source variables to the target variables.

• Functions SUM, MEAN, and SD operate only on numeric source variables. All other functions accept short and long string variables as well as numeric ones.

• The N and NU functions do not require arguments. Without arguments, they return the number of weighted and unweighted cases in a break group. If you supply a variable list, they return the weighted and unweighted number of valid cases for the variables specified.

• For several functions, the argument includes values as well as a source variable designation. PGT, PLT, FGT, and FLT take one value; PIN, POUT, FIN, and FOUT take two values.

• You can use either blanks or commas to separate the components of an argument list.

• String values specified in an argument should be enclosed in single quotes.

• The order used in aggregation functions with string values is alphabetical.

• For PIN, POUT, FIN, and FOUT, the first value should be less than or equal to the second. If the first is higher, AGGREGATE automatically reverses them and displays a warning message.

• If the two values are equal, PIN and FIN calculate the percentages and fractions, respectively, of values equal to the argument. POUT and FOUT calculate the percentages and fractions, respectively, of values not equal to the argument.

Example   `AGGREGATE OUTFILE='AGGEMP.SYS'`
                `  /BREAK=LOCATN82`
                `  /AVGSAL 'Average Salary' AVGRAISE=MEAN(SALARY82 RAISE82).`

• This example defines two aggregate variables, AVGSAL and AVGRAISE.

• AVGSAL is the mean of SALARY82 for each break group, and AVGRAISE is the mean of RAISE82.

• The label 'Average Salary' is assigned to AVGRAISE.

Example   `AGGREGATE OUTFILE=*`
                `  /BREAK=DEPT`
                `  /LOWVAC,LOWSICK=PLT(VACDAY SICKDAY,10).`

This example assigns the percentage of cases with values less than 10 for VACDAY to LOWVAC and for SICKDAY to LOWSICK.

Example   `AGGREGATE OUTFILE='GROUPS.SYS'`
                `  /BREAK=OCCGROUP`
                `  /COLLEGE=FIN(EDUC,13,16).`

This example assigns the fraction of cases having 13 to 16 years of education to COLLEGE.

Example   `AGGREGATE OUTFILE=*`
                `  /BREAK=CLASS`
                `  /LOCAL=PIN(STATE,"IL","IO").`

This example creates variable LOCAL, which is the percentage of cases in each break group whose two-letter state code represents Illinois, Indiana, or Iowa. (The abbreviation for Indiana, IN, is between IL and IO in an alphabetical sort sequence.)

Missing Values   By default, AGGREGATE uses all nonmissing values of the source variable to calculate aggregated variables. An aggregated variable will have a missing value only if the source variable is missing for every case in the break group. You can alter the default missing-value treatment by using the MISSING subcommand or by specifying the inclusion of missing values on any function.

• The COLUMNWISE keyword is the only specification available on MISSING.

• MISSING=COLUMNWISE declares the value of an aggregated variable as missing if the source variable is missing for any case in the break group.

• The MISSING subcommand must precede the BREAK subcommand.

• The MISSING subcommand does not affect the calculation of the N, NU, NMISS, or NUMISS functions.

You can force a function to include user-missing values in its calculations by specifying a period after the function name.

• AGGREGATE ignores periods used with functions N, NU, NMISS, and NUMISS if these functions have no argument.

• User-missing values are treated as valid when these four functions are followed by a period and have a variable as an argument. NMISS.(AGE) gives the number of cases for which AGE has the system-missing value only.

The effect of specifying a period with N, NU, NMISS, and NUMISS is illustrated by the following:

N = N. = N(AGE) + NMISS(AGE) = N.(AGE) + NMISS.(AGE)

NU = NU. = NU(AGE)+ NUMISS(AGE) = NU.(AGE) + NUMISS.(AGE)

• The function N (the same as N. with no argument) yields a value for each break group that equals the number of cases with valid values plus the number of cases with user- or system-missing values.

• This in turn equals the number of cases with either valid or user-missing values plus the number with system-missing values.

• The same identities hold for the NU, NMISS, and NUMISS functions.

Example
```
AGGREGATE OUTFILE='AGGEMP.SYS'
  /MISSING=COLUMNWISE
  /BREAK=LOCATN82
  /AVGSAL=MEAN(SALARY82).
```

• This example specifies that AVGSAL will be missing for an aggregate case if SALARY82 is missing for any case in the break group.

Example
```
AGGREGATE OUTFILE=*
  /BREAK=DEPT
  /LOVAC=PLT.(VACDAY,10).
```

• This function sets variable LOVAC to the percentage of cases within each break group with values less than 10 for VACDAY, even if some of those values are defined as user-missing.

Example
```
AGGREGATE OUTFILE='CLASS.AVG'
  /BREAK=GRADE
  /FIRSTAGE=FIRST.(AGE).
```

• This example assigns the first value of AGE in each break group to variable FIRSTAGE.

• If the first value of AGE in a break group is user-missing, that value will be assigned to FIRSTAGE. However, the value will retain its missing-value status since variables created with FIRST take their dictionary information from their source variables.

• Function LAST with a period operates in parallel fashion.

AUTORECODE

```
AUTORECODE VARIABLES=varlist

/INTO new varlist

[/DESCENDING]

[/PRINT]
```

Example
```
AUTORECODE VARIABLES=COMPANY
  /INTO RCOMPANY.
```

Overview
AUTORECODE recodes the values of both string and numeric variables to consecutive integers and puts the new values into a different variable called a *target variable*. AUTORECODE can recode long string variables into numeric variables, using the original string value as a label for the new numeric value. This is especially helpful when using long string variables in the TABLES procedure (see *SPSS/PC+ Tables* for more information). AUTORECODE can also recode the values of factor variables to consecutive integers, which is the form required by MANOVA, and which reduces the amount of workspace needed by other statistical procedures like ANOVA.

Options
Displaying Recoded Variables. You can display the values of the original and recoded variables (see PRINT subcommand below).

Ordering of Values. By default, values are recoded in ascending order (lowest to highest). You can recode values in descending order (highest to lowest). (See DESCENDING subcommand below.)

Basic Specification
• The basic specification is two subcommands: VARIABLES and INTO. VARIABLES specifies the variables to be recoded. INTO names the target variables that store the new values. VARIABLES and INTO must name or imply the same number of variables.

Subcommand Order
• VARIABLES must be specified first.
• INTO must immediately follow VARIABLES.
• The order of PRINT and DESCENDING is unimportant, provided each follows INTO.

Syntax Rules
• A variable cannot be recoded into itself. More generally, target variable names must not duplicate any variable names already in the file.

Operations
• AUTORECODE causes the data to be read.
• The values of each variable to be recoded are sorted and then assigned numeric values. By default, the values are assigned in ascending order: the value 1 is assigned to the lowest nonmissing value of the original variable, the value 2 to the second lowest nonmissing value, and so on for each value of the original variable.
• User-missing values are recoded into missing values higher than any nonmissing values, with their order preserved. For example, if the original variable has 10 nonmissing values, the value of the first missing value is recoded to 11. The value 11 is then a missing value on the new variable. System-missing values are not recoded. System-missing values in the new variable correspond to system-missing values in the variable to be recoded.
• Because the values of a variable to be recoded are sorted before they are assigned new values, AUTORECODE does *not* necessarily preserve the order of values as they were entered in the data file.
• Target variables are assigned the same variable labels as the original source variables. To change the variable labels, use the VARIABLE LABELS command after AUTORECODE.

• Value labels are automatically generated for each value of the target variables. If the original value had a label, that label is used for the corresponding new value. If the original value did not have a label, the old value itself is used as the value label for the new value. The old value is formatted according to its defined print format to create the new value label.

Example
```
DATA LIST / COMPANY 1-21 (A) SALES 24-29.
BEGIN DATA.
CATFOOD JOY             10000
OLD FASHIONED CATFOOD   11200
 . . .
PRIME CATFOOD           10900
CHOICE CATFOOD          14600
END DATA.
AUTORECODE VARIABLES=COMPANY
  /INTO=RCOMPANY
  /PRINT.
TABLES TABLE=SALES BY RCOMPANY
  /TTITLE='CATFOOD SALES BY COMPANY'.
```

• Because TABLES truncates string variables to eight characters, AUTORECODE is used to recode the string variable COMPANY, which contains the names of various hypothetical cat food companies.

• AUTORECODE recodes COMPANY into a numeric variable RCOMPANY. Values of RCOMPANY are consecutive integers beginning with 1 and ending with the number of different values entered for COMPANY. The values of COMPANY are used as value labels for RCOMPANY's numeric values. The PRINT subcommand displays a table to confirm the recodes.

• Variable RCOMPANY is used as the banner variable in the TABLES procedure to produce a table of sales figures for each cat food company. RCOMPANY's value labels display as column headings in the table and are not truncated because TABLES does not truncate value labels.

Example
```
AUTORECODE VARIABLES=REGION
  /INTO=RREGION
  /PRINT.
ANOVA Y BY RREGION (1,5).
```

• In statistical procedures, empty cells can reduce performance and increase memory requirements. In this example, assume factor REGION has only five nonempty categories, represented by the numeric codes 1, 4, 6, 14 and 20. AUTORECODE recodes those values into 1, 2, 3, 4, and 5 for target variable RREGION. The RECODE command can also be used to do this, but you would have to specify all five recodes. AUTORECODE automatically recodes the original values into consecutive integer values.

• Variable RREGION is used in ANOVA. If the original variable REGION were used, the amount of memory required by ANOVA would be 4429 bytes (because of all the empty cells in REGION). Using variable RREGION, ANOVA requires only 449 bytes of memory (because RREGION has no empty cells).

Example
```
DATA LIST / RELIGION 1-8 (A) Y 10-13.
MISSING VALUES RELIGION (' ').
BEGIN DATA.
CATHOLIC 2013
PROTEST  3234
JEWISH   5169
NONE      714
OTHER    2321
 . . .
END DATA.
AUTORECODE VARIABLES=RELIGION
  /INTO=NRELIG
  /PRINT
  /DESCENDING.
MANOVA Y BY NRELIG(1,5).
```

• Because MANOVA requires consecutive integer values for factor levels, string variable RELIGION is recoded into a numeric variable. Values for RELIGION are first sorted in descending order (Z to A), then assigned values 1, 2, 3, 4, 5, and 6 in target variable NRELIG. Value 6 is assigned to the ' ' specified as a missing value for RELIGION. In the PRINT table, value 6 is displayed as 6M for variable NRELIG to flag it as a user-defined missing value.

• Values of RELIGION are assigned as value labels to the corresponding new values in NRELIG.

• Target variable NRELIG is then used as a factor variable in MANOVA.

**VARIABLES
Subcommand**

VARIABLES names the variables to be recoded. The actual keyword VARIA-BLES is optional, unless the first name in the variable list begins with the letters *VAR*. VARIABLES is required and must be the first subcommand used.

• Keyword TO can be used to refer to consecutive variables in the active file.

• Values from specified variables are recoded and stored in the target variables listed on INTO. Values of the original variables are unchanged.

INTO Subcommand

INTO names the target variables that store the new values. INTO is required and must immediately follow VARIABLES.

• Keyword TO can be used to generate names for target variables.

• The number of target variables named or implied on INTO must equal the number of source variables listed on VARIABLES.

• Target variable names may not be the same as any variable names on the existing file.

Example

```
AUTORECODE VARIABLES=V1 TO V3
  /INTO=NEW_V1 TO NEW_V3
  /PRINT.
```

• AUTORECODE sequentially assigns the names implied by the inclusive list on INTO to the variables referenced on VARIABLES.

• INTO immediately follows VARIABLES, which must be the first subcommand specified on AUTORECODE.

PRINT Subcommand

PRINT displays a correspondence table of values for the original values of the source variable(s) and the new values of the target variable(s). The new value labels are also displayed.

• The only specification is the keyword PRINT. PRINT has no additional specifications.

• By default, or if the width is set to less than 132, the table is formatted to display in 80 columns. If the width has been previously set to 132 (by the SET WIDTH command), then the output is formatted to display in 132 columns.

• Only the first 18 characters of the values for the original variable and the first 48 characters of the value labels for the new variable are displayed.

**DESCENDING
Subcommand**

DESCENDING assigns the values to new variables in descending order (from highest to lowest) rather than in ascending order, which is the default. The largest value is assigned 1, the second largest 2, and so on.

• The only specification is the keyword DESCENDING. DESCENDING has no additional specifications.

C

Command Reference

BEGIN DATA—
END DATA

```
BEGIN DATA
lines of data
END DATA
```

Example:

```
BEGIN DATA.
1   3424   274 ABU DHABI 2
3 39932    86 AMSTERDAM 4
3  8889   232 ATHENS
2  3424   294 BOGOTA      3
END DATA.
```

Overview

The BEGIN DATA command signals the beginning of data lines in a command file, and the END DATA command signals the end of data lines. Both BEGIN DATA and END DATA must be used when data are part of an SPSS/PC+ command file (inline data). BEGIN DATA and END DATA are also used for inline matrix data or matrix materials.

Syntax

• BEGIN DATA, the data, and END DATA must appear before the first SPSS/PC+ procedure.

• Data lines must *not* have a command terminator.

• The BEGIN DATA command must be entered immediately before the first line of inline data.

• The END DATA command must be entered immediately after the last line of data, beginning in column 1.

• Only a single space is allowed between the words END and DATA.

• END DATA cannot be abbreviated to END. BEGIN DATA can be abbreviated to BEGIN (or BEG).

• Procedures and additional transformations can follow the END DATA command.

Operations

• When SPSS/PC+ encounters BEGIN DATA, it begins to read and process data on the next input line. All preceding transformation commands are processed as a file is built for use in SPSS/PC+ procedures.

• SPSS/PC+ continues to evaluate input lines as data until it encounters END DATA, at which point it begins evaluating input lines as SPSS/PC+ commands.

• No other SPSS/PC+ commands are recognized between BEGIN DATA and END DATA.

• You can use a file that contains BEGIN DATA, data lines, and END DATA with the INCLUDE command, provided you omit the FILE specification on your DATA LIST command (see INCLUDE).

Example

```
DATA LIST / XVAR 1 YVAR ZVAR 3-12 CVAR 14-22(A) JVAR 24.
BEGIN DATA.
1  3424  274 ABU DHABI 2
3 39932   86 AMSTERDAM 4
3  8889  232 ATHENS
2  3424  294 BOGOTA     3
4 11323  332 HONG KONG 3
3   323  232 MANILA     1
4  3234  899 CHICAGO    4
1 78998 2344 VIENNA     3
2  8870  983 ZURICH     5
END DATA.
MEANS XVAR BY JVAR.
```

• The DATA LIST command defines the names and column locations of the variables. The FILE subcommand is omitted because the data are inline.

• There are nine cases in the inline data.

• Each line of data is completed by pressing the enter key.

• The END DATA command begins in column 1, has only a single space between END and DATA, and signals the end of lines of data.

* **(Comment)**

```
* text
```

Example:

```
* CREATE A NEW VARIABLE AS A COMBINATION OF TWO OLD VARS.
COMPUTE XYVAR=0.
IF (XVAR EQ 1 AND YVAR EQ 1)XYVAR=1.
```

Overview

The comment facility allows you to insert text within your SPSS/PC+ job for the purpose of documentation.

Syntax

- The first line of a comment must begin with an asterisk (*) in column 1. The asterisk must be followed by a space.
- Comment text can extend for multiple lines. Continuation comment lines can start in any column and do not begin with an asterisk.
- You cannot specify a continuation line if the preceding line ends with a period. Instead, you must start a new comment with an asterisk.
- The comment text can contain any characters.
- Comments cannot be imbedded within data lines or within lines of multiple-line commands.
- A command terminator must be placed at the end of a comment. If you omit the command terminator, the first command following the comment is treated as a continuation of the comment.

Operations

- Comments are included in the command printback on the log file.

Example

```
* CREATE A NEW VARIABLE AS A COMBINATION OF TWO OLD VARIABLES.
COMPUTE XYVAR=0.
IF (XVAR EQ 1 AND YVAR EQ 1) XYVAR=1.
```

- The one-line comment will be included in the log file.

Example

```
DATA LIST / XVAR 1 YVAR ZVAR 3-12 CVAR 14-22(A) JVAR 24.
* THIS IS AN EXAMPLE OF A THREE LINE
COMMENT.   THE DATA BELOW ARE ENTERED
INTERACTIVELY.
BEGIN DATA.
1   3424   274 ABU DHABI 2
3 39932    86 AMSTERDAM 4
3  8889   232 ATHENS
2  3424   294 BOGOTA     3
4 11323   332 HONG KONG 3
3   323   232 MANILA     1
4  3234   899 CHICAGO    4
1 78998 2344 VIENNA      3
2  8870   983 ZURICH     5
END DATA.
MEANS XVAR BY JVAR
  /OPTIONS=1.
FINISH.
```

- The comment text begins just after the DATA LIST command and extends for two additional lines.

Command Reference

COMPUTE

COMPUTE target variable=expression

Arithmetic Operators:

+	Addition	−	Subtraction
*	Multiplication	/	Division
**	Exponentiation		

Numeric Functions:

ABS	Absolute value	RND	Round
TRUNC	Truncate	MOD10	Modulus
SQRT	Square root	EXP	Exponential
LG10	Base 10 logarithm	LN	Natural logarithm
SIN	Sine	COS	Cosine
ATAN	Arctangent		

Missing-Value Functions:

VALUE	Treat user-missing as valid
SYSMIS	Return 1 if system-missing
MISSING	Return 1 if missing

Cross-case Function:

LAG   Lag

Random-Number Functions:

UNIFORM	Uniform pseudo-random number
NORMAL	Normal pseudo-random number

Date Function:

YRMODA   Date function

Example:

```
COMPUTE YVAR1=RND((YVAR/ZVAR)*100).
COMPUTE NEWSTRNG='maxwidth'.
```

Overview

The COMPUTE transformation creates a new variable or modifies the values of an existing variable for each case in your active file. The variable name on the left of the equals sign is the *target variable*. The variables, values, and specifications on the right side of the equals sign form an *assignment expression*.

Numeric Transformations

You can use both arithmetic operations and functions in the transformation of numeric variables. The assignment expression can include combinations of arithmetic operations, constants, and functions. Parentheses are used to indicate the order of operations and to enclose the argument for a function.

String Transformations

You can create and modify short string variables using COMPUTE. A variable name can be set equal to a string constant or to an existing string variable. The LAG function is available for cross-case transformation of short string variables. All other functions are available for numeric transformations only.

Syntax

- The target variable is named first.
- The equals sign is required.
- You cannot mix numeric and string variables in an expression.
- Each function takes on at least one argument enclosed in parentheses.
- For a complete discussion of each function and its argument, see Universals: Functions.

Numeric Variables

- Parentheses are used to indicate the order of transformations and to set off the arguments for a function.
- To evaluate unary minus, the minus sign and the variable or constant must be enclosed in parentheses.
- Numeric functions can take on expressions, enclosed in parentheses, as arguments.

- The arc sine function is not available directly but can be computed as shown in the examples below.
- The VALUE, SYSMIS, MISSING, and LAG functions take only one variable name enclosed in parentheses as an argument.
- UNIFORM takes a single value or variable name, enclosed in parentheses, as an argument. The resulting random variable ranges between 0 and the value of the argument.
- NORMAL takes a single positive value or a variable name, enclosed in parentheses, as an argument. The resulting random variable has a mean of 0 and a standard deviation equal to the argument. The result is system-missing when the argument is negative.
- YRMODA requires three arguments that represent a year, month, and day, in that order. The arguments must yield integer values and can be in the form of variables, constants, or a combination of variables and constants.

String Variables

- Only short string variables, values, and constants can be used in an expression. Long string variables cannot be used.
- String values and constants must be enclosed in apostrophes or quotation marks.
- LAG is the only function available for strings.
- The LAG function takes only one variable enclosed in parentheses as an argument.

Operations

- COMPUTE is a transformation and is executed before the data are read for the next procedure.
- If the target variable already exists, its values are replaced.
- If the target variable does not already exist, it is created as a new variable.
- Invalid syntax stops all processing of the COMPUTE command. New variables are not created and existing target variables remain unchanged.

Numeric Variables

- New numeric variables created with COMPUTE are assigned a dictionary format of a width of eight characters with two decimal places.
- Existing numeric variables transformed with COMPUTE retain their original dictionary formats.
- You can change the format of a numeric variable using the FORMAT command.
- If a case is system-missing on any variable named in an assignment expression, SPSS/PC+ returns the system-missing value for that case since the operation is indeterminate.
- You can include user-missing values in computations by using the VALUE function.
- The MISSING function returns the value 1 if the variable named has either a user-missing or system-missing value.
- The SYSMIS function returns the value 1 if the variable named has a system-missing value.
- The YRMODA function returns the number of days since the beginning of the Gregorian calendar (October 15, 1582). The arguments for YRMODA must yield integers.
- The LAG function returns the value of the previous case for the named variable. The first case will have a system-missing value for the target variable.
- The UNIFORM and NORMAL functions return values with decimal places. Use the TRUNC or RND function to change these values to integers.
- You can change the seed value used by UNIFORM and NORMAL with the SEED specification on SET.
- All expressions are evaluated in the following order: first functions, then exponentiation, and then arithmetic operations. You can change the order of operations by using parentheses.

String Variables

- A new string variable created by setting a variable name equal to a string constant is assigned a dictionary format equal to the width of the string constant.

- A new string variable created by setting a variable name equal to an existing string variable has the same dictionary format as the existing variable.

- Existing string variables transformed with COMPUTE retain their original dictionary formats.

- All subsequent transformations on a string variable must use the format defined when the variable is first named. All leading or trailing blanks must be specified.

- You cannot change the format of string variables.

- The LAG function returns the value of the previous case for the named variable. The first case will have a system-missing value for the target variable.

Limitations

- Only 1 variable can be created or transformed per COMPUTE command.

- The number of variables created with COMPUTE, COUNT, and IF plus the number defined on DATA LIST, IMPORT, and GET cannot exceed the system maximum of 200 variables.

Numeric Examples

The following examples illustrate the use of the COMPUTE command with numeric variables.

Arithmetic Operations

```
COMPUTE XVAR=25.
COM YVAR1=(YVAR/XVAR)*100.
```

- XVAR is initialized to 25 for all cases.

- YVAR1 is computed as the percentage YVAR is of XVAR.

Numeric Functions

```
COMPUTE WTCHANGE=ABS(WEIGHT1-WEIGHT2).
COMPUTE YVAR1=RND((YVAR/ZVAR)*100).
COMPUTE ARCSINX=ARTAN(X/SQRT(1-X*X)).
```

- WTCHANGE is computed as the absolute value of WEIGHT1 minus WEIGHT2.

- YVAR1 is computed as a percentage of ZVAR and is rounded to an integer using the RND function.

- ARCSINX is computed as the arc sine of X, using the ARTAN and SQRT functions. This trigonometric identity is valid only if X is greater than -1 and less than $+1$.

Missing Values

```
MISSING VALUE XVAR1 XVAR2 XVAR3 (0).
COMPUTE FVAR1=XVAR1 + XVAR2 + XVAR3.
COMPUTE FVAR4=VALUE(XVAR1) + VALUE(XVAR2) + VALUE(XVAR3).
COMPUTE FVARSM=SYSMIS(XVAR1) + SYSMIS(XVAR2) + SYSMIS(XVAR3).
COMPUTE FVARM=MISSING(XVAR1) + MISSING(XVAR2) + MISSING(XVAR3).
```

- The MISSING VALUE command declares the value 0 as missing for XVAR1, XVAR2, and XVAR3.

- FVAR1 is computed as the sum of three variables only for cases with valid values for all three variables. FVAR1 is assigned the system-missing value for a case if any variable in the assignment expression has a system-missing or user-missing value.

- The VALUE function overrides user-missing value declarations. Thus, FVAR4 is the sum of XVAR1, XVAR2, and XVAR3 for each case, including cases with value 0 (the user-missing value) for any of the three variables. Cases with system-missing values are not included.

- The SYSMIS function on the third COMPUTE returns value 1 if the variable is system-missing. Thus, FVARSM ranges from 0 to 3 for each case, depending on whether the variables XVAR1, XVAR2, and XVAR3 are system-missing for the case.

- The MISSING function on the fourth COMPUTE returns the value 1 if the variable named is system-missing or user-missing. Thus, FVARM ranges from 0 to 3 for each case, depending on whether variables XVAR1, XVAR2, and XVAR3 are user- or system-missing for that case.

- Alternatively, you could use the COUNT command to create variables FVARSM and FVARM.

Across-Case Operations

```
COMPUTE LVAR1=LAG(LVAR).
COMPUTE LVAR2=LAG(LVAR1).
```

- The LAG function on the first COMPUTE sets LVAR1 equal to the value of LVAR for the previous case.
- The second COMPUTE sets LVAR2 equal to the value of LVAR1 for the previous case. In effect, LVAR2 is equal to the value of LVAR for two cases previous.
- This example demonstrates the use of successive LAG transformations to perform multiple-case LAG operations.

Random-Number Functions

```
COMPUTE QVAR=UNIFORM(10).
COMPUTE SVAR=NORMAL(1.5).
```

- The first COMPUTE sets QVAR equal to a pseudo-random number from a distribution with values ranging between 0 and the specified value of 10.
- The second COMPUTE sets SVAR equal to a pseudo-random number from a distribution with a mean of 0 and a standard deviation of the specified value of 1.5.
- You can change the seed value of the pseudo-random-number generator with the SEED specification on SET.

Date Function

```
COMPUTE AGER=(YRMODA(1980,08,23)-
YRMODA(YRBIRTH,MOBIRTH,DABIRTH))/365.25.
```

- The YRMODA function converts the current date (in this example, August 23, 1980) and birthdate to a number of days. Birthdate is subtracted from current date and the remainder is divided by the number of days in a year to yield age in years.

String Examples

The examples below illustrate the use of the COMPUTE command with string variables.

Equivalence

```
COMPUTE NEWSTR=YVAR.
COMPUTE DAYVAR='TODAY'.
```

- The first COMPUTE creates a new variable NEWSTR with the same values as YVAR. The format of NEWSTR is the same as YVAR.
- The second COMPUTE creates a new variable DAYVAR with the value 'TODAY' for each case. The width of DAYVAR is five characters.

LAG Operations

```
COMPUTE NEIGHBOR=LAG(HSHOLDER).
```

- COMPUTE creates a new short string variable NEIGHBOR as the value for HSHOLDER for the previous case. The first case will have the system-missing value for NEIGHBOR.

C

Command Reference

COUNT

```
COUNT varname=varlist (value list) varlist (value list)
      [/varname=...]
```

Keywords available for numeric value lists:

```
LO  LOWEST  HI  HIGHEST  THRU  SYSMIS  MISSING
```

Example:

```
COUNT RVAR=XVAR,YVAR,ZVAR (2).
```

Overview

The COUNT transformation creates a numeric variable that, for each case, counts the occurrences of the same value (or list of values) across a list of variables. The new variable is called the target variable. The variables and values that are counted are the criterion variables and values. You can create the target variable from numeric or string variables, or both.

Syntax

- The minimum specification is the target variable, an equals sign, a criterion variable, and a criterion value enclosed in parentheses.
- Only one target variable is allowed per specification.
- A variable can be specified more than once in the criterion variable list.
- The criterion variable list can include both string and numeric variables, provided they have separate value specifications.
- The TO keyword can be used to name consecutive criterion variables that have the same criterion value or values.
- You can specify more than one criterion value, separating each by a comma or space.
- String values must be enclosed in apostrophes.
- Keywords THRU, LOWEST (LO), and HIGHEST (HI) can be used in a numeric value list.
- SYSMIS counts system-missing values for numeric variables.
- MISSING counts both user- and system-missing values for numeric variables.
- You cannot specify any keywords with string variables.
- You can create more than one target variable on a single COUNT command by separating the specifications with a slash.

Operations

- COUNT is a transformation and is executed when the data are read for the next procedure.
- The target variable is numeric.
- The target variable is initialized to 0 for each case.
- If the target variable already exists, its previous values are replaced.
- Variables created with COUNT are assigned a dictionary format of eight columns with two decimal places.
- COUNT does not propagate missing values automatically. The target variable will never be system-missing. To declare missing-value flags, use the RECODE or MISSING VALUE command.

Limitations

- The number of variables created with COUNT combined with the number created with COMPUTE and IF and defined on DATA LIST, IMPORT, or GET cannot exceed the system maximum of 200 variables.

Example

```
COUNT RVAR=XVAR,YVAR,ZVAR (2).
```

- The value of RVAR for each case will be either 0, 1, 2, or 3, depending on the number of times the value 2 occurs across the three variables.
- RVAR is a numeric variable with a format of eight columns with two decimal places.

Example
```
COUNT QLOW=QVAR1 TO QVAR10 (LO THRU 0)
    /QSYSMIS=QVAR1 TO QVAR10 (SYSMIS).
```

- Assuming there are 10 variables between and including QVAR1 and QVAR10 on the active file, QLOW ranges from 0 to 10, depending on the number of times a case has a negative or 0 value across variables QVAR1 to QVAR10.

- QSYSMIS ranges from 0 to 10, depending on how many system-missing values are encountered for QVAR1 to QVAR10 for each case.

- Both QLOW and QSYSMIS are numeric variables and have a format of eight columns with two decimal places.

Example
```
COUNT SVARC=AVAR,BVAR ('male  ') CVAR, DVAR, EVAR ('female').
```

- SVARC ranges from 0 to 5, depending on the number of times a case has a value of 'male' for AVAR and BVAR and value 'female' for CVAR, DVAR, and EVAR.

- SVARC is a numeric variable with a format of eight columns with two decimal places.

Example
```
COUNT MIXVAR=SEX (2) EVAL ('good').
```

- MIXVAR ranges from 0 to 2, depending on the number of times a case has value 2 for variable SEX and value 'good' for variable EVAL.

- MIXVAR is a numeric variable with a format of eight columns with two decimal places.

CROSSTABS

General mode:

```
CROSSTABS [TABLES=]varlist BY varlist [BY...] [/varlist...]

  [/MISSING={TABLE** }]
            {INCLUDE}

  [/FORMAT={LABELS**  }   {AVALUE**}   {NOINDEX**}   {TABLES** }
           {NOLABELS  }   {DVALUE  }   {INDEX     }   {NOTABLES}
           {NOVALLABS }

     {BOX** }]
     {NOBOX}

  [/CELLS={COUNT**}   [ROW    ]  [EXPECTED]  [SRESID ]]
          {NONE  }    [COLUMN]   [RESID   ]  [ASRESID]
                      [TOTAL ]               [ALL    ]

  [/WRITE[={NONE** }]]
          {CELLS  }

  [/STATISTICS=[CHISQ]  [LAMBDA]  [BTAU]  [GAMMA]  [ETA ]]
               [PHI  ]  [UC    ]  [CTAU]  [D    ]  [CORR]
               [CC   ]  [NONE  ]  [RISK]  [KAPPA]  [ALL ]
```

Integer mode:

```
CROSSTABS VARIABLES=varlist(min,max) [varlist...]

  /TABLES=varlist BY varlist [BY...] [/varlist...]

  [/MISSING={TABLE** }]
            {INCLUDE}
            {REPORT }

  [/FORMAT={LABELS**  }   {AVALUE**}   {NOINDEX**}   {TABLES** }
           {NOLABELS  }   {DVALUE  }   {INDEX     }   {NOTABLES}
           {NOVALLABS }

     {BOX** }]
     {NOBOX}

  [/CELLS={COUNT**}   [ROW    ]  [EXPECTED]  [SRESID ]]
          {NONE  }    [COLUMN]   [RESID   ]  [ASRESID]
                      [TOTAL ]               [ALL    ]

  [/WRITE[={NONE** }]]
          {CELLS  }
          {ALL    }

  [/STATISTICS=[CHISQ]  [LAMBDA]  [BTAU]  [GAMMA]  [ETA ]]
               [PHI  ]  [UC    ]  [CTAU]  [D    ]  [CORR]
               [CC   ]  [NONE  ]  [RISK]  [KAPPA]  [ALL ]
```

**Default if the subcommand is omitted.

Example:

```
CROSSTABS  FEAR BY SEX
  /CELLS=ROW COLUMN EXPECTED RESIDUALS
  /STATISTICS=CHISQ.
```

Overview   CROSSTABS produces tables showing the joint distribution of two or more variables that have a limited number of distinct values. The frequency distribution of one variable is subdivided according to the values of one or more variables. The unique combination of values for two or more variables defines a cell, the basic element of all tables.

CROSSTABS operates in two different modes: *general* and *integer.* General mode operates via the TABLES subcommand and requires fewer specifications. Integer mode operates via the TABLES and VARIABLES subcommands and requires you to specify minimum and maximum values for the variables. This mode sometimes makes more efficient use of memory and offers a few additional features (see MISSING, STATISTICS, WRITE), but it requires more specification than general mode.

Defaults   By default, CROSSTABS displays a table containing the count of cases in each cell, with "marginal" totals and percentages for each row and column. Variable and value labels are displayed. Missing data are excluded from the table, but a count of missing cases is displayed.

Tailoring   You can request row, column, and total percentages, and also expected values and residuals (see CELLS Subcommand). In addition to the tables, you can obtain measures of association and tests of hypotheses for each subtable (see STATIS-TICS Subcommand). You can control the order in which rows are displayed and suppress the display of variable labels, value labels, and the table itself. In addition, you can display a list of the tables produced by CROSSTABS with the page number where each table begins (see FORMAT Subcommand). You can write cell frequencies to an ASCII file (see WRITE Subcommand).

Syntax   The basic specification is TABLES followed by a list of row variables, the keyword BY, and a list of column variables. You can optionally specify BY and one or more control variables. The actual keyword TABLES can be omitted in general mode.

For integer mode, specify the VARIABLES subcommand followed by a list of variables, each with its minimum and maximum value in parentheses. Then specify the TABLES subcommand. You must specify the keyword TABLES when you have specified VARIABLES.

• If keyword TABLES is omitted, the table list must be first.

• If keyword TABLES is explicitly used, subcommands can be specified in any order. The exception is VARIABLES in integer mode, which must precede TABLES.

Operations   • If a long string variable is used, only the short-string portion is tabulated.

• Statistics are calculated separately for each two-way table or two-way subtable. Missing values are reported for the table as a whole.

• If only percentages and/or cell counts are requested, the percentages are displayed without a percent sign and blanks are displayed instead of zero values for counts and percents.

• If percentages and any of the expected values or residuals are requested, the percent sign appears next to the percentage and zero values are displayed as zeros.

• Scientific notation is used for cell counts when necessary.

• The display uses the width defined on the SET command.

• The BOX subcommand on SET controls the characters used in the table display.

Specifications for CROSSTABS subcommands depend on whether *general mode* or *integer mode* is used to build tables. Each method has advantages and disadvantages in computational efficiency, available statistics, and additional options.

• General mode suffices for most purposes and is easier to use. It permits string or noninteger variables. Ranges do not have to be specified for variables, which makes general mode more convenient. The order of the variables in the active system file determines the positional order of variables in the table list.

• Integer mode uses less memory for tables with few empty cells, where the categories are coded as adjacent integers. It requires *more* space if the table has many empty cells. By specifying the appropriate ranges, you can select a subset of values for processing. You can include missing values in tables while excluding them from the calculation of statistics and percentages. Partial gammas are available only in integer mode. The order of the variables on VARIABLES determines the positional order of the variables on TABLES.

Limitations

The available memory places limits on the size and number of tables that can be built by CROSSTABS. If necessary, split your request among two or more CROSSTABS commands.

The following limitations apply to CROSSTABS in *general mode*:

• Maximum 200 variables named or implied with the TABLES subcommand.

• Maximum 250 nonempty rows or columns for each table.

• Maximum 20 table lists per CROSSTABS command.

• Maximum 10 dimensions per table.

• Maximum 400 value labels displayed on any single table.

The following limitations apply to CROSSTABS in *integer mode*:

• Maximum 100 variables named or implied with the VARIABLES subcommand.

• Maximum 100 variables named or implied with the TABLES subcommand.

• Maximum 250 nonempty rows or columns for each table.

• Maximum 20 table lists per CROSSTABS command.

• Maximum 8 dimensions per table.

• No more than 20 rows or columns of missing values can be displayed with MISSING=REPORT.

• Minimum value that can be specified is $-99,999$.

• Maximum value that can be specified is $999,999$.

Example

```
CROSSTABS  FEAR BY SEX
  /CELLS=ROW COLUMN EXPECTED RESIDUALS
  /STATISTICS=CHISQ.
```

• In general mode, the keyword TABLES has been omitted before the table list.

• CROSSTABS generates a bivariate table. Variable FEAR defines the rows of the table and variable SEX defines the columns.

• CELLS requests row and column percentages, expected cell frequencies, and residuals.

• STATISTICS requests the chi-square statistic.

Example

```
CROSSTABS  JOBCAT BY EDCAT BY SEX BY INCOME3.
```

• This table list produces a subtable of JOBCAT by EDCAT for each combination of values of SEX and INCOME3.

TABLES Subcommand

TABLES specifies the table lists. Use TABLES with CROSSTABS in both general and integer mode.

General Mode

The actual keyword TABLES can be omitted in general mode.

• Both numeric and string variables can be specified. Long strings are truncated to short strings for defining categories.

- Variables named before the first BY in a table list are row variables, and variables named after the first BY in a table list are column variables.
- Variables named after the second (or subsequent) BY are control variables.
- Each subsequent use of the keyword BY in a table list adds a new dimension to the tables requested and introduces a new order of control among the independent variables.
- You can name more than one variable in each dimension.
- You can use keyword ALL to include all user-defined variables in a dimension.
- When the table list specifies two dimensions, tables are produced that crosstabulate the first variable before BY with each variable after BY, then the second variable before BY with each variable after BY, and so forth.
- When the table list specifies more than two dimensions, a two-way subtable is produced for each combination of values of control variables.
- When the table list specifies more than three dimensions, the value of the last variable mentioned changes the most slowly in determining the order in which the tables are displayed.
- You can specify multiple TABLES subcommands on a single CROSSTABS command. The slash between the subcommands is required; the keyword TABLES is not.

Example   CROSSTABS FEAR BY SEX BY RACE.

- This example crosstabulates FEAR by SEX, controlling for RACE. In each subtable, FEAR is the row variable and SEX is the column variable.
- A subtable is produced for each value of the control variable RACE.

Example   CROSSTABS FEAR BY SEX BY RACE BY DEGREE.

- Assuming variables RACE and DEGREE have two values each, this command produces four subtables.
- The first subtable crosstabulates FEAR by SEX, controlling for the first value of RACE and the first value of DEGREE; the second subtable controls for the second value of RACE and the first value of DEGREE; the third subtable controls for the first value of RACE and the second value of DEGREE; and the fourth subtable controls for the second value of RACE and the second value of DEGREE.

Example   CROSSTABS CONFINAN TO CONARMY BY SEX TO REGION.

- This command produces CROSSTABS tables for all the variables between and including CONFINAN and CONARMY by all the variables between and including SEX and REGION.

Integer Mode   To run CROSSTABS in integer mode, the values of all the variables must be integers. Two subcommands are required. VARIABLES specifies all the variables to be used in the CROSSTABS procedure and the minimum and maximum values for building tables. TABLES specifies the table lists. Variables referenced on TABLES must be named on VARIABLES.

- TABLES has the same syntax in integer mode as it has in general mode; however, there is one important difference when you use the TO convention to specify a list of variables. In integer mode, the order of the variables implied on TABLES is established by the order of the variables named or implied on VARIABLES. In general mode, the order of variables implied on the table lists is established by their order in the active system file.
- Multiple TABLES subcommands can be used.
- When data values consist of consecutive integers, integer mode can produce more tables in a given amount of core storage space than general mode, and the processing is slightly faster. The values supplied as variable ranges do not have to include all values of the variables; thus, you have control from within CROSSTABS over the tabulated ranges of the variables. Some subcommand and keyword specifications are available only in integer mode.

Example `CROSSTABS  VARIABLES=FEAR (1,2) MOBILE16 (1,3)`
       `/TABLES=FEAR BY MOBILE16.`

- VARIABLES names two variables, FEAR and MOBILE16. Values 1 and 2 for FEAR are used in the tables, and values 1, 2, and 3 are used for variable MOBILE16.
- TABLES specifies a bivariate table with two rows (values 1 and 2 for FEAR) and three columns (values 1, 2, and 3 for MOBILE16). FEAR and MOBILE16 can be named on TABLES because they were named on the previous VARIABLES.

VARIABLES Subcommand

VARIABLES specifies a list of variables to be used in the crosstabulations. Specify the lowest and highest values in parentheses after each variable. These values must be integers. Noninteger values are truncated.

- Variables can appear in any order. However, the order in which they are named on VARIABLES affects their implied order on TABLES.
- A range must be specified for each variable. Several variables can have the same range.
- CROSSTABS uses the specified ranges to allocate tables. One cell is allocated for each possible combination of values of the row and column variables for a requested table before the data are read. Therefore, if you specify more generous ranges than the variables actually have, you are wasting space. If the table is sparse because the variables do not have values falling throughout the range specified, consider using general mode or recoding the variables. If the values of the variables fall outside the specified range, cases with these values are considered missing and are not used in the computation of the table.

Example `CROSSTABS  VARIABLES=FEAR SEX RACE (1,2)  MOBILE16 (1,3)`
       `/TABLES=FEAR BY SEX MOBILE16 BY RACE.`

- VARIABLES defines 1 as the lowest value and 2 as the highest value for FEAR, SEX, and RACE.

CELLS Subcommand

By default, CROSSTABS displays only the number of cases in each cell. Use CELLS to display row, column, or total percentages, and expected values and residuals. These are calculated separately for each bivariate table or subtable.

- CELLS specified without keywords displays cell counts plus ROW, COLUMN, and TOTAL percentages for each cell.
- If CELLS is specified with keywords, CROSSTABS displays only the requested cell information.
- The key located at the top left corner of each table describes the information contained in each cell.
- Scientific notation is used for cell contents when necessary.

COUNT	*Display cell counts.* This is the default if CELLS is omitted.
ROW	*Display row percentages.* Display the number of cases in each cell in a row expressed as a percentage of all cases in that row.
COLUMN	*Display column percentages.* Display the number of cases in each cell in a column expressed as a percentage of all cases in that column.
TOTAL	*Display two-way table total percentages.* Display the number of cases in each cell of a subtable expressed as a percentage of all cases in that subtable.
EXPECTED	*Display expected frequencies.* Display the number of cases expected in each cell if the two variables in the subtable are statistically independent.
RESID	*Display residuals.* Display the difference between the observed cell counts and the expected cell counts.
SRESID	*Display standardized residuals.* (Haberman, 1978).
ASRESID	*Display adjusted standardized residuals.* (Haberman, 1978).

ALL	*Display all cell information.* Display cell count; row, column, and total percentages; expected values; residuals; standardized residuals; and adjusted standardized residuals.
NONE	*Display no cell information.* You can use NONE when you use WRITE to send the tables to an ASCII file (see WRITE subcommand). This has the same effect as specifying FORMAT= NOTABLES.

STATISTICS Subcommand

STATISTICS requests measures of association and related statistics. There are no default statistics.

• STATISTICS without keywords displays the chi-square test.

• If STATISTICS is specified with keywords, CROSSTABS calculates only the requested statistics.

• If a range that excludes cases is specified for a variable in integer mode, the excluded cases are *not* used in the calculation of the statistics.

• If user-missing values are included with MISSING, cases with user-missing values are included in the tables as well as in the calculation of statistics.

CHISQ	*Chi-square.* Pearson chi-square, likelihood-ratio chi-square, and Mantel-Haenszel chi-square. Also, for 2×2 tables, Fisher's exact test is computed when a table that does not result from missing rows or columns in a larger table has a cell with an expected frequency less than 5; Yates' corrected chi-square is computed for all other 2×2 tables. This is the default if STATISTICS is specified with no keywords.
PHI	*Phi and Cramer's* V.
CC	*Contingency coefficient.*
LAMBDA	*Lambda, symmetric and asymmetric, and also Goodman and Kruskal's tau.*
UC	*Uncertainty coefficient, symmetric and asymmetric.*
BTAU	*Kendall's tau-b.*
CTAU	*Kendall's tau-c.*
GAMMA	*Gamma.* Partial and zero-order gammas for 3-way to 8-way tables are available in integer mode only. Zero-order gammas are displayed for 2-way tables and conditional gammas are displayed for 3-way to 10-way tables in general mode and 3-way to 8-way for integer mode.
D	*Somers'* d, *symmetric and asymmetric.*
ETA	*Eta.* Available for numeric data only.
CORR	*Pearson's* r, *and Spearman's correlation coefficient.* Available for numeric data only.
KAPPA	*Kappa coefficient* (Kraemer, 1982). Kappa can only be computed for square tables in which the row and column values are identical. If there is a missing row or column, use integer mode to specify the square table, since a missing column or row in general mode would keep the table from being square.
RISK	*Relative risk* (Bishop et al., 1975). Relative risk can only be calculated for 2×2 tables.
ALL	*All the statistics available for CROSSTABS.*
NONE	*No summary statistics.* This is the default if STATISTICS is omitted.

MISSING Subcommand

By default, CROSSTABS deletes cases with missing values on a table-by-table basis. A case missing on any of the variables specified for a table is not used either in the displayed table or in the calculation of the statistics. Use MISSING to control missing values.

• The only specification is a single keyword. TABLE is the default.

• When multiple table lists are specified, missing values are handled separately for each list.

- The number of missing cases is always displayed at the end of the table, following the last subtable, and after any requested statistics.
- If the missing values are not included in the range specifications on VARIABLES, they are excluded from the table regardless of the keyword you specify on MISSING.

TABLE *Delete cases with missing values on a table-by-table basis.* This is the default.

INCLUDE *Include user-missing values.*

REPORT *Report missing values in the tables* (integer mode only). This option includes missing values in tables but not in the calculation of percentages or statistics. The letter M is used to indicate that cases within a cell are missing.

FORMAT Subcommand

By default, CROSSTABS displays tables and subtables with variable labels and value labels when they are available. The values for the row variables display in order from lowest to highest and only the first 16 characters of a value label are displayed.

Use FORMAT to modify the default table display.

LABELS *Display both variable and value labels for each table.* This is the default.

NOLABELS *Suppress variable and value labels.*

NOVALLABS *Suppress value labels, display variable labels.*

AVALUE *Display row variables ordered from lowest to highest value.* This is the default.

DVALUE *Display row variables ordered from highest to lowest.*

NOINDEX *Suppress a table index.* This is the default.

INDEX *Display an index of tables.* The index lists all tables produced and the page number where each table begins. The index follows the last page of tables produced by the table list.

TABLES *Display the crosstabs tables.* This is the default.

NOTABLES *Suppress displayed tables.* If STATISTICS is used with FORMAT= NOTABLES, only the statistics are displayed. If STATISTICS is omitted and FORMAT=NOTABLES, CROSSTABS produces no output. Use NOTABLES to write the tables to a procedure file without displayed tables. This has the same effect as specifying CELLS=NONE.

BOX *Use box drawing characters around every cell.* This is the default.

NOBOX *Suppress the box drawing characters around each cell.* The banner and stub are still separated from the table by box drawing characters.

WRITE Subcommand

CROSSTABS can write cell frequencies to a file for subsequent use by either SPSS/PC+ or some other program. It can also use cell frequencies as input to reproduce tables and compute statistics. Use WRITE to write cell frequencies to an ASCII file.

- The only specification is a single keyword. Keyword ALL is available only in integer mode.
- The WRITE subcommand sends output to the *results file,* which by default is named SPSS.PRC. You can direct it to a different file by using SET RESULTS before CROSSTABS (see SET).
- If the results file already exists, the cell frequencies from CROSSTABS replace its existing contents.
- WRITE has two options for producing an output file of cell frequencies. You can write all the cells of the table, or only the nonempty cells. The file contains one record for each cell; each record contains a split-file group number and a table number, which identify the table, and the cell frequency and values, which identify the cell.

- If both CELLS and ALL are specified, CELLS is in effect and only the contents of the nonempty cells are written to the file.
- Use CELLS to write only nonempty cells. Combinations of values that include a missing value are not written to the output file. If you include missing values in the tables with keyword INCLUDE on MISSING, no values are considered missing and all nonempty cells will be written.
- Keyword ALL writes all defined cells and is available only with integer mode. A record for each combination of values defined by TABLES is written to the output file. If you include missing values in the tables with either keyword INCLUDE or keyword REPORT on MISSING, all defined cells are written whether or not a missing value is involved. If you exclude missing values on a table-by-table basis (the default), no records are written for combinations of values that include a missing value.
- If multiple tables are specified, the tables are written in the same order as they are displayed. The variable in the row variable list changes more slowly and the variable in the last control variable list changes more quickly.

The output record from each cell contains the following information:

Columns	Contents
1–4	Split-file group number, which always equals 1. This is written for compatibility with SPSS software on other operating systems.
5–8	Table number. A table is defined by taking one variable from each of the variable lists separated by the keyword BY.
9–16	Cell frequency. The number of times this combination of variable values occurred in the data, or, if case weights are used, the sum of case weights for cases having this combination of values.
17–24	The value of the row variable (named before the first BY).
25–32	The value of the column variable (named after the first BY).
33–40	The value of the first control variable (named after the second BY).
41–48	The value of the second control variable (named after the third BY).
49–56	The value of the third control variable (named after the fourth BY).
57–64	The value of the fourth control variable (named after the fifth BY).
65–72	The value of the fifth control variable (named after the sixth BY).
73–80	The value of the sixth control variable (named after the seventh BY).

- The split-file group number, table number, and frequency are written as integers.
- If the integer mode of CROSSTABS is used, the values of variables are also written as integers. If the general mode is used, the values are written in accordance with the PRINT FORMAT specified for each variable. Alphanumeric values are written at the left end of any field in which they occur.

Within each table, the records are written in the following order:

the value of the row variable, within
the value of the column variable, within
the value of the first control variable, within

.
.

.
the value of the fifth control variable

This order implies that the records are written from one column of the table at a time, and the value of the last control variable changes most slowly.

NONE   *Do not write the cell counts to the file.* This is the default.

CELLS   *Write the cell count for nonempty cells to a file.*

ALL   *Write the cell count for all cells to a file.* Available only in integer mode, since the possible cells are not known in general mode.

Example

```
CROSSTABS  VARIABLES=FEAR SEX (1,2)
   /TABLES=FEAR BY SEX
   /WRITE=ALL.
```

• CROSSTABS writes a record for each cell in the table FEAR by SEX to the file SPSS.PRC. Figure 1 shows the contents of SPSS.PRC.

Figure 1 Cell output records

```
1   1       55      1       1
1   1      172      2       1
1   1      180      1       2
1   1       89      2       2
```

Example

```
SET  RESULTS='CROSSTAB.DAT'.
CROSSTABS  TABLES=V1 TO V3 BY V4 BY V10 TO V15
   /WRITE=CELLS.
```

• CROSSTABS writes a set of records for each table to CROSSTAB.DAT, overwriting any existing contents of that file.

• All of the records for the table V1 BY V4 BY V10 are written first, the records for V1 BY V4 BY V11 second, and the records for V3 BY V4 BY V15 last.

WEIGHT Command with CROSSTABS

You can use the file created by the WRITE subcommand to reproduce a table and compute statistics for it. Each record in the file contains all the information used to build the original table.

Example

The following CROSSTABS command reads the SPSS.PRC file created by the commands in the previous section (see WRITE Subcommand). It reads the cell frequency as a weighting factor (WT), the value of the row variable (FEAR), and the value of the column variable (SEX):

```
DATA LIST  FILE='SPSS.PRC'/
   WT 9-16 FEAR 17-24 SEX 25-32.
VARIABLE LABELS  FEAR 'AFRAID TO WALK AT NIGHT IN NEIGHBOR-
HOODS'.
VALUE LABELS  FEAR 1 'YES' 2 'NO'/
             SEX 1 'MALE' 2 'FEMALE'.
WEIGHT  BY WT.
CROSSTABS  TABLES=FEAR BY SEX
   /STATISTICS=ALL.
```

• The WEIGHT command recreates the sample size by weighting each of the four cases (cells) by the cell frequency.

Example

This example assumes you do not have the original data for a published crosstabulation. The WEIGHT command is used to reproduce tables and compute statistics for the published tables.

```
DATA LIST / FEAR 1 SEX 3 WT 5-7.
VARIABLE LABELS  FEAR 'AFRAID TO WALK AT NIGHT IN NEIGHBORHOOD'.
VALUE LABELS  FEAR 1 'YES' 2 'NO'/
             SEX 1 'MALE' 2 'FEMALE'.
WEIGHT  BY WT.
BEGIN DATA
1 1   55
2 1  172
1 2  180
2 2   89
END DATA.
CROSSTABS  TABLES=FEAR BY SEX
   /STATISTICS=ALL.
```

• The values from the table are used as inline data between BEGIN DATA and END DATA.

• Each cell in the table becomes a case, and each record includes the row and column variables, and the cell frequency for weighting.

• You can define the variables for the cell frequency, row value, and column value in any order.

References   Bishop, Y. M. M., S. E. Feinberg, and P. W. Holland. 1975. *Discrete multivariate analysis: Theory and practice.* Cambridge: MIT Press.

Haberman, S. J. 1978. *Analysis of qualitative data,* vol. 1. London: Academic Press.

Kraemer, H. C. 1982. Kappa coefficient. In *Encyclopedia of statistical sciences,* ed. S. Kotz and N. L. Johnson. New York: John Wiley & Sons.

DATA LIST: Fixed Format

```
DATA LIST [FILE='filename'] [FIXED] [TABLE]

/varlist columns [{(0)}] [varlist columns ...]
                  {(n)}
                  {(A)}

[/ ...] [/ ...]
```

Format Meaning

(n)   Implied decimal places
      for numeric variables

(A)   String variable

Example:

```
DATA LIST / ID 1-3 SEX 5 (A) AGE 7-8 OPINION1 TO OPINION5 10-14.
BEGIN DATA.
001 m 28 12212
002 f 29 21212
003 f 45 32145
{lines of data}
128 m 17 11194
END DATA.
```

Overview

The DATA LIST command assigns names to variables and provides information about the column location and format. Data can be inline (entered with SPSS/PC+ commands) or stored in an external file. The DATA LIST command with keyword FIXED defines data arranged in fixed format. In fixed format, the values for each variable are found in the same location on the same record for each case. Fixed format is the default for DATA LIST.

See DATA LIST: Freefield Format for defining data organized in freefield format and DATA LIST: Matrix Materials for defining matrix materials.

- Use DATA LIST to read a data file containing ASCII data (numbers and other alphanumeric characters).

- Use the GET command, not DATA LIST, to read a *system file* created with the SAVE command (see GET and SAVE).

- Use the IMPORT command, not DATA LIST, to read a *portable file* created with the EXPORT command in SPSS/PC+ or SPSS (see IMPORT and EXPORT).

Defaults

By default, SPSS/PC+ assumes that data are inline, entered interactively, or contained in a file named on the INCLUDE command. (The file named on INCLUDE must also contain the BEGIN DATA command; see BEGIN DATA—END DATA and INCLUDE.) By default, all variables are assumed to be numeric without implied decimal places.

Tailoring

Data Source and Formats. You can use data from an external file. You can also define string variables and specify implied decimal places for numeric variables. **Summary Table.** You can ask SPSS/PC+ to display a table that summarizes your variable definitions.

Syntax

- The minimum DATA LIST specification for fixed format is a slash followed by at least one variable name and its location.

- The keyword FIXED is optional.

- The keyword TABLE is optional.

Operations

- Variable names are stored in the active file dictionary.

- The order of the variables in the active file dictionary is the order in which they are defined on the DATA LIST command, not their sequence on the input data file. This order is important if you later use the TO convention.

- By default, variables are assumed to be numeric. Alphabetical and special characters, except the decimal point and leading plus and minus signs, are not valid numeric values and are set to system-missing if encountered in the data.
- Blanks to the left or right of a number in the default format are ignored; embedded blanks are invalid.
- The system-missing value is assigned to a completely blank field for numeric variables. The value assigned to blanks can be changed using the BLANKS specification on the SET command.
- Formats are stored in the active file dictionary and are used to display the values. Use the FORMATS command to change formats of numeric variables defined on DATA LIST.

Limitations

- You cannot define more than 500 variables on a DATA LIST command.
- Each 8-character portion of a long string variable counts toward the 200-variable limit. For example, an 18-character long string counts as three short string variables (see Universals: Strings).
- The maximum length of an input record is 1024 characters.

Example

```
DATA LIST / ID 1-3 SEX 5 (A) AGE 7-8 OPINION1 TO OPINION5 10-14.
BEGIN DATA.
001 m 28 12212
002 f 29 21212
003 f 45 32145
lines of data
128 m 17 11194
END DATA.
```

- The data are assumed to be inline because no data file is specified.
- The data are in fixed format (the default).
- Variable definitions start with ID in columns 1 through 3.
- Variable SEX is a short string variable in column 5.
- AGE is a two-column variable in columns 7 and 8.
- Variables OPINION1, OPINION2, OPINION3, OPINION4, and OPINION5 are named using the TO convention (see Universals: Variable-Naming Conventions). Each is a one-column variable, with OPINION1 located in column 10 and OPINION5 located in column 14.
- The BEGIN DATA and END DATA commands enclose the inline data. Note that the values of SEX are in lowercase characters and must be specified as such on subsequent commands.

FILE Subcommand

- The FILE subcommand is required when data are contained in an external data file. It must not be used when the data are contained in a file included with an INCLUDE command or when the data are inline (see INCLUDE and BEGIN DATA—END DATA).
- The file specification must be enclosed in apostrophes.
- The file specification can be fully qualified, including drive, directory, filename, and extension.
- The FILE subcommand can be specified before or after the optional keyword FIXED.
- The FILE subcommand and keyword FIXED must be separated by at least one blank or comma.

Data on Floppy Diskettes

You can read an input data file from a floppy diskette.

- If you have two floppy diskette drives, insert the data diskette in B: and include the drive specification on the FILE subcommand, as in DATA LIST FILE= 'B:FLOPPY.DAT'.

• If you have one floppy diskette drive, you must start the system with the key diskette in that drive. When the security check is complete and the indicator light on the floppy drive has gone out, remove the key diskette and insert the data diskette. Enter the DATA LIST and other commands. SPSS/PC+ will read the data from the floppy diskette when it needs them for a procedure. Later in the session, SPSS/PC+ may request that you reinsert the key diskette into drive A:.

Example
```
DATA LIST FIXED FILE='\INVENTORY\MARCH.DAT'
   / NUTS3 1-2 BOLTS35 3-5 NAILS3P 6-10.
```

• Keyword FIXED indicates that the variables to be defined are on a fixed-format data file.

• The FILE specification directs SPSS/PC+ to read data from the file MARCH.DAT in directory \INVENTORY.

• Three numeric variables, NUTS3, BOLTS35, and NAILS3P, are defined for use in subsequent SPSS/PC+ procedures.

Keyword TABLE

• Keyword TABLE displays a table summarizing the variable definitions supplied on DATA LIST FIXED. For each variable, the table displays the variable name, record number, starting column, ending column, format, width, and number of decimal places. The table also includes the number of records per case.

• TABLE must be specified before the variable definitions (before the first slash).

• The TABLE keyword is only valid on DATA LIST FIXED.

Record Specification

• Records are indicated on the DATA LIST command by a slash, followed by the variables to be defined from that record.

• The first slash indicates the first (or only) record.

• The second and any subsequent slashes tell SPSS/PC+ to skip to a new record.

• You must specify a slash for every record, even if no variables are being defined from that record.

• Variables from each record can be named in any order, regardless of their sequence on the data file.

• All variables to be read from one record must be defined before proceeding to the next record.

Example
```
DATA LIST FILE='SOCSUR82.DAT'
   / ID 1-7 SEX 15 AGE 16-18
   / ANOMIA 15 LIKEPOL 17
   // OPIN1 76 OPIN2 77
   /.
```

• The DATA LIST command defines data in fixed format from file SOCSUR82.DAT in the current directory.

• Three variables, ID, SEX, and AGE, are defined from the first record.

• ANOMIA and LIKEPOL are defined from the second record.

• The third data record for each case is skipped; no variables are defined.

• The fourth record contains two variables, OPIN1 and OPIN2.

• The fifth record is skipped.

• The data file contains a total of five records per case. The DATA LIST command defines seven variables from three of these records.

Variable Names

• Variable names can contain up to eight characters.

• All variable names must begin with a letter or the @ character. System variables (beginning with a $) cannot be defined on DATA LIST.

• You can name a list of variables using the TO convention. For more information on the TO convention and other variable-naming rules, see Universals: Variable-Naming Conventions.

Variable Locations

- Each variable name is followed by its column location.

- If the variable is one column wide, specify the number of the column. If the variable is two or more columns wide, specify the number of the first column followed by a dash (–) and the number of the last column.

- The same column locations can be used to define different variables.

- If several variables are recorded in adjacent columns on the same record and have the same width and format type, you can use an abbreviated format for specifying column location. First list all variable names and then list the beginning column location of the first variable in the list, a dash, and the ending column location of the last variable in the list. SPSS/PC+ divides the total number of columns specified equally among the variables. If the number of columns do not divide equally, an error message is issued.

Example
```
DATA LIST FILE='AGES.DAT' TABLE / BIRTHDA 1-2 BIRTHMO 3-4
    BIRTHYR 5-8 BIRTHDAY 1-8 PRSNT1 TO PRSNT5 11-15
    CELEBRAT 65-68 CAKES 50-52 / WISHES 10-11.
```

- The DATA LIST command defines variables from the fixed-format file AGES.DAT in the current directory.

- Keyword TABLE generates a summary table of the names, formats, and locations of variables specified on the DATA LIST command.

- Three variables, BIRTHDA, BIRTHMO, and BIRTHYR, are read from the first eight columns on the first record. Variable BIRTHDAY is also read from the first eight columns as one variable.

- Variables PRSNT1, PRSNT2, PRSNT3, PRSNT4, and PRSNT5 are defined using the TO convention. Each of these variables is one column wide.

- Variable CELEBRAT is read from columns 65 through 68, and next CAKES is read from columns 50 through 52. The SPSS/PC+ active file dictionary will contain these variable names in the order they are defined on DATA LIST, even though this order differs from their order in the data file.

- Variable WISHES is read from columns 10 and 11 on the second data record.

Example
```
DATA LIST / LINENUM 1 ID 2-6 V1 TO V7 7-13
    OPINREL OPINSEX OPINDRUG OPINRAR 15-18
    LOCATN76 TO LOCATN83 20-35.
```

- The DATA LIST command defines inline data in fixed format.

- Variables V1, V2, V3, V4, V5, V6, and V7 are named using the TO convention. Each variable is one column wide.

- Four opinion variables, OPINREL, OPINSEX, OPINDRUG, and OPINRAR, are defined separately in columns 15 through 18. Each of these variables is one column wide.

- Eight location variables are defined by the LOCATN76 TO LOCATN83 specification. Each of these variables is two columns wide.

Variable Formats

- In the default format, variables are assumed to be numeric, either signed or unsigned integer or real numbers.

- String (alphanumeric) variables are indicated with an A in parentheses following the column specification.

- If a value is encountered that cannot be read according to the format type specified, it is assigned the system-missing value and a warning message is issued.

Numeric Formats

- When a decimal point is not actually coded in real data, the number of implied decimal places can be indicated in parentheses following the column specification.

- A coded decimal point in the data overrides the number of implied decimal places indicated on the DATA LIST command.

- The table below compares how values are interpreted for a four-column numeric variable when no decimal places are defined on DATA LIST and when two decimal places are defined.

C

Command Reference

Values in the data file	Default	Two defined decimal places
2001	2001	20.01
201	201	2.01
−201	−201	−2.01
2	2	.02
20	20	.20
2.2	2.2	2.2
.201	.201	.201
2 01	Undefined	Undefined

String Formats
- The values of string (alphanumeric) variables can contain any number, letter, or character, including special characters and embedded blanks. For further discussion of string variables, see Universals: Strings.

- String variables whose values contain eight characters or less are called *short string variables.*

- String variables with values longer than eight characters and up to 255 characters are called *long string variables.*

Example
```
DATA LIST FILE='\SPSSDAT\FILEX.DAT' TABLE
  / XVAR 1 YVAR 10-15 ZVAR 3-9(2) /
  / AVAR 25-30(A) BVAR 31-45(A).
```

- The data are defined from file FILEX.DAT in directory \SPSSDAT and are arranged in fixed format.

- Keyword TABLE generates a summary table of the variable names, formats, and locations specified on the command.

- Numeric variable XVAR is found in column 1 of the first record.

- The next variable defined is YVAR, found in columns 10 through 15.

- Variable ZVAR, found in columns 3 through 9, contains two implied decimal places, indicated by (2).

- No variables are defined on the second record for each case.

- Two variables are defined from the third record for each case.

- AVAR is a six-column short string variable.

- BVAR is a long string variable read from columns 31 through 45. BVAR counts as two variables toward the 200-variable system limit.

DATA LIST: Freefield Format

```
DATA LIST [FILE='filename'] FREE

        /variable [({A })] varlist
                   {Aw}
```

Format   Meaning

(Aw)   String of width w

Example:

```
DATA LIST FILE='MYFILE.DAT' FREE / XVAR YVAR.
```

Overview

The DATA LIST command assigns names to variables and provides information about their formats. The data can be inline or read from an external file. The DATA LIST command with keyword FREE identifies data arranged in freefield format. In freefield format, all variables are recorded in the same order for each case but not necessarily in the same column locations. Each value in the data file is separated by one or more blanks or by one comma.

See DATA LIST: Fixed Format for information on defining data in fixed format, and DATA LIST: Matrix Materials to define matrix materials.

Defaults

By default, SPSS/PC+ assumes that data are inline, entered interactively, or contained in a file named on the INCLUDE command. (The file named on INCLUDE must also contain the BEGIN DATA command; see BEGIN DATA—END DATA and INCLUDE.) All data values are assumed to be numeric.

Tailoring

You can use data stored on an external file. You can also define string variables.

Syntax

• The minimum specification for freefield data on DATA LIST is the keyword FREE, a slash, and at least one variable name.

• Variables must be named in the order they are entered on the data file.

• There is no record or column specification for freefield format.

Operations

• FREE can read freefield-format data with multiple cases recorded on one record or with one case recorded on more than one record.

• Variable names are stored in the active file dictionary.

• In the default format, variables are assumed to be numeric. Alphabetical and special characters, except the decimal point and leading plus and minus signs, are not valid numeric values and are set to the system-missing value.

• You can use BASIC conventions of delimiting data values. Two commas together or two commas separated by a blank indicate either numeric system-missing or a string blank.

Limitations

• You cannot define more than 200 variables on a DATA LIST command.

• The maximum length of an input record is 1024 characters.

• Each 8-character portion of a long string variable counts toward the 200-variable system limit. For example, an 11-character string variable counts as two short string variables (see Universals: Strings).

• The maximum number of format tokens, or syntactic elements, on the DATA LIST command is 600.

Example

```
DATA LIST FREE / XVAR YVAR.
BEGIN DATA.
1 3 2 15 3 16 4
156
5 22 6 -3
END DATA.
```

• The DATA LIST command indicates inline data in freefield format.

• Two variables, XVAR and YVAR, are named.

- The values for the first case are 1 for variable XVAR and 3 for variable YVAR. The second case has values of 2 and 15 for XVAR and YVAR. The third case has values 3 and 16, the fourth case has values 4 and 156, and so on. Note that in freefield format, a single line of data can include values for more than one case. Also, the values for one case can be split across lines, as for the fourth case. Individual values cannot be split across lines.

FILE Subcommand

- The FILE subcommand is required when data are contained in an external file. It is not required when the data are included using an INCLUDE command or when the data are inline (see INCLUDE and BEGIN DATA—END DATA).
- The file specification must be enclosed in apostrophes.
- The file specification can be fully qualified, including directory, filename, and extension.
- The FILE subcommand can be specified before or after keyword FREE.
- The FILE subcommand and keyword FREE must be separated by at least one blank or comma.

Example   `DATA LIST FILE='MYFILE.DAT' FREE / XVAR YVAR.`

- The freefield-format data file is read from MYFILE.DAT in the current directory.
- Two numeric variables are defined.

Variable Names

- Variable names can contain up to eight characters.
- All variable names must begin with a letter. System variables (beginning with $) cannot be defined on DATA LIST.
- Each variable name corresponds to one value per case.
- You can name a list of variables using the TO convention. For more information on the TO convention and other variable-naming rules, see Universals: Variable-Naming Conventions.

Example   `DATA LIST FREE / ID VAR1 TO VAR7.`

- The DATA LIST command indicates inline data in freefield format.
- Eight variables are defined: ID, VAR1, VAR2, VAR3, VAR4, VAR5, VAR6, and VAR7.

Variable Formats

- In DATA LIST with keyword FREE, formats can be specified for string variables only.
- All numeric variables are automatically assigned print and write formats of F8.2. Use the FORMATS command to specify any other format for numeric variables.
- All numeric variable digits are read and stored by SPSS/PC+.
- Numeric values with decimal points in the data preserve the decimal point and decimal digits.
- String variables are indicated by an *A* in parentheses after the variable name.
- By default, all string variables are assigned formats of A8 (width of eight characters). You can change the format of a string variable by specifying *A* and a width enclosed in parentheses, such as (A20).
- A format specification applies only to the variable immediately preceding it.
- If the string value in the data is longer than the specified length, the string is truncated and a warning message is displayed. Thus, you must specify formats for long string variables.
- If the string in the data is shorter than the specified format, it is right-padded with blanks and no warning message is displayed. All subsequent transformations require value specifications with the declared format width, including all padded values.

Example
```
DATA LIST FREE FILE='\MASTER\APRIL.DAT'
     / ID SEX (A1) NAME (A15) AGE TENURE ETHNIC (A).
FORMATS AGE (F2.0) TENURE (F3.1).
```

- The DATA LIST command defines data in freefield format from file AP-RIL.DAT in directory \MASTER.

- Six variables, ID, SEX, NAME, AGE, TENURE, and ETHNIC, are defined.

- ID, AGE, and TENURE are numeric variables.

- SEX is defined as a one-column short string variable. NAME is defined as a long string variable up to 15 columns wide. ETHNIC is a short string variable with an assumed width of eight columns.

- The FORMATS command changes the print and write formats of numeric variables AGE and TENURE.

Entering Freefield Data

- Values are read sequentially in the order variables are named.

- A value cannot be split across records.

- One data value is separated from another by any number of blanks or by a single comma.

- You can use both commas and blanks to distinguish data values in a single data file.

- Any number of consecutive blanks (except blanks specified within a string value) are interpreted as one delimiter.

- When commas are used as delimiters, two consecutive commas or commas separated by a blank indicate a system-missing numeric value or a blank string value.

- A blank field for a variable that is not delimited by commas causes values from that point on to be assigned to the wrong variable.

- String values that contain embedded blanks or commas must be delimited by apostrophes or quotation marks. The delimiters are not read as part of the string value (see Universals: Strings).

- You can include an apostrophe in string values by delimiting the value with quotation marks. You can include quotation marks by delimiting the value with apostrophes.

- You cannot use commas or blanks within numeric values.

- If there are not enough values to complete the last case, a warning is issued and the incomplete case is dropped.

Example
```
DATA LIST FREE / AVAR BVAR STATE (A) MAYOR(A10).
BEGIN DATA.
7500000 20000000 'S DAKOTA' "O'LEARY" 22222000 55000000
'INDIANA' 'JONES' 120000000 56000000 'NEW YORK' 'ALDRIDGE'
-1.2 2222.223 'MAINE' 'BURNS'
END DATA.
FORMATS AVAR (COMMA15.2) BVAR(DOLLAR14.2).
DISPLAY VAR=ALL.
FREQ VAR=ALL.
LIST VAR=ALL.
```

- The DATA LIST command defines inline data in freefield format.

- AVAR and BVAR are defined as numeric variables. STATE is defined as a string variable with the default width of eight columns. MAYOR is declared as a long string variable with a width of 10 columns (A10).

- The BEGIN DATA command indicates the beginning of data lines.

- The first case has a value of 7500000 for AVAR. BVAR has the value 20000000. STATE has the value 'S DAKOTA' enclosed in apostrophes to preserve the embedded blank. The value "O'LEARY" is enclosed in quotation marks to preserve the embedded apostrophe. The format for MAYOR indicates a width of 10 columns, so O'LEARY is right-padded with three blanks.

- The second case is split across two records. With freefield format, you can split cases but not individual values across records.

- Decimal values are included for AVAR and BVAR for the fourth case.

- The END DATA command indicates the end of inline data.

- The FORMATS command changes the print and write formats of numeric variables AVAR and BVAR from the default format (eight characters with two decimal places) to the specified formats (see FORMATS).

- The DISPLAY command shows the current print and write formats of the variables.

- The FREQUENCIES procedure produces tables for each of the variables. Because FREQUENCIES uses the internal representation of values in tables, the DOLLAR and COMMA formats do not appear on these tables.

- The LIST procedure produces a listing of the values of each variable. The DOLLAR and COMMA formats are preserved in the listing.

Example

```
DATA LIST FREE / AVAR BVAR STATE (A) MAYOR(A10).
BEGIN DATA.
7500000,20000000,'S DAKOTA',"O'LEARY",22222000,,
'INDIANA','JONES',120000000,,,'ALDRIDGE'
-1.2 2222.223 'MAINE' 'BURNS'
END DATA.
```

- This example shows the use of both commas and blanks to separate values.

- The two commas at the end of the first record indicate missing information for BVAR for the second case.

- In the second line of data, the three commas after value 120000000 indicate missing values for BVAR and STATE for the third case. A blank between the commas would also indicate missing information.

- The blanks after ALDRIDGE indicate the end of the value. The last line of data uses blanks as delimiters.

DATA LIST: Matrix Materials

```
DATA LIST [FILE='filename'] MATRIX [{FIXED}]
                                    {FREE }

          /varlist
```

Example:
```
DATA LIST MATRIX FILE='REG.MAT'/
   SUICIDE ANOMIE AGE.
N 488.
REG VAR=AGE SUICIDE ANOMIE
  /READ CORR
  /DEP=SUICIDE
  /METHOD=ENTER.
```

Overview

The DATA LIST command with keyword MATRIX provides variable names and a dictionary for matrix materials used as input in CLUSTER, FACTOR, ONEWAY, REGRESSION, and MANOVA. (For information on CLUSTER, FACTOR, and REGRESSION, see *SPSS/PC+ Statistics.* For information on MANOVA, see *SPSS/PC+ Advanced Statistics.)* The matrix materials can include correlation coefficients, covariance coefficients, a matrix of *n*'s, or group distance measures. Matrix materials can be read in fixed or freefield format but must conform to the requirements of the individual procedures (see each procedure for details). The matrix input can be inline or read from an external file.

For information on reading individual casewise data, see DATA LIST: Fixed Format or DATA LIST: Freefield Format.

Syntax

• The minimum specification is DATA LIST with keyword MATRIX, followed by a slash and a list of variable names.

• The slash (/) between keyword MATRIX and the variable names is required.

• Variable names must be eight characters or less and must begin with a letter or the @ character.

• You must supply names for all variables that will be used by the next procedure. If you specify more names on DATA LIST MATRIX than are specified for the procedure, the extra names are ignored.

• The order in which variables are named determines their order in the new active file but has no relation to the contents of the matrix.

• Format types are meaningless for matrix materials and cannot be specified.

• The FILE subcommand is required when the matrix materials are contained in an external file. The file specification must be enclosed in apostrophes.

• The FILE subcommand can be specified before or after keyword MATRIX.

• The FILE subcommand and keyword MATRIX must be separated by at least one blank or comma.

• You can specify files in directories other than the current directory by using fully qualified file spe :ifications.

Operations

• DATA LIST with keyword MATRIX defines variable names to be used in processing a variety of matrix materials arranged for specific procedures. Reading and interpreting the matrix are actually performed by the next procedure.

• Each procedure that can process matrix materials interprets them according to its own specifications. Thus, the format of a matrix to be read by SPSS/PC+ depends upon the procedure that will use it.

• Each procedure that reads matrix materials can accept its own matrix output in either FIXED or FREE format. Matrices entered directly and matrices that will be processed by a procedure other than the one that created them should normally be read in FREE format.

C

Command Reference

• DATA LIST with keyword MATRIX cannot read individual casewise data.
• You cannot use DATA LIST MATRIX with procedures that expect casewise data.
• You cannot perform any SPSS/PC+ transformations on matrix materials.
• The BASIC convention of using two commas in a row to indicate missing data is *not* supported with DATA LIST MATRIX.

Limitations
• You cannot define more than 200 variables on the DATA LIST command.
• The maximum number of format "tokens," or syntactic elements, on the DATA LIST command is 600.

Example
```
DATA LIST MATRIX FILE='REG.MAT'/
   SUICIDE ANOMIE AGE.
N 488.
REG VAR=AGE SUICIDE ANOMIE
   /READ CORR
   /DEP=SUICIDE
   /METHOD=ENTER.
```

• DATA LIST reads matrix materials from file REG.MAT in the current directory. The matrix was written to this file by procedure CORRELATION in a previous SPSS/PC+ session.
• The matrix materials are read in fixed format (the default). CORRELATION writes matrices in the same format as does REGRESSION. This matrix could also be read in freefield format.
• The variable names SUICIDE, ANOMIE, and AGE are defined for use in the REGRESSION command.
• The N command indicates that the matrix input is based on 488 cases. REGRESSION uses this information in computing significance tests.
• The VARIABLES subcommand on REGRESSION identifies the variables in the correlation matrix and their order.
• The READ subcommand on REGRESSION indicates that a correlation matrix will be read by the REGRESSION procedure.
• This example takes advantage of spelling permitted by three-character truncation of keywords.

Example
```
DATA LIST FREE MATRIX / AGE SUICIDE ANOMIE.
BEGIN DATA.
1.0 .5555555 .3333333
.5555555 1.0 .4555555
.3333333 .4555555 1.0
488
END DATA.
REGRESSION VARIABLES=AGE SUICIDE ANOMIE
   /READ CORR N
   /DEPENDENT=SUICIDE
   /METHOD=ENTER.
```

• The DATA LIST command specifies matrix materials in freefield format.
• Because no file is specified on DATA LIST, the matrix data are assumed to be inline.
• The variable names AGE, SUICIDE, and ANOMIE are defined for use in the REGRESSION command.
• The matrix materials are entered between the BEGIN DATA and END DATA commands. Each row vector begins on a new line. A final line contains a single number indicating the number of cases.
• The READ subcommand on REGRESSION indicates that a correlation matrix followed by the *n* (number of cases) will be read.

Matrix Data   The SPSS/PC+ procedures CORRELATION, CLUSTER, ONEWAY, FACTOR, and REGRESSION write matrix materials in a fixed format that automatically conforms to the requirements of the various procedures that read matrix materials. Some materials, such as factor matrices written by FACTOR and matrices written by ONEWAY and MANOVA, are specially formatted for a specific procedure. If you enter your own matrix materials, they must conform to these formats as well as to the requirements below.

- Matrix materials can be arranged in fixed or freefield format.
- A matrix written by an SPSS/PC+ procedure can always be read in fixed format by the same procedure.
- A matrix written by an SPSS/PC+ procedure can always be read in freefield format by any procedure that accepts that type of matrix. Factor matrices from FACTOR, and matrix materials from ONEWAY and MANOVA, are not accepted by other procedures.
- Each cell of the matrix must contain a value.
- Each element in a row in freefield format matrix materials is separated by at least one space or a comma.
- Each row of a matrix begins on a new line.
- Each type of matrix material begins on a new line.
- In fixed format, there is a maximum number of elements that can be entered in a row (see discussion of individual procedures). The format must conform to the requirements of the procedure that reads the matrix.
- If the elements for a vector do not fit in one row, the elements can be continued on the next row. Each row must be filled before continuing to the next in fixed format.
- Individual matrix elements cannot be split across input lines.
- Decimal points in the data must be entered explicitly. You cannot specify implied decimal places.

Matrix Input for Procedure CLUSTER
- Procedure CLUSTER reads matrix materials in both fixed and freefield format.
- Fixed-format matrix materials for CLUSTER must be arranged so that each matrix cell is 16 columns wide with up to 5 decimal places. You can have only 5 elements of a vector in each row.
- Freefield format matrix materials, such as a correlation matrix written by procedure CORRELATION, must conform to the requirements listed above under Matrix Data.

Example
```
DATA LIST MATRIX FREE/
   ABDEFECT ABHLTH ABNOMORE ABPOOR ABRAPE ABSINGLE.
BEGIN DATA.
 1.0000000    .6118418    .3936668    .3743177    .6284106    .3820830
  .6118418   1.0000000    .2870408    .3098805    .6097969    .2935045
  .3936668    .2870408   1.0000000    .7658386    .3806726    .7881280
  .3743177    .3098805    .7658386   1.0000000    .3847740    .7379326
  .6284106    .6097969    .3806726    .3847740   1.0000000    .3909586
  .3820830    .2935045    .7881280    .7379326    .3909586   1.0000000
END DATA.
CLUSTER ABDEFECT ABHLTH ABNOMORE ABPOOR ABRAPE ABSINGLE
   /READ=SIMILAR.
```

- The DATA LIST command specifies inline matrix materials in freefield format. The active file dictionary contains six variable names.
- In this case, the matrix is a correlation matrix. Each row vector begins on a new line.
- The READ subcommand on CLUSTER indicates that a square matrix based on a measure of similarity will be read (see CLUSTER).

Example

```
DATA LIST MATRIX / CASE1 TO CASE19.
BEGIN DATA
        0.0        19062.00391    17697.00781    17545.00781    19038.00781
    19050.00781    17742.00781    17964.00781    19125.00391      111.99998
    19230.00391    18041.00781    17693.00781    19023.00781     9635.00781
     9860.00781     9899.00781     9901.00781    10028.00781
    19062.00391        0.0        18485.00000    17867.00000    17904.00000
    17890.00000    18484.00000    18508.00000       49.00000    18536.00391
      109.99998    18537.00000    18193.00000    18009.00000     9427.00000
     9228.00000     9657.00000     9885.00000     9726.00000
        :             :             :             :             :
        :             :             :             :             :
    10028.00781     9726.00000     9929.00000     9659.00000     9502.00000
     9435.99609     9589.99609     9737.99609     9537.00000     9730.00781
     9476.00000     9660.99609     9449.00000     9261.00000       87.00000
       46.00000       40.99998       52.99998        0.0
END DATA.
CLUSTER ALL
   /MISSING INCLUDE
   /READ.
```

- The DATA LIST command specifies inline matrix materials in fixed format (the default). The active file dictionary contains 19 variable names.

- The distance matrix to be read was produced using procedure CLUSTER with the MISSING=INCLUDE and WRITE=DISTANCE subcommands. Here cases, not variables, are going to be clustered.

- The data are automatically arranged in the format required by the CLUSTER. Each column vector is 16 characters wide with 5 decimal values. There are 4 rows for each vector. Only the first two and last vectors are shown.

- The READ subcommand on CLUSTER indicates that a distance matrix will be read (see CLUSTER).

Matrix Input for Procedure FACTOR

- Procedure FACTOR can use matrix materials in either fixed or freefield format.

- Fixed-format matrix materials for FACTOR must be arranged so that each column vector entry is 10 columns wide with up to 3 decimal places. You can enter up to 8 values in each row.

- Matrix materials in freefield format must conform to requirements noted above under Matrix Data.

Example

```
DATA LIST MATRIX / X1 X2 X3 X4 X5.
N 100.
BEGIN DATA.
1.000
0.945    1.000
0.840    0.720    1.000
0.735    0.630    0.560    1.000
0.630    0.540    0.480    0.420    1.000
END DATA.
FACTOR READ=CORRELATION TRIANGLE
   /VARIABLES=X1 TO X5
   /ANALYSIS=X1 TO X5
   /PRINT=ALL
   /CRI=FAC(1)
   /EXT=ULS.
```

- The DATA LIST command specifies inline matrix materials in fixed format (the default). The active file dictionary contains five variable names.

- The N command tells SPSS/PC+ that the matrix input is based on 100 cases.

- The matrix data conform to the fixed-format requirements of FACTOR. Each row vector starts on a new line and each column entry occupies 10 columns.

- The READ subcommand on FACTOR indicates that a lower-triangular correlation matrix will be read (see FACTOR: Matrix Materials).

- This example takes advantage of spelling permitted by three-character truncation of keywords.

Example
```
DATA LIST FREE MATRIX / X1 TO X5.
N 100.
BEGIN DATA.
1.000
0.945,1.000
0.840,0.720,1.000
0.735,0.630,0.560,1.000
0.630,0.540,0.480,0.420,1.000
END DATA.
FACTOR READ=CORRELATION TRIANGLE
   /VARIABLES=X1 TO X5
   /ANALYSIS=X1 TO X5
   /PRINT=ALL
   /CRI=FAC(1)
   /EXT=ULS.
```

- The DATA LIST command specifies inline matrix materials in freefield format. The active file dictionary contains five variable names (X1, X2, X3, X4, and X5).

- The correlation matrix is entered with each coefficient separated by a comma.

- The READ subcommand on FACTOR indicates that a lower-triangular correlation matrix will be read (see FACTOR: Matrix Materials).

Matrix Input for Procedure ONEWAY

- Procedure ONEWAY reads matrix materials in either fixed or freefield format.

- If you use matrix materials in fixed format, you must specify Option 7 on the ONEWAY command.

- Each matrix cell entry has a width of 10 columns with up to 4 decimal places. You can enter up to 8 cells in each row.

Example
```
DATA LIST MATRIX / SCORE METHOD.
BEGIN DATA.
7          7          7
   4.4286     7.5714     6.7143
   1.2724     1.3973      .9512
END DATA.
ONEWAY SCORE BY METHOD(1,3)
   /OPTION 7.
```

- The DATA LIST command specifies inline matrix materials in the default fixed format. The active file dictionary contains two variable names, SCORE and METHOD.

- The data are arranged with each vector element occupying 10 columns. The vector of counts does not require decimal places.

- Option 7 on ONEWAY indicates that a matrix with a vector of counts, a vector of means, and a vector of standard deviations will be read (see ONEWAY).

Example
```
DATA LIST FREE MATRIX / YVAR XVAR.
BEGIN DATA.
65 95 181 82 40 37
2.6462 2.7737 4.1796 4.5610 4.6625 5.2297
6.2699
494
END DATA.
ONEWAY VARIABLES=YVAR BY XVAR(1,6)
   /OPTIONS=8.
```

- The DATA LIST command specifies inline matrix materials in freefield format. Two variable names, YVAR and XVAR, are in the active file dictionary.

- The data are arranged to conform to the requirements of Option 8 in ONEWAY, with one row of counts, a row of means, an entry for the pooled variance estimate, and an entry for the degrees of freedom.

- Option 8 on the ONEWAY command indicates that matrix materials arranged as a vector of counts, a vector of means, the pooled variance estimate (a single entry), and the degrees of freedom (a single entry) will be read (see ONEWAY).

C

Command Reference

Matrix Input for Procedure REGRESSION

- Procedure REGRESSION reads matrix materials in either fixed or freefield format.
- Materials arranged in fixed format must have 10 columns for each vector entry with up to 7 decimal places. You can enter up to 8 entries per line for each vector.
- Materials arranged in freefield format must conform to the requirements described above under Matrix Data.

Example

```
DATA LIST MATRIX / AGE SUICIDE ANOMIE.
BEGIN DATA.
1.0        0.555555   0.333333
0.555555   1.0        0.455555
0.333333   0.455555   1.0
488
END DATA.
REGRESSION VARIABLES=AGE SUICIDE ANOMIE
  /READ CORR N
  /DEPENDENT=SUICIDE
  /METHOD=ENTER.
```

- The DATA LIST command defines inline matrix materials in fixed format (the default). Three variable names are defined for the active file dictionary.
- The data are arranged to conform to the requirements of the REGRESSION procedure. Each row vector has 3 entries, each with a width of 10 columns. The last entry is the number of cases.
- The READ subcommand on REGRESSION reads the matrix of correlation coefficients and a value for the number of cases (see REGRESSION: Matrix Materials).

Example

```
DATA LIST MATRIX FREE / X1 X2 X3 X4 X5 Y.
BEGIN DATA.
35.0825 2.7315 40.9060 3.1405 25.0690 6.2550
5.8171 .4541 25.8985 9.6254 1.3138 .6543
33.8381250 .5079382 113.502300 51.9130250 2.5499079 2.7898921
.5079382 .2062029 2.1302800 1.0036676 .2998858 .0584658
113.502300 2.1302800 670.734846 206.202997 1.7372853 15.7105368
51.9130250 1.0036676 206.202997 92.6479839 2.3183584 5.1585079
2.5499079 .2998858 1.7372853 2.3183584 1.7260832 .1064316
2.7898921 .0584658 15.7105368 5.1585079 .1064316 .4281316
20
END DATA.
VAR LABELS X1 'STAFF SALARIES PER PUPIL'
           X2 '6TH GRADE PER CENT WHITE-COLLAR FATHERS'
           X3 'SES COMPOSITE'
           X4 'MEAN TEACHER VERBAL TEST SCORE'
           X5 '6TH GRADE MEAN MOTHER EDUCATION'
           Y  'VERBAL MEAN TEST SCORE, ALL 6TH GRADERS'.
REGRESSION READ=COV MEAN STDDEV N
  /DES DEF
  /VAR=Y,X1 TO X5
  /CRI TOL(.0001)
  /STATS ALL
  /DEP Y
  /ENT.
```

- The DATA LIST command specifies inline matrix materials in freefield format. Six variable names are specified for the active file dictionary.
- The data are arranged to conform to the requirements of the REGRESSION procedure. The first six rows form a covariance matrix, with each row starting on a new line. The seventh row forms a vector of means for each variable named. The eighth row is a vector of standard deviations. The last entry is the number of cases.
- The READ subcommand on REGRESSION indicates that matrix materials with a covariance matrix, a vector of means, a vector of standard deviations, and an entry for the number of cases will be read (see REGRESSION: Matrix Materials).

**Matrix Input for
Procedure MANOVA**

- Procedure MANOVA reads matrix materials in either fixed or freefield format.
- For complete information on the contents and format of matrix materials used by MANOVA, refer to WRITE Subcommand under MANOVA: Univariate in *SPSS/PC+ Advanced Statistics.*
- Because of the special requirements of MANOVA, this procedure cannot use matrix materials written by another procedure, nor can another procedure use the matrix materials written by MANOVA.

Example

```
DATA LIST MATRIX / Y1 Y2 Y3 EDUC SEX.
BEGIN DATA.
          6           54           2            3
        1           1
    2.09000000E+00    4.53000000E+00   3.56000000E+00
        1           2
    1.38000000E+00    4.17000000E+00   3.38000000E+00
        2           1
    2.12000000E+00    5.35000000E+00   3.59000000E+00
        2           2
    1.47000000E+00    4.89000000E+00   3.12000000E+00
        3           1
    2.13000000E+00    5.94000000E+00   3.51000000E+00
        3           2
    1.74000000E+00    5.37000000E+00   3.27000000E+00
          8           10          11          8      9      8
     1.00000
      .25689     1.00000
     -.07085      .13390     1.00000
    3.80000000E-01   6.30000000E-01   3.90000000E-01
END DATA.
MANOVA Y1 Y2 Y3 BY EDUC(1,3) SEX(1,2)
    /READ
    /ANALYSIS Y1 Y2 WITH Y3
    /DISCRIM
    /PRINT=ERROR(SSCP COR)
    /DESIGN.
```

- The DATA LIST command specifies inline matrix materials in fixed format (the default). The active file contains five variables (data from Tatsuoka, 1971).
- The matrix materials were produced by a WRITE subcommand in MANOVA, using the same variables specification as that used here to read the materials.
- The READ subcommand indicates that matrix materials should be read from the location specified or implied on the DATA LIST MATRIX command (inline, in this example).
- The ANALYSIS subcommand allows you to drop continuous variables that are in the matrix materials from the analysis or, as in this example, redefine them as covariates or dependent variables.
- The DISCRIM subcommand requests discriminant analysis, and the PRINT subcommand requests that two error matrices be displayed.

References   Tatsuoka, M. M. 1971. *Multivariate analysis.* New York: John Wiley & Sons.

C

Command Reference

DESCRIPTIVES

```
DESCRIPTIVES [VARIABLES=] {varlist}
                         {ALL    }

             [/OPTIONS=option numbers]

             [/STATISTICS={statistic numbers}]
                         {ALL             }
```

Options:

1 Include user-missing values	6 Serial format
2 Suppress variable labels	7 Narrow format
3 Save Z scores on active file	8 Suppress variable names
5 Exclude missing values listwise	

Statistics:

1	Mean	9 Range
2	Standard error of mean	10 Minimum
5	Standard deviation	11 Maximum
6	Variance	12 Sum
7	Kurtosis	13 Mean, standard deviation,
8	Skewness	minimum, and maximum

Example:

```
DESCRIPTIVES VARIABLES=YVAR ZVAR, AVAR1 TO AVAR5,
                       BETATEST, IOTATEST
  /STATISTICS=6 13
  /OPTIONS=5.
```

Overview

Procedure DESCRIPTIVES computes univariate statistics, including the mean, standard deviation, minimum, and maximum, for numeric variables. Because it does not sort values into a frequency table, DESCRIPTIVES is an efficient means of computing descriptive statistics for continuous variables. Other procedures that display descriptive statistics include FREQUENCIES and MEANS.

Defaults

The default table displays the variable name, variable label, mean, standard deviation, minimum, maximum, and number of cases with valid values on a single line for each variable. All cases with valid values for a variable are included in the calculation of statistics for that variable. The display uses the width set on the SET command.

Tailoring

Display Format. You can display statistics in serial format and restrict the width to narrow format regardless of the width defined on SET. DESCRIPTIVES also offers control over the display of variable labels and variable names.

Statistical Display. Optional statistics include the standard error of the mean, variance, kurtosis, skewness, range, and sum. DESCRIPTIVES does not compute the median or mode (see FREQUENCIES).

Z Scores. You can compute Z scores (standardized deviation scores from the mean) and add these to the active file as new variables.

Missing Values. You can include cases with user-missing values in the calculation of statistics. Optionally, you can exclude cases with missing values listwise.

Syntax

• The minimum specification is the VARIABLES subcommand with a list of variables. The actual keyword VARIABLES may be omitted.

• Subcommands are separated by slashes.

Operations

• DESCRIPTIVES causes the data to be read.

• If the STATISTICS subcommand is used, only those statistics explicitly requested are displayed.

• If a string variable is specified on the variable list, a warning is issued and no statistics are displayed for that variable.

• The available width and the statistics and options requested determine whether the statistics are displayed in tabular or serial form.

- If there is insufficient width to display the statistics requested, DESCRIPTIVES first truncates the variable label and then adopts serial format.
- If there is insufficient memory available to calculate statistics for all variables requested, DESCRIPTIVES truncates the variable list.
- Statistics that will fit within the allotted columns are displayed with two decimal places.

Limitations
- There is no fixed limit on the number of variables named or implied on DESCRIPTIVES.
- Maximum 1 each of the VARIABLES, OPTIONS, and STATISTICS subcommands.

Example
```
DESCRIPTIVES VARIABLES=YVAR ZVAR, AVAR1 TO AVAR5,
                       BETATEST, IOTATEST
     /STATISTICS=6 13
     /OPTIONS=5.
```

- This example requests statistics for all the variables named or implied by the TO keyword.
- The STATISTICS subcommand requests the variance (Statistic 6) and the defaults: mean, standard deviation, minimum, and maximum (Statistic 13).
- Option 5 specifies that cases with missing values for any variable on the variable list will be omitted from the calculation of statistics for all variables.

Example
```
DESCRIPTIVES VAR=RAGE RINC81.
```

- Because no STATISTICS subcommand is included, only the mean, standard deviation, minimum, and maximum for RAGE and RINC81 will be displayed.
- This example takes advantage of spelling permitted by three-character truncation of keywords.

VARIABLES Subcommand

The VARIABLES subcommand names the variables to be included in the table. The actual keyword VARIABLES may be omitted.

- You can use keyword ALL to refer to all user-defined variables on the active file.
- Variables named more than once appear in the display more than once.

Z Scores

The *Z*-score transformation standardizes variables to the same scale, producing new variables with a mean of 0 and a standard deviation 1. These variables are added to the active file. There are two methods for requesting *Z* scores. One is to use Option 3:

Option 3   *Add* Z *scores to the active file for all variables on the DESCRIPTIVES command.* SPSS/PC+ forms variable names for the new variables, using wherever possible the letter *Z* and the first seven characters of the old variable name.

Alternatively, you can obtain *Z* scores for any variable by specifying a new variable name in parentheses after the variable on the variable list.

- You must specify new names individually; a *list* in parentheses is not recognized.
- SPSS/PC+ creates variable labels for the new *Z*-score variables created with either method.
- Whenever *Z* scores are added to the file, a table is displayed showing the names of the new variables and of the original variables from which they were created.
- If you specify Option 3 and also enter variable names in parentheses for some variables, *Z* scores are calculated for all variables, using your names where you have supplied them and forming new names where you have not.
- If the new variables cause you to exceed the 200-variable limit, SPSS/PC+ displays an error message and does not process the DESCRIPTIVES command.

Example
```
DESCRIPTIVES VAR1 VAR2 SCORE (STDSCORE) INCOME
  /OPTIONS 3.
```

- *Z* scores are produced for four variables: VAR1, VAR2, SCORE, and INCOME.
- Since a name is specified only for one of the four variables, the other three are assigned names by the program.
- The variables ZVAR1, ZVAR2, STDSCORE, and ZINCOME are added to the end of the active file.

Display Format

By default, DESCRIPTIVES displays the statistics and a 40-character variable label for each variable on one line. If the statistics requested do not fit within the available width, DESCRIPTIVES first truncates the variable label and then uses serial format. Serial format provides larger field widths and permits more decimal places for very large or very small numbers than does the default format.

Optionally, you can request the following on the OPTIONS subcommand:

Option 2 *Suppress variable labels.*

Option 6 *Serial format.* The requested statistics are displayed below each variable name. This option is forced if the number of statistics requested does not fit within the available width.

Option 7 *Narrow format.* The display width is restricted to 79 columns regardless of the width defined on SET.

Option 8 *Suppress variable names.* The variable name will be displayed only if there is no variable label.

Statistical Display

DESCRIPTIVES automatically calculates the mean, standard deviation, minimum, and maximum for all variables in the variable list. The valid count on which statistics are based is always displayed. You can obtain additional statistics by specifying the following on the STATISTICS subcommand. If the STATISTICS subcommand is included, only statistics specifically requested are displayed.

Statistic 1 *Mean.*

Statistic 2 *Standard error of mean.*

Statistic 5 *Standard deviation.*

Statistic 6 *Variance.*

Statistic 7 *Kurtosis.* The standard error of the kurtosis is also displayed.

Statistic 8 *Skewness.* The standard error of the skewness is also displayed.

Statistic 9 *Range.*

Statistic 10 *Minimum.*

Statistic 11 *Maximum.*

Statistic 12 *Sum.*

Statistic 13 *Mean, standard deviation, minimum, and maximum.* This is the same as the default.

ALL *Display all statistics.*

Missing Values

By default, all cases with valid values for a variable are included in the calculation of statistics for that variable. You can alter the handling of cases with missing values by specifying the following on the OPTIONS subcommand:

Option 1 *Include cases with user-missing values.* Cases that have user-missing values will be included in the calculation of statistics for all variables named on the command.

Option 5 *Exclude cases with missing values listwise.* Cases missing on any variable named on the DESCRIPTIVES command are excluded from the calculation of statistics for all variables. The space reserved to display the valid counts for each variable is suppressed and the valid count is reported for the table as a whole.

DISPLAY

```
DISPLAY [{varlist}]
        {ALL    }
```

Example:

```
DISPLAY AVAR TO FVAR.
```

Overview

The DISPLAY command exhibits information about variables in the active file.

Syntax

- The minimum specification is simply the command keyword.
- When you specify a variable list, variable names can be separated by a comma or a space.

Operations

- DISPLAY information is directed to output destinations. This includes, by default, the screen and the listing file SPSS.LIS. You can also have it sent to the printer or to an alternate listing file (see SET).
- DISPLAY with no specifications provides a list of all variables in the active file and their variable labels.

Example

```
GET 'WEATHER.SYS'.
DISPLAY.
```

- DISPLAY displays a list of variables and variable labels defined in the system file WEATHER.SYS.

Variables Specification

You can request more detailed information on some or all of the variables in the active file by specifying either variable names or the keyword ALL.

- When a variables specification is entered, additional information is provided, including the variable name and label, value labels, missing-value flags, and variable type and width.
- You can specify keyword ALL to obtain detailed information on all variables in the active file.

Example

```
DISPLAY ALL.
```

- DISPLAY exhibits detailed information on all variables in the active file.

EXAMINE

```
EXAMINE VARIABLES=varlist [[BY varlist] [varname BY varname]]

    [/COMPARE={GROUP** }]
             {VARIABLE}

    [/SCALE={PLOTWISE**}]
           {UNIFORM   }

    [/ID={$CASENUM**}]
         {varname   }

    [/FREQUENCIES [FROM(initialvalue)] [BY(increment)]]

    [/PERCENTILES=[[{HAVERAGE  }] [NONE]]
                    {WAVERAGE  }
                    {ROUND     }
                    {AEMPIRICAL}
                    {EMPIRICAL }

    [/PLOT=[STEMLEAF**] [BOXPLOT**] [NPPLOT]]
           [SPREADLEVEL(value)] [HISTOGRAM]
           [{ALL }]
            {NONE}

    [/STATISTICS=[DESCRIPTIVES**] [EXTREME({5})]]
                                          {n}
                 [{ALL }]
                  {NONE}

    [/MESTIMATOR=[{NONE**}]]
                  {ALL   }

                 [HUBER({1.339})] [ANDREW({1.34!Pi}]
                        {c    }           {c      }

                 [HAMPEL({1.7,3.4,8.5})]
                         {a  ,b  ,c   }

                 [TUKEY({4.685})]
                        {c    }

    [/MISSING={LISTWISE**} [INCLUDE]]
             {REPORT   }
             {PAIRWISE }
```

**Default if subcommand is omitted.

Examples:

```
EXAMINE VARIABLES=ENGSIZE,COST.
```

```
EXAMINE VARIABLES=MIPERGAL BY MODEL,MODEL BY CYLINDERS.
```

Overview

EXAMINE provides stem-and-leaf plots, boxplots, robust estimates of location, tests of normality, and other descriptive statistics and plots. Separate analyses can be obtained for subgroups of cases.

Options.

Cells. Cases can be subdivided into cells based on their values for grouping (factor) variables.

Output. The display output is controlled by the COMPARE subcommand and the scale of plots by the SCALE subcommand. The FREQUENCY subcommand produces frequency tables and controls their output format. The computational method and breaking points for percentiles are specified with the PERCENTILES subcommand. ID assigns a variable to be used for labeling.

Plots. The PLOTS subcommand controls the output of plots. Available are stem-and-leaf plots, histograms, vertical boxplots, spread-versus-level plots with Levene statistic, and normal and detrended probability plots with accompanying statistics.

Statistics. Univariate statistical output and the output of M-estimators are controlled respectively by the STATISTICS and MESTIMATORS subcommands.

Basic Specification
- The basic specification is EXAMINE followed by VARIABLES= and at least one variable name from the active file.
- The default output includes univariate statistics (mean, median, standard deviation, standard error, variance, kurtosis, kurtosis standard error, skewness, skewness standard error, sum, interquartile range (IQR), range, minimum, maximum, and 5% trimmed mean), a vertical boxplot, and a stem-and-leaf plot.
- Outliers are labeled on the boxplot with the system variable $CASENUM.

Subcommand Order
- Subcommands can be named in any order.

Syntax Rules
- Only the VARIABLES subcommand is required.

Operations
- EXAMINE causes the data to be read.

Limitations
- String variables can be used as factors, but only the first eight characters are used to form cells. String variables are not allowed as dependent variables.

Caution
- Large amounts of output can be produced if many cells are specified. Many factors or factors with many values will result in a large number of separate analyses.

Example

```
EXAMINE VARIABLES=ENGSIZE,COST.
```

- ENGSIZE and COST are the dependent variables.
- EXAMINE produces univariate statistics, a vertical boxplot, and a stem-and-leaf plot for each dependent variable.

Example

```
EXAMINE VARIABLES=MIPERGAL BY MODEL,MODEL BY CYLINDERS.
```

- MIPERGAL is the dependent variable. The cell specification follows the first BY keyword. Cases will first be subdivided based on values of MODEL and then on the combination of values for MODEL and CYLINDERS. The keyword BY between factors indicates that all possible combinations are to be considered.
- EXAMINE produces univariate statistics, a vertical boxplot, and a stem-and-leaf plot for MIPERGAL for each cell defined by MODEL.
- EXAMINE generates univariate statistics, a vertical boxplot, and a stem-and-leaf plot for MIPERGAL for each combination of values for MODEL and CYLINDERS.
- Assuming that there are three values for MODEL and two values for CYLINDERS, this example produces separate output for all cases considered together, for the three cells defined by MODEL, and for the six cells defined by MODEL and CYLINDERS together.

VARIABLES Subcommand

VARIABLES specifies the dependent variables and the cells. A list of the dependent variables follows VARIABLES. The list of cells follows the first keyword BY.

- Only one VARIABLES subcommand is allowed.
- Cells formed by the combination of values of several factors are indicated with the keyword BY separating the factor names.
- Each value of a factor or combination of factors produces at least one separate page of output.

Example

```
EXAMINE VARIABLES=SALARY,YRSEDUC BY RACE,SEX,DEPT,RACE BY SEX.
```

- SALARY and YRSEDUC are dependent variables.
- The cells are formed first for the values of RACE, SEX, and DEPT individually and then by the combination of values for RACE and SEX.

• Univariate statistics, a boxplot, and a stem-and-leaf plot are generated for the sample as a whole and for each cell specified. That is, default output is produced for each separate value of RACE, SEX, and DEPT. In addition, default output is produced for each combination of values for RACE and SEX. If RACE and SEX each have two possible values and DEPT has three possible values, seven sets of output are produced for the variables individually and four sets of output for the combinations of values for RACE and SEX. Output for all cases together is also produced.

COMPARE Subcommand

COMPARE controls how boxplots are displayed. The default is GROUPS.

• COMPARE=VARIABLES and COMPARE=GROUPS are most useful if there is more than one dependent variable and if there is at least one factor in the design.

GROUPS   *Boxplots for all cells in same display.* Boxplots for all groups are displayed together, for each dependent variable. Comparisons across cells for a single dependent variable are easily made. This is the default.

VARIABLES   *Boxplots for all dependent variables in same display.* For each cell, boxplots for all dependent variables are displayed together. Comparisons of distributions of several dependent variables are easily made. This is useful in situations where the dependent variables are repeated measures of the same variable (see the following example) or when the dependent variable has very different values for different cells and plotting all cells on the same scale would cause information to be lost.

Example

```
EXAMINE VARIABLES=GPA1 GPA2 GPA3 GPA4 BY MAJOR
  /COMPARE=VARIABLE.
```

• The four GPA variables are summarized for each value of MAJOR.

• COMPARE=VARIABLES specifies that output for the four GPA variables be grouped together for each value of MAJOR. Thus, separate plots containing four GPA values are obtained for each of the majors.

Example

```
EXAMINE VARIABLES=GPA1 GPA2 GPA3 GPA4 BY MAJOR
  /COMPARE=GROUPS.
```

• COMPARE=GROUPS specifies that the boxplots for GPA1 be shown for all majors in the same display, then the values of GPA2 for all majors, and so on.

SCALE Subcommand

SCALE controls whether boxplots, stem-and-leaf plots, and histograms are constructed on the same scale for each cell in the analysis.

PLOTWISE   *Construct scales according to the values in each plot.* Boxplots for each cell are constructed on the basis of the values of the dependent variable for cases in that plot only. This is the default.

UNIFORM   *Display plots in a common scale.* Scales for boxplots and histograms are the same for each cell in the model. The common scale is constructed on the basis of dependent variable values of all cases.

• EXAMINE does not produce boxplots in a uniform scale for separate dependent variables unless they are plotted in the same plot using COMPARE= VARIABLE.

```
EXAMINE VARIABLES=SALARY BY SEX
  /SCALE=UNIFORM.
```

• The stem-and-leaf plots for SALARY are plotted on the same scale for both values of SEX.

```
EXAMINE VARIABLES=SALARY BONUS BY SEX
  /COMPARE=VARIABLES
  /SCALE=UNIFORM.
```

• SALARY and BONUS are plotted on the same boxplot for each value of SEX. The scale is the same for each boxplot.

ID Subcommand

ID assigns a variable from the active file to identify the cases in the analysis. By default the system variable $CASENUM is used for labeling boxplots and extreme-case listings.

• The first eight characters of the identifier are displayed adjacent to outliers or in a footnote for boxplots and for extreme cases if STATISTICS=EXTREME is requested.

• Only one label variable can be specified.

Example
```
EXAMINE VARIABLES=SALARY BY RACE BY SEX
   /ID=LASTNAME.
```

• ID displays the first eight characters of the value of LASTNAME for outliers in the boxplots and extreme-case listings.

FREQUENCIES Subcommand

The FREQUENCIES subcommand generates frequency tables. Frequency tables for values between the FROM cutoff value and the maximum value for the dependent variable are generated. By default, the FROM cutoff value is the minimum. If no BY value is specified for the size of increments, EXAMINE selects an increment size.

• Only one FREQUENCIES subcommand is permitted.

• Each bin is identified by its center.

FROM(value) *The lowest value for the frequency table.* The default is the minimum. All cases with values smaller than the FROM cutoff value are included in a separate bin.

BY (increment) *Specifies the increment for frequency display.* The default increment is the same as that used for the stems in the stem-and-leaf plot. If the increment is 0, a freqency table for each distinct value is produced.

Example
```
EXAMINE VARIABLES=DEGREES
   /FREQUENCIES FROM (90) BY (10).
```

• FREQUENCIES produces a frequency table for the dependent variable DEGREES.

• The FROM cutoff value for the frequency table is 90.

• Since BY specifies increments of 10, the first frequency bin contains all cases with values of 90 or greater, and less than 100. The next frequency increment contains all cases having a temperature of 100 or more, but less than 110.

• Frequencies continue in increments of 10 until the maximum value for DEGREES is included in a bin.

PERCENTILES Subcommand

PERCENTILES controls method and breaking points for percentile computations. If PERCENTILES is omitted, no percentiles are produced. If PERCENTILES appears without a keyword, the default method is HAVERAGE and the default breaking points are 5, 10, 25, 50, 75, 90, and 95.

• Values for breaking points are specified in parentheses following the subcommand.

• Keywords for computational method or suppressing PERCENTILE output follow the specifications for breaking point values.

In the following formulas, cases are assumed to be ranked in ascending order; W is the sum of the weights for all non-missing cases, p is the specified percentile divided by 100, i is the rank of each case, and X_i is the value of the ith case.

HAVERAGE	*Weighted average at* $X_{(W+1)p}$. The percentile value is the weighted average of X_i and X_{i+1} using the formula $(1-f)X_i + fX_{i+1}$ where $(W+1)p$ is decomposed into an integer part i and fractional part f. This is the default if PERCENTILES is specified without a keyword.
WAVERAGE	*Weighted average at* X_{Wp}. The percentile value is the weighted average of X_i and X_{i+1} using the formula $(1-f)X_i + fX_{i+1}$ where i is the integer part of Wp.
ROUND	*Observation closest to Wp.* The percentile value is X_i where i is integer part of $(Wp + 0.5)$.
EMPIRICAL	*Empirical distribution function.* The percentile value is X_i when the fractional part of Wp is equal to 0. The percentile value is X_{i+1} when the fractional part of Wp is greater than 0.
AEMPIRICAL	*Empirical distribution with averaging.* The percentile value is $(X_i + X_{i+1})/2$ when the fractional part of Wp equals 0. The percentile value is X_{i+1} when the fractional part of Wp is greater than 0.
NONE	*Suppresses the output of percentiles.* This is the default if PERCENTILES is omitted.

Example

```
EXAMINE VARIABLES=SALARY
   /PERCENTILES(10,50,90)=EMPIRICAL.
```

• PERCENTILES produces percentiles using the EMPIRICAL distribution for tenth, fiftieth, and ninetieth percentiles of the distribution of the dependent variable SALARY.

PLOT Subcommand

PLOT controls the output of plots. The default is a vertical boxplot and a stem-and-leaf plot for each dependent variable for each cell in the model.

BOXPLOT	*Vertical boxplot.* The boundaries of the box are Tukey's hinges. The median is identified by an asterisk. The length of the box is the interquartile range (IQR) computed from Tukey's hinges. Values more than three IQR's from the end of a box are labeled as extreme (**E**). Values more than 1.5 IQR's from the end of the box, but less than three IQR's are labeled as outliers (**O**).
STEMLEAF	*Stem-and-leaf plot.* Plot in which each observed value is divided into two components—leading digits (stem) and trailing digits (leaf).
HISTOGRAM	*Histogram.*
SPREADLEVEL(p)	*Spread-versus-level plot.* If the keyword appears alone, a plot is produced of the natural logs of the interquartile ranges against the natural logs of the medians for all cells. If the power for transforming the data(p) is given, the IQR and median of the transformed data are plotted. If p=0 is specified, a natural log transformation of the data is done. The slope of the regression line and Levene's test for homogeneity of variance are also displayed. Levene's test is based on the original data if no transformation is specified and on the transformed data if a transformation is requested.
NPPLOT	*Normal probability and detrended probability plots.* Shapiro-Wilks statistic and a Kolmogorov-Smirnov statistic with a Lilliefors significance level for testing normality are calculated. The Shapiro-Wilks statistic is not calculated when the sample size exceeds 50.
ALL	*All available plots.*
NONE	*Display no plots.*

Example

```
EXAMINE VARIABLES=CYCLE BY TREATMNT
   /PLOT=NPPLOT.
```

• PLOT produces normal probability plots and detrended probability plots for each value of TREATMNT.

```
EXAMINE VARIABLES=CYCLE BY TREATMNT
  /PLOT=SPREADLEVEL(.5).
```

• PLOT produces a spread-versus-level plot for medians and interquartile ranges of the square root of CYCLE. Each point on the plot represents one of the TREATMNT groups.

Example
```
EXAMINE VARIABLES=CYCLE BY TREATMNT
  /PLOT=SPREADLEVEL(0).
```

• PLOT generates a spread-versus-level plot for the medians and interquartile ranges of the natural-log-transformed values of CYCLE.

Example
```
EXAMINE VARIABLES=CYCLE BY TREATMNT
  /PLOT=SPREADLEVEL.
```

• PLOT generates a spread-versus-level plot for the logs of medians and the logs of the interquartile ranges of CYCLE for each TREATMNT group.

STATISTICS Subcommand

STATISTICS controls the output of univariate statistics.

DESCRIPTIVE *Univariate statistics only.* This includes the mean, median, mode, 5% trimmed mean, standard error, variance, standard deviation, minimum, maximum, range, interquartile range, skewness, skewness standard error, kurtosis, and kurtosis standard error. This is the default.

EXTREME(n) *The n largest and n smallest values.* If n is omitted, the five largest and five smallest values are displayed. Extreme values are labeled with their values on the label variable if the ID subcommand is used or with their values on the system variable $CASENUM if it is not.

ALL *Univariate statistics and top five and bottom five extreme values.*

NONE *Display neither univariate statistics nor extreme values.*

Example
```
EXAMINE VARIABLES=FAILTIME
  /ID=BRAND
  /STATISTICS=EXTREME(10)
  /PLOT=NONE.
```

• STATISTICS identifies the 10 cases with lowest values on FAILTIME and the 10 cases with highest values on FAILTIME. The output includes 20 cases labeled by the first 8 characters of their values for the variable BRAND.

MESTIMATORS Subcommand

The M-estimators are robust maximum-likelihood estimators of location. Four M-estimators are available. They differ in the weights they apply to the cases. The subcommand with no keywords produces Huber's M-estimator with c=1.339; Andrew's wave with c=1.34π; Hampel's M-estimator with a=1.7, b=3.4, c=8.5; and Tukey's biweight with c=4.685.

HUBER(c) *Huber's M-estimator.* Default with c=1.339. The value of the weighting constant c can be set by placing the desired value in parentheses following the keyword.

ANDREW(c) *Andrew's wave estimator.* Default is 1.34π. The value of the weighting constant c can be set by placing the desired value in parentheses following the keyword. Constants are multiplied by Π.

HAMPEL(a,b,c) *Hampel's M-estimator.* Default with a=1.7, b=3.4, and c=8.5. The values of the weighting constants a, b, and c can be set by placing the desired values in the appropriate order in parentheses following the keyword.

TUKEY(c) *Tukey's biweight estimator.* Default with c=4.685. The value of the weighting constant c can be set by placing the desired value in parentheses following the keyword.

ALL	*Output all four above M-estimators.* This is the default when MESTIMATORS is specified with no keyword.
NONE	*Suppress output of M-estimators.* This is the default if MESTIMATORS is omitted.

Example

```
EXAMINE VARIABLES=CASTTEST
    /MESTIMATORS.
```

• MESTIMATORS generates all four M-estimators computed with the default constants.

Example

```
EXAMINE VARIABLES=CASTTEST
    /MESTIMATORS=HAMPELS(2,4,8).
```

• MESTIMATOR produces Hampel's M-estimator. It is computed with the specified weighting constants a=2, b=4, and c=8.

MISSING Subcommand

MISSING controls the processing of missing values in the analysis. The default is LISTWISE. The keywords LISTWISE, PAIRWISE, and REPORT are mutually exclusive. Either of these three can be used with INCLUDE.

LISTWISE	*Listwise deletion of missing cases.* A case with user-missing or system-missing values on any dependent variable or any factor in the model specification is excluded from the computation of statistics or displaying of plots. This is the default.
REPORT	*Report missing values.* User-missing values and system-missing values for dependent variables are reported in frequency output and excluded from statistical computations and graphs. For factor variables, user-missing values and system-missing values are treated as valid factor categories with separate and complete statistical and graphic output labeled as missing.
PAIRWISE	*Pairwise deletion of missing cases.* A case is deleted from the analysis only if it has a user-missing or system-missing value for the dependent variable or factor being analyzed.
INCLUDE	*Include user-missing values.* Only system-missing values are excluded from the analysis.

Example

```
EXAMINE VARIABLES=RAINFALL MEANTEMP BY REGION.
```

• The absence of the MISSING subcommand produces the default listwise deletion of user-missing and system-missing values. Any case with a user-missing or system-missing value on RAINFALL, MEANTEMP, *or* REGION is excluded from the analysis.

Example

```
EXAMINE VARIABLES=RAINFALL MEANTEMP BY REGION
    /MISSING=PAIRWISE.
```

• MISSING=PAIRWISE requests that only cases with missing values for RAINFALL or REGION be excluded from the analysis of RAINFALL, and only cases with missing values for MEANTEMP or REGION be excluded from the analysis of REGION.

References

Frigge, M., D. C. Hoaglin, and B. Iglewicz. 1987. Some implementations of the boxplot. In *Computer science and statistics proceedings of the 19th symposium on the interface,* ed. R. M. Heiberger and M. Martin. Alexandria, Va: American Statistical Association.

Hoaglin, D. C., F. Mosteller, and J. W. Tukey. 1985. *Exploring data tables, trends, and shapes.* New York: John Wiley & Sons.

———. 1983. *Understanding robust and exploratory data analysis.* New York: John Wiley & Sons.

Tukey, J. W. 1977. *Exploratory data analysis.* Reading, Mass.: Addison-Wesley.

Velleman, P. F., and D. C. Hoaglin. 1981. *Applications, basics, and computing of exploratory data analysis.* Boston: Duxbury Press.

EXECUTE

```
EXECUTE {path\filename{.ext}} ['parameters']
        {               {.EXE}}
        {DOS                  }
```

Example:

```
EXECUTE '\SPSS\KERMIT.EXE'.
```

Overview
The EXECUTE command allows you to run other programs or execute DOS commands from within SPSS/PC+ and then return to your session at the point you left it. This is not intended to make SPSS/PC+ a regular operating environment: part of the system remains in memory, which limits the memory available for other programs. Rather, EXECUTE lets you run other programs briefly or execute DOS commands without having to reload SPSS/PC+ and recreate your active file and environment when you return.

SPSS/PC+ cannot control actions taken by other software that you invoke through EXECUTE and therefore cannot guarantee that any particular program will run safely. Read the cautions below before trying to use EXECUTE creatively.

Defaults
By default, the other program has approximately 128K of RAM in which to run. No parameters are passed to the other program.

Tailoring
RAM. You can allocate more RAM for use by other programs within your SPSS/PC+ session when you invoke SPSS/PC+ with the *SPSSPC* command from DOS.
Parameters. You can pass command-line parameters to the other program as if you were running it from DOS.

Syntax
• Specifications for EXECUTE consist of a file specification for an executable file with extension '.EXE' or '.COM'. The file specification should be in apostrophes.

• If you do not specify a file extension, the extension .EXE is assumed.

• Parameters in apostrophes following the file specification are passed to the program you invoke. For example, you could pass a filename to an editor.

• The keyword DOS is accepted as a synonym for COMMAND.COM, the DOS command processor. This provides access to any DOS command.

• The command *DOS* is accepted as a synonym for EXECUTE DOS. In this instance, the EXECUTE command itself is optional.

• To return from DOS to your SPSS/PC+ session, issue the DOS command *EXIT*.

• To return from any other program, issue the normal command used to leave that program.

Operations
• EXECUTE is an operation command and is performed immediately.

• SPSS/PC+ passes control to the program named on the EXECUTE command. By default, that program has approximately 128K of RAM available (see Memory Considerations, below).

• All files used by SPSS/PC+ are closed before control is passed to the other program.

• When the program terminates, you return to the SPSS/PC+ session and may continue, provided that you have observed the limitations below.

Limitations
• The program invoked must not leave anything resident in memory when it exits.

• The program must not attempt to redefine any of the interrupt vectors in low memory on the PC.

• The number of files that the program can open will be smaller than the FILES specification in CONFIG.SYS because of files that remain allocated for use by SPSS/PC+.

C

Command Reference

- Temporary files used by SPSS/PC+ should not be deleted in the middle of a session. These include files named SPSS.SY1 and SPSS.SY2, which hold the active file at various times.
- System files that have been read by the GET command should not be deleted unless data transformation or selection has created a new active file on disk.
- Entering some DOS commands will make it impossible to resume your session (such as erasing SPSS/PC+ modules or a system file that will be needed by a future procedure).

See Problems (below) for further discussion of these limitations.

Example   DOS.

- This command is a synonym for EXECUTE DOS and executes the DOS command processor, COMMAND.COM.
- DOS will issue its command prompt (for example, **C:\MYFILES>**). You can then issue any DOS command but must remember that you are still inside an SPSS/PC+ session.
- To return to SPSS/PC+, issue the DOS *EXIT* command. You will again see the **SPSSPC:** prompt, and any active file you created earlier in your session will be available.
- If you exit to SPSS/PC+ while printing, the printing is suspended.

File Specification   To invoke a program from SPSS/PC+, specify an executable file with extension '.COM' or '.EXE'.

- You can omit the extension if it is '.EXE'.
- If the file is in a directory other than your current directory, you can include a path specification.
- Paths defined with the DOS *PATH* command are searched just as if you were naming the file from DOS.
- To execute a batch (.BAT) file, specify EXECUTE DOS and then invoke the batch file by name.
- Most programs can be invoked indirectly by executing DOS and running the program from DOS. This method slightly increases memory requirements and substantially increases the possibilities for confusion.

Example   EXECUTE '\SPSS\KERMIT.EXE'.

- This command runs KERMIT from within an SPSS/PC+ session. You can use KERMIT to log on to a mainframe and download a portable file created by the EXPORT procedure in SPSS.
- After logging off the mainframe and leaving KERMIT with the KERMIT *EXIT* or *QUIT* command, you can continue the SPSS/PC+ session and IMPORT the file you have downloaded.

Parameters   Any text following the file specification is passed to the program you invoke.

- Parameters specified after the file specification should be enclosed in apostrophes.
- If you run a DOS *PRINT* command with parameters from SPSS/PC+ (DOS PRINT 'freq.lis', for example), the system prints no lines or only a few lines before suspending printing and going right back to SPSS/PC+. We recommend running the DOS command with no parameters—then, from the DOS prompt, issuing DOS commands such as *PRINT 'filename'* or *DIR*, and finally *EXIT*.

Example   This example shows how to use the DOS *PRINT* command to begin printing a
lengthy listing file and then continue with your SPSS/PC+ session while the file
prints. Prompts from DOS and SPSS/PC+ are shown in upper case and
commands given by the user in lower case.

```
C:\MYFILES>print
NAME OF LIST DEVICE [PRN]:
RESIDENT PART OF PRINT INSTALLED
PRINT QUEUE IS EMPTY.

C:\MYFILES>spsspc

...beginning of SPSS/PC!« session...

SPSS/PC:get file='bigfile.sys'.
SPSS/PC:set listing 'freq.lis'.
SPSS/PC:frequencies all.

...output from FREQUENCIES procedure...

SPSS/PC:dos.

C:\MYFILES>print freq.lis

        C:FREQ    :LIS IS CURRENTLY BEING PRINTED

C:\MYFILES>exit

SPSS/PC:crosstabs ....
```

- The DOS *PRINT* command is issued before entering SPSS/PC+ to install the
print driver (see Programs Remaining in Memory, below). Since no file is
specified, nothing is printed and DOS issues the message **PRINT QUEUE IS
EMPTY.**

- In the SPSS/PC+ session, the GET command specifies a system file, the SET
command specifies a file (FREQ.LIS) for the output listing, and the FRE-
QUENCIES command runs frequency distributions for all variables in the
system file. If the frequency distributions were printed at this time (with SET
PRINTER ON), you would have to wait for the printing to finish before
continuing your analysis.

- The SPSS/PC+ command DOS (an abbreviation for EXECUTE DOS) invokes
the DOS command processor, which responds with its prompt (in this case,
C:\MYFILES>).

- The DOS *PRINT* command prints the listing file containing the output from
FREQUENCIES.

- The DOS *EXIT* command returns to SPSS/PC+. If you exit before the printing
is complete, the printing is suspended. It will resume immediately after the
SPSS/PC+ session.

Problems   The following types of programs may make it impossible to return to your
SPSS/PC+ session.

Programs Remaining in   A program that leaves anything in RAM after exiting will cause SPSS/PC+ to
Memory   abort if that program is *first* invoked from an SPSS/PC+ session with the
EXECUTE command. Among the programs that can cause this problem are:

- *The DOS* PRINT *command.* The first time you print a file, DOS loads a print
driver into memory, where it remains. To use the DOS *PRINT* command during
an SPSS/PC+ session, you must first print something prior to entering
SPSS/PC+. This installs the print driver before SPSS/PC+ claims memory for
its own use. As shown in the example above, the *PRINT* command without any
filename will install the print driver.

- *The DOS* MODE *command.* Certain uses of the *MODE* command, including
those needed to configure a printer, cause additional code to be loaded into
memory (see your DOS manual). Do not attempt to do this when you are
executing DOS from within an SPSS/PC+ session.

• *Desk-accessory programs.* Such programs, after being started, remain in memory and can be called up with a few keystrokes to perform notepad, calendar, communications, and other functions. You can use these programs within SPSS/PC+ but cannot use the EXECUTE command to start them or you will abort the SPSS/PC+ session.

• *Keyboard utilities.* You must run a keyboard configuration utility before entering SPSS/PC+, not from within a session.

If you are uncertain whether any particular program remains in memory, run it before entering SPSS/PC+. You should then be able to use EXECUTE safely for the remainder of the session.

Programs Altering the Interrupt Vectors

Any program that alters the interrupt vectors stored in low memory of the PC and does not restore them before exiting will make it impossible for SPSS/PC+ to resume. Commercially available software is unlikely to do this.

Memory Considerations

Normally, SPSS/PC+ uses all available memory (beyond that occupied by SPSS/PC+ itself) as workspace. After obtaining this workspace, SPSS/PC+ will not give it up. Thus, only the 128K given up by SPSS/PC+ itself when you specify EXECUTE is available for use by another program.

If you intend to run a program that requires more than 128K, you must limit the amount of workspace SPSS/PC+ takes by means of a command-line *switch* specifying the size of the workspace SPSS/PC+ should request from DOS.

• The switch is specified when you invoke SPSS/PC+ from DOS with the *SPSSPC* command.

• The switch is entered as */S=nnnK,* where *nnnK* is the desired workspace size.

• A minimum of 20K is suggested for any productive work.

• To free up as much memory as possible (at the expense of not being able to do large tasks in SPSS/PC+), enter the system with the DOS command *SPSSPC /S=20K.*

• If you specify a filename on the *SPSSPC* command, put the size switch after the filename, as in *SPSSPC MYDATA.DEF /S=20K.*

If you know that a program will require a certain amount of memory (more than 128K) and you want SPSS/PC+ to use as much as possible of the remaining memory for workspace, you can:

1   Run SPSS/PC+ without the */S* switch, so that it will request the maximum possible workspace.

2   Use the SHOW command to find out how large this maximum workspace is.

3   Run SPSS/PC+ again, using the */S* switch to reduce the workspace sufficiently to leave the desired amount of memory free. Remember that your program will get about 128K of the SPSS/PC+ memory.

Example

To run a program requiring 192K with the EXECUTE command, you must reserve an additional 64K in addition to the 128K provided by SPSS/PC+. Suppose that the SHOW command reports a maximum workspace of 183K (this amount will vary from one machine to another). To reduce this by 64K, you would specify a workspace of 119K (or a bit less to be safe):

```
SPSSPC /S=115K
```

This will allow you to run SPSS/PC+ while leaving 192K for another program.

EXPORT

```
EXPORT OUTFILE='filename' [/KEEP={ALL    }] [/DROP=varlist]
                                 {varlist}


          [/RENAME=(old varlist=new varlist)...] [/MAP]


          [/DIGITS=number]
```

Example:

```
EXPORT OUTFILE='NEWDATA.POR'
   /RENAME=(V1 TO V3=ID,SEX,AGE)
   /MAP.
```

Overview   EXPORT produces a portable ASCII data file and dictionary that can be read with the IMPORT command in SPSS/PC+ or SPSS. You can upload EXPORT files to a mainframe using KERMIT, provided that KERMIT is installed on both the IBM PC and the receiving mainframe computer.

Defaults   EXPORT writes your active file, including all data and the data dictionary, to an external file. The dictionary contains variable and value labels, missing-value flags, and display formats for each variable. The portable file also contains the originating computer (IBM PC), the name and release number of SPSS/PC+, and the date and time the portable file was created.

Tailoring   You can save a subset of variables from your active file on the portable file and rename variables. You can also produce a record of all variables and their names on the exported file and specify the number of decimal digits of precision for the values of all numeric variables.

Syntax   • The minimum specification is the OUTFILE subcommand with a file specification enclosed in apostrophes.
                   • Subcommands can be named in any order and must be separated by a slash.

Operations   • EXPORT is a transformation and causes the data to be read.
                   • Portable files are written with 80-character record lengths.
                   • Portable files may contain some undisplayable characters.
                   • The active file is still available for SPSS/PC+ transformations and procedures after the portable file is created.
                   • The system variables $CASENUM and $DATE are assigned when the file is read by IMPORT. EXPORT specifies the weighting variable on the portable file.

Limitations   • Maximum 200 variables on a portable file. Each 8-character portion of a long string variable counts as 1 toward this limit.
                   • You may not have enough available memory on your PC to write a large portable file. Use the DROP or KEEP subcommand to exclude extraneous variables from the portable file.

Example
```
EXPORT OUTFILE='NEWDATA.POR'
   /RENAME=(V1 TO V3=ID,SEX,AGE)
   /MAP.
```
                   • The portable file is written to NEWDATA.POR in the current directory.
                   • Variables V1, V2, and V3 are renamed ID, SEX, and AGE for the portable file. Their names remain V1, V2, and V3 in the SPSS/PC+ active file. None of the other variables written to the portable file are renamed.
                   • The MAP subcommand requests a listing of the variables in the portable file.

C

Command Reference

OUTFILE Subcommand   The OUTFILE subcommand specifies the filename of the portable file.

- The filename must be enclosed in apostrophes.
- The file must be in the current directory. You cannot direct portable files to other directories.
- You can direct the portable file to another drive, including the A: drive. Replace the key diskette in the A: drive after the EXPORT command is finished.

Example   `EXP OUT='SALDATA.POR'.`

- The complete active file is written to file SALDATA.POR.
- This example takes advantage of spelling permitted by three-character truncation of keywords.

DROP and KEEP Subcommands   Use the DROP and KEEP subcommands to save a subset of variables on the portable file.

- DROP excludes a variable or list of variables from the portable file. All variables not named are included in the portable file.
- KEEP includes a variable or list of variables on the portable file. All variables not named are excluded.
- Variables can be specified on DROP and KEEP in any order.
- With the DROP subcommand, the order of variables in the portable file is the same as their order on the active file.
- With the KEEP subcommand, the order of variables in the portable file is the order they are named on KEEP. Thus, you can also use KEEP to reorder variables in the portable file.
- You can use both DROP and KEEP on the same EXPORT command, provided they do not name any of the same variables.
- You can use the TO keyword to specify a group of consecutive variables on the active file.
- The active file is not affected by DROP or KEEP.

Example   ```
EXPORT OUTFILE='NEWSUM.POR'
  /DROP=DEPT79 TO DEPT81.
```

- The portable file is written to NEWSUM.POR in the current directory.
- Variables between and including DEPT79 and DEPT81 on the active file are excluded from the portable file.
- All other variables are saved on the portable file.

**RENAME Subcommand**     Use the RENAME subcommand to rename variables being written to the portable file. The renamed variables retain their variable and value labels, missing-value flags, and display formats assigned in the SPSS/PC+ session.

- To rename a variable, specify the name of the variable in the active file, an equals sign, and the new name.
- The equals sign is required.
- You can specify lists of variables on both sides of the equals sign. The number of variables on both sides must be the same, and the entire specification must be enclosed in parentheses.
- You can use the TO convention for both variable lists (see Universals: Variable-Naming Conventions).

**Example**     ```
EXPORT OUTFILE='NEWSUM.POR'
  /DROP=DEPT79 TO DEPT81
  /RENAME=(DEPT82,SALARY82=DEPT,SALARY).
```

- The RENAME subcommand renames DEPT82 and SALARY82 to DEPT and SALARY.
- DEPT and SALARY retain the variable and value labels, missing-value flags, and display formats assigned to DEPT82 and SALARY82.

MAP Subcommand

If you use the RENAME, DROP, or KEEP subcommands to tailor your file, you may find it helpful to produce a listing of your changes with the MAP subcommand.

• The MAP subcommand can be specified as often as you wish.
• The MAP subcommand produces a listing of all actions taken up to that point.
• When the MAP subcommand is specified last, it produces a listing of the contents of the portable file.

Example

```
EXPORT OUTFILE='NEWSUM.POR'
  /DROP=DEPT79 TO DEPT81
  /MAP
  /RENAME DEPT82=DEPT SALARY82=SALARY
  /MAP.
```

• The first MAP subcommand produces a listing of the variables in the file after the DROP subcommand has dropped the specified variables.
• The RENAME subcommand renames DEPT82 and SALARY82.
• The second MAP subcommand shows the variables on the file after renaming. Since this is the last subcommand, the listing will show the variables as they are written on the portable file.

DIGITS Subcommand

The DIGITS subcommand lets you specify the degree of precision for all values of noninteger numeric variables written to the portable file.

• The DIGITS subcommand has the general form DIGITS=n, where n is the number of digits of precision you want. The default is 10 digits.
• The DIGITS subcommand applies to all numbers for which rounding is required.
• You cannot specify different degrees of precision for different variables. Thus, DIGITS should be set according to the requirements of the variable that needs the most precision.

Example

```
EXPORT OUTFILE='NEWSUM.POR'
  /DROP=DEPT79 TO DEPT81
  /RENAME=(DEPT82,SALARY82=DEPT,SALARY)
  /MAP
  /DIGITS=4.
```

• The DIGITS subcommand guarantees the accuracy of values to four significant digits.
• For example, 12.34567890876 will be rounded to 12.35.

FINISH

```
FINISH
```

Overview

The FINISH command terminates an SPSS/PC+ session and returns control to DOS.

Syntax

- The minimum specification is simply the command keyword. FINISH has no additional specifications.
- The commands BYE, EXIT, and STOP are accepted as aliases for FINISH.

Operations

- FINISH causes SPSS/PC+ to stop reading commands.
- Any commands following FINISH in an INCLUDE file are ignored.

Example

```
DATA LIST FILE='NEW.DAT'/
   NAME 1-15(A) V1 TO V15 16-30.
LIST.
FINISH.
```

- The DATA LIST and LIST commands are executed.
- The SPSS/PC+ session is ended with the FINISH command.

FLIP

```
FLIP [[VARIABLES=] {varlist}]
                   {ALL    }

     [/NEWNAMES=variable]
```

Example:

```
FLIP VARIABLES=WEEK1 TO WEEK52
   /NEWNAMES=DEPT.
```

Overview   SPSS/PC+ requires a file structure in which the variables are the columns and observations (cases) are the rows. If a file read with TRANSLATE is organized such that variables are in rows and the observations are in columns, you need to use procedure FLIP to reorganize it. FLIP transposes the rows and columns of the data on the active file, so that what was in row 1, column 2 is now in row 2, column 1, and so forth.

Defaults   By default, all rows and columns are transposed. A new variable named CASE_LBL is created, containing the variable names that existed before the transposition. The default names of the transposed variables in the new file are VAR001 to VARn. If the file to be transposed has a CASE_LBL variable on it as the result of a previous FLIP, the values of CASE_LBL are used as the variable names in the new file. A list of variable names is displayed in the output.

Tailoring   You can transpose specific variables (columns) from the original file by naming them on the VARIABLES subcommand. You can use the values of one of the variables from the original file as the variable names in the new file by specifying that original variable name on the NEWNAMES subcommand.

Syntax   • The minimum specification is the command keyword FLIP. All other specifications are optional.

Operations   • FLIP replaces the active file with one in which the original rows and columns have been exchanged.

• FLIP discards any previous variable labels, value labels, user-missing values, and WEIGHT settings. Values defined as user-missing in the original file are translated to system-missing in the transposed file.

• FLIP obeys any SELECT IF, N, USE, PROCESS IF, and SAMPLE commands in effect.

• PROCESS IF and SAMPLE are permanent transformations if followed by FLIP.

• String variables in the original file are assigned system-missing values (.) after transposition.

• Numeric variables are assigned a default format of F8.2 after transposition (with the exceptions of CASE_LBL and the variable specified on NEWNAMES).

• The variable CASE_LBL is created and added to the active file each time FLIP is executed.

• If CASE_LBL already exists as the result of a previous FLIP, its current values are used as the names of variables in the new file (if NEWNAMES is not specified).

Limitations   • There is a maximum of 500 variables (columns) and 499 cases (rows).

• FLIP will abort if there is insufficient memory. The amount of memory required by FLIP in bytes can be roughly calculated as (number of cases $\times$ number of variables $\times$ 8) + (number of cases $\times$ 8) + (number of variables $\times$ 8). An active file consisting of 200 variables and 199 cases requires about 314K.

Example 1   The following is LIST output for a data file arranged in a typical spreadsheet format, with variables in rows and observations in columns:

```
A               B          C          D

INCOME        22.00      31.00      43.00
PRICE         34.00      29.00      50.00
YEAR        1970.00    1971.00    1972.00
```

The command

```
FLIP.
LIST.
```

transposes all variables on the file. The LIST output for the transposed file is as follows:

```
CASE_LBL   VAR001     VAR002     VAR003

A             .          .          .
B           22.00      34.00    1970.00
C           31.00      29.00    1971.00
D           43.00      50.00    1972.00
```

- The values for the new variable CASE_LBL are the "variable" names from the original file.
- Case A has system-missing values since variable A had the string values INCOME, PRICE, and YEAR.
- The names of the variables in the new file are VAR001, VAR002, and VAR003.

VARIABLES Subcommand   The VARIABLES subcommand names one or more variables (columns) to be transposed. The specified variables become observations (rows) in the new active file.

- The VARIABLES subcommand is optional. If it is not used, all variables are transposed.
- The actual keyword VARIABLES can be omitted.
- If the VARIABLES subcommand is used, variables not named are discarded.

Example 2   Using the original, untransposed file from Example 1, the command

```
FLIP VARIABLES=A TO C.
LIST.
```

transposes only variables A through C. The LIST output for the transposed file is as follows:

```
CASE_LBL   VAR001     VAR002     VAR003

A             .          .          .
B           22.00      34.00    1970.00
C           31.00      29.00    1971.00
```

- Series D is not transposed and is discarded from the active file.

NEWNAMES Subcommand   The NEWNAMES subcommand specifies a variable whose values are used as the new variable names.

- The NEWNAMES subcommand is optional. If it is not used, the new variable names are either VAR001 to VAR*n*, or the values of CASE_LBL if it exists.
- Only one variable can be specified on the NEWNAMES subcommand.
- The variable specified on NEWNAMES does not become an observation (case) on the new active file, regardless of whether it is specified on the VARIABLES subcommand.
- If the variable specified is numeric, its values become a character string beginning with the prefix 'V'.
- If the variable specified is a long string, only the first eight characters are used.

• Lower-case character values of a string variable are converted to upper case, and any bad character values, such as blank spaces, are replaced with underscore (_) characters.

• If the variable's values are not unique, a numeric extension *n* is added to the end of a value after its first occurrence, where *n* increases by 1 at each additional occurrence.

Example 3   Using the original, untransposed file from Example 1, the command

```
FLIP NEWNAMES=A.
LIST.
```

uses the values for variable A as the names for variables in the new file. The LIST output for the transposed file is as follows:

```
CASE_LBL    INCOME     PRICE      YEAR

B           22.00      34.00      1970.00
C           31.00      29.00      1971.00
D           43.00      50.00      1972.00
```

• Note that variable A does not become an observation in the new file.

The following command transposes this file back to a form resembling its original structure:

```
FLIP.
LIST.
```

The LIST output for the transposed file is as follows:

```
CASE_LBL       B          C          D

INCOME        22.00      31.00      43.00
PRICE         34.00      29.00      50.00
YEAR        1970.00    1971.00    1972.00
```

• Since the NEWNAMES subcommand is not used, the values of CASE_LBL from the previous FLIP (B, C, and D) are used as variable names in the new file.

• The values of for CASE_LBL now become INCOME, PRICE, and YEAR.

C

Command Reference

FORMATS

```
FORMATS varlist (format) [varlist ...]
```

Format	Meaning
Fw.d	Numeric of width w and d decimal places
COMMAw.d	Numeric with commas and decimal places
DOLLARw.d	Numeric with dollar sign, commas, and decimal places

Examples:

```
FORMATS VARA (F4.2) VARB (DOLLAR9) VARC (COMMA7).

FORMATS VARD VARE VARF (F3.2).
```

Overview

The FORMATS command allows you to change the print and write formats of numeric variables. You can change the print width, specify additional decimal digits, and add commas and dollar signs. The values used in computations by SPSS/PC+ are not affected by the print and write FORMATS specification.

Syntax

• The syntax for specifying formats is Fw.d, COMMAw.d, or DOLLARw.d, where *w* specifies the total number of columns, including decimal point, commas, and dollar sign, and *d* specifies the number of decimal places. For example, to display the number 6543210 as $6,543,210, you must specify a dollar format of at least (DOLLAR10). The *d* specification is optional.

• Format specifications are enclosed in parentheses.

• You can specify format types for more than one variable on a single FORMATS command.

• You cannot use FORMATS with string variables.

Operations

• FORMATS is a transformation and is executed when the data are read for the next procedure.

• The FORMATS specification is saved on the active file dictionary.

• The FORMATS command specifies how values are printed in SPSS/PC+ procedures and how data values are written using the WRITE command.

• The formats specified on FORMATS are in effect for the duration of the session or until the variable is given a new FORMATS specification.

• Print and write formats are retained in system files (see SAVE) and portable files (see EXPORT).

• When a COMMA or DOLLAR format is incorrectly assigned, SPSS/PC+ attempts to display the value without commas or a dollar sign. If you have not allowed enough columns for printing a numeric value, SPSS/PC+ prints asterisks. The values in the active file are unchanged.

Limitations

• Some procedures are unable to print wide format values.

Example

```
DATA LIST / VARA 1-4 (3) VARB 6-10 VARC 12-17.
BEGIN DATA.
155  10500 429813
4309 25000 389213
6256 18750 35946
END DATA.
LIST.
FORMATS VARA (F4.2) VARB (DOLLAR9) VARC (COMMA7).
LIST VAR=ALL.
```

• The DATA LIST command indicates inline fixed-format data and defines three variables. VARA is four columns wide with three implied decimal places. VARB is five columns wide, and VARC is six columns wide.

- The first LIST command prints out all variables using the dictionary formats defined by the DATA LIST command. The results of the first LIST command are shown below:

```
VARA  VARB   VARC

 .155 10500 429813
4.309 25000 389213
6.256 18750  35946
```

- The FORMATS command defines new print formats for each variable. VARA is printed in four columns (including decimal point) with two decimal digits. VARB is printed in nine columns including dollar signs and commas. VARC is printed in seven columns including commas.

- The second LIST command prints out each of the variables using the new formats. The results of this LIST procedure are shown below:

```
VARA     VARB    VARC

 .15   $10,500 429,813
4.31   $25,000 389,213
6.26   $18,750  35,946
```

Example
```
DATA LIST FREE / VARA VARB VARC.
BEGIN DATA.
155 10500 429813 4309 25000 389213 6256 18750 35946
END DATA.
LIST.
FORMATS VARA (F4.0) VARB (DOLLAR11.2) VARC (COMMA9.1).
LIST VAR=ALL.
```

- The DATA LIST command identifies inline data in freefield format. By default, variables VARA, VARB, and VARC have print and write formats of eight columns with two decimal places.

- The first LIST command shows the default formats of the three variables:

```
  VARA     VARB     VARC

 155.00 10500.00 429813.0
4309.00 25000.00 389213.0
6256.00 18750.00  35946.00
```

- The FORMATS command specifies a print format of four columns with no decimal digits for VARA; eleven columns, including a dollar sign, commas, and two decimal digits for VARB; and nine columns, including commas and one decimal place for VARC.

- The LIST command uses the new print formats and is shown below:

```
VARA      VARB       VARC

 155   $10,500.00 429,813.0
4309   $25,000.00 389,213.0
6256   $18,750.00  35,946.0
```

C

Command Reference

FREQUENCIES

```
FREQUENCIES [VARIABLES=]{varlist}
                        {ALL    }

[/FORMAT=[{CONDENSE}] [{NOTABLE }] [NOLABELS]
          {ONEPAGE }   {LIMIT(n)}

          [{AVALUE}] [DOUBLE] [NEWPAGE]]
           {DVALUE}
           {AFREQ }
           {DFREQ }

[/MISSING=INCLUDE]

[/BARCHART=[MINIMUM(n)] [MAXIMUM(n)] [{FREQ(n)   }]]
                                     {PERCENT(n)}

[/HISTOGRAM=[MINIMUM(n)] [MAXIMUM(n)] [{FREQ(n)   }]]
                                      {PERCENT(n)}

            [{NONORMAL}] [INCREMENT(n)]]
             {NORMAL  }

[/HBAR=same keywords as HISTOGRAM]

[/GROUPED=varlist[{(width)        }]]
                  {(boundary-list)}

[/NTILES=n]  [/PERCENTILES=value list]

[/STATISTICS=[DEFAULT] [MEAN] [STDDEV] [MINIUM] [MAXIMUM]
             [SEMEAN] [VARIANCE] [SKEWNESS] [SESKEW] [RANGE]
[MODE]
             [KURTOSIS] [SEKURT] [MEDIAN] [SUM] [ALL] [NONE]]
```

Example:

```
FREQUENCIES VARIABLES=XVAR YVAR ZVAR1 TO ZVAR5
  /FORMAT=NOTABLE
  /STATISTICS=ALL
  /HISTOGRAM.
```

Overview

FREQUENCIES produces tables of frequency counts and percentages for the values of individual variables.

Defaults

The default output is a table that displays counts for each value of a variable, the counts percentaged over all cases and over all cases with nonmissing values, and the cumulative percentage over all cases with nonmissing values. Values of numeric variables are ordered from lowest to highest; values of string variables are ordered alphabetically. The number of cases with user-missing and system-missing values are displayed. The table is labeled with variable and value labels if these have been defined. Each page displays as many entire single-spaced tables as will fit.

Tailoring

Display Format. You can suppress all tables or only tables for variables with more than a specified number of categories. You can specify one table per page, a condensed format that fits more values in each table, or double spacing, and you can suppress label printing. Table contents can be ordered by values in descending order, by frequencies in ascending order, or by frequencies in descending order.

Statistical Display. You can display percentiles or ntiles and other optional statistics for each numeric variable. Available statistics include mean, median, mode, standard deviation, variance, skewness, kurtosis, and sum.

Plots. Histograms are available for numeric variables, and bar charts are available for numeric or string variables.

Missing Values. You can include user-missing values in statistical calculations and plots.

Syntax
- The minimum specification is a list of variables.
- Subcommands can be named in any order.
- Subcommands must be separated by slashes.
- Keyword order on subcommands is unimportant.
- VARIABLES names the variables to be tabulated.
- All optional subcommands apply to all variables named on the VARIABLES subcommand.
- Specify subcommands VARIABLES, FORMAT, MISSING, and STATISTICS only once.
- Specify only one of the following subcommands at a time: BARCHART, HISTOGRAM, and HBAR. If you specify any two of these together, HBAR is assumed.
- You can use subcommands PERCENTILES and NTILES more than once. Multiple requests for the same percentiles are consolidated.

Operations
- FREQUENCIES causes the data to be read.
- FREQUENCIES tabulates numeric variables with or without decimal values, short string variables, and the short string portion of long string variables.
- Variables are tabulated in the order that they are mentioned on the VARIABLES subcommand. If a variable is mentioned more than once, it will be tabulated more than once.
- Percentages in tables are displayed with one decimal place. Statistics are displayed with three decimal places.
- If a requested ntile or percentile cannot be calculated, a period (.) is displayed.
- The display always uses narrow format regardless of the width defined on SET.
- The HISTOGRAM subcommand on the SET command controls the character used to draw histograms.

Limitations
- The maximum number of variables on a FREQUENCIES command is the same as the system limit.
- The maximum unique observed values over all variables depends on available workspace and on available labels space (up to 5000 characters for all labels combined).

Example
```
FREQUENCIES VARIABLES=XVAR YVAR ZVAR1 TO ZVAR5
   /FORMAT=NOTABLE
   /STATISTICS=ALL
   /HISTOGRAM.
```
- This example requests FREQUENCIES for XVAR, YVAR, and all variables between and including ZVAR1 and ZVAR5.
- The FORMAT subcommand suppresses the display of frequency tables for all variables named on the VARIABLES subcommand.
- The STATISTICS subcommand requests that all statistics available be displayed for each variable named on the VARIABLES subcommand.
- The HISTOGRAM subcommand requests a histogram for each variable named on the VARIABLES subcommand.

VARIABLES Subcommand

VARIABLES names the variables to be tabulated and is the only required subcommand. The actual keyword VARIABLES can be omitted.

- You can use keyword ALL to refer to all user-defined variables in the active file.

FORMAT Subcommand

By default, FREQUENCIES displays as many single-spaced tables with complete labeling information as fit within the page length. The default table is ordered by ascending value (numeric variables) or in alphabetical order (string variables). Use FORMAT with the keywords listed below to change the defaults.

- If you specify FORMAT, only defaults that you explicitly alter are changed.

Table Formats

CONDENSE	*Condensed format.* Displays counts in three columns without value labels and with valid and cumulative percentages rounded to integers. Overrides ONEPAGE.
ONEPAGE	*Conditional condensed format.* Uses condensed format for tables that would otherwise require more than one page.
NEWPAGE	*Each table starts on a new page.*
NOLABELS	*No value labels.*
DOUBLE	*Double-space frequency tables.*

Table Order

AVALUE	*Sort categories in ascending order of values (numeric variables)* or in alphabetical order (string variables).
AFREQ	*Sort categories in ascending order of frequency.* Ignored when HISTOGRAM, HBAR, NTILES, or PERCENTILES are requested.
DFREQ	*Sort categories in descending order of frequency.* Ignored when HISTOGRAM, HBAR, NTILES, or PERCENTILES are requested.
DVALUE	*Sort categories in descending order of values (numeric variables)* or in reverse alphabetical order (string variables). Ignored when HISTOGRAM, HBAR, NTILES, or PERCENTILES are requested.

Table Suppression

LIMIT(n)	*No frequency tables with more than* n *categories.* The number of missing and valid cases and requested statistics are displayed for suppressed tables.
NOTABLE	*No frequency tables.* The number of missing and valid cases are displayed for suppressed tables. Overrides LIMIT.

BARCHART Subcommand

BARCHART produces a bar chart for each variable named on the VARIABLES subcommand. By default, the horizontal axis for each bar chart is scaled in frequencies and the interval width is determined by the largest frequency count for the variable being plotted. Bar charts are labeled with value labels or with the value if no value label is defined.

- If you omit the BARCHART subcommand, no bar charts are displayed.
- If no keywords are specified on the BARCHART subcommand, the default bar charts are displayed.
- Only defaults you explicitly alter with keywords are changed.

MIN(n)	*Lower bound* below which values are not plotted.
MAX(n)	*Upper bound* above which values are not plotted.
FREQ(n)	*Horizontal axis scaled in frequencies,* where optional *n* is the maximum. With no *n* or a too-small *n*, FREQUENCIES chooses 10, 20, 50, 100, 200, 500, 1000, 2000, and so forth, depending on the largest category. This is the default.

Example

```
FREQ VAR=JVAR
  /BAR=MAX(10).
```

- This command requests a bar chart with values through 10.
- This example takes advantage of spelling permitted by three-character truncation of keywords.

HISTOGRAM Subcommand

HISTOGRAM displays a plot for each numeric variable named on the VARIABLES subcommand. If there are no specifications on HISTOGRAM, the horizontal axis of each histogram is scaled in frequencies and the interval width is determined by the largest frequency count of the variable being plotted.

- If you omit the HISTOGRAM subcommand, no histograms are displayed.
- If no keywords are specified, the default histograms are displayed.
- Only defaults you explicitly alter with keywords are changed.

MIN(n)	*Lower bound* below which values are not plotted.
MAX(n)	*Upper bound* above which values are not plotted.
PERCENT(n)	*Horizontal axis scaled in percentages,* where optional *n* is the preferred maximum. With no *n* or a two-small *n*, FREQUENCIES chooses 5, 10, 25, 50, or 100, depending on the largest category.
FREQ(n)	*Horizontal axis scaled in frequencies,* where optional *n* is the scale. With no *n* or a too-small *n*. FREQUENCIES chooses 10, 20, 50, 100, 200, 500, 1000, 2000, and so forth, depending on the largest category. This is the default.
INCREMENT(n)	*Interval width,* where *n* is the size of the interval. Overrides the default number of intervals on the vertical axis, which depends on the system page length. For a variable that ranges from 1 to 100, INCREMENT(2) produces 50 intervals with 2 values each.
NORMAL	*Superimpose a normal curve.* Based on all valid values for the variable, including values excluded by MIN and MAX.
NONORMAL	Do not superimpose a normal curve.

Example

```
FREQS VAR=VARZ
    /HIST=NORMAL INCREMENT(4).
```

• This example requests a histogram with a superimposed normal curve and an interval width of 4.

• This example takes advantage of spelling permitted by three-character truncation of keywords.

HBAR Subcommand

HBAR produces a plot for each numeric and string variable named on the VARIABLES subcommand. For numeric variables, HBAR produces a bar chart if the number of categories fits within the page length (see SET). Otherwise, HBAR produces a histogram. HBAR produces bar charts for short string variables and for the short-string portion of long string variables, regardless of the number of values.

By default, the horizontal axis of each plot is scaled in frequencies and the interval is determined by the largest frequency count. All keyword specifications for HISTOGRAM and BARCHART work with HBAR.

GROUPED Subcommand

When the codes of a variable represent *grouped* or *collapsed* data, it is possible to estimate percentiles for the original, ungrouped data from the grouped data. The GROUPED subcommand lets you specify which variables have been grouped.

• When you use GROUPED, the codes in the data should equal the *midpoints* of the ranges that they represent. If people aged 10 through 20 are grouped together in a variable AGE, they should be coded 15. If necessary, you can use the RECODE command to assign the correct group midpoints before using FREQUENCIES.

• The GROUPED subcommand only affects the output from the PERCENTILES and NTILES subcommands, and the MEDIAN statistic from the STATISTICS subcommand.

• Multiple GROUPED subcommands can be used on a single FREQUENCIES command. Multiple variable lists, separated by slashes, can appear on a single GROUPED subcommand.

The specifications for GROUPED consist of a variable name or list of variable names, and an optional set of parentheses containing either a single value or a list of values. Values of the variables listed on GROUPED are treated as group midpoints rather than actual values.

• The variable(s) named on GROUPED must have been named on the VARIABLES subcommand.

Example
```
RECODE AGE (1=19) (2=25) (3=35) (4=45) (5=55)
          (6=65) (7=75) (8=85) (9=95)
      / INCOME (1=5) (2=15) (3=25) (4=35) (5=45)
               (6=55) (7=65) (8=75) (9=100).
FREQUENCIES VARIABLES=AGE, SEX, RACE, INCOME
 /GROUPED=AGE, INCOME
 /PERCENTILES=5,25,50,75,95.
```

The values of AGE and INCOME are recoded to category midpoints, and then the GROUPED subcommand on FREQUENCIES allows more accurate estimates of the requested percentiles. Note that data can be recoded to "category midpoints" on any scale; here AGE is recoded in years, but INCOME is recoded in thousands of dollars.

When you specify a single number in parentheses after the GROUPED variable list, that number is used as the width of each interval.

• When a width specification is provided on GROUPED, the actual data values must be separated by at least as much as the indicated width.

Example
Suppose that a clinic obtains patients' temperatures using an inexpensive digital thermometer whose readings are precise only to the nearest half degree.
```
FREQUENCIES VARIABLES=TEMP
 /GROUPED=TEMP (0.5)
 /NTILES=10.
```

The observed values of 97.5, 98, 98.5, 99, and so on, are treated as group midpoints, smoothing out the discrete distribution and yielding more accurate estimates of the deciles.

When you specify a list of numbers in parentheses after the GROUPED variable list, they are taken as interval boundaries.

• When interval boundaries are provided on GROUPED, it is not necessary to have recoded the data to interval midpoints. FREQUENCIES will treat the data as if they were recoded to interval midpoints, and will estimate percentiles accordingly.

• When interval boundaries are provided on GROUPED, the lowest boundary (the first number within the parentheses) must be lower than any value in the data. If any data values exceed the highest boundary specified (the last number within the parentheses), they will be assigned to an open-ended interval. In this case some percentiles cannot be calculated.

Example
Suppose that ages have been estimated, usually to the nearest five years, for questionnaire respondents who did not provide their age. Without actually recoding the data, you can treat them as grouped:
```
FREQUENCIES VARIABLES=AGE
 /GROUPED=AGE (17.5, 22.5, 27.5, 32.5, 37.5, 42.5, 47.5
              52.5, 57.5, 62.5, 67.5, 72.5, 77.5, 82.5)
 /PERCENTILES=5, 10, 25, 50, 75, 90, 95.
```

The artificial clustering of age estimates at multiples of five years is smoothed out by treating the age as grouped data. It is not necessary to recode the ages to category midpoints since the interval boundaries are explicitly given.

PERCENTILES Subcommand

PERCENTILES displays the value below which the specified percentage of cases falls.

• There are no default percentiles.

• If you omit the PERCENTILES subcommand, no percentiles are displayed.

Example
```
FREQUENCIES VARIABLES=VARZ
 /PERCENTILES=10 25 33.3 66.7 75.
```

• This example requests the values for percentiles 10, 25, 33.3, 66.7, and 75 for VARZ.

NTILES Subcommand

NTILES calculates the percentages that divide the distribution into the specified number of categories and displays the values below which the requested percentages of cases fall.

- There are no default ntiles for the NTILES subcommand.
- If you omit the NTILES subcommand, ntiles are not displayed.

Example

```
FREQUENCIES VARIABLES=VARZ
    /NTILES=4.
```

- This example requests quartiles (percentiles 25, 50, and 75) for VARZ.

STATISTICS Subcommand

The STATISTICS subcommand controls the display of statistics. By default, cases with missing values are excluded from the calculation of statistics.

- If you use the STATISTICS subcommand without any specifications, it produces the mean, standard deviation, minimum, and maximum (the same as produced by the keyword DEFAULT).
- If you use the STATISTICS subcommand with any specifications, only statistics requested are displayed.
- If you omit the STATISTICS subcommand, no statistics are displayed.

The following can be specified on the STATISTICS subcommand:

MEAN	*Mean.*
SEMEAN	*Standard error of the mean.*
MEDIAN	*Median.* Ignored with AFREQ or DFREQ on the FORMAT subcommand.
MODE	*Mode.* If there is more than one mode, the first (lowest) of the modes is displayed, with a warning note.
STDDEV	*Standard deviation.*
VARIANCE	*Variance.*
SKEWNESS	*Skewness.*
SESKEW	*Standard error of the skewness statistic.*
KURTOSIS	*Kurtosis.*
SEKURT	*Standard error of the kurtosis statistic.*
RANGE	*Range.*
MINIMUM	*Minimum.*
MAXIMUM	*Maximum.*
SUM	*Sum.*
DEFAULT	*Mean, standard deviation, minimum, and maximum.*
ALL	*Display all available statistics.*
NONE	*No statistics.*

Example

```
FREQS VAR=AGE
    /STATS=DEF MODE.
```

- The keyword DEFAULT on the STATISTICS subcommand produces the mean, standard deviation, minimum, and maximum of AGE.
- The keyword MODE requests the mode of AGE.
- This example takes advantage of spelling permitted by three-character truncation of keywords.

MISSING Subcommand

By default, both user- and system-missing values are labeled as missing in the table but are not included in the valid and cumulative percentages, in the calculation of descriptive statistics, or in bar charts and histograms. Use the MISSING subcommand and keyword to alter the handling of missing values.

INCLUDE *Include cases with user-missing values.* Cases with user-missing values will be included in the statistics and plots.

C

Command Reference

GET

```
GET [FILE={'SPSS.SYS'**}]
           {'filename'   }

    [/DROP=varlist]       [/KEEP=varlist]

    [/RENAME=(varlist=newlist) [(varlist=newlist] ]
```

**Default if subcommand is omitted.

Example:
```
GET FILE='NEWDATA.SYS'.
```

Overview

GET reads an SPSS/PC+ system file produced by the SAVE command. A system file contains data and a dictionary with variable and value labels, missing-value flags, and print formats for each variable on the system file. GET also reads older system files produced by SPSS/PC or SPSS/PC+.

Defaults

By default, GET retrieves the system file SPSS.SYS in the current directory.

Tailoring

You can retrieve system files other than SPSS.SYS. You can also retrieve only a subset of variables from a system file. You can rename variables while reading the system file.

Syntax

• The minimum specification is simply the command keyword.

• Subcommands are separated by an optional slash.

Operations

• GET causes the dictionary of the system file to be read.

• Data from the system file are copied into a separate active file on disk only if you use the DROP subcommand, or if you enter data transformation or selection commands. Otherwise SPSS/PC+ will read data from the system file repeatedly when executing procedures.

• You need not declare whether a system file is compressed.

• System files are designed to be read by SPSS/PC+ or SPSS Data Entry II only and should not be edited.

• A file saved with weighting in effect maintains the values of variable $WEIGHT. For a discussion of turning off weights, see WEIGHT.

• The order of cases in a system file depends on their order at the time the file was saved. The values of $CASENUM are those from the raw data file, before any selecting (see SELECT IF) or sorting (see SORT).

• The variable counts displayed by GET treat each 8-character portion of a long string variable as one variable. For example, a 17-character long string counts as three variables.

FILE Subcommand

Use the FILE subcommand to specify a system file other than the default SPSS.SYS.

• The only specification on FILE is the name of the file, which must be enclosed in apostrophes.

• You can specify files residing in other drives or directories by supplying a fully qualified filename (see Universals: Files).

Example

```
GET FILE = '\KL\SALDATA.NOV'.
```

• The system file SALDATA.NOV is retrieved from directory KL.

DROP and KEEP Subcommands

DROP and KEEP copy a subset of variables into the active file. DROP specifies the variables to drop from the active file; KEEP specifies the variables to keep on the active file.

- Variables may be specified in any order. The variable order on KEEP determines the variable order in the active file. Variable order on DROP does not affect the order of variables in the active file: the variables are copied in the same sequence in which they appear in the system file.
- Multiple DROP and KEEP subcommands are allowed.
- If a variable is referenced twice, only the first mention of the variable is recognized.

Reordering Variables

- The variable order on KEEP determines the variable order in the active file.
- Keyword ALL on KEEP refers to all remaining variables not previously specified. ALL must be the last specification on KEEP.

Example

```
GET FILE='D:HUBTEMP.SYS'
  /DROP=DEPT79 TO DEPT84 SALARY79.
```

- The active file is copied from system file HUBTEMP.SYS, which is in the current directory on drive D:. All variables between and including DEPT79 and DEPT84, as well as SALARY79, are excluded from the active file. All other variables are copied into the active file.
- Variables in the active file are in the same order as the variables in the original system file.

Example

```
GET FILE='PRSNL.SYS'
  /DROP=GRADE STORE
  /KEEP=LNAME NAME TENURE JTENURE ALL.
```

- DROP specifies that variables GRADE and STORE be dropped when file PRSNL.SYS is copied into the active file.
- KEEP determines that LNAME, NAME, TENURE, and JTENURE are the first four variables in the active file, followed by all remaining variables not specified on DROP. Variables not specified on KEEP are copied into the active file in the same sequence in which they appear in the original system file.

RENAME Subcommand

RENAME changes the names of variables as they are copied into the active file.

- Name changes can be specified within parentheses, in the form *(old varname =new varname)*. Multiple sets of variable specifications are allowed. Each set must be enclosed in parentheses.
- As an alternative to the above, name changes can be specified with a *list* of old variable names followed by an equals sign and a list of new variable names, all within parentheses. The same number of variables must be specified on both lists. Keyword TO can be used in either or both lists to refer to consecutive variables. A single set of parentheses enclosing the entire specification is required for this method.
- Old variable names need not be specified according to their order in the system file.
- Name changes take place in one operation. Therefore, variable names can be exchanged between two variables.
- Multiple RENAME subcommands are allowed.

Example

```
GET FILE='EMPL88.SYS'
  /RENAME (AGE=AGE88 JOBCAT=JOBCAT88).
```

- RENAME specifies two name changes for the active file. AGE is renamed to AGE88, and JOBCAT is renamed to JOBCAT88.

Example

```
GET FILE='EMPL88.SYS'
  /RENAME (AGE JOBCAT=AGE88 JOBCAT88).
```

- The name changes are identical to those in the previous example. AGE is renamed to AGE88, and JOBCAT is renamed to JOBCAT88.

C

Command Reference

GSET

GSET

```
GSET [PACKAGE={HARVARD}]   [optional specifications]
               {CHART  }
               {CMASTER}
               {3GTALK }
               {4GTALK }
               {DA     }
```

Optional specifications for Harvard Graphics with Trends:

```
[HIGHRES={OFF                 }]
         {'[d:\path\]rootname'*}

[LOWRES={AUTO}]
        {ON  }
        {OFF }

[GINVOKE={YES}]
         {NO }
```

Optional specifications for Chart-Master with GRAPH:

```
[SIZE=(h,v)]

[ORIGIN=(l,b)]

[PENS=n]
```

Optional specifications for GrafTalk with GRAPH:

```
[DEVICE={SCREEN }]
        {PRINTER}
        {PLOTTER}
        {OTHER  }
```

* Root for filenames, up to 5 characters.

Examples:

```
GSET PACKAGE=HARVARD
 /HIGHRES='GFILE'
 /LOWRES=OFF.

GSET PACKAGE=CHART.

GSET PACKAGE=CMASTER
 /SIZE=(6,6)
 /ORIGIN=(2,3).

GSET PACKAGE=4GTALK
 /DEVICE=PLOTTER.
```

Overview

The GSET command sets the graphics package and determines whether procedures in SPSS/PC+ Trends that support high-resolution graphics with Harvard Graphics will generate high- or low-resolution output.

Most subcommands of GSET apply to specific graphics packages. See the discussion of the individual subcommands for details.

Defaults

The default graphics package is Harvard Graphics.

Tailoring

In addition to Harvard Graphics, you can use Microsoft Chart, GrafTalk, Draw Applause, or Chart-Master. If you use Chart-Master, you can specify the size of the chart, the position of the plot on paper, and the number of pens. If you use GrafTalk, you can designate the display device.

Syntax
- Only one graphics package can be specified.
- The available subcommands depend on the specified graphics package.
- Slashes between subcommands are optional (but recommended).

Operations
- GSET is an operation command and takes effect immediately.
- GSET can be used more than once in an SPSS/PC+ session.
- The settings established with GSET are in effect until you enter another GSET command.
- Use GSHOW to display the current graphics system and other settings controlled by GSET.

PACKAGE Subcommand

The PACKAGE subcommand declares which graphics package you are using. The PACKAGE subcommand must be the first specification on GSET. Available options are:

HARVARD   *Harvard Graphics.* This is the default, so you do not have to specify it unless you have switched to another package with the GSET command. The optional subcommands HIGHRES, LOWRES, and GINVOKE are available to control graphics from SPSS/PC+ Trends procedures if PACKAGE is set to HARVARD, either explicitly or by default. These three subcommands do not affect the GRAPH command.

CHART   *Microsoft Chart.* No optional subcommands are available if you specify CHART.

DA   *Draw Applause.* No optional subcommands are available if you specify DA.

CMASTER   *Chart-Master.* The additional subcommands SIZE, ORIGIN, and PENS are available if you specify CMASTER. These three subcommands affect only the GRAPH command.

3GTALK   *GrafTalk* Version 3.27. The additional subcommand DEVICE is available if you specify 3GTALK. This subcommand affects only the GRAPH command.

4GTALK   *GrafTalk* Version 4.01. The additional subcommand DEVICE is available if you specify 4GTALK. This subcommand affects only the GRAPH command.

Example

```
GSET PACKAGE=CMASTER.
```

- This example designates Chart-Master as the default graphics package.

Harvard Graphics Specifications

With Harvard Graphics, you can get high-resolution plots from the GRAPH command and from SPSS/PC+ Trends procedures (other than X11ARIMA).

The optional subcommands HIGHRES, LOWRES, and GINVOKE are available when the package is set to HARVARD, either explicitly or by default. They affect only Trends procedures.

HIGHRES Subcommand

The HIGHRES subcommand serves two functions: it turns on high-resolution graphics output, and it furnishes a *rootname* for the files used to pass the graphics instructions to Harvard Graphics. You can specify the keyword OFF instead of a rootname.

- A rootname is specified in apostrophes or quotation marks.
- The rootname consists of from 1 to 5 letters and can optionally include drive and path specifications.
- Numbering of the output files begins at 1 each time you use the GSET HIGHRES specification, and any existing files with the same names are overwritten.
- This subcommand does not affect the GRAPH command. Use the OUTFILE subcommand of GRAPH to specify a filename.
- To suppress high-resolution graphics, specify HIGHRES=OFF. OFF is the default.

LOWRES Subcommand   The LOWRES subcommand controls the display of low-resolution (character) graphics. Its action is independent of HIGHRES. After LOWRES, specify ON, OFF, or AUTO.

- AUTO displays low-resolution graphics whenever high-resolution graphics cannot be displayed. AUTO is the default.
- ON always displays low-resolution graphics, even when high-resolution graphics are also generated.
- OFF never displays low-resolution graphics (except where important statistics appear on the low-resolution graph, as in the ACF command).

GINVOKE Subcommand   The GINVOKE subcommand determines whether SPSS/PC+ invokes Harvard Graphics immediately to display high-resolution plots. Specify YES or NO.

- YES is the default. When you invoke Harvard Graphics from within an SPSS/PC+ session, you return to SPSS/PC+ upon leaving Harvard Graphics.
- Specify NO to continue your SPSS/PC+ session. You can later load the graphics instruction files into Harvard Graphics and produce the charts.

Example
```
GSET HIGHRES='A:\REPORTS\FIG'
    /GINVOKE=NO.
```

- The HIGHRES subcommand causes SPSS/PC+ to generate high-resolution graphics instructions for Harvard Graphics from Trends procedures. Instructions for the first plot are written to A:\REPORTS\FIG1.CHT; for the second plot to A:\REPORTS\FIG2.CHT; and so on.
- Existing files with these names will be overwritten.
- The GINVOKE subcommand causes SPSS/PC+ *not* to invoke Harvard Graphics after a Trends procedure during the session.
- Do not enter a GRAPHICS specification on the TSET command in Trends if you wish to use Harvard Graphics with Trends commands.

Chart Specifications

No optional specifications apply to Microsoft Chart. With Chart, you can get high-resolution plots from the GRAPH command and from SPSS/PC+ Trends procedures.

To use Chart with SPSS/PC+ Trends, you must specify the TSET command as described in the Trends manual. Use the GRAPHICS, GOUT, and GINVOKE subcommands on TSET to control Microsoft Chart in Trends.

Example
```
GSET PACKAGE=CHART.
TSET GRAPHICS=CHART.
```

- The GSET command establishes Chart as the graphics package to be used by the GRAPH command.
- The TSET command establishes Chart as the graphics package to be used by Trends procedures.
- Either command can be used alone, but both are required to establish Chart as the graphics package for both GRAPH and Trends commands.
- Do not enter any of the GSET specifications that apply to Harvard Graphics (HIGHRES, LOWRES, GINVOKE) if you wish to use Chart with Trends commands.

Chart-Master Specifications

With Chart-Master, you can get high-resolution plots only from the GRAPH command.

The following optional subcommands are available if CMASTER is specified on the PACKAGE subcommand:

SIZE Subcommand   After SIZE, specify in parentheses the horizontal and vertical length of the plot, in inches. The defaults are 10.0 and 7.5.

ORIGIN Subcommand   After ORIGIN, specify in parentheses the coordinates that define the bottom left corner of the plot, in inches. The defaults are both 0.0.

PENS Subcommand   PENS=n

After PENS, specify the number of pens to be used. The default is 4.

Example   GSET PACKAGE=CMASTER
                        /SIZE=(5,4)
                        /PENS=6.

• This example designates Chart-Master as the default graphics package.

• Six pens will be used and the plot area will be 5 inches by 4 inches.

GrafTalk Specifications

With GrafTalk, you can get high-resolution plots only from the GRAPH command.

DEVICE Subcommand   The optional DEVICE subcommand is available if 3GTALK or 4GTALK is specified on the PACKAGE subcommand. Specify one of the following keywords:

SCREEN   *Display the chart on the screen.* This is the default.

PRINTER   *Print the chart on the printer.*

PLOTTER   *Plot the chart on a plotter.*

OTHER   *Produce the chart on another device.*

Example   GSET PACKAGE=3GTALK
                        /DEVICE=PLOTTER.

• This example designates GrafTalk Version 3.27 as the default graphics package.

• The graphics display will be directed to the plotter.

C

Command Reference

IF

```
IF (logical expression) target variable=assignment expression
```

Relational Operators:

EQ or =	Equal to	NE or ~= or <>	Not equal to
LT or <	Less than	LE or <=	Less than or equal to
GT or >	Greater than	GE or >=	Greater than or equal to

Logical Operators:

AND or &   OR or | NOT or ~

Missing-Value Functions:

SYSMIS	Selects the case if value is system-missing
MISSING	Selects the case if value is system- or user-missing
VALUE	Selects the case if value meets stated criteria, ignoring user-missing flags

Examples:

```
IF (SEX EQ 'F') EEOVAR=QUOTA+SXVAR.

IF (SYSMIS(QVAR)) RVAR=0.

IF (ABS(A-C) LT 100) INT=100.

IF (VALUE(AGE) = 99 OR VALUE(SEX) = 9) GROUP=9.
```

Overview

The IF command conditionally executes a single COMPUTE-like transformation based upon logical conditions found in the data. The transformation can create a new variable or modify the values of an existing variable for each case in your active file. You can create or modify the values of numeric and short string variables.

The IF command has three components. An expression enclosed in parentheses sets up the logical criteria and is called the *logical expression* (see Universals: Logical Expressions). The *target variable* (the one to be modified or created) is named next. Following the target variable is an equals sign and the *assignment expression.* The target variable's values are modified according to the assignment expression.

A series of IF commands testing the same variable can often be replaced by a single RECODE command, which is more efficient.

Syntax

- The minimum specification is a logical expression, followed by a target variable, an equals sign, and an assignment expression.
- Parentheses around the logical expression are required.
- The equals sign is required.
- Parentheses can also be used within the logical expression to specify the order of operations.
- The logical expression can contain short string variables, numeric variables, or both.
- To use a long string variable, you must convert it to numeric with the AUTORECODE command.
- At least one relation, SYSMIS function, or MISSING function must be included in the logical expression.
- A relation includes a variable name, the relational operator, and a value or variable.
- Relations cannot be abbreviated: (A EQ 2 OR 5) is invalid.
- String values used in relations must be specified in quotes and must include any leading or trailing blanks. Lowercase letters are considered distinct from uppercase letters.
- A relation cannot compare a string variable to a numeric value or variable, or vice versa.

• Both the logical expression and the assignment expression can use arithmetic operations and functions allowed in COMPUTE transformations (see COMPUTE and Universals: Functions).

Operations

• IF is a transformation and is executed when the data are read for the next procedure.
• Each IF command is evaluated independently.
• The logical expression is evaluated as true or false. The assignment is executed only if the logical expression is true.
• If the logical expression is false or if one of the variables used in the logical expression is system- or user-missing, the assignment is not made. Existing target variables remain unchanged; new numeric variables are assigned the system-missing value and new string variables are set to blanks.
• Logical expressions are evaluated in the following order: first numeric functions, then exponentiation, then arithmetic operations, then relations, and finally logical operators. You can change the order of operations using parentheses.
• For assignment expressions, the order of evaluation is numeric functions, then exponentiation, and then arithmetic operators.
• Relational and logical operators cannot be used in assignment expressions.
• Numeric variables created with IF are initially set to the system-missing value. Short string variables created with IF are initially set to a blank value of the specified width.
• Numeric variables created with IF are assigned a print format of eight characters with two decimal places.
• String variables created with IF are assigned a width equal to the number of characters used in the initial assignment.

Limitations

• The number of variables created with IF, COMPUTE, and COUNT plus the number defined on DATA LIST, IMPORT, or GET cannot exceed the system maximum of 200 variables.

Example

```
IF (XVAR EQ 5) YVAR=3.
```

• Numeric variable YVAR is set to 3 for cases where XVAR equals 5 (the expression is true).
• When the expression is false or missing, the value of YVAR remains unchanged. If YVAR has not been previously defined, it contains the system-missing value.

Example

```
IF (SEX EQ 'F') EEOVAR=QUOTA+SVAR.
```

• The logical expression tests string variable SEX for the value 'F'.
• When the expression is true (when SEX equals F), the value of numeric variable EEOVAR is assigned the value of QUOTA plus SVAR. Both QUOTA and SVAR must be previously defined numeric variables.
• When the expression is false or missing (for example, if SEX equals F), the value of EEOVAR remains unchanged. If EEOVAR has not been previously defined, it contains the system-missing value.

Example

```
COMPUTE SVAR=0.
IF ((QVAR-RVAR) LE 7))SVAR=QVAR**2.
IF (ABS(A-C) LT 100)INT=100.
```

• COMPUTE assigns SVAR the value 0.
• The logical expression tests whether QVAR minus RVAR is less than or equal to 7. If it is, the value of SVAR is assigned the value of QVAR squared. Otherwise, the value of SVAR remains at 0.
• The second IF command tests whether the absolute value of variable A minus variable C is less than 100. If it is, INT is assigned the value 100. Otherwise, the value is unchanged or, if INT has not been previously defined, system-missing.

C

Command Reference

Example
```
IF (SYSMIS(QVAR)) RVAR=0.
COM VALID=0.
IF (NOT(SYSMIS(VARA))) VALID=1.
```

- The first IF command tests whether QVAR is system-missing. If it is, RVAR is assigned the value 0. Otherwise RVAR is unchanged, or system-missing if RVAR has not been previously defined.
- COMPUTE assigns variable VALID a value of 0.
- The next IF command tests whether VARA is not system-missing. For each case where VARA contains a valid value (is not system-missing), the value of VALID is set to 1. For each case that contains a system-missing value for VARA, the value of VALID equals 0.
- The example takes advantage of spelling permitted by three-character truncation of keywords.

Example
```
IF (STATE EQ 'IL' AND CITY EQ 13) COST=COST + .07 * COST.
```

- The logical expression tests whether STATE equals IL and CITY equals 13.
- If the logical expression is true, numeric variable COST is assigned the original value of COST plus 7% of the original value of COST ($1.07 \times$ COST).
- For any other value of STATE or CITY, the value of COST remains unchanged.

Example
```
IF (VALUE(VARA) GT 0) QVAR=AVAR*BVAR.
```

- The logical expression tests whether the value of VARA is greater than 0. If it is, QVAR is assigned the value of AVAR times BVAR. This test will be true even if VARA is user-missing, provided that it is greater than 0.
- For values less than or equal to 0, QVAR remains unchanged.
- For system-missing values, QVAR remains unchanged.

Example
```
IF (QVAR EQ 'ok') AVAR='fine'.
```

- The new string variable AVAR is set to 'fine' when the value of QVAR is 'ok'.
- AVAR has format width of four characters.
- When QVAR is not equal to 'ok', AVAR is defined as a four-column blank field.

Example
```
IF (RECV GT DUE OR (REVNUES GE EXPNS AND BALNCE GT
0))STATUS='SOLVENT'.
```

- The IF command specifies a complex logical expression.
- First, SPSS/PC+ tests whether REVNUES is greater than or equal to EXPNS and whether BALNCE is greater than 0.
- Second, SPSS/PC+ evaluates if RECV is greater than DUE.
- If either of these expressions is true, STATUS is assigned the value 'SOLVENT'.
- If both expressions are false, STATUS remains unchanged. If STATUS has not been previously defined, it is defined as a seven-column blank field.

IMPORT

```
IMPORT FILE='filename' [/KEEP={ALL     }] [/DROP=varlist]
                              {varlist}
```

```
       [/RENAME=(old varlist=new varlist)...] [/MAP]
```

Example:

```
IMPORT FILE='NEWDATA.POR'
  /RENAME=(ID,SEX,AGE=V1 TO V3)
  /MAP.
```

Overview   IMPORT reads a portable ASCII data file and dictionary produced by the EXPORT command in SPSS/PC, SPSS/PC+ or SPSS. You can download files from SPSS on a mainframe to your IBM PC using KERMIT, provided KERMIT is installed on both the mainframe and the PC.

Defaults   IMPORT reads all data and dictionary information for all cases on the portable file. The data dictionary contains the variable and value labels, missing-value flags, and print formats for each variable on the portable file. The file also contains a message with the name, release, and version of the originating software, and the date and time the portable file was created. When the file originates from SPSS, it also includes the file label and the name of the originating installation. SPSS/PC+ assumes that the file is in the current directory.

Tailoring   You can import a subset of variables from the portable file, and you can rename the imported variables. You can also obtain a listing of the imported variables. You can read a portable file from a floppy disk.

Syntax   • The minimum specification on IMPORT is a file specification.

• Subcommands can be named in any order and must be separated by a slash.

Operations   • IMPORT causes SPSS/PC+ to read the data from the portable file.

• Most IBM/PC editors are unable to read a portable file.

• The portable data file and dictionary become the SPSS/PC+ active file.

• You cannot import a portable file directly from a directory other than your current directory on the hard disk. You can import a portable file from a floppy diskette.

• The SPSS/PC+ active file has a more restrictive dictionary than mainframe versions of SPSS. SPSS/PC+ IMPORT changes the dictionary to conform to internal conventions. In particular, if the SPSS file defined a range of missing values for a variable, only the bottom of the range is defined in SPSS/PC+.

• A file saved with weighting in effect automatically uses the case weights when the file is read.

Limitations   • You may not have enough available memory on your PC to read a portable file produced by SPSS on a mainframe. When you produce portable files on a mainframe for use on a PC, you should include only the variables you need for particular SPSS/PC+ sessions.

• You can import a file with up to 200 variables. Each 8-character portion of a long string variable counts as one variable.

Example
```
IMPORT FILE='NEWDATA.POR'
  /RENAME=(ID,SEX,AGE=V1 TO V3)
  /MAP.
```

• The portable file is read from NEWDATA.POR in the current directory.

• Variables ID, SEX, and AGE are renamed V1, V2, and V3 in the active file. Their names are unchanged on the portable file on NEWDATA.POR. None of the other variables read into the SPSS/PC+ active file are renamed.

• The MAP subcommand requests a listing of variables on the active file.

C

Command Reference

FILE Subcommand

The FILE subcommand specifies the name of the file that contains the portable file.

- The filename must be enclosed in apostrophes.
- You cannot specify a path on the IMPORT command. The portable file must be in your current directory, if any, for the drive on which it resides.
- You can use a portable file stored on a floppy diskette.

Example

```
IMP FIL='SALDATA.NOV'.
```

- The portable file is read from SALDATA.NOV in the current directory.
- This example takes advantage of spelling permitted by three-character truncation of keywords.

DROP and KEEP Subcommands

Use the DROP and KEEP subcommands to import a subset of variables from the portable file.

- DROP excludes a variable or list of variables from the active file. All variables not named on DROP are included.
- KEEP names a variable or list of variables to be included in the active file. All variables not named are excluded.
- Variables can be specified on DROP or KEEP in any order.
- With the DROP subcommand, the order of variables remaining on the active file is the same as their order on the portable file.
- With KEEP, the order of variables on the active file is the order in which they are named on KEEP. Thus, you can use KEEP to reorder variables.
- You can use both DROP and KEEP on the same IMPORT command, provided they do not name any of the same variables.
- You can use the TO keyword to specify consecutive variables on the portable file.
- The portable file is not affected by specifying DROP or KEEP on the IMPORT command.

Example

```
IMPORT FILE='NEWSUM.EXP'
 /DROP=DEPT79 TO DEPT81.
```

- The portable file is read from NEWSUM.EXP in the current directory.
- Variables between and including DEPT79 and DEPT81 are excluded from the active file. All other variables are on the active file.

RENAME Subcommand

Use the RENAME subcommand to rename variables being read from the portable file. The renamed variables retain the variable and value labels, missing-value flags, and print formats assigned in the session where the portable file was created.

- To rename a variable, specify the name of the variable in the active file, an equals sign, and the new name.
- The equals sign is required.
- You can specify lists of variables on both sides of the equals sign. The number of variables on both sides must be the same, and the entire specification must be enclosed in parentheses.
- You can use the TO convention for both variable lists (see Universals: Variable-Naming Conventions).

Example
```
IMPORT FILE='NEWSUM.POR'
  /DROP=DEPT79 TO DEPT81
  /RENAME=(DEPT82,SALARY82=DEPT,SALARY).
```

- The RENAME subcommand renames DEPT82 and SALARY82 to DEPT and SALARY.
- DEPT and SALARY retain the variable and value labels, missing-value flags, and print formats assigned to DEPT82 and SALARY82.

MAP Subcommand

If you use the RENAME, DROP, or KEEP subcommands to tailor your file, you may find it helpful to produce a listing of your changes with the MAP subcommand.

- The MAP subcommand can be specified as often as you wish.
- The MAP subcommand produces a listing of all actions taken *up to that point.*
- When the MAP subcommand is last, it produces a listing of the contents of the new active file.

Example
```
IMPORT FILE='NEWSUM.POR'
  /DROP=DEPT79 TO DEPT81
  /MAP
  /RENAME(DEPT82=DEPT SALARY82=SALARY)
  /MAP.
```

- The first MAP subcommand produces a listing of the variables after DROP has excluded the specified variables.
- The RENAME subcommand renames DEPT82 and SALARY82.
- The second MAP subcommand shows the variables after renaming. Since this is the last subcommand specified, it displays the variables that are contained in the active file.

SPSS Portable Files

SPSS EXPORT command writes a portable file that is read by a number of different mainframe computers as well SPSS/PC+. SPSS/PC+ uses a more restrictive dictionary than SPSS. If you are creating a portable file in SPSS that will be read by SPSS/PC+, keep the following in mind:

- After reading 200 variables, SPSS/PC+ stops processing variables. You can avoid this problem by dropping variables when you create the portable file, so that the portable file contains 200 or fewer variables.
- SPSS/PC+ only allows one missing-value flag per variable and accepts only the first of multiple missing-value declarations. You can override missing-value declarations prior to creating the portable file with SPSS.
- SPSS/PC+ prints values in one of the following formats: DOLLARw.d, COMMAw.d, Aw, or Fw.d. SPSS offers additional formats, which SPSS/PC+ attempts to translate. If the translation doesn't meet your purposes, you can change the print format of variables with the FORMAT command.

C

Command Reference

INCLUDE

```
{INCLUDE 'filename'}
{@filename        }
```

Examples:

```
INCLUDE '\MASTER\SET.CMD'.

INCLUDE 'DEFINE.INC'.

@CODEBOOK.RUN.
```

Overview

The INCLUDE command allows you to execute SPSS/PC+ commands from a file. With INCLUDE, you can prepare an entire session with your editor and leave SPSS/PC+ to execute unattended, as in batch-type processing. You can also use INCLUDE to execute all the file definition commands (such as DATA LIST and labeling commands) and then execute analysis commands interactively.

Another use for INCLUDE is to execute a "profile" for your machine configuration. For example, you can create a file containing a SET command that specifies printer characters, a prompt, and page size, and then include that file in any SPSS/PC+ session. A "profile" like this will be executed *automatically* when you enter SPSS/PC+ if you have named it SPSSPROF.INI and saved it in either your current directory (the one from which you work) or the directory in which the SPSS/PC+ system is saved.

You can nest INCLUDE commands so that one set of included commands includes another set of commands. This "nesting" can go five levels deep.

Syntax

• The only specification for INCLUDE is a filename enclosed in single quotes.

• You can include a file from another directory by using a fully qualified filename.

• The character @ is accepted as an alias for the INCLUDE command. With this form, the filename does not need to be in single quotes, although it can be. The space between @ and the filename is optional.

• You can use more than one INCLUDE command in a session, either in a series or nested.

• If you include a file of inline data, the first line of the data file must contain the BEGIN DATA command. The END DATA command can be specified as the last line of the included file or with your SPSS/PC+ commands.

Operations

• INCLUDE is an operation command and is executed immediately.

• INCLUDE identifies a file containing SPSS/PC+ commands that may include inline data.

• By default, each command from the INCLUDE file is displayed on your screen as it is processed. You can suppress this display by using the INCLUDE OFF specification on SET.

• Both the INCLUDE command and commands from the included file are copied to the LOG file. The INCLUDE command is executable from the LOG file. The commands from the included file are prefaced with an open bracket ([). These commands are treated as comments and are not executable. Thus, if you use the LOG file in a subsequent session, the INCLUDE command is read from the LOG file and the included commands are read from the original file. The included commands are executed only once.

• If an INCLUDE file contains a FINISH command, the SPSS/PC+ session ends and you are returned to DOS. No subsequent SPSS/PC+ commands are processed.

Limitations

• SPSS/PC+ will process only up to five levels of nested included files at a time.

• Only the first 80 characters of an included file are read. For data files with a record length exceeding 80 characters, you must use the FILE subcommand on DATA LIST. Command files can never have a record length longer than 80 characters.

Example   INCLUDE '\MASTER\SET.CMD'.

INCLUDE 'DEFINE.INC'.

@CODEBOOK.RUN.

• The first INCLUDE command processes the commands in file SET.CMD in directory \MASTER. SET.CMD contains the following:

```
SET DISK=ON
  /LENGTH=59
  /BOXST='-|+'
  /BEEP OFF.
```

• The second INCLUDE command processes commands in file DEFINE.INC in the current directory. DEFINE.INC contains the following:

```
DATA LIST FILE='CURRENT.DAT' /
   MONTH 1-2 (A) DAY 3-4 TEMP 6-7 PRESSURE 8-12 (2) WINSPED
13-14.
MISSING VALUE DAY (99) / WINSPED (-1).
INCLUDE 'TRANSFOR.INC'.
```

• DEFINE.INC includes another INCLUDE command, which processes commands in file TRANSFOR.INC from the current directory. TRANSFOR.INC contains some data transformation commands. This is an example of a nested INCLUDE.

• The next command (@) is the abbreviated form of INCLUDE. Since the quotation marks and the space separating the command from the filename are optional with this form, they are omitted here. Commands are read from file CODEBOOK.RUN in the current directory. CODEBOOK.RUN contains the following commands:

```
FREQ VAR=ALL
  /HBAR.
DESC VAR=ALL.
```

JOIN

```
[JOIN]  {MATCH}
        {ADD  }

 /{FILE }={file specification}
  {TABLE} {*                  }

 [/KEEP=varlist ]

 [/DROP=varlist ]

 [/RENAME (old varlist=new varlist) [(old varlist=...)]]

 /FILE=...
    ...

 [/FILE=...   ]
    ...

 [/MAP]

 [/BY=varlist]
```

Example:

```
JOIN MATCH FILE='UPDATE.SYS'
 /RENAME=(NEWPHONE,NEWID = PHONE,ID)
 /FILE='MASTER.SYS'
 /BY ID.
```

Overview   JOIN permits you to combine two or more system files. With keyword MATCH you can make parallel or nonparallel matches between different files or perform table lookups. With keyword ADD you can add more cases to an existing file. JOIN works with SPSS/PC+ system files created with the SAVE command or optionally with the current active file.

JOIN combines files to produce a new *active file*. Statistical procedures following JOIN use this combined file unless you replace it by building another active file. You must use the SAVE command if you want to write the combined file to disk as a system file.

Defaults   By default, all variables from all input files are included in the new active file.

Tailoring   **Variable Selection.** You can choose which variables from each input file will be retained on the new active file.

Variable Names. You can rename variables on each input file before joining the files. This permits you to join variables that are the same but whose names differ on different input files or to distinguish different variables whose names are the same on different input files.

Variable Map. You can request a map showing all the variables on the new active file, their order, and the input file(s) from which they came.

Syntax   • The minimum specification is keyword MATCH or ADD and two or more FILE subcommands specifying the names of files to be joined.

• With keyword MATCH, a TABLE subcommand can be used instead of one of the FILE subcommands.

• With MATCH or ADD, an asterisk can be substituted for one filename to indicate the active file.

• The first specification must be either MATCH or ADD.

• The command name JOIN is optional. MATCH is accepted as an alias for JOIN MATCH, and ADD is accepted as an alias for JOIN ADD.

• Subcommands are separated by slashes.

- The RENAME, KEEP, and DROP subcommands apply only to variables in the file named on the immediately preceding FILE or TABLE subcommand. They can be repeated after each FILE or TABLE subcommand.
- The BY subcommand can only be specified once. It must follow all other subcommands except MAP.
- The MAP subcommand can be placed anywhere and repeated as desired.

Operations

- JOIN causes all input files named on the FILE or TABLE subcommands to be read and builds a new active file that replaces any active file created earlier in the session.
- Keywords MATCH and ADD, which are mutually exclusive, determine the type of processing.
- If the active file is named as an input file, any N and SAMPLE commands you have specified are applied to the active file before files are joined.
- The PROCESS IF command has no effect on JOIN.

Limitations

- Maximum 5 files total can be specified on the FILE and TABLE subcommands.
- Maximum 1 TABLE subcommand specifying 1 table file.
- Maximum 10 variables on the BY subcommand. Each 8-character portion of a long string variable counts as 1 toward this limit.
- JOIN creates only uncompressed active files.

Keyword MATCH

In general, use MATCH to combine two or more files containing the same cases but different variables.

- Unless you specify otherwise, the new active file will contain all variables from all input files.
- The new active file will contain all cases that are in any of the input files named on FILE subcommands.
- When two or more files have a variable with the same name, values in the resulting file are taken from the file named first in the JOIN command, even if they are missing in that file. Dictionary information for that variable is taken from the first file for which the variable has either value labels, a variable label, or a declared missing value.
- Cases that are absent from one of the input files will be assigned missing values for variables that exist only in that file.
- If you do not enter a BY subcommand, SPSS/PC+ performs a "parallel" or sequential match, combining the first case from each file, then the second case from each file, and so on, without regard to any identifying values that may be present.
- The BY subcommand specifies that cases should be joined according to a common value on one or more "key" variables present in all input files. All input files must be sorted in ascending order of the key variables.
- When you use the BY subcommand with MATCH, one of the input files can be specified on a TABLE subcommand to indicate that it is a *table lookup* file.

Example

```
MATCH FILE='PART1.SYS'
  /FILE='PART2.SYS'
  /FILE=*.
```

- MATCH is used here as an alias for JOIN MATCH.
- This example combines three files (the active file and two system files) in a parallel match. Cases are combined according to their order in each file.
- The new active file will contain as many cases as are in the largest of the three input files.
- If the same variable name is used in more than one input file, data are taken from the file listed first: PART1.SYS, then PART2.SYS, and then the active file.

BY Subcommand with MATCH

When used with MATCH, the BY subcommand specifies one or more identification or "key" variables that determine which cases are to be combined. BY is required unless all input files are to be matched simply according to the order of cases.

- BY must be entered after all other file specifications. Only the MAP subcommand, which requests optional output, can follow BY.
- Specifications for the BY subcommand consist of the names of one or more *key variables*. The maximum is 10 keys.
- Key variables must be present in all input files.
- All input files must be sorted by the key variable(s), in ascending order. If necessary, use SORT CASES before JOIN.
- Missing values on key variables are handled like any other values.
- String variables are permitted on the BY subcommand. Each 8-character portion of a long string variable counts as 1 toward the limit of 10 key variables. A 16-character string counts as 2 toward the limit, while a 17-character string counts as 3.
- Unmatched cases are assigned system-missing values (in numeric variables) or blanks (in string variables) for variables from the files that do not contain a match.
- A message informs you if two or more cases from any input file have identical values for the key variable(s). Only one such message is generated, regardless of the number of duplicates encountered, since duplicate keys are expected in many applications.

Table Lookup

A *table file* for a MATCH operation is an input file whose cases are not to be added to the output file. Instead, variables from a table file are added to whatever cases are taken from the other input file(s).

- A table file is identified on the TABLE subcommand.
- The BY subcommand naming the key variable or variables according to which data can be "looked up" is required to process a table file.
- Only one table file can be specified on any JOIN command.
- A table file cannot contain cases with duplicate values for the key variable(s).

Duplicate Cases

Duplicate cases have the same values for the key variable(s) named on the BY subcommand. If no BY subcommand is specified, the question of duplicate cases does not arise.

- Duplicate cases are permitted in any input files except table files.
- When there is no table file, the first case in each file from a group of duplicates is joined with the first matching case (if any) from the other files; the second duplicate case is matched with a second matching duplicate, if any, and so on. In effect, a parallel (sequential) match is performed within groups of duplicate cases. Unmatched cases are assigned system-missing values (in numeric variables) or blanks (in string variables) for the variables from the absent files.
- When a table file is specified, data from the table file are added to *all* cases in the other files with matching values for the BY variable(s).

Keyword ADD

In general, use keyword ADD to combine two or more files containing different cases but the same variables.

- Unless you specify the BY subcommand (see below), the resulting file contains all cases from the first-named input file first, followed by all cases from the second input file, and so on.
- The number of cases in the new active file is the sum of the number of cases in all the input files. No cases are combined.
- The cases in the new active file contain all variables that appear in *any* input files. Cases from files without all the variables will have system-missing values (numeric variables) or blanks (string variables) for the extra variables.
- You cannot use the TABLE subcommand to specify an input file for ADD.

Example
```
JOIN ADD FILE='JAN.SYS'
    /FILE='FEB.SYS'
    /FILE='MAR.SYS'
    /FILE=*.
```

- This example combines cases from three system files saved previously on disk and from the current active file.
- Cases from JAN.SYS will be first in the new active file, followed by cases from FEB.SYS, then MAR.SYS, and then cases from the file that was active prior to the JOIN command.

BY Subcommand with ADD

If all input files are sorted by some variable, you can use the BY subcommand to interleave cases from the different files according to the values of that variable.

- All input files must be sorted in ascending order of the BY variable.
- You can specify up to 10 variables on the BY subcommand. Each 8-character portion of a long string variable counts as 1 toward this limit.
- A message informs you if two or more cases from any input file have identical values for the key variable(s). Only one such message is generated, regardless of the number of duplicates encountered, since duplicate keys are expected in many applications.
- Cases with identical values on the BY variable(s) are arranged in the order you name their input files.

Example
```
ADD FILE='SAMPLE1.SYS'
    /FILE=*
    /BY DATE.
```

- This example uses ADD as an alias for JOIN ADD.
- Cases from the system file SAMPLE1.SYS are interleaved with cases from the current active file in ascending order of their values for DATE.
- If cases have the same value for DATE, those from SAMPLE1.SYS will precede those from the current active file.

FILE Subcommand

The FILE subcommand identifies each input file (except a table file) for either a MATCH or an ADD operation.

- A maximum of five files total can be specified on the FILE and TABLE subcommands.
- Specifications on the FILE subcommand consist of either a filename in apostrophes or an asterisk to refer to the current active file.
- With MATCH, the order in which files are named on FILE subcommands determines the order of variables on the new active file. In addition, the order in which files are named determines which input file is used as the source for variables that can be taken from more than one input file (they are taken from the file named first).
- With ADD, the order in which files are named determines the order of cases in the new file (unless the BY subcommand is used).

TABLE Subcommand

One of the input files for a MATCH can be specified as a table file by entering its name on the TABLE subcommand instead of the FILE subcommand.

- A table file contributes variables, not cases, to the new active file.
- The BY subcommand is required when you specify a table file.
- A table file cannot contain duplicate cases (cases for which the key variable(s) have identical values).
- Variables from a table file are added to *all* of the cases from other file(s) that match on the key variable(s).

Example

```
JOIN MATCH FILE=*
  /TABLE='MASTER.SYS'
  /BY EMP_ID.
```

- This command adds variables from the system file MASTER.SYS to the current file, matching cases by the variable EMP_ID.
- No new cases are added to the current file as a result of the table lookup.
- Cases whose value for EMP_ID is not included in the table MASTER.SYS are assigned system-missing values for variables taken from the table.

RENAME Subcommand

Use the RENAME command to rename variables on the input files *before* they are processed by JOIN.

- Input system files are not changed on disk; only the copy of the file being joined is affected.
- RENAME applies only to the immediately preceding FILE or TABLE subcommand. To rename variables from more than one input file, enter a RENAME subcommand after each FILE or TABLE subcommand.
- Specifications for RENAME consist of a left parenthesis, a list of old variable names, an equals sign, a list of new variable names, and a right parenthesis. The two variable lists must have the same number of variables.
- You can enter more than one such specification, each enclosed in its parentheses, on a single RENAME subcommand.
- You can enter more than one RENAME subcommand for a single input file. Renaming variables is *not* cumulative: "old" variable names are always those on the input files, regardless of any previous RENAME subcommands.
- RENAME takes effect immediately. Any KEEP and DROP subcommands entered prior to a RENAME must use the old names, while KEEP and DROP subcommands entered after a RENAME must use the new names.
- The new name must be unique within that input file.
- All specifications within a single set of parentheses take effect simultaneously: the specification RENAME (A,B = B,A) is legal and swaps the names of the two variables.
- You can use RENAME to correct a situation where a key variable has different names on different input files. Since BY must be entered last, it always uses the new name of a key variable.
- The TO convention for variable lists is *not* valid on the RENAME subcommand.

Example

```
JOIN MATCH FILE='UPDATE.SYS'
  /RENAME=(NEWPHONE, NEWID = PHONE, ID)
  /FILE='MASTER.SYS'
  /BY ID.
```

- This example matches a master system file (MASTER.SYS) with an update system file (UPDATE.SYS).
- Two variables on UPDATE.SYS are renamed prior to the match. NEWPHONE is renamed PHONE to combine it with variable PHONE on the master file. NEWID is renamed ID so that it will have the same name as the identification variable in the master file and can be used on the BY subcommand.
- The BY subcommand ensures that only cases with the same ID will be joined.

DROP and KEEP Subcommands

Use DROP and KEEP to include only a subset of variables on the new active file. DROP specifies a set of variables to exclude, and KEEP specifies a set of variables to retain. One or the other will probably be easier to use, depending on how many variables you are excluding or keeping.

- Specifications consist of a list of variables on the input file separated by spaces or commas.
- DROP and KEEP apply only to the immediately preceding FILE or TABLE subcommand.

- The TO convention for variable lists is *not* valid on DROP or KEEP.
- KEEP does not affect the order of variables on the new active file. Variables that are kept retain their original order.

Example
```
MATCH FILE='THIS.SYS'
 /RENAME (ONE_VAR,TWO_VAR = VAR1,VAR2)
 /KEEP=ID,VAR1,VAR2
 /FILE='THAT.SYS'
 /KEEP=ID,ONE,TWO
 /RENAME (ONE,TWO = VAR1,VAR2)
 /BY ID.
```

- This example uses MATCH as an alias for JOIN MATCH.
- For the first file (THIS.SYS), the KEEP subcommand follows RENAME and therefore must use the new names.
- For the second file (THAT.SYS), the KEEP subcommand precedes the RENAME and therefore must use the old names.
- After the RENAME subcommands, each input file has variables named VAR1 and VAR2. These variables will therefore be combined, taking data from THIS.SYS for all cases present in that file and from THAT.SYS for cases absent in THIS.SYS.

Example
```
JOIN ADD FILE='SAMPLE1.SYS'
 /RENAME (SCALE=SCALE1)
 /FILE='SAMPLE2.SYS'
 /RENAME (SCALE=SCALE2)
 /FILE=*
 /RENAME (SCALE=SCALE3)
 /DROP=TEMP1 TEMP2 TEMP3
 /BY DATE.
```

- In this example, RENAME is used to give *different* names to variables that would otherwise be combined.
- The DROP subcommand lists each variable individually since the TO convention is not valid.
- The new active file will be sorted by DATE, assuming that each of the three input files is already sorted by DATE.

MAP Subcommand

The MAP subcommand produces a map showing which variables are on the new active file and from what file or files they may be taken.

- More than one MAP subcommand can be entered as part of a single JOIN command.
- MAP can be specified anywhere on the JOIN command. However, the map will reflect only the subcommands that precede the MAP subcommand.
- To obtain a map of the new active file in its final state, specify MAP last.

C

Command Reference

LIST

```
LIST [[VARIABLES=]{ALL**  }]
                  {varlist}

     [/CASES=[FROM {1**}] [TO {eof**}] [BY {1**}] ]
                   {n  }       {n   }      {n  }

     [/FORMAT=[{UNNUMBERED**}] [{WRAP**}] [WEIGHT] ]
               {NUMBERED    }   {SINGLE}
```

**Default if subcommand is omitted.

Example:
```
LIST VARIABLES=XVAR AVAR
  /CASES=FROM 10 TO 100 BY 2.
```

Overview   The LIST procedure displays the values of variables for cases in the active file.

Defaults   By default, all user-defined variables are listed for all cases in the active file. The listing for each case uses as many lines as needed.

Tailoring   You can specify a list of variables and request that the listing be numbered. You can also limit the listing to a particular sequence of cases. In addition, you can list values of system variables for each case in the active file and limit each case listing to a single line.

Syntax   • The minimum specification is simply the command keyword.

                  • All subcommands are optional.

                  • A subcommand or its abbreviation may not be recognized as such if a variable name is identical to it, unless the subcommand is followed by an equals sign.

                  • Subcommands can be specified in any order and are separated by slashes.

Operations   • LIST causes the data to be read.

                  • LIST uses the dictionary print formats (see Universals: Formats).

                  • If a value is longer than the format, the decimal portion will be rounded. If that fails, asterisks (*) are displayed.

                  • The LIST display uses the width specified on SET.

                  • If a long string variable cannot be listed within the page width, it is truncated.

                  • Values of the variables listed for a case are always separated by at least one blank.

                  • System-missing values are listed as a period (.).

                  • For case listings that fit on one line, the column width for each variable is determined by the length of the variable name or the format, whichever is greater. If the variable names do not fit on one line, they are displayed vertically.

                  • If case listings require more than one line, they are wrapped. LIST displays a table illustrating the location of the variables in the listing and prints the name of the first variable in each line at the beginning of the line.

                  • Each execution of LIST begins at the top of a new page.

                  • System variables will not be displayed unless explicitly requested.

Limitations   • Maximum 1 each of the VARIABLES, CASES, and FORMAT subcommands.

Example   ```
                  LIST VARIABLES=XVAR AVAR
                    /CASES=FROM 10 TO 100 BY 2.
                  ```

                  • This example produces a list of every second case starting with Case 10 and stopping at 100 for variables XVAR and AVAR.
                  ```

VARIABLES Subcommand

By default, all user-defined variables in the active file are listed. The optional VARIABLES subcommand allows you to limit the listing to variables you specify or to specify the default explicitly with keyword ALL.

• Variables named on VARIABLES must already exist.

• Variables are listed in the order they are named.

• If a variable is named more than once, it is listed more than once.

• The actual keyword VARIABLES is optional.

• You cannot enter the VARIABLES subcommand without specifications.

ALL   *List all user-defined variables.* Variables are listed in the order in which they appear in the active file. This is the default if the VARIABLES subcommand is omitted.

CASES Subcommand

By default, all cases in the active file are listed. Use the CASES subcommand to limit the number and pattern of cases listed.

• If you omit CASES or include it with no specifications, all cases in the file are listed.

• Defaults that you do not change remain in effect.

The following may be specified on CASES:

FROM n   *The case number of the first case to be listed.* The default is 1.

TO n   *Upper limit on the cases to be listed.* The default is the end of the active file. CASES 100 is interpreted as CASES TO 100.

BY n   *Increment used to choose cases for listing.* The default is 1.

FORMAT Subcommand

The default display does not number cases and uses more than one line per case if necessary. Use the optional FORMAT subcommand to change the defaults.

• If you omit the FORMAT subcommand or use it without any specifications, the default display is produced.

• Defaults that you do not change remain in effect.

The following specifications are available for FORMAT:

NUMBERED   *Include the sequence number of each case in the listing.* The sequence number is displayed to the left of the values listed. The default is UNNUMBERED.

SINGLE   *Limit each case listing to one line.* If the variables requested do not fit on a single line, LIST is not executed. The default is WRAP.

WEIGHT   *List the value of the case's weight in the active file.*

C

Command Reference

MEANS

```
MEANS [TABLES=] {varlist} BY varlist [BY varlist ...] [/varlist...]
                {ALL    }

       [/OPTIONS=option numbers]

       [/STATISTICS={statistic numbers}]
                    {ALL             }
```

Options:

1 Include user-missing values
2 Exclude cases with user-missing dependent values
3 Suppress all labels
5 Suppress group counts
6 Display group sums
7 Suppress group standard deviations
8 Suppress value labels
9 Suppress independent variable names
10 Suppress independent variable values
11 Suppress group means
12 Display group variances

Statistics:

1 One-way analysis of variance
2 Test of linearity

Example:

```
MEANS TABLES=VAR1 TO VAR5 BY GROUP
   /OPTIONS=9
   /STATISTICS=1.
```

Overview

MEANS displays means, standard deviations, and group counts for a dependent variable within groups defined by one or more independent variables. Other SPSS/PC+ procedures that display univariate statistics are FREQUENCIES and DESCRIPTIVES.

Defaults

By default, MEANS displays means, standard deviations, and number of cases. The default table is labeled with the variable name and label of the dependent and independent variables. Groups are labeled with the variable name, variable label, values, and value labels of the independent variables. Cases that have missing values on any variables that define a table are excluded from the statistics calculated for that table.

Tailoring

Display Format. You can suppress the display of all variable and value labels, value labels only, names of independent variables, and values of independent variables.

Statistical Display. Statistical display options allow you to display group sums and variances or to suppress group counts, group standard deviations, and group means. A one-way analysis of variance and a test of linearity are also available.

Missing Values. You can include cases with user-missing values on the dependent or independent variables. Alternatively, you can include cases with user-missing values on the independent variable only.

Syntax

- The minimum specification is a TABLES subcommand with a tables list. The actual keyword TABLES may be omitted.
- The minimum tables list specifies a dependent variable, the keyword BY, and an independent variable.
- Subcommands are separated by slashes.

Operations

- MEANS causes the data to be read.
- MEANS displays requested univariate statistics for the population as a whole and for each value of the first independent variable defined for the table in addition to statistics for groups.

• If an independent variable is a long string, only the short-string portion is used to identify groups in the analysis.

• Specifying a string variable as a dependent variable on any tables list stops execution of the MEANS procedure.

• Statistics are displayed with four decimal places where possible.

• The display uses the width defined on the SET command. If the statistics requested cannot fit within the available width, the command is not executed. You can use the OPTIONS subcommand to tailor the display to fit within the defined width.

Limitations

• The number of variables allowed per MEANS command is the same as the system limit.

• Maximum 250 tables can be produced.

• Maximum 30 TABLES subcommands.

• Maximum 1 each of the OPTIONS and STATISTICS subcommands.

• Maximum 6 dimensions (5 BY keywords) per TABLES subcommand.

• Maximum 200 value labels are displayed on any single table.

Example

```
MEANS TABLES=VAR1 TO VAR5 BY GROUP
    /OPTIONS=9
    /STATISTICS=1.
```

• In this example, the TABLES subcommand specifies that VAR1 through VAR5 are the dependent variables. GROUP is the independent variable.

• Assuming variables VAR2, VAR3, and VAR4 lie between VAR1 and VAR5 on the active file, five tables are produced: VAR1 by GROUP, VAR2 by GROUP, VAR3 by GROUP, and so on.

• Option 9 suppresses the display of variable name GROUP.

• Statistic 1 requests one-way analysis of variance tables of VAR1 through VAR5 by GROUP.

Example

```
MEA VARA BY VARB BY VARC / VAR1 VAR2 BY VAR3 VAR4 BY VAR5.
```

• This command contains two TABLES subcommands that omit the optional TABLES keyword.

• The first tables list requests one table. Statistics are produced for VARA within groups defined by each combination of values of VARB and VARC.

• The second tables list requests four tables: VAR1 by VAR3 by VAR5; VAR1 by VAR4 by VAR5; VAR2 by VAR3 by VAR5; and VAR2 by VAR4 by VAR5.

• This example takes advantage of spelling permitted by three-character truncation of keywords.

TABLES Subcommand

The TABLES subcommand specifies a tables list. The actual keyword TABLES may be omitted.

• The dependent variable is named first and must be numeric. The independent variables follow the BY keyword and can be numeric or string.

• You can specify more than one dependent variable in a tables list.

• Each use of the keyword BY in a tables list adds a dimension to the tables requested and introduces a new order of control among the independent variables.

• You can specify more than one independent variable in each dimension of a tables list.

• A table is built for each dependent variable by each combination of independent variables across dimensions.

• Each combination of values of the independent variables defined for a table defines a group.

- The order in which independent variables are displayed is the same as the order in which they are named. The values of the first independent variable defined for the table appear in the left-most column of the table and change most slowly in the definition of groups.
- You can use keyword ALL in each dimension to refer to all user-defined variables.
- You can specify multiple TABLES subcommands on a single MEANS command. The slash between the subcommands is required; the keyword is not.

Display Format

By default, MEANS displays the variable name and variable labels of both independent and dependent variables at the beginning of each table. Within the table, groups defined by the independent variables are identified by variable name, values, and value labels. Specify the following on the OPTIONS subcommand to change these defaults:

Option 3 *Suppress all labels.* No variable or value labels are displayed for either the independent or dependent variables.

Option 8 *Suppress value labels.* No value labels are displayed for the independent variables.

Option 9 *Suppress independent variable names.*

Option 10 *Suppress independent variable values.*

Statistical Display

By default, MEANS displays means, standard deviations, and number of cases. Statistics are displayed for groups and for the entire population. Specify the following on the OPTIONS and STATISTICS subcommands to change these defaults:

Option 5 *Suppress group counts.* The number of cases in each group is not displayed.

Option 6 *Display group sums.*

Option 7 *Suppress group standard deviations.*

Option 11 *Suppress group means.*

Option 12 *Display group variances.*

Statistic 1 *One-way analysis of variance including eta and eta^2.* The analysis of variance is performed for the first independent variable defined for the table only.

Statistic 2 *Test of linearity.* Produces a one-way analysis of variance in which the between-groups sum of squares is subdivided into linear and nonlinear components. Pearson's r and r^2 are displayed as part of the test of linearity. The analysis of variance is performed for the first independent variable defined for the table only, and the test of linearity is ignored if the independent variable is a string.

ALL *Display all statistics.* Produces the same display as Statistic 2. Specify ALL on the STATISTICS subcommand.

Example

```
MEANS TABLES=INCOME81 BY AGECAT BY SEX
    /STATISTICS=1.
```

- This example requests statistics for INCOME81 for groups defined by values of SEX within AGECAT.
- Statistic 1 requests an analysis of variance of INCOME81 by AGECAT.

Missing Values

By default, MEANS excludes cases that have missing values for any variables that define a table. You change the handling of missing values by specifying the following on the OPTIONS subcommand:

Option 1 *Include cases with user-missing values.* Cases with user-missing values on the independent or dependent variable are included.

Option 2 *Exclude cases with user-missing dependent values.* Cases with user-missing values for the dependent variable are excluded. Cases with user-missing values for independent variables are included.

MISSING VALUE

```
MISSING VALUE  {varlist}([value]) [[/]varlist ...]
               {ALL    }
```

Example:

```
MISSING VALUE XVAR (8) / YVAR ZVAR (0) / AVAR ('     ').
```

Overview   The MISSING VALUE command declares values for numeric and short string variables as user-missing. These values can then be treated specially in data transformations, statistical calculations, and case selection. By default, user-missing values are treated the same as the system-missing values. System-missing values are assigned automatically when no legal value can be assigned, as when input data for a numeric field are blank or when an illegal calculation is requested.

Syntax   • The minimum specification is a single variable followed by a value in parentheses.

• Each variable can have only one user-missing value.

• You can declare the same value as missing for more than one variable by specifying a variable list followed by the value in parentheses.

• You can declare different values as missing for different variables by specifying separate variable lists for each value. The slash between different specifications is optional.

• The missing-value specification must correspond to the variable type (numeric or string).

• You cannot assign missing values to long strings or system variables.

• Variable lists must have either all numeric or all string variables.

• Missing values for short string variables must be enclosed in apostrophes or quotation marks (see Universals: Strings).

• Keyword ALL can be used to refer to all user-defined variables in the active file provided the variables are either all numeric or all string.

• The TO keyword can be used to refer to consecutive variables on the active file.

• The missing-value specification for short string variables must include any leading or trailing blanks.

• More than one MISSING VALUE command can be specified per session.

Operations   • MISSING VALUE is a transformation command and is executed when the data are read for the next procedure.

• If a variable is mentioned more than once on one or more MISSING VALUE commands before a procedure, only the last specification is used.

• Missing-value specifications can be changed between procedures. New declarations replace previous ones.

• A variable list followed by an empty value specification (an empty set of parentheses) deletes any missing-value declarations for those variables.

• Missing-value declarations are saved in system files (see SAVE) and portable files (see EXPORT).

Example   ```
MISSING VALUE XVAR (8) / YVAR ZVAR (0) / AVAR ().
```

• Value 8 is declared missing for numeric variable XVAR.

• Value 0 is missing for numeric variables YVAR and ZVAR.

• Any previously declared missing values for AVAR are deleted by the empty value specification.

C

**Command Reference**
```

Example   `MIS VAL NAME1 TO NAME7 ('    ') / LIKE1 TO DLIKE7 (0).`

- Blanks are declared missing for the variables between and including NAME1 and NAME7. All these variables must be string variables four columns wide.
- The value 0 is declared missing for the variables between and including LIKE1 and DLIKE7. All variables in this list must be numeric.
- This example takes advantage of spelling permitted by three-character truncation of keywords.

MODIFY VARS

```
MODIFY VARS [/REORDER = [{FORWARD**}] [{POSITIONAL**}] [(varlist)]]
                        [{BACKWARD }] [{ALPHA       }] [(ALL**  ) ]


              [/DROP = varlist]    [/KEEP = {varlist}]
                                   [        {ALL**  }]

              [/RENAME = (old varlist = new varlist) [(...)] ]

              [/MAP]
```

**Default if subcommand is omitted.

Example:

```
MODIFY VARS
  /RENAME (V1 TO V3 = ID GROUP AGE)
  /MAP.
```

Overview

The MODIFY VARS command lets you change the names or the order of the variables in your active file or drop variables from your active file.

Syntax

- The minimum specification is any one subcommand.
- Subcommands can be entered in any order and must be separated by slashes.
- MAP is the only subcommand that can be entered more than once.
- Variable lists on all subcommands refer to the original variable names (before renaming) and the original variable order (before reordering).
- You cannot reorder, rename, or drop a system variable ($CASENUM, $WEIGHT, or $DATE).
- You cannot specify both DROP and KEEP.

Operations

- MODIFY VARS causes the data to be read if (and only if) you specify DROP, KEEP, or REORDER.
- Specifications on all subcommands use the original variable names and reference the original variable order. Thus, MODIFY VARS subcommands are *not* cumulative.
- Reordered or renamed variables retain variable labels, value labels, and missing-value and format specifications.
- MODIFY VARS affects your current active file. It does not affect any permanent disk file unless you use SAVE or some other command to write the file to disk.

Example

```
MODIFY VARS
  /RENAME (V1 TO V3 = ID GROUP AGE)
  /MAP.
```

- This example renames V1 to ID, V2 to GROUP, and V3 to AGE.
- SPSS/PC+ displays a map of the variable dictionary after renaming the three variables.

REORDER Subcommand

The REORDER subcommand allows you to change the order of the variables in your active file. This is useful in:

- Grouping related variables so you can refer to all of them together on other commands with the TO keyword.
- Simplifying the tabulation of variables in alphabetic or some other order.

The REORDER subcommand allows you to specify the *direction* of ordering, the *type* of ordering, and the *variables* to be ordered. You can enter one, two, or all three kinds of specification. If you enter more than one, you must enter the direction first, then the type, and then the variables.

Specify the direction of ordering with:

FORWARD   *For type POSITIONAL, the current order of variables in the active file. For type ALPHA, alphabetic order.* This is the default.

BACKWARD   *For type POSITIONAL, the opposite of the current order of variables in the active file. For type ALPHA, reverse alphabetic order.*

Specify the type of ordering with:

POSITIONAL   *The existing order of variables in the active file.* This is the default.

ALPHA   *Alphabetic order, according to the variable names in the input file.* (The RENAME subcommand has no effect on this order, even if it precedes the REORDER subcommand.) For variable names with numeric suffixes, such as V1 TO V100, ALPHA refers to the numeric order of the suffixes rather than to strict lexicographic order; thus, V9 precedes V10.

Specify the variables to be reordered in parentheses or specify ALL.

• The default is ALL.

• If you name one or more variables on REORDER, those variables are placed at the beginning of the new active file in the specified order. Variables not named are placed at the end of the new active file and retain their previous order among themselves.

Example   MODIFY VARS REORDER ALPHA (MAINE TO HAWAII)
    /MAP.

• This example arranges all of the variables from MAINE to HAWAII into alphabetic order.

After a variable list in parentheses, you can specify another direction and/or type of ordering and another variable list in parentheses, provided that the variable lists do not overlap. Variables named in the first set of parentheses precede those named in the second set of parentheses. Variables not named at all come at the end of the new active file.

Example   MODIFY VARS REORDER (ID SSNUMBER) ALPHA (GROUP TO SALARY).

• This example places ID and SSNUMBER at the beginning of the new active file. Since neither direction nor type of ordering is specified, the defaults FORWARD and POSITIONAL are used. Whichever of the two comes first in the old file will come first in the new file.

• After ID and SSNUMBER, all variables from GROUP to SALARY are arranged in alphabetic order by variable name.

• Any other variables in the file will come at the end of the new file, retaining their current order.

RENAME Subcommand

The RENAME subcommand allows you to assign new names to one or more variables in the active file.

• Specifications for RENAME consist of a list of existing variable names, an equals sign, and a list of new variable names (which must have as many names as the first list). All of these specifications must appear in parentheses.

• You can enter more than one set of parentheses containing old names, an equals sign, and new names on a RENAME subcommand.

• You cannot enter more than one RENAME subcommand on a MODIFY VARS command.

• All of the new names on a RENAME subcommand are assigned simultaneously. You can interchange variable names, as shown below.

• You can create a series of new names with numerical suffixes using the keyword TO, as shown below.

• SPSS/PC+ does *not* have to read the data to assign new names to variables.

Example   `MODIFY VARS RENAME (PLAN,ALTERNAT = ALTERNAT,PLAN)`
                            `(TASKA TO TASKJ = OLDJOB1 TO OLDJOB10)`
                            `(ALT1 TO ALT10 = TASKA TASKB TASKC TASKD`
                                           `TASKE TASKF TASKG TASKH`
                                           `TASKI TASKJ)`
       `/MAP.`

- This command switches the names of the two variables PLAN and ALTERNAT.
- Existing variables from TASKA to TASKJ are renamed as OLDJOB1, OLDJOB2, ..., OLDJOB10.
- Existing variables from ALT1 to ALT10 are renamed as TASKA, TASKB, ..., TASKJ. Note that TO cannot be used on this list of new variable names, since the new names do not have numeric suffixes.

KEEP Subcommand

The KEEP subcommand lets you specify which variables to retain in your active file. Reducing the number of variables in the active file speeds processing, saves the disk space used (temporarily) to hold the active file, and enables you to create additional variables without exceeding the system limit.

- After KEEP, enter the names of the variables you want to retain in the active file.
- KEEP is an alternative to DROP. Use whichever is easier, but not both.

DROP Subcommand

The DROP subcommand lets you specify which variables to drop from your active file. Reducing the number of variables in the active file speeds processing, saves the disk space used (temporarily) to hold the active file, and enables you to create additional variables without exceeding the system limit.

- After DROP, enter the names of the variables you want to drop from the active file.
- DROP is an alternative to KEEP. Use whichever is easier, but not both.

MAP Subcommand

The MAP subcommand displays a table showing the names and order of the variables in your file at the current point in the MODIFY VARS specifications and before you issued the MODIFY VARS command.

Use MAP to verify that MODIFY VARS has produced the results you expect.

- MODIFY VARS subcommands that you enter *after* MAP are not reflected in the table.
- You can use MAP more than once to see the state of the active file at different points in the MODIFY VARS specifications.
- You should normally place MAP at the end of the command, to see the "final" state of the new active file.

Example   `MODIFY VARS DROP ERR_1 TO ERR_40`
       `/RENAME (VSCORE MSCORE = SCOREV SCOREM)`
       `/MAP.`
    `MODIFY VARS`
       `/REORDER (ID DEPT) ALPHA (AREA TO EVAL87)`
       `/MAP.`

- Variables between ERR_1 and ERR_40 are dropped from the active file.
- The two variables VSCORE and MSCORE are renamed SCOREV and SCOREM. At this point, a table shows the results of the deletion and renaming of variables.
- The second MODIFY VARS command places ID and DEPT as the first two variables in the new file, followed by the variables between AREA and EVAL87 in alphabetic order, followed by any other variables in the file in their current order.
- A final table showing the names and order of variables in the new active file is displayed.

Two MODIFY VARS commands were required to alphabetize the variables using their new names since the REORDER subcommand uses the names as they existed prior to the command.

N

N n [ESTIMATED]

Example:

N 100.

Overview   The N command limits the number of cases in the active file to the first *n* cases. You can also use N with keyword ESTIMATED to provide SPSS/PC+ with information about the estimated number of cases in your data file. SPSS/PC+ uses the estimate to optimize use of memory. In this case, the number of cases processed is *not* limited to the estimated number.

Syntax   • The number of cases must be a positive integer.

• The N command keyword and the integer must be separated by at least one space.

• N can be entered at any point in an SPSS/PC+ session and can be used more than once.

• The keyword ESTIMATED is specified after the integer estimate of the number of cases.

Operations   • N is a transformation command and is executed when the data are read for the next procedure.

• N limits the number of cases analyzed by all subsequent procedures.

• Without the N command, SPSS/PC+ processes all cases.

• N controls the building of cases, not the reading of individual data records.

• SPSS/PC+ stops processing input data when N is reached. If keyword ESTIMATED is used, all input data are processed.

• Any SAMPLE, PROCESS IF, or SELECT IF commands are executed before cases are counted toward the limit specified on N.

• If N is specified more than once in an SPSS/PC+ session, each N command places a limit on the number of cases available for later procedures only if a new active file is created by data transformations. Otherwise, the eliminated cases are still on the active file and can be restored for subsequent procedures using the N command with a larger number.

• You cannot increase the size of the active file by specifying a value for N greater than the number of cases written to the active file. An active file is written when a raw data file is processed by a DATA LIST command and again when data transformations are processed.

• The keyword ESTIMATED allows SPSS/PC+ to optimize the allocation of memory for some procedures.

Example   N 100.

• This example limits the number of cases in the active file to the first 100 cases.

Example
```
DATA LIST FILE='INVENT.DAT' / ITEM1 TO ITEM30 1-60.
N 400 ESTIMATED.
FREQ VAR=ITEM24.
N 23.
SELECT IF (ITEM11 EQ 8).
LIST VAR=ITEM1, ITEM12 TO ITEM18, ITEM24.
```

• The DATA LIST command defines 30 variables in the file INVENT.DAT in the current directory.

• The N command with keyword ESTIMATED tells SPSS/PC+ to allocate memory for processing approximately 400 cases.

• The FREQUENCIES procedure produces a frequency table for ITEM24 that includes all cases.

- The second N command limits the number of cases in the active file to 23 after selecting cases that have a value of 8 for variable ITEM11, as specified on the subsequent SELECT IF command.
- The SELECT IF command causes a new active file to be created. Therefore, cases for which ITEM11 does not equal 8 and all cases beyond the 23rd case are lost to the session (unless the original active file is recreated with a new DATA LIST).
- LIST produces a listing of the values of ITEM1, ITEM24, and all variables between and including ITEM12 and ITEM18 for the remaining cases in the active file.

PLOT

```
PLOT [MISSING=[{PLOTWISE**}] [INCLUDE]]
                {LISTWISE }


    [/HSIZE={38**}]   [/VSIZE={16**}]
            {n   }            {n   }


    [/CUTPOINT={EVERY({1**})}]
              {      {n  }  }
              {value list   }


    [/SYMBOLS={ALPHANUMERIC**                        }]
              {NUMERIC                               }
              {'symbols'[,'overplot symbols']        }
              {X'hexsymbs'[,'overplot hexsymbs']}


    [/HORIZONTAL=['label'] [STANDARDIZE] [REFERENCE(vector)]]
                 [MIN(min)] [MAX(max)]
                 [UNIFORM]


    [/VERTICAL=['label'] [STANDARDIZE] [REFERENCE(vector)]]
               [MIN(min)] [MAX(max)]
               [UNIFORM]


    [/FORMAT={DEFAULT**        }]
             {CONTOUR[({10})]}
             {        {n }  }
             {OVERLAY         }
             {REGRESSION      }


    [/TITLE='title']

    /PLOT={varlist} WITH varlist [(PAIR)] [BY varname] [;varlist...]
          {ALL    }

    [/PLOT=...]
```

**Default if subcommand is omitted.

Example:
```
PLOT FORMAT=OVERLAY
  /SYMBOLS='MD'
  /VSIZE=12
  /HSIZE=60
  /TITLE='Marriage and Divorce Rates'
  /VERTICAL='Rates per 1000 population'
  /HORIZONTAL='Year' REFERENCE (1918, 1945)
                     MIN (1900) MAX (1983)
  /PLOT=MARRATE DIVRATE WITH YEAR.
```

Overview   Procedure PLOT produces two-dimensional line-printer plots, including simple
                bivariate scatterplots, scatterplots with a control variable, contour plots, and
                overlay plots. You can also request bivariate regression statistics. You can choose
                up to 36 ASCII or graphics symbols for the plot.

Defaults   By default, PLOT produces bivariate scatterplots within the page size specified on
                the SET command. Plots include all cases with valid values for both variables in
                the plot, with each symbol representing the count at that display position. The
                vertical and horizontal axes are labeled with variable labels. Default plot titles use
                either the names of the variables or type of plot requested.

Tailoring   **Types of Plots.** You can introduce a control variable for bivariate scatterplots or
                request regression plots with or without a control variable, contour plots, or
                overlay plots.

                Plot Format. You can specify a title for the plot, and you can scale and label the
                horizontal and vertical axes. You can request reference lines and plot standard-
                ized variables. You can also control the plot size and specify plotting symbols and
                the frequency they represent.

Missing Values. You can include cases with user-missing values and request that cases with missing values be deleted listwise from all plots named on the PLOT subcommand.

Syntax

- The minimum specification is the PLOT subcommand with a variable or variable list for the vertical (Y) axis, the keyword WITH, and a variable or variable list for the horizontal (X) axis.
- The PLOT subcommand can be specified more than once on a PLOT command.
- PLOT must be the last subcommand specified.
- Subcommands MISSING, VSIZE, HSIZE, CUTPOINT, and SYMBOLS apply to all plots requested and can be specified only once within any PLOT command. They must be entered *before* the final PLOT subcommand.
- Subcommands HORIZONTAL, VERTICAL, FORMAT, and TITLE can be specified more than once and apply only to the following PLOT subcommand.
- Subcommands are separated by slashes.

Operations

- PLOT causes the data to be read.
- The default plot frame size depends on the page size specified on SET. The HSIZE and VSIZE subcommands override the default plot size.
- A longer page length can produce longer default plots within the same width. A wider page does not produce a wider default plot unless the page length is changed accordingly.

Limitations

- No limitation on the number of plots requested.
- No limitation on the number of variables on a PLOT command.
- Maximum 20 overlay plots per FORMAT subcommand.
- Maximum 1 control variable per PLOT subcommand.
- Maximum 60 characters per TITLE subcommand.
- Maximum 36 symbols per SYMBOLS subcommand.
- Maximum 35 cutpoints per CUTPOINT subcommand.
- Maximum 10 reference points on each HORIZONTAL and VERTICAL subcommand.
- Maximum 40 characters per label on each HORIZONTAL and VERTICAL subcommand.
- Maximum 35 contour levels for each CONTOUR plot.

Example

```
PLOT FORMAT=OVERLAY
   /SYMBOLS='MD'
   /VSIZE=12
   /HSIZE=60
   /TITLE='Marriage and Divorce Rates'
   /VERTICAL='Rates per 1000 population'
   /HORIZONTAL='Year' REFERENCE (1918, 1945)
                      MIN (1900) MAX (1983)
   /PLOT=MARRATE DIVRATE WITH YEAR.
```

- This example produces an overlay plot of marriage and divorce rates by year.
- SYMBOLS selects the symbols M and D, respectively, for the two plots.
- VSIZE and HSIZE limit the vertical and horizontal axes to 12 lines and 60 columns, respectively.
- TITLE specifies a plot title, and VERTICAL provides a title for the vertical axis.
- HORIZONTAL provides a title for the horizontal axis. REFERENCE, MIN, and MAX provide reference lines at values 1918 and 1945 and minimum and maximum scale values on the horizontal axis.

PLOT Subcommand   The PLOT subcommand names the variables to be plotted on each axis. The PLOT subcommand can also name a control or contour variable.

- PLOT is the only required subcommand.
- You can enter multiple PLOT subcommands.
- No other subcommands can follow the last PLOT subcommand.
- Each plot list first specifies a list of variables to be plotted on the vertical axis, then the keyword WITH, and then a list of variables to be plotted on the horizontal axis.
- By default, PLOT creates separate plots for each combination of variables listed on the left side of WITH with variables on the right.
- Use semicolons to separate multiple plot lists on a single PLOT subcommand.
- Keyword ALL can be used to refer to all user-defined variables.
- Use keyword BY followed by a variable name to specify a control or contour variable.
- Only one control variable can be specified on any plot list.
- If a control variable is specified, PLOT uses the first character of the control variable's value label as the plot symbol. If value labels have not been specified, the first character of the value is used. The symbol $ indicates that more than one control value occurs in that display position.

You can also request special pairing of variables with the following keyword:

(PAIR)   *Plot corresponding pairs of variables.* The first variable before WITH is plotted against the first variable after WITH, and so on.

Example
```
PLOT PLOT=MARRATE WITH YEAR AGE;
         BIRTHS DEATHS WITH INCOME1 INCOME2 (PAIR);
         DIVRATE WITH AGE BY YEAR.
```

- This PLOT subcommand contains three plot lists. The first requests a plot of MARRATE with YEAR and of MARRATE with AGE.
- The second uses the keyword (PAIR) to request two plots: BIRTHS with INCOME1 and DEATHS with INCOME2.
- The third requests a plot of DIVRATE with AGE using YEAR as a control variable. The value labels for YEAR will be used to obtain plotting characters in this control plot.

FORMAT Subcommand   The FORMAT subcommand controls the type of plot produced.

- FORMAT can be specified only once before each PLOT subcommand and applies only to plots requested on that PLOT subcommand.
- If the subcommand is omitted or DEFAULT is specified, bivariate scatterplots are displayed.
- Only one keyword can be specified on each FORMAT subcommand.

The available keywords are:

DEFAULT   *Bivariate scatterplot.* When there is no control variable on the plot list, each symbol represents the case count at that plot position. When a control variable is specified, each symbol represents the first character of the value label of the control variable.

OVERLAY   *Overlay plots.* All bivariate plots on the next PLOT subcommand appear in one plot frame. PLOT selects a unique symbol for each plot to be overlaid, plus a symbol to represent multiple plot points in one display position.

CONTOUR(n)   *Contour plot with n levels.* Contour plots use a continuous variable as the control variable and *n* successive symbols to represent lowest to highest levels of the variable. Specify the control variable after BY on the PLOT subcommand. This variable is recoded into *n* equal-width intervals. If the levels specification is omitted, the default of 10 is used; the maximum is 35. When more than one level of the contour variable occurs at the same plot position, PLOT displays the value of the highest level.

REGRESSION *Regression of vertical-axis variable on horizontal-axis variable.* The regression-line intercepts on each axis are marked with the letter R. When there is no control variable, each symbol represents the frequency of cases at that plot position. If a control variable is specified, regression statistics are pooled over all categories and each symbol represents the first character of the value labels of the control variable.

Plot Symbols A wide range of alphabetical, numeric, and special ASCII graphic characters are available for use as PLOT symbols. Two subcommands control the display of symbols: the SYMBOLS subcommand controls the choice of plot symbols, and the CUTPOINT subcommand controls the frequencies represented by a symbol. SYMBOLS and CUTPOINT can each be specified only once and apply to all plots requested in a PLOT command. If you have more than one FORMAT subcommand within a PLOT command, the meaning of the plotting symbols can vary. The operation of SYMBOLS and CUTPOINT for each FORMAT specification is summarized below.

• *DEFAULT or REGRESSION plot, no control.* Each symbol represents the frequency of cases. Controlled by SYMBOLS and CUTPOINT.

• *DEFAULT or REGRESSION plot, control.* Each symbol represents one value of the control variable. SYMBOLS and CUTPOINT do not apply. The plot symbol is the first character of the control variable's value label or the first character of the actual value if no VALUE LABELS have been declared; the uniqueness of these symbols is not checked.

• *OVERLAY.* Each symbol represents one of the overlaid plots. SYMBOLS is applicable; CUTPOINT is not.

• *CONTOUR.* Each symbol represents one level of the contour variable. SYMBOLS is applicable; CUTPOINT is not.

CUTPOINT Subcommand By default, each frequency in a frequency plot is represented by a different plot symbol, and successive plotting symbols represent an interval width of 1. Use the CUTPOINT subcommand to alter the categories represented by plot symbols for bivariate and regression plots.

• CUTPOINT can be specified only once and applies to all frequency plots on the PLOT command.
• If the subcommand is omitted, the default interval of width 1 is in effect.
• Only one specification can be given on CUTPOINT.

The following specifications are available:

EVERY(n) *Frequency intervals of width* n. Each plot symbol represents the specified frequency interval. The default is an interval width of 1.

(value list) *Each value defines a cutpoint.* Successive plot symbols are assigned to each cutpoint. Up to 35 cutpoints can be specified. Specify values separated by blanks or commas. The number of cutpoints is one less than the number of intervals.

Example
```
PLOT CUTPOINT=EVERY(2)
  /PLOT=YVAR WITH XVAR.
PLOT CUTPOINT=(5,10,20)
  /PLOT=YVAR WITH XVAR.
```

• In the first PLOT command, 1 or 2 cases on a display position are represented by a 1, 3 or 4 cases by a 2, and so forth.
• In the second PLOT command, 1 to 5 cases on a display position are represented by a 1; 6 to 10 cases by a 2; 11 to 20 cases by a 3; and 21 or more cases by a 4.

SYMBOLS Subcommand

The SYMBOLS subcommand defines the plotting symbols for bivariate scatter-plots and bivariate regression, overlay, and contour plots. Successive symbols represent increasing frequencies in scatterplots or regression plots, successive subplots in overlay plots, and successive intervals in contour plots.

- SYMBOLS can be specified only once and applies to all plots requested except control plots.
- If the subcommand is omitted, the default alphanumeric symbol set is used.
- If SYMBOLS is specified, a table defining the plotting symbols is displayed.

The following specifications are available for SYMBOLS:

ALPHANUMERIC   *Alphanumeric plotting symbols.* Includes the characters 1 through 9, A through Z, and *. Thirty-six or more cases at a position are represented by a *. This is the default.

NUMERIC   *Numeric plotting symbols.* Includes the characters 1 through 9 and *. Ten or more cases at a plot position are represented by a *.

'symbols'[,'ovprnt']   *List of plot symbols.* Up to 36 symbols can be specified. Symbols are specified without any intervening blanks or commas. If specified, the list of overprint symbols is separated from the first symbol list by a comma or space. Indicate hexadecimal symbols on either list by specifying X before the list and enclosing the list in apostrophes. You can also specify any special ASCII graphic characters available on your terminal. See the SET command and your DOS manual for further reference.

- When overprint symbols are displayed (on the screen), only the symbols from the first list remain visible. Other characters in the plot may be erased. Overprinting will occur when the plot is printed.

Example
```
PLOT CUTPOINTS=EVERY(5)
  /SYMBOLS='.+O',' X'
  /PLOT=YVAR BY XVAR.
```

- This example uses a period (.) to represent 5 or fewer cases at one point, a plus sign (+) to represent 6 to 10 cases at the same position, and a symbol overprinting O and X to represent 11 or more cases at one position. Note the leading blanks in the list of overprint symbols.
- On the screen, the symbols .+O + X will remain visible to represent 1–5, 5–10, and 11 or more cases, respectively. The overprint of O and X will appear on printed output.

VSIZE and HSIZE Subcommands

Use the VSIZE and HSIZE subcommands to specify the vertical and horizontal frame size for the plot, respectively.

- VSIZE and HSIZE can each be used only once per PLOT command and apply to all plots requested.
- The default size of a plot depends on the current page size. If the SET command defines a width of 79 and a length of 24, the default plot width is 38 columns and the default plot length is 16 rows.
- VSIZE and HSIZE each use a single integer as their only specification.
- VSIZE and HSIZE values do not include display lines for the plot frame itself or for auxiliary information such as titles, axis scale numbers, regression statistics, or symbol table.
- If VSIZE is greater than the length specified on SET, the symbol table and other information are displayed on another page.
- If HSIZE is greater than the width specified on SET, the plot wraps on the screen if there is insufficient width for the plot.

VERTICAL and HORIZONTAL Subcommands

The VERTICAL and HORIZONTAL subcommands control labeling and scaling for the vertical and horizontal axes, respectively.

• VERTICAL and HORIZONTAL can each be specified once before each PLOT subcommand.

• VERTICAL and HORIZONTAL can each be specified once before each PLOT subcommand.

• VERTICAL and HORIZONTAL apply only to plots requested by the next PLOT subcommand.

• If VERTICAL and HORIZONTAL are omitted, all defaults are in effect. If VERTICAL and HORIZONTAL are included, only those defaults explicitly altered are changed.

'label'	*Label for axis.* The label can contain up to 40 characters. A label that will not fit in the plot frame is truncated. The default is the variable, label or the variable name if no variable label has been declared.
MIN (n)	*Minimum axis value.* If you specify a minimum value greater than the observed minimum value, some points will not be included in the plot. The default is the minimum observed value.
MAX (n)	*Maximum axis value.* PLOT may extend the scale value slightly in order to display integer scale values of equal width. The default is the maximum observed value.
UNIFORM	*Uniform values on axis.* All plots on the PLOT subcommand will have the same value scale on the axis. You imply a uniform scale when you specify both MIN and MAX. If you specify UNIFORM, PLOT determines the minimum and maximum observed values across all variables on the PLOT subcommand.
REFERENCE(values)	*Values at which reference lines will be drawn.* Specify the values separated by blanks or commas. The default is no reference lines.
STANDARDIZE	*Standardize variables on the axes.* Standardized variables are useful for overlay plots of variables with different scales. The default is to plot observed values.

TITLE Subcommand

Use the TITLE subcommand to label plots.

• TITLE can be specified once before each PLOT subcommand.

• TITLE applies to all plots named on the next PLOT subcommand.

• The default title is either the names of the variables in a bivariate plot or the type of plot requested on FORMAT.

• The title can be up to 60 characters long.

• The rules for specifying titles follow the usual conventions for strings (see Universals: Strings).

• The title is truncated if it exceeds the width specified on the HSIZE subcommand.

MISSING Subcommand

Use the MISSING subcommand to control the handling of cases with missing values.

• The MISSING subcommand can be specified only once on each PLOT command and applies to all plots.

• By default, cases with system-missing or user-missing values for any variables in a plot are omitted from that plot.

• The keywords LISTWISE and PLOTWISE (the default) are alternatives. Either one may also be specified with INCLUDE.

C

Command Reference

The following keywords are available for the MISSING subcommand:

PLOTWISE   *Delete cases with missing values plotwise.* The default. Cases with missing values for any variable in a plot are not included in that plot. In overlay plots, PLOTWISE applies separately to each overlaid plot in the frame, not to the full list specified on the PLOT subcommand.

LISTWISE   *Delete cases with missing values listwise.* Cases with missing values for any variable named on the PLOT subcommand are deleted from all plots specified on that PLOT subcommand.

INCLUDE   *Include cases with user-missing values.* Only cases with system-missing values are excluded according to the missing-value treatment specified (PLOTWISE, LISTWISE, or the default).

PROCESS IF

```
PROCESS IF [(]variable relational operator value[)]
```

Relational Operators:
EQ or =   NE or ~= or <>
LT or <   LE or <=
GT or >   GE or >=

Example:
```
PROCESS IF (TYPE EQ 1).
```

Overview

The PROCESS IF transformation temporarily designates cases for inclusion in the next procedure.

Syntax

- The specification is a simple logical expression that can be evaluated as true or false (see Universals: Logical Expressions).
- Parentheses enclosing the logical expression are optional.
- All six relational operators are permitted: EQ, NE, LT, LE, GT, GE. Symbolic forms (=, ~= or <>, <, <=, >, and >=) are also accepted.
- Only numeric or short string variables can be specified. Long string variables may not be used.
- String values must be enclosed in apostrophes or quotation marks.
- String values must match the length of the short string being tested.
- PROCESS IF can be entered anywhere in an SPSS/PC+ session, except between BEGIN DATA and END DATA.

Operations

- PROCESS IF is a temporary transformation and is executed when the data are read for the next procedure.
- PROCESS IF temporarily designates cases for inclusion in the next procedure.
- If the logical expression is true, the case is processed. If it is false or missing, the case is not processed in the next procedure.
- If multiple PROCESS IF commands are entered before a procedure, only the last one is in effect.
- PROCESS IF has no effect on SORT CASES, and is ignored if SORT CASES is the next procedure.

Limitations

- PROCESS IF can take only one simple expression; logical operators are not accepted.

Example

```
PROCESS IF (AGE GT 50).
```

- In the next procedure, only cases for which variable AGE is greater than 50 are included.

Example

```
PROCESS IF (SEX EQ 'MALE  ').
```

- SEX is a six-column left-justified variable. The trailing blanks must be included in the value specification.
- The next procedure uses cases in which the value of SEX is MALE with two trailing blanks.

Command Reference

RANK

```
RANK [VARIABLES=] varlist [({A**})] [BY varlist]
                           {D  }

[/TIES={MEAN**  }]
       {LOW     }
       {HIGH    }
       {CONDENSE}

[/FRACTION={BLOM**}]
           {TUKEY }
           {VW    }
           {RANKIT}

[/PRINT={YES**}]
        {NO  }

[/MISSING={EXCLUDE**}]
          {INCLUDE  }
```

The following rank function subcommands can each be specified once:

```
[/RANK**] [/NTILES(n)] [/NORMAL] [/PERCENT]
[/RFRACTION] [/PROPORTION] [/N] [/SAVAGE]
```

INTO can be used with any rank function subcommand:

```
[INTO=rankvarlist]
```

**Default if subcommand is omitted.

Example:

```
RANK SALARY JOBTIME.
```

Overview

RANK produces new variables containing ranks, normal scores, and Savage and related scores, for numeric variables.

Options

Methods. Ranking can be in ascending or descending order as specified by the A or D keyword following the variables list. Four methods of handling ties are available with the TIES subcommand. Eight ranking function algorithms can be specified by subcommand. The FRACTION subcommand supplies additional refinements for two of these, NORMAL and PROPORTION. MISSING allows the inclusion of user-missing values in computing ranks.

Output. The printing of the summary table that lists variables ranked with their associated new variables in the active file can be suppressed with the PRINT subcommand. Names of the new variables in the active file can be specified with the INTO keyword on the ranking function subcommands.

Basic Specification

- The basic specification is RANK followed by at least one variable from the active file.
- The output is a summary table that includes a list of ranked variables and each new variable in the active file into which computed ranks have been stored.
- The default ranking function is RANK. Direction is ascending. Missing values are excluded. Ties are handled by assigning the mean rank to tied values.

Subcommand Order

- The variable list must come first.
- Other subcommands may be named in any order.

Syntax Rules

- Only the variable list is required.

Operations

- RANK causes the data to be read.
- RANK does not change the way the active file is sorted.
- If new variable names are not specified with the INTO keyword on the ranking function subcommand, RANK creates default names (see RANK Function Subcommands).

Limitations
- String variables cannot be specified on RANK. AUTORECODE can be used to order string variables.

Example
```
RANK SALARY JOBTIME.
```
- RANK ranks SALARY and JOBTIME into two new variables in the active file, RSALARY and RJOBTIME.

Variables Specification

A list of variables to be ranked and the optional direction of ranking immediately follows the RANK command. The variable list is required.

- A or D in parentheses specifies the direction of the ranking as ascending or descending. Ascending is the default.
- The keyword BY causes ranking within groups defined by the variables listed after the BY.

Example
```
RANK MURDERS (D).
```
- RANK ranks MURDERS into a new variable in the active file, RMURDERS.
- D in parentheses specifies that the order of the ranking will be descending (largest value will get smallest rank).

Example
```
RANK MURDERS (D) ROBBERY (A) BY ETHNIC.
```
- RANK ranks MURDERS and ROBBERY into two new variables in the active file: RMURDERS AND RROBBERY.
- D in parentheses specifies that MURDERS is to be ranked in descending order.
- A in parentheses specifies that ROBBERY is to be ranked in ascending order.
- Ranks are computed within each group defined by ETHNIC.
- The active file does not have to be sorted by ETHNIC.

RANK Function Subcommands

The optional rank function subcommands specify methods for computing ranks. RANK is the default rank function.

- INTO follows the rank function and specifies variable names for the rank variables added to the active file.
- Any combination of rank function subcommands can be specified for a RANK procedure, but each rank function can be specified only once.

RANK   *Simple rank.* Value equals rank. Rank can either be ascending or descending (see Variables Specification).

RFRACTION   *Fractional ranks.* Value equals rank divided by the sum of the weights of the non-missing cases. For TIES=MEANS or TIES= HIGH, fractional rank values are an empirical cumulative distribution.

NORMAL   *Normal scores* (Lehmann, 1975). The new variable contains the inverse of the standard normal cumulative distribution of the proportion estimate defined by the FRACTION subcommand. The default is FRACTION=BLOM (see FRACTION Subcommand).

PERCENT   *Fractional rank as a percent.* The new variable contains fractional ranks multiplied by 100.

PROPORTION   *Proportion estimates.* Estimation method is specified by the FRACTION subcommand. The default is FRACTION=BLOM (see FRACTION Subcommand).

N   *Sum of case weights.* The new variable is a constant.

SAVAGE   *Savage score.* The new variable contains Savage (exponential) scores (Lehmann, 1975).

NTILES(n)   *Percentile groups.* The new variable contains values from 1 to n. Each group value is the integer that is equal to or less than y_i where $y_i = 1 + R_i n/(w+1)$ and where R_i is the rank of the ith case of the variable being ranked, n is the number of groups specified on the NTILES subcommand, and w is the sum of the case weights. Group values can be affected by the keyword specified on the TIES subcommand (see TIES Subcommand). There is no default value for n, the number of groups generated.

INTO varlist   *New variable(s) to be added to active file.* INTO can be used with any of the rank function subcommands. If INTO is not specified, RANK procedure creates default names for new variables according to the following rules:

- The first letter of the ranking function is added to the first seven characters of the original variable name.
- If some of the resulting names are not unique (in the dictionary or in an INTO new variables list), the non-unique variables are named XXXnnn. XXX represents the first three characters of the ranking function and nnn is a three-digit number starting with 001 and being increased by one for each variable. If the ranking function is N, XXX is reduced to N.
- If some of the names resulting from the first and second step are not unique, the non-unique variables are named RNKXXnn. XX is the first two characters of the ranking function and nn is a two-digit number starting with 01 and being increased by one for each variable.
- If it is not possible to generate unique names, an error results.

Example
```
RANK SALARY
  /NORMAL INTO SALNORM
  /SAVAGE INTO SALSAV.
```

- RANK generates two new variables from the variable SALARY.
- NORMAL produces the new variable SALNORM. SALNORM contains normal scores for SALARY computed with the default formula BLOM.
- SAVAGE produces the new variable SALSAV. SALSAV contains Savage scores for SALARY.

Example
```
RANK SALARY
  /NTILES(4) INTO SALQUART.
```

- The new variable SALQUART has values 1, 2, 3, or 4. For cases in the first (lowest-ranked) group of SALARY, the value of the new variable SALQUART is 1. The next three ranked groups are assigned values of 2, 3, and 4 for SALQUART according to the formula for group assignment.

TIES Subcommand

The optional TIES subcommand specifies how tied values are to be handled. The default method is MEAN.

MEAN   *Mean rank applied to tied values.*

LOW   *Lowest rank applied to tied values.*

HIGH   *Highest rank applied to tied values.*

CONDENSE   *Consecutive ranks with ties sharing a value.* Distinct values of the ranked variable are assigned consecutive ranks in the new variable. Ties share their value. The next untied value is assigned the value consecutive to the value assigned the ties.

Example
```
RANK BURGLARY
  /RANK INTO RMEAN
  /TIES=MEAN.
RANK BURGLARY
  /RANK INTO RCONDS
  /TIES=CONDENSE.
RANK BURGLARY
  /RANK INTO RHIGH
  /TIES=HIGH.
RANK BURGLARY
  /RANK INTO RLOW
  /TIES=LOW.
```

• The values of BURGLARY and the results of these four procedures are shown below.

```
COMMUNITY    BURGLARY    RMEAN    RCONDS    RHIGH    RLOW

    1            0          3         1         5        1
    2            0          3         1         5        1
    3            0          3         1         5        1
    4            0          3         1         5        1
    5            0          3         1         5        1
    6            1          6.5       2         7        6
    7            1          6.5       2         7        6
    8            3          8         3         8        8
```

FRACTION Subcommand

FRACTION specifies one of four ways to compute a proportion estimate P for the NORMAL and PROPORTION rank functions. This optional subcommand can only be used with rank function subcommands NORMAL or PROPORTION. With other rank function subcommands, FRACTION is ignored and a warning message is displayed. The default is BLOM.

• Only one formula can be specified for each RANK procedure. If more than one is specified, an error results.

Four formulas are available:

BLOM   *Blom's transformation,* defined by the formula $(r - 3/8) / (W + 1/4)$, where W is the sum of case weights and r is the rank, ranging from 1 to W (see Blom, 1958).

RANKIT *Uses the formula* $(r - 1/2) / W$, where $<W>$ is the sum of case weights and r is the rank, ranging from 1 to W (see Chambers et al., 1983).

TUKEY   *Tukey's transformation,* defined by the formula $(r - 1/3) / (W + 1/3)$, where W is the sum of case weights and r is the rank, ranging from 1 to W (see Tukey, 1962).

VW   *Van der Waerden's transformation,* defined by the formula $r / (W + 1)$, where W is the sum of case weights and r is the rank, ranging from 1 to W (see Lehmann, 1975).

Example

```
RANK MORTGAGE VALUE
  /FRACTION=BLOM
  /NORMAL INTO MORTNORM VALNORM.
```

• RANK generates new variables MORTNORM and VALNORM. MORTNORM contains normal scores for MORTGAGE, and ETHNNORM contains normal scores for VALUE.

PRINT Subcommand

The optional PRINT subcommand specifies whether the summary tables are to be written to the listing file. The default is YES.

YES *Print summary table.*

NO   *Do not print summary table.*

• RANK generates the new variable BURGRANK containing the ranks of BURGLARY.

• No summary table stating the name of ranked and new variable is generated as a result of the PRINT=NO subcommand.

MISSING Subcommand

The optional MISSING subcommand controls the treatment of cases with user-missing values. The default is EXCLUDE.

INCLUDE *Include all user-missing values.*

EXCLUDE *Exclude all missing values.*

Example
```
MISSING VALUE SALARY (0).
RANK SALARY
  /RANK INTO SALRANK
  /MISSING=INCLUDE.
```

- RANK generates the new variable SALRANK.
- MISSING=INCLUDE causes user-missing value 0 to be included in the ranking process.

References
Blom, G. 1958. *Statistical estimates and transformed beta variables.* New York: John Wiley & Sons.

Chambers, J. M., W. S. Cleveland, B. Kleiner, and P. A. Tukey. 1983. *Graphical methods for data analysis.* Belmont, Calif.: Wadsworth International Group; Boston: Duxbury Press.

Fisher, R. A. 1973. *Statistical methods for research workers,* 14th ed. New York: Hafner Publishing Company.

Frigge, M., D. C. Hoaglin, and B. Iglewicz. 1987. Some implementations of the boxplot. In *Computer science and statistics proceedings of the 19th symposium on the interface,* ed. R. M. Heiberger and M. Martin. Alexandria, Va.: American Statistical Association.

Lehmann, E. L. 1975. *Nonparametrics: Statistical methods based on ranks.* San Francisco: Holden-Day.

Tukey, J. W. 1962. The future of data analysis. *Annals of Mathematical Statistics* 33: 22.

RECODE

Numeric Recodes:
```
RECODE varlist (value list=value)...(value list=value)

        [/varlist...]
```
Input keywords available for numeric recodes are:
```
LO  LOWEST  HI  HIGHEST  THRU  MISSING  SYSMIS  ELSE
```
Output keywords available for numeric recodes are:
```
SYSMIS
```

String Recodes:
```
RECODE varlist ('string',['string'...]='string')

        [varlist...]
```
Input keywords available for string recodes are:
```
ELSE
```

Examples:
```
RECODE IVAR1 TO IVAR3 (0=1) (1=0) (2,3=-1) (9=9) (ELSE=SYSMIS).
RECODE STRINGVAR ('A','B','C'='A')('D','E','F'='B')(ELSE=' ').
```

Overview

The RECODE command changes the coding scheme of an existing numeric or short string variable on a value-by-value basis or for a range of values. Where it can be used, RECODE is much more efficient than the series of IF commands that produce the same transformation.

Syntax

• The variable(s) to be recoded must already exist.
• Each set of value specifications is enclosed in parentheses.
• Input values are specified first (to the left of the equals sign), followed by a single output value (to the right of the equals sign).
• More than one input value can be recoded to a single output value.
• Values in the value lists must be separated by blanks or commas.
• Only one output value per set of input values is allowed.
• Input values that are not mentioned remain unchanged, unless the ELSE keyword is used.
• ELSE refers to all input values not previously mentioned.
• The equals sign preceding the output value is required.
• You can recode more than one variable using the same value specifications by specifying a list of variables before the value specifications.
• More than one variable can be recoded differently in one command by specifying the variable and the value specifications for each transformation, separated by a slash.

Numeric Variables

• THRU specifies a value range, inclusive of specified end values.
• LOWEST and HIGHEST (LO and HI) specify the lowest and highest values encountered in the data.
• LOWEST and HIGHEST include user-missing values.
• LOWEST and HIGHEST do not include the system-missing value.
• ELSE includes all input values not already specified, including the system-missing value.
• MISSING specifies user- and system-missing values for recoding. MISSING is an input specification only.
• SYSMIS specifies the system-missing value and can be used as both an input and output value.

C

Command Reference

String Variables	• Only short string variables can be recoded. Long strings cannot be recoded.
	• Values must be enclosed in apostrophes or quotation marks.
	• Blanks are significant characters.
	• Input and output values must be specified according to the format width of the variable (see Universals: Strings).
Operations	• RECODE is a transformation and is executed when the data are read for the next procedure.
	• Recode value specifications are scanned left to right.
	• A value is recoded only once per RECODE command.
	• Invalid syntax stops processing of the RECODE command and cancels any recoding of variables named on the command.
Numeric Variables	• Blank fields for numeric variables are handled according to the SET BLANKS specification prior to recoding.
	• When you recode a value that was previously defined as user-missing on the MISSING VALUE command, the output value is not missing but is the new, recoded value.
String Variables	• If the input or output value is shorter or longer than the format width defined for that variable, it is an error.
Limitations	• You can recode (and count using the COUNT command) approximately 400 values prior to a data pass.
	• Invalid specifications on a RECODE command that result in errors stop all processing of that RECODE command.

Example

```
RECODE IVAR1 TO IVAR3 (0=1) (1=0) (2,3=-1) (9=9) (ELSE=SYSMIS) /
       QVAR(1 THRU 5=1)(6 THRU 10=2)(11 THRU HI=3)(ELSE=0).
```

• Values for the list of numeric variables between and including IVAR1 and IVAR3 are changed: input values 0 and 1 are switched to 1 and 0, respectively; 2 and 3 become −1; 9 remains 9; and any other value is changed to the system-missing value.

• Values for variable QVAR are also changed: input values 1 through 5 become 1; 6 through 10 become 2; 11 through the highest value become 3; and any other value, including system-missing, becomes 0.

Example

```
RECODE STRINGVAR ('A','B','C'='A')('D','E','F'='B')(ELSE=' ').
RECODE PET ('IGUANA', 'SNAKE ' = 'WILD  ').
```

• Values A, B, and C are changed to value A. Values D, E, and F are changed to value B. All other values are changed to a blank.

• Values IGUANA and SNAKE are changed to value WILD. The variable PET has a format width of six characters. Thus, values SNAKE and WILD include trailing blanks to total six characters.

• Note that each string value is enclosed within apostrophes.

REPORT   REPORT

```
[/FORMAT=[{MANUAL   }]† [{NOLIST   }] [ALIGN({LEFT  })]†
         {AUTOMATIC}    {LIST[(n)]}        {CENTER}
                                           {RIGHT }

         [TSPACE({1})] [CHDSPACE({1})] [FTSPACE({1})]
                {n}              {n}             {n}

         [SUMSPACE({1})] [COLSPACE({4})]† [BRKSPACE({1 })]
                  {n}             {n}               {n }
                                                    {-1}

         [LENGTH({1,length})] [MARGINS({1,width})]
                {n,n     }             {n,n    }
                {*,*     }             {*,*    }

         [CHALIGN({TOP    })]† [UNDERSCORE({OFF})]†
                 {BOTTOM*}                {ON*}

         [PAGE1({1})]† [MISSING {'.'}]]
               {n}             {'s'}

[OUTFILE=file]†

[/STRING=stringname (varname[(width)] [(BLANK)] ['literal...'])]

/VARIABLES=varname ({VALUE}) [+ varname({VALUE})] ['col head']
                   {LABEL}            {LABEL}
                   {DUMMY}            {DUMMY}
   [(option list)]

where option list can contain any of the following:

        width    OFFSET({0     })    {LEFT   }†
                       {n     }      {CENTER*}
                       {CENTER*}     {RIGHT  }

[/MISSING={VAR            }]
         {NONE           }
         {LIST(varlist{1})}
                      {n}

[/TITLE='line1' 'line2'...    ]    [/FOOTNOTE='line1' 'line2'...      ]
        or                                  or
[/TITLE=LEFT 'line1' 'line2'...]†  [/FOOTNOTE=LEFT 'line1' 'line2'...]†
[      CENTER 'line1' 'line2'...]  [        CENTER 'line1' 'line2'...]
[      RIGHT 'line1' 'line2'...]   [        RIGHT 'line1' 'line2'...]

        [)PAGE]†  [)DATE]†  [)var]†

[/BREAK=varlist [(TOTAL)] ['col head'] [(option list)]]

where option list can contain any of the following:

        width   {VALUE }   {NOTOTAL}  SKIP({1})   PAGE[(RESET†)]
                {LABEL*}   {TOTAL  }       {n}

        OFFSET({0     })   UNDERSCORE[(varlist)]†  {LEFT  }†  {NONAME}
              {n     }                             {CENTER*}  {NAME  }
              {CENTER*}                            {RIGHT }

[/SUMMARY=function...['summary title'][(break col #1)]

        [SKIP({0})]]
             {n}
```

```
or

[/SUMMARY=PREVIOUS[({1})]]
                    {n}

where function is

aggregate [(varname[(d)][({PLAIN })])[varname...])]
                          {DOLLAR}
                          {COMMA }

or

composite(agg(varname)...)[(report col[(d)][({PLAIN })])]]
                                            {DOLLAR}
                                            {COMMA }
```

* Default if FORMAT=AUTOMATIC.

Aggregate Functions:

VALIDN	VARIANCE	PCLT(n)
SUM	KURTOSIS	PCIN(min,max)
MIN	SKEWNESS	FREQUENCY(min,max)†
MAX	MEDIAN(min,max)	PERCENT(min,max)†
MEAN	MODE(min,max)	
STDDEV	PCGT(n)	

Composite Functions

DIVIDE(agg(varname) agg(varname)[factor])	&2
PCT(agg(varname) agg(varname))	&2
SUBTRACT(agg(varname) agg(varname))	&2
ADD(agg(varname) agg(varname)...)	&2
GREAT(agg(varname) agg(varname)...)	&2
LEAST(agg(varname) agg(varname)...)	&2
AVERAGE(agg(varname) agg(varname)...)	&2
MULTIPLY(agg(varname) agg(varname)...)	&2

Example:

```
REPORT FORMAT=AUTOMATIC LIST
  /VARIABLES=PRODUCT (LABEL) ' ' 'Retail' 'Products'
            SALES 'Annual' 'Sales' '1981'
  /BREAK=DEPT 'Department'
  /SUMMARY=VALIDN (PRODUCT) MEAN (SALES).
```

Overview

The REPORT procedure produces both case listings and summary statistics and gives you considerable control over the appearance of the output. REPORT calculates all the univariate statistics available in DESCRIPTIVES and the statistics and subpopulation means available in MEANS. In addition, REPORT calculates statistics not directly available in any other SPSS/PC+ procedure, such as computations involving aggregated statistics.

REPORT provides complete format defaults or lets you customize column widths, titles, footnotes, spacing, and other elements. Because REPORT is so flexible and its output can have so many components, it is often efficient to preview REPORT output using a small number of cases until you find the format that best meets your needs.

Defaults

A listing report without subgroup classification requires the FORMAT and VARIABLES subcommands. A listing report with subgroup classification requires the FORMAT, VARIABLES, and BREAK subcommands. A report with summary statistics requires the VARIABLES, BREAK, and SUMMARY subcommands.

By default, column heads use variable labels, or variable names if no variable labels have been specified. Default column widths are determined by REPORT using the maximum of the following for each variable:

• The widest print format in the column, whether it is a variable print format or a summary print format.

• The width of any temporary variable defined with the STRING subcommand.

• If a column heading is assigned, the length of the longest title line in that heading.
• If you specify (LABEL), the length of the variable's longest value label. (If MANUAL is in effect, REPORT uses the length of the variable's longest label, up to a maximum of 20 characters.)

Intercolumn spacing adjusts automatically, using a minimum of 1 and a maximum of 4 spaces between columns. By default, cases with user-missing values are excluded from the calculation of report statistics, and missing-value indicators are ignored for variables named on BREAK.

Many default settings depend on whether FORMAT=AUTOMATIC or MANUAL. Table A below shows the defaults according to both specifications.

Table A Keyword default settings

Subcommand	Keyword	Default for Automatic	Default for Manual
FORMAT	ALIGN	left	left
	BRKSPACE		
	summary report	1	1
	listing report	-1	1
	CHALIGN	bottom	top
	CHDSPACE	1	1
	COLSPACE	4	4
	FTSPACE	1	1
	LENGTH	1,system length	1,system length
	LIST|NOLIST	NOLIST	NOLIST
	MARGINS	1,system length	1,system length
	MISSING	'.'	'.'
	PAGE1	1	1
	SUMSPACE	1	1
	TSPACE	1	1
	UNDERSCORE	on	off
VARIABLES	LABEL|VALUE|DUMMY	VALUE	VALUE
	LEFT|CENTER|RIGHT	CENTER	RIGHT for numbers LEFT for strings
	OFFSET	CENTER	0
BREAK	LABEL|VALUE	LABEL	VALUE
	LEFT|CENTER|RIGHT	CENTER	RIGHT for numbers LEFT for strings
	NAME|NONAME	NONAME	NONAME
	OFFSET	CENTER	0
	PAGE	off	off
	SKIP	1	1
	TOTAL|NOTOTAL	NOTOTAL	NOTOTAL
	UNDERSCORE	off	off
SUMMARY	PREVIOUS	1	1
	SKIP	0	0

Tailoring

Display Format. REPORT provides full report format defaults and offers you optional control over page length, vertical spacing, margins and column widths, page titles and footnotes, and labels for statistics. The maximum width and length of the report are controlled by specifications on the SET command.

The FORMAT subcommand controls how the report is laid out on a page and whether case listings are displayed. The STRING subcommand concatenates variables to create temporary variables that can be referenced on the VARIABLES or BREAK subcommands. The VARIABLES subcommand names the report variables used to compute statistics and controls the titles, width, and contents of report columns. The BREAK subcommand specifies the variables that define groups and controls the titles, width, and contents of break columns.

The SUMMARY subcommand specifies statistics and controls the titles and spacing of summary lines. Additional subcommands control the specification and placement of multiple-line titles and footnotes.

Statistical Display. The statistical display is controlled by the SUMMARY subcommand. Statistics can be calculated for each category of a break variable and for the group as a whole. Available statistics include mean, variance, standard deviation, skewness, kurtosis, sum, minimum and maximum value, mode, median, and percentages. Composite functions perform arithmetic operations using two or more summary statistics calculated on single variables.

Missing Values. You can override the default to include user-missing values in report statistics and listings with the MISSING subcommand. You can also define a missing-value symbol to represent missing data on the FORMAT subcommand.

Syntax

- The minimum specification for REPORT is the VARIABLES subcommand, plus either FORMAT=LIST or the BREAK and SUMMARY subcommands.
- Only one each of the FORMAT, STRING, VARIABLES, and MISSING subcommands are allowed. If used, they must be entered in this order and must precede all BREAK and SUMMARY subcommands.
- Multiple BREAK subcommands are allowed, and multiple SUMMARY subcommands are allowed per BREAK.
- Each BREAK subcommand immediately precedes the SUMMARY subcommands that request statistics for that BREAK.
- To suppress subgroup classification when LIST is specified on FORMAT, omit the BREAK subcommand.
- TITLE and FOOTNOTE subcommands can appear anywhere after FORMAT except among the BREAK and SUMMARY subcommands.
- Keywords on REPORT subcommands have default specifications that are in effect if the keyword is not specified. Specify keywords only when you wish to change a default.
- Keywords are enclosed in parentheses if the subcommand takes variable names as arguments.
- Subcommands are separated from each other by slashes.

Operations

- REPORT causes the data to be read.
- REPORT processes cases sequentially. When the value of a break variable changes, REPORT displays a statistical summary for cases processed since the last set of summary statistics was displayed.
- The file must be sorted in order on the break variable or variables.
- The maximum width and page length of the report are the width and page length specified on the SET command.
- The format used to display values in case listings is controlled by the dictionary format of the variable. Each statistical function in REPORT has a default format.

Limitations

- The length of titles and footnotes cannot exceed the report width.
- The length of string variables created on the STRING subcommand cannot exceed the page width.
- There is no fixed limit on the number of BREAK and SUMMARY subcommands. However, the page width limits the number of variables displayed and thereby limits the number of break variables. The limit of 10 variables on SORT CASES often effectively acts as a limit on the number of breaks.
- The number of report variables that can be specified depends upon the width of the report, the width of the variable columns, and the number of BREAK subcommands.
- Maximum 10 dummy variables per VARIABLES subcommand.
- Maximum 50 strings per STRING subcommand.

- Maximum 20 MODE and MEDIAN requests per SUMMARY subcommand.
- Maximum 20 PCGT, PCLT, and PCIN requests per SUMMARY subcommand.
- Workspace is required to store all labeling information, frequency counts if summaries request MEDIAN or MODE, strings, and computed summary statistics.
- Memory requirements significantly increase if MEDIAN or MODE is requested for variables with a wide range of values. The amount of workspace required is $20 + 8*(\text{max} - \text{min} + 1)$ bytes per variable per function per break.
- If TOTAL is in effect, workspace requirements are almost doubled.
- Memory requirements also increase if value labels are displayed for variables with many value labels. The amount of workspace required is $4 + 24*(\text{number of labels})$ per variable.

Example

```
SORT CASES BY DEPT.
REPORT FORMAT=AUTOMATIC LIST
  /VARIABLES=PRODUCT (LABEL) ' ' 'Retail' 'Products'
            SALES 'Annual' 'Sales' '1981'
  /BREAK=DEPT 'Department'
  /SUMMARY=VALIDN (PRODUCT) MEAN (SALES) 'No.Sold,Mean Sales'.
```

- This report is a listing of products and sales by department. A summary of the total number of products sold and the average sales by department is also produced.
- Cases are first sorted by DEPT to ensure that cases are appropriately grouped for the calculation of statistics.
- FORMAT requests AUTOMATIC format and a report that includes a listing of cases within each break group.
- VARIABLES specifies PRODUCT and SALES as the report variables and requests that the value labels identifying products be displayed. Three-line column headings are provided for each report column. The first line of the column head is blank for the variable PRODUCT.
- BREAK identifies DEPT as the break variable and provides a one-line column title for the break column.
- SUMMARY requests the calculation of the valid number of cases for PRODUCT and the mean of SALES for each value of DEPT. A title is provided for the summary line to override the default title, VALIDN.

FORMAT Subcommand

```
FORMAT=[AUTOMATIC|MANUAL]  [NOLIST|LIST[(n)]]
      [PAGE(n)]  [LENGTH(t,b)]  [MARGINS(l,r)]
      [ALIGN(LEFT|CENTER|RIGHT)]  [COLSPACE(n)]
      [CHALIGN(TOP|BOTTOM)]  [UNDERSCORE(ON|OFF)]
      [TSPACE(n)]  [CHDSPACE(n)]  [BRKSPACE(n)]
      [SUMSPACE(n)]  [FTSPACE(n)]  [MISSING 's']
```

The optional FORMAT subcommand controls the overall width and length of the report and vertical spacing.

- Keyword specifications and their arguments can be named in any order.

The following can be specified on FORMAT:

AUTOMATIC
MANUAL
The default settings. AUTOMATIC facilitates report design by doing the following: displays labels for break variables; centers all data; centers column headings but left-justifies column headings if value labels or string values exceed the width of the longest word in the heading; bottom aligns and underscores column headings; extends column widths to accommodate the longest word in a variable label or the variable's longest value label; shrinks a report that is too wide for its margins. MANUAL does the following: displays values for break variables; right-justifies numeric values and their column headings; left-justifies value labels and string values and their column headings; top aligns and does not underscore column headings; extends column widths to accom-

C

Command Reference

modate the variable's longest value label (but not the longest word in the variable label), up to a width of 20; generates an error message when a report is too wide for its margins. MANUAL is the default.

NOLIST
LIST[(n)]   *Listing of individual cases.* List the values of all variables named on the VARIABLES subcommand for each case. The optional *n* indicates that a blank line be inserted after each *n* cases; the default is not to insert blank lines. Values for cases are listed using the default formats for the variables. The default is the alternative NOLIST, which requests that no case listing be produced.

PAGE(n)   *The number for the first page of the report.* The default is 1.

LENGTH(t,b)   *The top and bottom lines of the report.* The value for the bottom line cannot be greater than the system page length. The system page length is controlled by SET. By default, the top of the report begins at line 1 and the bottom of the report is the last line of the system page length. You can use an asterisk to indicate a default value.

MARGINS(l,r)   *The columns for the left and right margins.* By default, the left margin is print column 1 and the right margin is the rightmost print column of the system page width, which is controlled by the SET WIDTH command. The right column cannot be beyond the width specified on SET. You can use an asterisk to indicate a default value.

ALIGN   *The report's placement relative to its margins.* The specification is either (LEFT), (CENTER), or (RIGHT). (LEFT) left justifies the report. (CENTER) centers the report between its margins. (RIGHT) right justifies the report. The default is (LEFT).

COLSPACE(n)   *The number of spaces between each column.* The default is the lesser of either 4 or the result obtained by first subtracting the combined column widths of the break and report variables from the REPORT margins and then dividing the difference by the number of columns minus one. When AUTOMATIC is in effect, REPORT overrides the specified column spacing if necessary to fit the report between its margins.

CHALIGN   *Alignment of column headings.* The specification is either (TOP) or (BOTTOM). (TOP) aligns all column headings with the first, or top, line of multi-line headings. (BOTTOM) aligns headings with the last, or bottom, line of multi-line headings. The default when AUTOMATIC is in effect is (BOTTOM); when MANUAL is in effect, it is (TOP).

UNDERSCORE   *Heading underscores.* The specification is either (ON) or (OFF). (ON) underscores the bottom line of each column heading for the full width of the column. (OFF) does not underscore column headings. The default when AUTOMATIC is in effect is (ON); when MANUAL is in effect, it is (OFF).

TSPACE(n)   *The number of blank lines between the report title and the column heads.* The default is 1.

CHDSPACE(n)   *The number of blank lines beneath the longest column head.* The default is 1.

BRKSPACE(n)   *The number of blank lines between the break head and the next line.* The next line is a case if LIST is in effect or the first summary line if NOLIST is in effect. BRKSPACE(−1) places the first summary statistic or the first case listing on the same line as the break value. When a summary line is placed on the same line as the break value, the summary title is suppressed. When AUTO-MATIC is in effect, the default is -1; when MANUAL is in effect, it is 1.

SUMSPACE(n) *The number of blank lines between the last summary line at the lower break and the first summary line at the higher break when they break simultaneously.* SUMSPACE also controls spacing between the last case listed and the first summary line if LIST is in effect. The default is 1.

FTSPACE(n) *The minimum number of blank lines between the last listing on the page and the footnote.* The default is 1.

MISSING 's' *Missing-value symbol.* The symbol can be only 1 character and is used to represent both system- and user-missing values. The default is a period (.).

Example   `/FORMAT=AUTOMATIC LIST MARGINS(1,60) LENGTH(5,30) MISSING ('*')`

• This FORMAT subcommand requests a case listing, defines a new page size smaller than the system page size, and specifies an asterisk as the missing-value symbol.

Page Layout   Figure A displays the complete page layout and subcommand specifications used to control the basic structure of the report.

Figure A Page layout for REPORT

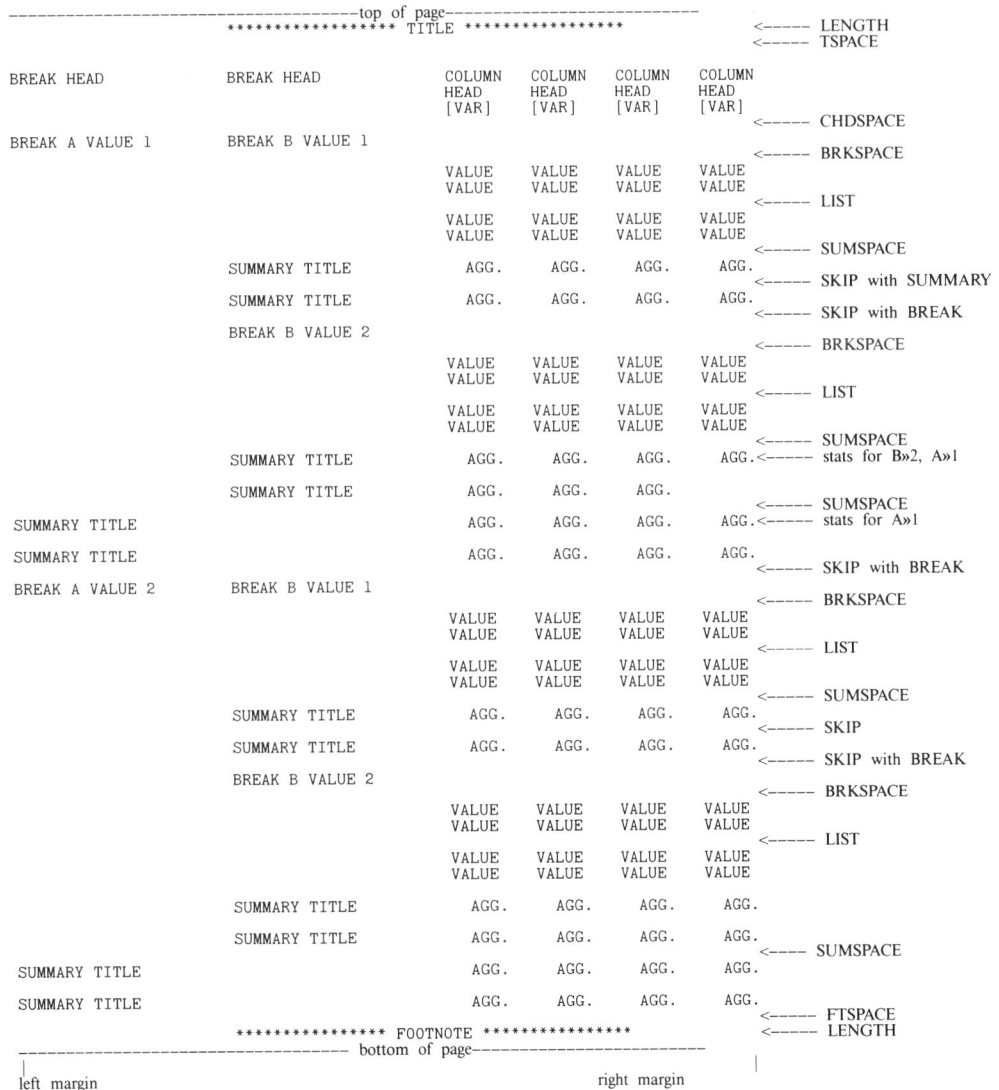

```
----------------------------------------top of page----------------------------
                     ****************** TITLE ******************          <----- LENGTH
                                                                          <----- TSPACE
BREAK HEAD           BREAK HEAD              COLUMN  COLUMN  COLUMN  COLUMN
                                            HEAD    HEAD    HEAD    HEAD
                                            [VAR]   [VAR]   [VAR]   [VAR]
                                                                          <----- CHDSPACE
BREAK A VALUE 1      BREAK B VALUE 1
                                                                          <----- BRKSPACE
                                            VALUE   VALUE   VALUE   VALUE
                                            VALUE   VALUE   VALUE   VALUE
                                                                          <----- LIST
                                            VALUE   VALUE   VALUE   VALUE
                                            VALUE   VALUE   VALUE   VALUE
                                                                          <----- SUMSPACE
                     SUMMARY TITLE          AGG.    AGG.    AGG.    AGG.
                                                                          <----- SKIP with SUMMARY
                     SUMMARY TITLE          AGG.    AGG.    AGG.    AGG.
                                                                          <----- SKIP with BREAK
                     BREAK B VALUE 2
                                                                          <----- BRKSPACE
                                            VALUE   VALUE   VALUE   VALUE
                                            VALUE   VALUE   VALUE   VALUE
                                                                          <----- LIST
                                            VALUE   VALUE   VALUE   VALUE
                                            VALUE   VALUE   VALUE   VALUE
                                                                          <----- SUMSPACE
                     SUMMARY TITLE          AGG.    AGG.    AGG.    AGG. <----- stats for B»2, A»1
                     SUMMARY TITLE          AGG.    AGG.    AGG.
                                                                          <----- SUMSPACE
SUMMARY TITLE                               AGG.    AGG.    AGG.    AGG. <----- stats for A»1
SUMMARY TITLE                               AGG.    AGG.    AGG.    AGG.
                                                                          <----- SKIP with BREAK
BREAK A VALUE 2      BREAK B VALUE 1
                                                                          <----- BRKSPACE
                                            VALUE   VALUE   VALUE   VALUE
                                            VALUE   VALUE   VALUE   VALUE
                                                                          <----- LIST
                                            VALUE   VALUE   VALUE   VALUE
                                            VALUE   VALUE   VALUE   VALUE
                                                                          <----- SUMSPACE
                     SUMMARY TITLE          AGG.    AGG.    AGG.    AGG.
                                                                          <----- SKIP
                     SUMMARY TITLE          AGG.    AGG.    AGG.    AGG.
                                                                          <----- SKIP with BREAK
                     BREAK B VALUE 2
                                                                          <----- BRKSPACE
                                            VALUE   VALUE   VALUE   VALUE
                                            VALUE   VALUE   VALUE   VALUE
                                                                          <----- LIST
                                            VALUE   VALUE   VALUE   VALUE
                                            VALUE   VALUE   VALUE   VALUE
                     SUMMARY TITLE          AGG.    AGG.    AGG.    AGG.
                     SUMMARY TITLE          AGG.    AGG.    AGG.    AGG.
                                                                          <---- SUMSPACE
SUMMARY TITLE                               AGG.    AGG.    AGG.    AGG.
SUMMARY TITLE                               AGG.    AGG.    AGG.    AGG.
                                                                          <----- FTSPACE
                     *************** FOOTNOTE ****************             <----- LENGTH
------------------------------------ bottom of page------------------------
left margin                                          right margin
```

OUTFILE Subcommand

The OUTFILE subcommand allows you to direct the report to a disk file other than the SPSS/PC+ listing file. You can later print this file from DOS without having to delete the extraneous material that would be present in the listing file.

- OUTFILE must follow the FORMAT subcommand.
- Specifications on OUTFILE consist of a filename in apostrophes.
- You can send the report to a directory or drive other than your current defaults by specifying an appropriate DOS file specification.
- You can print the report with the DOS *PRINT* command at the end of your session.
- The report does not appear on your screen when you specify OUTFILE.

Example

```
REPORT FORMAT=LIST
  /OUTFILE='B:SALES.RPT'
  /VARIABLES=SALES,QUOTA
  /BREAK=REGION
  /SUMMARY=MEAN.
```

- The report is written to SALES.RPT on the floppy diskette in drive B:.

VARIABLES Subcommand

```
/VARIABLES=var|var TO var [(VALUE|LABEL|DUMMY)] ['col head']
           [(LEFT|CENTER|RIGHT)] [(width)]
           [(OFFSET(n|CENTER))] [varname...]
```

The required VARIABLES subcommand names the variables to be listed and summarized in the report. Optionally, you can use VARIABLES to control column titles, column widths, and the contents of report columns.

- The minimum VARIABLES specification is a list of variables. These are the report variables. The number of variables that can be named is limited by the system page width.
- Variables named on the BREAK subcommand can also be named on VARIABLES.
- Each report variable defines a report column. Each report column can be thought of as having the name of the variable that defines it.
- The value of the variable or an aggregate statistic calculated on the variable is displayed in that variable's report column.
- Variables are assigned to columns in the order in which they are named on the VARIABLES subcommand.
- When FORMAT=LIST, variables can be stacked in a single column by linking them with + signs on the VARIABLES subcommand. If no column heading is specified, REPORT uses the default heading from the first variable on the list. Only values from the first variable in the stacked list are used to calculate summaries.
- Optional specifications can be given in any order following the variable name to which they apply.
- Optional specifications apply only to the immediately preceding variable or list of variables implied by the TO keyword.

The following options can be specified:

(VALUE)
(LABEL)
(DUMMY)

Contents of the report column assigned to the variable. If no specification is given, the keyword (VALUE) is in effect. (VALUE) specifies that values of the variable be displayed in the column. The alternative keyword (LABEL) displays value labels if value labels are defined, and values otherwise. (VALUE) and (LABEL) have no effect unless LIST has been specified on the FORMAT subcommand.

(DUMMY) defines a report column for a variable that does not exist in the active file. Such dummy variables are used to control spacing or to reserve space for statistics computed upon other variables. Do not name an existing SPSS/PC+ variable as a dummy variable.

When AUTOMATIC is in effect, value labels or string values are centered in the column based on the length of the longest string or label; numeric values are centered based on the width of the widest value or summary format. When MANUAL is in effect, value labels or string values are left-justified in the column; numeric values are right-justified.

'column title'   *Title used for the report column assigned to the variable.* Specify multiple-line titles by enclosing each line in a set of apostrophes or quotes, using the conventions for strings (see Universals: Strings). Separate the specifications for title lines with at least one blank.

If no column title is specified, the default column title is the variable label, or the variable name if no variable label has been specified.

Default column titles wrap for as many lines as are required to display the entire label. If AUTOMATIC is in effect, user-specified column titles appear exactly as specified, even if the column width must be extended. If MANUAL is in effect, user-specified titles wrap to fit within the column width.

(LEFT)   *Alignment of the column heading.* If AUTOMATIC is in effect,
(CENTER)   column headings are centered within their columns; if value labels
(RIGHT)   or string values exceed the width of the longest word in the heading, the heading is left-justified. If MANUAL is in effect, column headings are left-justified for value labels or string values, and right-justified for numeric values.

(width)   *Width for the report column.* If no width is specified for a variable, REPORT determines a default width using the criteria described under Defaults, above. If you specify a width that is not wide enough to display numeric values, REPORT first rounds decimal digits, then converts to scientific notation if possible, and then displays asterisks. Value labels or string values that exceed the width are truncated.

(OFFSET)   *Adjust the position of the report column contents.* The specification is either (n) or (CENTER). (OFFSET(n)) indicates the number of spaces to offset. Contents are offset from the left for value labels or string values, and from the right for numeric values. (OFFSET(CENTER)) centers contents within the center of the column. If AUTOMATIC is in effect, the default is CENTER. (However, entering a number on OFFSET offsets the contents from the justified position, not from the center.) If MANUAL is in effect, the default is 0.

Example
```
/VARIABLES=V1 TO V3 (LABEL) (15)
            V4
            V5 (LABEL)(OFFSET (2))(10)
            SEP1 (DUMMY) (2) ''
            V6 'Results using' "Lieben's Method" 'of Calculation'
```

- The variables from V1 through V3 have report columns with a width of 15 each. Values are listed in the case listing. Value labels are displayed for these variables in the case listing.

- Variable V4 has a report column with the default width. Values are listed in the case listing.

- Value labels are displayed for variable V5. The column has a width of 10 columns. Column contents are offset two spaces from the left.

- SEP1 is a dummy variable. The column width is 2, and there is at least one space column on each side of SEP1. Thus, there are at least 4 blanks between the columns for V5 and V6. SEP1 is given a null title to override the default column title SEP1.

- V6 is given a three-line title. Its column has the default width, and values are listed in the case listing.

STRING Subcommand

```
/STRING=stringname (varname [(width)] [(BLANK)] ['literal'])
```

```
[stringname...]
```

The optional STRING subcommand concatenates variables and user-specified strings into temporary string variables that exist only within REPORT.

• The minimum specification is a name for the string variable followed by a variable name or a user-specified string enclosed in parentheses.

• The name assigned to the string variable must be unique.

• Any combination of string variables, numeric variables, and user-specified strings can be used enclosed in parentheses to define the string.

• The keyword TO cannot be used within the parentheses to imply a variable list.

• More than one string variable can be defined on the STRING subcommand.

• If a variable within the parentheses has a missing value, the string has a system-missing value, and the missing-value symbol is used for that value in case listings.

• A string variable defined in REPORT cannot exceed the system page width.

• String variables defined on the STRING subcommand can be used on the VARIABLES or BREAK subcommand.

The following options can be specified:

(width) *Column width within the string of the preceding variable.* The default width is the dictionary width of the variable.
  If the width specified is less than required by the value, asterisks are displayed for numeric values, and string values are truncated on the right. If the width exceeds the width of a value, values of numeric variables are padded with zeros on the left and values of string variables are padded with blanks on the right.
  The maximum width for numeric variables within the string definition is 16. The maximum width for a string variable is the system page width.

(BLANK) *Left-pad values of the preceding numeric variable with blanks.* If the specification is omitted, the default is to left-pad values of numeric variables with zeros. If a numeric variable has a DOLLAR or COMMA format, it is automatically left-padded with blanks.

'literal' *A user-specified string.* Any combination of characters can be specified, enclosed in apostrophes or quotes.

Example
```
/STRING=JOB1(AVAR VARN)
       JOB2(AVAR(2) VARN(3))
       JOB3(AVAR(2) VARN(BLANK) (4))
```

• This STRING subcommand defines three string variables to be used within the report.

• Assume that AVAR is a string variable read from a four-column field using the FIXED keyword on DATA LIST, and that VARN is a computed numeric variable with the default format of 8 columns with 2 implied decimal places.

• If a case has the value 'KJ ' for AVAR and the value 241 for VARN, JOB1 displays the value KJ 00241.00, JOB2 the value KJ241, and JOB3 the value KJ 241.

Example
```
/STRING=SOCSEC(S1 '-' S2 '-' S3)
```

• This STRING subcommand concatenates the three variables S1, S2, and S3, which each contain a portion of the social security number.

• Hyphens are inserted between the portions when the values of SOCSEC are displayed.

• This example assumes that the variables S1, S2, and S3 were read from three-column, two-column, and four-column fields respectively, using the FIXED keyword on DATA LIST. These variables have format widths of 3, 2, and 4 columns, and are not left-padded with zeros.

BREAK Subcommand

```
/BREAK=[varlist] [(VALUE|LABEL)] ['col title']
       [(LEFT|CENTER|RIGHT)] [(width)] [(OFFSET(n|CENTER))]
       [(UNDERSCORE(ON|OFF))] [(NOTOTAL|TOTAL)]
       [(NONAME|NAME)] [(SKIP(n|PAGE))]
```

The BREAK subcommand specifies the variables that define the subgroups for the report display, or specifies summary totals for reports with no subgroups. BREAK also allows you to control the titles, width, and contents of break columns and to begin a new page for each level of the break variable.

• A break occurs when any one of the break variables named on BREAK changes value. Cases must be presorted by the values of all BREAK variables on all BREAK subcommands.

• The keyword TO can be used to specify an implied variable list.

• To obtain summary totals without any break levels, use the keyword (TOTAL) on BREAK without listing any variables.

• Optional specifications can be given in any order following the last variable named.

• Multiple BREAK subcommands can be used.

• When you use more than one BREAK subcommand, specify (TOTAL) on only one BREAK to get a summary for the entire file. Otherwise, redundant statistics may be displayed. (Use as many SUMMARY subcommands as you need to specify the statistics to be totaled.)

• Missing-value specifications are ignored for variables named on the BREAK subcommand. There is one break category for system-missing values and one for user-missing values. The values are displayed using the missing-value symbol controlled by the FORMAT subcommand.

• The BREAK subcommand must precede the SUMMARY subcommand that defines the summary line for the break.

• A break column is reserved for each BREAK subcommand.

• If more than one variable is specified on a BREAK subcommand, a single break column is used. The value or value label for each variable is displayed on a separate line, in the order in which the variables are named on BREAK. The first variable named changes most slowly. The default column width is the longest of the default widths for any of the break variables.

• Optional specifications apply to all variables in the break column and to the break column as a whole.

The following can be specified on BREAK:

(VALUE)
(LABEL) *Contents of the break column.* (VALUE) specifies that values of the break variables be displayed in the column. The alternative keyword (LABEL) displays value labels if value labels have been defined, and values otherwise. The value is displayed only once for each break change and is not repeated at the top of the page in a multiple-page break group. When AUTOMATIC is in effect, the default is (LABEL); when MANUAL is in effect, it is (VALUE).

When AUTOMATIC is in effect, value labels and string values are centered in the column based on the length of the longest string or label; numeric values are centered based on the width of the widest value or summary format. When MANUAL is in effect, value labels and string values are left-justified in the column; numeric values are right-justified.

'column head' *Title used for the break column.* Specify multiple-line titles by enclosing each line in a set of apostrophes or quotes, following the conventions for strings (see Universals: Strings). Separate the specifications for title lines with at least one blank.

The default title is the variable label of the break variable or the variable name if no label has been defined. If the break column is defined by more than one variable, the label or name of the first variable is used.

Default column titles wrap for as many lines as are required to display the entire label. If AUTOMATIC is in effect, user-specified column titles appear exactly as specified, even if the column width must be extended. If MANUAL is in effect, user-specified titles wrap to fit within the column width.

(LEFT)
(CENTER)
(RIGHT)

Alignment of the column heading. When AUTOMATIC is in effect, column headings are centered within their columns. However, if value labels or string values exceed the width of the longest word in the heading, the heading is left-justified. When MANUAL is in effect, column headings are left-justified for value labels or string values, and right-justified for numeric values.

(width)

Column width for the break column. If no width is specified for a variable, REPORT determines a default width using the criteria described under Defaults, above. If you specify a width that is not wide enough to display numeric values, REPORT first rounds decimal digits, then converts to scientific notation if possible, and then displays asterisks. Value labels or string values that exceed the width are truncated.

(OFFSET)

Adjust the position of the break column contents. The specification is either (*n*) or (CENTER). (OFFSET(*n*)) indicates the number of spaces to offset. Contents are offset from the left for value labels or string values, and from the right for numeric values. (OFFSET(CENTER)) centers contents within the center of the column. If AUTOMATIC is in effect, the default is CENTER. (However, entering a number on OFFSET offsets the contents from the justified position, not from the center.) If MANUAL is in effect, the default is 0.

(UNDERSCORE) *Heading underscores.* The specification is either (ON) or (OFF). (UNDERSCORE(ON)) underscores the bottom line of each column heading for the full width of the column. (UNDER-SCORE(OFF)) does not underscore column headings. The default when AUTOMATIC is in effect is (ON); when MANUAL is in effect, it is (OFF).

(TOTAL)
(NOTOTAL)

(TOTAL) calculates summary statistics specified on the next SUMMARY subcommand for all the cases on the report. (NOTOTAL) is the default and displays summary statistics only for each break.

(SKIP)
(PAGE)

The vertical spacing between the last summary line for a break and the next break. The specification is either (*n*) or (PAGE). If (SKIP(*n*)) is specified, each break begins following *n* blank lines. The default is 1. If (PAGE) is specified, each break begins on a new page. If (RESET) is specified on (PAGE), the page counter resets to the PAGE1 setting on the FORMAT subcommand every time the break value changes for the specified variable. (PAGE(RESET)) is not allowed on listing reports with no break levels.

(NAME)
(NONAME)

Display the name of the break variable alongside each value or value label of the break variable. (NAME) requires 10 spaces (the maximum eight-character length of SPSS/PC+ variable names plus two parentheses) in addition to the space needed to display break values or value labels. (NAME) is ignored if the break-column width is insufficient. If the default keyword (NONAME) is specified, the name of the break variable is omitted.

Example

```
SORT DIVISION BRANCH DEPT.
REPORT FORMAT=AUTOMATIC MARGINS (1,70) BRKSPACE(-1)
  /VARIABLES=SPACE(DUMMY) ' ' (4)
              SALES 'Annual' 'Sales' '1981' (15) (OFFSET(2))
              EXPENSES 'Annual' 'Expenses' '1981' (15)
(OFFSET(2))
  /BREAK=DIVISION
          BRANCH (10) (TOTAL) (OFFSET(1))
      /SUMMARY=MEAN
  /BREAK=DEPT 'Department' (10)
      /SUMMARY=MEAN.
```

- This example creates a report that breaks on three variables. BRANCH breaks within values of DIVISION, and DEPT breaks within values of BRANCH.
- FORMAT sets margins to a maximum of 70 columns and requests that the summary line be displayed on the same report line as the break values. Because LIST is not specified on FORMAT, only summary statistics are displayed.
- VARIABLES defines three report columns, each occupied by a report variable: SPACE, SALES, and EXPENSES.
- The variable SPACE is a dummy variable that exists only within REPORT. It has a null title and a width of 4. It is used as a space holder to separate the break columns from the report columns.
- SALES is given a three-line title and a width of 15. The values of SALES are offset 2 spaces from the right.
- EXPENSES is the third report variable and has the same width and offset specifications as SALES.
- The leftmost column in the report is reserved for the first two break variables, DIVISION and BRANCH. The break column has a width of 10, and the value labels are offset 1 space from the left. Any value label more than 9 characters long is truncated. The default column title is used. (TOTAL) requests that the BRANCH summary line be displayed when all values of DIVISION and BRANCH have been cycled through; that is, at the end of the report.
- The summary line for the first BREAK subcommand consists of the mean of each report variable, displayed in its own report column. This line is displayed each time the value of DIVISION or BRANCH changes.
- The third break variable, DEPT, occupies the second column from the left in the report. The break column has a width of 10 and has a one-line title. The first 10 characters of the value labels are displayed in the break column.
- The second SUMMARY subcommand displays the mean for each report variable when the value of DEPT changes.

SUMMARY Subcommand

```
/SUMMARY={function...['summary title'][(break col #)] [SKIP(n)]}
         {PREVIOUS[(n)]                                         }
```

where function is

```
aggregate [(varname[(d)][(PLAIN|DOLLAR|COMMA)][varname...])]
```

or

```
composite(agg(varname)...)[(report col[(d)][(PLAIN|DOLLAR|
COMMA)])]
```

The SUMMARY subcommand calculates a wide range of aggregate and composite statistics.

- A SUMMARY subcommand must be specified unless LIST is specified on the FORMAT subcommand.
- Each SUMMARY subcommand following a BREAK subcommand specifies a new summary line.
- The minimum specification is an aggregate function or a composite function and its arguments. This must be the first specification on SUMMARY.
- The default format can be altered for any function. Format specifications in an aggregate modify only the immediately preceding result.
- The default location of the summary title is the column of the break variable to which the summary applies.
- When more than one function is named on the SUMMARY subcommand, the default summary title is that of the function named first.
- Both the title and the default column location of the title can be altered.
- SUMMARY subcommands apply only to the preceding BREAK subcommand. If there is no SUMMARY subcommand after a BREAK subcommand, no statistics are displayed for that break level.
- Specify the keyword PREVIOUS on SUMMARY to use the summary specifications from a previous BREAK subcommand for the current BREAK subcommand.

C

Command Reference

- More than one function can be specified on SUMMARY as long as you do not attempt to place two results in the same column.
- Multiple summary statistics requested on one SUMMARY subcommand are all displayed on the same summary report line.
- Use the SKIP keyword to insert blank lines when more than one summary line is requested for a break.
- An implicit or explicit attempt to place the result of two or more functions in the same report column stops execution of REPORT. Use multiple SUMMARY subcommands to place results of more than one function in the same report column.
- Summary lines can combine any composite functions and aggregrate functions (except FREQUENCY and PERCENT).

Aggregate Functions

Use the aggregate functions to request descriptive statistics on report variables.

- If no variable names are given as arguments to an aggregate function, the statistic is calculated for all variables named on the VARIABLES subcommand; that is, for all report variables.
- To request an aggregate function for a subset of the report variables, specify the list of report variables in parentheses after the function keyword.
- All variables specified on an aggregate function must have been named on the VARIABLES subcommand.
- The keyword TO cannot be used to specify a list of variables for an aggregate function.
- The result of an aggregate function is always displayed in the report column reserved for the variable on which the function was calculated.
- To use several aggregate functions on the same report variable, specify multiple SUMMARY subcommands. The results are displayed on different summary lines.
- The aggregate functions FREQUENCY and PERCENT have special display formats and cannot be placed on the same summary line with other aggregate or composite functions.
- Aggregate functions use only cases with valid values.

The following aggregate functions are available:

VALIDN	*Valid number of cases.* This is the only function that operates on string variables.
SUM	*Sum of values.*
MIN	*Minimum value encountered.*
MAX	*Maximum value encountered.*
MEAN	*Mean.*
STDDEV	*Standard deviation.* Aliases are SD and STDEV.
VARIANCE	*Variance.*
KURTOSIS	*Kurtosis.*
SKEWNESS	*Skewness.*
MEDIAN(min,max)	*Median value for values within the range.* MEDIAN sets up integer-valued bins for counting all values in the specified range. Noninteger values are truncated when the median is calculated.
MODE(min,max)	*Modal value for values within the range.* MODE sets up integer-valued bins for counting all values in the specified range. Noninteger values are truncated when the mode is calculated.
PCGT(n)	*Percentage of cases with values greater than specified value.*
PCLT(n)	*Percentage of cases with values less than specified value.*

PCIN(min,max)   *Percentage of cases within the inclusive value range specified.*

FREQUENCY(min,max)   *Frequency counts for values within the inclusive range.* FREQUENCY sets up integer-valued bins for counting all values in the specified range. Noninteger values are truncated when the frequency is computed. FREQUENCY cannot be mixed with other aggregate statistics on a summary line.

PERCENT(min,max)   *Percentages for values within the inclusive range.* PERCENT sets up integer-valued bins for counting all values in the specified range. Noninteger values are truncated when the frequency is computed. PERCENT cannot be mixed with other aggregate statistics on a summary line.

Example
```
SORT CASES BY BVAR AVAR.
REPORT FORMAT=AUTOMATIC LIST
  /VARIABLES=XVAR YVAR ZVAR
  /BREAK=BVAR
    /SUMMARY=SUM
    /SUMMARY=MEAN (XVAR YVAR ZVAR)
    /SUMMARY=VALIDN(XVAR)
  /BREAK=AVAR
    /SUMMARY=PREVIOUS.
```

• The FORMAT subcommand requests a case listing, and the VARIABLES subcommand establishes a report column for variables XVAR, YVAR, and ZVAR. The report columns have default widths and titles.

• Both break variables, BVAR and AVAR, have default widths and titles.

• Every time the value of BVAR changes, three summary lines are displayed. The first line contains the sums for variables XVAR, YVAR, and ZVAR. The second line contains the means of all three variables. The third line displays the number of valid cases for XVAR in the report column for XVAR.

• Every time the value of AVAR changes within each value of BVAR, the three summary lines requested for BVAR are displayed. These summary lines are based on cases with the current value of BVAR that also have the current value of AVAR.

Example
```
SORT CASES BY DEPT.
REPORT FORMAT=AUTOMATIC
  /VARIABLES=WAGE BONUS TENURE
  /BREAK=DEPT (23)
  /SUM=SUM(WAGE BONUS) MEAN(TENURE) 'Sum Income: Mean Tenure'.
```

• The SUMMARY subcommand defines a summary line consisting of the sums of WAGE and BONUS and the mean of TENURE. The result of each aggregate function is displayed in the report column of the variable on which the function is calculated.

• A title is assigned to the summary line. A width of 23 is defined for the break column to accommodate the right-justified summary-line title.

Composite Functions   Use composite functions to obtain statistics based on aggregated statistics, to place a summary statistic in a column other than that of the report variable on which it was calculated, or to manipulate variables not named on the VARIABLES subcommand.

• Composite functions can be computed upon constants and any variable in the active file.

• The following aggregate functions can also be arguments to composite functions: VALIDN, SUM, MIN, MAX, MEAN, STDEV, VARIANCE, KURTOSIS, and SKEWNESS. When used within composite functions, aggregate functions can have only one variable as an argument.

• A composite function and its arguments cannot be separated from each other by other SUMMARY specifications.

• By default, the results of a composite function are placed in the report column of the first variable named on the composite function that is also named on the VARIABLES subcommand.

- The result of a composite function can be placed in any report column, including columns of dummy or string variables, by specifying a target column. To specify a target column, enclose the variable name of a report column in parentheses after the composite function and its arguments.
- The format for the result of a composite function can be specified in parentheses after the name of the column location and within the parentheses that enclose the column-location specification.

The following composite functions are available:

DIVIDE(agg() agg() [factor]) *Divide the first argument by the second and multiply by the optional factor.*

MULTIPLY(agg() ... agg()) *Multiply the arguments.*

PCT(agg() agg()) *Percentage of the first argument over the second.*

SUBTRACT(agg()agg()) *Subtract the second argument from the first argument.*

ADD(agg() ... agg()) *Add the arguments.*

GREAT(agg() ... agg()) *Give the maximum of the arguments.*

LEAST(agg() ... agg()) *Give the minimum of the arguments.*

AVERAGE(agg() ... agg()) *Give the average of the arguments.*

Example
```
SORT CASES BY DEPT.
REPORT FORMAT=AUTOMATIC BRKSPACE(-1)
  /VARIABLES=WAGE BONUS SPACE1 (DUMMY) ''
             BNFT1 BNFT2 SPACE2 (DUMMY)''
  /BREAK=DEPT
    /SUMMARY=MEAN(WAGE BONUS BNFT1 BNFT2)
             ADD(VALIDN(WAGE)) (SPACE2)
    /SUMMARY=ADD(SUM(WAGE) SUM(BONUS))
             ADD(SUM(BNFT1) SUM(BNFT2)) 'Totals' SKIP(1)
    /SUMMARY=DIVIDE(MEAN(WAGE) MEAN(BONUS)) (SPACE1 (COMMA)(2))
             DIVIDE(MEAN(BNFT1) MEAN(BNFT2)) (SPACE2 (COMMA)(2))
             'Ratios' SKIP(1).
```

- The VARIABLES subcommand defines six report columns. The columns called WAGE, BONUS, BNFT1, and BNFT2 contain aggregate statistics based on those variables. The variables SPACE1 and SPACE2 are dummy variables that are created for use as space holders; each is given a blank title to suppress the default column head.
- The first SUMMARY computes the means of the variables WAGE, BONUS, BNFT1, and BNFT2. Because BRKSPACE=−1, this summary line will be placed on the same report line as the break value and will have no summary title. The means are displayed in the report column for each variable. SUMMARY also computes the valid number of cases for WAGE inside a composite function and places the result in SPACE2 column.
- The second SUMMARY adds the sum of WAGE to the sum of BONUS. Since no location is specified, the result is displayed in the WAGE column. In addition, the sum of BNFT1 is added to the sum of BNFT2, and the result is placed in the BNFT1 column. One line is skipped before the summary line requested by this SUMMARY subcommand is displayed.
- The third summary line divides the mean of WAGE by the mean of BONUS and places the result in SPACE1. The ratio of the mean of BNFT1 to the mean of BNFT2 is displayed in the SPACE2 column. Because locations are specified, formats can also be given. The results are displayed with commas and 2 decimal places. One line is skipped before the summary line requested by this SUMMARY subcommand is displayed.

Summary Titles   The default titles for summary lines are listed below:

Keyword	Title
VALIDN	N
VARIANCE	Variance
SUM	Sum
MEAN	Mean
STDDEV	StdDev
MIN	Minimum
MAX	Maximum
SKEWNESS	Skewness
KURTOSIS	Kurtosis
PGT(n)	<n
PLT(n)	<n
PIN(n1,n2)	In n1 to n2
FREQUENCY(min,max)	Total
PERCENT(min,max)	Total
MEDIAN(min,max)	Median
MODE(min,max)	Mode

- You can specify a summary title enclosed in apostrophes or quotes, following the conventions for strings (see Universals: Strings).

- The summary title must be specified after the first function and its arguments. It cannot separate any function from its arguments.

- A summary title can be only one line long.

- A summary title wider than the break column extends into the next break column to the right. If the title is wider than all of the available break columns, it is truncated.

- Only one summary title applies per summary line. If more than one is specified, the last is used.

- The summary title is left- or right-justified depending upon whether the break title is left- or right-justified.

- The default location for the summary title is the column of the BREAK variable to which the summary applies.

- With multiple breaks, you can override the default placement of the title by specifying the break-column number in which you want the summary title to be displayed in parentheses following the title.

- In a report with no break levels, REPORT displays the summary title above the summary line at the left margin.

Summary Print Formats   All functions have default formats that are used to print results (see Table B). You can override these defaults by specifying a format keyword and/or the number of decimal places.

- A format specification must be enclosed in parentheses.

- For aggregate functions, one or both format specifications are placed after the variable name, within the parentheses that enclose the variable name. The variable must be explicitly named as an argument.

- For composite functions, one or both format specifications are placed after the variable name of the column location, within the parentheses that enclose the variable name. The column location must be explicitly specified.

- If the report column is wide enough, SUM, MEAN, STDDEV, MIN, MAX, MEDIAN, and MODE use DOLLAR or COMMA format if one has been declared for the variable on the FORMATS command.

- If the column is not wide enough to display the decimal digits for a given function, REPORT displays fewer decimal places. If the column is not wide enough to display the integer portion of the number, REPORT adopts scientific notation and then displays asterisks.

- An exact value of zero is displayed with one zero to the left of the decimal point and as many 0 digits to the right as specified by the format. A number less than 1 in absolute value is displayed without a zero to the left of the decimal point, except with DOLLAR and COMMA formats.

C

Command Reference

The following format keywords are available:

(DOLLAR) *Display the value using DOLLAR format.*

(COMMA) *Display the value using COMMA format.*

(PLAIN) *Override DOLLAR or COMMA dictionary formats.* PLAIN is the default for all functions except MEAN, STDDEV, MIN, MAX, MEDIAN, and MODE. For these functions, the default is the dictionary format.

Example

```
/SUMMARY=MEAN(INCOME (DOLLAR)(2))
         ADD(SUM(INCOME)SUM(WEALTH) (WEALTH(DOLLAR)(2))
```

• SUMMARY displays the mean of INCOME with dollar format and two decimal places. The format can be specified because INCOME is specified as an argument to the MEAN function. The result is displayed in the INCOME column.

• The sums of INCOME and WEALTH are added and the result is displayed with dollar format and two decimal places. The format can be specified because an explicit location is given for the results of ADD. The result is displayed in the WEALTH column.

Table B Default print formats for functions

Function	Width	Decimal places
VALIDN	5	0
SUM	Dictionary print format + 2	Dictionary print format
MEAN	Dictionary print format	Dictionary print format
STDDEV	Dictionary print format	Dictionary print format
VARIANCE	Dictionary print format	Dictionary print format
MIN	Dictionary print format	Dictionary print format
MAX	Dictionary print format	Dictionary print format
SKEWNESS	5	2
KURTOSIS	5	2
PGT	6	1
PLT	6	1
PIN	6	1
MEDIAN	Dictionary print format	Dictionary print format
MODE	Dictionary print format	Dictionary print format
PERCENT	6	1
FREQUENCY	5	0
DIVIDE	Dictionary print format	0
PCT	6	2
SUBTRACT	Dictionary print format	0
ADD	Dictionary print format	0
GREAT	Dictionary print format	0
LEAST	Dictionary print format	0
AVERAGE	Dictionary print format	0
MULTIPLY	Dictionary print format	0

Other SUMMARY Keywords

Spacing between multiple summary lines for a single break and references to previously defined summary lines are controlled by the following keywords:

SKIP(n) *Blank lines before the summary line.* SKIP is not enclosed in parentheses. The default is 0. SKIP on the first SUMMARY subcommand for a BREAK skips the specified lines after skipping the number of lines specified for BRKSPACE on FORMAT.

PREVIOUS(n) *Use the SUMMARY subcommands for the nth BREAK.* If no specification is given in parentheses, PREVIOUS points to the set of SUMMARY subcommands for the previous BREAK. If an integer specification is given, the SUMMARY subcommands from the *n*th BREAK are used.

No other specification can be used on SUMMARY with PREVIOUS. For a multiple-break report for which you want the same sets of summaries, specify SUMMARY subcommands for the higher BREAK subcommand and keyword PREVIOUS for lower breaks.

TITLE and FOOTNOTE Subcommands

```
/TITLE ='title' (centered head)
/FOOTNOTE='title' (centered foot)
```

or

```
/TITLE=LEFT 'title' (left-justified head)
/TITLE=CENTER 'title' (centered head)
/TITLE=RIGHT 'title' (right-justified head)
/FOOTNOTE=LEFT 'title' (left-justified foot)
/FOOTNOTE=CENTER 'title' (centered foot)
/FOOTNOTE=RIGHT 'title' (right-justified foot)
```

```
[)PAGE]    [)DATE]    [)var]
```

- The TITLE and FOOTNOTE subcommands are optional and can be placed anywhere after the FORMAT subcommand except among the BREAK and SUMMARY subcommands.
- TITLE subcommands should be specified before any FOOTNOTE subcommands.
- The default REPORT title is the title specified on the TITLE command. If there is no TITLE command specified in your SPSS/PC+ session, the default REPORT title is the first line of the SPSS/PC+ header.
- A title or footnote is specified by providing a string in apostrophes or quotes on one of the TITLE or FOOTNOTE subcommands.
- If the title or footnote is more than one line, enclose each line in apostrophes or quotes and separate the specifications for each line by at least one blank.
- The positional keywords LEFT, CENTER, and RIGHT can each be specified only once.
- Titles are displayed beginning in the first line of the system page.
- Footnotes end in the last line of the system page.
- Centered titles and footnotes are centered within the report page width.
- Titles and footnotes are repeated on each page of a multiple-page report.
- If the total width requested for the combined titles or foonotes for a line exceeds the page width, REPORT generates an error message.

Three keywords can be used in a title or footnote. *You must specify)PAGE and)DATE in upper case, as shown here.*

)PAGE *Display the page number right-justified in a five-character field.*

)DATE *Display the current date in the form* dd/mmm/yy *right-justified in a nine-character field.*

)var *Print this variable's value label in this relative position.* If you specify a variable that has no value label, the value itself will print, formatted according to its print format. You cannot specify a scratch or system variable, nor can you specify a variable you create with the STRING subcommand. In addition, you cannot use variables named DATE or PAGE in the)var argument because they will only print the current date or a page number. If you want to use a variable named DATE or PAGE, change the variable's name with the RENAME VARIABLES command before you use it in the)var argument.

Each variable you specify with)var must be one you've defined in the active file, though it does not need to be a variable you've included as a column on your report. One label or value from each variable specified in a)var argument prints on every page of the report. The label printed for each varies from page to page and is chosen from cases determined as follows:

C

Command Reference

- If a new page starts with a case listing, REPORT takes the value label from the first case listed.
- If a new page starts with a BREAK line, REPORT takes the value label from the first case of the new break group.
- If a new page starts with a summary line, REPORT takes the value label from the last case of the break group being summarized.
- If you specify the same variable in both a title and a footnote, REPORT takes the title value from the top case on the page, and the footnote value from the last case on the page.

Example

```
/TITLE=LEFT 'Personnel Report' 'Prepared on )DATE'
/TITLE=RIGHT 'Page )PAGE'
```

- The TITLE=LEFT subcommand provides a two-line title. The second line of this title contains the date on which the report was processed. This title is displayed left-justified at the top of each page of the report.
- The TITLE=RIGHT subcommand displays the page number following the string Page, right-justified at the top of each page.
- The keywords)DATE and)PAGE are entered in upper case.

MISSING Subcommand

```
/MISSING=VAR|NONE|LIST [([varlist][n])]
```

Use the optional MISSING subcommand to control the handling of cases with missing values on the VARIABLES and SUMMARY subcommands. By default, cases with missing values are included in case listings but are excluded from the calculation of functions on a function-by-function basis.

- MISSING specifications apply to variables named on VARIABLES and SUMMARY as well as to strings created with the STRING subcommand.
- The character used to indicate missing values is controlled by the FORMAT subcommand.

The following keywords are available for the MISSING subcommand:

VAR   *Missing values are treated separately for each variable.* Missing values are displayed in case listings but are not included in summary statistics. This is the default.

NONE   *User-missing-value indicators are ignored.* Applies to all variables named on the VARIABLES subcommand.

LIST[([varlist][n])]   *Eliminates any case with the specified number of missing values among the specified list of variables.* If no *n* is specified, the default is 1. If no variables are specified, all variables named on the VARIABLES subcommand are assumed.

Example

```
/MISSING=LIST (XVAR,YVAR,ZVAR 2)
```

- Any case with a missing value for two or more of the variables XVAR, YVAR, and ZVAR is omitted from the report.

REVIEW

```
REVIEW [{SCRATCH                }]
        {LISTING                }
        {LOG                    }
        {BOTH                   }
        {'filename' ['filename']}
```

Example:

```
REVIEW.
```

Overview   The REVIEW command initiates a REVIEW editing session. REVIEW is a full-screen editor specifically designed for editing SPSS/PC+ scratch pad and listing files. It allows you to edit two files at once in separate windows. It also allows you to submit revised command lines directly to SPSS/PC+ for execution.

The REVIEW command places you in a full-screen editing environment, complete with the Menu and Help system. In REVIEW, you can build your SPSS/PC+ commands in three ways: by selecting from the Menu and Help windows; by browsing the menus and then typing commands yourself; or by clearing the menus and typing complete commands in the scratch pad. REVIEW's editing commands are issued by selecting options from mini-menus called up with the function keys on your keyboard. For example, pressing (F4) calls up a mini-menu from which you can choose to insert, delete, or undelete lines.

Defaults   If no keywords are specified, REVIEW initiates an editing session of the current scratch pad and listing files. The Menu and Help windows initially cover up the listing file in the upper window. The scratch pad is displayed in the bottom window. On color monitors, REVIEW uses a default color scheme of (1,2,4) for lower-window (or only window) background color, upper-window background color, and frame color, respectively. See the manual for your monitor for the actual colors that correspond to these numbers. The default selection for each mini-menu is highlighted when the menu is called up.

Tailoring   You can edit any file or pair of files that consist of legible characters (see Limitations below). On color monitors, you can choose colors for the two editing windows and frame. You can also turn color off.

Syntax   • The minimum specification is the word REVIEW followed by the command terminator.

• Only one keyword (SCRATCH, LISTING, LOG, or BOTH) can be specified.

• Use the SCRATCH keyword to edit your SPSS/PC+ scratch pad file.

• Use the LISTING keyword to edit your SPSS/PC+ listing file.

• Use the LOG keyword to edit your SPSS/PC+ log file.

• Use the BOTH keyword to edit both the log and listing files simultaneously.

• If you do not use a keyword, you can specify one or two filenames within apostrophes to edit files other than your scratch pad, listing, and log files.

• At least one space must separate the keyword REVIEW and its specifications.

• When you enter REVIEW, the Menu and Help system is displayed in the upper window, concealing the listing file. (Alt) (M) reveals the listing file.

• Issue the SET RCOLOR command before entering REVIEW to set nondefault colors (see SET).

• Specify SET COLOR OFF before entering REVIEW to turn color off.

• As an alternative to using the mini-menus, you can perform some editing functions by using the (Alt) key in combination with various other keys.

• Some commands cause REVIEW to prompt for additional information, such as a filename, at the bottom of the screen. To cancel such commands when the prompt appears, press (Esc).

C

Command Reference

Operations

- You can enter REVIEW from SPSS/PC+ or directly from DOS.
- If you edit two files at once, REVIEW divides your screen into upper and lower windows. The file named first occupies the upper window and the file named second occupies the lower window. At first, the Menu and Help windows cover the upper window. You can clear the menus (or recall them) with (Alt) (M).
- To keep the menus up while you type in the other window, press (Alt) (E). To redirect your typing back to the menus, press (Esc).
- When you first enter REVIEW and the menus are on screen, the system searches the menu for a match to every character you type. The cursor moves to the first menu entry that matches what you've typed. This is called *incremental search.* To direct your keystrokes to the other window, press (Alt) (E).
- Editing occurs at the current line and character as determined by the position of the cursor.
- There are two editing modes: insert mode and overtype mode. In *insert mode,* entered text is inserted to the left of the current character. In *overtype mode,* entered text replaces existing text.
- A two-digit number in the lower-right corner of the screen displays the column location of the cursor.
- To enter extended ASCII characters in the Edit window, activate (NumLck) and use (Alt) with the numeric keypad. If (NumLck) is not activated, the keypad controls cursor movement, and when used with (Alt) scrolls the Help window.

Limitations

- You can edit only ASCII files with REVIEW. Do not attempt to edit formatted (non-ASCII) files used by spreadsheet, word-processing, or other software. If the listing of a file that results from a DOS *TYPE* command is meaningful, the file is probably an ASCII file.
- REVIEW displays only the first 80 characters of any line. Use the Split Line command to view lines longer than 80 characters.
- REVIEW works on files held in memory. It starts with the *last* lines in the file in memory and reads additional lines as required. You may not be able to edit very large files.

Example

```
REVIEW 'A:PLOT.INC' 'PLOT.LIS'.
```

Entering REVIEW from DOS

To enter REVIEW directly from DOS, specify:

```
SPSSPC/RE filename1 [filename2] [/La] [/Ub] [/Fc]
[/B]
```

- Place the names of the files you wish to edit in place of filename1 and filename2.
- If you wish to edit only one file, omit the second filename.
- The /La, /Ub, and /Fc options allow you to change the colors used for the lower (or only) window, upper window, and frame, respectively. Specify integers from 0 to 6 in place of a, b, and c. See the manual for your monitor for the colors that correspond to numbers 0 through 6.
- To turn off color use, specify /B on the command line.

If you plan to use REVIEW frequently from outside SPSS/PC+ with nondefault colors, create a batch file (a file with a .BAT extension) that contains the following single line:

```
SPSSPC /REVIEW /La /Ub /Fc %1 %2
```

- Specify the desired color numbers in place of a, b, and c.
- The batch file should be in the directory that holds your SPSS/PC+ program files.
- After you create the batch file, you can enter REVIEW by typing the name of the batch file followed by the names of the files you wish to edit. The colors you have specified in the batch file will take effect automatically.

	Command Name	**Key Combination/Function**
Setting and Information Commands	REVIEW help*	F1 followed by R (or Alt R) reveals the Help screen for REVIEW function keys and Menu system commands. Pressing F1 again reveals the Help screen for motion commands. When pressed in response to a prompt, F1 provides a short message explaining the prompt.
	Menus*	F1 followed by M (or Alt M) invokes the SPSS/PC+ Menu and Help system.
	Glossary*	F1 followed by G (or Alt G) calls up the online glossary. You are prompted for the term to look up; press ← to look up the term currently under the cursor, or enter another term before pressing ←. The glossary displays the closest alphabetic match.
	Filelist*	F1 followed by F (or Alt F) switches the Files menu on and off. The Files menu displays all (or a specified subset) the files in your current directory. When you need a filename to execute an SPSS/PC+ command, you can select the name from this menu. Esc clears the menu.
	Varlist*	F1 followed by V (or Alt V) switches the Variables menu on and off. The Variables menu displays all the variables defined in your active file. You can select variable names from this menu. Esc also clears the menu.
	Switch windows*	F2 followed by S (or Alt S) causes the editor to switch windows.
	Change window size*	F2 followed by C allows you to change the relative sizes of the two windows.

	Command Name	**Key Combination/Function**
Menu Commands	menu Hlp on*	F1 followed by H (or Alt H or Alt ?) switches the Help window on and off. The Help window contains an explanation of the currently highlighted menu item.
	Incremental Search	When the Menu and Help windows are displayed, the cursor automatically moves to the first item on the menu that matches what you type. If you type an *s*, the cursor moves to the first item that begins with *s*. If you then type an *e*, the cursor moves to the first item that begins with *se*.
	Get Typing Window	Alt T opens a narrow window at the bottom of the Menu and Help system window. You can type anything you want in this window and when you press ← the contents of this typing window are pasted in the Edit window.
	Down Menu	↓ moves the cursor down one item on the menu.
	Up Menu	↑ moves the cursor up one item on the menu.
	Bottom of Menu	End moves the cursor to the bottom of the menu.
	Top of Menu	Home moves the cursor to the top of the menu.
	Down Help Window	Alt ↓ moves you down one line in the Help window. Alt PgDn moves you down one page in the Help window.
	Up Help Window	Alt ↑ moves you up one line in the Help window. Alt PgUp moves you up one page in the Help window.
	Bottom of Help Window	Alt End moves you to the bottom of the Help window.
	Top of Help Window	Alt Home moves you to the top of the Help window.

C

Command Reference

Paste Menu Item, Descend Menus	⊢ pastes the highlighted menu item into the Edit window and descends to a lower-level menu (if any). If the menu item is followed by empty parentheses or apostrophes, you'll be prompted to fill in the space before descending to a lower menu, unless lower menu selections fill in the space.
Browse Menus	→ or Tab selects the highlighted menu item without pasting the item in the Edit window. Therefore you can descend through the lower menus, browsing, before deciding what to paste into your Edit window. Your selections are stored in a memory buffer in case you later decide to paste them. You can climb back out of the menus, and clear the buffer, with either ⊢ or Esc.
Clear Memory Buffer	Alt K clears ("kills") the memory buffer. When you browse through the menus without pasting items into the Edit window, your selections are stored in a memory buffer. If you had already typed part of a command, for example, and you wanted to paste just one keyword instead of a complete command, you would first clear the buffer, then paste the keyword you need.
Remove Window, Ascend Menus	Esc either returns you to the Main Menu or brings you one step closer to the Main Menu. Esc removes the Variables and Files menus and the typing window. If you've descended several levels into the menus, Esc brings you up one level at a time. If you're typing in the Edit window, Esc returns you to the Menu and Help window.
Jump to Main Menu	Alt Esc returns you to the Main Menu from any level in the Menu and Help system.
Standard/Extended Menus	Alt X switches you back and forth between standard and extended menus. The *standard menus* contain the procedures and operations that you will use most of the time. The *extended menus* contain keywords that you may need, but probably not as often. A note at the bottom of the screen says either **STD** or **EXT**.

File Commands

Command Name	Key Combination/Function
write Marked area*	F9 followed by M writes the current marked area to disk under a name you specify. The default name is REVIEW.TMP.
write Whole file*	F9 followed by W (or Alt W) saves the current file to disk under a name you specify. The default is the current name. The original copy is renamed with an extension of .BAK.
Delete file on disk*	F9 followed by D allows you to delete any file from a DOS directory.
Insert File*	F3 followed by I inserts the contents of a DOS file into the current file below the current line.
Edit different file*	F3 followed by E replaces the file in the current window.
run marked Area*	F10 followed by A (or Alt A) submits a marked area to SPSS/PC+ for execution. This command is available only if REVIEW was entered from SPSS/PC+. If unsaved changes have been made in either window, you're prompted to save or abandon the changes.

run from Cursor*	F10 followed by C (or Alt C) submits the commands beginning with the one containing the cursor and continuing to the end of the file to SPSS/PC+ for execution. This command is available only if REVIEW was entered from SPSS/PC+. If unsaved changes have been made in either window, you're prompted to save or abandon the changes.
Exit to prompt*	F10 followed by E exits REVIEW. If unsaved changes have been made in either window, you're prompted to save or abandon the changes.
exit Fastgraf*	F10 followed by F exits Fastgraph. If unsaved changes have been made in either window, you're prompted to save or abandon the changes.

Editing Commands

Command Name	Key Combination/Function
	Key Combination/Function
Change Edit Mode	Ins changes the editing mode from overtype to insert and from insert to overtype.
Insert after*	F4 followed by I (or Alt I) inserts a blank line after the current line. The blank line becomes the current line.
insert Before*	F4 followed by B (or Alt B) inserts a blank line before the current line. The blank line becomes the current line.
Delete*	F4 followed by D deletes the current line. The line below becomes the current line.
Undelete*	F4 followed by U restores the most recently deleted line and places it immediately above the current line. It is only possible to restore the single most recently deleted line.
Split Line	← in insert mode splits the current line at the current character. In overtype mode, it moves the cursor to the next line.
Join Line	Del joins the line below to the current line if the cursor is at the end of a line.
Delete Current Character	Del deletes the current character. The text to the right of the cursor moves left one space.
Delete Previous Character	The backspace key deletes the character to the left of the cursor. The cursor and righthand text move left.
fOrward change*	F5 followed by O replaces one character string with another following the current cursor position. At each occurrence, prompts for C to change the occurrence and move to the next one, A to change all occurrences without individual prompting, N to move to the next occurrence without changing the current one, S to stop the search, or X to change the occurrence and then stop the search. The previous search and replacement strings are the defaults but can be typed over. Upper and lower case are distinguished in searches. To identify only those occurrences of the string that begin in column 1, place a tilde (~) at the beginning of the search string. It is not possible to change a character string that begins with a tilde.
bAckward change*	F5 followed by A works the same as forward change moving backward through the file to the earliest line in memory.

Command Reference

The following commands deal with marking or unmarking areas:

Command Name	Key Combination/Function
Lines*	[F7] followed by [L] marks an area of lines for subsequent action. Press [F7] followed by [L] at the first or last line of an area and [F7] again at the opposite border to mark the area. Press [F7] a third time to unmark the area. Areas of lines consist of *whole* lines.
Rectangle*	[F7] followed by [R] marks any rectangle for subsequent action. Press [F7] followed by [R] at one corner of the rectangle, and [F7] again at the other corner. A rectangle consists of a given number of lines of the marked width, which may be shorter than the width of the longest line. When you have marked a rectangular area, place the cursor at the *top left* of the area to which you want to copy or move it.
Command*	[F7] followed by [C] marks the current command for subsequent execution. Place the cursor anywhere within the command and press [F7] followed by [C]. Press [F7] again to unmark the command.

The following commands apply to marked areas:

Command Name	Key Combination/Function
Copy*	[F8] followed by [C] copies a marked area to the line below the current line; it copies a marked rectangle to the right of and below the cursor. In insert mode, a rectangle pushes existing text to the right; in overtype mode, a rectangle replaces existing text. Areas of lines, commands, and rectangles can be copied between windows.
Move*	[F8] followed by [M] moves a marked area to the line below the current line; it moves a marked rectangle to the right of and below the cursor. In insert mode, a rectangle pushes existing text to the right; in overtype mode, a rectangle replaces existing text. Areas of lines, commands, and rectangles can be moved between windows.
Delete*	[F8] followed by [D] deletes a marked area or rectangle.
Round*	[F7] followed by [R] rounds all numeric values in the marked area or rectangle to a specified number of decimal places. When you press [F7] followed by [R], REVIEW prompts you for the desired number of decimal places. There is no way to reverse this command after execution; save important files before you round them in case the results are not what you expected. To round columns of numbers that are adjacent to one another, mark and round each column separately as a rectangle. Do not try to round numbers with imbedded commas (REVIEW will round each group of three digits) or numbers in scientific notation.

Motion Commands

Command Name	Key Combination/Function
Left	[←] moves the cursor left one space.
Right	[→] moves the cursor right one space.
Up	[↑] moves the cursor up one line.
Down	[↓] moves the cursor down one line.
Start of Line	[Ctrl] [←] moves the cursor to the first character of the current line.

End of Line	Ctrl → moves the cursor to the last character of the current line.
Tab Forward	Tab moves the cursor eight characters to the right.
Tab Backward	⇧ Tab moves the cursor eight characters to the left.
Previous Page	PgUp moves the cursor to the last line of the preceding page.
Next Page	PgDn moves the cursor to the first line of the following page.
Top of Page	Home moves the cursor to the start of the first line in the window.
Bottom of Page	End moves the cursor to the end of the last line in the window.
Top of File	Ctrl Home moves the cursor to the first line of the file.
Bottom of File	Ctrl End moves the cursor to the last line of the file.
Top of Memory	Ctrl PgUp moves the cursor to the first line of the portion of the file currently in memory.
Put Line at Top	Ctrl PgDn moves the current line to the top of the window.
Start of Next Line	← moves the cursor to the first character of the next line in overtype mode.
Forward search*	F5 followed by F moves the cursor to the first occurrence of a specified character string on or below the current line. Upper and lower case are not distinguished in searches. If you want to locate the string only when it appears at the beginning of a line, specify a tilde (~) at the beginning of the search string. The search continues to the end of the file and the search string defaults to the last specified string. It is not possible to search for a string that begins with a tilde.
Backward search*	F5 followed by B works the same as Forward search, moving backward through the file to the earliest line in memory.

The following commands tell the cursor to go to the indicated location:

Command Name	Key Combination/Function
Marked area*	F6 followed by M moves the cursor to the top left corner of the marked area. If the cursor is already at the top left corner, this command moves it to the bottom right corner. If you are editing two files, this command may switch the cursor from one window to the other.
after executed Line*	F6 followed by L (or Alt L) moves the cursor to the line below the last one executed.
Error line*	F6 followed by E moves the cursor to the line below the first one that caused an error when the commands where executed.
Output page*	F6 followed by O moves the cursor to a specified page in the listing file. REVIEW prompts you for the page number. The cursor must be located in the listing file when you use this command. Some types of output are not saved in listing files; thus some page numbers may be missing.

* These commands are mini-menu items that can be selected by highlighting the item with the cursor arrows and pressing ←.

SAMPLE

```
SAMPLE {sampling fraction          }
       {sample size FROM file size}
```

Example:

```
SAMPLE .25.
```

Overview

The SAMPLE transformation temporarily draws a random sample of cases for processing in the next procedure. Sampling is based on a pseudo-random-number generator.

Syntax

- A decimal value between 0 and 1 selects an approximate percentage of cases.
- A positive integer value less than the file size followed by keyword FROM and the file size selects an exact-sized random sample.
- SAMPLE can be entered anywhere in an SPSS/PC+ session, except between BEGIN DATA and END DATA.

Operations

- SAMPLE is a temporary transformation and is executed when the data are read for the next procedure.
- By default, the initial seed value is randomly assigned. Use the SEED subcommand on SET to assign a specific seed value.
- A proportional sample (a sample based on a decimal value) usually does not produce the exact proportion specified.
- If the number (n) following FROM is less than the actual file size, the sample is drawn only from the first n cases.
- If the number following FROM is greater than the actual file size, SPSS/PC+ will sample an equivalent proportion of cases from the active file (see Example below).
- If SAMPLE follows SELECT IF or PROCESS IF, it samples only cases selected by SELECT IF or PROCESS IF.
- If SAMPLE precedes SELECT IF or PROCESS IF, cases are selected from the sample.
- SAMPLE does not affect SORT CASES, and is ignored if the next procedure is SORT CASES.
- If more than one SAMPLE is specified before a procedure, only the last SAMPLE command is executed.
- If the same SAMPLE specification is used for different procedures in the same session or in different sessions, the two samples may be different because of the random assignment of the seed value. To obtain the same sample for different procedures, use the SET command specifying the same seed value before entering the SAMPLE command.

Example

```
SAMPLE .25.
```

- This command samples approximately 25% of the cases in the active file.

Example

```
SAMPLE 500 FROM 3420.
```

- In this example, the active file must have 3,420 cases or more to obtain a random sample of exactly 500 cases.
- If the file contains fewer than 3420 cases, approximately 15% of the cases are sampled.
- If the file contains more than 3420 cases, a random sample of 500 cases would be drawn from the first 3420 cases.

SAVE

```
SAVE [OUTFILE={'SPSS.SYS'**}]
               {'filename'  }

     [/DROP=varlist]    [/KEEP=varlist]

     [/RENAME=(varlist=newlist) [(varlist=newlist)] ]

     [/{COMPRESSED   }]
       {UNCOMPRESSED}
       {QUICK        }
```

**Default if subcommand is omitted.

Example:

```
SAVE DROP V1 TO V20.
```

Overview   SAVE produces an SPSS/PC+ system file. The system file includes all data and a data dictionary with variable and value labels (if specified), missing-value flags, and print formats for each variable. System files are read with the GET command.

System files saved by SPSS/PC+ *cannot* be read by SPSS/PC Release 1.0 or 1.1. To transfer a system file to SPSS/PC, use the EXPORT command from SPSS/PC+ and the IMPORT command in SPSS/PC. System files from SPSS/PC *can* be read directly by SPSS/PC+.

Defaults   SAVE writes all variables in your active file to the file SPSS.SYS in the current directory. To save processing time, the system file is normally written in compressed form if and only if the active file is currently in compressed form (that is, COMPRESS=ON has been specified on SET).

Tailoring   You can direct the system file to a file of your choosing. You can save a subset of variables on the system file. You can rename variables while writing the system file. You can specify that the system file be written in compressed or uncompressed form.

Syntax   • The minimum specification is simply the command keyword.

• Subcommands, if used, must be separated by a slash.

• Only one of the subcommands COMPRESSED, UNCOMPRESSED, or QUICK can be specified per SAVE command.

Operations   • The system file created by SAVE includes the system variables $CASENUM, $DATE, and $WEIGHT.

• The system file dictionary is arranged in the same order as the active file.

• System files are binary files designed to be read and written by SPSS/PC+ only and cannot be edited.

• The active file remains available for SPSS/PC+ transformations and procedures after a SAVE file is created.

• SAVE messages that display variable counts treat each 8-character portion of a long string variable as one variable.

Example   `SAVE DROP=V1 TO V3.`

• The system file is written to SPSS.SYS in the current directory.

• Any variables between and including V1 and V3 on the active file are excluded from the system file.

OUTFILE Subcommand

Use OUTFILE to direct the system file to a file other than the default SPSS.SYS.

- The only specification on OUTFILE is the name of the file.
- The file specification must be enclosed in apostrophes.
- You can save a system file in another directory or on a drive other than the default by specifying a fully qualified filename (see Universals: Files).

Example

```
SAVE OUT='\NSDIR\SALDATA.SYS'.
```

- The complete active file is written to file SALDATA.SYS in directory NSDIR.
- This example takes advantage of spelling permitted by three-character truncation of keywords.

DROP and KEEP Subcommands

DROP and KEEP save a subset of variables. DROP specifies the variables not to save in the new system file; KEEP specifies the variables to save in the new system file.

- Variables may be specified in any order. The variable order on KEEP determines their sequence in the system file. Variable order on DROP does not affect the order of variables in the system file: the variables are saved in the same sequence in which they appear in the active file.
- Multiple DROP and KEEP subcommands are allowed.
- If a variable is referenced twice, only the first mention of the variable is recognized.

Reordering Variables

- The variable order on KEEP determines variable order in the output system file.
- Keyword ALL on KEEP refers to all remaining variables not previously specified. ALL must be the last specification on KEEP.

Example

```
SAVE OUTFILE='A:PERSONL.SYS'
  /DROP=DEPT79 TO DEPT84 SALARY79.
```

- The system file is saved as file PERSONL.SYS on drive A:. All variables between and including DEPT79 and DEPT84, as well as SALARY79, are excluded from the system file. All other variables are saved in the system file.

RENAME Subcommand

RENAME changes the names of variables as they are copied into the system file.

- Name changes can be specified within parentheses in the form *(old varname =new varname)*. Multiple sets of variable specifications are allowed. Each set must be enclosed in parentheses.
- As an alternative to the above, name changes can be specified with a *list* of old variable names followed by an equals sign and a list of new variable names, all within parentheses. The same number of variables must be specified on both lists. Keyword TO can be used in either or both lists to refer to consecutive variables. A single set of parentheses enclosing the entire specification is required.
- Old variable names need not be specified according to their order in the active file.
- Name changes take place in one operation. Therefore, variable names can be exchanged between two variables.
- Multiple RENAME subcommands are allowed.

Example

```
SAVE OUTFILE='EMPL88.SYS'
  /RENAME (AGE=AGE88 JOBCAT=JOBCAT88).
```

- RENAME specifies two name changes for file EMPL88: AGE is renamed to AGE88, and JOBCAT is renamed to JOBCAT88.

Example

```
SAVE OUTFILE='EMPL88.SYS'
  /RENAME (AGE JOBCAT=AGE88 JOBCAT88).
```

- The name changes are identical to those in the previous example: AGE is renamed to AGE88, and JOBCAT is renamed to JOBCAT88.

COMPRESSED Subcommand

The optional COMPRESSED subcommand tells SPSS/PC+ to save the system file in compressed form. In a compressed file, small integers (from -99 to 155) are stored in one byte, instead of the usual eight bytes.

- Compressed system files occupy less disk space than do uncompressed system files.
- Compressed system files can take slightly longer to read than uncompressed system files.
- No additional specification is required on the GET command to read a compressed system file.

Example

```
SAVE OUTFILE='EMPLOY.SYS'
  /COMPRESSED.
```

- The system file is written to EMPLOY.SYS in the current directory.
- The system file is saved in compressed form.

UNCOMPRESSED Subcommand

The optional UNCOMPRESSED subcommand tells SPSS/PC+ to save the system file in uncompressed form.

- Uncompressed system files can be slightly quicker to read than compressed system files.
- Uncompressed system files occupy more disk space than do compressed system files.
- No additional specification is required on the GET command to read an uncompressed system file.

QUICK Subcommand

The optional QUICK subcommand tells SPSS/PC+ to save the system file in the same form as that of the active file. This minimizes the time required to save the system file.

- QUICK is the default.
- If the active file is uncompressed, the system file is saved in uncompressed form.
- If the active file is compressed, the system file is saved in compressed form.
- Use the SET COMPRESS command at any time during an SPSS/PC+ session to set the active file to either compressed or uncompressed form. The default for COMPRESS is OFF.
- No declaration that a system file is either compressed or uncompressed is ever required by other SPSS/PC+ commands.

C

Command Reference

SELECT IF

```
SELECT IF  (logical expression)
```

Relational Operators:

EQ or =	Equal to	NE or ~= or <>	Not equal to
LT or <	Less than	LE or <=	Less than or equal to
GT or >	Greater than	GE or >=	Greater than or equal to

Logical Operators:

AND or &   OR or | NOT or ~

Missing-Value Functions:

SYSMIS   Selects the case if value is system-missing
MISSING   Selects the case if value is system- or user-missing
VALUE   Selects the case if value meets stated criteria,
          ignoring user-missing flags

Examples:

```
SELECT IF (SEX EQ 'MALE   ').

SELECT IF (AVAR GE BVAR).

SELECT IF (SYSMIS(VARA)).
```

Overview

The SELECT IF transformation permanently selects cases for analysis based upon logical conditions found in the data. These conditions are specified in a *logical expression.* The logical expression can contain relational operators, logical operators, missing-value functions, and arithmetic operations and functions allowed in COMPUTE transformations (see COMPUTE, Universals: Logical Expressions, and Universals: Functions). For temporary case selection, see PROCESS IF.

Syntax

- The logical expression must be enclosed in parentheses.
- Parentheses also may be used to specify the order of evaluation.
- Relational operators are EQ, NE, LT, LE, GT, and GE (and their symbolic equivalents).
- Each relational operator must be preceded and followed by a variable name or an expression.
- Abbreviated syntax such as (AGE GE 18 AND LE 65) is *not* allowed.
- Logical operators are AND, OR, and NOT (and their symbolic equivalents).
- At least one relation, SYSMIS function, or MISSING function must be included in the logical expression.
- A relation includes a variable name, a relational operator, and a value or variable.
- Long string variables cannot be used in the SELECT IF command.
- SELECT IF can be entered anywhere in an SPSS/PC+ session, except between BEGIN DATA and END DATA.

Operations

- SELECT IF is a transformation and is executed when the data are read for the next procedure.
- SELECT IF permanently selects cases.
- The logical expression is evaluated as true or false.
- If a logical expression is true, the case is selected; if it is false or missing, the case is not selected.
- Multiple SELECT IF commands issued prior to a procedure command must all be true for a case to be selected.
- SELECT IF should be placed before other transformations for efficiency considerations.

• Logical expressions are evaluated in the following order: first numeric functions, then exponentiation, then arithmetic operators, then relational operators, and finally logical operators.

• Use parentheses to change the order of evaluation.

Limitations   • The complexity of logical expressions is limited by available memory.

Example   SELECT IF (SEX EQ 'MALE ').

• All subsequent procedures will use only cases in which the value of SEX is equal to MALE.

• SEX is a short string variable with a format width of six characters. The specification for value MALE includes trailing blanks to fill the field.

• Since upper and lower case are different in comparisons of string variables, cases for which SEX equals 'male ' are not selected.

Example   SELECT IF (INCOME GT 75000 OR INCOME LE 10000).

• The logical expression tests whether a case has a value greater than 75000 or less than 10000. If either relation is true, the case is used in subsequent analyses. Note that the variable name INCOME is repeated before the second relational operator.

Example   SELECT IF (AVAR GE BVAR).

• This example selects cases where variable AVAR is greater than or equal to BVAR.

Example   SELECT IF (SEX = 'F' & INCOME <= 10000).

• The logical expression tests whether short string variable SEX is equal to F and if numeric variable INCOME is less than or equal to 10000. Cases that meet both conditions are included in subsequent analyses.

Example   SELECT IF (SYSMIS(VARA)).

• The logical expression tests whether VARA is equal to the system-missing value. If the value of VARA is system-missing, the case is selected for subsequent analyses.

Example   SELECT IF (VALUE(VARA) GT 0).

• Cases are selected if VARA is greater than 0, even if the value of VARA has been declared user-missing.

SELECT IF (VARA GT 0).

• In this example, cases are not selected if VARA is user-missing, even if its value is greater than 0.

Example   SEL IF (RECEIV GT DUE OR (REVNUS GE EXPNS AND BALNCE GT 0)).

• The expression uses parentheses to change the order of evaluation. First, SPSS/PC+ tests whether variable REVNUS is greater than or equal to variable EXPNS and variable BALNCE has a value greater than 0. Second, SPSS/PC+ tests whether RECEIV is greater than DUE. If either of these conditions are met, the case is included in the active file for subsequent analyses.

Example   SELECT IF ((V1-15) LE (V2*(-0.001))).

• The logical expression compares whether V1 minus 15 is less than or equal to V2 multiplied by −0.001. If the expression is true, the case is selected for subsequent analyses.

Example   SELECT IF ((YRMODA(84,13,0) - YRMODA(YVAR,MVAR,DVAR)) LE 30).

- The logical expression subtracts the number of days representing the date YVAR (year), MVAR (month), and DVAR (day) from the number of days representing the last day in 1984. If the difference is less than or equal to 30, the case is selected for subsequent analyses.

SET

```
SET [SCREEN={ON  }]/  [PRINTER={OFF}]/  [LISTING={'SPSS.LIS'}]/
            {OFF}            {ON }              {ON        }
                                               {OFF       }
                                               {'filename'}

    [RUNREVIEW={AUTO  }]/†  [AUTOMENU={ON }]/†
              {MANUAL}                {OFF}

    [MENUS={STANDARD}]/†     [HELPWINDOWS={ON }]/†
          {EXTENDED}                     {OFF}

    [LENGTH={24}]/  [WIDTH={79    }]/  [EJECT={OFF}]/
           {n }          {132   }           {ON }
                         {n     }
                         {NARROW}
                         {WIDE  }

    [VIEWLENGTH={MINIMUM}]/†    [ERRORBREAK={ON }/†
               {MEDIUM }                   {OFF}
               {MAXIMUM}
               {number }

    [LOG={'SPSS.LOG'}]/  [RESULTS={'SPSS.PRC'}]/
         {ON        }            {'filename'}
         {OFF       }
         {'filename'}

    [HISTOGRAM={'■'   }]/  [BLOCK={'■'   }]/
              {'char'}           {'char'}

    [BOXSTRING={ -|+└┌┐H┬┴ }]/ [PTRANSLATE={ON }]/
              {'11 char'   }              {OFF}
              {' 3 char'   }

    [INCLUDE={ON }]/  [ECHO={ON }]/
            {OFF}           {OFF}

    [PROMPT={'SPSS/PC:'}]/   [CPROMPT={'      :'}]/  [MORE={ON }]/
           {'string'  }             {'string' }           {OFF}

    [ENDCMD={'.'   }]/  [NULLINE={ON }]/
           {'char'}             {OFF}

    [BEEP={ON }]/
         {OFF}

    [COLOR={(15,1,1) }]/  [RCOLOR={(1,2,4)   }]/
          {ON        }           {(a,b[,c])}
          {OFF       }
          {(a,b[,c]) }

    [COMPRESS={OFF}]/  [WORKDEV=device]/
             {ON }

    [BLANKS={'.'     }]/  [SEED={RANDOM}]/
           {real num}           {number}

    [CPI={6    }]/  [LPI={10   }]
        {chars}          {lines}
```

When SCREEN is OFF, the following defaults are in effect:

```
LENGTH=59 EJECT=ON
BOXSTRING='-|+++++++++'  HISTOGRAM='X'  BLOCK='X'
```

Example:

```
SET MORE=OFF /ECHO=ON /LENGTH=59 /EJECT=ON.
```

Overview   The SET command changes SPSS/PC+ running options. To see the current running options, use the SHOW command.

Defaults   The default running options include the command prompt **SPSS/PC:** , the continuation prompt   : , the period (.) and blank line as command terminators, and a prompt of **MORE** after each page of output. To remind you to move to the next screen of output, a high-pitched beep is sounded. Error messages are accompanied by a low-pitched beep. The default foreground, background, and border colors are 15, 1, and 1, respectively. On many color monitors this corresponds to white on blue. However, your monitor may interpret 15, 1, 1 differently. The default environment is the Menu and Help system within REVIEW, displaying the standard menus and their help windows.

SPSS/PC+ directs the output from statistical and reporting procedures to your screen, with a length of 24 rows and a width of 79 columns. Output does not go automatically to the printer and no blank lines are left between pages. In addition to appearing on the screen, procedure output is sent to a listing file whose default name is SPSS.LIS. Command lines are not sent to the listing file. If you write out a data set or matrix materials, SPSS/PC+ writes the results to the file SPSS.PRC.

Any commands you enter are sent to a log file. By default, this file is SPSS.LOG. Commands processed from a command file with the INCLUDE command are shown on the screen. If a command causes an error, processing stops.

Crosstabulation tables use special characters for the screen display. Histograms (available in FREQUENCIES) use a solid bar. Icicle plots (available in CLUSTER) use a solid box. By default, special characters are translated to simpler ones when output is sent directly to a printer.

The SAMPLE transformation and UNIFORM and NORMAL functions (available in COMPUTE) use a random seed obtained from the clock. Numeric blanks are interpreted as system-missing values and printed as a period (.) in output. Active files are kept in uncompressed form on the current device.

Tailoring   **Output Destination.** You can send your output to multiple destinations (screen, disk, and printer), and you can change destinations or turn off any of them throughout the course of an SPSS/PC+ session.

Output Form and Layout. You can change the length and width of output. Additionally, you can include printer carriage-control characters for page ejects in disk file output.

Optional Output. You can write data from the WRITE procedure or matrix materials from REGRESSION, CORRELATION, CLUSTER, ONEWAY, and FACTOR procedures to either SPSS.PRC or to a file of your choice.

Environment. Instead of beginning in the Menu and Help system environment, you can begin at the SPSS/PC+ command prompt, or in REVIEW without the Menu and Help system. If you do use the Menu and Help system, you can suppress the help windows and/or use extended menus.

Error Processing. You can direct the system to try to continue processing commands after one causes an error.

Special Characters. You can change the characters SPSS/PC+ uses to print crosstabulation table grids. You can also specify the symbols SPSS/PC+ uses in histograms (available in FREQUENCIES) and in icicle plots (available in CLUSTER).

Character Translation. SPSS/PC+ automatically translates special characters to simpler ones for output going directly to a printer. You can suppress this translation if you have a printer that can handle special characters.

Command Printback. You can direct all your SPSS/PC+ commands to your output file and/or printer. You can also suppress the screen printback of commands included with the INCLUDE command.

Prompts. You can specify your own command prompt and continuation prompt. You can turn off the prompt that appears by default after each screen of output.

Command Terminators. You can change the default command terminator from a period to a character of your choice. You can specify either that a blank line be ignored or taken as a command terminator.

Sound and Color. You can suppress the paging and error-message beeps. On a color monitor, you can choose colors for the type, the background, and the border.

Active and Scratch Files. You can direct your active and scratch files to any disk. You can specify that the active file be kept in compressed or uncompressed form.

Treatment of Numeric Blanks. You can substitute a numeric value for blank fields in numeric variables. All numeric blanks encountered are translated to this value.

Random Number Seed. You can change the initial seed value to a particular number or have SPSS/PC+ select a random number.

Syntax
- Subcommands on SET can be named in any order.
- Subcommands can be separated by an optional slash.
- Only one keyword or argument can be specified for each subcommand.
- SET can be used more than once in an SPSS/PC+ session.
- Each time SET is entered, only the named specifications are affected. All others remain at their previous settings or the default.
- YES is accepted as an alias for keyword ON.
- NO is accepted as an alias for keyword OFF.

Operations
- SET is an operation command and takes effect immediately.
- Since SPSS/PC+ output, by default, is primarily directed to the screen, the default character settings use graphics characters that may not be available on your printer.
- SPSS.LIS and SPSS.LOG are erased at the *beginning* of each SPSS/PC+ session. If you want to preserve their contents, use the DOS *RENAME* command to rename them before reentering SPSS/PC+.
- If you use multiple log, listing, or results files, you should not start with one file, go to another file, and then return to the first file. SPSS/PC+ will *not* append new information to the first file. It will *write over* the previous contents.
- The results file can be directed only to the current directory. The log and listing files may be sent to any directory.

Limitations
- Some characters used in screen displays are not available on all printers. Additionally, some of the characters used for the screen do not have a printable equivalent.
- A screen display length of 35 or 43 lines can only be used with an EGA or VGA adapter. A length of 43 may not be compatible with an ANSI.SYS file.

Example
`SET MORE=OFF /ECHO=ON /LENGTH=59 /EJECT=ON.`

- The specification MORE=OFF requests that SPSS/PC+ send output to the screen continuously, without pausing to give the *MORE* prompt when the screen fills. (Use REVIEW to examine output when a procedure is finished.)
- The specification ECHO=ON integrates all input commands in the output *listing* file. This is independent of whether commands are written to a log file.
- SPSS/PC+ uses a page length of 59 for both screen and disk output.
- EJECT=ON inserts a page-eject carriage-control character in the disk output file after each 59 lines of output and suppresses the dashed line between pages.

Output Destination
By default, SPSS/PC+ directs output both to the screen and to a listing file named SPSS.LIS in the current directory. You can change the name of the listing file. Additionally, you can direct output directly to a printer.

- When SCREEN=ON is in effect, the output is, by default, formatted especially for screen-by-screen displays and includes special graphics characters that are available only on the screen.

- If you turn screen display off, SPSS/PC+ uses different defaults for output. The defaults for SCREEN=ON and SCREEN=OFF are listed in Table A below. You can change these options with other SET subcommands.
- When you direct output to both the screen and printer or disk file, you must specify format options that are compatible with your printer.
- The keywords ON and OFF on subcommand LISTING apply to the current listing file, regardless of its name. You can suspend sending output to a file and then resume sending output to the same file, as long as you do not specify a different listing file in the interim.
- The output from different procedures can be directed to different disk files by naming a different file on the LISTING subcommand prior to a procedure command.
- When you use multiple disk files, you cannot send output to one file, then to another file, and then resume sending output to the first file. If you do, SPSS/PC+ writes over the first set of output. It cannot append output to a file once another file has been named.

The subcommands for controlling output destinations are:

SCREEN   *Screen output.* SCREEN=ON is the default. You can suppress screen display by specifying SCREEN=OFF and then restart screen display by specifying SCREEN=ON.

PRINTER   *Printer output.* PRINTER=OFF is the default. With PRINTER=ON, output is sent directly to your printer in addition to any other destinations. Your printer must be turned on if you specify PRINTER =ON. You can stop sending output to the printer by specifying PRINTER=OFF.

LISTING   *Disk output.* LISTING=ON is the default. You can suppress the copying of your output to a disk file by specifying LISTING=OFF. The default disk output file is SPSS.LIS in the current directory. You can direct the output to another disk file in a directory of your choice by specifying a filename on the LISTING subcommand. Enclose the filename in apostrophes. The keyword DISK is accepted as an alias for LISTING.

Example

```
GET FILE='MARCH.SYS'.
LIST VAR=V1 TO V10.
SET LISTING='MEANS.LIS'
MEANS V1 TO V5 BY V7.
SET LISTING=OFF.
FREQ VAR=V1,V3,V4
   /HISTOGRAM.
SET LISTING=ON
   /HISTOGRAM='X'.
FREQ VAR=V3
   /HISTOGRAM.
FINISH.
```

- Output is initially routed to the default file SPSS.LIS in the current directory.
- The GET command reads the SPSS/PC+ system file MARCH.SYS from the current directory.
- The LIST procedure output is directed to the screen and to SPSS.LIS.
- The second SET command directs output to the file MEANS.LIS in the current directory.
- The output from the MEANS procedure is directed to MEANS.LIS and to the screen.
- The next SET command suspends sending output to the file MEANS.LIS. Procedure display continues coming to the screen.
- The FREQUENCIES command requests frequency tables and histograms for three variables. The histograms use the default histogram characters for the screen.
- The next SET command with LISTING=ON resumes sending output to the file MEANS.LIS. The character used in any histogram on the screen and in the disk file is X.

• The FREQUENCIES command produces a table and histogram for the variable V3. Output is directed to both the screen and to the disk file.

• The FINISH command ends the SPSS/PC+ session.

• The file SPSS.LIS contains the results from the LIST procedure. The file MEANS.LIS contains output from the MEANS procedure and from the last FREQUENCIES procedure.

Output Form and Layout

SCREEN=ON and SCREEN=OFF set up different defaults for output format (see Table A). You can change these defaults with the LENGTH, VIEWLENGTH, WIDTH, and EJECT subcommands.

• The LENGTH subcommand affects the page length for the screen, the printer, and for the listing file.

• On the screen, the **MORE** prompt appears after the specified number of lines have been displayed.

• For printer and listing-file output, a dotted line is printed or a page eject occurs at the end of the specified number of lines.

• The VIEWLENGTH subcommand determines the display of lines on the screen. Computers with special adapters can display more than 25 lines at a time by making the lines appear smaller.

• The PC must have a special graphics adaptor (EGA or VGA) to use any VIEWLENGTH other than MINIMUM (25 lines).

• If the CONFIG.SYS file contains the specification DEVICE=ANSI.SYS, a VIEWLENGTH of 43 may not work.

• The WIDTH subcommand affects screen, printer, and listing-file output.

• The screen allows a width of only 79 characters. Lines longer than 79 characters are normally wrapped onto two lines. Some SPSS/PC+ output is produced by special-purpose routines that do not support the wrapping of long lines. To examine the portion of such lines that is off the screen, either specify SET WIDTH 79, print the listing file, or use an editor that wraps or allows horizontal scrolling to view the listing file (REVIEW does not do this).

• Printer and disk output can contain lines longer than 79 characters.

• To print long lines (from 80 to 132 characters), use the DOS *MODE* command to reduce the size of characters on your printer.

• The EJECT subcommand affects only printer and disk file output. With LENGTH=59 and EJECT=ON, insert printer paper with perforations one-half inch above the type head; SPSS/PC+ will print each page with skips over subsequent perforations.

Table A   Defaults for SCREEN settings

SCREEN	LENGTH	BOXSTRING	HISTOGRAM	BLOCK	EJECT
ON	24	-|+ ⌐¬ Н ┬┴	■	■	OFF
OFF	59	-|+++++++++	X	X	ON

The subcommands for controlling output, form, and layout are:

LENGTH   *The page length* (the number of lines before the MORE prompt, and before a page eject is sent to the listing file and the printer). Specify a positive integer. LENGTH is normally set to one line less than VIEWLENGTH. When you intend to print the listing file, you may want to set LENGTH to a suitable value for your printer. A standard printer page length is 59 lines.

VIEWLENGTH *The number of lines shown on the screen.* Specify MINIMUM, MEDIUM, MAXIMUM, or a number. Available settings depend upon your display adapter. MDA and CGA allow only MINIMUM (25 lines). EGA allows 25, 35, and 43 line displays. VGA likewise honors all three keywords, with 50 lines displayed for MAXIMUM. If you specify an inappropriate number, SPSS/PC+ rounds it to the nearest available number.

WIDTH *The page width.* Specify an integer or keywords NARROW (79 characters) or WIDE (130 characters). Most SPSS/PC+ output is formatted to fit in a page width of 79 characters. For procedures that let you specify your own width, the width specified in the procedure should agree with the width specified on SET.

EJECT *Carriage control for page ejects for printer and disk output.* Specify ON or OFF. With EJECT=OFF, output sent to the printer and/or to a disk file contains a dotted line indicating page breaks. With EJECT=ON, no dotted line is printed, and pages are printed with margins between each page. When SCREEN=ON, the default is EJECT=OFF.

Example
```
SET LISTING='REG.LIS' /VIEWLENGTH=MAXIMUM
  /LENGTH=59 /WIDTH=130 /EJECT=ON.
REG VAR=SAVINGS POP15 POP75 INCOME GROWTH
  /SELECT IN2 NE 1
  /DEP SAVINGS /ENTER POP15 /RES SEPARATE
  /CASEWISE DEP OUTLIER (3) ALL PLOT (RESID)
  /DEP SAVINGS /ENTER INCOME /RES POOLED.
```

• The SET command directs output to the file REG.LIS in addition to the screen; the latter will display the maximum number of lines possible for the display adapter. The output is formatted with 59 lines for each page with an eject after each page. The width of each page is 130 characters.

• The REGRESSION procedure uses 130 characters on each line of the output display.

• If REG.LIS is printed, each page includes top and bottom margins to skip over the perforations. No lines are wrapped in printed output.

Optional Output

SPSS/PC+ provides two types of additional output: a log file, which includes all commands processed in a session; and a results file, which contains matrix or casewise data produced by options on SPSS/PC+ procedures.

LOG Subcommand

By default, SPSS/PC+ copies all the commands you enter into log file SPSS.LOG in the current directory.

• You can send the log file to a file other than SPSS.LOG by specifying a different filename, in apostrophes, on the LOG subcommand.

• You can suppress the building of the log file by specifying LOG=OFF.

• You can resume sending commands to the file SPSS.LOG or to the log file last specified by specifying LOG=ON. Any existing contents of that file will be overwritten.

• The log file contains each command processed during a session.

• If you enter a command with errors, the log file contains a comment line after that command indicating the error.

• The log file can be edited to remove erroneous lines for use as a command file (see INCLUDE). REVIEW allows you to do this without leaving SPSS/PC+.

• When you use a log file from a completed session as a command file, you must initially send the log file to a file other than SPSS.LOG or rename the log file using the DOS *RENAME* command, since SPSS.LOG is initialized at the start of each session.

When you use INCLUDE in your session, the commands from the included command file are preceded by a square bracket ([) in the log file. If this log file is then used as a command file in a subsequent session, only the INCLUDE command is processed, not the commands preceded by the square bracket. This avoids double processing of commands. You cannot enter the square bracket yourself in interactive sessions.

Example
```
SET LOG='DATADEF.FIL'.
DATA LIST FILE='MARCH.DAT' / OP1 TO OP7 1-14.
VARIABLE LABELS OP1 'Opinion on sex' /
                OP2 'Opinion on religion' /
                OP7 'Opinion on divorce'.
VALUE LABELS OP1 TO OP7 1 'Agree' 2 'Disagree'.
MISSING VALUE OP1 TO OP7(9).
INCLUDE 'DES.INC'.
FIN.
```

- The SET command directs the log file to DATADEF.FIL in the current directory.
- The DATA LIST, VARIABLE LABELS, VALUE LABELS, MISSING VALUE, and INCLUDE commands and their specifications are copied to the file. Each of the commands processed from the INCLUDE file, DES.INC, is copied to the log file prefaced with a square bracket.
- The file DATADEF.FIL can be used as a command file in a subsequent SPSS/PC+ session.

RESULTS Subcommand
Some SPSS/PC+ procedures produce data that can be used in other sessions. WRITE produces a rectangular data file of individual values. Procedures CORRELATION, ONEWAY, REGRESSION, CLUSTER, FACTOR, MANOVA, SURVIVAL, and QUICK CLUSTER produce summary data in the form of matrix materials. SPSS/PC+ writes these data files to the default file SPSS.PRC in the current directory.

- You can direct these data files to other files in the current directory by specifying a filename in apostrophes on the RESULTS subcommand.
- The results file is always written to the current directory.
- The results file can be used as input (named on the DATA LIST or, after editing, on the INCLUDE command) at a later time or in a subsequent SPSS/PC+ session.
- SPSS/PC+ does *not* append data to the results file. If two procedures write results to the same file, the second set of data will overwrite the first set.

Example
```
SET LISTING 'NEWDAT.LIS'
   /RESULTS='NEWDAT.DAT'.
GET FILE='INVENT.SYS'.
COMPUTE TOTCOST=V1+V7+V9.
SELECT IF (V3 LT 7).
WRITE VARIABLES=ID TO V15, TOTCOST.
FINISH.
```

- The SET command specifies that procedure output be sent to the disk file NEWDAT.LIS and that data results be written on the file NEWDAT.DAT. Both files are written in the current directory.
- The GET command reads the system file INVENT.SYS from the current directory.
- The COMPUTE command creates (or modifies) the variable TOTCOST.
- The SELECT IF command tells SPSS/PC+ to select cases in which the value of variable V3 is less than 7.
- The WRITE command writes the values of variable TOTCOST and variables between and including ID and V15 (provided the value of V3 is less than 7). The data are written on the file NEWDAT.DAT.

Environment
SPSS/PC+ provides three environments in which to enter commands: the Menu and Help system; the REVIEW text editor; and the command prompt. The default environment when you enter SPSS/PC+ is the Menu and Help system within REVIEW. You can make one of the other environments the default; additionally, you can alter the default settings of the Menu and Help system environment.

Default Environment
- To make the default environment the REVIEW text editor *without* the Menu and Help system, use the subcommand AUTOMENU=OFF. You can still call up the menus whenever you like by pressing (Alt) (M).

Example

Menu Settings

Example

Error Processing

Example

Special Characters

• To make the default environment the SPSS/PC+ command prompt, use the subcommand RUNREVIEW=MANUAL. To get into REVIEW from the command prompt, use the REVIEW command.

`SET RUNREVIEW MANUAL.`

• The default environment becomes the SPSS/PC+ command prompt. If commands are entered and run from REVIEW, the system returns to the command prompt upon completion of processing, not to REVIEW.

• To automatically display menus with all possible keywords, use the subcommand MENUS=EXTENDED. The alternative, MENUS=STANDARD, omits seldom-used keywords. You can switch between standard and extended menus at any time by pressing (Alt) (X).

• To display the menus without the help windows that annotate each menu selection, use the subcommand HELPWINDOWS=OFF. (This speeds up the display of menus on slow machines.) You can bring back the help windows at any time by pressing (Alt) (H).

```
SET MENUS=EXTENDED
   /HELPWINDOWS=OFF.
```

• When the menus display, all keywords are included, but the help windows do not appear.

To direct the system to continue processing commands after one causes an error, use the subcommand ERRORBREAK=OFF. This is useful when initial commands are not essential for the processing of subsequent commands. Regardless of the setting of ERRORBREAK, when the system returns to REVIEW after processing commands that caused errors, the cursor is always positioned at the first command that caused an error.

```
SET ERRORBREAK=OFF.
VRIABLE LABELS OP1 'Opinion on sex' /
               OP2 'Opinion on religion' /
               OP7 'Opinion on divorce'.
LIST.
```

• The SET command directs the system to continue processing even if errors are encountered.

• The VRIABLE LABELS command is misspelled and causes an error.

• The LIST command is processed even though the preceding command caused an error, because ERRORBREAK is set to OFF. However, the listing does not include variable labels.

SPSS/PC+ uses special graphic characters in tables and plots. These graphic characters appear on the screen but may not print correctly (depending upon the type of printer you are using) or may be interpreted as special printer escape sequences. Three subcommands, HISTOGRAM, BLOCK, and BOXSTRING, are used to specify other characters.

HISTOGRAM *The character used in histograms and barcharts.* Specify a single character in apostrophes. If output is directed to the screen, the default is a lower-half solid block (ASCII decimal 220). If output is not directed to the screen, X is the default.

BLOCK *The character used in icicle plots.* Specify a single character in apostrophes. If output is directed to the screen, the default is a full solid block (ASCII decimal 219). If output is not directed to the screen, the default is X.

BOXSTRING *Box-building characters.* Specify the characters to be used in building boxes. You can specify a set of three characters or a full set of eleven. Enclose either set in apostrophes.

A set of three characters comprises the horizontal bar, vertical bar, and intersection characters, in that order. The intersection character is used for all types of intersections.

A set of eleven characters comprises the following characters: horizontal bar, vertical bar, intersection, lower-left corner, upper-left corner, lower-right corner, upper-right corner, left T, right T, top T, bottom T. The characters must be specified in this order.

If the display is going to the screen, the defaults are the eleven single-stroke graphics characters (see Table B). If the display is not directed to the screen, '-|+++++++++' are the default BOX-STRING characters.

You can enter special characters by holding down (Alt) and entering the ASCII decimal value for the character desired on the numeric keypad on the right side of the keyboard. For example, to enter the lightest-shade block character, press (Alt) and hold it down while entering 176. Then release (Alt). Depending upon the editor you use to build command files, you may be able to enter special characters in the same manner.

A complete list of characters and their ASCII decimal values is available in the DOS BASIC manual. Table B below documents some of the more useful characters and their ASCII decimal codes.

Table B Special characters

Character	ASCII value	Character	ASCII value
Single-stroke horizontal bar	196	Double-stroke horizontal bar	205
Single-stroke vertical bar	179	Double-stroke vertical bar	186
Single-stroke intersection	197	Double-stroke intersection	206
Single-stroke lower-left corner	192	Double-stroke lower-left corner	200
Single-stroke upper-left corner	218	Double-stroke upper-left corner	201
Single-stroke lower-right corner	217	Double-stroke lower-right corner	188
Single-stroke upper-right corner	191	Double-stroke upper-right corner	187
Single-stroke left T	195	Double-stroke left T	204
Single-stroke right T	180	Double-stroke right T	185
Single-stroke top T	194	Double-stroke top T	203
Single-stroke bottom T	193	Double-stroke bottom T	202
Light-intensity block	176	Lower-half solid block	220
Medium-intensity block	177	Upper-half solid block	223
Heavy-intensity block	178	Left-half solid block	221
Solid block	219	Right-half solid block	222
Small solid block	254		

Character Translation

Many printers cannot print the special characters used by SPSS/PC+ for histograms, plots, and tables. By default, SPSS/PC+ translates these characters to simpler ones when output is sent directly to a printer (PRINTER=ON). If your printer can print special characters, you may want to turn off this translation.

PTRANSLATE *Character translation for output to printers.* Specify ON or OFF. PTRANSLATE=ON (the default) translates special characters to simpler ones when PRINTER=ON. PTRANSLATE=OFF prevents this translation.

Example SET PTRANSLATE=OFF.

• Translation of special characters to simpler ones is turned off. When PRINTER=ON, the printer will receive unsimplified characters.

Command Printback

SPSS/PC+ provides two options for printing back commands either on the screen or in output: the INCLUDE and ECHO subcommands.

• If you don't want to see SPSS/PC+ commands from an INCLUDE file on your screen, specify INCLUDE=OFF prior to using the INCLUDE command.

• If you do not want SPSS/PC+ commands (from whatever source) copied to your listing file, specify ECHO=OFF.

INCLUDE   *Printback of commands from command files on the screen.* Specify ON or OFF. INCLUDE=ON (the default) displays commands on your screen from any command file that you include. Inline data from included command files is never sent to the screen.

ECHO   *Printback of commands in output.* By default ECHO=ON, and SPSS/PC+ sends SPSS/PC+ commands along with results of statistical and reporting procedures to listing and printer files. Specify ECHO=OFF if you want only results of statistical and reporting procedures sent to these files. This does not affect screen output.

Example
```
SET ECHO=OFF.
GET FILE='MUFILE.SYS'.
CROSSTABS TABLES=AVAR BY BVAR BY CVAR.
SET SCREEN=OFF.
INCLUDE 'REG.INC'.
FIN.
```

- The first SET command specifies that the listing file commands should not include the command printback.
- The second SET command stops sending output display to the screen. Output is still sent to the listing file.
- The INCLUDE command processes commands from file REG.INC in the current directory. By default, all commands from REG.INC are sent to the screen as they are processed. If INCLUDE=OFF is specified in REG.INC, further commands from that file are not sent to the screen as they are processed.

Prompts

Use the PROMPT, CPROMPT, and MORE subcommands to control the characters used for prompts and to suppress page prompting.

- SPSS/PC+ uses two types of prompts for command input: a command prompt and a continuation prompt. The command prompt prompts for a new command and the continuation prompt prompts for the next line of a command.
- The continuation prompt is always issued if a command terminator has not been used on the previous input.
- You can specify special characters for both PROMPT and CPROMPT.
- By default, SPSS/PC+ pauses after each screen of output and displays the **MORE** prompt. You must press a key to see the next screen of output. The MORE subcommand lets you eliminate the pause and prompt between screens of output.

PROMPT   *The command prompt.* Specify a string of up to 8 characters in apostrophes. The default is SPSS/PC: .

CPROMPT   *The continuation prompt.* Specify a string of up to 8 characters in apostrophes. The default is   : .

MORE   *The full screen prompt.* Specify ON or OFF. MORE=ON (the default) causes SPSS/PC+ to pause between screens of output and display the **MORE** prompt. MORE=OFF eliminates the prompt, and output is displayed continuously across the screen.

Example
```
SET PROMPT='===> '
  /CPROMPT='this it?'
  /MORE=OFF.
```

- The command prompt is changed to '===> '.
- The continuation prompt becomes, 'this it?'.
- Pausing and prompting between screens of output is turned off.

Command Terminators

Use the ENDCMD and NULLINE subcommands to control command termination.

- Every SPSS/PC+ command must end with a command terminator.

• By default, the terminator is a period, but you can change it with the ENDCMD. SPSS/PC+ continues to read lines as part of the current command until it encounters the command terminator.

• When NULLINE is ON (the default), a completely empty input line is accepted as an alternative command terminator. If you SET NULLINE OFF, you must enter the character specified for ENDCMD.

• The ENDCMD specification should be a printable character.

• Do not specify a command terminator that is the last character in any of your variable names, nor a character with special syntactic meaning in SPSS/PC+ (such as a slash). Such specifications will often result in syntactic ambiguity.

ENDCMD *The command terminator.* Specify a character in apostrophes. The default is a period.

NULLINE *Empty lines as an alternative command terminator.* Specify ON or OFF. The default is NULLINE=ON.

Example
```
SET ENDCMD='!'
   /NULLINE=OFF.
```

• The command terminator is set to '!'.

• A blank line will not be accepted as a command terminator.

Sound and Color

Use the BEEP subcommand to suppress the beep that signals the next screen of output and errors. Use the COLOR subcommand to control the text, background, and border colors on color monitors. On some monochrome monitors, you can use the COLOR subcommand to control the patterns and shading that may appear in place of colors. The RCOLOR subcommand allows you to set the background colors in REVIEW, the SPSS/PC+ text editor.

• A high-pitched beep reminds you to page to the next screen of output.

• A low-pitched beep is sounded when an error occurs.

• On most color displays, it is possible to assign one color to text, another color to the background on which the text appears, and a third color to a border surrounding the central text area.

• In REVIEW, you can assign colors to the primary and secondary text windows, and to the frame surrounding them.

BEEP *Beep.* To suppress the beep, specify OFF. To turn it on, specify ON. The default is ON.

COLOR *Color.* Specify a set of two or three integers in parentheses or specify ON or OFF. A set of three integers represents text color, background color, and border color, in that order. An asterisk in place of an integer retains the existing color. If you specify the first two integers only, the border color is taken to be the same as the background color. The default color scheme is COLOR=(15,1,1), which on many color monitors corresponds to white text on a blue background with a blue border. Check your monitor manual for the colors available on your monitor and the integers that represent these colors. Colors for the standard IBM color monitor are shown in Table C.

RCOLOR *Color in REVIEW.* Specify a set of three integers in parentheses, representing background color in the lower (or only) window, background color in the upper window (when present), and frame color, in that order. The three integers must be between 0 and 6. An asterisk in place of an integer retains the existing color. The default color scheme is RCOLOR=(1,2,4). Text is always white in REVIEW. The keywords OFF and ON are not recognized for RCOLOR, but if you SET COLOR OFF, REVIEW will use a monochrome display.

• The SET RCOLOR command must be issued from the SPSS/PC+ environment; you cannot change colors from within REVIEW itself.

• On some monochrome monitors, colors may be interpreted as patterns and shading. Your monitor manual will tell you how to control these patterns.

- You can specify COLOR=OFF (on color or monochrome monitors) to eliminate all color representation.
- COLOR=OFF affects REVIEW as well as the SPSS/PC+ command environment; however, the specific colors used by REVIEW when COLOR is on are determined by RCOLOR rather than COLOR.
- Specify COLOR=ON to return to the color patterns that were in effect before color was turned off.
- Put the command SET COLOR=OFF in your automatic profile SPSS-PROF.INI to force a monochrome display if you prefer it to the default display.
- The high-intensity colors 8–15 can only be used for the first (text) color in SPSS/PC+. Only colors 0–6 are used in REVIEW.

Table C Color selection for standard IBM color monitor

0	Black	8	Gray
1	Blue	9	Light Blue
2	Green	10	Light Green
3	Cyan	11	Light Cyan
4	Red	12	Light Red
5	Magenta	13	Light Magenta
6	Brown	14	Yellow
7	White	15	High Intensity White

Example

```
SET BEEP=OFF.
GET FILE='AUTO.SYS'.
SET COLOR=(6,1,3).
FREQUENCIES VARIABLES=COSTCAT,SIZE,POWER.
SET COLOR OFF.
CROSSTABS TABLES=MANUFACT BY POWER.
SET COLOR ON.
FREQUENCIES VARIABLES=COSTCAT.
FINISH.
```

- The first SET command turns off beeps for this session.
- Prior to the first SET COLOR command, the default color pattern (15,1,1) is in effect.
- The first SET COLOR command sets the text color to 6, the background color to 1, and the border color to 3.
- The second SET COLOR command turns color off, creating a monochrome display.
- The third SET COLOR command restores the text, background, and border colors to their previous values of 6, 1, and 3, respectively.

Active and Scratch Files

Use COMPRESS subcommand to indicate whether the active file for an SPSS/PC+ session should be kept in compressed or uncompressed form. Use WORKDEV to direct the active and scratch files to a specific block device (disk drive).

- A compressed active file occupies less space in your directory than does an uncompressed active file.
- A compressed active file takes longer to access when you run a procedure than does an uncompressed active file.
- When you perform transformations during a session, SPSS/PC+ creates a new active file but both the new and old active files exist simultaneously. Thus, the space you save by keeping your active file compressed doubles if you do any transformations during an SPSS/PC+ session.
- If you save a system file from a compressed active file, the system file is saved in compressed form unless you have issued commands that modify the active file before it is saved.
- SPSS/PC+ can write the active files for a session to any disk drive.

COMPRESS   *Compression of the active file.* Specify ON or OFF. COMPRESS=ON causes SPSS/PC+ to keep the active file in compressed form. COMPRESS=OFF causes SPSS/PC+ to keep the active file in uncompressed form. COMPRESS=ON is the default.

WORKDEV   *Location of active files.* Specify a device letter that corresponds to one of your disk drives. The active file and most scratch files for the session will be kept on that device. The default device is that of the current directory. Once an active file has been written during the session, you cannot change the WORKDEV.

Example

```
SET COMPRESS=ON
 /WORKDEV=B.
```

- The active file for this session will be kept in compressed form.
- The active file and other scratch files for the session will be kept on device B. If an active file has already been written during the session, WORKDEV will generate an error message.

Treatment of Numeric Blanks

By default, SPSS/PC+ translates entirely blank fields read with a numeric format to the system-missing value. You can use the BLANKS subcommand to specify some other value.

- BLANKS controls only the translation of numeric fields.
- If a blank field is read with an A format, the resulting value is a blank.
- The BLANKS specification controls all numeric-variable blanks. You cannot have different specifications for different variables.
- BLANKS must be specified before data are read, since blanks in numeric fields are converted to system-missing as they are read.

BLANKS   *Blanks for numeric fields.* Specify any number. Blanks are translated to this number. The number is not automatically defined as missing. The default, however, is the system-missing value.

Example

```
SET BLANKS=-1.
```

- The SET command translates all numeric-variable blanks to the value −1.

Random Number Seed

SPSS/PC+ has a random number generator used by the SAMPLE command and the NORMAL and UNIFORM functions. By default, the seed is a random seed generated from the clock. Optionally, you can specify a seed on the SEED subcommand.

- You can change the random number seed any number of times within a session.
- To replicate samples across sessions or procedures, specify the same seed each time.

SEED   *The random number seed.* Specify a positive integer or keyword RANDOM. The default is RANDOM. If you specify an integer, it must be no larger than 2147483647.

Example

```
SET SEED=200000000.
```

- The random number seed is set to the value 200000000.

Categories Plots

The optimal-scaling procedures in the SPSS/PC+ Categories option compute square plots. Square plots (as opposed to rectangular ones) are easier to interpret geometrically. Occasionally, certain printers might make the plots appear rectangular because their print density is different than what SPSS/PC+ expects. If your printer is producing rectangular ones, you need to specify the characters-per-inch and lines-per-inch parameters. SET CPI and SET LPI specify the characters-per-inch and lines-per-inch, respectively. You can use the SHOW command to see what the current settings are.

Your correct CPI and LPI values can be found in your printer manual or can easily be calculated with a ruler and some output. The CPI is simply the number of characters per inch moving horizontally across the page. The LPI is the number of lines per inch moving vertically down the page. SPSS/PC+ uses these values when plotting output from ANACOR, HOMALS, PRINCALS, and OVERALS. Plots from other procedures are unaffected.

CPI *Characters per inch horizontally.* The default is 6.

LPI *Lines per inch vertically.* The default is 10.

SHOW

SHOW

Overview   The SHOW command displays a table of all the current specifications on the SET command.

Syntax   • The minimum specification is simply the command keyword. SHOW has no additional specifications.

Operations   • SHOW is an operation command and is executed immediately.
• SHOW lists every current SET specification, including the default settings.

Limitations   • BOXSTR and HISTOGRAM graphics characters that are displayed on the screen can be printed on graphics printers but may not be printable on nongraphics printers.

Example   SHOW.

• The SHOW command produces a table similar to the one below of the current specifications on the SET command.
• In this example, the settings shown are the default settings.

```
SPSS/PC+ V4.0 (14-221)        Workspace:  227.7K + 64K Expanded
Machine:  IBM                 Free disk space: 14704K
Coprocessor not installed     Work Device D:     995K
Current directory:  C:\MYFILES
SPSS/PC+ directory:  c:\spss

LISTING  SPSS.LIS      SCREEN    ON      INCLUDE  ON
LOG      SPSS.LOG      PRINTER   OFF     BEEP     ON
RESULTS  SPSS.PRC      PTRANSL   ON      MORE     ON
NULLINE  ON            ECHO      ON      EJECT    OFF

PROMPT   SPSS/PC:      LENGTH    24      WIDTH    79
CPROMPT       :        BLOCK     ■       BOX      -|+└┘┐┠┰┸
ENDCMD   .             HIST      ■       SEED     1105152293
COLOR    (15, 1, 1)    CPI       10.00   LPI      6.00
WEIGHT   OFF           COMPRESS  OFF     BLANKS
                       ERRORBREAK ON     VIEWLENGTH 25
_____ Review Settings _____?

AUTOMENU  ON           HELPWINDOWS ON    MENUS    EXTENDED
RCOLOR  ( 1, 2, 4)                       RUNREVIEW AUTO
```

SORT CASES

```
SORT CASES [BY] varlist [({A})] [varlist...]
                        {D}
```

Example:
```
SORT CASES BY XVAR (A) YVAR (D).
```

Overview
The SORT CASES procedure reorders the sequence of cases in the active file based on the values of one or more variables.

Defaults
By default, cases are sorted in ascending order for each variable, starting with the first variable named. For each subsequent variable, cases are sorted in ascending order within categories of previously named variables.

Tailoring
Optionally, you can sort cases in descending order or use combinations of ascending and descending order for different variables.

Syntax
• The minimum specification is a list of variables that are used as sort keys.

• Variables can be numeric or string.

• Keyword BY is optional.

• You can explicitly request the default sort order (ascending) by specifying A in parentheses after the variable name.

• To sort cases in descending order, specify (D).

• An order specification (A or D) applies to all variables to its left until it reaches a previous order specification. Thus, if you combine ascending and descending order on the same specification, you may need to specify the default (A) explicitly.

Operations
• SORT CASES causes the data to be read.

• SORT CASES begins by sorting the file according to the first variable named. For subsequent variables, cases are sorted within categories of previously named variables.

• For string variables, the sort order is the ASCII collating sequence (see the IBM *BASIC* manual). An ascending (A) sort order places numeric characters first, then uppercase letters in alphabetical order, then lowercase letters in alphabetical order; a descending (D) sort order does the reverse.

• The values of system variable $CASENUM are not changed from their original values as the file is sorted. You can use the variable $CASENUM as a sorting key to restore the original order.

• The temporary transformation commands SAMPLE and PROCESS IF are ignored by SORT CASES.

Limitations
• Up to 10 variables can be used as sort keys.

• SORT CASES uses intermediate scratch files for which sufficient disk space must be available on the default device. SET WORKDEV does not control the drive to which scratch files for SORT CASES are written.

Example
```
SORT CASES BY XVAR (A) YVAR (D).
```

• Cases are sorted in ascending order of variable XVAR.

• Cases are further sorted in descending order of YVAR within categories of XVAR.

Example
```
SORT CASES XVAR YVAR (A) ZVAR (D).
```

• Cases are sorted in ascending order of XVAR.

• Cases are further sorted in ascending order of YVAR within values of XVAR. Specification A applies to both XVAR and YVAR.

• Cases are further sorted in descending order of ZVAR within values of YVAR and XVAR.

SPSS MANAGER

```
SPSS MANAGER

{REMOVE  =procedure-name [;procedure-name...] }
{INSTALL =procedure-name [;procedure-name...] }
{STATUS [=procedure-name [;procedure-name...]]}


[/{CONFIRM  }]
  {NOCONFIRM}


[/FROM={'device or path specification'}]
       {"A:"                          }
```

Example:

```
SPSS MANAGER REMOVE=TABLES;MANOVA.
```

Overview

SPSS MANAGER allows you to reduce the disk space requirements of the SPSS/PC+ system by removing seldom-used procedures from the hard disk. If you need a procedure that is not on the hard disk, use SPSS MANAGER to install it from either the original distribution diskette or a backup copy.

• You can install and remove a module as many times as you wish.

• You can make backup copies of the distribution diskettes in case the originals are damaged. You are strongly advised to do so.

• SPSS MANAGER removes and installs modules in the SPSS/PC+ system directory. By default this is C:\SPSS. If you have issued the DOS environment command *SET SPSS,* the system is assumed to reside in the directory named on that command.

Most of the program modules that hold the SPSS/PC+ system contain more than one procedure. For such modules, you cannot remove one of these procedures without removing all of them. As of the initial release of SPSS/PC+ 4.0, procedures are grouped into modules as follows:

• DATA LIST, GET, SAVE, IMPORT, EXPORT, JOIN, all transformation commands, plus DESCRIPTIVES, FREQUENCIES, GSET, LIST, MEANS, MODIFY VARS, REVIEW, SPSS MANAGER, TRANSLATE, and WRITE make up the *central system.* This module must be installed at all times.

• AGGREGATE, AUTORECODE, CROSSTABS, EXAMINE, FLIP, PLOT, RANK, REPORT, SORT, and SYSFILE INFO. These procedures are part of the base system, but can be removed.

• ANOVA, CLUSTER, CORRELATIONS, FACTOR, NPAR TESTS, ONEWAY, QUICK CLUSTER, REGRESSION, RELIABILITY, T-TEST. These procedures are in the Statistics option.

• HILOGLINEAR, LOGISTIC REGRESSION. These procedures are in the Advanced Statistics option.

• DSCRIMINANT, LOGLINEAR, MANOVA. These procedures are in the Advanced Statistics option.

• DERIVATIVES, MODEL PROGRAM, NLR, PROBIT, SURVIVAL. These procedures are in the Advanced Statistics option.

• TABLES and PRINT TABLES. These procedures are in the Tables option.

• DE. This procedure is in the Data Entry option.

• CREATE, READ MODEL FILE, RMV, SAVE MODEL FILE, SPECTRA, WLS, and 2SLS. These procedures are in the Trends option.

• CASEPLOT, CURVEFIT, EXSMOOTH, NPPLOT, SEASON, and TSPLOT. These procedures are in the Trends option.

• ACF, AREG, ARIMA, CCF, and PACF. These procedures are in the Trends option.

• X11ARIMA. This procedure is in the Trends option.

• CONJOINT, ORTHOPLAN, and PLANCARDS. These procedures are in the Categories option.

C

Command Reference

- GRAPH. This procedure is in the Graphics option. To install or remove GRAPH, you must use the INSTALL program.
- MAP. This procedure is in the Mapping option. To install or remove MAP, you must use the INSTALL program.

It is not guaranteed that this arrangement of procedures into modules will remain constant. To find out which procedures are grouped with a given procedure use the STATUS subcommand (see below).

Syntax

- One and only one of the subcommands INSTALL, REMOVE, or STATUS can be specified. Invoke SPSS MANAGER once for each type of action you need.
- Unless the NOCONFIRM subcommand is entered, SPSS MANAGER will request confirmation before installing or removing any modules.
- Subcommands are separated by slashes.
- Semicolons are required to separate procedure names on the INSTALL, REMOVE, and STATUS subcommands.
- Drive or path specifications on the FROM subcommand should be enclosed in apostrophes and may not contain embedded blanks.
- A colon is required after a drive specification.

Operations

- SPSS MANAGER always reports the names of all procedures affected by an INSTALL or REMOVE operation before taking action, unless you have specified NOCONFIRM.
- SPSS MANAGER displays the name of each file as it installs or removes it.
- The (Ctrl) (C) and (Ctrl) (Break) interrupts are not accepted during the processing of an INSTALL or REMOVE operation.

Example

```
SPSS MANAGER REMOVE=MANOVA.
SPSS MANAGER INSTALL=TABLES.
```

- The first SPSS MANAGER command removes the MANOVA procedure from the hard disk. DSCRIMINANT and LOGLINEAR are removed at the same time, since they are in the same module.
- The second SPSS MANAGER command installs the TABLES procedure on the hard disk. You will be prompted to insert the necessary diskettes into the A: drive.

REMOVE Subcommand

The REMOVE subcommand deletes modules from the directory in which the system is stored on the hard disk.

- Specifications for REMOVE consist of the names of one or more SPSS/PC+ procedures separated by semicolons. Procedure names can be abbreviated to three characters.
- REMOVE cannot be specified along with INSTALL or STATUS. Invoke the SPSS MANAGER once for each type of action you need.
- You cannot remove the central system, nor can you remove procedures that are in the same module as the central system.
- SPSS MANAGER first tells you if any procedures you specify are already absent from the hard disk. It then displays the following: the names of all remaining procedures requested and of other procedures that are packaged in the same module(s); the disk space required to hold these modules; and the available disk space.
- After confirmation by the user (unless NOCONFIRM is specified), SPSS MANAGER simply deletes the appropriate modules from disk. If you attempt to use a procedure from a deleted module, you will receive a message stating that the procedure must be installed before use.

INSTALL Subcommand

The INSTALL subcommand places the module(s) containing one or more procedures requested by the user into the directory with the rest of the system on the hard disk.

- Specifications for INSTALL consist of the names of one or more SPSS/PC+ procedures separated by semicolons. Procedure names can be abbreviated to three characters.

- INSTALL cannot be specified along with REMOVE or STATUS. Invoke the SPSS MANAGER once for each type of action you need.

- SPSS MANAGER first tells you if any procedures you specify are already on the hard disk. It then displays the following: the names of all remaining procedures requested and of other procedures that are packaged in the same module(s); the disk space required to hold these modules; and the available disk space.

- After confirmation by the user (unless NOCONFIRM has been specified), SPSS MANAGER will prompt for the insertion of the necessary diskettes into the A: drive (unless you have used the FROM subcommand described below). Diskettes are requested by number.

- By default, SPSS MANAGER expects to install procedures from diskettes in the A: drive. The FROM subcommand, described below, allows you to install from a different drive, which can be another hard disk or similar device.

STATUS Subcommand

The STATUS subcommand reports on the presence or absence of requested procedures and the other procedures grouped together in modules with them.

- Specifications for STATUS consist of the names of one or more SPSS/PC+ procedures separated by semicolons. Procedure names can be abbreviated to three characters.

- If no procedure is listed on the STATUS subcommand, all procedure names are listed in alphabetical order.

- To find what is grouped with any particular procedure in your system, specify STATUS and the name of that procedure.

- STATUS cannot be specified along with INSTALL or REMOVE. Invoke the SPSS MANAGER once for each type of action you need.

- For every procedure named, SPSS MANAGER displays whether that procedure is installed and the names of other procedures that are packaged in the same module.

- Files are never added to or deleted from the hard disk when the STATUS subcommand is specified. The CONFIRM and NOCONFIRM subcommands are therefore ignored with STATUS.

CONFIRM and NOCONFIRM Subcommands

CONFIRM and NOCONFIRM control whether or not the user must confirm a REMOVE or INSTALL specification before it is executed.

- CONFIRM requests that no action be taken without confirmation from the user. CONFIRM is the default.

- Confirmation is requested after the SPSS MANAGER has reported on the procedures involved, their disk space requirements, and the available space on the hard disk.

- NOCONFIRM requests that the specified action be carried out without further prompting, aside from prompts for the insertion of diskettes during installation.

- The NOCONFIRM subcommand is intended for batch processing.

- You will have to press ⏎ once before installing procedures, even if you have specified NOCONFIRM.

C

Command Reference

FROM Subcommand

The FROM subcommand allows you to install procedures from a drive other than A:, which is the default. For example, you can install procedures from backup copies kept on high-density floppy diskettes or a removable-cartridge storage device.

• Specifications on FROM consist of a device or path specification in apostrophes. The apostrophes and the colon following a device specification are required.

• FROM is ignored unless the INSTALL subcommand is entered.

• If the modules containing the requested procedures cannot be found at the location specified on the FROM subcommand, the SPSS MANAGER will display a message explaining the problem and terminate. After determining the correct drive or directory, enter the SPSS MANAGER command again.

• The specified device and directory should contain copies of all files on the distribution diskettes. For example, use the DOS command

```
COPY  A:*.*  D:
```

when copying the distribution diskettes to a cartridge system on the D: drive.

• When making backup copies of the distribution diskettes, back up the diskettes in numerical order and do not divide the files distributed on a single diskette. All files on diskette B4, for example, should be copied to the same high-density diskette or removable cartridge.

Example

```
SPSS MANAGER INSTALL FACTOR
  /FROM 'D:\SPSSBACK'.
```

• The module containing the FACTOR procedure will be installed from directory \SPSSBACK on the D: drive.

• CONFIRM, the default, is in effect.

SUBTITLE

SUBTITLE [$\{{' \atop "}\}$] text [$\{{' \atop "}\}$]

Example:

SUBTITLE FREQUENCIES FOR SEX=FEMALE..

Overview

The SUBTITLE command inserts a left-justified subtitle on the second line from the top of each page of the display file. The default subtitle is a blank line.

Syntax

• The only specification on SUBTITLE is the subtitle itself.

• The subtitle can include any characters.

• The subtitle can be up to 64 characters long. Subtitles longer than 64 characters are truncated.

• You can specify the subtitle as a string by enclosing it within either apostrophes or quotation marks (see Universals: Strings). This allows you to include quotation marks, apostrophes, and lowercase text within the subtitle.

• A subtitle entered without apostrophes or quotation marks is converted to uppercase.

• More than one SUBTITLE command is allowed in a single session.

Operations

• Each SUBTITLE command overrides the previous one and takes effect on the next display page.

• SUBTITLE is independent of TITLE and can be changed separately.

Example

TITLE 'Preliminary analysis of Santa Survey'.
SUBTITLE FREQUENCIES FOR SEX=FEMALE..

• This SUBTITLE command includes a period for the subtitle as well as the required command terminator.

Example

SUB "Crosstabs of Respondent's Age by Gift Preference".

• This subtitle is specified within quotation marks to allow the use of an apostrophe in the subtitle and to preserve upper and lower case.

• This example takes advantage of spelling permitted by three-character truncation of keywords.

SYSFILE INFO

```
SYSFILE INFO [FILE =] 'file specifications'
```

Example:
```
SYSFILE INFO '\DATA\MYSTERY.SYS'.
```

Overview

The SYSFILE INFO command allows you to determine the contents of an SPSS/PC+ system file without having to use GET, which replaces your active file. SYSFILE INFO works only with SPSS/PC+ system files that were created with the SAVE command in SPSS/PC+, in SPSS/PC+ Data Entry or SPSS Data Entry II, or by an SPSS/PC+ procedure such as AGGREGATE.

Syntax

The sole specification on SYSFILE INFO is a DOS file specification in apostrophes.

• The file specification can include a drive and/or a path.

Operations

SPSS/PC+ determines if the specified file exists and if it is an SPSS/PC+ system file. If so, it displays:

• The filename, creation date, and creation time.
• The file title, if any.
• The number of cases and variables.
• The use of case weights.
• Whether the file is compressed or not.
• Whether the file contains special information for use by SPSS Data Entry II.
• The names and variable labels of all user-defined variables in the file.

The variable names in the file are particularly useful prior to a JOIN command. The following are error conditions:

• If SPSS/PC+ cannot find or obtain access to the specified file, it displays a message indicating that an error occurred while referencing the file.
• If the file is found but is not an SPSS/PC+ system file, SPSS/PC+ displays a message indicating this.

TITLE

TITLE [{'}] text [{'}]
      {"}   {"}

Example:

TITLE This run will contain preliminary analyses.

Overview
The default page heading on SPSS/PC+ output contains the date, SPSS/PC+, and the display page number. The TITLE command replaces the centered title portion (SPSS/PC+) of the default display heading with user-supplied text. The date and page number remain.

Syntax
- The only specification on TITLE is the title itself.
- The title can include any characters.
- The title can be up to 58 characters long. Titles longer than 58 characters are truncated.
- You can specify the title as a string by enclosing it within either apostrophes or quotation marks (see Universals: Strings). This allows you to include quotation marks, apostrophes, and lowercase text within the title.
- A subtitle entered without apostrophes or quotation marks is converted to upper case.
- More than one TITLE command is allowed in a single session.

Operations
- Each TITLE command overrides the previous one and takes effect on the next display page.
- TITLE does not cause a new page.

Example
TITLE This run will contain preliminary analyses.

- This title will replace the default title on subsequent output pages.
- Since the title is not enclosed in apostrophes or quotation marks, it is converted to upper case.
- Note that the period (.) is the command terminator and will not appear as part of the title.

Example
TITLE "Regression on Nora's Dissertation Data".

- This title is specified within quotation marks to allow the use of an apostrophe in the title and to preserve upper and lower case.

TRANSLATE

```
TRANSLATE {FROM = 'filename.ext'}[/RANGE={name      }]*
          {TO   = 'filename.ext'}        {start..stop}
                                         {start:stop }


[/TYPE={WKS}]              [/REPLACE]
       {WK1}
       {WK3}
       {WRK}
       {WR1}
       {SLK}
       {DBF}
       {DB2}
       {DB3}
       {DB4}


[/DROP=variable list]

[/KEEP=variable list]

[/FIELDNAMES]**

[/MAP]
```

*RANGE is available only for translating from spreadsheet files.
**FIELDNAMES is available only for spreadsheet files.

Keyword	Foreign file
WKS	1-2-3 Release 1A
WK1	1-2-3 Release 2.0,2.01,2.2
WK3	1-2-3 Release 3
WRK	Symphony 1.0,1.01
WR1	Symphony 1.1,1.2,2.0
SLK	Multiplan, Excel (symbolic format only)
DBF	all dBASE (with FROM)
DB2	dBASE-II (with TO)
DB3	dBASE-III, dBASE-III PLUS (with TO)
DB4	dBASE-IV (with TO)

Examples:

```
TRANSLATE FROM='PROJECT.WKS'
   /FIELDNAMES
   /RANGE=D3..J279.

TRANSLATE FROM='ANNUAL.DBF'
   /DROP=JANUARY TO MARCH
   /MAP.

TRANSLATE TO='SALESREP.SLK'
   /KEEP=SALES, UNITS, MONTHS, PRICE1 TO PRICE20
   /FIELDNAMES
   /MAP.
```

Overview   Procedure TRANSLATE either creates an active file from a foreign file (subcommand FROM) or translates the SPSS/PC+ active file into a foreign file (subcommand TO). Supported formats are 1-2-3 (1A through 3.0), Symphony, Excel, Multiplan, dBASE-II, dBASE-III, dBASE-III PLUS, and dBASE-IV. Excel and Multiplan are supported via the symbolic (SYLK) format.

Defaults   By default, all data are translated from the input file into the resulting file. The format of the input or output file is inferred from the file extension (except for translating to database files; see TO Subcommand—Databases).

Tailoring   You can use the DROP and KEEP subcommands to specify variables to omit or retain in the resulting active file. You can use the RANGE subcommand to translate a subset of cells from a spreadsheet file. You can use the FIELDNAMES subcommand to translate field names in the spreadsheet file to SPSS/PC+ variable names or to translate SPSS/PC+ variable names to field names. The optional MAP subcommand displays the names of variables retrieved from a foreign file.

Syntax
- The minimum specification is subcommand FROM or TO with an associated filename. FROM or TO must precede any other specifications.
- The TYPE subcommand is required for translating from the SPSS/PC+ active file to a dBASE file, since the file extension DBF is shared by all dBASE database files.
- The file specification is enclosed in apostrophes and can be fully qualified, including drive, directory, filename, and extension.
- The RANGE subcommand can be used only for translating spreadsheet files into SPSS/PC+ active files.
- The FIELDNAMES subcommand is available for spreadsheet files only.
- Subcommands are separated by slashes.

Operations
- TRANSLATE FROM replaces an existing active file. If TRANSLATE FROM is not successful, the current active file is not changed and is still available.
- After TRANSLATE TO is executed, the active file remains available for SPSS/PC+ transformations and procedures.
- TRANSLATE TO will *not* overwrite an existing file with the same name unless you use the REPLACE subcommand.
- Commands N, SAMPLE, PROCESS IF, SELECT IF, and any transformations are executed prior to TRANSLATE TO.

Limitations
TRANSLATE tries to avoid creating a database or spreadsheet that is too big to load into the target software product.

- The number of variables translated into the active file is limited by the source file. Thus, you cannot retrieve more than 256 columns from a 1-2-3, Symphony, or .SLK file.
- Maximum 2048 cases can be translated to 1-2-3 (Release 1A); maximum 8192 cases to 1-2-3 (Release 2.0, 3.0) or Symphony files; and maximum 16384 cases to .SLK files.
- Maximum 32 variables and 65,535 cases can be translated to a dBASE-II file.
- Maximum 128 variables and 1 billion cases (subject to disk space availability) to a dBASE-III or dBASE-III PLUS file.
- Maximum 256 variables and 1 billion cases (subject to disk space availability) to a dBASE-IV file.

FROM Subcommand
TRANSLATE FROM reads a foreign file and translates it into the active file. The only required specification on FROM is the name of the foreign file enclosed in apostrophes.

Spreadsheets
A spreadsheet file suitable for SPSS/PC+ should be arranged so that each row represents a case and columns indicate variables.

- By default, the new active file contains all rows and up to 256 columns from 1-2-3, Symphony, and SYLK (Excel or Multiplan) files.
- Only one worksheet at a time can be translated from a WK3 (1-2-3 Release 3) file. By default, the first (A:) worksheet is translated.
- By default, TRANSLATE FROM uses the column letters as variable names in the active file.
- The first row of a spreadsheet or specified range may contain field labels immediately followed by rows of data. These names can be transferred as SPSS/PC+ variable names (see FIELDNAMES Subcommand).
- The current value of a formula is translated to the active file.
- Blank, ERR, and NA values in 1-2-3 and Symphony are translated as system-missing in the SPSS/PC+ active file.
- Hidden columns and cells in 1-2-3 and Symphony files *are* translated into the SPSS/PC+ active file.

- Column width and format type are transferred to the active file dictionary.
- The format type is assigned from values in the first data row. By default, the first data row is row 1. If RANGE is specified, the first data row is the first row in the range. If FIELDNAMES is specified, the first data row follows immediately after the single row containing field names.
- If a cell in the first data row is empty, the variable is assigned the global default format from the spreadsheet.
- The formats from 1-2-3, Symphony, and Multiplan are translated by default as follows:

1-2-3/Symphony	Multiplan	SPSS/PC+
Fixed	Fixed	Number
	Integer	Number
Scientific	Exponent	Number
Currency	$ (dollar)	Dollar
,(comma)		Comma
General	General	Number
+/−	* (bargraph)	Number
Percent	Percent	Number
Date		String
Time		String
Text		Number
Label	Alpha	String

- If a string is encountered in a column with numeric format, the active file contains the system-missing value.
- If a numeric value is encountered in a column with string format, the active file contains a blank.
- TRANSLATE FROM creates string variables for 1-2-3 and Symphony variables with DATE format. The SPSS/PC+ variable is in the form MM/DD/YY if the spreadsheet column has a width of 9 or less. If the width of the spreadsheet column is greater than 9, the SPSS/PC+ variable is in the form MM/DD/YYYY.
- Values with the Percent format in 1-2-3 files *earlier than WK3* and in Symphony files are multiplied by 100 so that the value in the SPSS/PC+ active file is the same as the value displayed in 1-2-3. This is not done in translating from WK3 files.
- Values longer than 255 characters in label cells from WK3 files are truncated to 255 characters.
- Blank lines are translated as cases containing the system-missing value for numeric variables and blanks for string variables.
- 1-2-3 and Symphony date and time indicators (shown at the bottom of the screen) are not transferred from WKS, WK1, WK3, or WRK files. The values for system variables $CASENUM, $WEIGHT, and $DATE are assigned by TRANSLATE as each case is written to the active file.

Example

```
TRANSLATE FROM='PROJECT.WKS'.
```

- TRANSLATE creates an active file from the 1-2-3 Release 1A spreadsheet with the name PROJECT.WKS.
- The active file contains all rows and uses the column letters as variable names.
- The format for each variable is determined by the format of the value in the first row of each column.

Databases

Database files are logically very similar to SPSS/PC+ data files.

- By default, all fields and records from dBASE-II, dBASE-III, or dBASE-IV files are included in the SPSS/PC+ active file.
- Field names are automatically translated to SPSS/PC+ variable names.
- If the FIELDNAMES subcommand is used with database files, it is ignored.

- Field names to be translated should comply with SPSS/PC+ variable-naming conventions.
- Field names longer than eight characters are converted into valid and unique variable names. Field names longer than eight characters are first truncated; if duplicate names result, the final characters of the name are modified to produce unique names.
- Colons used in dBASE-II field names are translated to underscores.
- If you have marked records for deletion in dBASE-II, dBASE-III, or dBASE-IV but have not actually purged them, the records *are* included in the active file.
- TRANSLATE creates a new string variable D_R when converting dBASE files, which contains an asterisk for cases marked for deletion. Other cases contain a blank for D_R.
- Character and numeric fields are transferred directly to SPSS/PC+ variables. Date and logical fields are converted into string variables. Memo fields are ignored. The following table shows how dBASE formats are translated to SPSS/PC+:

dBASE	SPSS/PC+
Character	String
Logical	String
Date	String
Numeric	Number
Float	Number
Memo	Ignored

Example   TRANSLATE FROM='ANNUAL.DBF'.

- TRANSLATE creates an active file from the database file ANNUAL.DBF.
- All cases are translated and each field becomes a variable in the active file.

TO Subcommand   Procedure TRANSLATE with the TO subcommand converts a SPSS/PC+ active file to a foreign file. The only required specification on TO is the name to be used for the foreign file.

- User-missing values are transferred as the actual values.
- The three system variables, $DATE, $WEIGHT, and $CASENUM, are translated only if they are specified explicitly on the KEEP subcommand. $DATE is passed as a short string value with an A8 format; $WEIGHT and $CASENUM are passed as numeric values with formats of F8.2 and F8.0.

Spreadsheets   Variables in the active file become columns and cases become rows in the spreadsheet file.

- If you specify FIELDNAMES, variable names become the first row and indicate field names.
- String variable values are left-justified and numeric variable values are right-justified.
- The resulting spreadsheet file is given the range name of SPSSPC.
- System-missing values are translated to NA in spreadsheet files.
- SPSS/PC+ formats are translated as follows:

SPSS/PC+	1-2-3/Symphony	Multiplan
Number	Fixed	Fixed
Comma	Comma	Fixed
Dollar	Currency	$ (dollar)
String	Label	Alpha
$DATE	Date	Alpha

Example   TRANSLATE TO='STAFF.WRK'.

- TRANSLATE TO creates a Symphony spreadsheet file containing all variables in the active file. The variable names are *not* transferred to the Symphony file.

C

Command Reference

Databases   Variables in the active file become fields and cases become records in the database file.

- You must use the TYPE subcommand with keyword DB2, DB3, or DB4 when translating from SPSS/PC+ to a dBASE file.
- Characters that are allowed in SPSS/PC+ variable names but are not allowed in dBASE field names are translated to colons in dBASE-II and underscores in dBASE-III or dBASE-IV. If requested, the system variables $CASENUM, $WEIGHT, and $DATE are translated to fields PC:CASENUM, etc. for dBASE-II and PC_CASENUM, etc. for dBASE-III and dBASE-IV.
- SPSS/PC+ numeric variables containing the system-missing value are translated to **** in dBASE-III or dBASE-IV, and to 0 (zero) for dBASE-II.
- SPSS/PC+ variable formats are translated to dBASE formats as follows:

SPSS/PC+	dBASE
Number	Numeric
String	Character
Dollar	Numeric
Comma	Numeric
$DATE	Date

Example
```
TRANSLATE TO='STAFF.DBF'
  /TYPE=DB3.
```

- TRANSLATE TO creates a dBASE-III file called STAFF.DBF. The TYPE subcommand is required.

TYPE Subcommand

The TYPE subcommand indicates the format of a foreign file.

- You can use the TYPE subcommand with both FROM and TO subcommands.
- The TYPE subcommand can be omitted for translating to and from spreadsheet files if the file extension named on the TO or FROM subcommand corresponds to the format keyword.
- The TYPE subcommand with keyword DB2, DB3, or DB4 is required for translating the SPSS/PC+ active file into a dBASE file. TYPE is optional for translating dBASE files into SPSS/PC+ if the file extension named on FROM corresponds to the format keyword.
- The TYPE subcommand takes precedence over the file extension.
- You can create a Lotus format file in Multiplan and translate it to a SPSS/PC+ active file with TYPE=WKS.
- Available keywords on TYPE are:

WKS   *1-2-3 Release 1A.*

WK1   *1-2-3 Release 2.0, 2.01, 2.2.*

WK3   *1-2-3 Release 3.*

WRK   *Symphony Release 1.0, 1.01.*

WR1   *Symphony Release 1.1, 1.2, 2.0.*

SLK   *Symbolic format for use with Excel or Multiplan.*

DBF   *dBASE files.* Use DBF as the file extension or on the TYPE subcommand when translating any dBASE file into an SPSS/PC+ active file.

DB2   *dBASE-II.* Specify DB2 on TYPE when translating to a dBASE-II file.

DB3   *dBASE-III.* Specify DB3 on TYPE when translating to a dBASE-III or dBASE-III PLUS file.

DB4   *dBASE-IV.* Specify DB2 on TYPE when translating to a dBASE-IV file.

Example
```
TRANSLATE FROM='PROJECT.OCT'
  /TYPE=SLK.
```

- TRANSLATE creates an active file from the Multiplan spreadsheet PROJECT.OCT.

FIELDNAMES Subcommand

When used with the FROM subcommand, the optional FIELDNAMES subcommand translates spreadsheet field names into SPSS/PC+ variable names. When used with TO, FIELDNAMES translates SPSS/PC+ variable names into field names in the spreadsheet.

- FIELDNAMES can be used with spreadsheets only. FIELDNAMES is ignored when used with database files.
- SPSS/PC+ variable names are transferred to the first row of the spreadsheet file.
- For translating spreadsheet field names to SPSS/PC+, each cell in the first row of the spreadsheet file or range must contain a field name. If a column does not contain a name, the column is dropped.
- Field names to be translated into SPSS/PC+ should conform to the SPSS/PC+ variable-naming conventions.
- Variable names that exceed eight characters are truncated.
- If two or more columns in the spreadsheet have the same field name, new unique variable names are assigned to the second and later of such columns.
- Illegal characters in field names are changed to underscores in SPSS/PC+.
- If duplicate variable names occur, the final characters of the name are modified to produce unique names.
- If you use SPSS/PC+ reserved words (ALL, AND, BY, EQ, GE, GT, LE, LT, NE, NOT, OR, TO, or WITH) as field names in a spreadsheet file, TRANSLATE FROM appends a dollar sign ($) to the variable name. For example, 1-2-3 columns named GE, GT, EQ, and BY are named GE$, GT$, EQ$, and BY$ in the SPSS/PC+ active file.

Example
```
TRANSLATE TO='STAFF.WRK'
  /FIELDNAMES.
```

- TRANSLATE TO creates a Symphony spreadsheet file containing all variables in the active file. The variable names *are* transferred to the Symphony file.

Example
```
TRANSLATE FROM='MONTHLY.WRK'
  /FIELDNAMES.
```

- TRANSLATE creates an active file from a Symphony spreadsheet. The first row in the spreadsheet contains field names that are used as variable names in the active file.

RANGE Subcommand

The RANGE subcommand translates a specified set of cells from a spreadsheet file.

- The RANGE subcommand cannot be used with subcommand TO or for translating from database files.
- For 1-2-3 or Symphony, specify the beginning of the range with a column letter and row number, two periods, and the end of the range with a column letter and row number, as in A1..K14.
- For 1-2-3 Release 3 files of type WK3, you can specify a range of cells in a worksheet other than the first by including a worksheet specification in the range, separated from the column specification by a colon. See the example below. *The entire range must be within a single worksheet.* If the second worksheet specification differs from the first, the entire range is taken from the worksheet first specified.
- For Multiplan spreadsheets, specify the beginning and ending cells of the range separated by a colon, as in R1C1:R14C11.
- You can also specify the range using range names supplied in Symphony, 1-2-3, or Multiplan.
- If you specify FIELDNAMES with RANGE, the first row of the range must contain field names. If you do not, it must contain data.

Example
```
TRANSLATE FROM='PROJECT.WKS'
  /FIELDNAMES
  /RANGE=D3..J279.
```

- TRANSLATE FROM creates an active file from the 1-2-3 Release 1A file PROJECT.WKS.
- Variable names are assigned from the field names in the first row of the range, in this case row 3.
- Data from cells D4 through J279 are transferred to the active file.

Example
```
TRANSLATE FROM='PROJECT.WK3'
  /FIELDNAMES
  /RANGE=C:D3..C:J279.
```

- This example takes the same range as above from the third worksheet of the 1-2-3 Release 3 file PROJECT.WK3.

DROP and KEEP Subcommands

Use DROP or KEEP to include only a subset of variables in the resulting file. DROP specifies a set of variables to exclude, and KEEP specifies a set of variables to retain.

- Use DROP or KEEP with TO or FROM file translation.
- Specifications consist of a list of variable, column, or field names separated by commas or spaces.
- When SPSS/PC+ alters field names to form valid and unique variable names, you must specify the SPSS/PC+ variable names on the DROP and KEEP subcommands.
- You can use TO to refer to adjacent variables or columns.
- You can use keyword ALL to specify all user-defined (not system) variables.
- KEEP=ALL is equivalent to omitting the KEEP subcommand.
- KEEP does not affect the order of variables in the resulting file. Variables are kept in their original order.
- If FIELDNAMES is specified when translating from a spreadsheet, the DROP and KEEP subcommands must refer to the field names, not the default column letters.
- If you specify both RANGE and KEEP, the resulting file contains only variables that are both within the range and specified on KEEP.
- If you specify both RANGE and DROP, the resulting file contains only variables within the range and excludes those mentioned on the DROP subcommand, even if they are within the range.

Example
```
TRANSLATE FROM='ADDRESS.DBF'
  /DROP=PHONENO, ENTRY.
```

- TRANSLATE creates an active file from the dBASE file ADDRESS.DBF, omitting the fields named PHONENO and ENTRY.

Example
```
TRANSLATE FROM='PROJECT.OCT'
  /TYPE=WK1
  /FIELDNAMES
  /KEEP=NETINC, REP, QUANTITY, REGION, MONTH, DAY, YEAR.
```

- TRANSLATE creates an active file from the 1-2-3 Release 2.0 file called PROJECT.OCT.
- Subcommand FIELDNAMES indicates that the first row of the spreadsheet contains field names, which will be translated into variable names in the active file.
- Subcommand KEEP translates columns with the field names NETINC, REP, QUANTITY, REGION, MONTH, DAY, and YEAR to the active file.

REPLACE Subcommand   In previous versions of SPSS/PC+, TRANSLATE TO would not replace an existing spreadsheet or database file. Starting with SPSS/PC+ 4.0, you can replace an existing file by specifying the REPLACE subcommand. This subcommand should be used with caution.

Example
```
TRANSLATE TO='WEEKLY.WK1'
    /REPLACE.
```

• If WEEKLY.WK1 already exists, it is replaced without warning.

MAP Subcommand   Subcommand MAP produces a listing of the variables transferred from or to a foreign file.

• MAP displays a listing of the names of the variables, the variable type (string or numeric), the width of the variable, and the number of decimal places.

• If TRANSLATE has changed the name of a variable, the original name (up to 10 characters) is also displayed.

• MAP can be specified anywhere in the TRANSLATE command.

Example
```
TRANSLATE TO='STAFF.DBF'
    /TYPE=DB3
    /MAP.
```

• The keyword MAP requests a listing of the variables translated to the dBASE-III database.

C

Command Reference

VALUE LABELS

```
VALUE LABELS  varlist value 'label' value 'label' ...

              [/varlist ...]
```

Example:

```
VALUE LABELS XVAR TO ZVAR   0 'NORTH' 1 'CENTRAL' 2 'WEST'
                            3 'SOUTH' 4 'EAST'
 / RESIDE 'URBAN    '  "Within city proper"
          'SUBURBAN'  "Metro area"
          'EXURBAN '  "Outside SMSA".
```

Overview

The VALUE LABELS command provides descriptive labels for individual values of a variable.

Syntax

• The VALUE LABELS command is followed by a variable name (or variable list) and the individual values with associated labels.

• The variable must have been previously defined, either on a DATA LIST, GET, JOIN, AGGREGATE, or IMPORT command, or on a transformation command.

• Value labels must be specified as strings enclosed in apostrophes or quotation marks (see Universals: Strings).

• The values of short string variables as well as their labels are specified as strings.

• You cannot assign value labels to long string variables.

• The same labels can be assigned to the same values of several variables by listing all of the variables followed by the values and associated labels.

• The value labels for one variable or variable list must be separated from the next variable or variable list by a slash.

• More than one VALUE LABELS command is allowed.

Operations

• Value labels are stored in the active file dictionary.

• If any value label is assigned to a variable that already has value labels, the new assignment completely replaces the old assignment. This is true even if the new label is assigned to a previously unlabeled value.

Limitations

• Each value label can be up to 60 characters long, although most procedures only display 20 characters.

• Some procedures display fewer than 20 characters in labels.

• Only the TABLES procedure (available in SPSS/PC+ Tables) will display all 60 characters of a label.

Example

```
VALUE LABELS XVAR TO ZVAR   0 'NORTH' 1 'CENTRAL' 2 'WEST'
                            3 'SOUTH' 4 'EAST'
 / AVAR 'X' 'SALES STAFF'  'S' 'SUPERVISORY STAFF'
        'M' 'MANAGERIAL STAFF'.
```

• Labels are assigned to the values 0, 1, 2, 3, and 4 of the variables between and including XVAR and ZVAR on the active file.

• Following the required slash, labels for values X, S, and M of variable AVAR are specified. X, S, and M are string values and must be enclosed in apostrophes or quotes.

Example
```
DAT LIS / ID 1-3 SOCROLE 4-5 OPIN1 TO OPIN5 6-10.
VAL LAB SOCROLE 1 'MOTHER' 2 'FATHER' 3 'SISTER'
                4 'BROTHER' 5 'COUSIN' 10.0 'NEIGHBOR'
                97 'REFUSED TO ANSWER' 98 "DON'T KNOW"
 / OPIN1 TO OPIN5 1 'STRONGLY AGREE' 3 'NO OPINION'
                5 'STRONGLY DISAGREE'.
BEG DAT.
0012 12121
0021033333
0039845541
lines of data
END DAT.
```

- The DATA LIST command defines ID as a three-column variable, SOCROLE as a two-column variable, and each of the five OPIN variables as one-column variables.

- The VALUE LABELS command assigns labels to variables SOCROLE, OPIN1, OPIN2, OPIN3, OPIN4, and OPIN5.

- The value label for value 98 is enclosed in quotation marks to allow the embedded apostrophe.

- Three values of the OPIN variables are assigned labels.

- This example takes advantage of spelling permitted by three-character truncation of keywords.

String Value Labels

- Both the values and the labels for short string variables must be enclosed in apostrophes or quotation marks.

- The *values* of a short string variable must be specified with the correct width of that variable, including any leading or trailing blanks that are in the data.

Example
```
DATA LIST / REGION 1 RESIDE 2-9 (A) V1 TO V15 10-24.
VAL LAB RESIDE "URBAN   " "Within city proper"
               "SUBURBAN" "Metro area"
               "EXURBAN " "Outside SMSA".
```

- The DATA LIST command defines one short string variable, RESIDE, which is eight characters wide.

- The VALUE LABELS command assigns labels to three values of RESIDE. Each value and each label is specified in quotation marks. The value URBAN contains three trailing blanks in order to match the format width of eight characters. The value EXURBAN contains one trailing blank in order to match data values.

C

Command Reference

VARIABLE LABELS

```
VARIABLE LABELS  varlist 'label' [[/]varname ...]
```

Example:

```
VARIABLE LABELS XVAR 'SALES TERRITORY X'
              / YVAR "John's Territory"
              / ZVAR 'SALES TERRITORY Z'.
```

Overview

The VARIABLE LABELS command assigns a descriptive label of up to 60 characters to a variable.

Syntax

- The variable name or list of variables is followed by at least one blank or comma and the associated label.
- Variable labels must be specified within apostrophes or quotation marks (see Universals: Strings).
- The variable must have been previously defined, either on a DATA LIST, GET, JOIN, AGGREGATE, or IMPORT command, or on a transformation command.
- The slash separating a variable name and its label from subsequent names and labels is optional.
- More than one VARIABLE LABELS command is allowed per session.
- Individual variable labels cannot be specified across multiple lines.

Operations

- If a label is assigned to a variable that already has a label assigned to it, the new label completely replaces the old label.
- Variable labels are stored in the active file dictionary.
- If a list of variables precedes a label specification, the label is assigned to each of them.

Limitations

- Variable labels are limited to 60 characters, although most procedures only display 40 characters.
- Some procedures show fewer than 40 characters of a label.
- Only the TABLES procedure (available in SPSS/PC+ Tables) will display all 60 characters of a variable label.

Example

```
VARIABLE LABELS XVAR 'SALES TERRITORY X'
              / YVAR "John's Territory"
              / ZVAR 'SALES TERRITORY Z'.
```

- This command assigns labels to variables XVAR, YVAR, and ZVAR.
- The label for YVAR is enclosed in quotation marks to allow the inclusion of an apostrophe in the label.

WEIGHT

```
WEIGHT  {BY varname}
        {OFF       }
```

Example:

```
WEIGHT BY AVAR.
FREQ VAR=VAR1.
```

Overview   The WEIGHT transformation reassigns the value of the system variable $WEIGHT for each case (see Universals: System Variables). With WEIGHT, you can arithmetically alter the sample size or its distribution.

Syntax
- Only one variable can be specified.
- The WEIGHT variable must be numeric.
- If the keyword BY is omitted, the first word following WEIGHT is taken to be the weighting variable.
- WEIGHT OFF turns weighting off. You cannot weight the file by a variable named OFF.

Operations
- WEIGHT is a transformation and is executed when data are read for the next procedure.
- The default value of $WEIGHT for each case is 1.0.
- To list the values of $WEIGHT or any other system variable, you must request it explicitly on the LIST command.
- Weighting is permanent during a session unless it is changed or turned off with the WEIGHT OFF specification.
- Each WEIGHT command overrides the previous one.
- WEIGHT tells SPSS/PC+ to use the value of the specified variable to arithmetically replicate cases for subsequent procedures.
- Weight values do not need to be integer.
- Cases are *not* physically replicated.
- System-missing, user-missing, and negative values for the weighting variable are treated as 0 in the computation of weights.
- A file saved with EXPORT or SAVE when weighting is in effect maintains the weighting in the system variable $WEIGHT. When the file is reread, weighting is maintained.
- If the weighted number of cases exceeds the sample size, tests of significance are inflated; if it is smaller, they are deflated.

Example
```
WEIGHT BY AVAR.
FREQ VAR=VAR1.
```
- The frequency counts for the values of variable VAR1 will be weighted (multiplied) by the values of variable AVAR.

Example
```
COMPUTE WVAR=1.
IF (GROUP EQ 1) WVAR=.5.
WEIGHT BY WVAR.
```
- Variable WVAR is initialized to 1 with the COMPUTE command. The value of WVAR is changed to 0.5 with the IF command for cases where GROUP equals 1.
- Subsequent procedures will use a case base in which cases from Group 1 only count half as much as other cases.

C

Command Reference

WRITE

```
WRITE [VARIABLES={ALL**  }]
                 {varlist}

[/CASES=[FROM {1**}] [TO {eof**}]
              {n  }      {n    }

      [BY {1**}]]
          {n }

[/FORMAT=[{UNNUMBERED**}] [{WRAP**}] [WEIGHT]]
          {NUMBERED    }   {SINGLE}
```

**Default if subcommand is omitted.

Example:
```
WRITE VARIABLES=XVAR AVAR
  /CASES=FROM 10 TO 100 BY 2.
```

Overview

The WRITE procedure writes cases to an ASCII file. The cases are written to the results file specified on SET (by default, SPSS.PRC). SPSS/PC+ automatically specifies the format of the case file that is written using the dictionary formats and a record length of 80. In addition to writing the file, WRITE displays a table that shows the names and the record and column locations of the variables on the written file.

Defaults

By default, all user-defined variables are written for all cases in the file. Each case is written on as many records as are needed.

Tailoring

You can limit the written file to specified variables or a specified sequence of cases. In addition, you can include each case's weight or sequence number in the file. You can also limit each case to a single record.

Syntax

• The minimum specification is simply the command keyword.
• All subcommands are optional.
• A subcommand or its abbreviation may not be recognized as such if a variable name is identical to it, unless the subcommand is followed by an equals sign.
• Subcommands can be specified in any order and must be separated by slashes.

Operations

• WRITE is a procedure and causes the data to be read.
• WRITE uses the dictionary print formats (see Universals: Formats). If a value is greater than the format allows, asterisks (*) are written.
• Records are written with 80 characters regardless of the width defined on SET.
• If a long string variable cannot be written within the record length of 80, it is truncated.
• Records are always written with a single blank between variables.
• System-missing values are written as blanks.
• System variables are only written when explicitly requested.
• Records are written to the results file named on SET. The default is SPSS.PRC.
• If you write to the same file with more than one procedure in the same session, the file will contain only the results of the last procedure.
• Use the SET command to change the results file if you write output more than once in a session.

Limitations

• The VARIABLES, FORMAT, and CASES subcommands can each be specified only once.

Example
```
DATA LIST FILE='EMPLOYEE.DAT'
  / XVAR 1 YVAR 10-15 ZVAR 3-9(2)
  / AVAR 25-30(A).
WRITE VARIABLES=XVAR AVAR
  /CASES=FROM 10 TO 100 BY 2.
```

• This example writes a file containing every second case starting with Case 10 and stopping at 100 for variables XVAR and AVAR.

• The records are written to the default results file SPSS.PRC.

• A display table describing the format of the written file is sent to the screen and to the default listing file SPSS.LIS.

VARIABLES Subcommand

By default, all user-defined variables in the active file are included. Use the optional VARIABLES subcommand to control the variables to be written for each case.

• If you use the VARIABLES subcommand, a list of variables must be specified and only specified variables are written.

• Variables named on VARIABLES must already exist.

• Variables are written in the order named on VARIABLES.

• If a variable is named more than once it is written more than once.

• The actual keyword VARIABLES is optional.

Optionally, you can specify keyword ALL on the VARIABLES subcommand:

ALL   *Write all user-defined variables.* Variables are written in the order in which they appear in the active file. This is the default if the VARIABLES subcommand is omitted.

• ALL does not include the system variables $CASENUM, $WEIGHT, and $DATE. You must request them explicitly to write them.

CASES Subcommand

By default, all cases in the active file are written. Use the CASES subcommand to limit the number and pattern of cases written.

• If you omit CASES or use it without specifications, all cases in the active file are written.

• Only defaults that you change are altered.

The following can be specified on CASES:

FROM n   *The case number of the first case to be written.* The default is 1.

TO n   *Upper limit on the cases to be written.* The default is the end of the file. CASES 100 is interpreted as CASES TO 100.

BY n   *Increment used to choose cases for writing.* The default is 1.

FORMAT Subcommand

By default, the written file does not include the case weight or sequence number for each case, and each case uses as many records as it needs. Use the FORMAT subcommand to specify format options for the written file.

• If the FORMAT subcommand is omitted or if it is included without specifications, the file is written with the default format.

• Only defaults that you change are altered.

The following may be specified on FORMAT:

NUMBERED   *Include the sequence number of the case.* The sequence number is the first item written for each case and is labeled **Case#** in the display table. The default is UNNUMBERED.

SINGLE   *Limit each case to one record.* If variables requested cannot be written on a single record, WRITE is not executed. The default is to WRAP the case, using as many records as necessary.

WEIGHT   *Write the value of the case's weight in the active file.*

Examples

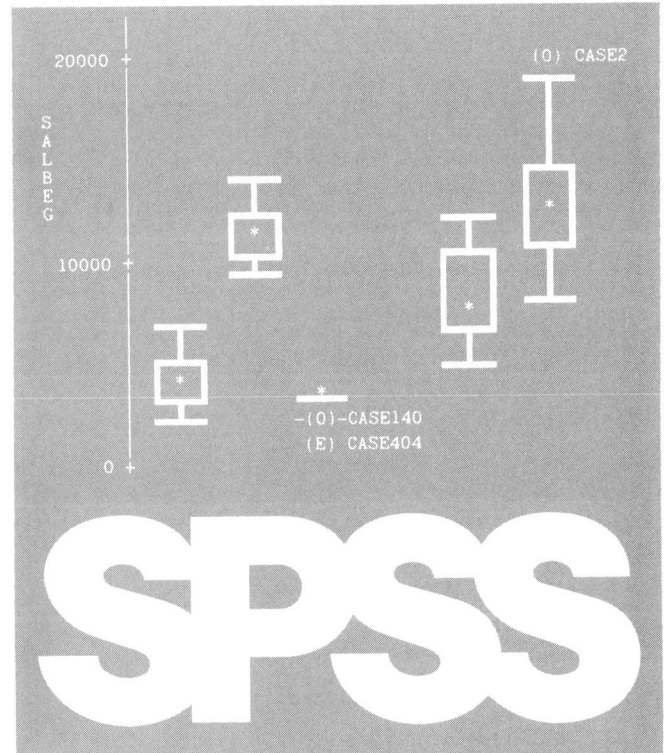

Contents

Examples

AGGREGATE and JOIN

This example creates a file that can be used to produce a report of product sales by different sales representatives. The file contains data on the individual sales of each product by each representative, the average and total sales for each product, and the performance of each representative relative to the product average and total. On two system files for the first and second quarters of a year, the original input variables are

- SALESREP—the name of the sales representative who closed a sale.
- PRODUCT—the product, coded 1=Primo, 2=Mocha, 3=Blend, and 4=Special.
- NUMBER—the quantity sold of each product.
- MONTH—the month of a sale, coded as a number with a value label.
- DAY—the day of a sale, coded as a number.
- YEAR—the year of a sale.

The two system files, containing data on individual sales by each representative, are combined. The resulting active file is sorted and aggregated to produce variables summarizing the sales of each product. The summary variables are appended to the individual sales data so that variables can be computed for the sales of each representative in comparison to the summarized sales. Finally, the REPORT command produces a report displaying all the desired information. The SPSS/PC+ commands in the command file named on the INCLUDE command are:

```
GET FILE='FSTQTR.SF'.
SORT CASES BY PRODUCT MONTH.
SAVE OUTFILE='FSTQTRSO.SF'.

GET FILE='SECQTR.SF'.
SORT CASES BY PRODUCT MONTH.

JOIN ADD FILE='FSTQTRSO.SF'/FILE=*
  /BY PRODUCT MONTH/MAP.

AGGREGATE OUTFILE='AGGSALES.SF'/BREAK=PRODUCT
  /TOTAL=SUM(NUMBER)
  /AVSALES=MEAN(NUMBER).

JOIN MATCH FILE=*/TABLE='AGGSALES.SF'/BY PRODUCT/MAP.

SORT BY PRODUCT SALESREP.

COMPUTE CONTRIB=NUMBER/TOTAL*100.
COMPUTE DIFF=RND(NUMBER-AVSALES).
FORMATS DIFF(F4.0).

REPORT FORMAT=MANUAL LIST BRKSPACE(-1)
  /TITLE 'Mid Year Sales Report'
  /VARIABLES=NUMBER 'Number of' 'Units Sold' (10)
             MONTH (label) 'Month' (5)
             DIFF 'Deviation' (9)
             CONTRIB '% of Total' (10)
  /BREAK=PRODUCT (label) 'Product' 'Name' (12)
  /SUMMARY=SUM '    Total' (NUMBER CONTRIB)
  /SUMMARY=MEAN '  Average' (NUMBER)
  /BREAK=SALESREP 'Sales' 'Rep' (SKIP(0)).
```

- The first GET command retrieves the system file FSTQTR.SF. The cases are ordered according to months within product categories, as specified on the SORT command. The SAVE command saves a copy of the sorted system file, named FSTQTRSO.SF.

- The second GET command retrieves the system file SECQTR.SF, and SORT again orders the cases by months within product categories. The sorted system file is the current active file.

- ADD (synonym for JOIN ADD) combines cases from FSTQTRSO.SF and the active file, interleaving the cases according to values of the key variables, PRODUCT and MONTH. The MAP subcommand produces a listing of the variables contained on the resulting active file (Figure A).

- The AGGREGATE command writes an aggregated system file called AGGSALES.SF. The file contains one case for each category of the variable PRODUCT, named on the BREAK subcommand. Each case contains a value for PRODUCT; a value for TOTAL, representing the sum of variable NUMBER for each break group; and a value for AVSALES, representing the mean of NUMBER for each break group. Figure B shows the variables in the system file AGGSALES.SF.

- MATCH (a synonym for JOIN MATCH) combines variables from the active file and from the aggregated file, which has been declared a TABLE. Cases with matching values of PRODUCT are joined. The MAP subcommand requests a listing of the variables that are in the resulting active file (Figure B).

- The SORT command orders the file according to SALESREP within categories of PRODUCT. The subsequent REPORT command requires that the input file be sorted on each variable named on a BREAK subcommand.

- The two COMPUTE commands create two new variables, CONTRIB and DIFF, based on variables from the combined files. The FORMATS command assigns four columns for DIFF.

- The REPORT command requests a case-listing report of the variables SALESREP, NUMBER, MONTH, DIFF, and CONTRIB for each category of product. For each category, two summary measures are computed. Figure C shows the report.

The exact appearance of the following printed displays will depend on the characters available on the printer used.

A ADD MAP display

```
RESULT          FSTQTRSO.SF    *

SALESREP        SALESREP       SALESREP
PRODUCT         PRODUCT        PRODUCT
NUMBER          NUMBER         NUMBER
MONTH           MONTH          MONTH
DAY             DAY            DAY
YEAR            YEAR           YEAR
```

B Table look-up MAP display

```
RESULT          *              AGGSALES.SF

SALESREP        SALESREP
PRODUCT         PRODUCT        PRODUCT
NUMBER          NUMBER
MONTH           MONTH
DAY             DAY
YEAR            YEAR
TOTAL                          TOTAL
AVSALES                        AVSALES
```

C REPORT display

```
                             Mid Year Sales Report
Product         Sales          Number of     Month    Deviation    % of Total
Name            Rep            Units Sold
Primo           Brennan               6      Feb          -3          23.08
                                      1      Jun          -8           3.85
                Walsh                19      Feb          10          73.08

    Total                            26                              100.00
    Average                        8.67

Mocha           Curtis                6      Feb          -9           5.08
                                      6      Mar          -9           5.08
                                     14      May          -1          11.86
                                     26      Jun          11          22.03
                Feyerherd            11      Feb          -4           9.32
                                      3      Jun         -12           2.54
                Sullivan             24      Mar           9          20.34
                Walsh                28      May          13          23.73

    Total                           118                              100.00
    Average                       14.75

Blend           Brennan               5      Feb          -6           6.58
                                     13      Jun           2          17.11
                Curtis               11      Feb           0          14.47
                                     10      May          -1          13.16
                Feyerherd             1      Jun         -10           1.32
                James                18      Jan           7          23.68
                Schultz              18      Jan           7          23.68

    Total                            76                              100.00
    Average                       10.86

Special         Brennan               6      Apr          -6           7.06
                James                10      Mar          -2          11.76
                                      9      Jun          -3          10.59
                Schultz               5      Jan          -7           5.88
                                     12      May           0          14.12
                Sullivan             29      Jun          17          34.12
                Walsh                14      Mar           2          16.47

    Total                            85                              100.00
    Average                       12.14
```

CROSSTABS   This example uses CROSSTABS to examine how respondents in different age groups answer a question on alcohol-drinking habits. The data are drawn from a 500-case sample from the 1980 General Social Survey. The variables are

- AGE—the respondent's age recoded to four categories.
- DRUNK—the response to the question, Did you ever drink too much?

The raw data are stored in an external file named AXTABS.DAT. The SPSS/PC+ commands in the command file named on the INCLUDE command are:

```
DATA LIST FILE='AXTABS.DAT'/
   DRUNK 1 AGE 2-3.
RECODE AGE (LOW THRU 29=1) (29 THRU 40=2) (40 THRU 58=3)
           (58 THRU HI=4) /DRUNK (1=1) (2=2) (ELSE=8).
MISSING VALUE DRUNK(8).
VARIABLE LABELS AGE 'Age in Four Categories'/
                DRUNK 'Ever Drink Too Much'.
VALUE LABELS AGE 1 'YoungestQuarter' 4 'Oldest  Quarter'/
             DRUNK 1 'Yes' 2 'No' 8 "Don't Drink/NA".
CROSSTABS TABLES=DRUNK BY AGE
  /CELLS=COUNT, ROW, COLUMN
  /STATISTICS=CHISQ, LAMBDA, BTAU, CTAU, GAMMA, D.
FINISH.
```

- The DATA LIST command identifies the data file, and gives the names and locations of the variables to be analyzed (see DATA LIST).
- The RECODE command redefines the variable AGE into four categories and recodes all missing values for the variable DRUNK to one missing value (see RECODE).
- The VARIABLE LABELS, VALUE LABELS, and MISSING VALUE commands complete the data definition for AGE and DRUNK (see VARIABLE LABELS, VALUE LABELS, and MISSING VALUE). The value labels for AGE are formatted to display appropriate labels for a column variable. Note that the label "Youngest-Quarter" has no blanks between the words and the label "Oldest Quarter" has two blanks separating the words.
- The CROSSTABS command sets up the table. It requests a table with DRUNK as the row variable and AGE as the column variable.
- The CELLS command requests row and column percentages.
- The STATISTICS subcommand requests chi-square, lambda, Kendall's tau-*b*, Kendall's tau-*c*, gamma, and Somers' *d*.

The results produced by CROSSTABS are on the following page. The exact appearance of a printed display will depend on the characters available on the printer used.

CROSSTABS display

```
DRUNK  Ever Drink Too Much  by  AGE  Age in Four Categories
                        AGE                           Page 1 of 1
              Count
              Row Pct | Youngest                Oldest
              Col Pct | Quarter                 Quarter    Row
                      |      1 |      2 |      3 |      4 | Total
DRUNK         --------+--------+--------+--------+--------+
                  1   |     62 |     33 |     36 |     16 |   147
Yes                   |   42.2 |   22.4 |   24.5 |   10.9 |  38.5
                      |   57.9 |   34.7 |   37.9 |   18.8 |
              --------+--------+--------+--------+--------+
                  2   |     45 |     62 |     59 |     69 |   235
No                    |   19.1 |   26.4 |   25.1 |   29.4 |  61.5
                      |   42.1 |   65.3 |   62.1 |   81.2 |
              --------+--------+--------+--------+--------+
               Column     107       95       95       85      382
               Total     28.0     24.9     24.9     22.3    100.0
```

Chi-Square	Value	DF	Significance
Pearson	31.57230	3	.00000
Likelihood Ratio	32.49043	3	.00000
Mantel-Haenszel test for linear association	26.54495	1	.00000

Minimum Expected Frequency - 32.709

Statistic	Value	ASE1	T-value	Approximate Significance
Lambda :				
symmetric	.09716	.04043	2.34152	
with DRUNK dependent	.11565	.06617	1.64929	
with AGE dependent	.08727	.03709	2.26282	
Goodman & Kruskal Tau :				
with DRUNK dependent	.08265	.02707		.00000 *2
with AGE dependent	.02808	.00970		.00000 *2
Kendall's Tau-b	.24165	.04394	5.46443	
Kendall's Tau-c	.28768	.05265	5.46443	
Gamma	.39632	.06875	5.46443	
Somers' D :				
symmetric	.23546	.04281	5.46443	
with DRUNK dependent	.19222	.03519	5.46443	
with AGE dependent	.30381	.05511	5.46443	

*2 Based on chi-square approximation
Number of Missing Observations: 118

DESCRIPTIVES   This example analyzes 1979 prices and earnings in 45 cities around the world, compiled by the Union Bank of Switzerland. The variables are:

- NTCPUR—the city's net purchasing-power level, calculated as the ratio of labor expended (measured in number of working hours) to the cost of more than 100 goods and services, weighted by consumer habits. NTCPUR is expressed as a percentage above or below that of Zurich, where Zurich equals 100%.
- FOOD—the average net cost of 39 different food and beverage items in the city, expressed as a percentage above or below that of Zurich, where Zurich equals 100%.
- RENT—the average gross monthly rent in the city, expressed as a percentage above or below that of Zurich, where Zurich equals 100%.
- APPL—the average cost of six different household appliances, expressed as a percentage above or below that of Zurich, where Zurich equals 100%.
- SERVICE—the average cost of 28 different goods and services in the city, expressed as a percentage above or below that of Zurich, where Zurich equals 100%.
- WCLOTHES—the cost of medium-priced women's clothes, expressed as a percentage above or below that of Zurich, where Zurich equals 100%.
- MCLOTHES—the cost of medium-priced men's clothes, expressed as a percentage above or below that of Zurich, where Zurich equals 100%.
- CLOTHES—the average cost of medium-priced women's and men's clothes, expressed as a percentage above or below that of Zurich, where Zurich equals 100%.

In this example, we obtain univariate summary statistics about purchasing power and the costs of various goods and services in cities. The data are in an external file named ADESC.DAT. The command file specified on the INCLUDE command contains the following SPSS/PC+ commands:

```
DATA LIST FILE='ADESC.DAT'/
    NTCPUR 1-3 FOOD 12-14 RENT 23-25 APPL 34-36
    SERVICE 45-47 WCLOTHES 56-58 MCLOTHES 67-69.
VARIABLE LABLES NTCPUR 'Net Purchasing Level'/
             FOOD 'Avg Food Prices'/
             RENT 'Normal Rent'/
             APPL 'Price of Appliances'/
             SERVICE 'Price for Services'/
             WCLOTHES "Medium-Priced Woman's Clothes"/
             MCLOTHES "Medium-Priced Men's Clothes"/.
COMPUTE CLOTHES=(WCLOTHES + MCLOTHES)/2.
VARIABLE LABELS CLOTHES 'Ave. Cost of W and M Clothes'.
DESCRIPTIVES VARIABLES=NTCPUR, FOOD, RENT TO SERVICE, WCLOTHES,
            MCLOTHES, CLOTHES
  /STATISTICS=1,5,9
  /OPTIONS=5.
FINISH.
```

- The DATA LIST command defines the names and locations of the variables to be analyzed (see DATA LIST).
- The VARIABLE LABELS command completes the definition of the variables (see VARIABLE LABELS).
- The COMPUTE command creates the variable CLOTHES by adding the values for WCLOTHES and MCLOTHES and dividing by 2 (see COMPUTE).
- The VARIABLE LABELS command assigns a label to the new variable CLOTHES (see VARIABLE LABELS).
- The DESCRIPTIVES command requests statistics for the variables named.
- The associated STATISTICS subcommand requests the mean, standard deviation, and range for each variable in the analysis.
- Option 5 specifies listwise deletion of missing values. A case missing on any variable specified on the DESCRIPTIVES command is excluded from the computation of statistics for all variables.
- Because the default width of 79 is used, DESCRIPTIVES displays the statistics and variable labels for each variable on one line using only 79 columns.

The display produced by DESCRIPTIVES is shown below. The exact appearance of the printed display will depend on the characters available on the printer used.

DESCRIPTIVES display

```
Number of Valid Observations (Listwise) =        44.00

Variable      Mean    Std Dev    Range   Label

NTCPUR        58.70     28.81    100.00   Net Purchasing Level
FOOD          71.00     18.61     90.00   Avg Food Prices
RENT         121.75     94.65    413.00   Normal Rent
APPL          78.70     22.23    111.00   Price of Appliances
SERVICE       73.68     18.80     71.00   Price for Services
WCLOTHES      81.20     30.36    153.00   Medium-Priced Woman's Clothes
MCLOTHES      87.86     25.91    125.00   Medium-Priced Men's Clothes
CLOTHES       84.53     26.75    139.00   Ave. Cost of W and M Clothes
```

EXAMINE This example uses EXAMINE to compare salaries and bonuses among male and female bank employees. The variables are:

- SALNOW—Current salary for each employee.
- JOBCAT—Job category for each employee. The value labels for variable JOBCAT are:

  1 Clerical Staff
  2 Office Trainee
  3 Security Officer
  4 College Trainee
  5 Exempt Employee
  6 MBA Trainee
  7 Technical Staff

- SEX—Employee sex. The value labels for variable SEX in the data are 0 Male, and 1 Female.

The SPSS/PC+ commands for the analysis are:

```
GET FILE='BANK.SYS'.
SET WIDTH=132 /LENGTH=60.
EXAMINE VARIABLES = SALNOW BY JOBCAT
  /STATISTICS=ALL /PLOT=BOXPLOT /ID=SEX.
```

- GET reads an existing SPSS/PC+ system file, which defines the variables for the session.
- SET increases the page width to 132 and the page length to 60 for larger and more readable plots. This command is optional. With it, long lines "wrap" on the screen, but the listing file, when printed on a suitable printer, shows the larger plots.
- EXAMINE specifies one dependent variable (SALNOW) and one independent variable (JOBCAT). The STATISTICS subcommand specifies all statistics available on EXAMINE. The PLOT subcommand specifies boxplots. EXAMINE will print the statistics and plots for all employee salaries, then separate statistics and boxplots for salaries within each job category. The ID subcommand specifies that extreme values and outliers in the salary ranges will be identified according to employee sex.
- Figure 1 shows the statistics for overall salaries. The extreme values indicate that the five bank employees with the highest salaries all are male, and the five employees with the lowest salaries all are female.
- Figure 2 shows the boxplot for overall salaries. Again, from the plot you can see that the extreme values and higher outliers all are males. The only two female outliers are very close to the whisker of the box. Figure 3 shows the footnote that prints on the page following the boxplot. The footnote explains that the multiple occurrences of the outlier at the salary range of about $24,000 (this outlier is indicated by **note 1** in the plot) represent 1 male and 1 female employee.
- Figure 4 shows the statistics for three of the job categories: clerical staff, office trainees, and security officers. Comparing mean, median, and 5% trim values for clerical staff and office trainees, you can see there is very little difference in the salaries offered by each job category. Among clerical staff, the highest salaries are mixed between males and females; the lowest salaries are all females. Among office trainees, all the highest salaries are paid to men and all the lowest salaries to women.
- Among security officers, all the highest and all the lowest salaries are paid to males, suggesting that all the security officers might be males. (This might prompt you to run a CROSSTABS of JOBCAT by SEX to see the distribution of males and females in each job category.) Notice the small interquartile range ($480) for security officers. Because the $47,700 range in salary values imposes a broad scale on the vertical axis, an interquartile range of only $480 causes the boxplot that prints for security officers (value 3 along the horizontal axis) to collapse into one spot. All you can see are the lower corners of the box.
- Looking at the number of cases in each job category (see Figure 5), you can see that there are a high number of clerical workers and office trainees, a small number of security officers, college trainees, and exempt employees, and very few MBA trainees and technical staff members.

Figure 1 Overall statistics for variable SALNOW

```
   SALNOW    Current Salary

Valid cases:        474.0   Missing cases:        .0   Percent missing:        .0


Mean       13767.83   Std Err    313.7244   Min       6300.000   Skewness   2.1246
Median     11550.00   Variance   46652514   Max       54000.00   S E Skew    .1122
5% Trim    12982.08   Std Dev    6830.265   Range     47700.00   Kurtosis   5.3778
                                            IQR       5265.000   S E Kurt    .2238

                                        Extreme Values
                                      _____  _____

   5    Highest    SEX                    5    Lowest    SEX

            54000    Males                        6300    Females
            44250    Males                        6360    Females
            41500    Males                        6480    Females
            41400    Males                        6540    Females
            40000    Males                        6600    Females
      SALNOW    Current Salary

Valid cases:        474.0   Missing cases:        .0   Percent missing:        .0
```

Figure 2 Boxplot for overall salaries

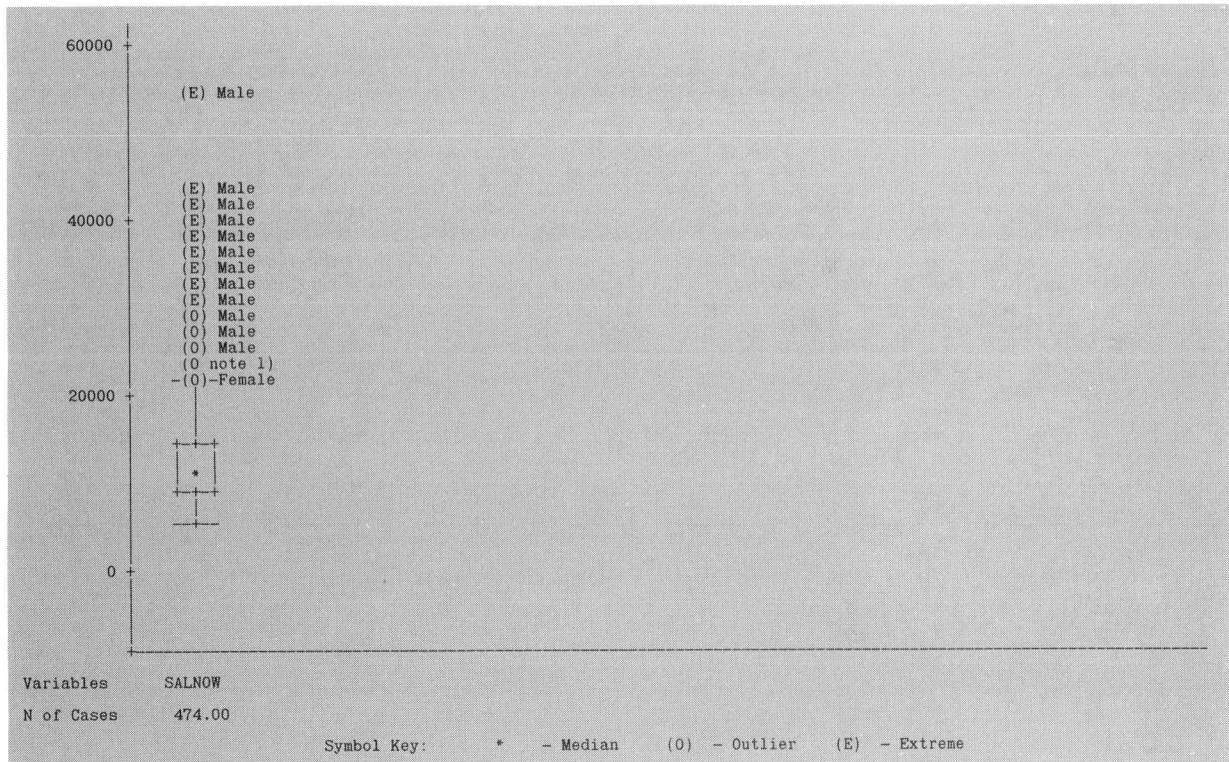

```
  60000 +

          (E)  Male


          (E)  Male
          (E)  Male
  40000 +  (E)  Male
          (E)  Male
          (E)  Male
          (E)  Male
          (E)  Male
          (0)  Male
          (0)  Male
          (0)  Male
          (0 note 1)
         -(0)-Female
  20000 +

            +-+-+
            |   |
            | * |
            +-+-+

            -+-+

      0 +



Variables     SALNOW
N of Cases    474.00

          Symbol Key:        *  — Median    (0) — Outlier    (E) — Extreme
```

Figure 3 Footnote on the first page following the boxplots

```
Boxplot footnotes denote the following:
   1)    Female, Male
```

Figure 4 Salary statistics broken down by job category

```
     SALNOW    Current Salary
By   JOBCAT    1        Clerical

Valid cases:        227.0   Missing cases:        .0   Percent missing:      .0


Mean      11134.82  Std Err   212.1638  Min     6300.000  Skewness   1.2922
Median    10500.00  Variance  10218056  Max    26750.00   S E Skew    .1615
5% Trim   10903.13  Std Dev   3196.569  Range  20450.00   Kurtosis   2.7254
                                        IQR     3660.000  S E Kurt    .3217

                        Extreme Values
                        -------  ------

   5    Highest   SEX                5    Lowest    SEX

          26750    Males                   6300     Females
          21600    Females                 6360     Females
          21060    Males                   6480     Females
          20400    Females                 6540     Females
          20220    Males                   6600     Females


     SALNOW    Current Salary
By   JOBCAT    2        Office Trainee

Valid cases:        136.0   Missing cases:        .0   Percent missing:      .0


Mean      11136.41  Std Err   234.3188  Min     7260.000  Skewness   3.5272
Median    10950.00  Variance  7467119   Max    32000.00   S E Skew    .2078
5% Trim   10913.92  Std Dev   2732.603  Range  24740.00   Kurtosis  24.2175
                                        IQR     3075.000  S E Kurt    .4127

                        Extreme Values
                        -------  ------

   5    Highest   SEX                5    Lowest    SEX

          32000    Males                   7260     Females
          17364    Males                   7680     Females
          16800    Males                   7860     Females
          15960    Males                   8040     Females
          15660    Males                   8160     Females


     SALNOW    Current Salary
By   JOBCAT    3        Security Officer

Valid cases:         27.0   Missing cases:        .0   Percent missing:      .0


Mean      12375.56  Std Err   162.7832  Min     9720.000  Skewness   -.3680
Median    12300.00  Variance  715456.4  Max    14100.00   S E Skew    .4479
5% Trim   12403.09  Std Dev   845.8466  Range   4380.000  Kurtosis   3.6515
                                        IQR      480.0000  S E Kurt    .8721

                        Extreme Values
                        -------  ------

   5    Highest   SEX                5    Lowest    SEX

          14100    Males                   9720     Males
          13800    Males                  11400     Males
          13500    Males                  11820     Males
          12780    Males                  12000     Males
          12480    Males                  12120     Males
```

Figure 5 Salary boxplots broken down by job category

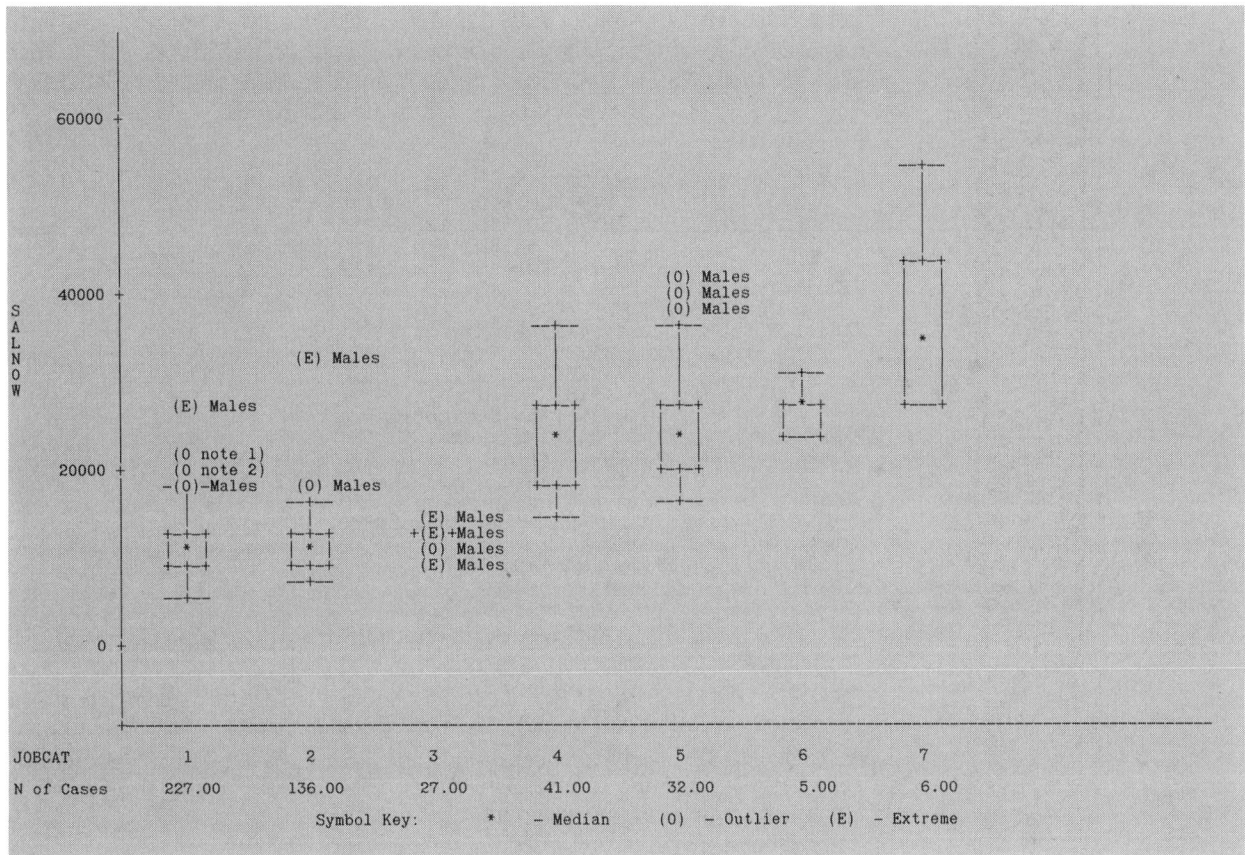

FREQUENCIES

The following example demonstrates the use of FREQUENCIES to do some preliminary checks on a newly defined file. The file is based on employment data from Hubbard Consultants Inc. Variables include: date employee was hired, employee's department, salary, job category, name, age, and sex, as well as salary increases from 1980 to 1982. The data are in an external file named AFREQ.DAT. The SPSS/PC+ commands in the command file named on the INCLUDE command are:

```
DATA LIST FILE='AFREQ.DAT'
                / MOHIRED YRHIRED 12-15 DEPT79 TO DEPT82 SEX 16-20
                / SALARY79 TO SALARY82 6-25
                  AGE 54-55 RAISE80 TO RAISE82 56-70
                / JOBCAT 6 EMPNAME 25-48 (A).
MISSING VALUE   SALARY79 TO SALARY82 AGE (0)
                JOBCAT (9).
VARIABLE LABELS  SALARY79 'Salary in 1979'
                SALARY80 'Salary in 1980'
                SALARY81 'Salary in 1981'
                SALARY82 'Salary in 1982'
                JOBCAT 'Job Categories'.
VALUE LABELS  SEX 1 'Male' 2 'Female'/
                JOBCAT 1 'Officials & Managers' 2 'Professionals'
                3 'Technicians' 4 'Office & Clerical' 5 'Craftsmen'
                6 'Service Workers'.
FREQUENCIES   VARIABLES=SALARY79 TO SALARY82 SEX AGE JOBCAT
  /FORMAT=LIMIT(10)
  /STATISTICS=DEFAULT MEDIAN.
FINISH.
```

- The DATA LIST command assigns variable names and gives column locations for the variables in the analysis (see DATA LIST).
- MISSING VALUE, VARIABLE LABELS, and VALUE LABELS complete the file definition (see MISSING VALUE, VARIABLE LABELS, and VALUE LABELS).
- FREQUENCIES displays frequency tables for variables having 10 or fewer categories and statistics for all the variables named. The default statistics are the mean, standard deviation, minimum, and maximum.
- The output uses the default format of 79 characters.

The FREQUENCIES display produced by this job is on the following page. The exact appearance of the printed display will depend on the characters available on the printer used.

FREQUENCIES display

```
SALARY79  Salary in 1979

Mean        12247.323      Median      10140.000      Std Dev      6665.182
Minimum      6337.000      Maximum     45500.000

Valid Cases       158      Missing Cases    117
- - - - - - - - - - - - - - - - - - - - - - - - - - - - - - - - - - - - - -

SALARY80  Salary in 1980

Mean        12123.725      Median      10400.000      Std Dev      6316.356
Minimum      5720.000      Maximum     48100.000

Valid Cases       273      Missing Cases      2
- - - - - - - - - - - - - - - - - - - - - - - - - - - - - - - - - - - - - -

SALARY81  Salary in 1981

Mean        15096.212      Median      12359.500      Std Dev      8074.387
Minimum      7605.000      Maximum     52000.000

Valid Cases       160      Missing Cases    115
- - - - - - - - - - - - - - - - - - - - - - - - - - - - - - - - - - - - - -

SALARY82  Salary in 1982

Mean        17161.552      Median      15132.000      Std Dev      8695.734
Minimum      5830.000      Maximum     50700.000

Valid Cases       145      Missing Cases    130
- - - - - - - - - - - - - - - - - - - - - - - - - - - - - - - - - - - - - -

SEX

                                                    Valid      Cum
     Value Label          Value  Frequency  Percent  Percent  Percent

Male                        1         83     30.2     30.2     30.2
Female                      2        192     69.8     69.8    100.0
                                    -----    -----    -----
                         TOTAL      275    100.0    100.0

Mean         1.698      Median       2.000      Std Dev       .460
Minimum      1.000      Maximum      2.000

Valid Cases       275      Missing Cases      0
- - - - - - - - - - - - - - - - - - - - - - - - - - - - - - - - - - - - - -

AGE

Mean        37.158      Median      34.000      Std Dev      11.335
Minimum     20.000      Maximum     69.000

Valid Cases       272      Missing Cases      3
- - - - - - - - - - - - - - - - - - - - - - - - - - - - - - - - - - - - - -

JOBCAT    Job Categories

                                                    Valid      Cum
     Value Label          Value  Frequency  Percent  Percent  Percent

Officials & Managers        1         48     17.5     17.5     17.5
Professionals               2         62     22.5     22.5     40.0
Technicians                 3         98     35.6     35.6     75.6
Office & Clerical           4         67     24.4     24.4    100.0
                                    -----    -----    -----
                         TOTAL      275    100.0    100.0

Mean         2.669      Median       3.000      Std Dev      1.030
Minimum      1.000      Maximum      4.000

Valid Cases       275      Missing Cases      0
```

LIST This example demonstrates the use of LIST to display values of selected cases in a newly defined file. The file is based on employment data from Hubbard Consultants Inc. Variables include: date employee was hired, employee's department, salary, job category, name, age, and sex, as well as salary increases from 1979 to 1982. The data are in an external file named ALIST.DAT. The SPSS/PC+ commands in the command file named on the INCLUDE command are:

```
SET WIDTH=WIDE.
DATA LIST FILE='ALIST.DAT'
   / EMPLOYID 1-5 MOHIRED YRHIRED 12-15 DEPT79 TO DEPT82 SEX 16-20
   / SALARY79 TO SALARY82 6-25 HOURLY81 HOURLY82 40-53(2) PROMO81 72
     AGE 54-55 RAISE82 66-70
   / JOBCAT 6 NAME 25-48 (A).
LIST VARIABLES=MOHIRED YRHIRED DEPT82 SALARY79 TO SALARY82 NAME/
   CASES FROM 50 TO 100 BY 5/ FORMAT=SINGLE,NUMBERED.
FINISH.
```

- The SET command requests a width of 132 (WIDE) so the column titles will all be horizontal (see SET command).
- The DATA LIST command assigns variable names and gives column locations for the variables in the analysis. The variable NAME is defined as a string variable (see DATA LIST).
- LIST displays values for the variables MOHIRED, YRHIRED, DEPT82, SALARY79 to SALARY 82, and NAME. Beginning with the 50th case, every 5th case will be listed. The display is forced to have only one line per case, and the sequence number for each case will be displayed.

The LIST display produced by this job is shown below. The exact appearance of the printed display will depend on the characters available on the printer used.

LIST display

```
Cas MOHIRED YRHIRED DEPT82 SALARY79 SALARY80 SALARY81 SALARY82 NAME

 50       1      79      0    14300    14300    15730        0 EVA ELDER
 55       6      79      0        0    15600        0        0 EDWARD GREEN
 60      12      79      0        0     8840     9503        0 LOVEY E. HUDSON
 65       5      80      0        0    13520        0        0 PATRICIA SMITH
 70       8      79      0        0     8255        0        0 HELEN D. SMITH
 75      10      70      4    14300    18850    21450    26182 MONICA C. RIVERS
 80       1      79      0        0     7442        0        0 THOMAS P. JOHNSON
 85       4      80      3        0    18200    18395    19682 ANN JOHNSON
 90      10      79      0        0     5720        0        0 CHRISTINA P. NORRIS
 95       5      79      0     7670     9490        0        0 M. ELLIOT KRAFT
100       2      70      3    11830    12545    13799    18083 FANNIE SMITH


Number of cases read =      100   Number of cases listed =        11
```

MEANS   This example uses MEANS to analyze personnel data from Hubbard Consultants Inc. 1981 salaries are analyzed by sex, within departments and grades. The data are in an external file named AMEANS.DAT. The SPSS/PC+ commands in the command file named on the INCLUDE command are:

```
DATA LIST FILE='AMEANS.DAT'
   /SALARY81 1-5 DEPT81 6 GRADE81 7-8 SEX 9.
VARIABLE LABELS SALARY81 'Yearly Salary in 1981'/
                DEPT81 'Department Code in 1981'/
                SEX "Employee's Sex".
VALUE LABELS DEPT81 1 'Admin' 2 'Project Directors'
             3 'Chicago Operations' 4 'St Louis Operations'/
             SEX 1 'Male' 2 'Female'.
COMPUTE GRADE81S=GRADE81.
RECODE GRADE81S (1 THRU 4=1) (5 THRU 7=2) (8 THRU 15=3) (ELSE=0).
VALUE LABELS GRADE81S 1 'Grades 1-4' 2 'Grades 5-7' 3 'Grades 8-15'.
MISSING VALUE GRADE81S(0).
MEANS TABLES=SALARY81 BY DEPT81 BY GRADE81S BY SEX
  /OPTIONS=6,9,10,12.
FINISH.
```

- The DATA LIST command identifies the column locations of the four variables used in the analysis (see DATA LIST).
- The VARIABLE LABELS and VALUE LABELS commands complete the file definition (see VARIABLE LABELS and VALUE LABELS).
- The COMPUTE command creates the variable GRADE81S as a copy of GRADE81 (see COMPUTE).
- The RECODE command recodes the variable GRADE81S into three values which contain the 15 valid values of GRADE81. Other values of GRADE81S are recoded into the value 0 (see RECODE).
- The VALUE LABELS and MISSING VALUE commands provide dictionary definitions for the new variable GRADE81S (see VALUE LABELS and MISSING VALUE).
- The MEANS command specifies a three-way breakdown of salaries with SALARY81 as the dependent variable.
- Since no missing-value option is specified, MEANS deletes cases with missing values on a tablewide basis.
- The OPTIONS subcommand requests that group sums and variances be displayed. OPTIONS are used to suppress display of the independent variable names and values so that the output will fit within the default width of 79 columns.

The display produced by MEANS is on the following page. The exact appearance of the printed display depends on the characters available on the printer used.

D

Examples

MEANS display

```
Summaries of    SALARY81   Yearly Salary in 1981
By levels of    DEPT81     Department Code in 1981
                GRADE81S
                SEX        Employee's Sex


Label                       Sum      Mean    Std Dev   Variance   Cases

For Entire Population  2415394.00 15096.2125  8074.3872 65195729.2   160

Admin                   590438.000 15537.8421  9810.5522 96246934.7    38
  Grades 1-4            120922.000 10076.8333  1685.2658 2840120.70    12
    Male                111172.000 10106.5455  1764.2221 3112479.67    11
    Female                9750.0000  9750.0000     0.0       0.0        1

  Grades 5-7            179291.000 11952.7333  2019.7453 4079371.07    15
    Male                 13910.0000 13910.0000     0.0       0.0        1
    Female              165381.000 11812.9286  2019.2662 4077435.92    14

  Grades 8-15           290225.000 26384.0909 12759.5664  162806534    11
    Male                170625.000 34125.0000 15498.1047  240191250     5
    Female              119600.000 19933.3333  4858.3605 23603666.7     6

Project Directors       428804.000 15314.4286  8146.9522 66372830.5    28
  Grades 1-4            181449.000 11340.5625  1999.6042 3998416.80    16
    Male                105839.000 10583.9000  1143.2161 1306942.99    10
    Female               75610.0000 12601.6667  2566.9469 6589216.27     6

  Grades 5-7             38480.0000 12826.6667  2015.3494 4061633.33     3
    Female               38480.0000 12826.6667  2015.3494 4061633.33     3

  Grades 8-15           208875.000 23208.3333 10558.8272  111488831     9
    Male                143065.000 28613.0000 11587.9159  134279795     5
    Female               65810.0000 16452.5000  2953.7674 8724741.67     4

Chicago Operations      940294.000 14925.3016  7705.3167 59371905.9    63
  Grades 1-4            168677.000  9922.1765  1536.2349 2360017.78    17
    Male                 20917.0000 10458.5000   836.5073 699744.500     2
    Female              147760.000  9850.6667  1612.6409 2600610.67    15

  Grades 5-7            197356.000 12334.7500  2190.5735 4798612.47    16
    Male                 40924.0000 13641.3333  3333.0827 11109440.3     3
    Female              156432.000 12033.2308  1903.0008 3621412.19    13

  Grades 8-15           574261.000 19142.0333  9294.0232 86378866.9    30
    Male                142090.000 28418.0000 15680.5949  245881058     5
    Female              432171.000 17286.8400  6471.7384 41883398.6    25

St Louis Operations     455858.000 14705.0968  6624.5319 43884422.6    31
  Grades 1-4             66118.0000  9445.4286   680.5620 463164.619     7
    Male                 18395.0000  9197.5000   873.2769 762612.500     2
    Female               47723.0000  9544.6000   679.0183 461065.800     5

  Grades 5-7            160420.000 12340.0000  1925.6254 3708033.33    13
    Male                 35100.0000 11700.0000  1357.2398 1842100.00     3
    Female              125320.000 12532.0000  2087.3897 4357195.56    10

  Grades 8-15           229320.000 20847.2727  7667.4707 58790106.8    11
    Male                 21775.0000 21775.0000     0.0       0.0        1
    Female              207545.000 20754.5000  8075.7134 65217146.9    10

  Total Cases =     275
Missing Cases =     115 OR  41.8 PCT.
```

PLOT

Example 1: An Overlay Plot

Overlay plots are useful when several variables represent the same type of measurement, or the same variable is measured at different times. This example overlays two time series: marriage and divorce rates, 1900–1981. The data are drawn from the 1983 *Information Please Almanac.* Rates are specified for five-year periods for 1900–1940 and annually after 1943. The variables are

- MARRATE—Marriage rate per 1,000 population, excluding armed forces overseas.
- DIVRATE—Divorce rate (including annulments) per 1,000 population. (The rates for 1941-1946 include armed forces overseas.)

The data are in an external file named APLOT1.DAT. The SPSS/PC+ commands in the command file named on the INCLUDE command are:

```
DATA LIST FILE='APLOT1.DAT'
        / YEAR 1-4 MARRATE 6-9 (1) DIVRATE 11-13 (1).
PLOT SYMBOLS='MD'/
     VSIZE=30 /HSIZE=70/
     FORMAT=OVERLAY/
     TITLE 'MARRIAGE AND DIVORCE RATES  1900-1981'/
     VERTICAL='RATES PER 1000 POPULATION'/
     HORIZONTAL='YEAR' REFERENCE (1918,1945) MIN (1900) MAX (1983)/
     PLOT=MARRATE DIVRATE WITH YEAR.
FINISH.
```

- The DATA LIST command defines the variables to be used in the overlay plot.
- The PLOT subcommand, placed last within the PLOT command, requests two bivariate plots: marriage rate by year and divorce rate by year.
- The SYMBOLS subcommand specifies the symbol M for the plot of marriage rate with year. The divorce rate by year plot is represented by the symbol D.
- The VSIZE and HSIZE subcommands establish the plot frame size of 30 lines high and 70 columns wide.
- The FORMAT subcommand requests an overlay plot of the variables specified on the PLOT subcommand.
- The VERTICAL subcommand supplies a label for the vertical axis.
- The HORIZONTAL subcommand supplies a label for the horizontal axis. The REFERENCE keyword requests reference lines to be drawn at the dates on which World War I and World War II ended. These lines point out the time period following the wars in which a sharp increase in marriage and divorce rates occurred. The MIN and MAX keywords specify the horizontal scale. SPSS/PC+ automatically divides the scale into equal-width intervals.

The PLOT display produced by this job follows. The exact appearance of the printed display will depend on the characters available on the printer used.

D

Examples

Overlay plot

```
                  MARRIAGE AND DIVORCE RATES   1900-1981

   M:MARRATE WITH YEAR   D:DIVRATE WITH YEAR   $:Multiple occurrence
            48 cases                48 cases
                          MARRIAGE AND DIVORCE RATES   1900-1981
           +---+----+----+----+----+----+----+----+----+----+----+----+----+
     16.5+                                          M                         +
   R
   A
   T
   E  13.75+                                        M                         +
   S                                                M
   P                                    M         M M
   E                                              M
   R   11+                    M   M         M        M  M      MM             +
                         M                     M M   M    MMMM M  MMMM
   1                   M                    M     M   MM            MMM
   0                                              MMM
   0    8.25+                                    M  MMM                       +
   0                                             MMM
   P
   O
   P                                                                    D D
   U    5.5+                                                          DDDD D  +
   L                                                             D  D
   A                                                   D          D
   T                                                              DD
   I                                          D  D            DDD
   O    2.75+                               DD  DDDDDD          DDD          +
   N                                          D      DDDDDDDDDD
                            D  D  D  D    D
                    D  D                      .
         0+   D  D                                                            +
           +---+----+----+----+----+----+----+----+----+----+----+----+----+
              1902      1914      1926      1938      1950      1962      1974
                  1908      1920      1932      1944      1956      1968      1980

                                      YEAR
```

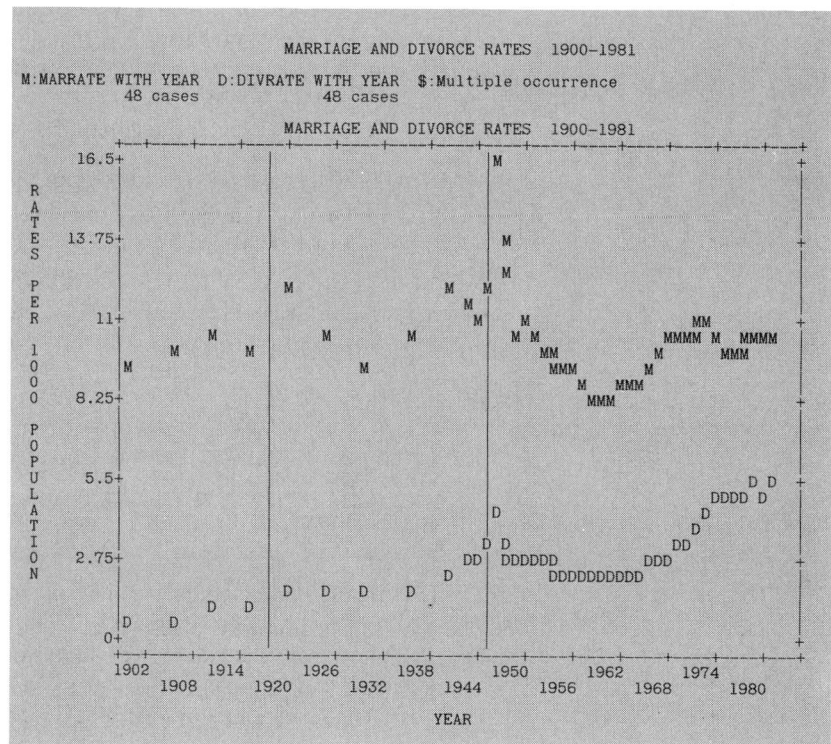

Example 2: A Regression Plot

Regression plots display a set of basic regression statistics below your plot and mark the regression-line intercepts on each axis. The statistics include the correlation coefficient, slope and intercept values, standard errors, and significance level.

This example examines the relationship of beginning salary to current salary as a first step in an analysis of salary differentials between race and sex groups. The data are drawn from bank employees hired between 1969 and 1971. The variables are

- SALBEG—annual starting salary of bank employees.
- SALNOW—current annual salary.

The data are in an external file named APLOT2.DAT. The SPSS/PC+ commands in the command file named on the INCLUDE command are

```
DATA LIST FILE='APLOT2.DAT'
        / SALNOW 1-5 SALBEG 6-10.
PLOT    HSIZE=35/ VSIZE=40/
        CUTPOINTS=EVERY (4)/
        SYMBOLS='+X*'/
        TITLE='SALARY REGRESSION'/
        VERTICAL='CURRENT ANNUAL SALARY'/
        HORIZONTAL= 'ANNUAL STARTING SALARY'/
        FORMAT=REGRESSION/
        PLOT=SALNOW WITH SALBEG.
FINISH.
```

- The DATA LIST command defines the variables to be used in the regression plot.
- The PLOT subcommand, the last specification on the PLOT command, names the variables to be plotted.
- The HSIZE subcommand requests a horizontal size of 35 display positions. VSIZE requests a vertical size of 40.

- The CUTPOINTS subcommand requests that each successive symbol represent accumulated frequency intervals of 4.
- The SYMBOLS subcommand defines the symbols to be plotted in accordance with the frequency cutpoints specified on the CUTPOINTS command. Thus, the symbol + represents positions with 4 or fewer cases; X, positions with 5 to 8 cases; and *, positions with 9 or more cases.
- The TITLE subcommand supplies a plot title. Note that the title is less than 35 display positions because of the HSIZE specification.
- The VERTICAL subcommand supplies an extended label for the vertical axis. The HORIZONTAL subcommand supplies an extended label for the horizontal axis.
- The FORMAT subcommand requests a regression plot. The following display shows the regression statistics generated by the FORMAT subcommand. The regression intercepts for the regression of SALNOW on SALBEG are displayed on the top and bottom horizontal axis lines.

The display produced by the above commands is shown below. The exact appearance of the printed display will depend on the characters available on the printer used.

Regression plot

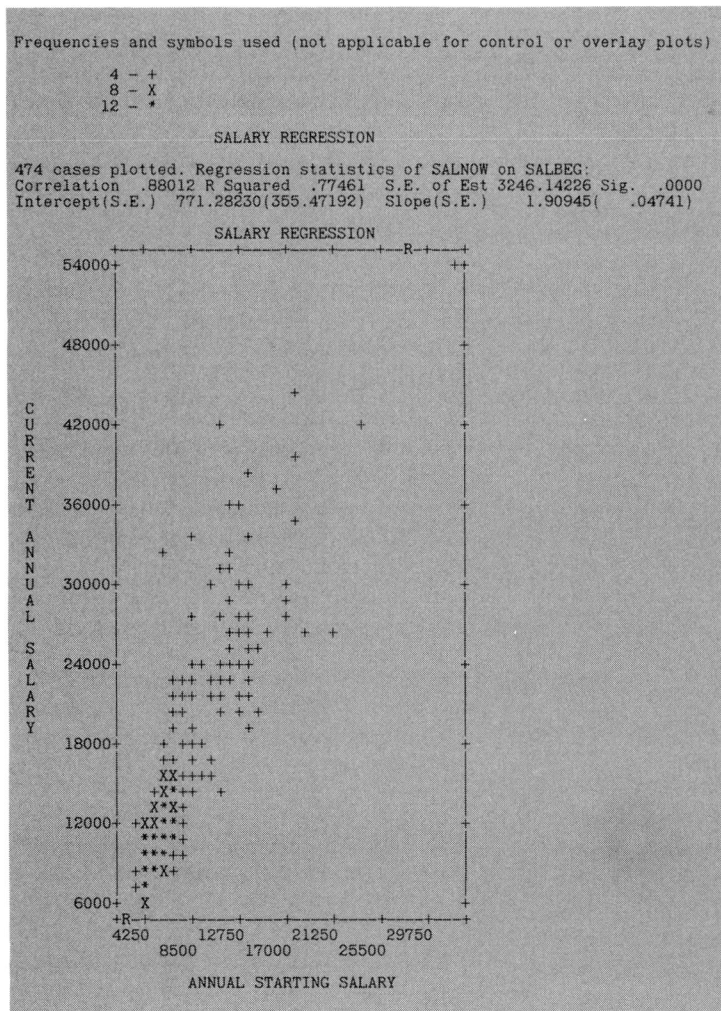

```
Frequencies and symbols used (not applicable for control or overlay plots)
          4 - +
          8 - X
         12 - *
                        SALARY REGRESSION
474 cases plotted. Regression statistics of SALNOW on SALBEG:
Correlation  .88012 R Squared  .77461  S.E. of Est 3246.14226 Sig.   .0000
Intercept(S.E.)  771.28230(355.47192)  Slope(S.E.)   1.90945(   .04741)
                        SALARY REGRESSION
              +---+----+----+----+----+----+----+---R-+----+
       54000+                                        ++
   C
   U   48000+                                         +
   R
   R                           +
   E   42000+          +                  +           +
   N                                +
   T                         +
                              +
       36000+            ++                            +
   A                  +       +
   N           +        +
   N                   ++
   U   30000+      +  ++    +                          +
   A                 +    +
   L             +  + ++   +
                  +++  +   +  +
   S               + ++
   A   24000+     ++ ++++                              +
   L            +++ +++ +
   A            +++ ++ ++
   R            ++   + + +
   Y            + +     +
       18000+    + +++                                 +
                ++ + +
                XX++++
                +X*++  +
                X*X+
       12000+ +XX**+                                   +
              ****+
              ***++
              +**X+
              +*
        6000+  X                                       +
              +R-+----+----+----+----+----+----+----+
              4250   12750   21250   29750
                 8500    17000   25500
                        ANNUAL STARTING SALARY
```

REPORT

Example 1: A Report with Summaries

This example produces a report that summarizes information from a retail company's personnel file. It reports summary statistics for employees in each division of the company within each store. The variables are:

- AGE—age of employee in years.
- TENURE—length of employment at the company in months.
- JTENURE—length of employment in job grade in months.
- SALARY—annual salary in dollars.

The data are in an external file named AREPORT.DAT. The SPSS/PC+ commands are:

```
DATA LIST FILE='AREPORT.DAT' /
    AGE 4-8 TENURE 13-16 JTENURE 21-24 SALARY 25-29
    STORE 30 DIVISION 31.
VARIABLE LABELS TENURE 'Tenure in Company' JTENURE 'Tenure in Grade'
                DIVISION 'Product Division' SALARY 'Annual Salary'
                STORE 'BRANCH STORE' age 'Age'.
VALUE LABELS DIVISION  1  'CARPETING'  2  'APPLIANCES'  3
'FURNITURE'
                       4  'HARDWARE' / STORE 1 'SUBURBAN' 2
'DOWNTOWN'.
FORMATS AGE (F2.0) TENURE JTENURE (F3.1).
SORT CASES  BY STORE DIVISION.
REPORT FORMAT=AUTOMATIC MARGINS(1,72) LENGTH(1,24) BRKSPACE(-1)/
       VARIABLES=AGE TENURE JTENURE SPACE(DUMMY)' '(4) SALARY /
       TITLE='Chicago Home Furnishing'/
       FOOTNOTE=LEFT 'Tenure measured in months'/
       BREAK=STORE /
           SUMMARY=MEAN 'AVERAGE:' (2) /
           SUMMARY=VALIDN (AGE) ' Count:' (2) /
       BREAK=DIVISION (SKIP(0))/
       SUMMARY=MEAN.
FINISH.
```

- The DATA LIST command assigns variable names and gives column locations for the variables, which are in the file AREPORT.DAT (see DATA LIST).
- The VARIABLE LABELS command defines labels for the variables; these appear on the report as column headings.
- The VALUE LABELS command defines labels for the break variables' values. These labels will be displayed in upper case since they are entered in upper case on this command (see VALUE LABELS).
- The FORMATS command overrides the default print formats (see FORMATS).
- The SORT CASES command sorts the file into the major and minor breaks required for REPORT (see SORT CASES).
- The FORMAT subcommand implements the AUTOMATIC settings, sets the left margin at column 1 and right margin at column 72, sets the top of the report page on the first line and defines the last line of the page as line 24, and places the break-group label on the first line of summary statistics.
- The VARIABLES subcommand defines five columns in the body of the report. AGE, TENURE, JTENURE, and SALARY are SPSS/PC+ variables. SPACE defines a 4-column-wide dummy column, for spacing purposes, with a blank column heading.
- The TITLE subcommand defines a one-line centered title.
- The FOOTNOTE subcommand defines a left-justified one-line footnote.
- The first BREAK subcommand defines the major break in this two-break report. Variable STORE breaks the file into two categories: the downtown store and the suburban store.
- The first two SUMMARY subcommands display two lines of summary statistics for each store. The first SUMMARY subcommand computes means for AGE, TENURE, JTENURE, and SALARY. The second SUMMARY subcommand computes the number of employees in each store. Titles are specified for each summary line.
- The second BREAK subcommand breaks the file into divisions within each store. The SKIP specification suppresses blank lines between the summary for each division.
- The last SUMMARY subcommand computes means for the report variables for each division.

Summary report

```
                            Chicago Home Furnishing

                                        Tenure       Tenure
                                          in           in
  BRANCH        Product                 Company      Grade              Annual
  STORE         Division       Age                                     Salary
  ------        --------       ---      -------      ------            ------

  SUBURBAN      CARPETING       40        2.4          2.4              20869
                APPLIANCES      35        2.3          2.3              16105
                FURNITURE       38        2.4          2.4              18821
                HARDWARE        35        2.3          2.4              15234

                AVERAGE:        36        2.3          2.4              17011
                Count:          97

  DOWNTOWN      CARPETING       37        2.3          2.4              14207
                APPLIANCES      37        2.3          2.4              14130
                FURNITURE       38        2.3          2.4              14403
                HARDWARE        37        2.3          2.4              14469
                AVERAGE:        37        2.3          2.4              14307
                Count:         153

  Tenure measured in months
```

Example 2: A Report Using LIST

This example produces a report using data from the October 1980 issue of *Runner's World* magazine. It lists the top-rated shoes in the survey, organized by manufacturer. Measures used by the raters to determine an overall evaluation for each shoe are reported. The data are in an external file named AREPT.DAT. The SPSS/PC+ commands are:

```
SET WIDTH=132/LENGTH=45.
DATA LIST FILE='AREPT.DAT' FIXED /
               TYPE 1 MAKER 2-3 QUALITY 5-9
               REARIMP FOREIMP FLEX SOLEWEAR 10-29
               REARCONT SOLETRAC 31-40 WEIGHT 42-46 LASTYEAR 48
               PREFER 50-53 STARS 55 NAME 57-72 (A).
VARIABLE LABELS NAME 'SHOE' STARS 'RATING'
               REARIMP 'REARFOOT IMPACT'
               FOREIMP 'FOREFOOT IMPACT'
               SOLEWEAR 'SOLE WEAR' REARCONT 'REARFOOT CONTROL'
               SOLETRAC 'SOLE TRACTION' LASTYEAR '1979 STARS'
               PREFER 'READER PREFERENCE'.
VALUE LABELS MAKER 1 'ADIDAS'  2 'AUTRY'  3 'BROOKFIELD'  4 'BROOKS'
               5 'CONVERSE'  6 'REEBOK'  7 'NEW BALANCE'  8 'PUMA'
               9 'OSAG'
               10 'PONY'  11 'ETONIC'  12 'NIKE'  13 'SAUCONY'
               14 'WILSON-BATA'  15 'VOL SHOE CORP'
               16 'SPECS INTERNATIONAL'  17 'POWER SPORT'
               18 'THOM MCAN JOX'  19 'REGAL SHOES'  20 'SHOE CORP'
               21 'ASICS'  22 'INTL FOOTWEAR'  23 'EB SPORT INTL'
               24 'VAN DOREN'/
               TYPE 1 'MALE'  2 'FEMALE'/
               STARS 6 '******'  5 '*****'/.
FORMATS   QUALITY (F5.3)/REARIMP FOREIMP SOLEWEAR (F4.1)/
               FLEX SOLETRAC (F4.2)/REARCONT WEIGHT (F5.1)/
               PREFER (F4.3).
SELECT IF (STARS GE 5).
SORT CASES MAKER STARS(D).
REPORT  FORMAT=AUTOMATIC LIST MISSING ' '  /
               VARIABLES=TYPE(LABEL) NAME STARS(LABEL)
                       SEP1(DUMMY)(1)' '
                       REARIMP FOREIMP
                       FLEX 'FLEXI-' 'BILITY'
                       SOLEWEAR REARCONT SOLETRAC WEIGHT
                       LASTYEAR PREFER /
               TITLE='RATINGS OF TRAINING SHOES'
                       "RUNNER'S WORLD MAGAZINE - OCTOBER, 1980"/
               FOOTNOTE=LEFT '****** HIGHLY RECOMMENDED'
                           '***** RECOMMENDED'/
                       RIGHT ' ' 'PAGE )PAGE'/
               BREAK=MAKER 'MANUFACTURER'.
FINISH.
```

- Because there are many variables, the SET command sets the WIDTH to 132 columns, the maximum, and the LENGTH to 45 lines (see SET).
- The DATA LIST command assigns variable names and gives column locations for the variables in the analysis (see DATA LIST).
- The VARIABLE LABELS command defines labels for the variables; these appear on the report as column headings.
- The VALUE LABELS command supplies value labels for the manufacturer, type of shoe, and rating. These labels are used in the report (see VALUE LABELS).
- The FORMATS command overrides the default print formats (see FORMATS).
- The SELECT IF command selects shoes with the top two ratings (see SELECT IF).
- The SORT CASES command sorts cases in descending order of ranking for each manufacturer. They are sorted by manufacturer so that the report can group them by manufacturer. They are sorted by descending order of ranking so that the top-rated shoes for the manufacturer are listed first (see SORT).
- In REPORT, the FORMAT subcommand implements the AUTOMATIC settings and specifies a case listing. In a listing report, AUTOMATIC places the first case for each break on the same line as the break value, so BRKSPACE(−1) is not needed. The MISSING keyword displays a blank in place of the period for variables with missing values.
- The VARIABLES subcommand names all the variables to be listed as well as a dummy column (SEP1) to separate the measurements from the rating. Value labels are displayed in place of values for variables TYPE and STAR. The column heading specified for FLEXIBILITY splits the variable name so that the column is narrower.
- The TITLE subcommand displays a two-line centered title.
- The FOOTNOTE subcommand displays a two-line left-justified footnote, and a two-line right-justified footnote in which the first line is blank while the second line uses the special keyword)PAGE to display page numbers.
- The BREAK subcommand groups the shoes by manufacturer.

The report produced by these commands is shown below and on the following page.

Report on running-shoe data—page 1

RATINGS OF TRAINING SHOES
RUNNER'S WORLD MAGAZINE – OCTOBER, 1980

MANUFACTURER	TYPE	SHOE	RATING	REARFOOT IMPACT	FOREFOOT IMPACT	FLEXI-BILITY	SOLE WEAR	REARFOOT CONTROL	SOLE TRACTION	WEIGHT	1979 STARS	READER PREFERENCE
SAUCONY	MALE	TC84	******	9.3	15.1	1.56	6.5	5.2	.85	278.0	0	.028
	MALE	HORNET 84	******	9.9	13.1	2.65	7.6	3.0	.68	265.0	4	.097
	FEMALE	MS TRAINER	******	10.2	13.3	1.58	6.4	22.4	.86	237.7	5	.053
	MALE	JAZZ	*****	8.9	12.7	2.04	7.6	-7.0	.64	270.8	0	
	MALE	TRAINER 80	*****	10.5	14.5	2.18	4.1	11.5	.82	307.6	5	.232
	FEMALE	JAZZ	*****	9.0	12.2	1.86	6.1	-7.5	.63	223.0	0	.013
	FEMALE	TC 84	*****	9.3	14.6	1.46	7.5	1.3	.77	231.1	0	
	FEMALE	MS HORNET	*****	9.8	13.2	2.59	6.4	6.5	.67	224.0	4	.046
NIKE	MALE	DAYBREAK	******	10.8	15.4	2.17	3.7	7.8	.54	304.2	5	.6
	MALE	YANKEE	*****	10.9	13.7	1.93	2.0	9.8	.66	276.6	0	
	FEMALE	LIBERATOR	*****	10.6	14.7	2.20	5.8	6.5	.52	254.2	5	.503
ETONIC	MALE	ECLIPSE TRAINER	******	10.0	12.9	1.65	10.0	-2.6	.51	237.4	0	
	FEMALE	ECLIPSE TRAINER	******	9.6	12.8	1.78	10.0	1.4	.57	204.1	0	
	MALE	STABILIZER	*****	10.3	15.5	2.25	1.2	-.6	.53	283.1	4	.232
	MALE	STREETFIGHTER	*****	10.8	15.5	2.28	1.4	-.4	.61	266.1	4	.222
	FEMALE	STREETFIGHTER	*****	10.7	15.5	1.66	.7	-7.7	.70	214.1	4	.3
	FEMALE	STABILIZER	*****	10.8	14.4	2.09	2.6	-6.9	.67	235.3	4	.298
PONY	MALE	TARGA FLEX	******	9.6	14.3	1.32	2.5	-22.7	.86	253.0	3	
	MALE	SHADOW	*****	9.9	13.8	1.53	2.5	-17.9	.77	270.2	0	
	FEMALE	LADY SHADOW	*****	10.6	17.4	.91	3.0	-7.1	.90	211.8	0	
OSAG	MALE	FAST RIDER	*****	10.5	14.0	2.48	4.9	1.9	.66	296.7	5	.025
	FEMALE	KT-26	*****	10.7	17.3	1.66	5.5	8.1	.60	223.1	2	
NEW BALANCE	MALE	420	*****	9.8	14.8	2.09	1.8	-17.7	.46	267.9	0	.516
	MALE	620	*****	12.0	14.6	2.73	1.1	-3.5	.41	242.0	5	.475
	FEMALE	420	*****	9.9	13.9	1.94	1.6	-.7	.46	219.3	0	.411
REEBOK	MALE	AZTEC	******	10.9	12.6	2.07	2.5	3.7	.65	260.8	5	.065
	MALE	SHADOW I	*****	10.7	13.1	1.79	1.9	-8.7	.63	253.0	0	
	FEMALE	SHADOW III	*****	10.2	12.9	1.63	2.4	-24.6	.66	212.8	0	
	FEMALE	AZTEC PRINCESS	*****	10.2	12.8	2.18	5.9	-20.3	.70	221.3	5	.033

****** HIGHLY RECOMMENDED
***** RECOMMENDED

PAGE   1

Report on running-shoe data—page 2

RATINGS OF TRAINING SHOES
RUNNER'S WORLD MAGAZINE – OCTOBER, 1980

MANUFACTURER	TYPE	SHOE	RATING	REARFOOT IMPACT	FOREFOOT IMPACT	FLEXI-BILITY	SOLE WEAR	REARFOOT CONTROL	SOLE TRACTION	WEIGHT	1979 STARS	READER PREFERENCE
CONVERSE	MALE	ARIZONA 84	*****	10.1	13.6	1.90	6.6	-5.1	.55	302.9	4	.006
	FEMALE	WORLD CLASS 84	*****	9.4	14.0	2.19	4.3	-.3	.65	234.7	3	.020
BROOKS	MALE	VANTAGE	******	8.3	11.0	1.33	10.0	-13.6	.55	232.4	5	.531
	MALE	VANTAGE SUPREME	******	8.5	10.9	1.31	10.0	-16.5	.58	239.1	5	
	MALE	HUGGER GT	******	8.5	11.2	1.32	9.4	-11.7	.60	234.5	5	.488
	MALE	NIGHTHAWK	******	8.7	13.5	1.57	3.1	-8.6	.45	216.7	0	
	MALE	SUPER VILLANOVA	******	10.0	14.1	1.07	10.0	14.4	.61	238.7	5	.155
	FEMALE	VANTAGE	******	8.1	11.0	1.27	10.0	-13.1	.58	199.9	5	.563
	FEMALE	HUGGER GT	******	8.2	11.1	1.28	10.0	-12.7	.60	203.8	0	.126
	FEMALE	VANTAGE SUPREME	******	8.2	11.1	1.34	10.0	.6	.62	201.4	3	.205
	FEMALE	SUPER VILLANOVA	******	9.0	13.4	1.01	10.0	11.9	.62	195.1	5	.298
	FEMALE	NIGHTHAWK	*****	8.6	13.1	1.54	2.4	-9.3	.45	189.0	0	
BROOKFIELD	MALE	COLT	*****	12.4	17.4	2.31	3.5	21.5	1.13	289.3	4	
AUTRY	MALE	MACH III	*****	8.7	13.0	2.13	3.0	-37.6	.66	250.2	4	
	MALE	NEW JET	*****	9.1	14.5	1.88	4.0	-37.9	.69	242.4	4	
	MALE	CONCORDE	*****	9.2	13.2	2.41	2.0	-33.9	.61	261.7	5	.023
	FEMALE	CLOUD 9	*****	9.4	17.6	1.79	2.3	-27.3	.63	198.6	3	
ADIDAS	MALE	TRX TRAINER	*****	10.5	16.8	2.07	2.1	-.6	.72	309.0	5	.143
	MALE	MARATHON TRAINER	*****	13.0	17.2	2.75	10.0	14.5	.63	302.3	5	.315
	FEMALE	MARATHON TRAINER	*****	11.7	16.5	2.14	10.0	17.5	.58	243.6	5	.298

****** HIGHLY RECOMMENDED
***** RECOMMENDED

PAGE   2

Glossary

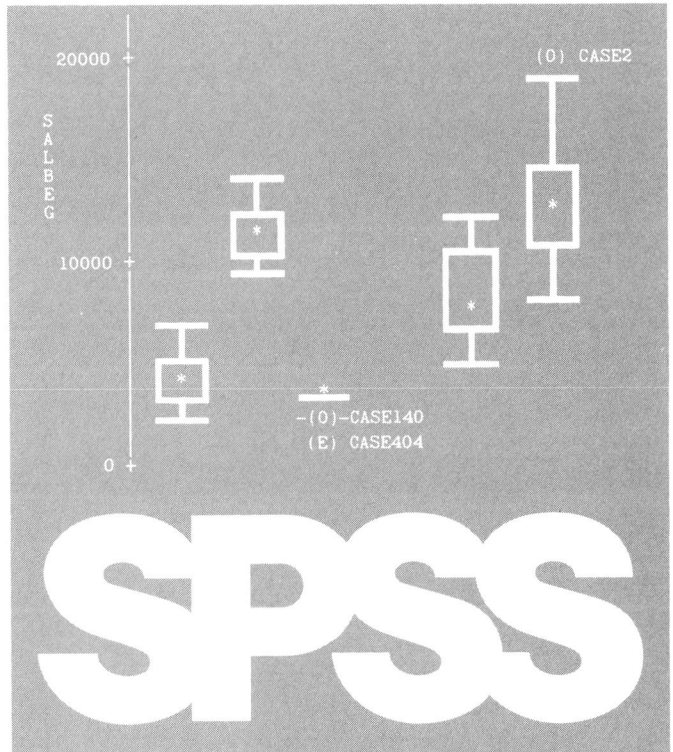

Glossary

active default   Options that are in effect when an optional subcommand is included but is not followed by any keywords. For example, in REGRESSION, including the subcommand DESCRIPTIVES without any modifying keywords requests the active defaults MEAN, STDDEV, and CORR. See also *passive default*.

active file   The file defined in a session by a DATA LIST command or called by a GET or IMPORT command. Consists of the data and a dictionary and is the file that you modify using transformations, and analyze using any of the procedures.

active window   In REVIEW, the portion of the screen that accepts file modifications. Two windows of different sizes can be accessed, but only the active window can be modified.

alias   A keyword that is a synonym for another SPSS/PC+ keyword. For example, XTABS is an alias for CROSSTABS.

alphanumeric variable   A variable whose values are stored as characters and are not available for arithmetic operations. The values may contain letters or special characters as well as numbers. Also known as *string variable*. Compare *numeric variable*.

analysis list   Portion of an SPSS/PC+ command that requests an analysis (such as a correlation matrix) or a set of related analyses (such as a set of crosstabs that use the same variables).

argument   An expression (usually within parentheses) following a function or another SPSS/PC+ keyword that is the object of the operation. For arithmetic function SQRT(X), variable X is the argument. For REPORT function PCGT(150), the value 150 is the argument.

arithmetic operators   Graphic symbols used in a variable transformation to represent arithmetic functions such as addition (+), subtraction (−), multiplication (*), division (/), and exponentiation (**).

ASCII file   A data or command file containing characters conforming to the American Standard Code for Information Interchange standards. These files contain a carriage control line-feed sequence at the end of each line and a CTRL−Z at the end of the file. SPSS/PC+ reads and writes ASCII files.

assignment expression   The expression following the equals sign in the COMPUTE and IF commands that assigns a value for each case to the target variable. See also *target variable*.

batch processing   Using the INCLUDE command to process SPSS/PC+ commands stored in a file. While SPSS/PC+ is processing the commands from the file, you cannot change any of the specifications given on the commands in the file. See also *interactive operation*.

case identifier   Unique code assigned to each case.

case, observation   Basic unit of analysis for which measurements are taken.

categorical variable   A variable that has a limited number of values that form categories of cases. See also *continuous variable*.

code   A numeric or alphabetical value that represents the status of a case on a variable.

codebook   Document that describes each variable, its name, label, values and value labels, formats, and missing values. Also known as a coding form.

command   A specific instruction that controls the execution of SPSS/PC+.

command file   A file that contains SPSS/PC+ commands and sometimes includes data. Use the INCLUDE command to process command files. See also *batch processing*.

command line   A line of specifications for one SPSS/PC+ command. It may take more than one line to enter all of the instructions for a single command (see *continuation line*).

conditional transformation   Changing the values of a variable contingent upon logical conditions found in the data; e.g., altering variables one way for one subset of cases and other ways for other subsets. See the IF command.

constant   A value that is the same for every case. For example, in the expression B=A+12, 12 is a constant. Constants can be either numeric or string values.

contingency table   A table containing the joint frequency distribution of two or more variables. See the CROSSTABS command.

continuation line   The second or any subsequent line of specifications for one SPSS/PC+ command.

continuous variable   A variable that does not have a fixed number of values. For example, the variable INCOME, measured in dollars, can take on many different values.

control variable   The variable whose values are used to separate cases into subgroups. In a crosstabulation, the variable whose values form subtables.

CPU   The abbreviation for central processing unit. The CPU performs tasks based on instructions from SPSS/PC+ commands.

current character   The character highlighted by the cursor.

current line   The line containing the cursor.

cursor   The highlighted symbol on the screen indicating the current location.

data   Information organized for analysis.

data line   A line of information for a single case recorded on a disk. It may take more than one line to enter all the data for a case.

default   Instruction assumed when no other specification is stated.

delimiter   A symbol or a blank used by SPSS/PC+ to detect when one specification on a command ends and another one begins (blanks between keywords, commas between arguments, slashes between subcommands, and so on).

dictionary   Descriptive information about variables on the active file. Includes variable names and labels, print formats, value labels, missing-value flags, and a positional index.

directory (DOS)   The type of structure used for storing files. Your personal computer uses a tree structure of directories. The primary level is the root directory. SPSS/PC+ is loaded into the directory \SPSS. This is a subdirectory under the root. See your *DOS* manual, "Using Tree-Structured Directories."

discrete variable   A variable that has a limited number of values. The values can have nominal or ordinal properties. For example, INCOME with values high, medium, and low is a discrete variable. Compare *continuous variable*.

disk   Oxide-coated plastic disk that stores data magnetically. See also *hard disk, diskette*.

diskette   A flexible disk (5 1/4 inches in diameter for the IBM PC) that can be removed from the drive.

drive   A device for reading data or commands from a disk or diskette. The floppy disk drive is usually called the A: drive. The hard disk drive is usually called the C: drive.

editor   A program that allows you to enter text or data from your keyboard into the computer, to edit text or data, and to save files on disk. A text editor named REVIEW is integrated into the SPSS/PC+ system. A simpler text editor, EDLIN, is supplied with DOS.

external file   A file residing on the hard disk that can be called in during an SPSS/PC+ session. SPSS/PC+ can read external files that contain data or commands. The term is generally not used in this manual to refer to system files or portable files.

file   A physical organization of records, usually stored on a disk. Refer to Command Reference: Universals for files used by SPSS/PC+.

file definition   Description of file characteristics. Points SPSS/PC+ to the data file and indicates the format of the file and the number of records SPSS/PC+ should read per case from fixed-format data files. See also *variable definition*.

floppy disk   A flexible disk.

format   The way values of a variable are represented to the computer and the way these values are displayed. The DATA LIST and FORMATS commands assign formats that SPSS/PC+ uses to write or display values. The components of a format are the variable type (string or numeric), the variable width, and the number of decimal places.

fully qualified name   A filename that includes the drive, directory, and name of a file.

hard disk   Rigid, oxide-coated plastic disk that stores data magnetically. Generally holds more information than a floppy.

implied decimal places   The number of digits that are placed to the right of a decimal point in the stored value for a value that contains no decimal places when it is read. Implied decimal places are declared on the DATA LIST command when fixed-format data are read.

include file   A file of SPSS/PC+ commands and/or data to be processed in an SPSS/PC+ session via the INCLUDE command. See also *batch processing*.

initialization   The assignment of a value to a new variable before a data transformation assigns a computed value. New numeric variables are initialized with the system-missing value. New string variables are initialized with blanks. See the IF and COMPUTE commands.

inline data   Data included as lines in a command file or entered from the terminal during a session. The BEGIN DATA command precedes the first data line and the END DATA command follows the last data line.

input   Information entered into the computer.

input data file   Contains data in almost any format stored on a disk. This file can be included within an SPSS/PC+ command file as inline data, or it can be a separate file defined on the DATA LIST command.

interactive operation   Entering commands (and sometimes data) directly into SPSS/PC+, as opposed to entering a file of SPSS/PC+ commands using the INCLUDE command. See also *batch processing*.

key diskette   A floppy disk inserted in the A: drive to unlock SPSS/PC+. The key diskette is required to operate SPSS/PC+.

keyword   A word already defined by SPSS/PC+ to identify a command, subcommand, or specification. See Command Reference: Universals for rules for using keywords.

label   A string that contains an extended description associated with a file, a variable, or a value of a variable. See also *dictionary*.

line   A line of SPSS/PC+ command text or a line of data. See *command line*, *continuation line*, *data line* (or *record*).

listing file   A file that contains the statistical and tabular output from SPSS/PC+ procedures, diagnostic information, and messages about the session. The default listing file is SPSS.LIS. This default can be changed with the SET command.

listwise deletion   Cases that have missing values for any of the variables named are omitted from the analysis.

literal   The value of a string variable or a label, enclosed within apostrophes or quotation marks. See also *string*.

log file   A file that contains all commands entered and processed by SPSS/PC+. The default log file is SPSS.LOG. This default can be changed using the SET command.

logical expression   Expression composed of logical operators and relations comparing two or more variables, or a compound expression. Results in assignment as true or false (or missing).

logical operator	Symbol that joins two or more relations logically in a conditional transformation. The SPSS/PC+ logical operators are AND (both relations must be true) and OR (either relation can be true). The NOT logical operator reverses the outcome of the expression that immediately follows.
logical variable	A numeric variable whose values are 0 (false), 1 (true), or missing.
long string variable	A string variable that has more than 8 and up to 255 alphanumeric characters.
map	Lists variable names from the active-file dictionary, showing the result of the IMPORT or EXPORT command.
matrix materials	Summary data used as input to procedures CLUSTER, FACTOR, ONEWAY, and REGRESSION. The data can contain correlation coefficients, covariance coefficients, standard deviations, distance measures, counts, means, standard deviations, as well as other summary measures. See these commands and DATA LIST: Matrix Materials in the Command Reference for more information.
memory	The internal storage area of the CPU where SPSS/PC+ operates and where calculations are performed. See also *workspace*.
missing value	A code that indicates that the true value of the variable could not be obtained, or a code that you would like to have ignored during statistical calculations. These values are defined on the MISSING VALUE command and are then flagged in the dictionary of the active file. The SPSS/PC+ statistical procedures and transformation commands recognize this flag. See also *user-missing value*, *system-missing value*.
module	A portion of SPSS/PC+ software. SPSS/PC+ is stored on the hard disk as a set of modules. Each module contains different parts of the whole system.
narrow format	The default width, 79 characters, of SPSS/PC+ display. Narrow format is designed to fit on your screen. Compare *wide format*.
numeric expression	An expression consisting of numeric variables, constants, and operators.
numeric function	A function that operates on a numeric expression and returns a number or system-missing value. The expression to be transformed by a function is called an *argument* and usually consists of a variable name or a list of variable names.
numeric variable	A variable whose values are numbers. Compare *string* (or *alphanumeric*) *variable*.
operating system	A collection of programs that supervise the operation of the computer and handle files and sessions. SPSS/PC+ uses MSDOS.
option numbers	Numbers used on the OPTIONS subcommand to request that options be in effect for a procedure.
output	Results produced by a computer from specific input. SPSS/PC+ produces several types of output (statistics, tables, reports, plots, data, matrices, and so forth). The output destination is controlled by the SET command.
output file	Contains data formatted to be read by a computer. Some procedures create output files containing matrix or other materials. The WRITE command produces a rectangular file to your specifications. SAVE produces a system file that is read by SPSS/PC+. EXPORT produces a portable file that can be read by SPSS/PC+ or SPSS.
pairwise deletion	Cases that have valid values on both variables used in a calculation are included in the calculation. Other cases are deleted.
passive default	Options that are in effect when an optional subcommand is omitted. Passive defaults are indicated by two asterisks (**) in the syntax diagrams. For example, in REGRESSION, when the optional subcommand STATISTICS is omitted, the passive defaults R, COEFF, ANOVA, ZPP, and OUTS are requested. See also *active default*.
portable file	An ASCII file produced by SPSS/PC+ or SPSS EXPORT. Portable files contain data and a dictionary of labels and variable formats. See also *system file*.
print format	Format used for displaying and printing the values of a variable. Controlled by the DATA LIST and FORMATS commands. See also *dictionary*.

procedure	Any SPSS/PC+ command that reads data from the active file. Procedures cause preceding transformations to be executed. Most SPSS/PC+ procedures produce statistical results.
prompt	The string that SPSS/PC+ displays to indicate that it is ready to receive your commands. The default prompt is SPSS/PC: for the first line of a command and : for a continuation line. You can change the prompts by using the SET command.
record	Line of machine-readable information.
rectangular data file	A file in which each case contains one and only one value for each variable and in which each case is the same type of unit of analysis throughout the entire file. The variables are in the same order for each case.
relational operator	Symbol that compares two values of a logical expression in a conditional transformation such as EQ (equal to), LT (less than), LE (less than or equal to), and so forth.
reserved keyword	Keywords that cannot be used as variable names since they can appear in variable lists (e.g., TO, EQ, WITH, BY).
scientific notation	Expression of a number as a fractional part and a power of ten. 350,000,000 can be expressed as 0.3500E9 or 3.5000E8.
scratch file	A file used by SPSS/PC+ to hold intermediate results from transformation and procedure commands. You cannot directly access this file.
scrolling	The phenomenon of watching your results fly by on your screen when you set the page length too long.
session	An SPSS/PC+ session begins with the SPSSPC command given in response to the DOS prompt, and ends with the SPSS/PC+ FINISH command.
short string variable	A string variable with a width of 8 or fewer alphanumeric characters.
specifications	Instructions added to a command. May include subcommands, keywords, numbers, strings, arithmetic operators, variable names, special delimiters, and spacing as needed to separate these elements. Specifications begin at least one space after the command keyword and continue for as many lines as necessary.
statistic number	A number that is included on the STATISTICS subcommand to request optional statistics from a procedure.
status area	The area in the upper right-hand corner of your screen that contains messages about what SPSS/PC+ is doing. The status area informs you when modules are swapped and when data are read into memory.
string	One or more alphanumeric characters. Strings are specified in apostrophes or quotation marks in SPSS/PC+ commands. See also *alphanumeric variable, string variable, literal.*
string variable	A variable whose values contain letters or special characters (as well as numbers). Also known as *alphanumeric variable.* Compare *numeric variable.*
subcommand	Additional instructions that further specify SPSS/PC+ commands. A command may contain one or more subcommands, each with specifications to that subcommand. Defined in Command Reference: Universals.
syntax	General rules for the structure of the SPSS/PC+ language.
system-missing value	Value assigned by SPSS/PC+ when a value in your data is undefined according to the format type that you have specified, when a numeric field is blank for the default format type, or when a value resulting from a transformation command is undefined. See also *user-missing value.*
system file	A binary file specially formatted for use by SPSS/PC+, containing both data and the dictionary that is written by the SPSS/PC+ SAVE command. See also *portable file.*
system variable	Special variables assigned by SPSS/PC+ that determine the number of cases read by the system, compare the system-missing value, obtain the current date, and so forth. System variable names begin with a dollar sign. You cannot modify system variables or use them in most procedures, but you can use them in transformations.

E

Glossary

table list	The portion of an SPSS/PC+ command that requests tables using a subset of variables.
tabulation	Counting, arranging, or listing values and cases in table format.
target variable	A variable that contains the result of a transformation. See COMPUTE, IF, and COUNT commands in Command Reference. See also *assignment expression*.
terminator	The character used to indicate the end of an SPSS/PC+ command. The default terminator is a period.
transformation	Changing the values of a variable to correct coding errors, modify the coding scheme, create new variables, or construct an index.
truncation	The convention that allows you to enter only the first three characters of an SPSS/PC+ keyword.
unary operator	The algebraic operation of using the minus sign before a numeric variable or value to reverse the sign, or using the plus sign, which does not produce a reversal.
user-missing value	A value that indicates missing information. Defined on the MISSING VALUE command. See also *system-missing value*.
valid	Not missing (having neither the system-missing value nor a value defined as missing).
value	A numeric or alphabetical code that represents the status of a case on a variable.
variable	Observable entity that can take on more than one value or characteristic.
variable definition	The portion of the DATA LIST command that assigns a name to each variable you intend to analyze and provides information about the location and format of the variables in the data file.
variable name	A name assigned to a variable. The name can be up to 8 characters in length. It must begin with a letter (A–Z) or the character @. The remaining characters in the name can be any letter, any digit, a period (.), an underscore (_), and the symbols @, #, or $. See also *reserved keyword*.
wide format	The display is 132 columns wide. Usually for printed output. See also *narrow format*.
window	A portion of the screen used for displaying parts of a file. REVIEW allows access to two windows for displaying two files.
workspace	The amount of memory available to SPSS/PC+ to perform procedures and transformations.

Appendixes

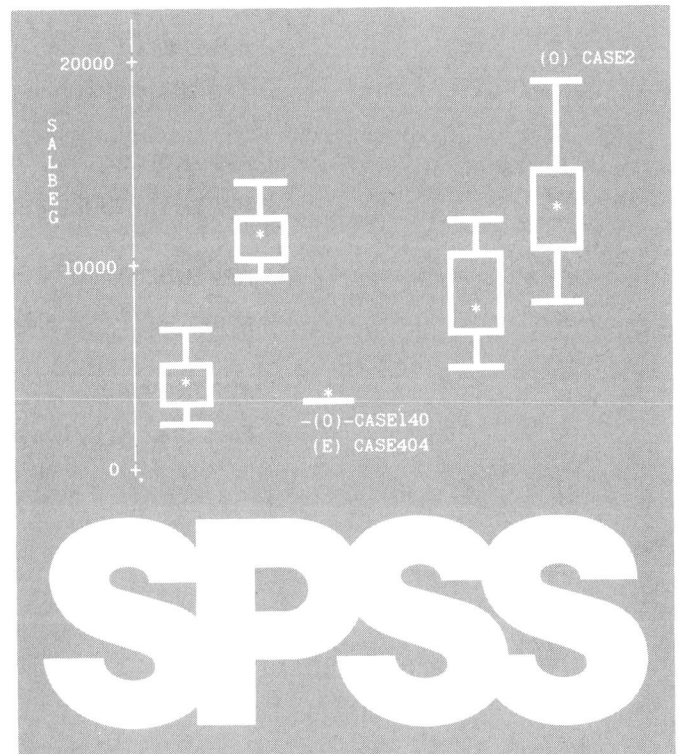

- *SPSS/PC+ Graph-in-the-Box*
- *SPSS/PC+ Graph-in-the-Box Executive*
- *Using SPSS/PC+ with RAM Disks*
- *Files Created by Other Software*

Contents

Appendix
1

SPSS/PC+ Graph-in-the-Box

SPSS/PC+ Graph-in-the-Box is a quick way to add graphical impact to SPSS/PC+ results. Graph-in-the-Box captures data directly from the screen and quickly converts the numbers into a choice of bar, line, or pie charts. Whether you have produced a simple table or conducted a complex statistical analysis, Graph-in-the-Box helps you visualize the results and convey them more forcefully to others.

Overview   Graph-in-the-Box is a memory-resident program distributed by SPSS Inc. through an agreement with New England Software. It comes with full documentation from New England Software (referred to here as "the manual"). The appendix you're reading tells how to use Graph-in-the-Box within SPSS/PC+. It also provides some examples specific to SPSS/PC+ and some hints for making the most out of the graphics software. If you have the Graph-in-the-Box Executive option, see Appendix 2.

To provide flexible screen-capture and graphics capabilities, Graph-in-the-Box requires a significant amount of random-access memory. For this reason, SPSS/PC+ loads Graph-in-the-Box into memory only when you are reviewing the results of your analyses. SPSS/PC+ then removes Graph-in-the-Box to free up memory for your analyses or other applications. Here's how it works:

- Install Graph-in-the-Box on your hard disk according to the instructions in the manual. Make sure you have a path to the directory in which it is installed. Use GBINSTALL to set up your monitor, printer, and plotter if you have one. Do not put the GB command in your AUTOEXEC.BAT file.

- *Do not* issue the GB command.

- Start and run SPSS/PC+ as you ordinarily would. When you obtain results that you'd like to see graphically, run the SPSS/PC+ command

 FASTGRAF.

- SPSS/PC+ loads Graph-in-the-Box and places you into REVIEW with your most recent results showing (just as though you had used the command REVIEW LISTING). Move around in REVIEW as always until you have on the screen the results you want to convert into a graph. Press (Alt) (G). You're now in Graph-in-the-Box, ready to capture and display data as described in the Graph-in-the-Box manual. You can quit and re-enter Graph-in-the-Box as often as you want while you're still in REVIEW.

- When you're done looking over your results and have viewed (and optionally printed or saved) as many charts as you want, exit from REVIEW normally, using either (Alt) (F10) if you just want to exit or (F10) if you've marked a block for SPSS/PC+ to run. SPSS/PC+ removes Graph-in-the-Box from memory as you go back into the SPSS/PC+ session.

- As you'll see in the examples in this booklet, when you quit Graph-in-the-Box, it retains your chart. The data, labels, and layout are all preserved and available the next time you press (Alt) (G). But when you leave REVIEW, Graph-in-the-Box is removed from memory, and the chart disappears. If you want to get it back, save it as described in the manual.

If you load Graph-in-the-Box yourself, using the GB command, SPSS/PC+ will not attempt to load or remove it for you. It will remain in memory until you specifically remove it (using GBKILL as described in the manual) or reboot your system—regardless of whether you use the FASTGRAF command. This takes away about 130K of the memory available to SPSS/PC+.

An Example Using Frequency Tables

One hundred husbands and wives were asked to evaluate how likely they would be to buy each of twenty products, one of which was a hands-free telephone effective up to twenty feet. Frequency tables for their responses can be obtained with the SPSS/PC+ command

```
FREQUENCIES VAR=W11S H11S.
```

Capturing Data and Labels

After running the FREQUENCIES procedure, run

```
FASTGRAF.
```

1 You're now in REVIEW. Go to the frequency table for **Phone Wife Self** and press ⌊Alt⌋ ⌊G⌋ to wake up Graph-in-the-Box.

2 Graph-in-the-Box expects you to start by capturing data. Move the cursor to one corner (it doesn't matter which) of the column containing frequencies and press ⌊←⌋. Use the arrow keys to move the cursor to the opposite corner of the column and press ⌊←⌋ again. Graph-in-the-Box immediately draws a quick chart of the frequencies. (For scaling purposes, you might want to capture the percentages instead of the frequencies. This file has 100 valid cases, so it doesn't matter.)

3 The initial plot has no labels showing which values the frequencies apply to. You can capture the labels also. Press the space bar to clear the graph. The main menu appears at the bottom of the screen with your data. Select **Capture**. (Press the space bar until **Capture** is highlighted and press ⌊←⌋, or just press ⌊C⌋.) You can capture the block containing the value labels, but they'll overlap in a vertical column chart, so capture the column of values. Figure 1 shows the way the screen appears with the values and frequency counts captured.

Figure 1

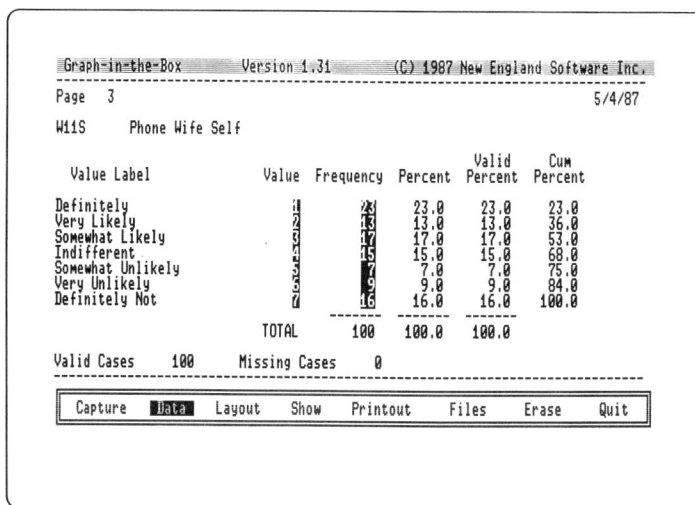

4 Because you already have data captured in your chart, this time Graph-in-the-Box takes you to the Data screen so you can show it where you want the captured data placed. The Data screen contains columns of data, a column on the left for labels for each row, and some rows at the top for labels and other information about each column. The values you captured are labels for the rows, so use the arrow keys to move the cursor to the top of the left-hand column and press ⏎. Figure 2 shows the Data screen with the labels in place.

Figure 2

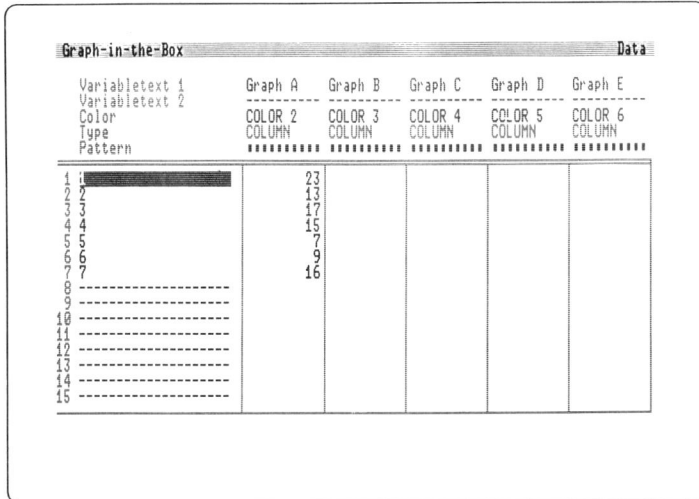

5 If you press [F10] to display the chart, you'll see that the labels appear along the horizontal axis; but it would be better if the endpoints were labeled to indicate which value means *yes* and which means *no*. Also, the label **Graph A** is not very helpful.

6 To change the label, press [Ctrl] [D] to go to the Data screen. Move the cursor to where that text appears and press [Del] until it's gone.

7 To label the base axis, press [Ctrl] [L] to go to the Layout screen. Move the cursor to the **X-axis label** line and type in the label. (*Hint:* to get **Definitely Not** at the far right end of the line, it's easiest to type the words, back up with the arrow keys, and insert spaces until the label arrives at the end of the line.) While on the Layout screen, add a title for the graph. The completed screen is shown in Figure 3.

Figure 3

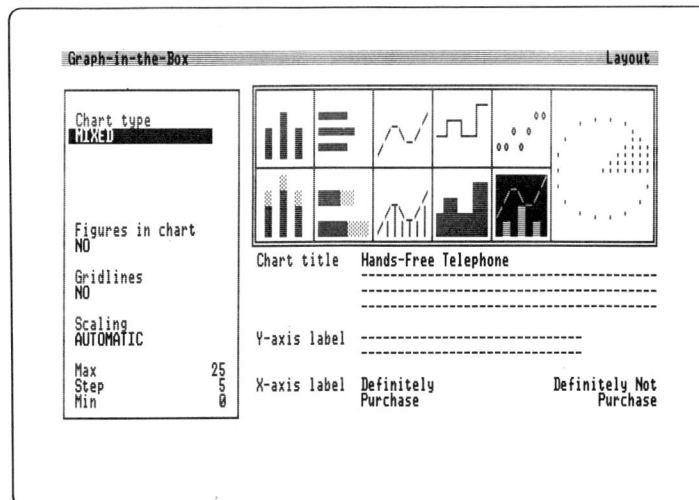

F

Appendixes

8 Press F10 to display the graph (Figure 4).

Figure 4

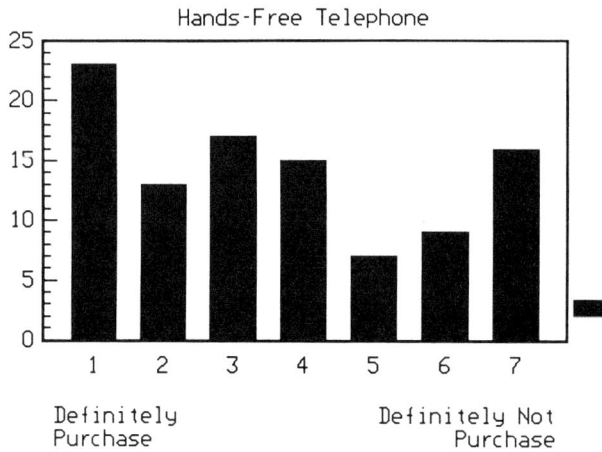

Adding Data   Although Graph-in-the-Box provides more formatting options, the chart just created doesn't contain any more information than you can obtain simply by adding the BARCHART subcommand to the FREQUENCIES command. The power of Graph-in-the-Box becomes useful when you combine information or when you get creative about graphing output for which plots are not already available. Let's combine the information from two frequency tables into a single chart.

1 Go to the main menu (Esc takes you there) and quit Graph-in-the-Box. Quitting does not affect your current chart; when you press Alt G again, the data, labels, and layout information are just as you left them.

2 You can now use REVIEW as usual. Go to the frequency table for **Phone Husband Self.**

3 Press Alt G and proceed to capture the frequency data. When Graph-in-the-Box takes you to the Data screen, you'll find the data from the previous chart still in place. Move the cursor to the top of the second data column and press ↵ to place the data there, as shown in Figure 5.

4 Above the two data columns, type in labels to distinguish husband and wife data, as shown in Figure 5.

Figure 5

```
┌─────────────────────────────────────────────────────────────────┐
│                                                                   │
│  Graph-in-the-Box                                          Data   │
│                                                                   │
│   Variabletext 1       Wife's    Husband's Graph C  Graph D  Graph E │
│   Variabletext 2       Intent    Intent                           │
│   Color                COLOR 2   COLOR 3  COLOR 4  COLOR 5  COLOR 6 │
│   Type                 COLUMN    COLUMN   COLUMN   COLUMN   COLUMN │
│   Pattern              ■■■■■■■■■  - - - -  ■■■■■■■■ ■■■■■■■■ ■■■■■■■■ │
│                                                                   │
│  1 1                        23       15                           │
│  2 2                        13       14                           │
│  3 3                        17       16                           │
│  4 4                        15       22                           │
│  5 5                         7       13                           │
│  6 6                         9       12                           │
│  7 7                        16        8                           │
│  8   ────────                                                     │
│  9   ────────                                                     │
│ 10   ────────                                                     │
│ 11   ────────                                                     │
│ 12   ────────                                                     │
│ 13   ────────                                                     │
│ 14   ────────                                                     │
│ 15   ────────                                                     │
│                    ↑                                              │
│                                                                   │
│                                                                   │
└─────────────────────────────────────────────────────────────────┘
```

5 Press (F10) to display the graph (Figure 6).

Figure 6

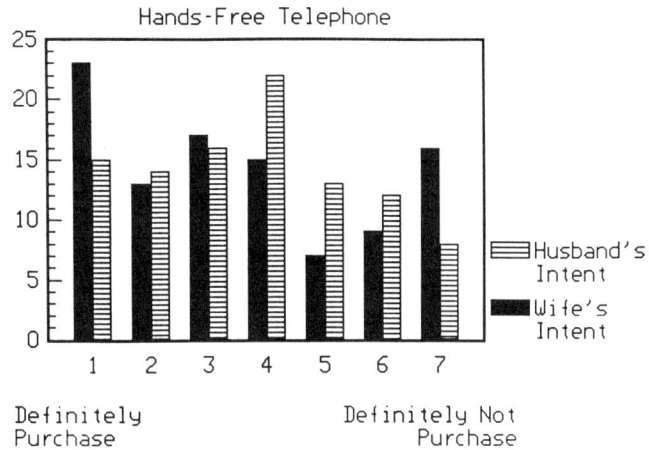

Varying the Style Graph-in-the-Box makes it easy to find different ways of viewing the data. Just go to the Layout screen ((Ctrl) (L)), highlight **Chart type,** and press the space bar to view different chart types you would like to see.

Figure 7

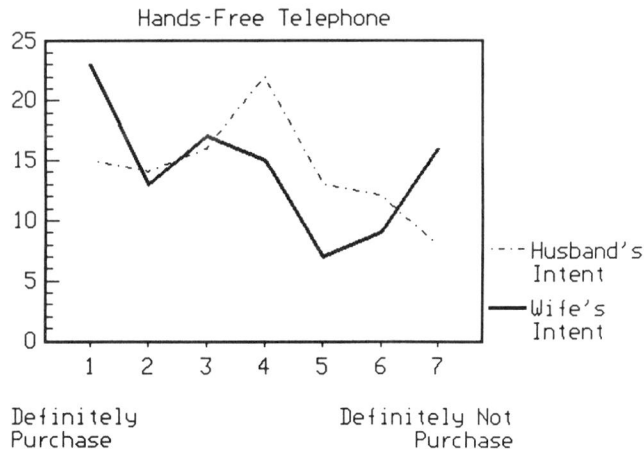

• To create the line chart shown in Figure 7, simply go to the Layout screen ((Ctrl) (L)), make sure the highlight is under **Chart type,** press the space bar until **LINE** is highlighted, and press (↵).

When you select chart type **MIXED** from the Layout screen, you can then select the chart type to use for each column of numbers. You can also omit columns of numbers by telling Graph-in-the-Box to ignore them.

F

Appendixes

1 To create the chart shown in Figure 8, go to the Layout screen (Ctrl L) and select chart type **MIXED.**

Figure 8

Hands-Free Telephone

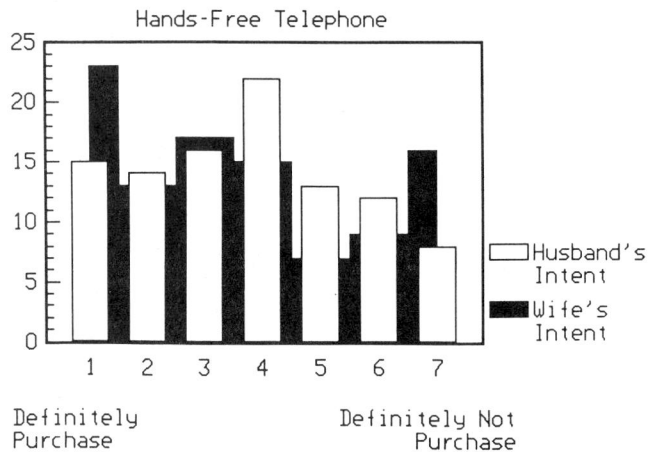

2 Go to the Data screen (Ctrl D) and move the cursor up to the top of the columns where the chart type is shown for each column. You can change the type by placing the cursor on the field for each column and pressing the space bar until the right type appears. Choose **STEP,AREA** for the first column, and **BAR** for the second (Figure 9).

Figure 9

Rotating the Data

The pie chart in Figure 10 provides another way of looking at the same frequency data, but it requires a different arrangement of the data. Graph-in-the-Box creates a pie for just the top row of data—each column becomes one slice. This requires you to capture a vertical column of frequencies into a horizontal row.

Figure 10

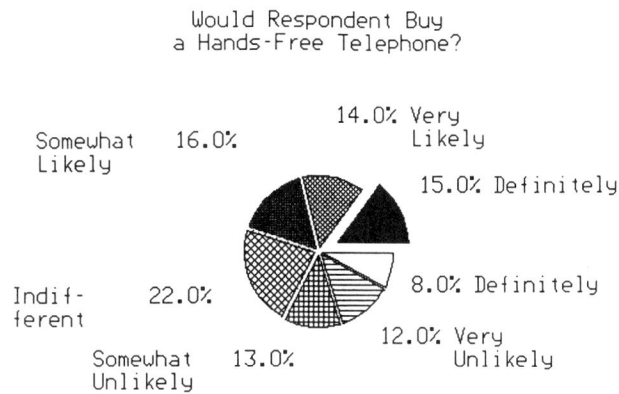

Would Respondent Buy
a Hands-Free Telephone?

1 Get rid of the current chart by selecting **Erase** from the main menu. You can verify the erasure by checking the Data screen.

2 Press F4 to display the current option settings, and then use the space bar to change the capturing mode to **ROTATED**. You can do this from any screen. Figure 11 shows the settings at the bottom of the Data screen.

Figure 11

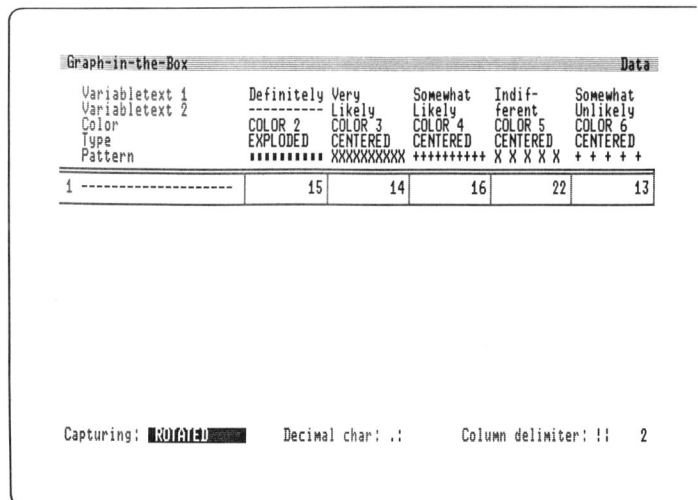

3 Capture the frequencies as before. They will now appear as shown in Figure 11.

4 Capture the value labels to the left of the frequency table and place them in the top row of the column labels (where **Graph A** appears). Some are too long for the space provided, so you'll have to edit them; but capturing them gives you a head start.

5 Go to the Layout screen and select chart type **PIE**. Add a title. To get values to print in the chart, change the specification for **Figures in chart** to **YES** (Figure 12).

Figure 12

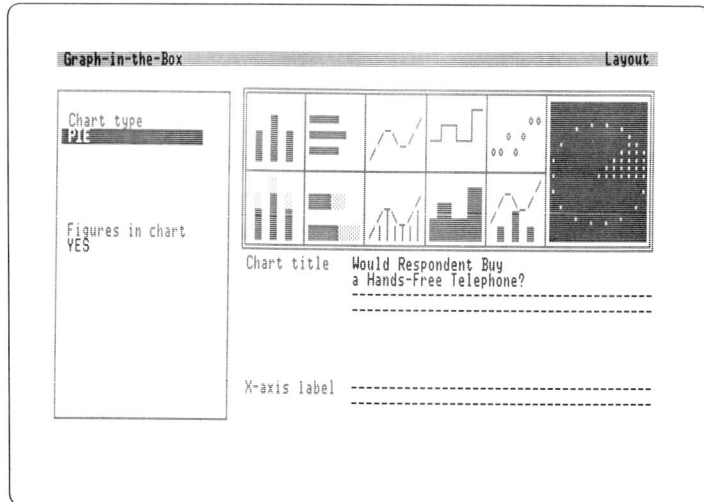

6 Press $\boxed{\text{F10}}$ to display the chart (Figure 10).

Working with Tables

It's usually very easy to work with boxed tables such as those produced by CROSSTABS or the TABLES option. In capturing data, Graph-in-the-Box ignores most characters that are not alphanumeric, so you can capture a whole table and not worry about blank lines or boxing characters. It also allows you to specify certain characters that divide columns in your table, so you can capture multiple columns that are separated by something like vertical bars rather than spaces. The default vertical boxing characters in CROSSTABS and TABLES are default delimiters for Graph-in-the-Box. If you change the defaults in SPSS/PC+ (or SET SCREEN=OFF, which also changes the box characters), you might want to change the column delimiters in Graph-in-the-Box. Use $\boxed{\text{F4}}$ to call up the system settings and type in the delimiter you want to use.

The following example shows how easy it can be to capture and graph output from TABLES. The data file is the same as in the previous examples. The SPSS/PC+ command

```
TABLES TABLE = (LABELS) BY W11S + H11S + W11O + H11O.
```

produces the table shown in Figure 13.

Figure 13

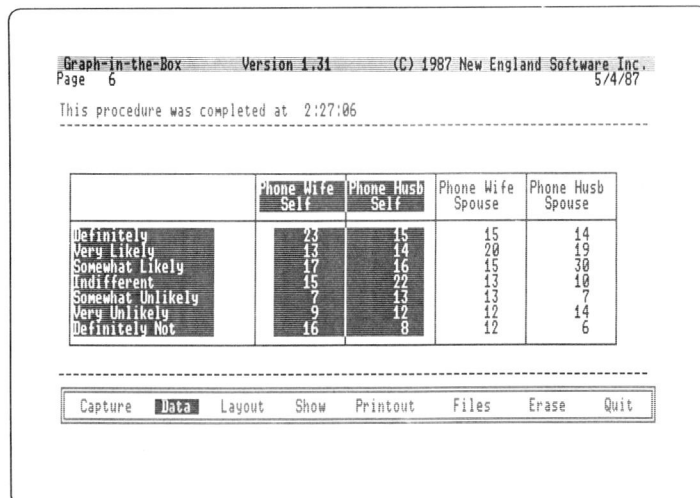

1 Capture both columns of data as one block.

2 Capture the value labels from the stub as row labels.

3 Capture the headings from the banner as column labels. The Data screen now appears as shown in Figure 14.

Figure 14

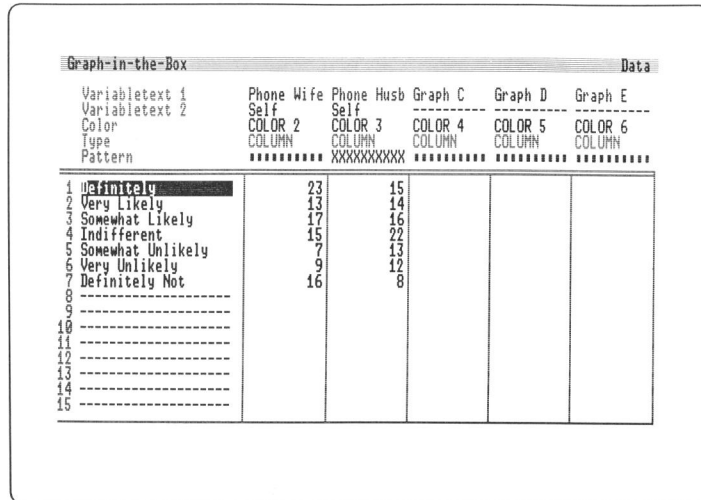

4 The long value labels will overlap in a vertical column chart, so go to the Layout screen and select one of the horizontal bar charts. Add a chart title and an X-axis label.

5 Press (F10) to display the graph (Figure 15).

Figure 15

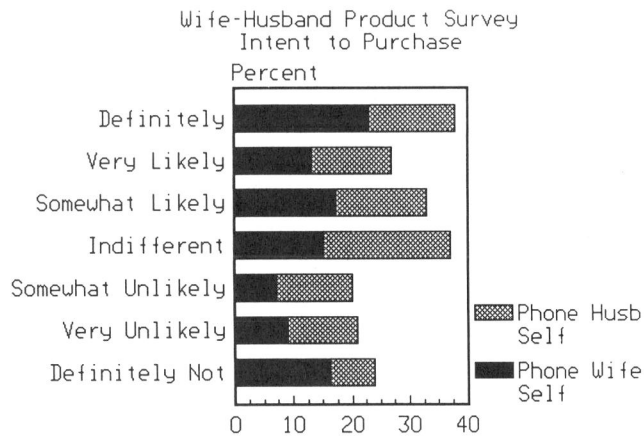

An Example from the SPSS/PC+ Statistics Option

A worldwide economic study collected information on prices and salaries in 45 major cities. A large number of price and salary variables were collected. The SPSS/PC+ FACTOR procedure can help you see whether there are groups of very similar economic variables, and Graph-in-the-Box can help you visualize how each variable contributes to the underlying factors. This example also contains a few additional variations on Graph-in-the-Box operations.

Figure 16 shows the rotated factor matrix containing the coefficients that relate the individual variables to each of two factors. The highlighted areas are those to be captured into Graph-in-the-Box.

Figure 16

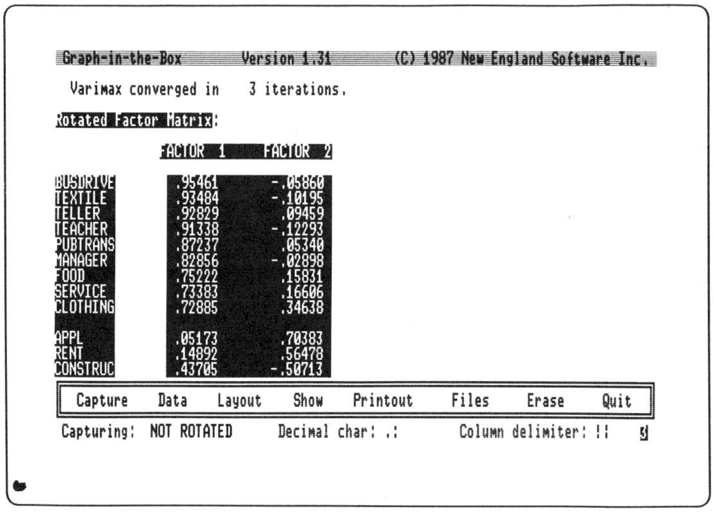

1 Capture the entire matrix of coefficients. Graph-in-the-Box simply ignores the blank line.

2 Capture the variable names as row labels. Again, Graph-in-the-Box ignores the blank line.

3 Capture the column headings as column labels. This requires a little extra effort. Note that there are two spaces in **FACTOR 1** and **FACTOR 2**. Graph-in-the-Box interprets two or more spaces as the delimiter between labels, so it would read the column heads as labels for four columns. You can fix this by editing out one space in REVIEW before capturing the column heads (you have to quit Graph-in-the-Box, edit, and then press (Alt) (G)), or you can raise the number of spaces Graph-in-the-Box interprets as a delimiter. Before initiating the capture, press (F4) to display the option settings, move the cursor to the far right, and change 2 to 3 (Figure 16). Press (↵) and proceed with the capture. The captured data and labels are shown in Figure 17.

Figure 17

```
┌─────────────────────────────────────────────────────────────────────────┐
│                                                                           │
│   Graph-in-the-Box                                                   Data │
│                                                                           │
│        Variabletext 1          FACTOR  1  FACTOR  2  Graph C   Graph D   Graph E │
│        Variabletext 2          ---------  ---------  --------  --------  -------- │
│        Color                   COLOR 2    COLOR 3    COLOR 4   COLOR 5   COLOR 6  │
│        Type                    COLUMN     COLUMN     COLUMN    COLUMN    COLUMN   │
│        Pattern                 ▪▪▪▪▪▪▪▪▪  ▪▪▪▪▪▪▪▪▪  ▪▪▪▪▪▪▪▪  ▪▪▪▪▪▪▪▪  ▪▪▪▪▪▪▪▪ │
│                                                                           │
│     1 BUSDRIVE                 0.95461    -0.0586                         │
│     2 TEXTILE                  0.93484    -0.10195                        │
│     3 TELLER                   0.92829     0.09459                        │
│     4 TEACHER                  0.91338    -0.12293                        │
│     5 PUBTRANS                 0.87237     0.0534                         │
│     6 MANAGER                  0.82856    -0.02898                        │
│     7 FOOD                     0.75222     0.15831                        │
│     8 SERVICE                  0.73383     0.16606                        │
│     9 CLOTHING                 0.72885     0.34638                        │
│    10 APPL                     0.05173     0.70383                        │
│    11 RENT                     0.14892     0.56478                        │
│    12 CONSTRUC                 0.43705    -0.50713                        │
│    13 --------------------                                                │
│    14 --------------------                                                │
│    15 --------------------                                                │
│                                                                           │
└─────────────────────────────────────────────────────────────────────────┘
```

4 Capture the title **Rotated Factor Matrix** for use in labeling the axis of your chart. When the Data screen appears after you highlight the block to capture, press (Ctrl) (L) to go to the Layout screen. Move the cursor to the **X-axis label** line and press (↵) to execute the capture.

5 If you want to include in your chart the actual SPSS/PC+ command that produced the result (to document the model you used), SET ECHO=ON (the default) in SPSS/PC+ before running the procedure. The command will then appear in the listing file, and you can move to it in REVIEW (quit and re-enter Graph-in-the-Box) and capture it, as shown in Figure 18.

Figure 18

```
┌─────────────────────────────────────────────────────────────────────────┐
│                                                                           │
│   Graph-in-the-Box        Version 1.31      (C) 1987 New England Software Inc. │
│              TEACHER  -        Teacher Salary                             │
│              CONSTRUC -        Construction Worker Salary                 │
│              MANAGER  -        Manager Salary                            │
│              TELLER   -        Bank Teller Salary                        │
│              WORLD    -        Economic Class for Country                │
│              CONT     -        Continent                                 │
│              CASEID   -        CASE SEQUENCE NUMBER                       │
│              BUSDRIVE -        Bus Driver Salary                         │
│              TEXTILE  -        Textile Worker Salary                     │
│              CLOTHING -        Clothing Prices                           │
│                                                                           │
│   ┌──────────────────────────────────────────┐                          │
│   │factor var=food to teller                  │                          │
│   │         busdrive to clothing              │                          │
│   │/format=sort /criteria=factors(2).         │                          │
│   └──────────────────────────────────────────┘                          │
│   This FACTOR analysis requires    18696 (    18.3K) BYTES of memory.    │
│   --------------------------------------------------------------          │
│   Page   4                    SPSS/PC+                        5/6/87      │
│                                                                           │
│               - - - -   F A C T O R   A N A L Y S I S   - - - -          │
│    ┌──────────────────────────────────────────────────────────────┐     │
│    │ Capture   Data   Layout   Show   Printout   Files   Erase   Quit │   │
│    └──────────────────────────────────────────────────────────────┘     │
│                                                                           │
└─────────────────────────────────────────────────────────────────────────┘
```

F

Appendixes

6 As with the captured X-axis label, highlight the area to be captured, go to the Layout screen, and capture the text into the chart title lines of your choice. You can type in additional lines or edit the text once you've completed the capture (Figure 19).

Figure 19

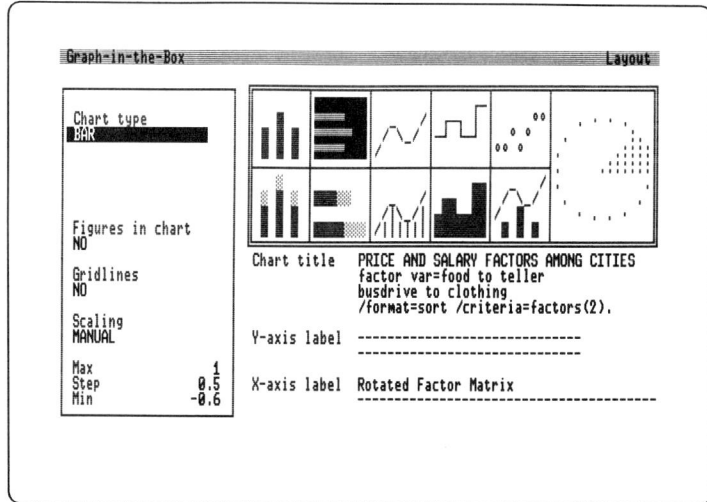

7 With many row labels (12 in this case), a horizontal bar chart avoids the overlapping labels that occur in a vertical column chart. Select chart type **BAR**.

8 Press (F10) to display the chart (Figure 20).

Figure 20

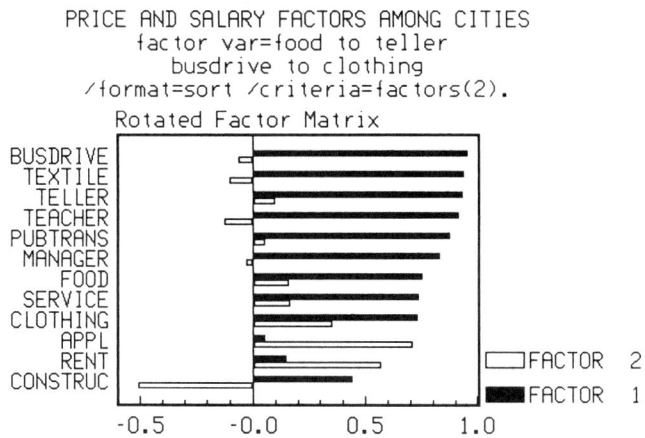

The Importance of Scale

The next example uses REGRESSION to predict sales from a leading indicator. The data are part of a series from Box and Jenkins' *Time Series Analysis: Forecasting and Control.* (For a more complete treatment, see *SPSS/PC+ Trends.*) REGRESSION coefficients are used along with values of the leading indicator to calculate predicted values, and these are displayed with LIST.

```
LIST VARIABLES = SALES PREDICT.
```

The LIST command produces two long columns containing the sales and predicted sales (Figure 21).

Figure 21

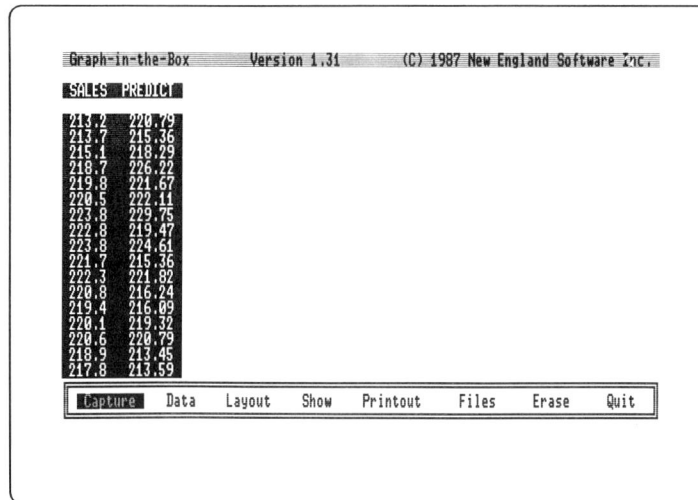

1   Capture the two columns of data. Because the listing covers several screens, you have to quit Graph-in-the-Box, move down in the text, wake up Graph-in-the-Box, and begin another capture. Just scroll down the Data screen after you've marked the second block for capture and start the capture right below the last line of the first capture—and so on (Figure 22).

Figure 22

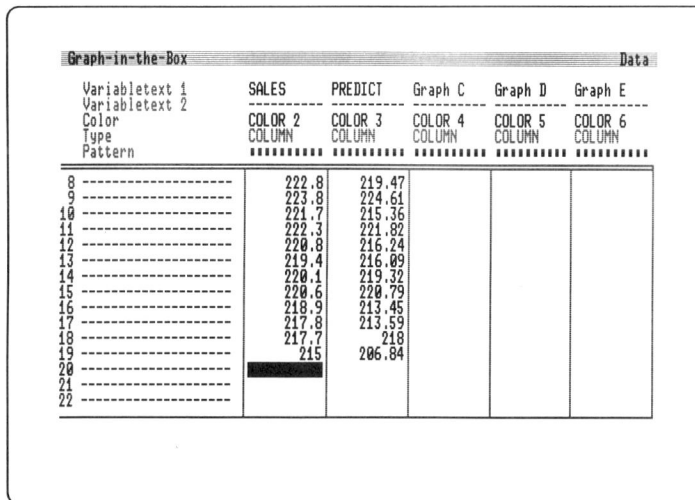

2   Capture the column headings from the top of one page.

3   Go to the Layout screen and select chart type **LINE**. Add a title.

4   Press F10 to display the chart as shown in Figure 23. The lines are compressed against the top of the chart and the curves are indistinct because the default scaling starts at 0 while the actual values being plotted are all well within the range of 200 to 250.

F

Appendixes

Figure 23

Predicting Sales
with a Leading Indicator

———— PREDICT
━━━ SALES

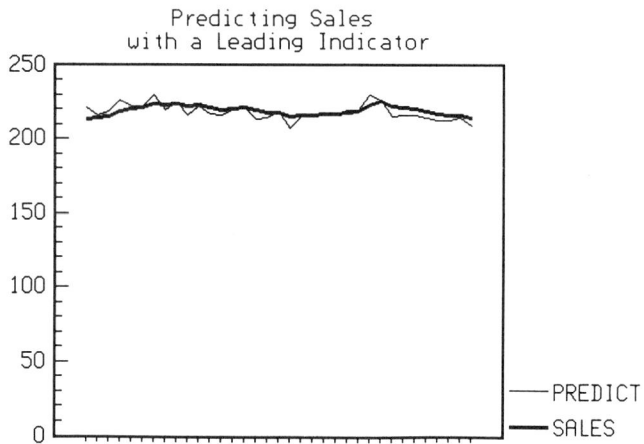

5 Return to the Layout screen. Change the **Scaling** specification from **AUTOMATIC** to **MANUAL**. You can then change the **Min**(imum) value to **200** and the **Step** to **10** (Figure 24).

Figure 24

6 Press F10 to redisplay the chart as shown in Figure 25.

Figure 25

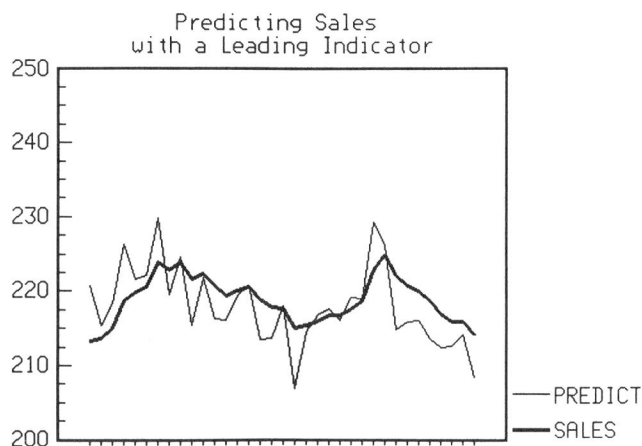

Predicting Sales
with a Leading Indicator

A Few Final Notes

The preceding examples contain most of the special cases you should be aware of when using Graph-in-the-Box within SPSS/PC+. Here are a few additional hints:

* Watch for empty cells when capturing tables or multiple columns of data. Graph-in-the-Box skips over blanks, getting data out of order. If you know that a blank equals 0 or some other value, insert that value in REVIEW before waking up Graph-in-the-Box.

* Graph-in-the-Box does not create a scatterplot with scaling of both axes. The Y-axis is scaled, but the X-axis gets one equal interval for each row of data—regardless of the actual values. The values *1, 2, 5, 6*, and *20* will be equally spaced along the X-axis. For some data it may be possible to add intervening values to correct the X-axis scale.

* SPSS/PC+ uses exponential notation for some values that will not fit into the allocated display area. Graph-in-the-Box will not capture values expressed in exponential notation.

* If you want to capture columns separated by just one space, change the delimiter from the default of two spaces to one.

Appendix 2

SPSS/PC+ Graph-in-the-Box Executive

SPSS/PC+ Graph-in-the-Box Executive is a quick and easy way to add graphical impact to SPSS/PC+ results. Graph-in-the-Box Executive captures data directly from the screen and quickly converts the numbers into a choice of bar, line, scatterplot, or pie charts. Whether you have produced a simple table or conducted a complex statistical analysis, Graph-in-the-Box Executive helps you visualize the results and convey them more forcefully to others.

Graph-in-the-Box Executive is a memory-resident program distributed by SPSS Inc. through an agreement with New England Software. It comes with full documentation from New England Software (referred to here as "the manual"). The appendix you're reading tells how to use Graph-in-the-Box Executive within SPSS/PC+. It also provides some examples specific to SPSS/PC+ and some hints for making the most out of the graphics software. If you have Graph-in-the-Box (not Executive), see Appendix 1.

Installation

1 Install Graph-in-the-Box Executive on your hard disk according to the instructions in the manual. Make sure you have a path to the directory in which it is installed.

2 Use the Setup screen in Graph-in-the-Box Executive to set up your printer and plotter (if you have one).

3 On the Setup screen, specify another set of keys in the **Keys to activate** field. (Ctrl) (G) is a good choice; it will be used in the examples in this appendix. If you do not change the activation keys, pressing (Alt) (G) in SPSS/PC+ will activate Graph-in-the-Box Executive, not the SPSS/PC+ glossary.

   Whatever keys you specify here will activate Graph-in-the-Box Executive in other programs, not just SPSS/PC+.

4 Put the GBX command in your AUTOEXEC.BAT file and reboot the computer. Graph-in-the-Box Executive requires a very small part of random-access memory when not activated. When activated, it uses a swap technique, as explained in the manual. Therefore, we recommend that you load Graph-in-the-Box Executive in your AUTOEXEC.BAT file. It will then be ready to wake up whenever you are running SPSS/PC+. As an alternative, you could load Graph-in-the-Box Executive by running the GBX command from the DOS prompt before starting SPSS/PC+. Either way, it will remain in memory until you specifically remove it (as described in the manual).

FASTGRAF Command. The FASTGRAF command is primarily for use with Graph-in-the-Box (not Executive). *Note:* FASTGRAF does not load Graph-in-the-Box Executive. If Graph-in-the-Box Executive is loaded and you run the FAST-GRAF command in SPSS/PC+, you switch into REVIEW. You can then use (Ctrl) (G) (or whatever activation keys you specified) to activate Graph-in-the-Box Executive. When you are ready to leave REVIEW, press (Alt) (F10) (or run the FASTGRAF command again), which takes you back to the SPSS/PC+ session.

Memory Problems. Graph-in-the-Box Executive uses extended or expanded memory (if you have any on your PC). If memory-related problems arise from conflicts with other software using this memory, you can easily disable the use of extended or expanded memory by Graph-in-the-Box. When you load GBX, use the /D option:

```
GBX /D.
```

This instructs Graph-in-the-Box Executive to use disk space instead of extended or expanded memory. If you put the GBX command with the /D option in your AUTOEXEC.BAT file, the memory problems should go away, although the program's operation will be slower.

Typical Session

The steps below give a brief overview of a typical session. Detailed examples follow.

- Start and run SPSS/PC+ as you ordinarily would. When you obtain results that you'd like to see graphically, switch to the listing file (press [F2] and [↵] if you are using the Menu and Help system) and move around until you have on the screen the results you want to convert into a graph.

- Press [Ctrl] [G] (the keys specified on the Setup screen, as described in the previous section). You're now in Graph-in-the-Box Executive, ready to capture and display data as described in the manual. You can quit and re-enter Graph-in-the-Box Executive as often as you want.

- When you're done looking over your results and have viewed (and optionally printed or saved) as many charts as you want, exit from the listing normally. For example, if you were using the Menu and Help system, press [F2] and [↵]. You will switch back to the SPSS/PC+ scratch pad in the bottom window.

- Graph-in-the-Box Executive retains the current chart (even if you leave SPSS/PC+) until you erase it, remove Graph-in-the-Box Executive from memory, or switch off your computer. If you want to save the chart permanently, follow the instructions in the manual.

Files Used in this Appendix

The following system files are used in the examples in this appendix:

```
PHONES.SYS
SALPRICE.SYS
SALEPRED.SYS
```

They were delivered with your SPSS/PC+ system.

An Example Using Frequency Tables

One hundred husbands and wives were asked to evaluate twenty products and give their rating of how likely they were to buy each of the twenty products, and their rating of how likely their spouses were to buy the products. To try the analysis as you are reading this appendix, you can GET the file PHONES.SYS that came with your system. This file contains data only for a hands-free telephone effective up to twenty feet. You can run the commands from the Menu and Help system or you can run them from the prompt:

```
GET FILE 'PHONES.SYS'.
FREQUENCIES
   /VARIABLES = HUSBSELF WIFESELF.
```

The following instructions assume you are using the Menu and Help system. Alternatively, you can capture the data while you are running the SPSS/PC+ commands or later from the listing file by running REVIEW LISTING from the prompt. Another assumption is that there is no current chart in Graph-in-the-Box Executive. Either you have not awakened Graph-in-the-Box Executive since turning on your computer or you have erased any current chart.

Capturing Data and Labels

1 After running the FREQUENCIES procedure, switch from the scratch pad to the listing file (press [F2] and [↵]). Press [F2] again, and then [Z] to zoom to a full screen. Go to the frequency table for **Phone Wife Self** and press [Ctrl] [G] to wake up Graph-in-the-Box Executive. (We reset the keys for activation earlier, on the Setup screen.)

2 Graph-in-the-Box Executive expects you to start by capturing data. Move the cursor to one corner (it doesn't matter which) of the column containing frequencies and press (↵). Use the arrow keys to move the cursor to the diagonally opposite corner of the column and press (↵) again. Graph-in-the-Box Executive immediately draws a quick chart of the frequencies. (When you have another data file, for scaling purposes you might want to capture the percentages instead of the frequencies. This file has 100 valid cases, so it doesn't matter.)

3 The initial plot has no labels showing which values the frequencies apply to. You can capture the labels also. Press the space bar to clear the graph. A Data screen appcars showing function kcys at thc bottom of the screen. The Data screen contains a column on the left for labels for each row and data columns with some fields at the top for labels and other information about the individual columns. Move the cursor to the left and then to the top of the **T** column, which is where you want the labels. Press (F2) (Capture). Move the cursor to one corner of the block containing the value labels and capture them as before. Figure 1 shows the way the listing screen appears with the value labels and frequency counts captured.

Figure 1

```
WIFESELF  Phone Wife Self
                                                        Valid      Cum
Value Label                   Value  Frequency  Percent  Percent  Percent

Definitely                        1         23     23.0     23.0     23.0
Very Likely                       2         13     13.0     13.0     36.0
Somewhat Likely                   3         17     17.0     17.0     53.0
Indifferent                       4         15     15.0     15.0     68.0
Somewhat Unlikely                 5          7      7.0      7.0     75.0
Very Unlikely                     6          9      9.0      9.0     84.0
Definitely Not                    7         16     16.0     16.0    100.0
                                         -------  -------  -------
                              Total        100    100.0    100.0
Valid cases      100     Missing cases       0
------------------------------------------------------------------------
Page    7                      SPSS/PC+                          7/2/90

This procedure was completed at  9:57:18
------------------------------------------------------------------------
Page    8                      SPSS/PC+                          7/2/90


---------------------------------------------Ins----Num-Ext Menus- 81
                                              spss.lis
```

4 Because you pressed (F2) from the Data screen, this time Graph-in-the-Box Executive takes you to the Data screen to place the captured data. Figure 2 shows the Data screen with the labels in place.

Figure 2

```
Graph-in-the-Box EXECUTIVE          Chart type: Vert. bar              Data
    Variable text 1      Graph A     Graph B     Graph C     Graph D     Graph E
    Variable text 2      ----------  ----------  ----------  ----------  ----------
    Type                 BAR         BAR         BAR         BAR         BAR
    Color                RED     L2  BLUE    L3  MAGENTA L4  GREEN   L5  CYAN    L6
    Pattern              1 ■■■■■■■■  2 XXXXXXXX  3 ////////  4 X X X X   5 / / / /
    Axis                 LEFT Y      LEFT Y      LEFT Y      LEFT Y      LEFT Y
  ---------- T ---------|---- A ----|---- B ----|---- C ----|---- D ----|---- E ----
 1|Definitely           |        23|           |           |           |
 2|Very Likely          |        13|           |           |           |
 3|Somewhat Likely      |        17|           |           |           |
 4|Indifferent          |        15|           |           |           |
 5|Somewhat Unlikely    |         7|           |           |           |
 6|Very Unlikely        |         9|           |           |           |
 7|Definitely Not       |        16|           |           |           |
 8|                     |          |           |           |           |
 9|---------------------|          |           |           |           |
10|---------------------|          |           |           |           |
11|---------------------|          |           |           |           |
12|---------------------|          |           |           |           |
13|---------------------|          |           |           |           |
14|---------------------|          |           |           |           |
F1-Help  F2-Capture  F3-Calc                       F9-Layout  F10-View  Esc-Quit
```

5 If you press (F10) to display the chart, you'll see that the labels appear along the horizontal axis; but they are staggered and hard to read. Press (Esc) to go to the Data screen, highlight label **2**, and press the space bar to delete it. In a like manner, delete labels **3** to **6**.

6 Also, the label **Graph A** is not very helpful. To change the label, tab to column **A** and press the (↑) until the highlight is on **Graph A**. Then press the space bar to delete it. The label will be gone when the graph is displayed. You can also change the pattern, which determines the type of hatching that will fill the bars.

7 Now add some titles. Press (F9) to go to the Layout screen and type a title. Next, move the cursor to the **Axis title 1** field in the **X-axis** column and type *Purchase*, which will complete the labeling of the axis. The completed Layout screen is shown in Figure 3.

Figure 3

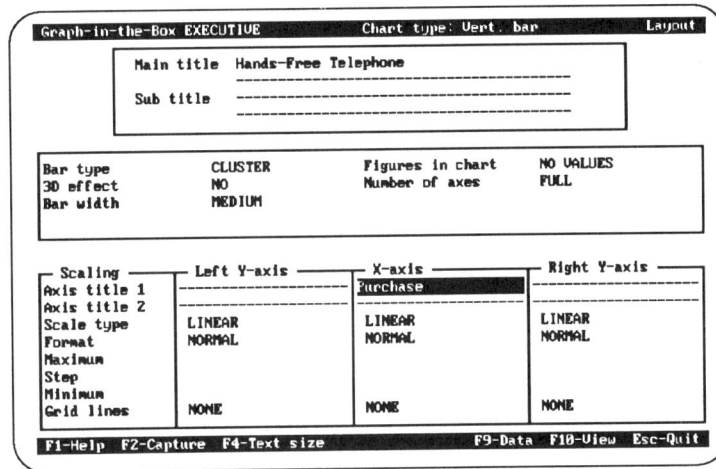

8 Press (F10) to display the graph (Figure 4).

Figure 4

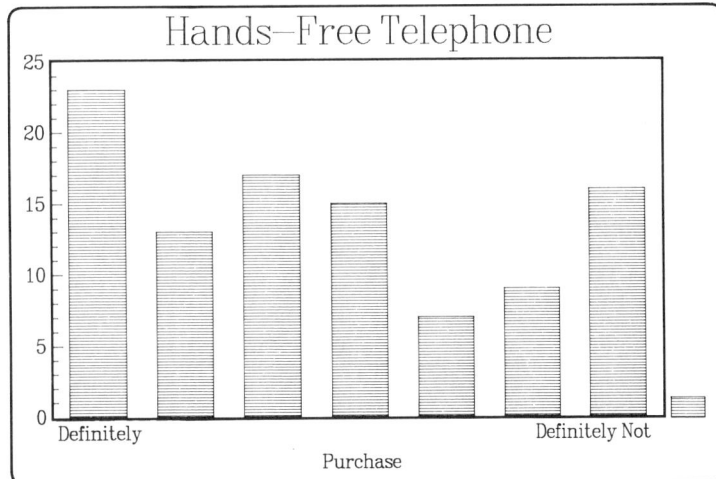

Adding Data Although Graph-in-the-Box Executive provides more formatting options, the chart just created doesn't contain any more information than you can obtain simply by adding the BARCHART subcommand to the SPSS/PC+ FREQUENCIES command. The power of Graph-in-the-Box Executive becomes useful when you combine information or when you get creative about graphing output for which plots are not already available. Let's combine the information from two frequency tables into a single chart.

1 On the Data screen, move the cursor to the top of the empty **B** column, the position for inserting the next set of frequencies (from the Husband data).

2 Go to the *main menu* (Esc) takes you there) and quit Graph-in-the-Box Executive. Quitting does not affect your current chart or data. If you were to press F2 (Capture) from the Data screen, you would be in the listing file at the **Phone Wife Self** table, unable to move to another table.

3 In the listing file, go to the frequency table for **Phone Husb Self**.

4 Press Ctrl G and capture the frequency data. Graph-in-the-Box Executive draws a new chart, showing both the Husband and the Wife data. Press Esc to get to the Data screen.

5 Above the two data columns, type in labels to distinguish Husband and Wife data, as shown in Figure 5.

Figure 5

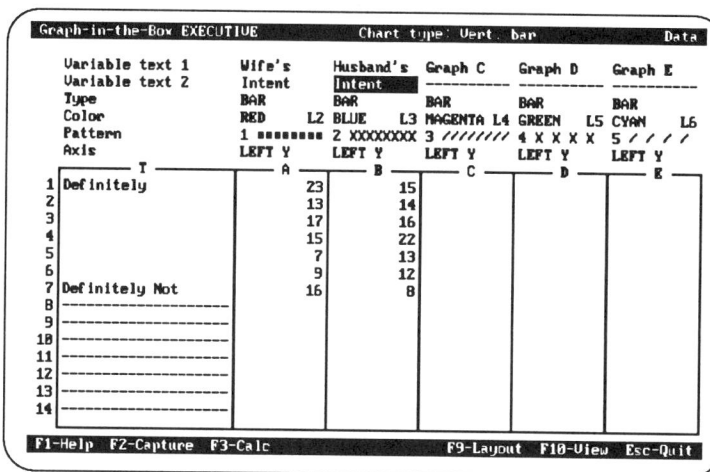

6 Press F10 to display the graph (Figure 6).

Figure 6

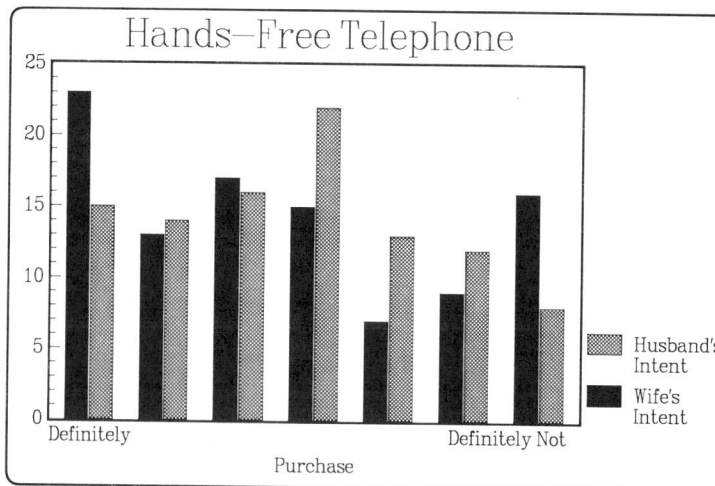

Varying the Style   Graph-in-the-Box Executive makes it easy to find different ways of viewing the data. Just go to the Chart type screen (press (Esc) twice to get to the main menu, and press (C) for chart type). Then press the space bar or the arrow keys to select the type of chart and press (↵).

Figure 7

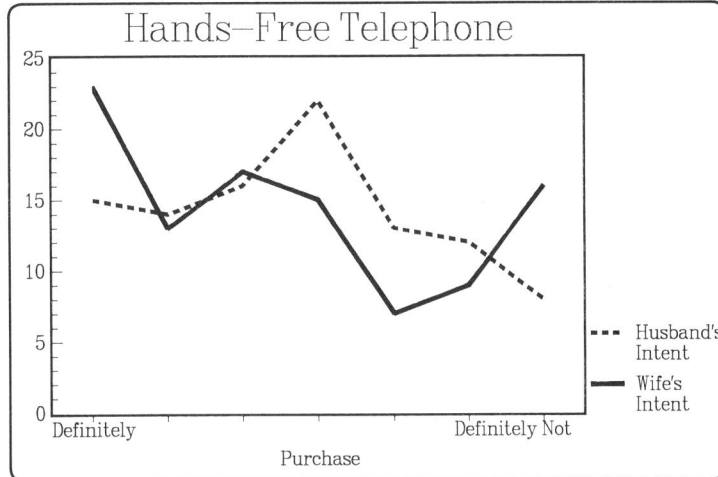

Hands—Free Telephone

- To create the line chart shown in Figure 7, simply go to the Chart type screen, select **Line**, and press (↵).

When you select **Mixed** from the Chart type screen, you can then select a different chart type to use for each column of numbers. You can also omit columns of numbers by telling Graph-in-the-Box Executive to ignore them.

Figure 8

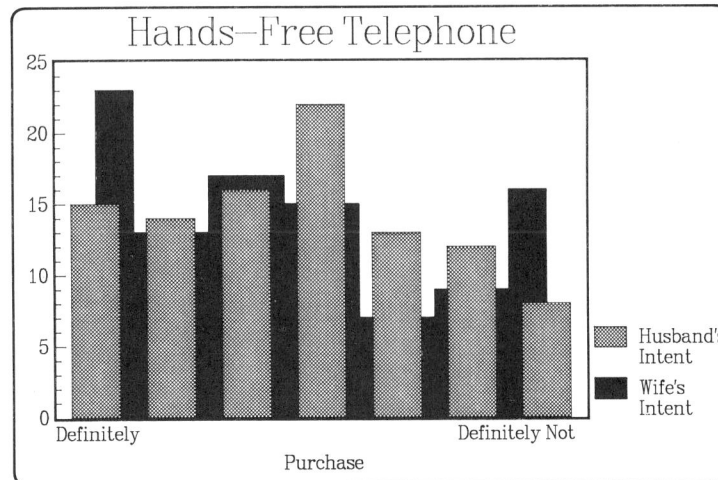

Hands—Free Telephone

1   To create the chart shown in Figure 8, go to the Chart type screen and select **Mixed.**

2 Go to the Data screen and move the cursor up near the top of the columns where the **Type** is shown for each column. You can change the type by placing the cursor on the field for each column and pressing the space bar until the right type appears. To see the whole list of choices, press F2. Choose **STEP,AREA** for the wife's intent and **BAR** for the husband's intent (Figure 9).

Figure 9

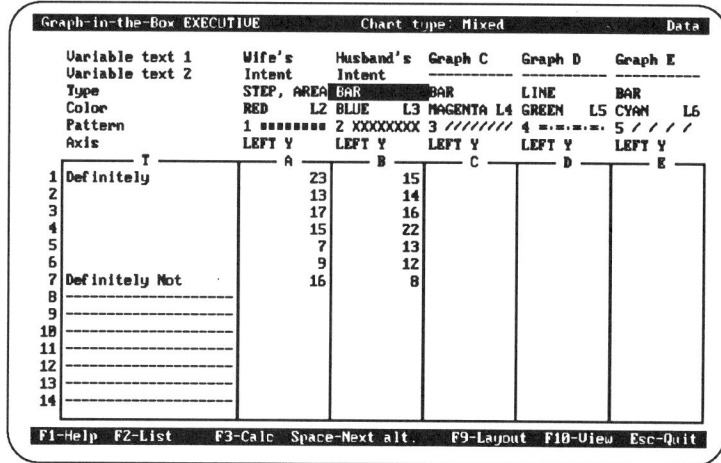

Rotating the Data

The pie chart in Figure 10 provides another way of looking at the same frequency data, but it requires a different arrangement of the data. Graph-in-the-Box Executive creates a pie for just the row of data containing the cursor—the value in each column becomes one slice. This requires you to capture a vertical column of frequencies into a horizontal row.

Figure 10

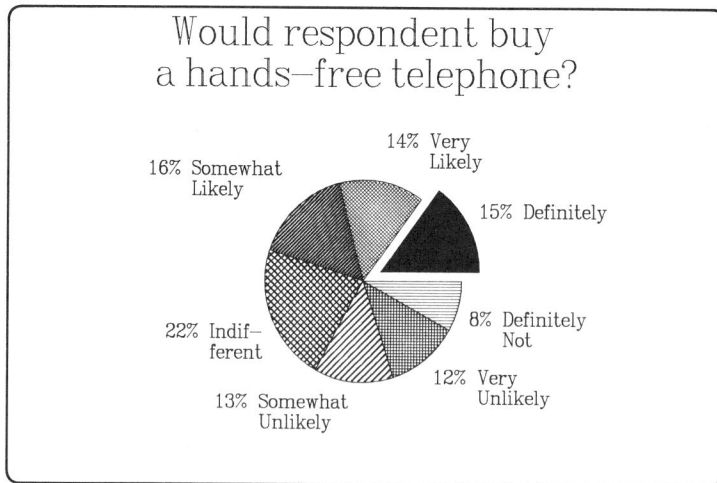

Would respondent buy a hands-free telephone?

14% Very Likely
16% Somewhat Likely
15% Definitely
22% Indif-ferent
8% Definitely Not
13% Somewhat Unlikely
12% Very Unlikely

1 Get rid of the current chart by selecting **Erase** from the Chart type screen. Press ← for **Erase: COMPLETE CHART.** Then move to **Pie** on the Chart type screen.

2 Go to the main menu and select **Setup**. Highlight **NOT ROTATED** in the **Capture** field (in the **Miscellaneous** box) and press the space bar to change to **ROTATED**. Figure 11 shows the Setup screen.

Figure 11

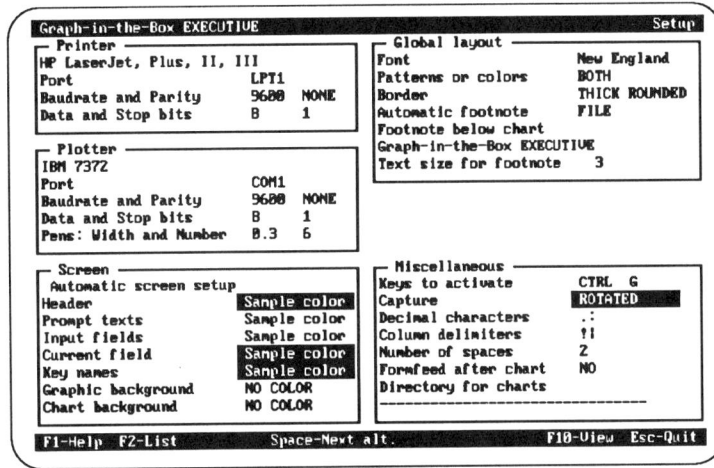

3 Go to the Data screen, position the cursor in the first row of column **A**, and press ⌷F2⌷ to capture the frequencies as before. They will now appear in the first row.

4 Move the cursor to **Graph A** in the top row and press ⌷F2⌷. Capture the column of value labels to the left of the frequency table. They will be entered in the top row (**Variable text 1**). Some are too long for the space provided, so you'll have to edit them; but capturing them gives you a head start. Be sure all seven columns have unique names.

5 After you have edited the labels, move the cursor to highlight **CENTERED** in the **Definitely** column (**A**) and press the space bar until **EXPLODED** appears. This will move the sector out from the center along a radius (see Figure 12).

Figure 12

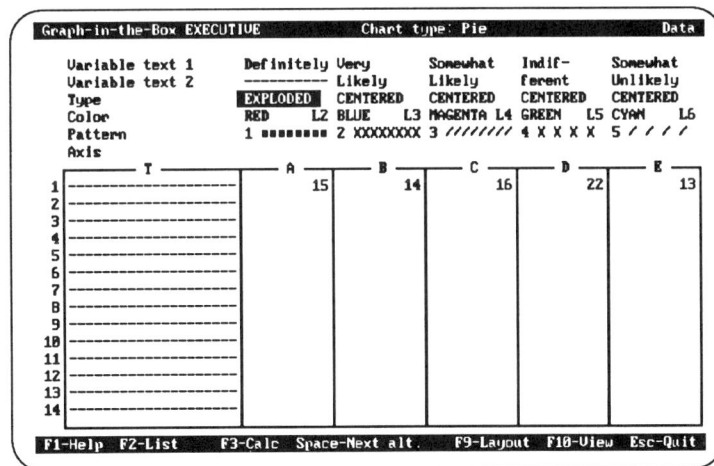

6 Go to the Layout screen and type a title for the chart. To display percentages in the chart, move the cursor to the **Figures in chart** field and press the space bar until **0 DEC PERCENT** appears (see Figure 13).

Figure 13

```
Graph-in-the-Box EXECUTIVE                 Chart type: Pie                    Layout

          Main title  Would respondent buy
                      a hands-free telephone?
          Sub title   ----------------------------------------
                      ----------------------------------------

  3D effect        NO           Figures in chart   0 DEC PERCENT
  Number of pies   1            Show legend        AROUND CHART




          Footnote    ----------------------------------------
                      ----------------------------------------
  F1-Help  F2-List            Space-Next alt.        F9-Data  F10-View  Esc-Quit
```

7 Press F10 to display the chart (Figure 10).

Another Rotation Method. Another way to rotate data for a pie chart is to use the **Calc**(ulate) function on the Data screen after the data are already in vertical columns. With the cursor on a data value, press F3. Type **rotate** after the equals sign and press ↵. The first 15 values of all columns will be swapped into rows, and the labels in row **Variable Text 1** will be exchanged with the labels in column **T**. This method does not change the **Capture** field on the Setup screen. You can view a pie chart for any of the rows by placing the cursor on a value in that row (if the chart type is **Pie**) and pressing F10. The position in the row determines the orientation of the pie.

Working with Tables

It's usually very easy to work with boxed tables such as those produced by CROSSTABS or the TABLES option. In capturing data, Graph-in-the-Box Executive ignores most characters that are not alphanumeric, so you can capture a whole table and not worry about blank lines or boxing characters. It also allows you to specify certain characters that divide columns in your table so you can capture multiple columns that are separated by something like vertical bars rather than spaces. The default vertical boxing characters in CROSSTABS and TABLES are ignored by Graph-in-the-Box Executive. If you change the defaults in SPSS/PC+ (or SET SCREEN=OFF, which also changes the box characters), you might want to change the column delimiters in Graph-in-the-Box Executive. Choose **Setup** from the main menu, and in the **Miscellaneous** box, type the column delimiter you want to use.

If you have been working with rotated data for the pie chart, change the **Capture** specification to **NOT ROTATED**. Also, go to the Chart type screen and erase any current chart.

The following example shows how easy it can be to capture and graph output from TABLES. The data file is the same as in the previous examples, PHONES.SYS. The SPSS/PC+ command

```
TABLES TABLE = (LABELS) BY WIFESELF + HUSBSELF + WIFESP + HUSBSP.
```

produces the table shown in Figure 14.

Figure 14

	Phone Wife Self	Phone Husb Self	Phone Wife Spouse	Phone Husb Spouse
Definitely	23	15	15	14
Very Likely	13	14	20	19
Somewhat Likely	17	16	15	30
Indifferent	15	22	13	18
Somewhat Unlikely	7	13	13	7
Very Unlikely	9	12	12	14
Definitely Not	16	8	12	6

Page   6   SPSS/PC+   7/2/90

This procedure was completed at 11:25:01

Page   7   SPSS/PC+   7/2/90

Ins   Ext Menus 01
spss.lis

1   Switch to the listing file in REVIEW (F2 ⏎ F2 Z) and find the table. Then press Ctrl G.

2   Capture the first two columns of data as one block. Graph-in-the-Box Executive draws the vertical bar chart with grouped bars.

3   Press F9 to display the Data screen and move the cursor to the top of column **T**. Then press F2 and capture the value labels from the stub as row labels.

4   Move the cursor to **Graph A** on the Data screen. Then press F2 and capture the first two headings from the banner as column labels. The Data screen now appears as shown in Figure 15.

Figure 15

```
Graph-in-the-Box EXECUTIVE              Chart type: Vert. bar         Data

     Variable text 1   Phone Wife  Phone Husb  Graph C     Graph D     Graph E
     Variable text 2   Self        Self        ---------   ---------   ---------
     Type              BAR         BAR         BAR         BAR         BAR
     Color             RED     L2  BLUE    L3  MAGENTA L4  GREEN   L5  CYAN    L6
     Pattern           1 ■■■■■■■■ 2 XXXXXXXX 3 ///////  4 X X X X  5 / / / /
     Axis              LEFT Y      LEFT Y      LEFT Y      LEFT Y      LEFT Y
            ── T ──           ── A ──     ── B ──     ── C ──     ── D ──     ── E ──
     1│Definitely              23          15
     2│Very Likely             13          14
     3│Somewhat Likely         17          16
     4│Indifferent             15          22
     5│Somewhat Unlikely        7          13
     6│Very Unlikely            9          12
     7│Definitely Not          16           8
     8│────────────────
     9│────────────────
    10│────────────────
    11│────────────────
    12│────────────────
    13│────────────────
    14│────────────────

  F1-Help  F2-Capture  F3-Calc              F9-Layout  F10-View  Esc-Quit
```

5   The long value labels will overlap in a vertical bar chart, so go to the Chart type screen and select **Hor. bar.** Then go to the Layout screen, add a title, and in the **Bar type** field press the space bar until **STACK** appears.

6   Press F10 to display the graph (Figure 16).

F

Appendixes

Figure 16

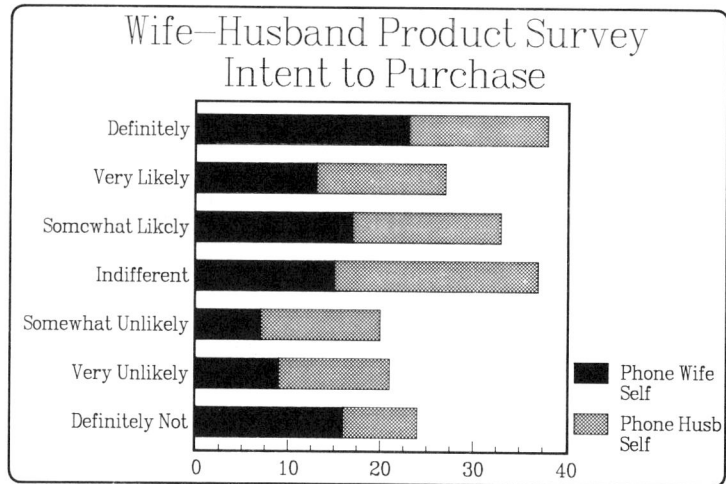

An Example Using the SPSS/PC+ Statistics Option

A worldwide economic study collected information on prices and salaries in 45 major cities. A large number of price and salary variables were collected. The SPSS/PC+ FACTOR procedure can help you see whether there are groups of very similar economic variables, and Graph-in-the-Box Executive can help you visualize how each variable contributes to the underlying factors. This example also contains a few additional variations on Graph-in-the-Box Executive operations. If you want to run the commands, first GET the file SALPRICE.SYS.

Exploring with a Simple Scatterplot

Before doing analysis of several factors, let's look at a scatterplot of two of the variables: the price of food and the price of services in the various cities. List them and then capture the data in Graph-in-the-Box Executive.

1 Run the commands:

```
GET FILE 'SALPRICE . SYS'.
LIST FOOD SERVICE.
```

2 Capture both lists together into Graph-in-the-Box Executive. Because the listing covers several screens, you have to quit Graph-in-the-Box Executive, move down in the listing file, wake up Graph-in-the-Box Executive with (Ctrl) (G), and begin another capture. Start the second capture on the next line of data below the last line of the first capture—and so on. Label the columns *Food* and *Service*.

3 Go to the Chart type screen and select **Scatter.** The points for both variables are plotted against the case numbers. On the Data screen, you can see that both columns are designated **LEFT Y** in the **Axis** field. In the **Food** column, highlight **LEFT Y** and press the space bar until **X AXIS** appears. Now, each variable has its own axis, and after you add titles on the Layout screen, the graph looks like Figure 17.

Figure 17

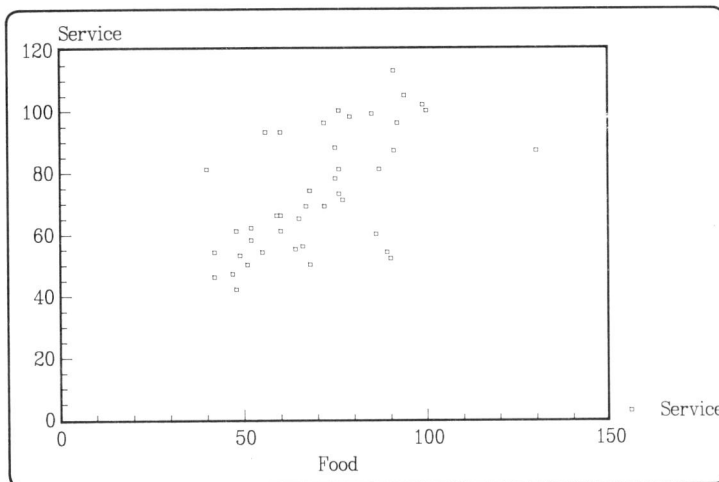

When you are finished with the scatterplot, erase it before starting the next chart (go to the Chart type screen and select **Erase**).

Charting Factors   To produce a factor analysis of the data, you can run the command

```
FACTOR VAR=ALL
    /FORMAT=SORT
    /CRITERIA=FACTORS(2).
```

Figure 18 shows the rotated factor matrix containing the coefficients that relate the individual variables to each of two factors. The highlighted areas are those to be captured into Graph-in-the-Box Executive.

Figure 18

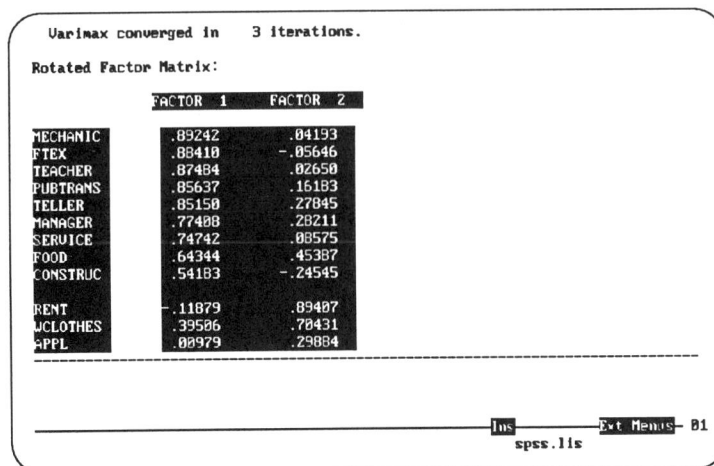

1   Capture the entire matrix of coefficients (the two columns of numbers). Graph-in-the-Box Executive simply ignores the blank line.
2   Capture the variable names as row labels. Again, Graph-in-the-Box Executive ignores the blank line.

3 Capture the column headings as column labels. This requires a little extra effort. Note that there are two spaces in **FACTOR 1** and **FACTOR 2**. Graph-in-the-Box Executive interprets two or more spaces as the delimiter between labels, so it would ordinarily read the column heads as labels for four columns. You can fix this by editing out one space in the listing file before capturing the column heads (you have to quit Graph-in-the-Box Executive, edit, and then press (Ctrl) (G)). or you can raise the number of spaces Graph-in-the-Box Executive interprets as a delimiter. Before initiating the capture, press (Esc) and then (S) to go to the Setup screen. Move the cursor to the **Number of spaces** field (in the **Miscellaneous** box) and change **2** to **3** (Figure 19).

Figure 19

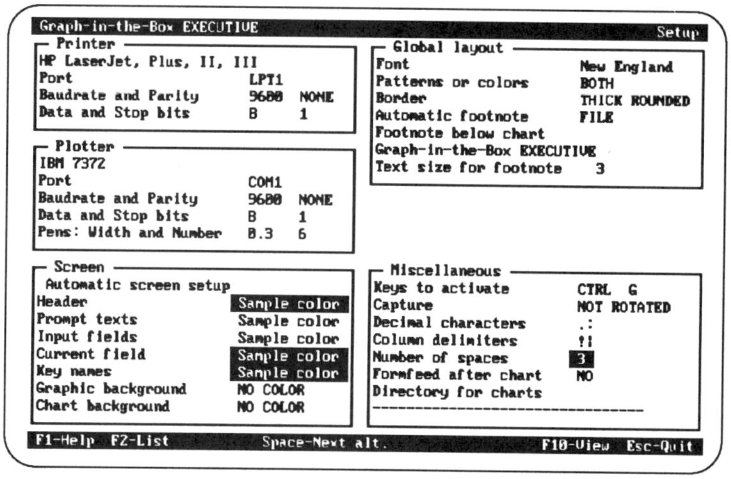

4 Go back to the **Data** screen, place the cursor on **Graph A**, and proceed with the capture. The captured data and labels are shown in Figure 20.

Figure 20

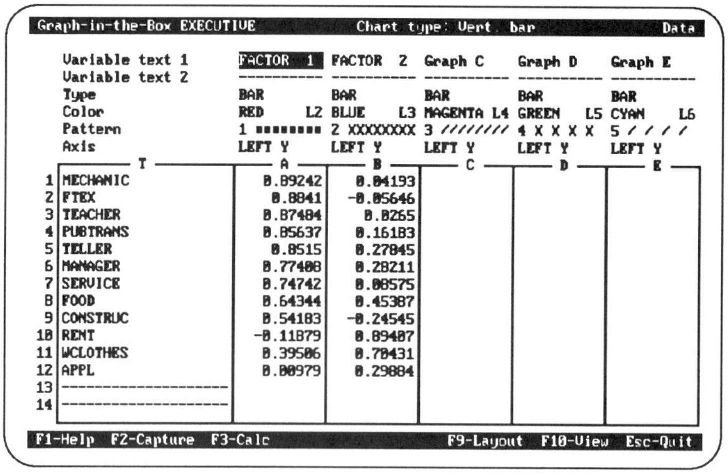

5 Press (F9) to access the Layout screen and move the cursor to the **Axis title 1** field. Capture (press (F2)) the title **Rotated Factor Matrix.** You will have to type **Matrix** on the second line, since it doesn't fit on the first line. Move the cursor up to the **Main title** field and type a title.

6 If you want to include in your chart the actual SPSS/PC+ command that produced the result (to document the model you used), you can position the cursor in the **Sub title** field on the Layout screen and capture the command from the listing file as shown in Figure 21. Since the FACTOR command is long, you should capture it in sections.

Figure 21

```
    48.00   61.00
    68.00   74.00

Number of cases read =      45    Number of cases listed =      45
------------------------------------------------------------------------
Page   8                      SPSS/PC+                          7/3/90

This procedure was completed at   9:18:28
------------------------------------------------------------------------
Page   9                      SPSS/PC+                          7/3/90
FACTOR /VARIABLES ALL
    /FORMAT SORT /CRITERIA FACTORS (2).
This FACTOR analysis requires      18696 (     18.3K) BYTES of memory.
------------------------------------------------------------------------
Page  10                      SPSS/PC+                          7/3/90
          - - - -  F A C T O R   A N A L Y S I S  - - - -

Analysis Number  1  Listwise deletion of cases with missing values
                                                    Ins       Ext Menus  B1
                                                      spss.lis
```

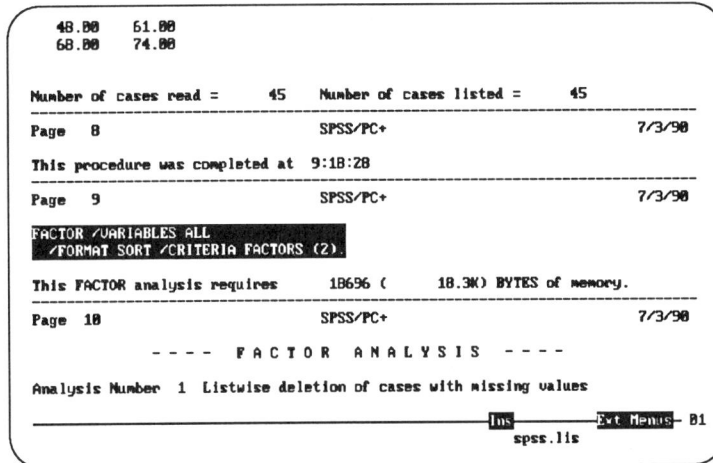

7 You can type in additional lines or edit the text once you've completed the capture (Figure 22).

Figure 22

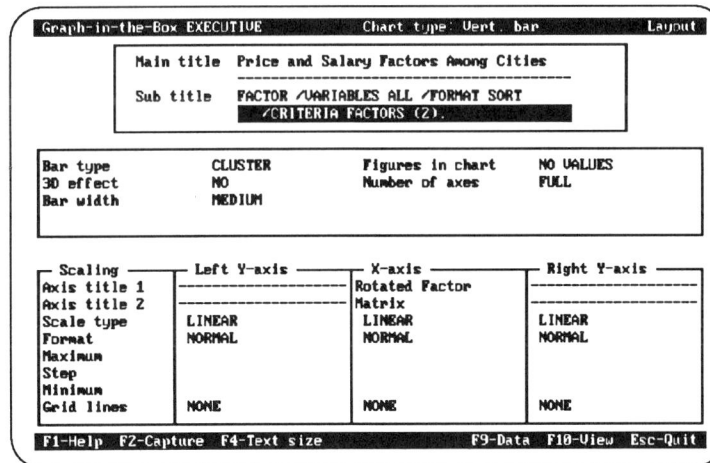

8 With many row labels (12 in this case), a horizontal bar chart avoids the overlapping labels that occur in a vertical bar chart. Go to the Chart type screen and select **Hor. bar.**

9 Press F10 to display the chart (Figure 23).

Figure 23

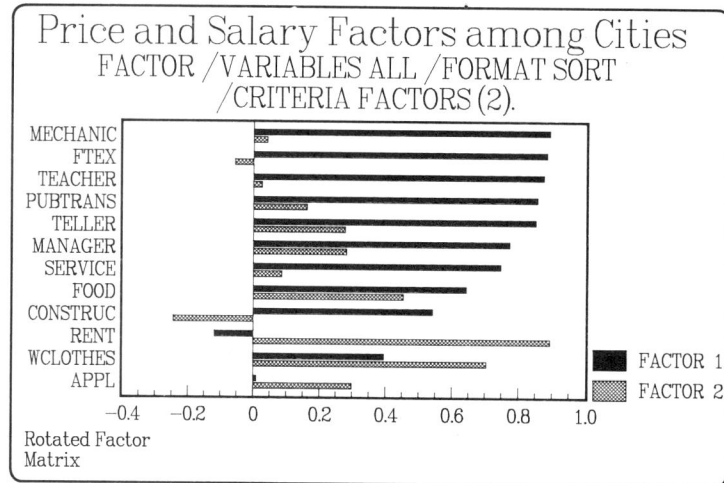

The Importance of Scale

The next example uses REGRESSION (in the SPSS/PC+ Statistics option) to predict sales from a leading indicator. The data are part of a series from Box and Jenkins' *Time Series Analysis: Forecasting and Control.* (For a complete treatment of this analysis, see *SPSS/PC+ Trends.*) REGRESSION coefficients are used along with values of the leading indicator to calculate predicted values. To follow along with this example, GET the file SALEPRED.SYS, which contains the resulting values.

```
GET FILE 'SALEPRED.SYS'.
LIST VARIABLES = SALES PREDICT.
```

The LIST command produces two long columns containing the sales and predicted sales (Figure 24). If you plot the data using the TSPLOT command from SPSS/PC+ Trends in low resolution, the resulting character plot cannot be adjusted. Plotting the data in Graph-in-the-Box Executive and adjusting the scale makes it much easier to see relationships.

Figure 24

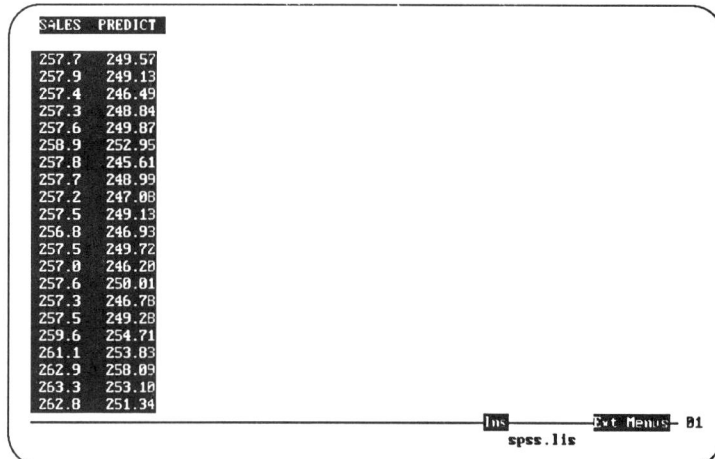

1 Capture the two columns of data, quitting Graph-in-the-Box Executive and going back to the listing file as many times as necessary (as in the previous scatterplot). Start capturing with the fourth case, since the first three cases don't have valid values.

2 When all the data have been transferred, position the cursor on **Graph A** on the Data screen and capture the column headings from the top of one page (see Figure 25).

Figure 25

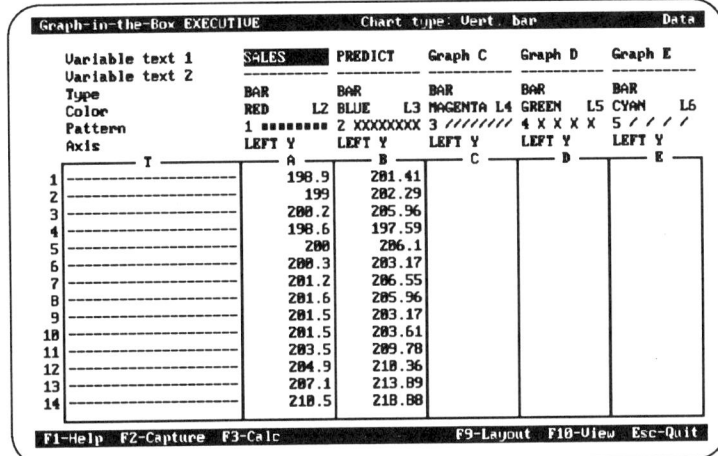

3 Go to the Chart type screen and select **Line**. Graph-in-the-Box Executive draws the line chart. With the current format, the lines are compressed near the top of the chart and the curves are indistinct because the default scaling starts at 0 while the actual values being plotted are all well within the range of 190 to 270 (see Figure 26).

Figure 26

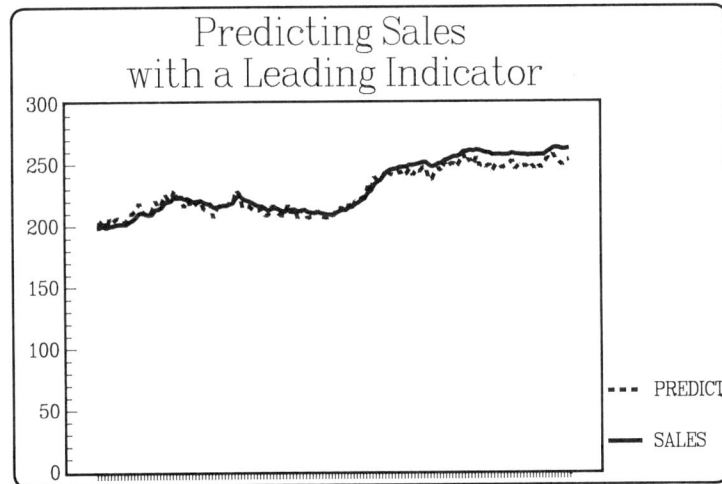

4 Return to the Layout screen and type a title. Then move the cursor down to the **Left Y-axis** box and enter the values **270** for **Maximum**, **10** for **Step**, and **190** for **Minimum** (Figure 27).

Figure 27

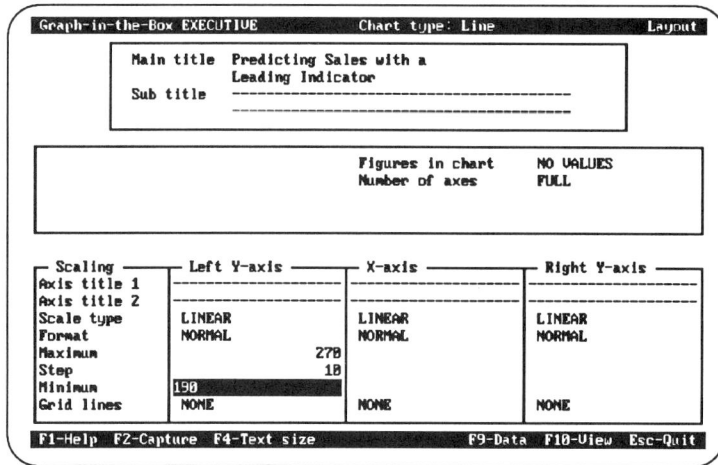

5 Press F10 to redisplay the chart as shown in Figure 28.

Figure 28

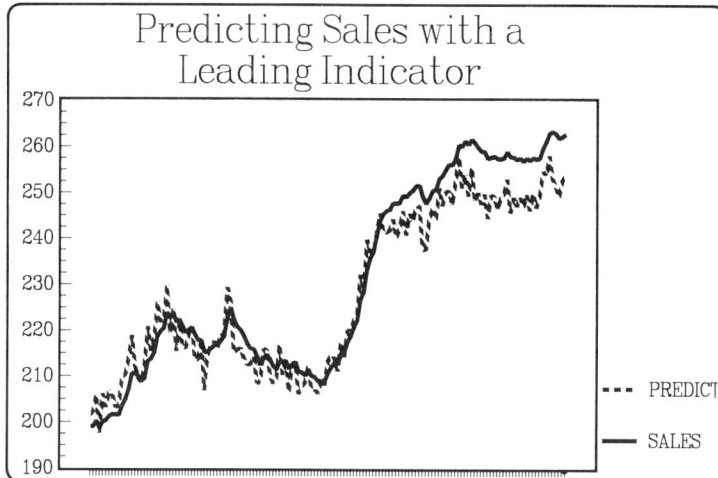

A Few Final Notes   The preceding examples contain most of the special cases you should watch for in using Graph-in-the-Box Executive within SPSS/PC+. Here are a few additional hints:

- Watch for empty cells when capturing tables or multiple columns of data. SPSS/PC+ may put periods in empty cells. Graph-in-the-Box Executive skips over blanks or periods, getting data out of order. If you know that a blank equals 0 or some other value, insert that value in REVIEW before waking up Graph-in-the-Box Executive.

- When you are leaving Graph-in-the-Box Executive to capture data, before pressing F2 or quitting, be sure to position the cursor on the Data screen or Layout screen where you want the new data to go.

- For scatterplots, Graph-in-the-Box Executive initially creates a scatterplot with scaling of the Y-axis only, and cases equally spaced on the X-axis. If you want one column of data scaled on the X-axis, change the **Axis** specification for that column on the Data screen. You can also change the scale for that axis on the Layout screen.

- SPSS/PC+ uses exponential notation for some values that will not fit into the allocated printing area. Graph-in-the-Box Executive will capture values expressed in exponential notation.

- If you want to capture columns separated by just one space, change the delimiter from the default of two spaces to one.

- A quick way to rotate data for a pie chart is to place the cursor on a value in the data matrix, press F3, and type *rotate*. When you press ↵, the rows and columns are swapped. (To do this, the number of rows must be 15 or fewer.) You can then create a pie chart from the row containing the cursor. You can also create up to three more pie charts from the succeeding rows by changing the number of pies on the Layout screen.

Appendix 3

Using SPSS/PC+ with RAM Disks

If your PC has an extended or expanded memory board and RAM-disk software—software that makes some of your memory (RAM) appear to be an extremely fast disk drive—you can put the RAM disk to good use in SPSS/PC+.

- You should not use a RAM disk in regular DOS memory (below 640K). Such memory is best used directly by SPSS/PC+.
- The following examples assume that the RAM disk is drive D: and that SPSS/PC+ is installed into its default location (the \SPSS directory) on your default drive.

Use the RAM disk for your active file, for REVIEW, or for both.

THE ACTIVE FILE
Whenever you read a raw data file or transform your active file, SPSS/PC+ writes the data in binary format to a scratch file, called the *active file*. You can control the location of these scratch files with the SPSS/PC+ command SET WORKDEV. When you are going to be processing a file large enough so that reading the data occupies substantial time, begin your session with the SPSS/PC+ command:

```
SET WORKDEV=D:.
```

SPSS/PC+ will write one and perhaps two copies of the active file to the RAM disk. Be certain that they will fit before giving this command. You cannot set the work device after the active file has been created in a session.

You may want to put the SET WORKDEV command in your automatic SPSS/PC+ profile, SPSSPROF.INI.

REVIEW
You can also put REVIEW onto a RAM disk. If you go in and out of REVIEW frequently (for example, using the default RUNREVIEW AUTO setting), you can speed up the automatic return to REVIEW considerably. Use the DOS command *SET SPSSR=path* and place REVIEW on a RAM disk. Here is a sample batch file to place REVIEW on drive D:.

```
ECHO OFF
IF EXIST D:SPSSRV.EXE GOTO RUN
COPY C:\SPSS\SPSRV4.EXE D:
:RUN
SET SPSSR=D:\
SPSSPC %1 %2 %3 %4 %5
SET SPSSR=
```

- The *IF* command checks whether REVIEW has already been copied to the RAM disk. (If you had executed this batch file earlier in the same session, it would already be there.)
- The *COPY* command places REVIEW on the RAM disk, if it is not already there. REVIEW occupies approximately 180,000 bytes of space on the RAM disk. *Do not* invoke REVIEW by the name of this .EXE file. To invoke REVIEW from DOS, use the command:

```
SPSSPC/RE file1 [file2]
```

- The *SET SPSSR* command sets a DOS environment variable so that SPSS/PC+ will know that REVIEW is in drive D:.

- The *SPSSPC* command invokes SPSS/PC+, passing any parameters that you may have used when calling the batch file (such as the name of a command file).
- The second *SET SPSSR* command deletes the string SPSSR from the DOS environment area. There should be nothing—not even a blank space—after the equals sign.

CAUTIONS

- SPSS Inc. does not distribute or support any RAM-disk software.

Neither of the two applications suggested above places anything on the RAM disk that needs to be copied to a physical disk at the end of your session. Nevertheless, if you use a RAM disk

- Use reliable RAM-disk software and be aware of its limitations.
- Be sure that your RAM disk has enough room for the application. If you place your active file on the RAM disk, you need enough room for two copies of the data in binary form. If you place REVIEW on the RAM disk, you need enough room to hold the file SPSSRV.EXE.

Appendix 4

Files Created by Other Software

SPSS/PC+ reads and writes several types of files. This section discusses the use of these files with other text editors typically used in the personal computing environment. You probably will use an editor to prepare command files and data files. The REVIEW editor that is part of SPSS/PC+ allows you to prepare these files, but many other editors are available as well.

You may also want to analyze data stored in a database or spreadsheet program. SPSS/PC+ has the ability to translate files produced by several popular spreadsheet or database packages into its own active file format—and the ability to translate files into formats used by the same packages. SPSS/PC+ can do this with one command: TRANSLATE. See TRANSLATE Command (Part C) for a description of this command and a list of the database and spreadsheet packages supported.

EDITORS

An editor is software used to create or modify files containing text or data. SPSS/PC+ processes command and data files created with editors.

SPSS/PC+ itself contains an editor called REVIEW. However, you can use another editor to create SPSS/PC+ command and data files, as long as you produce an ASCII file that conforms to the following criteria:

- Each line in the file must end with a carriage-return line-feed sequence. (This is typical of most DOS files.)
- The file must end with a `Ctrl` `Z` for SPSS/PC+ to read the last line correctly. (This is typical of most DOS files.)
- The file must not contain special format codes or other information specific to the program from which it was created. (An example of this is the use of control characters to indicate special document formatting options, such as `Ctrl` `B` for boldface.)
- The maximum line length for files containing SPSS/PC+ commands and inline data is 80 characters. Anything past column 80 is ignored.
- The maximum line length for data files named on the DATA LIST command is 1,024 characters.

The REVIEW Editor

The REVIEW editor (in Part A, see REVIEW: The SPSS/PC+ Editor) allows you to edit the ASCII files produced by SPSS/PC+ and to produce data and command files that can be read by SPSS/PC+. If you use REVIEW for editing related to SPSS/PC+, you don't have to worry about problems of compatibility between SPSS/PC+ and the editor.

You can use REVIEW as your general-purpose editor, creating and modifying files for other applications.

Other Editors

Some editors store files in a special format that combines text with escape sequences and/or control characters. The escape sequences and control characters are usually used to perform font shifts when printing, or to format text for display. For example, the editor might add a special character to the end of every line, paragraph, and page. Editors designed for word processing are more likely to use such special formats than are editors designed for programming. If you INCLUDE a file created with an editor that inserts escape sequences, SPSS/PC+ reads the escape sequences literally and cannot interpret them. Fortunately, these types of editors usually have a special mode or translate program to produce files readable by programs such as SPSS/PC+. For example, WordStar™ has a "non-document" mode for creating files. Other word processors typically let you specify ASCII or "text" format when you save a file.

How do you find out whether your favorite editor is going to work with SPSS/PC+? Use the DOS *TYPE* command to type a file created with your editor. If the file does not look the same when typed as when viewed within the editor, then it probably cannot be read correctly by SPSS/PC+. Beware of special symbols that are not directly available on the keyboard. The one exception to this rule is the use of tabs. If your editor permits tabs, and it places an ASCII 09 character into the file, SPSS/PC+ interprets it as *one* blank. Although the file does not look the same when echoed by SPSS/PC+ (since the interpretation of tabs is always context specific), it is interpreted correctly.

Another potential problem is the requirement for a carriage-return line-feed sequence at the end of the line. If an editor has an automatic word-wrap procedure that automatically creates a new line while you continue typing, it may not insert the end-of-line sequence required by SPSS/PC+. To obtain the carriage-return line-feed sequence required by SPSS/PC+, you may need to use the enter key after typing in each line. Some editors may not even wrap to start a new line but appear to do so because they are displaying a line longer than 80 characters in an 80-character window. In general, you should avoid using the word-wrap facilities of your editor when preparing files to read with SPSS/PC+ unless your editor explicitly documents that it inserts the carriage-return line-feed sequence. If your editor's documentation provides special instructions for preparing files for use with other applications such as language compilers, follow them.

With the exception of forms control for listing files, ASCII files written by SPSS/PC+ do not contain special escape sequences, tabs, etc., and are generally readable and editable by most editors. The one exception is a file produced by SPSS/PC+ that does not contain a (Ctrl)(Z) at the end because a session was not ended normally. Some editors can read such a file (although they might issue a read error warning); other editors have great difficulty. If you terminate an SPSS/PC+ session normally, you should be able to *TYPE*, *PRINT*, or otherwise display listing and log files written by SPSS/PC+. Follow your editor's discussion for editing "foreign" files.

COMMUNICATIONS PROGRAMS

Communications programs such as CROSSTALK™ and PC-TALK III can be used to transfer ASCII files read and written by SPSS/PC+. However, they should not be used with SPSS/PC+ system files or portable system files. ASCII files containing special graphics characters used in SPSS/PC+ output cannot be transferred correctly to mainframes or to other types of personal computers.

F

Appendixes

Index

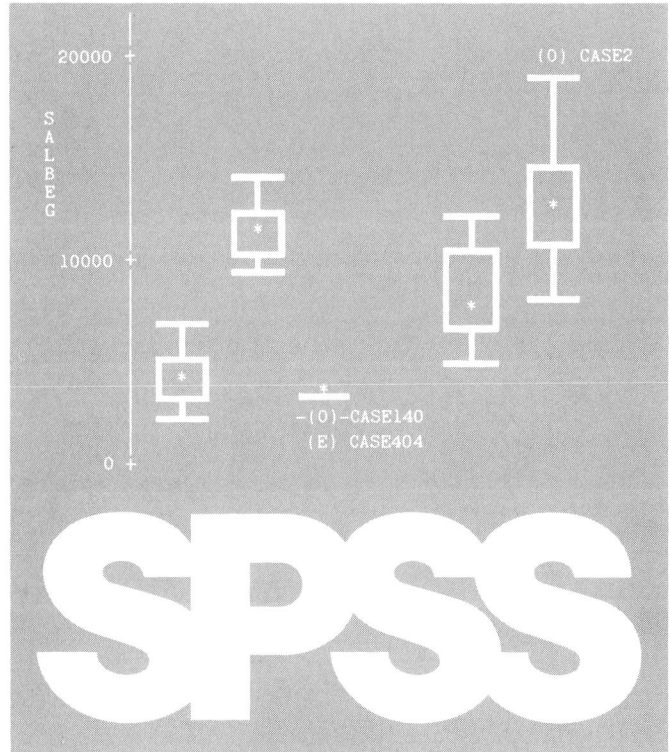

Index